Affirmative Action
and
Representation

Affirmative Action
and
Representation

Shaw v. Reno and the Future
of Voting Rights

Edited by
Anthony A. Peacock

CAROLINA ACADEMIC PRESS
Durham, North Carolina

Library of Congress Cataloging-in-Publication Data

Affirmative action and representation: Shaw v. Reno and the future
of voting rights/ [edited by] Anthony A. Peacock.
    p.   cm.
Includes index.
ISBN 0–89089–883–9
ISBN 0–89089–884–7 paperback
1. Afro-Americans—Suffrage. 2. Apportionment (Election law)—
United States. 3. Election districts—United States.
4. Representative government and representation—United States.
5. United States—Race relations. I. Peacock, Anthony A., 1959–
KF4893.A75A34   1997
342.73'07—dc21   96-39532
                                             CIP

The following chapters in this book are reprinted with the permission of the law
reviews and publishers listed below. These organizations retain the copyright in the
articles referred to. Chapter 3, Shaw v. Reno: *The Shape of Things to Come*, by
Timothy G. O'Rourke, originally appeared in the *Rutgers Law Journal*, 26 Rutgers L.J. 723 (1995). Chapter 4, *More Notes from a Political Thicket*, by Abigail
Thernstrom, originally appeared in the *Emory Law Journal*, 44 Emory L.J. 911
(1995). Chapter 8, *Groups, Representation, and Race-Conscious Districting: A
Case of the Emperor's Clothes*, is reprinted with the permission of The Free Press,
a division of Simon & Schuster, from The Tyranny of the Majority: Fundamental Fairness in Representative Democracy, Copyright, 1994, by Lani
Guinier. Chapter 11, *Equal Justice: Applying the Voting Rights Act to Judicial
Elections*, by Frederick G. Slabach, originally appeared in the *University of Cincinnati Law Review*, 62 U. Cin. L. Rev. 823 (1994).

North Carolina map with 12th congressional district copyright 1992 by the
Institute of Government. Used with permission.

Carolina Academic Press
700 Kent Street
Durham, North Carolina 27701
Phone (919) 489-7486
Fax (919) 493-5886

Printed in the United States of America

Contents

Acknowledgments

This book would never have been completed without the perseverance of all of the contributors. I am particularly grateful to Ralph Rossum and Mark Rush, who provided sound advice throughout. Terrie Bissonnette, Boyle Ke, and Jeremy Roper provided invaluable help on the computers, as well as with the Table of Cases and the Index. The generous financial assistance of the Lynde and Harry Bradley Foundation of Milwaukee, Wisconsin, and of the Faculty Research Committee, Claremont McKenna College, which provided me a summer research grant for 1996, allowed me the opportunity to work on this book at length. Special thanks are owed to Keith Sipe, the Publisher at Carolina Academic Press, who had confidence in this book from the beginning and who resolved all problems from start to finish expeditiously and with an effervescence that should serve as the standard for all of us who survive by the printed word. Special thanks are also due to Russ Bahorsky, Greta Strittmatter, Tim Colton, and Miranda Bailey, also of Carolina Academic Press, for their first rate assistance producing and marketing the book.

The following law reviews and publishers have graciously provided me permission to reprint four chapters in this book. These organizations retain the copyright in the articles referred to. Chapter 3, *Shaw v. Reno: The Shape of Things to Come*, by Timothy G. O'Rourke, originally appeared in the *Rutgers Law Journal*, 26 RUTGERS L.J. 723 (1995). Chapter 4, *More Notes from a Political Thicket*, by Abigail Thernstrom, originally appeared in the *Emory Law Journal*, 44 EMORY L.J. 911 (1995). Chapter 8, "Groups, Representation, and Race-Conscious Districting: A Case of the Emperor's Clothes," is reprinted with the permission of The Free Press, a division of Simon & Schuster, from THE TYRANNY OF THE MAJORITY: FUNDAMENTAL FAIRNESS IN REPRESENTATIVE DEMOCRACY, Copyright, 1994, by Lani Guinier. Chapter 11, *Equal Justice: Applying the Voting Rights Act to Judicial Elections*, by Frederick G. Slabach, originally appeared in the *University of Cincinnati Law Review*, 62 U. CIN. L. REV. 823 (1994). I am particularly grateful to Sue Haverkos, Executive Editor of the *University of Cincinnati Law Review*, for digging out the appropriate diskette from the University archives, thus saving me much grief.

Anthony A. Peacock
Claremont, California

Notes on Contributors

RICHARD L. ENGSTROM is Research Professor of Political Science at the University of New Orleans. His research on electoral systems has been published in the *American Political Science Review*, the *Journal of Politics*, *Electoral Studies*, *Social Science Quarterly*, and other journals. He currently serves as the Chair of the Representation and Electoral Systems Section of the American Political Science Association.

BERNARD GROFMAN is Professor of Political Science and Social Psychology at the University of California, Irvine. He is a specialist in the theory of representation. His major fields of interest are in American politics, comparative election systems, and social choice theory. He has edited numerous books, including, most recently, *Quiet Revolution in the South: The Impact of the Voting Rights Act, 1965–1990* (co-edited with Chandler Davidson), and *Legislative Term Limits: Public Choice Perspectives*.

LANI GUINIER is Professor of Law at the University of Pennsylvania Law School. She has published widely on voting rights and representation. Her articles have appeared in such law journals as the *Texas Law Review*, the *Virginia Law Review*, and the *Michigan Law Review*. In 1994 she published *The Tyranny of the Majority: Fundamental Fairness in Representative Democracy*.

SAMUEL ISSACHAROFF is the Charles Tilford McCormick Professor of Law at the University of Texas Law School. He is a 1983 graduate of Yale Law School and practised law extensively in the area of voting rights before joining the Texas faculty in 1989. He writes extensively in the areas of voting and electoral law, employment law, civil procedure, and the economic analysis of law.

JASON F. KIRKSEY is the Hannah D. Atkins Endowed Chair for Political Science at Oklahoma State University. His research has been published in *Women and Politics*, the *Voting Rights Review*, and *Oklahoma Politics*.

TIMOTHY G. O'ROURKE is the Teresa M. Fischer Professor of Citizenship Education at the University of Missouri-St. Louis. He is the author of *The Impact of Reapportionment* (1980), named by *Choice* as one of the Outstanding Academic Books of 1980, and his articles on the federal Voting Rights Act have appeared in such journals as the *Virginia Law Review* and the *Journal of Law & Politics*. In recent years, he has testified before both U.S. House and Senate committees on various voting issues and also has served as an expert witness in voting rights litigation.

ANTHONY A. PEACOCK is a visiting assistant professor in the Department of Government, Claremont McKenna College. He is a member of the Bar of Ontario and recently edited *Rethinking the Constitution: Perspectives on Canadian Constitutional Reform, Interpretation, and Theory* (1996).

RALPH A. ROSSUM is the Henry Salvatori Professor of American Constitutionalism at Claremont McKenna College and a member of the faculty of the Claremont Graduate School. He has written over 50 articles in law and professional journals and is the author of six books, including *American Constitutional Law* (with G. Alan Tarr), a two-volume work now in the fourth edition, *Reverse Discrimination: The Constitutional Debate*, and *The Politics of the Criminal Justice System: An Organizational Analysis*. He is currently at work on a book on the textualist jurisprudence of Justice Antonin Scalia.

MARK E. RUSH is Associate Professor of Politics at Washington and Lee University, where he teaches constitutional law. He received his Ph.D. from the Johns Hopkins University in 1990. His book, *Does Redistricting Make a Difference?*, was published by the Johns Hopkins University Press in 1993. His areas of research include voting rights, political parties, civil liberties, and comparative constitutionalism.

FREDERICK G. SLABACH is the Associate Dean of Whittier Law School. He has served as the Assistant Secretary of Agriculture in Washington, D.C., the Associate Dean for Academic Affairs at Mississippi College School of Law, the Legislative Counsel to the President Pro Tempore of the United States Senate, an Associate Attorney with the Washington, D.C., law firm of Akin, Gump, Strauss, Hauer and Feld, and as law clerk to former Chief Judge William C. Keady of the United States District Court for the Northern District of Mississippi. He is also the 1995 recipient of the Elmer B. Staats Public Service Award presented by the Harry S. Truman Scholarship Foundation in Washington, D.C.

EDWARD STILL is a member of the Alabama State Bar and practices employment and civil rights law in Birmingham. He has sued more than 200 jurisdictions in Alabama in voting rights cases, including the redistricting of the Alabama Legislature during the last two decades. He is the author and co-author of several political science and law review articles on alternative election systems. He has been a guest lecturer at several universities in the United States and is an adjunct professor of law at the University of Alabama School of Law, where he teaches American Legal History and Election Law.

ABIGAIL THERNSTROM is a Senior Fellow at the Manhattan Institute and an adjunct professor at the School of Education, Boston University. Her book, *Whose Votes Count? Affirmative Action and Minority Voting Rights* (1987) won four awards, including the Anisfield-Wolf Book Award for the best book on race and ethnicity in 1987, and the 1988 American Bar Association's certificate of merit. She writes frequently for a variety of journals and newspapers, including *The New Republic, Commentary, The Wall Street Journal, The Washington Post,* and *The Public Interest.* With her husband, Harvard historian Stephan Thernstrom, she is now working on a book on the problem of race in modern America entitled *America in Black and White.*

Affirmative Action
and
Representation

Part I

INTRODUCTION

CHAPTER 1

Voting Rights, Representation, and the Problem of Equality

Anthony A. Peacock

The Supreme Court's 1993 decision, *Shaw v. Reno*,[1] was a bellwether in equal protection litigation, marking a significant turn away from earlier voting rights jurisprudence. Forecasts immediately following the decision had speculated that *Shaw* would not lay "the foundation for a major attack on the Voting Rights Act"[2] or was "best read as an exceptional doctrine for aberrational contexts rather than as a prelude to a sweeping constitutional condemnation of race-conscious redistricting."[3] Subsequent jurisprudence made clear, however, that the new cause of action created in *Shaw*, one that found an equal protection violation where states have used race to separate voters into electoral districts, was not limited to bizarre shaped districts, such as the North Carolina 12th Congressional District at issue in *Shaw*. In *Miller v. Johnson* (1995), the Court clarified that "Although it was not necessary in *Shaw* to consider further the proof required in ... more difficult cases, the logical import of our reasoning is that evidence other than a district's bizarre shape can be used to support [an equal protection] claim."[4] Did this signal the end to affirmative action in redistricting, the beginning of a wholesale re-examination of the Voting Rights Act of 1965 (VRA)?[5]

The essays in this collection address this question, and related issues, with a view to assessing the implications of the Supreme Court's 1990s voting rights jurisprudence. Is there a trend in constitutional and noncon-

---

1. 113 S.Ct. 2816 (1993).

2. Bernard Grofman, *High Court Ruling Won't Doom Racial Gerrymandering*, CHICAGO TRIBUNE, 9 July 1993, section 1, p. 19.

3. Richard H. Pildes and Richard G. Niemi, *Expressive Harms, "Bizarre Districts," and Voting Rights: Evaluating Election-District Appearances After* Shaw v. Reno, MICHIGAN L. REV. 92 (1993): 483, 495.

4. 115 S.Ct. 2475, 2487, Kennedy, J.

5. Voting Rights Act of 1965, Pub. L. No. 89-110, 79 Stat. 445 (codified as amended at 42 U.S.C. §§ 1971, 1973 to 1973bb-1 (1988)).

stitutional equality rights litigation that helps explain developments under the VRA?[6]

In a controversial series of decisions in 1988 and 1989, the Court modified the legal doctrines applicable to race conscious affirmative action under Title VII of the Civil Rights Act. Disparate impact analysis was altered, making it more difficult for employees to assert claims.[7] The Court also allowed for judicial review of affirmative action consent decrees to which white plaintiffs were not a party.[8] These decisions justifiably caused consternation among members of the civil rights community and resulted in Congress effectively overturning them in the Civil Rights Act of 1991.[9]

This did not occur, however, before the Court further reined in affirmative action in its equal protection jurisprudence. In 1989, the Court rejected the "benign" purposes of a Richmond set-aside program for minority businesses, maintaining that strict scrutiny under the Equal Protection Clause applied equally to all groups, regardless of race.[10] In 1990, the effects of this decision were temporarily limited to state affirmative action programs when the Court determined that two race-conscious policies applied by the Federal Communications Commission were not subject to strict scrutiny but only to intermediate scrutiny.[11]

Repose from the Court's assault on affirmative action was short-lived, however. On June 12, 1995, the Court released *Adarand Constructors, Inc. v. Pena*,[12] consolidating its affirmative action jurisprudence, ruling that strict scrutiny applied both to state *and* federal law, and to all racial classifications, benign and otherwise.[13] In the absence of strong evidence showing a compelling governmental interest in maintaining racial classifications and that proposed legislative measures were narrowly tailored to meet such interests, state and federal affirmative action programs would now fall before the exacting standards of strict scrutiny.

Shaw and *Miller* were consistent with these developments in equality rights jurisprudence, reflecting a new, harder line toward affirmative ac-

---

6. *See, generally*, HERMAN BELZ, EQUALITY TRANSFORMED: A QUARTER-CENTURY OF AFFIRMATIVE ACTION (Transaction Publishers, 1991), esp. 209–32.

7. *Watson v. Fort Worth Bank*, 108 S.Ct. 2777 (1988) and *Wards Cove v. Antonio*, 109 S.Ct. 2115 (1989).

8. *Martin v. Wilks*, 109 S.Ct. 2180 (1989).

9. P.L. 102–166.

10. *Richmond v. J.A. Croson Co.*, 109 S.Ct. 706 (1989).

11. *Metro Broadcasting v. Federal Communications Commission*, 497 U.S. 547 (1990).

12. 115 S.Ct. 2097 (1995).

13. *Id.*, 2112–13.

tion. But as Justice O'Connor, writing for the majority in *Shaw*, acknowledged, voting rights litigation is qualitatively distinct from other types of equal protection jurisprudence. Emphasizing that the "Court never has held that race-conscious state decisionmaking is impermissible in *all* circumstances,"[14] O'Connor highlighted that

> redistricting differs from other kinds of state decisionmaking in that the legislature always is *aware* of race when it draws district lines, just as it is aware of age, economic status, religious and political persuasion, and a variety of other demographic factors. That sort of race consciousness does not lead inevitably to impermissible race discrimination.[15]

If it did not, what sort of race consciousness did? What was the constitutional cut off point?

O'Connor never answered this question, and perhaps for good reason. To the extent that the VRA guarantees more than the right to cast a ballot, allowing claims for minority vote dilution, it protects group rights. Vote dilution only makes sense in the context of group identification and group interests. Measuring political effectiveness cannot be achieved through the medium of individuals, who afford no measure of comparison. Yet as the Court has emphasized time and again, the provisions of the Fourteenth Amendment are "personal rights" guaranteed to the individual and not to groups.[16] The question arises: how is a group model of equality, which focuses on race, to be reconciled with an individualist model, which proscribes considerations of race except in increasingly rare circumstances? In addition, how is a concept of representation that concentrates on the distribution of political power between racial groups to be reconciled with a concept of representation that divides the electorate territorially?

Although *Shaw* was not a vote dilution case, the plaintiffs asserting a claim "analytically distinct" from a vote dilution claim,[17] the Court nevertheless recognized the principle of vote dilution developed in *Allen v. State Board of Elections* (1969).[18] The Court also acknowledged that in response to the problem of vote dilution, Congress had, in 1982, "amended § 2 of the Voting Rights Act to prohibit legislation that *results* in the dilution of a minority group's voting strength, regardless of the leg-

---

14. 113 S.Ct. 2824, emphasis in original.

15. *Id.*, 2826, emphasis in original.

16. See, for instance, *Shelley v. Kraemer*, 334 U.S. 1, 22 (1948); *University of California Regents v. Bakke*, 438 U.S. 265, 289 (1978); and *Richmond v. J.A. Croson Co.* 488 U.S. at 493.

17. 113 S.Ct. at 2830, O'Connor, J., opinion of the Court.

18. *Id.*, 2823.

islature's intent."[19] The 1982 section 2 amendments underscored the novel approach that would now have to be taken in section 2 analysis. As Justice Brennan observed in *Thornburg v. Gingles* (1986): it is "the *correlation* between race of voter and the selection of certain candidates [that] is crucial to [a section 2] inquiry;"[20] "the *difference* between choices made by blacks and whites—not the reasons for that difference."[21] If it was the correlation between the selections made by voters and not the reasons for those selections that was crucial to a section 2 inquiry, was this incarnation of voting rights compatible with the Court's individualistic equal protection jurisprudence, specifically requiring justification or "reasons" for race-based legislative classifications? Would state legislatures subject to the "narrow tailoring" or "compelling state interest" components of equal protection review have to explain the causes of racial group voting, go beyond the mere recitation of the existence of racially polarized voting, to defend redistricting plans drafted in compliance with the VRA? Were the requirements of the VRA constitutional?

In *Johnson v. De Grandy*[22] and *Holder v. Hall*,[23] decided one year after *Shaw*, the Court addressed the problem of finding a benchmark by which to measure vote dilution, this time in the context of section 2 of the VRA. Ironically, the Court's attempt in *De Grandy* to loosen the three preconditions for establishing vote dilution—preconditions delineated in *Gingles*[24]—emphasizing that these preconditions were necessary but not sufficient for success in such a case, may have muddied, not clarified, section 2 jurisprudence. As a number of voting rights commentators have acknowledged, once groups are recognized as the criterion of political effectiveness, the simplest gauge of political or electoral success is results—equal group results. It is reasonable that proportional representation should become the measure of vote discrimination in cases under section 2 and section 5 of the VRA. If what counts under the new language of section 2 is the difference between the choices made by mi-

---

19. *Id.*
20. 106 S.Ct. 2752, 2773 (1986), opinion of the Court, emphasis added.
21. *Id.*, emphasis in original.
22. 114 S.Ct. 2647 (1994).
23. 114 S.Ct. 2581 (1994).
24. See *Gingles*, 106 S.Ct. at 2766–67, Brennan, J., opinion of the Court:
    First, the minority group must be able to demonstrate that it is sufficiently large and geographically compact to constitute a majority in a single-member district....Second, the minority group must be able to show that it is politically cohesive....Third, the minority must be able to demonstrate that the white majority votes sufficiently as a bloc to enable it—in the absence of special circumstances...usually to defeat the minority's preferred candidate.

norities and whites, not the causes of those choices, then the focus of analysis will be numerical differences. Vote dilution remedies, as Justice O'Connor pointed out in *Gingles*, will have to provide for minority electoral success in rough proportion to the minority population.[25] Similarly, in cases involving section 5, federal courts and the Department of Justice, restrained by the principle of nonretrogression,[26] will have to provide remedies to VRA violations that provide no less than what minorities had enjoyed under earlier electoral schemes. There will be a proclivity toward providing for increasingly proportionate representation of minority groups, since only an increase and not a decrease of such representation will pass the retrogression test. The Court's attempt, in *De Grandy*, to modify a strict proportionality test in the direction of a more lenient "totality of circumstances" test, where "substantial proportionality" appears to become the new litmus test of vote dilution, is consistent with the spirit of *Shaw* and the attempt to rein in affirmative action in voting rights. The decision, however, will likely provide little assistance to lower courts in search of a more judicially manageable standard than has prevailed since *Gingles*.

In *Holder*, the Court rejected the plaintiffs' claim because, among other things, there was no alternative practice which could be used as a benchmark against which to assess the voting practice at issue. But the question of what benchmark might contribute to a "fair" system of representation in cases in which a section 2 action was available was again left unresolved.

Ultimately, *De Grandy* and *Holder* invite speculation on whether the language of section 2(b) of the VRA is not itself inconsistent, providing, on the one hand, that the right to vote is violated where it can be shown that members of protected groups "have less opportunity than other members of the electorate to participate in the political process and to elect representatives of their choice," while, on the other hand, stipulating that nothing in section 2 grants a right to equal or proportional representation. Does the legislative history of the 1982 section 2 amendments reflect a compromise between antithetical theories of equality and representation—between an understanding of equality that provides for equal opportunity and unequal electoral results, and an understanding of equality that requires equal or proportional representation? If section 2 jurisprudence since 1982 has been inchoate, certainly blame for such a development cannot rest solely with the federal judiciary.

---

25. *Id.* at 2787, O'Connor, J., concurring.

26. See *Beer v. United States*, 425 U.S. 130, 141 (1976), establishing that proposed voting changes will not be precleared under section 5 if they lead to "a retrogression in the position of racial minorities with respect to their effective exercise of the electoral franchise" (opinion of the Court).

The intractable nature of voting rights jurisprudence, the inability of the Court to solve the riddle of equality and representation, providing coherent legal standards that will reconcile the Equal Protection Clause with the VRA, will likely persist into the next millennium. The numerous opinions in *Shaw v. Hunt* (*Shaw II*, 1996)[27] and *Bush v. Vera* (1996),[28] released immediately prior to this book going to press, highlight the difficulties future courts and legislators will likely have deciphering, as well as complying with, the Court's VRA law.

The essays in this collection, balancing contributions from advocates and critics of affirmative action in voting rights, focus on three issues that have emerged as determinative in 1990s voting rights litigation. The first, examined in Part II, is the significance of *Shaw* and post-*Shaw* jurisprudence. What does *Shaw* and its legacy augur for the future of voting rights? The second issue, addressed in Part III, examines alternative models of representation. This issue has become increasingly important as the Supreme Court has intensified its scrutiny of racial redistricting. Part IV investigates the little known, but significant, issue of the applicability of the VRA to judicial elections, an issue left unaffected by *Shaw*. Part V provides a brief postscript discussing the Court's rulings in *Shaw II* and *Bush*, with particular emphasis on Justice O'Connor's plurality and concurring opinions in *Bush*, the latter opinion being perhaps the most significant, if not curious, of any voting rights decision post-dating *Shaw*.

PART II
Shaw v. Reno and its Legacy

In the first chapter, Mark Rush argues that *Shaw* sent forth contradictory and confusing signals regarding how far states could take racial redistricting in their attempts at complying with the VRA. Reversing a trend that the Court appeared to establish in two decisions decided earlier in the 1993 term,[29] *Shaw* indicated a willingness on the part of the Court to challenge state attempts at compliance with the VRA where such attempts violated traditional districting principles and failed to provide compelling justification for doing so. Creating a new cause of action, an equal protection claim based on the bizarre shape of electoral districts, Rush maintains that determining the consistency of *Shaw* with earlier ju-

---

27. 64 U.S.L.W. 4437.
28. 64 U.S.L.W. 4452.
29. *Growe v. Emison*, 113 S.Ct. 1075 (1993) and *Voinovich v. Quilter*, 113 S.Ct. 1149 (1993).

risprudence is difficult because voting rights precedents themselves are muddled and inconsistent.

In addition to addressing old problems, *Shaw* created new problems of its own. Finding, for instance, that plaintiffs need only prove that a redistricting scheme was racially motivated and that palpable, direct injury did not have to be established, *Shaw* raised the issue of who would enjoy standing in voting rights cases, a question left open by the failure of the Court to define what precisely the right to vote consisted of.

Defining the right to vote remains the irresolvable dilemma of VRA litigation. Resurrecting old dissents from previous decisions to form a new basis for voting rights, *Shaw*, Rush contends, failed to resolve the tensions that have characterized voting rights litigation for over a generation, tensions between what does and does not constitute fair and effective representation, and, above all, between individual and group voting rights. By reasserting limits on remedial redistricting grounded on individual rights, while simultaneously upholding the constitutionality of race-based redistricting, making geographical coherence one of the indicia of constitutionally acceptable districting, *Shaw* insured that courts in future, compelled to assess state redistricting plans, would have to venture deeper into the political thicket of representational politics.

Timothy O'Rourke joins issue with Rush, advancing three propositions with respect to *Shaw*.

First, *Shaw* is wholly consistent with the core values of thirty years of reapportionment jurisprudence, both in emphasizing voting as an individual, as opposed to a group-based, right, and in recognizing the constitutional relevance of "traditional districting criteria." Thus, the dissenters in *Shaw* were wrong on two counts: in their insistence on gauging the fairness of redistricting plans solely in terms of racial proportionality (suggesting that if white voters enjoyed representation in proportion to their numbers, they had no cognizable grievance); and in their assertion that, in the absence of a constitutional requirement of compactness and contiguity, the shape of legislative districts is beyond judicial notice.

Second, O'Rourke argues that the shape of the districts at issue in *Shaw* attracted the Court's attention precisely because post-1990 redistricting had produced a "new look," which was the product of the convergence of three factors: (1) the constitutional requirement for virtually perfect population equality across congressional districts; (2) innovations in census and redistricting technology; and (3) the Justice Department's (mis)reading of the VRA to require maximization of majority-minority districts without regard to the limits imposed by traditional districting criteria.

O'Rourke's third proposition emerges from his application of traditional criteria to the districts in contention in *Shaw* and to those at issue in legal challenges to state congressional maps in Georgia, Louisiana, and Texas. A radical departure from traditional criteria, these districts violate the expectation—central to representative government—that districts be "cognizable" (to use Bernard Grofman's term) and facilitate communication between representative and constituents. To require, as the Justice Department did, the creation of geographically contorted, racially configured districts or to seek to legitimize such districts, as did the dissenters in *Shaw*, in terms of usual politics or racial justice is to challenge basic notions of fair representation and equal protection.

In Abigail Thernstrom's opinion, *Shaw* represents a change in judicial focus symbolic of a broader change in American society. Implicit in the Court's decision was an acknowledgement that racism is no longer the major threat to America's social and political health. Rather, racial and ethnic fragmentation, aggravated by policies such as racial redistricting, is the principal infirmity, threatening to transform the United States from a nation of individuals into a confederation of racial and ethnic groups.

Shaw represented a rejuvenation of constitutional actions that had been more or less absent from the Supreme Court's docket since its landmark decision in *City of Mobile v. Bolden* (1980).[30] But *Shaw* was a constitutional action with a twist, the issue no longer being fair and effective representation for racial and ethnic minorities, but whether the Equal Protection Clause placed constitutional limits on the very race-conscious redistricting that had been the remedy of choice in equal protection litigation and section 2 lawsuits after 1982.

Shaw's significance, according to Thernstrom, lays in its implicit challenge to Justice Blackmun's statement, in *Regents of the University of California v. Bakke*, that "In order to get beyond racism, we must first take account of race."[31] Although not altogether clear, Justice O'Connor's opinion nonetheless emphasized that districting that could "be viewed only as an effort to segregate the races for purposes of voting, without regard for traditional districting principles and without sufficiently compelling justification,"[32] was problematic. In *Miller*, Justice Kennedy further clarified that *Shaw* was not limited to evidence regarding a district's geometry but allowed plaintiffs to establish an equal protection claim on the basis of any evidence sufficiently establishing the assignment of voters to a district on the basis of race.

Thernstrom maintains that the Department of Justice has misconstrued sections 2 and 5 of the VRA and has been remiss in its administrative duties by turning over the enforcement of the act to civil rights

---

30. 446 U.S. 55.

31. 438 U.S. at 407, Blackmun, J., concurring.

32. *Shaw*, 113 S. Ct. at 2832, opinion of the Court.

groups, a development not lost on lower courts which have criticized the DOJ's excessively intimate relationship with advocates such as the ACLU. But the real issue at the heart of voting rights disputes is more fundamental than these problems of interpretation and enforcement. The real issue, Thernstrom claims, concerns the nature of American society. "At issue between the opposing sides are entirely different views of white racial attitudes, black opportunity, the nature of democratic representation, and the costs of race-conscious policies." Voting rights proponents often regard blacks as "a nation within a nation, a people apart." Although this may have been true in the past, it is not today. Racial redistricting risks becoming a permanent fixture in America's political landscape not only because few whites are willing to challenge black incumbents in black majority districts, exposing themselves to certain media criticism, or because the retrogression test of section 5, prohibiting a decline in black legislative seats once they have been created, will make it difficult to dismantle racially gerrymandered districts once established. Most precariously, racial redistricting risks becoming a permanent fixture because its underlying assumption—that America is comprised of two societies, one black and one white—may become a reality. To prevent such an eventuality, Thernstrom admonishes, judicial intervention is imperative.

For Anthony Peacock, the difficulty of reconciling the apparently antithetical concepts of equality underlying the VRA and the Equal Protection Clause goes a long way to explaining the split between the majority and minority in *Shaw*, and also goes some distance to explaining why the Court has been unable to expound a theory of representation consistent with VRA-equal protection jurisprudence. On Peacock's reading, if the Court is to overcome the conflict between the VRA and the Equal Protection Clause, it will have to settle upon a single constitutional understanding of equality.

Yet this will not resolve the problem of representation in voting rights litigation. An adequate account of representation, while accommodating the demands of group interests and individual constituents (the concern in most voting rights scholarship and jurisprudence), must also account for the role of the public interest in American representative government. The public interest and the problem of factious strife appeared to occupy the center of attention in *Shaw*, where the majority focused more on the structures or forms of representative government than on the political or electoral results of the representational process, the focus of attention in vote dilution jurisprudence. *Shaw* is unique in voting rights jurisprudence because, for the first time, the Court appeared to recognize the paradoxical effects of vote dilution law on the formal processes of representative government: that the desire to achieve certain electoral results had distorted the process or structure of political representation itself.

The very procedures that had developed to give minorities more political power through assured electoral outcomes were themselves creating political or structural inequalities. The task of future courts would be to insure that these inequalities were not further aggravated through the continuing erosion of the structural underpinnings of American republican government.

In *Shaw*, the Rehnquist Court grappled with the challenge to the constitutional forms of equality and representation that the VRA, in its post-1982 incarnation, presented. Displacing the source of decisionmaking power with respect to such fundamental political issues as the meaning of equality and the role of representation in American politics, the VRA, Peacock concludes, should not be approached as one choice among many about how to deal with the problem of voting rights, given a fixed constitutional regime. Rather, the act represents a choice between regime types themselves.

Contrary to VRA critics who suggest that racial redistricting is no longer necessary, Bernard Grofman objects that race-conscious remedies are still required because race-conscious voting continues to persist. To outlaw black majority districts on the pretence that they violate the Equal Protection Clause may not only misconstrue the intent of the Fourteenth Amendment but may retard the integration of legislative halls throughout the United States.

The new test for equal protection violations that *Shaw* created, one not based on reverse discrimination but on geographic aesthetics, established a new constitutional right with no clear standard of enforcement, threatening the electoral gains blacks and Hispanics have recently achieved. On Grofman's reading, *Shaw* raised a host of problems that have yet to be resolved. How are courts to determine when districts should be subject to strict scrutiny? How are they to determine when race is the predominant or exclusive factor determining the configuration of districts under challenge? When is a redistricting plan narrowly tailored to meet a compelling state interest? Is *Shaw* compatible with *Gingles* and subsequent VRA enforcement?

Although *Shaw* could have been decided on non-racial grounds, setting more exacting standards with respect to district contiguity and geographic cognizability, the decision nevertheless does not pose as serious a threat to minority representation as many voting rights experts believe because *Shaw*'s effects will not be that great on municipal and local districting. That said, the reasoning underlying *Shaw* may be misguided. The idea that minority-majority districts are politically or constitutionally unnecessary requires a harder look at the evidence.

Cataloguing the legislative gains of blacks and Hispanics, focusing on congressional elections since 1990, Grofman illustrates how the few cases in which black candidates succeeded in non-black majority districts were anomalies to the general rule that such districts were a precondition for black electoral success. This was particularly the case in the South, where in the absence of majority-minority districts, no black members of Congress would have been elected in 1990, 1992, or 1994.

Grofman concludes that the obvious danger that *Shaw* and subsequent *Shaw*-based jurisprudence poses is that courts may strip American legislatures of what little minority representation they currently enjoy— and this arguably on the basis of false assumptions about the source of such representation or the constitutionality of race-conscious remedies. As much as Americans may dislike the notion that race-based remedies are, in the 1990's, still necessary, racial redistricting is the only solution that provides for fair representation while recognizing the reality that underlies American electoral patterns.

In the last essay of Part II, Samuel Issacharoff suggests that the *Shaw* majority's attempt to rein in the excesses of race-based redistricting may not be confined to the excesses but may actually undermine the very essence of the districting process, challenging the system by which representatives are elected and dislodging thereby a fundamental building block of the American political order.

Failing to provide any real content to its invocation that the redistricting process must respect "traditional principles of districting" and exposing the Court's institutional integrity to suspicion by denying minority representation at the very moment African Americans appeared to have succeeded in figuring out the redistricting game, *Shaw* nevertheless addressed one of the most controversial aspects of voting rights jurisprudence, the unseemliness of "essentialism." Defined as state action that assumes "that individuals will share outlooks and interests simply on the basis of a single characteristic, such as race," essentialism was at the heart of the Supreme Court's 1977 decision, *United Jewish Organizations v. Carey*.[33] There the Court denied a claim by Hasidic Jews in Williamsburgh, New York, who had had their community split in half when a portion of their population was used to fill a majority black district in compliance with the terms of the VRA. The Court' logic, that the Hasidic community could take solace in the fact that, despite the dilution of its electoral power, it would be "virtually represented" in the state legislature by white Gentiles from other parts of the state, made the dubious assumption that the Hasidim was an undifferentiated group, indistinguishable from other white people.

Reexamining the logic of *UJO*, and challenging the last twenty years of voting rights jurisprudence, *Shaw* rejected the principle that race-conscious state action engaged to benefit disadvantaged groups was a per-

---

33. 430 U.S. 144.

missible state objective. Of particular concern to the *Shaw* majority was what Issacharoff refers to as the "filler people," those individuals who provide the "numerical chaff to the representational wheat of another group." This was the plight of two of the plaintiffs in *Shaw* who were used to fill the interstices between the African American population base of the North Carolina 12th Congressional District.

The irony of *Shaw* was that once the issue of the filler people was raised, the very process of districting, in which governmental actors determine who shall be the dominant groups in any constituency, became the focus of attention, subjecting the representational process to previously unparalleled scrutiny. In *Shaw*, the real issue was not so much "community" or "geography" but the unseemliness of any governmental authority drawing lines expressly designed to confer power on one group while suppressing another. Exposing the potential balkanizing effects of the VRA— an act that, following *Gingles*, paradoxically rewarded, rather than discouraged, racial segregation—*Shaw* accentuated the dilemma that all geographic districting poses where there are winners and losers. In raising the issue of the fairness of districting to heightened attention, the decision may have loosened a pillar of American representational politics.

PART III
Alternative Systems of Representation

The fairness of geographic representation is addressed by Lani Guinier. Guinier criticizes territorial districting and provides a defense of proportional representation. For her, the principal shortcoming of critics of racial redistricting is not so much that they have failed to identify a problem with the current state of representational politics, but that they have not thought the problem through to its logical conclusion. The problem is not race-conscious districting. It is districting *per se*. Winner-take-all territorial districting is unfair. The dominant group within a district gets all of the power, while the votes of nondominant groups are wasted. The inflated advantage of district control that the winner-take-all system allows, awards electoral majorities power disproportionate to their numbers. This creates incentives to determine who the electoral majority will be in any particular district—rendering, in effect, all districting, at some level, gerrymandering.

Guinier proposes a system of "one-vote, one-value," where each vote counts towards someone's election. The unit of representation is political, not regional, and the aggregating principle is proportionality, not winner-take-all.

Territorial districting cannot respect the natural contours of group representation because groups tend to be defined by a cultural and political community that extends beyond geographic boundaries. Although representational politics is necessarily group oriented—groups of voters electing representatives, not individuals—the individual right to vote must be respected in any system of representation. Territorial districting cannot realize individual autonomy because individuals often do not choose where they live. Even when they do, the range or salience of their interests is not geographically limited. Proportional or semi-proportional representation reconciles individual rights with group-based representation by eliminating the "losers" from the winner-take-all system, giving each vote the same value. In addition, proportional representation systems avoid the problem of partisan or racial gerrymandering by allowing voters to "district" themselves. By determining who their representatives will be from the bottom-up, voters self-district rather than relying on political incumbents, federal judges, and others to draft district lines on the basis of presumed group preferences and community interests.

Guinier observes that in systems respecting the principle of one-vote, one-value, voters choose their representational identity. The unit of representation is transformed from territorial or racial constituencies into political or psychological constituencies. One-person, one-value eliminates gerrymandering because it removes the disproportionate power of incumbents and others to determine electoral districts. Political participation is enhanced because everyone has an equal opportunity to influence political outcomes. The purpose of the VRA, to extend equal opportunities to minority groups to elect candidates of their choice, is attained in a way that does not offend the principles of equal protection or that denies non-minority voters a say in electoral outcomes. When all things are considered, non-territorial, proportional representation systems, even if periodically destabilizing by promoting legislative stalemate and chaos, are more principled, more equitable, systems of representation than what currently prevails in American politics.

Richard Engstrom, Jason Kirksey, and Edward Still propose that in the wake of the *Shaw* decision, which has rendered majority-minority districts an "endangered species," cumulative voting is a defensible alternative medium through which to provide minorities with electoral opportunities they otherwise would not enjoy.

Examining exit poll data from the 1992 November election of the Board of Commissioners in Chilton County, Alabama, the authors argue that the importance of the Chilton County cumulative voting experiment lays in its complexity. Whereas previous uses of cumulative voting were limited to three candidates and nonpartisan elections, the Chilton

County Commissioners election involved seven members elected at-large and parties running full slates of candidates.

Contrary to what many critics of cumulative voting assume, the exit poll data from the Chilton County election indicated that voters were neither confused nor dissatisfied with the new method of election. Under a cumulative voting system, voters get as many votes as there are seats in the election. They can cast more than one vote for the candidate of their choice and can "plump" votes—cast them all—for a single candidate. Significantly, over 90 percent of African-Americans participating in the Chilton County poll cast more than a single vote for at least one candidate, while less than 75 percent of whites did. 87.4 percent of African Americans reported plumping all seven votes for a single candidate compared to only half that number, 44.4 percent, for whites. Blacks exercised the cumulative voting option to support two black candidates. In the absence of cumulative voting, there is little likelihood that Chilton County's only black commissioner would have been reelected.

The authors also examined the Chilton County election data to determine how political parties that failed to attract a plurality of votes, as well as women, might fare under the cumulative voting system. Party identity appeared to have little effect on the evaluation of the cumulative system. Support for the only woman candidate in the election did not appear to be affected by the cumulative voting option, although white women were much less negative in their evaluation of the system than were white men.

Finally, the authors maintain that unlike single member districts, cumulative voting is not a race-specific remedy for minority vote dilution. Cumulative voting in elections such as the Chilton County experiment may generate white resentment and resistance because such systems, like that in Chilton County, are often imposed as a remedy for racial vote dilution. However, the only study that conducted similar polls during two consecutive cumulative voting elections found majority hostility to the cumulative system to decline over time. Chilton County, the authors contend, illustrates how cumulative voting can provide minority voters the opportunity to elect candidates of their choice, while at the same time enhancing, rather than inhibiting, the ability of other voters to express the intensity of their electoral preferences through the ballot.

PART IV
Judicial Elections and the Voting Rights Act

Although *Shaw* affected future voting rights jurisprudence in a way that no other decision since 1982 arguably has, the decision did not address whether judicial elections should continue to be covered by the VRA. In *Chisom v. Roemer* (1991),[34] the Supreme Court imperiled the process of judicial selection in 29 states by determining that the "results" test of section 2 of the act applied to the election of judges.

In the first chapter of Part IV, Ralph Rossum criticizes Justice Stevens' majority opinion in *Chisom* for misconstruing the language of section 2 and misreading its legislative history.

Section 2 provides that an election "standard, practice, or procedure" has a discriminatory result if minority citizens are found to "have less opportunity than other members of the electorate to participate in the political process and to elect representatives of their choice." Rossum highlights that Justice Stevens read section 2 in a manner contrary to lower federal court decisions that had determined that judges were not "representatives." Finding that the functions of judges were analytically distinct from the functions of representatives, courts in the Fifth and Sixth circuits had held that judges administer and interpret the law, whereas representatives make the law. Representatives are expected to be partisan and to re-present the views of their constituents. To the extent that judges represent anyone, they are not judges but partisans.

The federal appellate courts, hearing these cases on appeal, rejected this reasoning as too simple. Justice Stevens concurred. The spirit of the VRA and the 1982 amendments, he surmised, required a broad construction of section 2: if Congress had intended to withdraw judicial elections from the purview of the amended section, either it would have made such an intention explicit in the body of the statute or there would have been evidence of such an intention in the extensive legislative history of the section. The reference to "representatives" in section 2 would therefore be better read as referring to "the winners of representative popular elections," rather than as referring to the functions they perform. Judges were, Stevens concluded, covered by section 2.

Writing in dissent, Justice Scalia responded that Stevens' interpretation of section 2 was the product of judicial contrivance. Neither the ordinary meaning of the word "representatives" nor the text or structure of the VRA warranted Stevens' interpretation. Moreover, the absence, in the legislative history, of any discussion of the applicability of section 2 to judicial elections was perfectly understandable, since at no point in the discussions was it ever suggested that section 2 should apply to judges. To infer from this silence that Congress intended the VRA to apply to judges was to get legislative intent perfectly backwards. As Scalia emphasized: "[I]f the dog of legislative history has not barked

---

34. 111 S.Ct. 2354.

nothing of great significance can have transpired.... We have forcefully and explicitly rejected the Conan Doyle approach to statutory construction in the past.... We are here to apply the statute, not legislative history, and certainly not the absence of legislative history."[35]

Rossum suggests that the *Chisom* decision is exemplary of what Justice Thomas observed in *Holder*: that the Supreme Court's construction of section 2 has been based not on the words of the statute but on a partisan and misleading history of the legislation. Thomas' observation is especially apt in the case of judicial elections, which are exempt from the one-person, one-vote rule applicable to representatives.

The *Chisom* majority thought it knew better what Congress intended in amending section 2 than Congress itself knew. It suggested that the solution to subjecting judicial elections to the scrutiny of the VRA was to opt for judicial appointments and to do away with judicial elections altogether, a solution the irony of which was palpable: to ensure that minorities had an equal opportunity to elect judges of their choice, the Court condemned minorities as well majorities to having judges appointed for them. Failing the basic test of judicial construction, Rossum concludes, *Chisom* should be overturned.

Contrary to this conclusion, Frederick Slabach argues that judicial elections should be covered by the VRA. In three cases decided during the 1990 Supreme Court term, *Chisom, Clark v. Roemer*,[36] and *Houston Lawyers' Ass'n v. Attorney General*,[37] the Court erased any doubt that both section 2 and section 5 of the VRA applied to judicial elections. This was a salutary development in light of the history of the VRA and the 1982 amendments to the act. In addition, the history of judicial elections, which dates back to the nineteenth century, confirms that they were intended to make judges representatives of the people, responsive to the popular will.

Slabach observes that when the VRA was originally passed in 1965, Congress did not establish separate rules for kinds of elections based upon their purpose or object. Nor did it recognize such a distinction in the 1982 amendments to the act. As a unanimous Court in *Clark* pointed out, there is nothing in the language or history of section 5 that allows for distinctions to be made between judicial elections and other types of elections. Similarly, the *Chisom* Court highlighted that section 2, like the Fifteenth Amendment which it codifies, protects the right to vote without regard to the object of voting. Thus, any distinctions made respecting the applicability of section 2 to judicial elections are unwar-

35. *Id.*, 2370, dissenting.
36. 111 S.Ct. 2096 (1991).
37. 111 S.Ct. 2376 (1991).

ranted. *Houston Lawyers'* further clarified that section 2 was unitary, applying to all types of judicial elections.

To date, the Supreme Court has failed to provide a standard for measuring vote dilution in challenges to judicial elections. Does the same standard apply to judicial as to nonjudicial elections? This problem could be resolved, Slabach maintains, if the Court applied the one-person, one-vote principle to both types of elections. Failing that, the Court could apply the totality of circumstances test, as set out in *White v. Regester*[38] and *Zimmer v. McKeithen*,[39] and as codified in section 2(b) of the VRA.

In *Chisom*, the Court admonished that if jurisdictions did not want the VRA to apply to judicial elections, they could choose an appointive method of selection. Slabach cautions, however, that this alternative to judicial elections could be problematic. Changing from an electoral to an appointive method of judicial selection may be subject to the provisions of the VRA. On the Court's own logic—even though it apparently failed to recognize this—an electoral change, such as that contemplated here, would require either preclearance under section 5 or a vote dilution assessment under section 2. Such an eventuality, as undesirable as state governments might find it, would nevertheless be consistent with the spirit and letter of the VRA.

PART V
Postscript

The book concludes with a brief discussion by Anthony Peacock of *Shaw II* and *Bush*. Peacock focuses on Justice O'Connor's plurality and concurring opinions in *Bush*, anticipating that the latter may be both the most perplexing and the most significant opinion of any voting rights decision post-dating *Shaw*. In *Bush*, O'Connor determined that compliance with the "results test" of section 2 is a compelling state interest. The significance of this for future voting rights is not merely its apparent incommensurability with earlier equal protection law but its potential to undermine the ruling in *Shaw*, as well as the Court's later rulings in *Miller* and *Adarand*, should the four dissenting justices from the Texas and North Carolina cases join O'Connor in her assessment.

---

38. 412 U.S. 755 (1973).
39. 485 F.2d 1297 (5th Cir. 1973).

Part II

SHAW v. RENO
AND ITS LEGACY

CHAPTER 2

The Price of Unclear Precedents: *Shaw v. Reno* and the Evolution of Voting Rights Jurisprudence

Mark E. Rush

Shaw v. Reno,[1] where the Supreme Court remanded North Carolina's congressional redistricting plan because its excessive use of racial considerations was found to be violative of the Fourteenth Amendment, quickly garnered its fair share of criticism from both scholars and federal judges.[2] These criticisms focused primarily on two issues: 1) the role of the federal judiciary in supervising state redistricting processes and 2) the standards and rules that the courts will use in applying the Voting Rights Act (VRA) to vote dilution claims. With regard to the Court's role, *Shaw* seems to reverse the course taken in two decisions handed down earlier in the same term, *Growe v. Emison* and *Voinovich v. Quilter*,[3] where the Court contended that the state legislatures and courts were certainly capable of handling the VRA's intricacies and, therefore, the federal courts should give them a lot of leeway when they are seeking to comply with the Act. In *Shaw*, however the Court forayed back into the political thicket of representation rights despite indications by several of the Supreme Court justices that they wish to extract themselves from it and that they do not perceive the VRA to be an "all purpose" anti-discrimination tool.[4]

The lengths to which the Court has re-entered the thicket notwithstanding, *Shaw* was criticized as well because of the vagueness of the measures it established in order to determine whether a given redistricting plan was constitutional. According to one lower federal court, the

---

1. 113 S. Ct. 2816 (1993)

2. See, e.g., Pamela Karlan, *All Over the Map: The Supreme Court's Voting Rights Trilogy*, THE SUPREME COURT REVIEW (1994): 245; Symposium: *The Future of Voting Rights after Shaw v. Reno*, MICHIGAN LAW REVIEW (December, 1993).

3. 113 S. Ct. 1075 (1993) and 113 S. Ct. 1149 (1993), respectively.

4. See *Presley v. Etowah County*, 112 S. Ct. 820, 832 (1992); see also Thomas' dissent in *Holder v. Hall*, 114 S. Ct. 2581, 2602 (1994).

standard set forth by *Shaw* can be described as a "minuet" between the state and the plaintiff:

> if a plaintiff comes into court with a map bearing hideously contorted districts and evidence that the state legislature drew those districts on the basis of race, and if the plaintiff complains that those districts lack a non-racial explanation—i.e., cannot be explained or understood without hypothesizing racial gerrymandering—then the plaintiff has stated a prima facie case under *Shaw*. If the state then introduces evidence that tends to show that the legislature was actuated by other motives that can explain the bizarre contours of the districts without resorting to race, the state has created a competing inference. The factfinder must then decide, on the basis of all available evidence, who is right.[5]

These criteria require judges to decide whether a district's outline is so irregular as to be unexplainable on any grounds other than race. If the district is sufficiently bizarre, then, according to *Shaw*, the judges must continue their investigation in order to decide whether the racial considerations were justifiable in light of the VRA and whether, in seeking to comply with the VRA, the state tailored its remedial redistricting plan as narrowly as possible. The issue of narrow tailoring was especially controversial; while the *Shaw* majority contended essentially that individuals have a right to participate in a colorblind electoral process, the dissenters responded that the Court created a new cause of action whereby any voter could challenge remedial redistricting legislation. Whether this was a new cause of action or merely the Court's bringing its voting rights decisions in line with the rest of its equal protection jurisprudence remained a matter of debate among the Justices. Similarly, the extent to which the *Shaw* decision breaks with precedent or merely augments it formed the focus of the disputes among the Justices and a subject of scholarly criticism.

It is my contention that *Shaw*'s fidelity to precedent is not a fruitful topic of debate precisely because the precedents are so unclear regarding the Court's role in voting rights cases, the definition and balancing of individual and group voting rights, and the establishment of a clear notion of representational denial, that it is hard to discern what precedent would require. Justice O'Connor contended that *Shaw* addressed nothing less than "the meaning of the constitutional "right" to vote, and the propriety of race-based state legislation designed to benefit members of historically disadvantaged racial minority groups."[6] Yet, despite this acknowledgment, the Court came no closer to stating clearly what, *exactly*,

---

5. *Hays v. Louisiana*, 839 F. Supp 1188, 1198 (1993).
6. *Shaw* at 2819.

comprised its vision of the right to vote than it had in previous cases. There is no doubt that the Court added to the right's substance by creating, in the words of Justice Souter, a "new cause of action"[7] by which any individual voter could challenge the constitutionality of a remedial redistricting scheme under the equal protection clause. However, the debates which developed among the Justices indicated clearly that they have yet to reach a consensus regarding the substance of the right to vote, the right to fair and effective representation, and the use of measures to determine when either has been breached.

The Meandering Course of *Shaw's* Precedents

A significant part of the debate between Justices O'Connor and White addressed whether the Court adhered to *Whitcomb v. Chavis* and *UJO v. Carey*,[8] where the Court had addressed vote dilution claims, and to *Thornburg v. Gingles*[9] in which it established its three-prong test for assessing the merits of minority challenges to multimember districts brought under the auspices of the VRA. These precedents are vague and characterized by strong differences of opinion that were stated in language similar to that used by the Justices in *Shaw*. In fact, the language of old dissents was resurrected to form the basis for the new opinion of the Court in *Shaw*. Thus, it is not accurate to look upon the decision as a break with precedent; instead, it can be regarded as another step in the Court's development of a voting rights jurisprudence. Even if the Court were able to resolve the immediate issue in *Shaw*—that of ascertaining a set of consistent districting criteria—the larger issue of deciding what exactly counts as fair representation remains. The Court's decisions since *Baker v. Carr* have provided, in a piecemeal manner, statements which indicate the sort of representational structures we *do not* want—or which the Court will not tolerate. The Court has struck down malapportioned legislative districts,[10] the poll tax,[11] racial or partisan gerrymandering,[12] limited the hurdles that states may place in the path of voter registration,[13] and suggested that some electoral systems may have discriminatory impacts on

---

7. *Id.* at 2845.

8. 403 US 124 (1971) and 430 US 144 (1976), respectively.

9. 478 US 30 (1986).

10. *Baker v. Carr*, 369 US 186 (1962) and *Reynolds v. Sims* 377 US 533 (1964).

11. *Harper v. Virginia Board of Elections*, 383 US 663 (1966).

12. *Davis v. Bandemer* 478 US 109 (1986).

13. *Katzenbach v. Morgan*, 384 US 641 (1966).

particular voting groups.[14] But, this ad hoc process of weeding out the bad has not been complemented with either firm or consistent assertions about good districting criteria or clear statements about representation rights in general.

Shaw's Impact on Thornburg v. Gingles

According to *Shaw*, "a state [has] the right to create a majority-minority congressional district by racial gerrymandering...but only if the state does it right."[15] Insofar as the Court was willing to consider a challenge to the North Carolina districting map on the grounds that two of the districts were so bizarrely shaped that they could be explained only on the basis of race, it concluded in this case that North Carolina had not, in fact, done it right. It *did not*, however, argue that remedial gerrymandering was always unconstitutional. Instead, the Court contended that there were limits to the measures a state could employ in seeking to enhance opportunities for minority representation: "This Court never has held that race-conscious state decisionmaking is impermissible in *all* circumstances. What appellants object to is redistricting legislation that is so extremely irregular on its face that it rationally can be viewed only as an effort to segregate the races for purposes of voting without regard for traditional districting principles and without compelling justification."[16] Thus, a redistricting plan could not be the product simply of a desire to create racially safe districts:

> In some exceptional cases, a reapportionment plan may be so highly irregular that, on its face, it rationally cannot be understood as anything other than an effort to "segregate...voters" on the basis of race...*Gomillion*, in which a tortured municipal boundary line was drawn to exclude black voters, was such a case. So, too, would be a case in which a State concentrated a dispersed minority population in a single district by disregarding traditional districting principles such as compactness, contiguity, and respect for political subdivisions. We emphasize that these criteria are important not because they are constitutionally required—they are not...but because they are objective factors that may serve to defeat a claim that a district has been gerrymandered on racial lines.[17]

---

14. *Thornburg v. Gingles*, 478 US 60 (1986) and *White v., Regester*, 412 US 735 (1973).

15. *Hays*, at 1188.

16. *Shaw* at 2824.

17. *Shaw* at 2826–27.

While this was a clear statement of principle, it ensured confusion because, in *Shaw*, the Court sustained this *individual* claim as a basis for restricting the attempts taken by North Carolina to advance minority *group* voting rights under the auspices of the VRA. In so doing, it employed the test it had established in *Thornburg v. Gingles*, but arrived at a radically different outcome.

In *Gingles*, the Court set forth criteria for determining whether a minority had made a feasible claim under section 2 of the VRA. In order to bring a viable vote dilution claim under section 2 of the VRA, a plaintiff minority group must prove that "first...it is sufficiently large and geographically compact to constitute a majority in a single member district...Second, the minority group must be able to show that it is politically cohesive...Third, the minority must be able to demonstrate that the white majority votes sufficiently as a bloc to enable it—in the absence of special circumstances...usually to defeat the minority's preferred candidate."[18] *Gingles* actually dealt with the constitutionality of multimember districts, however the Court had also applied essentially the same criteria to single-member districts (such as those at issue in *Shaw*) in *Growe v. Emison*.[19]

The *Shaw* Court relied heavily on the *Gingles* compactness criterion to strike down North Carolina's congressional districting plan. The Court's rationale was deceptively simple: there *are* limits to the VRA's applicability,[20] and a redistricting plan that would not be feasible under the *Gingles* three-prong test will not withstand the rigors of strict scrutiny. Put differently, if it could be argued that a minority group was too dispersed to make a viable vote dilution claim under *Gingles'* section 2 test, then a state which attempted to draw districts in a manner that would aggregate such a dispersed minority in order to make it a district-wide majority would be in violation of the Fourteenth Amendment's equal protection clause.

While this use of the *Gingles* test was controversial because it used the test's criteria *against* a state that was attempting to comply with the VRA, it was also quite confusing because it signaled a further foray into the voting rights thicket despite the decisions in *Growe* and *Voinovich*

---

18. *Thornburg*, 478 US at 50–51.

19. 113 S. Ct. at 1084 (1993); See also *Voinovich* at 1157 (1993).

20. See the Court's discussion in *Presley v. Etowah County*, 112 S. Ct. 820, 832 (1992): "The Voting Rights Act is not an all-purpose antidiscrimination statute. The fact that the intrusive mechanisms of the Court do not apply to other forms of pernicious discrimination does not undermine its utility in combating the specific evils it was designed to address."

which evinced a judicial desire to retreat. As the Court stated in *Voinovich*: "Federal courts are barred from intervening in state apportionment in the absence of a violation of federal law precisely because it is the domain of the States, and not the federal courts, to conduct apportionment in the first place."[21] Thus, while *Growe* and *Voinovich* may have signaled a desire on the Court's part to extract itself and the federal courts from the voting rights thicket, *Shaw* indicated that the Court was not willing to do so if the methods by which the states sought to implement and adhere to the VRA presented other, *bona fide* questions of electoral fairness.

Despite the mixed signals concerning the Court's role in redistricting cases, the opinion of the Court in *Shaw* did have firm roots in *Gingles*. In fact, O'Connor drew from her concurrence in *Gingles* in order to set forth the limits she prescribed in *Shaw*. In the former, she contended:

> The Court's definition of the elements of a vote dilution claim is simple and invariable: a court should calculate minority voting strength by assuming that the minority group is concentrated in a single-member district in which it constitutes a voting majority. Where the majority group is not large enough, geographically concentrated enough, or politically cohesive enough for this to be possible, the minority group's claim fails.[22]

In *Shaw*, O'Connor reminded us that a minority group *could* fail the *Gingles* test. Thus, a state could not create a district which would not be regarded as feasible if it had been proposed by a minority plaintiff under the auspices of section 2 of the VRA.

Equal Protection and the Resuscitation of Individual Voting Rights

The majority's acceptance of the premise that *Shaw* presented an equal protection issue is indeed a turning point in the development of the Court's jurisprudence of voting rights. Asserting that the race of the *plaintiffs* was not an issue, the Court cited a long line of equal protection precedents which "require[d] state legislation that expressly distinguishes among citizens because of their race to be narrowly tailored to further a compelling governmental interest.[23] The key consideration was not

---

21. 113 S. Ct. at 1156.
22. *Gingles*, 478 US at 90.
23. *Shaw* at 2825.

whether the plaintiffs could show a palpable injury,[24] but that the redistricting scheme was racially motivated:

> [W]e believe that reapportionment is one area in which appearances do matter. A reapportionment plan that includes in one district individuals who belong to the same race, but who are otherwise widely separated by geographical and political boundaries, and who may have little in common with one another but the color of their skin, bears an uncomfortable resemblance to political apartheid.[25]

Having said this, the Court spoke for the first time in some years of *individual* voting rights and representation and urged that the unrestrained creation of majority-minority districts was "antithetical to our system of representative democracy." Citing Justice Douglas' dissent in *Wright v. Rockefeller*, the Court took a decidedly individualistic stance regarding voting rights: "Here the individual is important, not his race, his creed or his color. The principle of equality is at war with the notion that District A must be represented by a Negro, as it is with the notion that District B must be represented by a Caucasian, District C by a Jew, District D by a Catholic, and so on..."[26]

Justice Souter, in dissent, contended that the Court had always maintained a special equal protection approach to redistricting cases *precisely* because racial considerations were naturally involved and because, as the majority noted, appearances do matter. However, Souter maintained that this exceptional approach to matters of equal protection in gerrymandering claims was not problematic. The key distinction in redistricting cases, he stated, is the impact of the VRA: "in electoral redistricting there frequently are permissible uses of race, such as its use to comply with the Voting Rights Act, as well as impermissible ones. In determining whether a use of race is permissible in cases in which there is a bizarrely-shaped district, we can readily look to its effects, just as we would in any other electoral districting scheme."[27]

The equal protection standard erected by the *Shaw* majority resembles that set forth by Justice Powell in *Bakke*[28] where the Court declared racial quotas unconstitutional but then turned and permitted the use of race as a consideration in the medical school admissions process. *Shaw* states that too much racial consideration is unconstitutional, but fails to say exactly where the line between the permissible and impermissible use

---

24. See Karlan, *All Over the Map*, 278.

25. 113 S. Ct. at 2827.

26. 376 US 52, 66–67 (1964).

27. *Shaw* at 2848, note 7.

28. *Regents of Universtiy of California v. Bakke*, 438 US 265 (1978).

of race lies. Whereas *Bakke* could claim to have been injured by the University of California's employment of quotas, there appeared to be no basis for such a claim in *Shaw* because, as Justice Souter pointed out, the plaintiffs were *not* denied their right to vote: "In districting...the mere placement of an individual in one district instead of another denies no one a right or benefit provided to others. All citizens may register, vote, and be represented. In whatever district, the individual voter has a right to vote in each election, and the election will result in the voter's representation."[29] Accordingly, the issue of standing arose insofar as the Court had to establish a cause of action for the *Shaw* plaintiffs.

Any controversy concerning standing first addresses whether a given plaintiff has suffered a palpable and distinct injury. However, since the Court has never clearly stated what it considers to be the substance of the voting right *per se*, the question of who has standing in a voting rights case remains open. In *Shaw* the majority's vision seems to be a hybrid drawn from *Gomillion v. Lightfoot*[30] and *Bakke*. The white plaintiffs in *Shaw* had as much of an equal protection claim as the black plaintiffs did in *Gomillion*. The right to vote was abridged in neither case: only the right to vote *in a particular jurisdiction* was.[31] Whereas, *Gomillion*'s egregiousness was clear, the Justices' rationale in that case was not. Although *Gomillion* appeared to have been decided as a vote *denial* case on the basis of the Fifteenth Amendment, the Justices did in fact approach—and later regard—it as a Fourteenth Amendment case. In *Karcher v. Daggett*, Justice Stevens pointed this out:

> Although the [*Gomillion*] Court explicitly rested its decision on the Fifteenth Amendment, the analysis in Justice Whittaker's concurring opinion—like Justice Clark's in *Wesberry*—is equally coherent...Moreover the Court has subsequently treated *Gomillion* as though it had been decided on equal protection grounds...
>
> *Gomillion* involved complete geographical exclusion of a racially identified group. But, in case after case arising under the Equal Protection Clause the Court has suggested that "dilution" of the voting strength of cognizable *political* as well as racial groups may be unconstitutional.[32]

---

29. *Id.* 2846.

30. 364 US 339 (1960).

31. See Mark E. Rush, DOES REDISTRICTING MAKE A DIFFERENCE, 18 (Johns Hopkins, 1993); see also Justice Whittaker's assertion in *Gomillion*: "No one has the right to vote in a political division," 364 US at 349 (1960).

32. *Karcher* at 748–49, citations omitted, emphasis in original.

Insofar as the Justices decided that denial of the opportunity to vote as part of a local majority in a given municipality constituted an injury and justifiable claim, the plaintiffs in *Gomillion* had standing to sue.

In *Shaw* the justifiable claim had to be ascertained in a similar manner. The showing of injury is similar to that manifested in taxpayer lawsuits, such as *Flast v. Cohen*[33] and equal protection cases such as *Bakke*. In *Flast*, the Court sustained a challenge to government programs which provided religious education funding even though the plaintiffs could not show that they suffered any direct injury. However, the Court maintained that if it could be shown that the government was behaving in a patently unconstitutional manner—in this case, in violation of the First Amendment—then plaintiffs would be regarded as having standing. Although the *Shaw* plaintiffs could not show that they had suffered any tangible damage, the Court regarded the excessive use of racial considerations in redistricting as a breach of the 14th Amendment equatable with the breach of the First that occurred in *Flast*.

Of course, a key difference between *Gomillion* and *Shaw* lay in the fact that the VRA had been passed and amended in the period between the two. The Justices in *Shaw* all acknowledged that the VRA imposed a special burden—one that did not exist at the time of *Gomillion*—on the states to pass remedial redistricting legislation. However, the Court maintained as well that compliance with the VRA did not give states "*carte blanche* to engage in racial gerrymandering in the name of nonretrogression."[34] Accordingly, in *Shaw*, Congress' desire to enhance group rights to representation under the auspices of the VRA encountered the limits established in *Gomillion* upon any such race-conscious legislation.

The Price of Unclear Precedents: The Ghosts of *UJO* and *Whitcomb*

The differences of opinion in the *Shaw* Court indicate little more than that the Court was as divided a quarter-century ago as it is now regarding representation rights. A key point of contention was whether or not *UJO v. Carey* should or could have controlled *Shaw*. In *UJO*, the Court dispensed with a challenge to the New York state legislative apportionment scheme brought by Hasidic Jews on grounds similar to those upon which the plaintiffs brought their case in *Shaw*. Justice White argued

---

33. 398 US 83 (1968).
34. *Shaw* at 2831.

that the *Shaw* majority chose not to overrule but to "sidestep" the *UJO* decision by creating an artificial distinction between the two cases. Justice O'Connor described *UJO* as a white vote-dilution complaint and *Shaw* as an equal protection claim:

> [N]othing in the Court's highly fractured decision in *UJO* . . . forecloses the claim that we recognize today . . . it resembles [*Shaw*] [b]ut the cases are critically different in another way. The plaintiffs in *UJO* . . . did not allege that the plan, on its face, was so highly irregular that it rationally could be understood only as an effort to segregate voters by race . . . The *UJO* plaintiffs [claimed] that the New York plan impermissibly 'diluted' their voting strength."[35]

However, if we look at the opinion of the Court in *UJO*, we find that, in fact, the *Shaw* majority is either misinformed or disingenuous. Intriguingly, Justice White wrote the *UJO* opinion where he stated: "Petitioners argue that the New York Legislature, although seeking to comply with the Voting Rights Act as construed by the Attorney General, has violated the Fourteenth and Fifteenth Amendments by deliberately revising its reapportionment along racial lines."[36]

Thus, O'Connor and White's disagreement about the meaning of *UJO* is central to understanding *Shaw*. Insofar as the Court stated in *UJO* that "the Constitution does not prevent a State subject to the Voting Rights Act from deliberately creating or preserving black majorities in particular districts in order to ensure that its reapportionment plan complies with section 5,"[37] it would seem to support states' attempts to draw district lines. The *Shaw* Court, however, contended that

> *UJO* set forth a standard under which white voters can establish unconstitutional vote dilution. But it did not purport to overrule *Gomillion* or *Wright*. Nothing in the decision precludes white voters (or voters of any other race) from bringing the analytically distinct claim that a reapportionment plan rationally cannot be understood as anything other than an effort to segregate citizens into separate voting districts on the basis of race without sufficient justification.[38]

In this respect, *Shaw did* break with *UJO* because the Court contended that it would not regard a redistricting plan as "narrowly tailored" if it did more than the VRA required to enhance minority representation. In contrast, White argued in *UJO* that "the permissible use of

---

35. *Id.* at 2830.
36. 430 US 144, 155.
37. *Id.* at 161.
38. *Shaw* at 2829–2830.

racial criteria is not confined to eliminating the effects of past discriminatory districting or apportionment."[39]

A closer inspection of *UJO* indicates, however, that the *Shaw* Court paid closer attention to it than White suggests. While *UJO* found that the New York reapportionment scheme was acceptable, the Court still maintained that a tension did exist between the VRA's goals and the Constitution: "Whether or not the plan was authorized by or was in compliance with section 5 of the Voting Rights Act, New York was free to do what it did as long as it did not violate the Constitution, particularly the Fourteenth and Fifteenth Amendments."[40] Thus, in *UJO*, White made essentially the same argument that he made in *Shaw*:

> There is no doubt that in preparing the 1974 [reapportionment] legislation, the State deliberately used race in a purposeful manner. But its plan represented no racial slur or stigma with respect to whites or any other race, and we discern no discrimination violative of the Fourteenth Amendment nor any abridgment of the right to vote on account of race within the meaning of the Fifteenth Amendment.
>
> It is true that New York deliberately increased the nonwhite majorities in certain districts in order to enhance the opportunity for election of nonwhite representatives from those districts. Nevertheless, there was no fencing out of the white population from participation in the political process of the county, and the plan did not minimize or unfairly cancel out white voting strength.[41]

In response, however, Chief Justice Burger urged that the opposite was, indeed, the case: "The record before us reveals—and it is not disputed—that this is precisely what took place here. In drawing up the reapportionment scheme, the New York Legislature did not consider racial composition as merely *one* of several political characteristics; on the contrary, race appears to have been the one and only criterion applied."[42] Thus, despite Justice White's contention, *Shaw* does not necessarily represent a new cause of action. Instead, it represents a reconsideration of a cause of action that failed to win the sympathy of a majority of the Justices in the *UJO* decision.

In *Shaw*, White found himself in the same position in which Justices Frankfurter and Rutledge found themselves in cases such as *Baker*, *Reynolds* and *White v. Regester*: positions which once enjoyed the support of a majority of the Court were now relegated to lonely dissents.

---

39. *UJO* at 161.
40. *Id.*, at 165.
41. *Id.*
42. *Id.* at 181.

While White complains because key precedents which he wrote were being overturned or ignored by *Shaw*, he fails to acknowledge that those same cases served to overrule prior opinions which have been resurrected in *Shaw* by O'Connor.

Whitcomb and the Question of Denial of Representation

Although *Whitcomb* differs from *Shaw* because the former concerned the constitutionality of the use of *multimember, state legislative* districts by Indiana, the opinion of the Court, again delivered by Justice White, addressed a central question of the latter: what constitutes 1) a fair electoral process and 2) viable grounds to have standing to challenge a districting scheme on the basis that it is unfair? Insofar as the black plaintiffs in *Whitcomb* were unable to show that the multimember district scheme in that case had actually diminished their ability to elect a favored candidate, White argued that there were no grounds for challenging it: "The mere fact that one interest group or another concerned with the outcome of Marion County elections has found itself outvoted and without legislative seats of its own provides no basis for invoking constitutional remedies where, as here, there is no indication that this segment of the population is being denied access to the political system."[43]

Here, we have another key connection to *Shaw*. White argues in the latter decision that the white plaintiffs in *Shaw* could not show that they had experienced a dilution of their influence or ability to elect their candidates. Furthermore, insofar as the white plaintiffs could do nothing more than prove that they might vote for a candidate who loses an election, White argued in *Shaw*—as he did in *Whitcomb* that there is no right to gain legislative influence when you fail to win an election: "a group's power to affect the political process does not automatically dissipate by virtue of an electoral loss. Accordingly, we have asked that an identifiable group demonstrate more than mere lack of success at the polls to make out a successful gerrymandering claim."[44]

White made this same point in both *UJO* and *Whitcomb*, where he contended that "the individual voter in the *district with a nonwhite majority* has no constitutional complaint merely because his candidate has lost out at the polls and his district is represented by a person for whom he did not vote. Some candidate, along with his supporters, always

---

43. 403 US 154–155.
44. *Shaw* at 2835.

loses."[45] Similarly, Justice Souter echoed this sentiment in his *Shaw* dissent. Instead of focusing on group rights as the basis for representation, he addressed representation as an *individual* issue in order to dispense with the plaintiffs' claim that they had somehow been denied a fair representational opportunity by being subjected to a racially-motivated remedial gerrymander: "in whatever district, the individual voter has a right to vote in each election, and the election will result in the voter's representation."[46]

In reflecting various elements from *Gomillion, Whitcomb* and *UJO*, *Shaw* exposes the tension that exists among the three. The respective precedents' vision of the voting right are not easily reconciled, because they maintain, yet do not resolve the doctrinal strain between individual and group voting rights.

The Multifaceted Voting Right

While the Court maintained that remedial gerrymandering was necessary to counter the existence of group vote dilution that formed the underpinning of the decisions in *UJO, Whitcomb* and *Gingles*, it cast this as being in tension with the *individual* right to participate in a fair electoral process which the Court established in *Gomillion*. Critics may argue that by passing the VRA, Congress has endorsed a group-based vision of representation rights.[47] However, the VRA does not extend to all aspects of the Court's electoral process jurisprudence. If we expand our focus, it becomes clear that the Court has established and protected a durable individual voting right independent of its VRA decisions.[48]

In cases such as *Burdick v. Takushi, Tashjian v. Republican Party of Connecticut*, and *Williams v. Rhodes*,[49] the Court established and protected the individual voter's rights to participate in an open and essentially unencumbered political process. While these cases all usually addressed the conflict between individual voters' access to the ballot or to party primaries on the one hand and political parties' associational

---

45. *UJO* at 166, citing *Whitcomb* at 153–160, italics added.

46. *Shaw* at 2846.

47. See, generally, Lani Guinier, *(E)racing Democracy: The Voting Rights Cases*, HARVARD LAW REVIEW 108: (1994) 109.

48. See, e.g., Mark E. Rush, *Voters' Rights and the Legal Status of American Political Parties*, THE JOURNAL OF LAW AND POLITICS 9: (Spring, 1993) 487; see also Daniel Hays Lowenstein, *Associational Rights of Major Political Parties: A Skeptical Inquiry*, TEXAS LAW REVIEW 71: (June 1993) 1741.

49. 112 S. Ct. 2059 (1992), 479 US 208 (1986) and 393 US 23 (1968), respectively.

rights on the other, the one unifying theme running throughout the decisions is that *voters qua individuals* have certain inalienable rights which exist independent of their group affiliations.[50] In *Shaw*, this individual right to an open and meaningful political process collided with the VRA's desire to enhance group rights.

Shaw thus exposes the tension between group and individual voting rights as well as the Court's desire not to sacrifice one or the other. For the most part, the Court has spoken of group voting rights only in terms of *their not being diluted*. Hence in *Gingles* and *Davis v. Bandemer*,[51] it set forth standards concerning the grounds on which a claim of group vote dilution by gerrymander could be lodged. Nonetheless, such assertions about what fair representation *is not* do not form the basis for a coherent jurisprudence.

Any discussion of the wisdom of the Court's foraging through the political thicket of representation must be conducted against a backdrop colored by the observations and warnings made by Justice Frankfurter some thirty years ago. In *Baker v. Carr*, he contended that in reapportionment cases, "[w]hat is actually asked of the Court...is to choose among competing bases of representation—ultimately, really, among competing bases of political philosophy—in order to establish an appropriate frame of government for the state of Tennessee and thereby for all the States in the Union."[52] Frankfurter's concerns about the limits of the Court's ability to resolve the representation issue have been vindicated by both the issues' complexity and the Court's development of confusing and contradictory lines of precedents. Insofar as "the Court...is in part the maker of the tradition that influences it,"[53] the *Shaw* decision exposes a Court which appears to have cornered itself.

There is, however, no obvious or uncontroversial method for balancing the two rights. On the one hand, *Shaw* suggests that the Justices may be ready to go further into the political thicket in order to reassess the vision of representation which has underpinned their approach to redistricting cases. By suggesting that the limits on the use of remedial redistricting were grounded on individual rights, the majority not only contradicted the spirit of *Gingles*, but also ensured that it would remain active in VRA decisions despite its contentions in *Voinovich* and *Growe* that it was willing to give states the benefit of the doubt.

---

50. See, e.g., Rush, *Voters' Rights* and Lowenstein, *Associational Rights of Major Political Parties*.

51. 478 US 109 (1986).

52. *Baker* at 300.

53. Bickel, THE SUPREME COURT AND THE IDEA OF PROGRESS (Yale University Press, 1978), 87.

The Continued Absence of Coherence

Currently, the Court seems to be caught between the conflicting desires to back out of the thicket and to continue to balance its protection of group and individual voting rights. The Court's dicta also cover so much ground that it is hard to tell exactly what it envisions as the nature and substance of the voting right. For example, in *Shaw* the Court engaged in broad but telling discussions about the nature and form of representation. In contending that racial gerrymandering's balkanization of constituencies sends the wrong message to legislators, the *Shaw* Court moved even further away from a group-oriented approach to redistricting: "when a district obviously is created solely to effectuate the perceived common interests of one racial group, elected officials are more likely to believe that their primary obligation is to represent only the members of that group rather than their constituency as a whole."[54] Such a statement risks deeper and more complicated entanglement in the political thicket by suggesting that the relationship between a representative and his constituents is now fair game for the Court to consider in weighing the merits of a redistricting claim. It also indicates that the Court may in fact be adding new dimensions to its reasoning that, heretofore, had been the province of lower courts and courts of other nations.[55] Already, the implications of this mindset are manifesting themselves in the lower courts.

In *Prosser v. Elections Board*,[56] for example, Republican legislators challenged the reapportionment of the Wisconsin legislature on the grounds that it violated the VRA by wasting black votes and because it was characterized by unacceptably large population discrepancies. In ordering the draft of a new apportionment plan, the court discussed the relationship between a district's size and other characteristics and the representative's ability to speak for it in the assembly:

> To be an effective representative, a legislator must represent a district that has a reasonable homogeneity of needs and interests; otherwise, the

---

54. *Shaw* at 2827. For a further discussion of the relationship between a district's shape and the behavior of its representative, see Daniel Polsby and Robert D. Popper, *The Third Criterion: Compactness as a Procedural Safeguard against Partisan Gerrymandering*, 9 YALE LAW AND POLICY REVIEW 301 (1991).

55. In several recent Canadian cases concerning the drawing of electoral boundaries, the issue of a representative's ability to cater to the needs of constituents who lived in a very large, but sparsely populated district was addressed at several points. See, *Ref. re: Electoral Boundaries Commission Acts* 81 D. L. R. (4th) 16 (1991); *Re: Dixon and Attorney-General of British Columbia* 59 D. L. R. (4th) 246 (1989).

56. 793 F. Supp. 859 (W. D. Wis. 1992).

> policies he supports will not represent the preferences of most of his constituents...Compactness and contiguity...reduce travel time and costs, and therefore make it easier for candidates in the legislature to campaign for office and once elected to maintain close and continuing contact with the people they represent. (793 F. Supp 863 (W. D. Wis. 1992).

While this clearly represents a new line of judicial inquiry, the fact that it exists at all indicates that courts have expanded their vision of what constitutes fair and effective representation to include more than simply the attempt to maintain group representational opportunity.

In *Shaw*'s wake, the Fifth Circuit court not only challenged the direction in which the Court had moved in the wake of *Gingles*, but sought as well to resurrect the measure of vote dilution employed by Justice White in *Whitcomb*. In *LULAC v. Clements*,[57] Judge Higginbottom challenged the rationale set forth in *Thornburg* by Justice Brennan. Brennan had argued that "it is the difference between choices made by blacks and whites *alone*...that is the central inquiry of section 2 [of the Voting Rights Act]." Thus, other factors which may have led to a minority's defeat at the polls were rendered virtually irrelevant. Higginbottom challenged the insularity of this approach:

> failures of a minority group to elect representatives of its choice that are attributable to "partisan politics" provide no ground for relief. Section 2 is "a balm for racial minorities, not political ones—even though the two often coincide...." The Voting Rights Act does not guarantee that nominees of the Democratic Party will be elected, even if black voters are likely to favor that party's candidates." Rather, section 2 is implicated only where Democrats lose because they are black, not because they are Democrats. (855)

When we recall that same court's description of the *Shaw* standard as a minuet,[58] it becomes clear that the Supreme Court's voting rights decisions have done little to propagate a coherent jurisprudence and much to elicit frustrated responses from lower courts.

The frustration is hardly novel. In the wake of the *UJO* decision, the Fifth circuit complained as well. In *Kirksey v. Board of Supervisors of Hinds County*, Judge Gee expressed his frustration with the *UJO* decision.

> Doubtless, the Court holds a coherent vision of better things to come which is denied me. At any rate, I am sustained by the recollection that it is not for us to pursue matters of national policy in competition with

---

57. 999 F.2d 831 (5th Cir. 1993). Although *LULAC* dealt specifically with judicial elections, its reading of the impact of the Voting Rights Act resonates well with the opinion of the Court in *Shaw*.

58. *Hays* at 1198.

or obstruction of the Court. Where relevant precedent exists, our duty is to ascertain and obey that which is closest and most recent. For the time being, that is *United Jewish Organizations*. Since it is, I concur in the en banc court's judgment invalidating those of our panel and the district court, though not in its opinion.[59]

Summary: The Limits of Representation?

Justice Frankfurter's augury in *Baker* still haunts the Court's redistricting decisions: "a hypothetical claim resting on abstract assumptions is now for the first time made the basis for affording illusory relief for a particular evil even though it foreshadows deeper and more pervasive difficulties in consequence."[60] The *Shaw* majority's willingness to reassess the use of remedial gerrymandering indicates perhaps, that the Court may now be reconsidering whether or not the relief afforded by such measures is indeed illusory. What remains to be seen is whether the Court will seek to exit the political thicket gracefully or cast Frankfurter's prophecies to the wind.

So long as the Court emphasizes group voting rights, the continued use by the states and Congress of single member districts as the basis for their legislative representation will sustain the gerrymandering controversy. The tension with which the Court is now confronted could be relaxed by either a de-emphasis of group rights in favor of the individual concerns resurrected in *Shaw* or a conversion to some form of proportional representation. Doubtless any move to PR with multimember districts would assuage the gerrymandering issue because there would be correspondingly fewer districts to be drawn and thus, fewer lines to divide groups. Furthermore, PR systems would force group leaders actually to encourage their constituents to cohere and become more politically active because they could no longer rely on mapmakers to create special majority-minority districts.

Nonetheless, resolving the gerrymandering issue would not necessarily resolve the problem of assuring of fair and effective representation. Thirty years of jurisprudence indicates that we cannot ignore political groups; however a system of proportional representation would bestow only limited benefits upon minorities.[61] Insofar as representation issues

---

59. 554 F. 2d 139, 156–57 (1977).

60. *Baker* at 267.

61. See Karlan, *Undoing the Right Thing*, 77 VIRGINIA LAW REVIEW 1, (February, 1991), and Guinier, *The Triumph of Tokenism: The Voting Rights Act and the Theory of Black Electoral Success*, 89 MICH. L. R. 1077, 1136 (March, 1991).

are as much the province of political theory as they are of constitutional law, the courts are not especially well equipped to address them. In seeking to limit the use of remedial gerrymandering, the *Shaw* Court exacerbated the tension between individual voting rights and group representation. Whether this signals a strategic retreat from the thicket remains to be seen.

CHAPTER 3

Shaw v. Reno: The Shape of Things to Come

Timothy G. O'Rourke[*]

> Q. Would it be true, then, that it would be impossible to go from the eastern side of the 3rd District to the western side of the 3rd District— if I were walking there,...without going through the 1st District?
>
> A. It would certainly be true that somebody the size of a human being to go from one district to another at that point, that some part of their body would be in the 3rd District and another part of their body would be in the 1st District.
>
> Q. Now, let's even go beyond human beings. There have been references to snakes at various times.... It would even be impossible for a serpent to slither from the eastern part of the 3rd District to the western part...without physically going through some part of the 1st District; wouldn't that be true?
>
> (Witness and counsel confer.)
>
> A. Any living creature would be greater than the width... at that point at which the two parts of the district meet.
>
> Colloquy on the Metaphysics of North Carolina's 1st and 3rd Congressional Districts.[1]

---

[*] *A very preliminary version of this article was presented as Timothy G. O'Rourke, Crazy Quilts Then and Now: Shaw v. Reno and the Legacy of Baker v. Carr, at the* Annual Meeting of the Western Political Science Association, Albuquerque, New Mexico (March 10-12, 1994). A much briefer presentation of some of these ideas with substantially less emphasis on legal principles has been published as Timothy G. O'Rourke, *Shaw v. Reno and the Hunt for Double Cross-Overs,* 28 PS: POL. SCI. & POL., Mar. 1995, at 36-41. I served, without compensation, as an expert witness for the plaintiffs in *Shaw v. Hunt,* 861 F. Supp. 408 (E.D.N.C. 1994), and, with compensation, as an expert for the plaintiffs in *Johnson v. Miller,* 864 F. Supp. 1354 (S.D. Ga. 1994).

1. Deposition of Gerry F. Cohen at vol. I, 63-64, *Shaw v. Hunt,* 861 F. Supp. 408 (E.D.N.C. 1994) (No. 92-202-CIV-5-BR) (on file with author).

Introduction

In *Shaw v. Reno*,[2] the Supreme Court held that a group of voters stated a "cognizable claim"[3] against a North Carolina districting plan that "sent black representatives to Congress for the first time since Reconstruction."[4] Specifically, the voters in *Shaw* complained that the "plan, which contains district boundary lines of dramatically irregular shape, constitutes an unconstitutional racial gerrymander."[5]

Reduced to its barest essentials, *Shaw v. Reno* casts doubt on many recently established African-American and Hispanic majority congressional districts, which led to the election of an additional thirteen African-American members and six Hispanic members to the House of Representatives in 1992.[6] The immediate effect of *Shaw*, some suggest, is to threaten the historic electoral gains that minorities made in the 1992 congressional elections.[7] Others have described the litigation as "a serious assault on Black political power."[8]

Yet the *Shaw* progeny has produced mixed outcomes. Since the Supreme Court's decision in 1993, the district court on remand ruled North Carolina's congressional map constitutional.[9] On the other hand,

---

2. U.S. 113 S. Ct. 2816 (1993).

3. *Id.* at 2820.

4. *Id.* at 2843 (Blackmun, J., dissenting). The Court refused to rule on the merits of the claim, and instead remanded the case to a lower court for trial. *Id.* at 2832.

5. *Id.* at 2820.

6. These gains occurred in 13 states—Alabama, California, Florida, Georgia, Illinois, Louisiana, Maryland, New Jersey, New York, North Carolina, South Carolina, Texas, and Virginia. Bob Benenson, *GOP's Dreams of a Comeback Via the New Map Dissolve*, 50 CONG. Q. WKLY. REP. 3580 (1992).

The Voting Rights Act Amendments of 1982, widely interpreted as requiring the creation of majority-minority districts wherever possible, prodded state legislatures to carve out black and Hispanic constituencies in a wave of post-1990 redistricting. Voting Rights Amendments of 1982, Pub. L. No. 97-205, 96 Stat. 131 (1982). The Voting Rights Act was originally passed in 1965. Voting Rights Act of 1965, Pub. L. No. 89-110, 79 Stat. 437 (codified as amended at 42 U.S.C. §§ 1971, 1973 to 1973bb-1 (1988 & Supp. V 1993)). This article is primarily concerned with Section 2, (codified as amended at 42 U.S.C. § 1973 (1988)), and Section 5 (codified as amended at 42 U.S.C. § 1973c (1988)) of the Act.

7. Peter Applebome, *Suits Challenging Redrawn Districts That Help Blacks*, N.Y. TIMES, Feb. 14, 1994, at A1, A14.

8. Kenneth J. Cooper, *Dismantling Black Political Power*, 5 EMERGE: BLACK AMERICA'S NEWSMAGAZINE, Apr. 1994, at 30.

9. *Shaw v. Hunt*, 861 F. Supp. 408, 417 (E.D.N.C.), appeal. filed, 63 U.S.L.W. 3439 (Nov. 21, 1994) (No. 94-923).

in other post-*Shaw* actions, courts have invalidated districting plans in Georgia, Louisiana, and Texas—although the Supreme Court blocked the implementation of new congressional lines until after the 1994 elections.[10]

But the results of 1994 elections, in fact, greatly complicate attempts to assess the ramifications of *Shaw*. The Republican party seized majority control of the House of Representatives for the first time since 1954 by picking up more than fifty seats. These Republican additions in 1994 could be partly attributed to the same redistricting that spawned African-American and Hispanic gains in 1992.[11] The concentration of

---

10. *Johnson v. Miller*, 864 F. Supp. 1354 (S.D. Ga.), *stay granted*, 115 S. Ct. 36 (1994), *and prob. juris. noted*, 115 S. Ct. 713 (1995); *Vera v. Richards*, 861 F. Supp. 1304 (S.D. Tex.) (postponing relief order until after 1994 elections), *appeal filed*, 63 U.S.L.W. 3388 (Nov. 2, 1994) (No. 94-806), *and appeal filed*, 63 U.S.L.W. 3476 (Dec. 1, 1994) (No. 94-988); *Hays v. Louisiana*, 839 F. Supp. 1188 (W.D. La. 1993), *vacated as moot and remanded*, 114 S. Ct. 2731, *on remand*, 862 F. Supp. 119 (W.D. La.), *prob. juris. noted sub nom. United States v. Hays*, 115 S. Ct. 687 (1994). Another district court rejected a challenge to a districting design creating majority-minority constituencies, because it was outside the *Shaw* framework. *DeWitt v. Wilson*, 856 F. Supp. 1409 (E.D. Cal.), *appeal filed*, 63 U.S.L.W. 3127 (Aug. 8, 1994) (No. 94-275). Because *DeWitt* does not concern bizarrely-shaped districts, it is not included in this analysis.

11. Steven A. Holmes, Did Racial Redistricting Undermine Democrats? N.Y. Times, Nov. 13, 1994, § 1, at 32. Holmes, referring to various analysts who suggest that race-based redistricting cost the Democrats five seats in 1992 and another ten seats in 1994, noted:

> They argue that reapportionment not only siphoned solid Democratic votes from white districts, but also helped Republicans attract higher-caliber candidates and raise more money by giving them a better shot at winning those districts. In addition, when black voters were removed from marginally Republican districts, the Democrats' chances of winning such seats became that much slimmer.

Id. See also Juan Williams, *Blacked Out in the Newt Congress: The Black Caucus Regroups as Jesse Mulls a Third Party Bid*, WASH. POST, Nov. 20, 1994, at C1 (arguing that redistricting added 15 Republican seats in Alabama, Florida, Georgia, and North Carolina in 1992 and 1994).

The NAACP Legal Defense and Educational Fund has challenged the view that race-based redistricting accounted, even in small measure, for the loss of Democratic seats in 1994. The Fund's analysis contends that 47 of the seats lost by Democrats were either in states without majority-minority districts, in white districts surrounded by other white districts, or in districts in which the percentage of minority voters in post-1990 redistricting either increased or remained constant. The Legal Defense and Educational Fund also argues that race-based redistricting caused a Democratic loss in only one district, North Carolina's Second District. Furthermore, the Fund argues, the creation of majority-minority seats in Georgia, Mississippi, and North Carolina prevented additional Democratic losses in 1994. Steven A. Holmes, *Civil Rights Group Disputes Election Analyses*

predominantly Democratic African-American and Hispanic voters in majority-minority districts tends to place more Republicans in surrounding districts. The impact was most evident in Georgia and North Carolina, where Republicans picked up three and four seats, respectively.[12]

---

on Black Districts, N.Y. TIMES, Dec. 1, 1994, at A15. The NAACP's view has received some support from a Democratic party task force established to assess the impact of redistricting on Democratic losses in the 1992 and 1994 congressional elections. Thomas B. Edsall, *Racial Redistricting Had Minor Role Nov. 8, Analysts Say,* WASH. POST, Dec. 27, 1994, at A4.

The analysts cited by Edsall, however, put 1994 Democratic losses attributable to redistricting at somewhere between five and nine seats. *Id.* While noting that at least one Republican insider thought race-based redistricting had cost Democrats as many as two dozen House seats, commentator Richard E. Cohen suggested that most analysts put the loss at about a dozen seats, roughly the Republicans' margin of control at the beginning of the 1995 session of the House of Representatives. Richard E. Cohen, *Did Redistricting Sink the Democrats?*, 26 NAT'L J. 2984, 2984 (1994).

Thus, it would appear that the NAACP Legal Defense Fund grossly underestimates the number of Democratic seats lost to race-based redistricting, both overall and in specific states. *See infra* note 12. The Fund's analysis also ignores the larger lessons of the 1994 elections: that the efficacy of race-based redistricting is heavily dependent on Democratic hegemony at the national level and that the pursuit itself of race-based remedies may have contributed to the Republican sweep. Indeed, Juan Williams has suggested "that the black liberal demands for more seats in Congress, more special programs for minorities and more support for a black separatist movement have pushed black America out of the mainstream of the national political dialogue." Williams, *supra*, at C1; *see also* Stephen Chapman, *Redistricting by Race May Be No Boon to Minorities*, CHIC. TRIB., Nov. 20, 1994, Perspective Section, at 3 ("Racial gerrymandering may simultaneously increase minority representation and diminish minority influence.").

12. In 1994, race-based redistricting netted Republicans one to three seats in North Carolina. Republicans took a seat away from the Democrats in the Second District, from which post-1990 redistricting took substantial segments of the black population in order to create the majority black First District. Republicans also took the Third District, where redistricting marginally reduced the black population percentage and significantly altered the district's boundaries. The Fifth District went from Democrat to Republican as well; here the black percentage changed little; nevertheless redistricting might have affected the District's political disposition. MICHAEL BARONE & GRANT UJIFUSA, THE ALMANAC OF AMERICAN POLITICS 1994, 955 (1994) ("[R]edistricting took black constituents away [from the Fifth District] to create the new black-majority 12th District, although the legislature tried to compensate elsewhere."). That redistricting plainly contributed to Republican gains in North Carolina is reinforced by Edward Walsh. Edward Walsh, *North Carolina Reflects Voting Shift in South: GOP Takeover Nov. 8 Both Wide and Deep*, WASH. POST, Nov. 26, 1994, at A1; *see also North Carolina and the New Solid South: Turning to the GOP*, VIRGINIAN- PILOT, Nov. 25, 1994, at A22. *See generally* BARONE & UJIFUSA, *supra*, at 945-56; Benenson, *supra* note 6, at 3581. As a result of the 1994 elections the North Carolina congressional delegation went from eight

While the number of African-Americans in the House did not change with the 1994 elections,[13] the Congressional Black Caucus, all but one of whose 1994 members was a Democrat, suffered a precipitous decline in power. The Republican takeover of the House displaced a sizable contingent of African-American committee and subcommittee chairmen.[14] His-

---

Democrats and four Republicans to eight Republicans and four Democrats.

In Georgia, redistricting probably netted Republicans four or five seats over two election cycles, 1992 and 1994. The new redistricting plan created three majority-black districts in an eleven-person delegation. The plan in effect in 1990 had one majority-black district out of ten. The GOP took control of the First, Third and Fourth Districts in 1992, and won the Eighth and Tenth Districts in 1994. In each case redistricting pulled out significant segments of the black population in order to create the new majority-black districts. Kevin A. Hill, *Does the Creation of Majority Black Districts Aid Republicans?, An Analysis of the 1992 Congressional Elections in Eight Southern States*, 57 J. OF POL. 384, 388, table 1 (1995). Hill used a computer simulation to run the 1992 election returns in the districts in place in 1990; he concluded that race-based redistricting accounted for the Republican takeover of Georgia's First, Third and Fourth Districts. *Id.* at 397-98. Hill correctly predicted that race-based redistricting would lead to GOP wins in Georgia's Eighth and Tenth Districts in 1994. *Id.* at 399. *See also* Charles S. Bullock, *Affirmative Action Districts: In Whose Face Will They Blow Up?*, 16 CAMPAIGNS & ELECTIONS, April 1995, at 22-23; Ben Smith II, *Redrawn districts sparked GOP gains*, ATLANTA J. & CONST., Nov. 1994, at B4. On April 10, 1995 Ninth District Congressman Nathan Deal switched from the Democrat to the Republican party so that the Georgia congressional delegation now has eight white Republicans and three African-American Democrats (who represent black-majority districts). Before the 1992 elections, the delegation was composed of nine Democrats (one of whom was African-American) and one Republican. Juliana Gruenwald, *Deal's Switch to GOP Exposes Erosion of Once Solid South,* 53 CONG. Q. WKLY REP. 1084, 1084 (1995).

13. Prior to the 1994 elections, the House had 39 African-American members, including Eleanor Holmes Norton, a non-voting delegate from the District of Columbia. In 1994, this increased to 40 with the election of an African-American non-voting delegate from the Virgin Islands. The number of African-American Congressmen eligible to vote remained at 38; two African-American freshmen stepped into seats held previously by other African-Americans. In other developments, J.C. Watt won in Oklahoma, becoming only the second African-American Republican in the House. But in Missouri, Congressman Alan Wheat gave up his seat to run, unsuccessfully, for the U.S. Senate. *See Special Report: The Freshmen-Elect,* 52 CONG. Q. WKLY. REP. 10-11 (Nov. 12, 1994) (Supp.).

14. Williams, *supra* note 11 at C1. I confirmed this by examining information in the *Players, Politics and Turf of the 103rd Congress,* 52 CONG. Q. WKLY REP. 52-97 (Mar. 5, 1994) (Supp.) [hereinafter *Players*]. Three chairmanships were lost: Armed Services (Ronald V. Dellums of California); Government Operations (John Conyers, Jr. of Michigan); and Post Office and Civil Service (William L. Clay of Missouri). *Id.* at 58, 70, 80.

panics also failed to increase their numbers in the House in the 1994 elections, and the Republican tidal wave removed six Hispanic committee and subcommittee chairmen.[15]

It is notable, however, that African-American and Hispanic Democrats, for the most part, coasted to victory in their 1994 House races, while white Democrats, especially white Southern Democrats, either struggled in victory or sank in defeat.[16] The 1994 elections confirm that majority-minority districts are a particularly effective device for ensuring that minorities are represented in some way in Congress. But at the same time, the results also support a proposition that has profound implications for the manner and extent to which minorities will be represented. Redistricting designed to increase the number of African-American and Hispanic congressmen also seems to aid Republicans[17]—a relationship that was of little political significance so long as Democrats were an apparently permanent majority in the House of Representatives. The elections of 1994 have surely tested the political wisdom of creating majority-minority districts, even as *Shaw v. Reno* raised legitimate legal questions about the unfettered pursuit of majority-minority districts.

In the second part of this article, I review the holding of *Shaw*, asserting that it is compatible with the letter and spirit of three decades of reapportionment jurisprudence. In the third part I undertake a comparative overview of the facts and law in the four post-*Shaw* congressional districting cases decided by lower courts. My thesis is that the creation of these challenged districts was driven partly by an improper interpretation of both Sections 2 and 5 of the Voting Rights Act, and partly by a cynical embrace of new redistricting technology. In the forth part, I judge

---

15. *Players, supra* note 14, at 52-97. For example, E. "Kika" de la Garza of California lost the chairmanship of Agriculture, and Henry B. Gonzales of Texas lost the chairmanship of Banking, Finance and Urban Affairs. *Id.* at 52, 60. Before the 1994 elections, there were 20 Hispanics in the House, including non-voting delegates from Puerto Rico and the Virgin Islands. The retirement of a delegate from the Virgin Islands reduced the present number to 19. *Special Report: The Freshmen-Elect, supra* note 13, at 10-11.

16. A post-election analysis, noted:

> The most consistently Democratic districts in the South are its 23 majority-minority districts—17 black-majority seats plus six Texas districts with Hispanic majorities. Members from these districts usually win reelection with 60 percent of the vote. In 1994, all but six topped 60 percent; nine received more than two-thirds of the vote.

Southern Democrats: A Dying Breed, 52 CONG. Q. WKLY. REP. 3356 (1994).

17. Abigail Thernstrom, *Redistricting in Black and White: By Any Name, It's a Quota,* N.Y. TIMES, Dec. 7, 1994, at A23. *See generally* Kimball Brace et al., *Does Redistricting Aimed to Help Blacks Necessarily Help Republicans?* 49 J. POL. 169 (1987); Hill, *supra* n.12.

the contested districts by "traditional" redistricting criteria. My contention is that the challenged lines represent truly radical departures from the past. Precisely because they are so extraordinary—as racial gerrymanders that cast traditional redistricting criteria to the wind—they are patently unconstitutional. Finally, in the fifth section, I offer concluding observations about the significance of *Shaw*-type litigation, which encourages state legislatures to create "functional [and] cognizable"[18] congressional districts.

The Road to Reno

The Supreme Court's Holding

The North Carolina Assembly created the plan at issue in *Shaw v. Reno* primarily because of pressure from the U.S. Department of Justice. Forty of the State's 100 counties are subject to the preclearance provisions of Section 5 of the Voting Rights Act;[19] therefore, the legislature could not implement a new redistricting plan until the Justice Department had determined that the plan would not discriminate against African-Americans, who constitute nearly 22 percent of the State population. The plan in effect in the 1980's did not create a district with an African-American majority. As a result of the 1990 census, the State picked up a twelfth seat and, in 1991, the legislature enacted a plan calling for one majority African-American district. The Justice Department objected to the plan,[20] and the General Assembly responded by crafting

---

18. The term "cognizable" was coined by Professor Bernard Grofman. *See infra* part IV.E.

19. 42 U.S.C. § 1973c (1988). A listing of North Carolina's covered counties appears in 28 C.F.R. app. § 51 (1994).

20. The objection letter noted:

> The proposed congressional plan contains one majority black congressional district drawn in the northeast region of the state. The unusually convoluted shape of that district does not appear to have been necessary.... [but] the irregular configuration of that district did not have the purpose or effect of minimizing minority voting strength in that region.... [T]he proposed configuration of the district boundary lines in the south-central to southeastern part of the state appear [sic] to minimize minority voting strength given the significant minority population in this area of the state. In general, it appears that the state chose not to give effect to black and Native American voting strength in this area, even though it seems that boundary lines that were no more irregular than found elsewhere in the proposed plan could have been drawn to recognize such minority concentration in this part of the state.

the revised plan at issue in *Shaw*. The new plan created two majority African-American districts: the First District, which roughly followed the contours of the majority African-American district in the discarded 1991 plan, and the Twelfth District, a narrow 160-mile-long band from Durham to Greensboro to Winston-Salem to Charlotte that connected the African-American population concentrated in those urban centers.[21] Both the First and Twelfth Districts elected African-American representatives in 1992, Eva M. Clayton and Melvin L. Watt, respectively.

The *Shaw* plaintiffs sued both the United States Attorney General[22] and North Carolina, contending that the 1992 plan amounted to an unconstitutional racial classification of voters.[23] A district court unanimously dismissed the suit against the Justice Department, and, in a narrow decision, dismissed the action against the state as well.[24]

Viewing reapportionment as "one area where appearances do matter," a majority of the Supreme Court in *Shaw*[25] recognized a new voting right: "the right to participate in a 'color-blind' electoral process."[26] The Court elaborated:

> What appellants object to is redistricting legislation that is so extremely irregular on its face that it rationally can be viewed only as an effort to segregate the races for purposes of voting, without regard for traditional districting principles and without sufficiently compelling justification.... [W]e conclude that appellants have stated a claim upon which relief can be granted under the Equal Protection Clause.[27]

Letter from John R. Dunne, Assistant Attorney General, Civil Rights Division, U.S. Department of Justice, to Tiare B. Smiley, Special Deputy Attorney General, State of North Carolina 4-5 (Dec. 18, 1991) (on file with author) [hereinafter Dunne Letter, Dec. 18].

21. African-Americans comprised 57.26 percent of the total population in the First District and 50.53 percent of registered voters. In the Twelfth District, African-Americans comprised 56.63 percent of total population and 53.54 percent of registered voters. *See* Memorandum from Gerry F. Cohen, Director of Legislative Drafting, North Carolina General Assembly, to Members of the North Carolina General Assembly, 1992 Congressional Base Plan #10-Explanation/Statistics (Jan. 23, 1992) (on file with author).

22. William Barr, the original named Attorney General, was followed by Janet Reno.

23. *Shaw*, 113 S. Ct. at 2821. Plaintiffs made constitutional claims under Article I, §§ 2, 4, both the Privileges and Immunities and Equal Protection Clauses of the Fourteenth Amendment, and the Fifteenth Amendment. *Id.* at 2822.

24. *Id.* at 2821-22.

25. Justice O'Connor wrote the majority opinion and was joined by Chief Justice William H. Rehnquist and Justices Antonin Scalia, Anthony M. Kennedy, and Clarence Thomas. *Id.* at 2819.

26. *Id.* at 2824.

27. *Id.*

The Court held that such claims demand strict scrutiny, which means redistricting legislation survives judicial review only if the state advances a compelling interest and shows that the use of race as a classification is narrowly tailored to advance that interest.[28]

Four Justices dissented[29]—assailing the creation of a new kind of voting rights claim and the holding that a redistricting plan designed to ensure fair representation for a racial minority would trigger "strict scrutiny."[30] For Justice White (joined by Justices Blackmun and Stevens) the voting rights precedents authorized only a claim against "outright deprivations" of the right to vote or a claim that an electoral arrangement results in vote dilution (i.e., a denial of the opportunity to participate equally in the electoral process). The claim in *Shaw* fit neither category, according to Justice White. He argued that the question of the right to participate in a color-blind electoral process had already been presented in *United Jewish Organizations v. Carey*[31] ("*UJO*"). According to Justice White, that question "was in plain view" and had been rejected in *UJO*.[32]

Justice Stevens made three points in dissent. First, he argued that the Constitution imposes no "compactness and contiguity" standard on legislative districts.[33] Next, "uncouth boundaries" violate Equal Protection only when adopted "for the sole purpose" of disadvantaging the chances of a racial or political minority to win elections.[34] Finally, he argued that affirmative efforts to ensure fair representation for a racial minority do

---

28. *Id.* at 2825.

29. Separate dissenting opinions were delivered by Justice Byron R. White, *Id.* at 2834, Justice Harry A. Blackmun, *Id.* at 2843, Justice John Paul Stevens, *Id.*, and Justice David H. Souter. *Id.* at 2845.

30. The dissenters argued that strict scrutiny was inappropriate, but even if strict scrutiny were applied, North Carolina had a compelling interest in complying with the Voting Rights Act. *Id.* at 2842 (White, J., dissenting); *Id.* at 2847-48 (Souter, J., dissenting).

31. 430 U.S. 144 (1977).

32. *Shaw*, 113 S. Ct. at 2839 (White, J., dissenting). In *UJO*, the Justice Department, relying on Section 5 of the Voting Rights Act, pressured New York to enhance the size of nonwhite majorities in four state legislative districts. *UJO*, 430 U.S. at 162. The new districts fractured an Hasidic Jewish community, which had challenged the state legislative plan as an impermissible use of race. *Id.* at 152-53. In her opinion in *Shaw*, Justice O'Connor rightly viewed *UJO* as a suit on behalf of "white voters" whose influence as a group was diluted by the plan at issue, thus distinguishing the group-based claim in *UJO* from the individual-based claim in *Shaw*. *Shaw*, 113 S. Ct. at 2829-30.

33. *Shaw*, 113 S. Ct. at 2843 (Stevens, J., dissenting).

34. *Id.* at 2844.

not violate the Equal Protection Clause.[35] Justice Souter, like Justice White, contended that the *Shaw* plaintiffs suffered no real injury since white voters were fairly represented in the distribution of seats in the North Carolina delegation. "I would not respond to the seeming egregiousness of the redistricting now before us," he wrote, "by untethering the concept of racial gerrymander in such a case from the concept of harm exemplified by dilution."[36]

Shaw v. Reno and the Ghost of *Baker v. Carr*

Shaw v. Reno is remarkably similar to the Court's plunge into the political thicket in *Baker v. Carr*.[37] Both *Shaw* and *Baker* centered on questions of standing and justifiability. Moreover, both cases focused on districting plans that could be aptly described as "a crazy quilt," or "a topsy-turvical of gigantic proportions."[38] In both instances, the Court ultimately defined political rights on a highly individualized basis, implicitly rejecting an analysis focusing on groups.

In *Baker*, according to Justice William J. Brennan's majority opinion, the Court had been "present[ed] a justifiable constitutional cause of action."[39] In a concurring opinion, Justice William O. Douglas described the core question as "the extent to which a State may weight one person's vote more heavily than it does another's."[40] Justice Frankfurter, in dissent, rejected the notion that what was at issue was an individual right, with a separate existence outside the context of group politics. He reasoned, "[T]his charge of discrimination based on legislative underrepresentation is given the appearance of a more private, less impersonal claim, than the assertion that the frame of government is askew....However, the discrimination relied on is the deprivation of what appellants conceive to be their proportionate share of political influence."[41]

This claim, according to Justice Felix Frankfurter, made no sense unless it was viewed as a group claim. Since *Baker* was not a member of a clearly identifiable class of citizens, such as African-Americans disenfranchised by legislative action, his was "[a] hypothetical claim resting on

---

35. *Id.* at 2843-45 (Stevens, J. dissenting).
36. *Id.* at 2849 (Souter, J., dissenting).
37. 369 U.S. 186 (1962).
38. *Id.* at 254 (Clark, J., concurring).
39. *Id.* at 237.
40. *Id.* at 242 (Douglas, J., concurring).
41. *Id.* at 298-99 (Frankfurter, J., dissenting).

abstract assumptions."[42] Justice Frankfurter found no support in the Fourteenth Amendment for "the assurance of equal weight to every voter's vote."[43]

In language reminiscent of Justice Frankfurter's, the *Shaw* dissenters emphasized that the plaintiffs lacked standing. The plaintiffs, in Justice White's characterization, "have not presented a cognizable claim, because they have not alleged a cognizable injury."[44] He noted that white voters controlled ten of twelve congressional districts, a percentage of seats greater than their share of the population; therefore, they could not "complain of discriminatory treatment."[45] Similarly, Justice Stevens argued that the fairness of the North Carolina plan ultimately should be assessed with reference to its treatment of groups.

> The duty to govern impartially is abused when a group with power over the electoral process defines electoral boundaries solely to enhance its own political strength at the expense of any weaker group. That duty, however, is not violated when the majority acts to facilitate the election of a member of a group that lacks such power because it remains underrepresented in the state legislature—whether that group is defined by political affiliation, by common economic interests, or by religious, ethnic, or racial characteristics.[46]

Justice Stevens was correct in pointing out that some forms of racial gerrymandering are legitimate. The majority did not dispute this, noting that "race-conscious redistricting is not always unconstitutional."[47] However, a major defect in the approach of Justice Stevens (and the other dissenters) is its emphasis on representation as a group-based right—an orientation essentially at odds with modern redistricting law and the doctrine of "one person, one vote."

Voting as an Individual Right

To be sure, the Court recognized within a few years after *Baker* that a plan that satisfied the test of equal numbers might nevertheless discrimi-

---

42. *Id.* at 267.
43. *Id.* at 300 (Frankfurter, J., dissenting).
44. 113 S. Ct. at 2834 (White, J., dissenting).
45. *Id.* at 2838.
46. *Id.* at 2844 (Steven, J., dissenting).
47. *Id.* at 2824.

nate against a racial or ethnic minority.[48] But *Whitcomb v. Chavis*[49] made it clear that a group could not sustain a claim of discrimination merely by showing that it did not have legislative seats in proportion to its percentage of the population.[50] Even as the Court held in *White v. Regester*[51] that multimember state legislative districts in Texas discriminated against blacks and Hispanics,[52] it reaffirmed that there was no right to proportional representation.[53] The 1982 amendments to the Voting Rights Act embody the same principles set out in the Court's decisions in *Whitcomb* and *White*.[54]

There is no right to proportional representation because the protection against vote dilution is an individual right with a group dimension, but not a group right. An election system cannot discriminate against individuals because of their membership in a protected group, but the group has no presumptive claim on some share of legislative seats.[55] Indeed, in dealing with the matter of racial discrimination in voting, the

---

48. *See, e.g., Burns v. Richardson*, 384 U.S. 73, 88 (1966); *Fortson v. Dorsey*, 379 U.S. 433, 439 (1965). Of course, *Gomillion v. Lightfoot*, 364 U.S. 339 (1960), usually considered the first racial gerrymandering case, preceded *Baker* by two years. Both the majority and the dissenters in *Shaw v. Reno* devoted significant attention to the symbolism of *Gomillion*, but that discussion is beyond the scope of this article.

49. 403 U.S. 124 (1971).

50. *Id.* at 149.

51. 412 U.S. 755 (1973).

52. *Id.* at 765.

53. *Id.* at 765-66.

54. Section 2 of the Voting Rights Act, provides, in part, that an election practice is illegal if, "based on the totality of the circumstances, it is shown that the political processes leading to nomination or election in the State or political subdivision are not equally open to participation" by a minority group (principally blacks, Hispanics, or Native Americans) "in that its members have less opportunity...to participate in the political process and to elect representatives of their choice." 42 U.S.C. § 1973(b) (1988). While electoral success is one measure of equal opportunity, Section 2 states "[t]hat nothing in this section establishes a right to have members of a protected class elected in numbers equal to their proportion in the population." *Id.* According to the architects of Section 2, "In adopting the 'result standard' as articulated in *White v. Regester*, the [Senate] Committee [on the Judiciary] has codified the basic principle in that case as it was applied prior to the *Mobile [v. Bolden*, 446 U.S. 55 (1980)] litigation." S. REP. No. 417, 97th Cong., 2d Sess. 28 (1982), *reprinted in* 1982 U.S.C.C.A.N. 177, 205.

55. *See* Paul W. Jacobs, II & Timothy G. O'Rourke, *Racial Polarization in Vote Dilution Cases Under Section 2 of the Voting Rights Act: The Impact of* Thornburg v. Gingles, 3 J. L. & POL. 295, 299-300 (1986). *See also* Katharine I. Butler, *Reapportionment, the Court, and the Voting Rights Act: A Resegregation of the Political Process?* 56 U. Colo. L. Rev. 1, 84-85 (1984).

Court has been as much concerned with perfecting geographic districting as guaranteeing fair treatment. Thus, the creation of the doctrine of minority vote dilution was fashioned largely in the context of challenges either to multimember legislative districts or local at-large elections.[56] As this doctrine evolved, the Court came to see single-member districting as the remedy for racially discriminatory multimember schemes.[57] Beyond the realm of racial claims, the Court has endorsed single-member districts more generally, requiring that federal judges crafting redistricting remedies rely wholly on single-member districts.[58]

In short, the Court's racial gerrymandering cases do not create a right to group representation, so much as they effectuate a refinement of the individualistic analysis of "one person, one vote," in order to prevent the use of multimember districts or district lines to treat voters unequally because of race or membership in some other group. At bottom, this is how we can understand the Court's reluctance to enter into the thicket of partisan gerrymandering, notwithstanding its holding that such claims are justiciable.[59]

The dissenters in *Shaw* turned the Supreme Court's prior holdings on their head, not only in contending that group fairness is the touchstone of voting rights law, but also in contending that group fairness overrides all other considerations (save for that of equal population). Thus, Justice Souter asserted that "the mere placement of an individual in one district instead of another denies no one a right or benefit provided to others."[60] Elaborating, he asserted:

> The majority's use of "segregation" to describe the effect of districting here may suggest that it Carries effects comparable to school segregation making it subject to like scrutiny. But a principal consequence of school segregation was inequality in educational opportunity provided, whereas use of race (or any other group characteristic) in districting does not without more deny equality of political participation.[61]

Whether considered within the context of the Court's school desegregation precedents or within the realm of its voting rights jurisprudence,

---

56. *See, e.g.*, Timothy G. O'Rourke, *Constitutional and Statutory Challenges to Local At-Large Elections*, 17 U. RICH. L. REV. 39 (1982).

57. *See, e.g., Thornburg v. Gingles*, 478 U.S. 30, 50 (1986).

58. *See Connor v. Johnson*, 402 U.S. 690, 692 (1971); *Connor v. Finch*, 431 U.S. 407, 415 (1977).

59. *See Davis v. Bandemer*, 478 U.S. 109 (1986).

60. *Shaw*, 113 S. Ct. at 2846.

61. *Id.* at 2846 n.4.

Justice Souter's argument is unpersuasive. It is useful to recall the question posed and answered by *Brown v. Board of Education*:[62] "Does segregation of children in public schools solely on the basis of race, even though the physical facilities and other "tangible" factors may be equal, deprive the children of the minority group of equal educational opportunities? We believe that it does."[63] Segregation *per se*, according to *Brown*, is inherently unequal. The harm flows from the fact of racial classification. In suggesting that the plaintiffs had suffered no injury because their group (white voters) was fairly treated, Justice Souter missed the point. What the plaintiffs were asserting is the right to be treated as individual voters, rather than with reference to their putative membership in a group. "In their complaint," Justice O'Connor noted, the plaintiffs "did not even claim to be white."[64]

---

62. 347 US. 483 (1954).

63. *Id.* at 493.

64. *Shaw*, 113 S. Ct. at 2824. After the remand of *Shaw* and the subsequent trial on the merits, the district court gave considerable attention to the question of whether the plaintiffs had, in fact, established standing to bring the action at issue. "Their primary claim is that the Plan 'injures' them...because it threatens to perpetuate archaic racial stereotypes and to increase racial divisions in society." *Shaw v. Hunt*, 861 F. Supp. 408, 424. While the district court suggested that elements of the plaintiffs' claim appeared to be "abstract, theoretical, and merely speculative, not concrete and palpable" the court concluded, nevertheless, that what plaintiffs were asserting was a kind of "'stigmatic' injury," which the Supreme Court had recognized in *Allen v. Wright*, 468 U.S. 737, 755 (1984), *Regents of the Univ. of Calif. v. Bakke*, 438 U.S. 265, 281 n.14, (1978) and *Northeastern Fla. Contractors v. Jacksonville*, 113 S. Ct. 2297, 2303 (1993). *Hunt*, 861 F. Supp. at 424-25. Although the district court rightly found support for standing in the Supreme Court's racial classification cases, it should be noted that the plaintiffs' claim is not reducible simply to a racial discrimination claim. Their claim has a voting component as well, which would hold that contorted districts, predicated on race, preclude a more conventional—and functional—kind of political representation built around geographic proximity and common political and economic interests not tied to race.

The Court, in *Shaw v. Reno*, hinted at the dimensions of this component, observing that "When a district is obviously created solely to effectuate the perceived common interests of one racial group, elected officials are more likely to believe that their primary obligation is to represent only the members of that group, rather than their constituency as a whole." *Shaw*, 113 S. Ct. at 2822. As the district court noted in the Texas congressional redistricting case, "*Shaw* implicitly reaffirms the important interconnection of community and geography and effective representative government in drawing its distinction between those ideal districting criteria [such as compactness, contiguity, and respect for political subdivisions] and a racial gerrymander that ignores them." *Vera v. Richards*, 861 F. Supp. 1304, 1335 (S.D. Tex. 1994). The claim that sprawling, bizarrely shaped districts intrude on the process of fair representation is no more or no less abstract than the claim made by plaintiffs in *Baker v. Carr* that unequally populated districts enhance the influence of some

Traditional Redistricting Criteria

Not only did the dissenters in *Shaw v. Reno* incorrectly analyze the nature of the injury at issue in the case, they also misapprehended the significance of "traditional redistricting criteria" in assessing the constitutionality of the North Carolina congressional district lines. Justice Stevens focused on the significance of the contours of the districts at issue, arguing that shape might provide a clue both to legislature's "ulterior purpose" and to the legitimacy of that purpose. Since the North Carolina legislature clearly had intended to draw majority black districts and these districts benefited a heretofore underrepresented minority, Justice Stevens viewed shape, first, as "irrelevant" as to the existence of purpose and, second, as benign with respect to the impact of that purpose.[65] Except as an indicia of purpose, shape has no value at all since "[t]here is no independent constitutional requirement of compactness or contiguity."[66]

At most, however, this assertion means only that the Constitution does not offer a precise prescription for the shape of districts in the same way that it mandates a specific standard with respect to the population of legislative districts. It cannot mean that shape has no constitutional significance. Even Justices Stevens and White concede that the bizarre district lines can provide a clue to illicit purpose.[67] But it is not the hint of illicit purpose that makes the lines bizarre. The lines appear bizarre precisely be-

---

voters at the expense of others. To the charge that the *Shaw* plaintiffs' claim is too abstract to merit standing, it is useful to recall that an individual voter would have standing to challenge a congressional redistricting plan on "one person, one vote" grounds even if the variations in district populations were less than the margin of error in the census count itself. *See Karcher v. Daggett*, 462 U.S. 725, 727 (1983) (holding unconstitutional a plan including congressional districts which varied by a mere 0.69 percent).

65. *Shaw*, 113 S. Ct. at 2844 (Stevens, J., dissenting).

66. *Id.* at 2843. *Gaffney v. Cummings*, 412 U.S. 735 (1973), is the principal authority for the proposition that the Constitution does not impose an "independent...requirement" on district shape. *Id.* at 752 n.18. But *Gaffney* refers to "compactness or attractiveness," *Id.*, not "compactness or contiguity," as Justice Stevens would have it. Given the contiguity problems in the North Carolina plan (discussed later in this article) the distinction may be important. Justice White's analysis of the importance of shape is virtually identical to Justice Stevens':

> [W]hile district irregularities may provide strong indicia of a potential gerrymander, they do no more than that. In particular, they have no bearing on whether the plan ultimately is found to violate the Constitution. Given two districts drawn on similar, race-based grounds, the one does not become more injurious than the other simply by virtue of being snake-like....

Shaw, 113 S. Ct. at 2841 (White, J., dissenting).

67. *Shaw*, 113 S. Ct. at 2834 (White, J., dissenting); *Id.* at 2843 (Stevens, J., dissenting).

cause, under most circumstances, one would expect district lines to create constituencies that facilitate communication between representatives and represented. One's expectation is that district lines will follow familiar landmarks—natural features or subdivision boundaries—and encompass constituencies of compact area with populations of shared interests. Put simply, bizarre districts look that way because both tradition and experience suggest that they are, indeed, both uncommon and dysfunctional.[68] If bizarrely shaped districts were the rule, they would not be bizarre.[69]

In this respect, it is significant that the Justice Department's own regulations provide that the Department, in reviewing redistricting plans under Section 5 of the Voting Rights Act, will consider, "[t]he extent to which the plan departs from objective redistricting criteria set by the submitting jurisdiction, ignores other relevant factors such as compactness and contiguity, or displays a configuration that inexplicably disregards available natural or artificial boundaries."[70] For instance, the Justice Department in 1992 objected to "a slender finger"[71] and "a land

---

68. It is true, of course, that compact or attractive districts may be dysfunctional or that they may, as Justice White observed, mask the most vicious forms of partisan and racial gerrymandering. *Id.* at 2841. But I think, as a rule, that looks are revealing. Tellingly, Justice White provided no examples of attractive-looking gerrymanders.

69. Hearings on the Voting Rights Acts Amendments of 1982 generated testimony on a number of examples, historical and contemporary, of ill-shaped districts that evidenced discrimination against minority voters. Frank R. Parker, before the House Subcommittee on Civil and Constitutional Rights, noted that county redistricting had produced districts shaped like a "Tyrannosaurus Rex," "baby elephant," and "turkey," while city redistricting produced lines not "related to...achieving compactness or regularity of shape." *Extension of the Voting Rights Act: Hearings Before the Subcomm. on Civil and Constitutional Rights of the House Comm. on the Judiciary,* 97th Cong., 1st Sess. Pt. 1, 517, 521, 528 (1981) (prepared statement of Frank R. Parker). In his written testimony, Dr. J. Morgan Kousser described late nineteenth century examples of "[r]acially motivated gerrymandering" including a district that was "contiguous at one point only by considering the Atlantic Ocean a land mass" and another district known as the "Shoestring District." *Id.* at pt. 3, 2013 (written testimony of Dr. J. Morgan Kousser).

70. 28 C.F.R. § 51.59(f) (1994). One must assume that compactness and contiguity contribute to fair representation in order to use their relative absence as an indication that something is amiss.

71. Letter from John R. Dunne, Assistant Attorney General, Civil Right Division, U.S. Department of Justice, to Mark H. Cohen, Senior Assistant Attorney General, State of Georgia 4 (Jan. 21, 1992) (on file with author) [hereinafter Dunne Letter, Jan. 21]. The Department's letter noted "[c]oncerns" that the boundary was "drawn to avoid control by black voters' representatives." *Id.* Thus, one might argue that the Department's objection was not to shape *per se,* but to the racial effect or purpose associated with the shape. Nevertheless, my point remains: there would be no reason to pay special attention to

The Supreme Court, on occasion, has paid attention to district configurations, even if shape itself was never dispositive. As Justice O'Connor pointed out in *Shaw v. Reno*, the Court's prior holding in *UJO* turned, at least in part, on New York's reliance on "traditional districting principles."[73] In *Connor v. Finch* (1977),[74] the Court engaged in a fairly extensive discussion of the criteria of compactness and adherence to political subdivision boundaries within the context of a Mississippi state legislative redistricting plan fashioned by a district court. Curiously, the allegation in that case was that departures from compactness tended to dilute black voting strength, leading the Supreme Court to instruct the lower court to "draw legislative districts that are reasonably contiguous and compact, so as to put to rest suspicions that Negro voting strength is being impermissibly diluted, or explain why in a particular instance the goal cannot be accomplished."[75] Justice Blackmun, writing a concurring opinion, thought the instruction misdirected. Describing "contiguity and compactness" as "desirable characteristics of a districting plan,"[76] he did not believe that blind adherence to these criteria would guarantee "fair representation for racial or other minority groups."[77] Instead, he suggested that "[a] better constraint on potential gerrymandering, is imposed by the use of established political boundaries."[78]

The dialogue in *Connor* illustrates both that traditional criteria have been invoked on behalf of minority representational interests[79] and that

---

peculiar configurations unless there must be some presumption in favor of *usual* shapes.

72. Letter from John R. Dunne, Assistant Attorney General, Civil Right Division, U.S. Department of Justice, to Mark H. Cohen, Senior Assistant Attorney General, State of Georgia 2 (Mar. 20, 1992) (on file with author) [hereinafter Dunne Letter, Mar. 20].

73. 113 S. Ct. at 2829. See *supra* note 32 for a summary of the facts of *UJO*. While Justice White announced the judgment of the Court in favor of the New York plan at issue in *UJO*, no part of his opinion (except Part I on the background of the case) commanded a majority of the Court. In a portion of his opinion joined by Justices Stevens and Rehnquist, Justice White asserted that "a State, employing sound districting principles such as compactness and population equality [could] attempt to prevent racial minorities from being repeatedly outvoted by creating" majority-minority districts for "members of those racial groups who are sufficiently numerous and whose residential patterns afford the opportunity of creating districts in which they will be in the majority." *UJO v. Carey*, 430 U.S. 144, 168 (1977). In *Shaw*, this language was cited approvingly by Justice O'Connor. *Shaw*, 113 S. Ct. at 2829.

74. 431 U.S. 407 (1977).

75. *Id.* at 425-26.

76. *Id.* at 428, (Blackmun, J. concurring).

77. *Id.* at 429.

78. *Id.*

79. See *Major v. Treen*, 574 F. Supp. 325 (E.D. La. 1983) (invalidating, based on

the Court's consideration of apportionment questions has not been limited by a narrow focus on population criteria alone. Thus, *Karcher* v. *Daggett*,[80] which holds that there is no *de minimis* population deviation for congressional districts,[81] also allows that "[a]ny number of consistently applied legislative policies might justify some variance, including, for instance, making districts compact, respecting municipal boundaries, preserving the core of prior districts, and avoiding contests between incumbent Representatives."[82]

The district court, then, in *Shaw* v. *Hunt* was surely wrong in suggesting that traditional redistricting criteria have virtually no relevance to contemporary redistricting. Asserting that "compactness, contiguity, and

---

revised Section 2 of the Voting Rights Act, a Louisiana congressional districting scheme.) The court's discussion of district configurations is illuminating:

> Districts One and Two of Act 20, with their distorted shapes and irregular, indented perimeters, are not geographically compact. These unusual configurations are not necessary to ensure adherence to the one person, one vote rubric....Act 20 deviates from the natural geographic barrier formed by the Mississippi River....
>
> New Orleans' traditional political subunit, the ward, has been selectively fragmented by Act 20....
>
> By disregarding parish lines and uniting populated segments of Orleans and Jefferson Parishes with mutually exclusive, often discordant needs and concerns, Act 20 effectively ignores both historic boundaries and obvious communities of interest.
>
> *Id.* at 335-36.

80. 462 U.S. 725 (1983).

81. *Id.* at 734.

82. *Id.* at 740. In this case, the Court upheld a lower court's invalidation of a congressional districting plan enacted by the New Jersey legislature. *Id.* On remand the lower court, at the request of the contending parties, selected a new plan from among several proposals. The lower court chose a plan that "achieved lower population deviations and more compact districts" than another plan that more closely resembled the invalidated plan (and thus, arguably, more nearly approximated state policy). *Karcher v. Daggett*, 466 U.S. 910, 910 (1984) (Stevens, J., concurring), *denying stay of Daggett v. Kimmelman*, 580 F. Supp. 1259 (D.N.J. 1984). The district court did not abuse its discretion because compactness "is a legitimate consideration in reapportionment." *Id.* Moreover, the district court's action was not inconsistent with *White v. Weiser*, 412 U.S. 783, 797 (1973) (holding a "[d]istrict [c]ourt should defer to [otherwise constitutional] state policy in fashioning" a redistricting plan) since New Jersey had "identified no state policy...that justifies the bizarre district lines in the original reapportionment plan." *Karcher*, 466 U.S. at 911. The Supreme Court subsequently affirmed on appeal the district court's action. *Karcher v. Daggett*, 467 U.S. 1222 (1984).

respect for political subdivisions have little inherent value in the district-ing process,"[83] the *Hunt* court went on to argue:

> As the [Supreme] Court explained in *Reynolds*, arguments that "geo-graphic considerations" should receive primary emphasis in redistrict-ing, while perhaps valid at one point in our history, are "unconvincing" today, because "[m]odern developments and improvements in trans-portation and communications" mean that small and compact legisla-tive districts are no longer necessary to insure that all citizens have access to their representatives.[84]

The full passage in *Reynolds*, however, conveys a rather different impres-sion from the one suggested by the district court:

> Considerations of area alone provide an insufficient justification for devi-ations from the equal-population principle. Again, people, not land or trees or pastures, vote. Modern developments in transportation and commu-nication make rather hollow...most claims that deviations from popu-lation-based representation can be validly based *solely* on geographical considerations. Arguments for allowing such deviations in order...to prevent legislative districts from becoming so large that the availability of access of citizens to their representatives is impaired are today, for the most part, unconvincing.[85]

Plainly, the Court did not rule out the use—or relevance—of geo-graphic considerations in redistricting; instead, it rejected geographic considerations as an excuse for drawing districts of substantially unequal population. In the paragraph immediately preceding the paragraph in which the above quoted passage appears, the Court noted:

> A State may legitimately desire to maintain the integrity of various polit-ical subdivisions, insofar as possible, and provide for compact districts of contiguous territory....Valid considerations may underlie such aims. Indiscriminate districting, without any regard for political subdivision or natural or historical boundary lines, may be little more than an open invitation to partisan gerrymandering.[86]

Thus, not only did the district court in *Hunt* mischaracterize the teaching of *Reynolds*, it also advanced a logical *non sequitur*, suggesting that be-cause compactness does not guarantee fairly representative districts,

---

83. *Shaw v. Hunt*, 861 F. Supp 408, 451 (E.D.N.C. 1994).
84. *Id.* at 451 (quoting *Reynolds v. Sims*, 377 U.S. 533, 580 (1964)).
85. *Reynolds v. Sims*, 377 U.S. 533, 580 (1964) (emphasis added).
86. *Id.* at 578-79.

compactness is irrelevant. The point is tantamount to the argument that sending children to school does not guarantee that they will be educated; therefore schools don't matter.

In addition to arguing that compactness is irrelevant because it is ineffective as a guarantee of fair districting, the district court in *Hunt* also contended that the absence of federal statutory requirements for compactness, contiguity, and fidelity to subdivision boundaries support the proposition that these criteria are "no longer appropriate today."[87] The court observed that, from 1842 to 1929, federal law required that districts be contiguous, that from 1901 to 1929 the law called for compact districts, that the requirements of contiguity and compactness were repealed in 1929, and that successive congresses have resisted the re-establishment of these requirements.[88] Interestingly, Justice John Marshall Harlan, in his dissenting opinion in *Wesberry v. Sanders*,[89] made much the same argument with respect to the requirement for equally-populated districts. Since Congress had adopted an equal population rule for congressional districts in 1872, dropped it in 1929,[90] and refused to reinstate it thereafter, Justice Harlan asserted that Congress intended "to leave the problem [of the population of congressional districts] and its solution to the States."[91] The *Hunt* court's analysis, therefore, is as much an argument against a constitutional requirement of "one person, one vote" as it is a case against a constitutional test of compactness.[92] Viewed in this light, the argument is unpersuasive.

Challenged Districts and the Voting Rights Act

An Overview of Cases

Since *Shaw v. Reno*, federal district courts, sitting in three judge panels, have issued rulings on *Shaw*-based attacks of congressional districts

---

87. *Shaw*, 861 F. Supp. at 452 n.45.

88. *Id.*

89. 376 U.S. 1, 42-45 (1964) (Harlan, J., dissenting).

90. *Id.* at 42-43.

91. *Id.* at 45. See also *Colegrove v. Green*, 328 U.S. 549, 555-56 (1946) (plurality opinion of Frankfurter, J.).

92. Thus, the Hunt court, like the dissenters in *Shaw v. Reno*, seems to take on the posture of the dissenters in *Baker v. Carr*, instead of the majority opinion in *Baker*.

in Georgia,[93] Louisiana,[94] North Carolina,[95] and Texas.[96] All four states are subject to the preclearance provisions of Section 5 of the Voting Rights Act[97] and their legislatures crafted the challenged plans under the watchful eye of the Justice Department. As previously detailed,[98] the North Carolina General Assembly created that state's contested congressional plan—with two majority black districts—after the Justice Department had objected to a plan providing for only one black district. Like North Carolina, Georgia gained a seat as a result of the 1990 census, and its legislature adopted a plan with three majority black districts only after the Justice Department had issued Section 5 objections to earlier plans providing for only two majority black districts.[99]

Texas picked up three congressional seats in the 1990 census,[100] but, in contrast to North Carolina and Georgia, was able to craft, on the first try,

93. *Johnson v. Miller*, 864 F. Supp. 1354 (S.D. Ga. 1994).

94. *Hays v. Louisiana*, 862 F. Supp. 119 (W.D. La. 1994).

95. *Shaw v. Hunt*, 861 F. Supp. 408 (E.D.N.C. 1994).

96. *Vera v. Richards*, 861 F. Supp. 1304 (S.D. Tex. 1994).

97. 28 C.F.R. app. § 51 (1994).

98. See *supra* notes 19-21 and accompanying text.

99. Data on the racial composition of districts in the three Georgia plans appears in *Johnson v. Miller*, 864 F. Supp. 1354, 1363 n.5, 1364 n.9, 1366 n.12 (S.D. Ga. 1994). The first plan, adopted in September 1991, provided for two majority black districts: the Fifth (57.84 percent black VAP); and the Eleventh (56.61 percent black VAP). *Id.* at 1363 n.5. The Justice Department complained that this plan might suggest that "the Georgia legislative leadership was predisposed to limit black voting potential to two black majority districts" and that it "did not make a good faith attempt to recognize the concentrations of black voters in the southwest." Dunne Letter, Jan. 21 supra note 71, at 5. The second plan, enacted in February 1992, provided for two majority black districts (the Fifth with a 57.7 percent black VAP and the Eleventh with a 57.97 percent black VAP) and one near black-majority district (the Second with a 45.01 percent black VAP). *Johnson*, 864 F. Supp. at 1364 n.9. The Justice Department again assailed this plan for continuing to reflect the legislative leadership's predisposition in favor of two majority black districts. The Department's letter strongly suggested that the black percentage in the Second should be enhanced by taking Bibb County (Macon) out of the Eleventh; the black percentage of the Eleventh, in turn, could be maintained by shifting that district southward to Savannah. Dunne Letter, Mar. 20, supra note 72, at 3. The final plan adopted the configuration proposed by the Department and thus created three majority-black districts: the Second (52.23 percent black VAP), Fifth (57.47 percent black), and the Eleventh (60.36 percent black). Johnson, 864 F. Supp. at 1366 n.12. The Second and Eleventh districts in 1992 elected black representatives, while the Fifth reelected a black incumbent. The three, all Democrats, retained their seats in the 1994 elections. BARONE & UJIFUSA, *supra* note 12, at 336-37, 343-44, 356-57.

100. *Vera*, 861 F. Supp. at 1311.

a congressional redistricting plan that the Justice Department pre-cleared.[101] The success of the plan might be attributed to the determination of the legislative leadership to use the State's three new seats to fashion a new majority black district and two new Hispanic districts.[102] Louisiana, unlike the other three states, lost a congressional seat in the 1990 census, thereby reducing the State's delegation to seven members.[103] With one black majority district in the New Orleans area, the state legislature decided that the Voting Rights Act required the formation of a second and so fashioned the sprawling, Z-shaped 4th District.[104]

Aside from their status as majority-minority districts, the challenged districts share another common feature: all are bizarrely shaped. The three Texas districts virtually defy description. The 30th District, according to the *Vera* court,

> sprawls throughout Dallas County, deliberately excludes the wealthy white neighborhoods of Highland Park and University Park and extends fingers into Collin County ... and picks up a small African-American neighborhood. The district extends into Tarrant County only to pick up

---

101. *Id.* at 1314.

102. *Id.* at 1315. Before the 1991 redistricting, there were four Hispanics and one African-American in the 27-member Texas congressional delegation. The 1992 elections resulted in the election of an additional Hispanic and another black. *Id.* at 136. An Anglo Democrat, however, won the 29th District, which was designed to elect an Hispanic. BARONE & UJIFUSA, *supra*, note 12, at 1275-77.

103. *Hays v. Louisiana*, 839 F. Supp. 1188, 1190 (W.D. La. 1993) (*"Hays I"*).

104. *Id.* at 1196. In this case, a three-judge court invalidated the 4th District as an unconstitutional racial gerrymander. *Id.* at 1218. The Louisiana legislature subsequently adopted a new redistricting plan that retained two majority black districts but created a less bizarrely shaped, less sprawling 4th District. On June 27, 1994, the U.S. Supreme Court vacated the judgment in *Hays I* and remanded the case "for further consideration in light of Act 1 of the Second Extraordinary Session of the 1994 Louisiana Legislature," a reference to the new plan. *Louisiana v. Hays*, U.S. 114 S. Ct. 2731 (1994). As the district court noted in *Shaw v. Hunt*, 861 F. Supp. 408, 427 n.15 (E.D.N.C. 1994), it is not clear whether the Supreme Court vacated *Hays I* because the new plan made that decision moot or because the decision itself was flawed. The three-judge court subsequently invalidated the new plan, relying on the rationale of its original opinion. *Hays v. Louisiana*, 862 F. Supp. 119 (W.D. La. 1994) (*"Hays II"*). In *Hays II*, the court emphasized that the new plan still "classified citizens along racial lines and segregated them into voting districts accordingly." *Id.* at 121. The court imposed its own plan, an action which the Supreme Court stayed. *Louisiana v. Hays*, U.S. 115 S. Ct. (1994). In the analysis in the text, I focus primarily on the configuration of the 4th District at issue in *Hays I*. For a useful comparison of the plans at issue in *Hays I* and *II*, *see* Dave Kaplan, *Redrawn Map Still Features Two Minority Districts*, 52 CONG. Q. WKLY. REP. 1083, 1083-84 (1994).

a small border area with a high African-American concentration. It also reaches out to claim Hamilton Park, an affluent African-American neighborhood surrounded by whites.[105]

Justice O'Connor offered this description of North Carolina's 12th District in *Shaw v. Reno.*

> It is approximately 160 miles long and, for much of its length, no wider than the [Interstate]-85 corridor. It winds in snake-like fashion through tobacco country, financial centers, and manufacturing areas "until it gobbles in enough enclaves of black neighborhoods." Northbound and southbound drivers on I-85 sometimes find themselves in separate districts in one county, only to "trade" districts when they enter the next county. Of the ten counties through which District 12 passes, five are cut into three different districts; even towns are divided. At one point the district remains contiguous only because it intersects at a single point with two other districts before crossing over them.[106]

A three-judge district court described Louisiana's 4th District in the following way: "Like the functional swordsman Zorro, when making his signature mark, District 4 slashes a giant but somewhat shaky 'Z' across the state, as it cuts a swath through much of Louisiana."[107] *The Almanac of American Politics 1994* characterized Georgia's 11th District in this fashion: "Geographically, it is a monstrosity, stretching from Atlanta to Savannah. Its core is the plantation country in the center of the state,

---

105. *Vera*, 861 F. Supp. at 1337. Of the 18th and 29th Texas Districts, the court observed that they "are so tortuously drawn that an 8 x 11" map does not begin to show their block- by-block district lines.... The districts literally meander from one side of the street to the other and cross major thoroughfares, like Shepherd Drive, numerous times." *Id.* at 1340. Michael Tomasky suggested that the 29th District "looks a bit like a jigsaw puzzle in progress." Michael Tomasky, *Out-of-Bounds Lines?* HARPER'S, Mar. 1992, at 56, 56.

106. *Shaw*, 113 S. Ct. at 2820-21 (quoting Shaw v. Barr, 808 F. Supp. 461, 476-77 (E.D.N.C. 1992) (Voorhees, C.J., dissenting)).

107. *Hays*, 839 F. Supp. at 1199. The revised 4th District at issue in Hays II is a kind of twisted dagger that runs diagonally across the state, extending from the northwest corner across the heart of the state for about four-fifths of the distance to New Orleans. Chief Judge Shaw described the new 4th District at issue in *Hays II* in this way:

> Though it may be less bizarre than the [original plan]..., the physiognomy of [the new] District 4 still strongly suggests that the Legislature engaged in racial gerrymandering in creating the district. Looking at District 4 on a map of Louisiana, it appears as if someone knocked over an inkwell somewhere around Waskom, Texas, spilling ink aimlessly across the map of Louisiana. There is simply nothing regular about the contours of District 4.

Hays, 862 F. Supp. at 126 (Shaw, C.J., concurring).

lightly populated, but heavily black. It links by narrow corridors the black neighborhoods in Augusta, Savannah, and southern DeKalb County."[108]

The Voting Rights Act and the New Technology

Despite the differences among the contested districts, it is their shared characteristics—shape and racial composition—that are the twin concerns of *Shaw*-based challenges. The contested districts reflect the confluence of three forces. First is the constitutional mandate to create congressional districts that are, as nearly as practicable, equal in population. *Karcher* v. *Daggett*,[109] holds that any deviation from absolute population equality must be justified.[110] Second is the prevailing view, discussed at greater length below, that the Voting Rights Act requires the creation of majority-minority districts. Third is the impact of a new redistricting technology that has revolutionized the task of political cartography. The district court in *Shaw* v. *Hunt* offered this richly detailed description of the dimensions of the new technology:

> [T]he critical redistricting data—total population, voting age population by race or national origin, voter registration by party and race— was now made available by the Census Bureau and state legislative staff not only down to townships and precincts, but even further down to the level of the "census block." ... Incorporated into a newly acquired computer software program along with digital map files, these allowed the rapid call-up and visual display on computer terminals of critical demographic and statistical data down to the census block level, along with geographic features—highways, streets, rivers, railroads—and political boundaries. ... [P]recinct election results in a number of recent statewide elections were included in the computer database, making available at the precinct level partisan voting patterns that might affect particular candidacies in potential districts.[111]

In the early 1980's, the North Carolina legislature, seeking to draw congressional districts that followed county boundary lines, used the state's 100 counties as building blocks.[112] In the 1990's, the legislature

---

108. BARONE & UJIFUSA, *supra* note 12, at 356.
109. 462 U.S. 725 (1983).
110. *Id.* at 734.
111. *Shaw v. Hunt*, 861 F. Supp. 408, 457 (E.D.N.C. 1994).
112. The 1982 plan divided only 4 counties. Act of Feb. 11, 1982, ch. 7, 1982 N.C. Sess. Laws 13.

readily disregarded county lines, working with some 2,417 precincts[113] and ultimately having access to some 229,000 census blocks.[114] But for some Texas districts, such as the 18th and 29th in Houston, "[t]easing out the actual boundaries between the two districts was done block by block, home by home, to ensure a 'majority minority' in both [districts]."[115] So many precincts were divided that Harris County had to "increase its number of precincts from 672 to 1,224."[116]

Faced with the parallel commands of "one person, one vote" and the Voting Rights Act, and aided by the new districting technology, legislatures and other redistricting agencies in the 1990's began to create districts that were previously unimaginable. Since the new technology made it possible to create mathematically perfect districts, the logic of "one person, one vote," especially as applied to congressional districting, seemed to mandate such districts. But states such as North Carolina and Georgia could have easily met the requirement of perfectly equipopulous districts without resort to wildly contorted districts. It was the conjunction of the "one person, one vote" rule with the requirement to create black majority districts wherever possible that demanded the abandonment of traditional redistricting criteria. Once these criteria were cast aside, legislatures were free to pursue other goals, such as partisan advantage and incumbent protection, unconstrained by considerations of district shape and notions of community.[117]

The Transformation of Section 5

At this point, it must be said that the legal foundation for the Justice Department's demand that North Carolina and Louisiana craft two majority black districts or that Georgia draw three black districts is, at best, dubious. Before the 1982 amendments to the Voting Rights Act, a jurisdiction subject to the preclearance provisions of Section 5 needed to show only that a proposed voting change, otherwise free of discriminatory intent, did not have a *retrogressive* effect on a covered minority popula-

---

113. Beth Donovan, *North Carolina Computer Draws Some Labyrinthine Lines*, 49 CONG. Q. WKLY REP. 1916 (July 13, 1991).

114. *Hunt*, 861 F. Supp. at 457.

115. Tomasky, *supra* note 105, at 56. That the "home by home" reference is not hyperbole is confirmed by the district court's account of the line drawing process. *See Vera v. Richards*, 861 F. Supp. 1304, 1309 (S.D. Tex. 1994).

116. *Vera*, 861 F. Supp. at 1325.

117. *See* the text at p. 82.

tion.[118] For Georgia, for instance, the congressional map in effect in the 1980's provided for one majority black district, so a two-district plan, which the state adopted in 1991 (but to which the Justice Department objected) would have been nonretrogressive. In the case of North Carolina, since its 1982 plan had no majority black district and the 1991 plan created one, the state's 1991 plan was plainly nonretrogressive. In her majority opinion in *Shaw*, Justice O'Connor pointedly reiterated that retrogression is the appropriate test of discriminatory effect under Section 5,[119] and went on to observe that a plan, having been precleared under Section 5, could still be challenged as unconstitutional.[120] As Justice O'Connor emphasized, North Carolina could not use Section 5 as "*carte blanche* to engage in racial gerrymandering in the name of nonretrogression."[121]

---

118. *Beer v. United States*, 425 U.S. 130, 141 (1976) ("[T]he purpose of § 5 has always been to insure that no voting procedure changes would be made that would lead to a retrogression in the position of racial minorities with respect to their effective exercise of the electoral franchise."). For discussion of the retrogression rule, see Abigail M. Thernstrom, Whose Votes Count, Affirmative Action And Minority Voting Rights at 144-56 (1987).

119. *Shaw*, 113 S. Ct. at 2831.

120. *Id.* at 2830.

121. *Id.* 2831. Justice O'Connor's assertion that preclearance does not insulate a plan against a constitutional challenge presents a new twist on an old theme. Section 5 itself provides that preclearance "shall [not] bar a subsequent action to enjoin enforcement" of a plan. 42 U.S.C. § 1973c (1988). In *Beer*, the Court viewed this *proviso* as leaving the door open for minority voters or the Justice Department to challenge precleared, nonretrogressive plans on constitutional grounds. *Beer*, 425 U.S. at 142-43. At the same time, the *Beer* Court indicated that the plan at issue—which created, at most, two majority black seats on a seven- member council in a city 45 percent black—would "not remotely approach a violation of the constitutional standards" of *Whitcomb v. Chavis*, 402 U.S. 124 (1971) and *White v. Regester*, 412 U.S. 755 (1973), among other cases. *Beer*, 425 U.S. at 142. The Court's embrace of an intent standard for 14th and 15th Amendment vote dilution cases in *Mobile v. Bolden*, 446 U.S. 55 (1980), made constitutional challenges to precleared plans even more problematic. *Id.* at 74. After Congress amended Section 2 of the Voting Rights Act in 1982, nonretrogressive plans precleared under Section 5 became vulnerable to lawsuits based on the statutory results test of Section 2. *See Gingles v. Edmisten*, 590 F. Supp. 345, at 375-76 (E.D.N.C. 1984) (holding, *inter alia*, that preclearance of a redistricting plan does not preclude a Section 2 challenge), *aff'd in part and rev'd in part on other grounds sub. nom. Thornburg v. Gingles*, 478 U.S. 30 (1986) (affirming the district court's invalidation of four multimember districts and reversing the district court's invalidation of a fifth). *See also Major v. Treen*, 574 F. Supp. 325 (E.D. La. 1983) (invalidating precleared congressional redistricting plan on Section 2 grounds). Conceivably, a state might win preclearance and foreclose a Section 2 lawsuit by a single-mindedly maximizing safe minority seats. Under *Shaw*, however, a state that pursued a maximization strategy would run the risk of committing

But the State had argued to the Court, said Justice O'Connor, that its principal redistricting concern was not to avoid retrogression but "to avoid dilution of black voting strength in violation of Section 2, as construed by *Thornburg v. Gingles*."[122] The state's argument was, at once, both misleading and true. It was misleading because the driving force behind the state's adoption of the 1992 plan was not compliance with Section 2, but preclearance under Section 5. Whatever its concerns about Section 2, the State would not have created the 1992 plan if the Justice Department had not objected to the 1991 plan. It was true because the 1991 objection clearly signaled to the State that the Justice Department wanted a plan that created two majority black districts, an outcome presumably required by Section 2; nonretrogression would not do. After the 1991 objection, then, the state's principal concern remained Section 5 preclearance, but preclearance took on the coloration of Section 2. It is important to ask, therefore, whether the Justice Department's objection to the 1991 plan was based on a results-oriented analysis.

In the wake of the 1982 Voting Rights Act Amendments, the Justice Department adopted regulations that provide:

> In those instances in which the Attorney General concludes that, as proposed, the submitted change is free of discriminatory purpose and retrogressive effect, but also concludes that a bar to implementation of the change is necessary to prevent a clear violation of amended Section 2, the Attorney General will withhold Section 5 preclearance.[123]

The addition of the Section 2 results test to the purpose or effect language of Section 5 altered the terms of the Voting Rights Act in two fundamental ways: (1) with regard to burden of proof, and (2) with respect to the substantive standard governing preclearance. Under Section 5, a covered jurisdiction bears the burden of proof in demonstrating that a voting change is not discriminatory. Under Section 2, a minority plaintiff challenging an election practice bears the burden of proof. By reading results into Section 5, the Department effectively could shift the burden of proof in a Section 2 action to the jurisdiction and thereby require a cov-

---

a constitutional voting rights violation, for which preclearance would offer no shield against litigation.

122. *Shaw*, 113 S. Ct. at 2831.

123. 28 C.F.R. § 51.55(b)(2) (1994). Since Congress had not amended the language of Section 5 itself, the incorporation depended on an attenuated reading of the 1982 amendments' legislative history. *Proposed Changes to Regulations Governing Section 5 of The Voting Rights Act: Oversight Hearings Before the Subcomm. on Civil and Constitutional Rights of the House Comm. on the Judiciary*, 99th Cong., 1st Sess. 29-42 (1982) (testimony of Timothy G. O'Rourke).

ered state to draw majority-minority seats wherever voting allegedly was racially polarized. Not only could the Department demand that majority-minority districts be drawn, it also could demand, based on its assessment of local conditions, that such districts have some requisite percentage of minority population designed to ensure a majority-minority electorate on election day.[124] Thus, the 1987 regulations helped to fuel the expectation, widely reported before and during states' post-1990 redistricting, that the Justice Department would require covered states to create majority-minority districts wherever possible.[125] In fact, the Justice Department apparently encouraged this expectation. Thus, in the Louisiana case, the court concluded that "[t]he testimony at the Trial and at the Evidentiary Hearing reflected overwhelmingly that the Attorney General's Office ("AGO") had let it be known that preclearance would not be forthcoming for any plan that did not include at least *two* 'safe' black districts out of seven."[126]

While the results test apparently underlay the Justice Department's pressure on covered states to create new black and Hispanic majority districts after the 1990 census, the Department's objection letters often do not clarify the basis for the objection. The regulation cited above suggests that the Justice Department might invoke the results test to object to a plan that is free of discriminatory purpose or effect. In fact, the Department appears to have developed a different, hybrid approach, which is to find discriminatory purpose in plans that fail to achieve the appropriate, proportional results. Thus, the *Hunt* court interpreted the Justice Department's objection to the 1991 North Carolina plan to mean "that

---

124. The Justice Department objected to the 1991 North Carolina congressional redistricting plan and to redistricting plans for both houses of the General Assembly. With regard to state House District 8, the Department complained: "In spite of the 58 percent black population majority, serious concerns have been raised as to whether black voters in this district will have an equal opportunity to elect their preferred candidate, particularly given the fact that only 52 percent of the registered voters in the district are black." Dunne Letter, Dec. 18, *supra* note 20, at 3.

125. *See e.g.,* Phil Duncan, *Creating Black Districts May Segregate Voters,* 48 CONG. Q. WKLY REP. 2462 (1990) ("In the 1990s round of redistricting, the Justice Department and the courts are expected to demand that mapmakers prove they have done all they can to maximize the voting strength of minority groups."); Robert W. Merry, *The New Commitment To Gerrymandering,* 49 CONG. Q. WKLY. REP. 2346 (1991) ("Wherever feasible, states must create a district in which a minority group enjoys majority status."); *see also* BARONE & UJIFUSA, *supra* note 12, at 1265 ("[Congressman David] Frost is a Democrat [from Texas's 24th District] whose tenure was threatened more than anyone else's by the interpretation of the 1982 amendments to the Voting Rights Act requiring a maximum number of black-majority districts.").

126. *Hays v. Louisiana,* 839 F. Supp. 1188, 1196 n.21 (W.D. La. 1993).

two such districts meeting the *Gingles* requirements demonstrably could be created, and that the plan's failure to do so represented a *deliberate effort* to dilute minority voting strength."[127] Similarly, in the Georgia case, the Justice Department did not rely on a results test, but rather—in the view of the three-judge court—found that the state had only offered "pretextual reasons" for failing to adopt various configurations that would result in the creation of three majority-black districts.[128]

In essence, what the Justice Department appears to be doing is dressing a results analysis in the clothes of purpose. From the Department's perspective, the approach offers a variety of advantages. First, it provides the Department with an alternative to the "relatively toothless" retrogression test,[129] which is the standard for assessing discriminatory effect under Section 5. Second, the hybrid analysis grounds objections in the more traditional purpose prong of Section 5 (in this respect, it matters a great deal that the purpose language appears in Section 5 and the results test does not). Third, it sidesteps the issues associated with a full-blown results approach. Since the Department's own regulations require that a results-based objection flow only "from a clear violation of amended section 2,"[130] the hybrid analysis excuses the Department from specifying exactly what it is that Section 2 requires in a particular instance. Precisely because the Section 2 vote dilution claims have been delimited to a minority group that is geographically concentrated,[131] the Justice Department would be hard pressed to define "clear violation" without defining, in the first instance, whether a minority was sufficiently concentrated to constitute a majority in a reasonably compact district.[132] In the Georgia

---

127. *Shaw v. Hunt*, 861 F. Supp. 408, 464 (E.D.N.C. 1994) (emphasis added).

128. *Johnson v. Miller*, 864 F. Supp. 1354, 1368. The Justice Department, in its representations to the district court, "denied that the max-black plan [which provided for three black districts] was the 'benchmark' against which" it assessed Georgia's proposed plans. *Id.* at 1364. The court found the denial disingenuous. *Id.* at 1375.

129. *Hunt*, 861 F. Supp. at 441 (describing the retrogression test).

130. 28 C.F.R. § 51.55(b)(2) (1994).

131. According to the Court in *Thornburg v. Gingles*, 478 U.S. 30, 48-50 (1986), a minority group can make out a Section 2 claim only by showing that it is politically cohesive, that its candidates are regularly defeated by white bloc voting, and that "it is sufficiently large and geographically compact to constitute a majority in a single-member district." *Id.* at 50-51. As the district court noted in *Hays v. Louisiana*, 839 F. Supp. 1188, 1196, n.21, the Supreme Court applied these criteria to single-member districts in *Growe v. Emison*, U.S. 113 S. Ct. 1075, 1084-85 (1993).

132. During the hearings on the 1982 Amendments, Yale Professor Drew Days, III, who served as the Assistant Attorney General for Civil Rights from 1977 to 1980, offered this portrait of the preclearance process under Section 5:

Take the case of redistricting plans. In a community with a 25 percent minority

case, the Department's position then was not that Section 2 requires three black majority districts, but instead that the state had not given valid reasons for the lines that produced fewer than three.[133] In North Carolina, the Department's objection to the 1991 plan did not build on the premise that two compact, majority black districts could be created; the Department contended, instead, that the state could have drawn a second majority-minority district, with "lines that were no more irregular than [those] found elsewhere in the proposed plan."[134]

The results-dressed-as-purpose analysis yields a fourth advantage, especially in the context of *Shaw*-type litigation, by finessing troubling issues associated with a purely results-based approach. Whether Congress intended Section 5 to incorporate the results test of Section 2 remains an open question.[135] Even if Section 5 were read to encompass a results test, it is doubtful that it can be interpreted to support a maximization theory of minority representation.[136] If the results test is excluded from Section 5, then it is difficult to see how the Justice Department could press for changes beyond retrogression.[137]

---

population, let us assume that local officials can create a compact and contiguous set of four city council districts where minorities are likely to have a sizable population advantage in one district. When the jurisdiction submits instead, however, a plan that is not compact or contiguous[,] reflects substantial population deviations from district to district or is otherwise drawn in a fashion that frustrates any prospect that minorities will gain control of one district in the plan, the Department is likely to object. On the other hand, we might assume another set of facts in which it can be shown that no fairly-drawn redistricting plan will result in minority control of one district, because of dispersed minority residential patterns, for example. The Department's response is not to demand that the jurisdiction adopt a crazy-quilt, gerrymandered districting plan to ensure that proportional minority representation.

Extension of the Voting Rights Act: Hearings Before the Subcomm. on Civil and Constitutional Rights of the House Comm. on the Judiciary, 97th Cong., 1st Sess. pt. 3, 2119 (1981) (prepared statement of Professor Drew S. Days III). Arguably, Professor Days' reading of Section 5 was the one that Congress expected to be enforced in the wake of the 1982 Amendments.

133. *See Johnson v. Miller*, 864 F. Supp. 1354, 1390-92 (S.D. Ga.).

134. Dunne Letter, Dec. 18, *supra* note 20, at 4.

135. *See Shaw v. Hunt*, 861 F. Supp. 408, 441 n.30.

136. *See Johnson v. De Grandy*, U.S. 114 S. Ct. 2647, 2651 (1994) (rejecting the contention that Section 2 of the Voting Rights Act requires the creation of a maximum number of majority-minority districts).

137. The three-judge court in *Hays*, severely criticized both the Justice Department's reading of the Voting Rights Act and its specific actions in the Louisiana setting. The court asserted, "[N]either Section 2 nor Section 5 of the Voting Rights Act justify the [Attorney General's Office's] insistence that Louisiana adopt a plan with two safe, black

But, in truth, the problem with the Justice Department's enforcement of a rule that requires covered states to draw majority-minority districts wherever possible has less to do with the Department's reading of the law than with its viewing of the maps. In other words, it was not so much the Department's insistence on the creation of black and Hispanic districts, as it was the Department's definition of what constitutes a *bona fide* district. As the *Hays* court noted, the Justice Department "cannot rely on Section 2 of the Voting Rights Act to force a state to adopt a plan containing an additional majority-minority district with a geographically dispersed black majority."[138] In short, the Justice Department is obliged to do more than to define compactness simply in terms of whatever majority-minority district it is willing to approve.[139] In like vein, a state should not be able to defend a plan as compact merely because the Justice Department has approved it.

The Link Between Section 5, Section 2 and Compelling Interest

Faced with *Shaw*-type challenges, courts must decide two basic questions: whether racial gerrymandering has occurred and, if so, whether such districting "is narrowly tailored to further a compelling governmental interest."[140] In the four congressional redistricting cases decided to date, the first question has been remarkably easy to answer. The documentary record is replete with statements of legislators who readily ex-

---

majority districts." *Hays v. Louisiana*, 839 F. Supp. 1188, 1196 n.21. The court complained that "[i]n one letter the [Assistant Attorney General] went so far as to suggest *how* the plan should be drawn." *Id.* at 1197. The court charged that the Justice Department had "arrogated the power to use Section 5 preclearance as a sword to implement forcibly its own redistricting policies." *Id.*

138. *Id.* at 1196 n.21. *See also Jeffers v. Tucker*, 847 F. Supp. 655, at 662 (E.D. Ark. 1994) (three-judge court). In the context of a Section 2 action against state legislative districts, the court noted that "[w]hile [plaintiffs' proposed senate districts] are nowhere nearly so unusual in shape as the I-85 district at issue in *Shaw*, [they] are anything but compact.... precisely due to the lack of the compact minority population required by *Gingles*." *Id.*

139. The case law on which the results test of Section 2 is based dealt primarily with the evils associated with multimember districts. *See Whitcomb v. Chavis*, 403 U.S. 124, at 157- 58 (1971). A problem with such districts is that their very size may inhibit political access. Thus, one of the factors for assessing a Section 2 violation is whether election districts are "unusually large." S. REP. No. 417, 97th Cong., 2d Sess. 29 (1982), *reprinted in* 1982 U.S.C.C.A.N. 177, 206. The defect of great size would appear to characterize sprawling single-member districts.

140. *Shaw*, 113 S. Ct. at 2832.

pressed their intention to craft majority-minority districts that would meet with Justice Department approval.[141] And the cartographic evidence[142] clearly demonstrates that contested districts essentially collected concentrations of minority voters without serious regard for traditional redistricting criteria. All four courts, therefore, found the existence of racial gerrymandering.[143]

With respect to the second set of questions—whether racial gerrymandering is supported by a compelling interest and is narrowly tailored—it is evident that neither Section 5 nor Section 2 provide a compelling interest for the plans under analysis here. *Shaw v. Reno* holds that compliance with Section 5 does not give states *"carte blanche"* to engage in racial gerrymandering; the basic test of Section 5 is retrogression. It follows, as noted above, that the Justice Department has misread and misapplied Section 5, objecting to plans that satisfied the terms of the Voting Rights Act; indeed, this is the view of three of the four courts that have ruled on *Shaw*-type congressional redistricting cases.[144] States cannot, therefore, invoke the text of Section 5 as a source of compelling interest, nor can they rely on a Justice-Department-made-us-do-it defense.

It is equally clear, in view of *Thornburg v. Gingles*, that states cannot invoke Section 2 of the Act for a compelling interest to create radically

---

141. *See Johnson v Miller*, 864 F. Supp. 1354, 1377 (S.D. Ga. 1994) (quoting testimony of Georgia House Speaker Thomas Murphy on the final version of Eleventh Congressional District: "'What we did is we went into counties and precincts and picked up pockets of African-Americans to make a strong district with voting age black population so that it would guarantee a black would be elected from there.'"); *Hays v. Louisiana*, 839 F. Supp. 1188, 1204 (W.D. La. 1993) (quoting testimony of "Mr. Willie Hunter, a black state legislator," that the legislature, in designing the 4th District, "'looked at numbers [of black voters] period'"); *Shaw v. Hunt*, 861 F. Supp. 408, 473 (E.D.N.C. 1994) (noting that the North Carolina General Assembly "deliberately created two districts... that would have narrow, but effective voting majorities of African-American citizens"); *Id.* at 481 n.9. (Voorhees, C.J., dissenting) (quoting testimony of one North Carolina state senator who said African- Americans "'deserve two black districts'"); *Vera v. Richards* 861 F. Supp. 1304, 1321 (S.D. Tex. 1994) (quoting testimony of Texas Representative Fred Blair on the creation of the 30th Congressional District, which "'was crafted in a manner that we sought to pick up those precincts, those communities, those areas we thought were stable areas that would present an opportunity to elect an African-American'").

142. *See* the discussion in the text at p. 77.

143. *Johnson*, 864 F. Supp. at 1377-78; *Hays*, 839 F. Supp. at 1204-05; *Vera*, 861 F. Supp. at 1345; *Shaw v. Hunt*, 861 F. Supp. 408, 476 (E.D.N.C.).

144. *Johnson*, 864 F. Supp. at 1384-86; *Hays*, 839 F. Supp. at 1196; *Vera*, 861 F. Supp. at 1342.

uncompact districts that connect widely dispersed clusters of minority voters. Again, this is the holding of three of the four courts (and nine of twelve judges) that have looked at the issue.[145]

Because there is, in the cases under examination, no compelling interest in creating highly contorted districts that effectuate a racial sorting of voters, the question of narrow tailoring is immaterial. It should be noted, however, that the plans at issue—to the extent they depart from traditional redistricting criteria—are not narrowly tailored. Moreover, it is transparently clear in at least two cases that the state legislatures, having decided to do whatever was necessary to create majority-minority districts, also decided to do whatever was necessary to mitigate the undesirable partisan effects associated with race-based redistricting. In order to protect white Democratic incumbents against the political dislocations occasioned by racial gerrymandering, the Democratic-controlled Texas and North Carolina legislatures drew majority-minority congressional districts that were far less compact than those that would have resulted had each state tried simply or solely to create majority-minority districts. In North Carolina, for instance, the creation of the majority black First District threatened to undermine Democratic incumbents in adjacent districts. Among the adjustments that the legislature made in order to remove this threat were the following:

> Though the home precincts of both Congressman [Tim] Valentine in Nash County in the existing Second District and of Congressman [H. Martin] Lancaster in the Third were heavily (45%) African-American and were geographically situated for ready inclusion in the First District, they were retained, as were their entire counties, in their existing districts. To compensate, the First District had to be extended much further southward to include rural portions of Columbus and Bladen Counties with comparable African-American populations.[146]

In the Texas case, the district court cited numerous examples of jagged lines tied to incumbency protection.[147] The *Vera* court summed up the situation in language equally applicable to North Carolina:

---

145. *See supra* note 10. With respect to Louisiana, the fact that the state was able to draw, after *Hays I*, a new black majority district less than half as long as the infamous Z-district clearly demonstrates that the earlier version of the 4th was, indeed, not narrowly tailored. *See Hays v. Lousianna*, 862 F. Supp. 119,122 n.1 (*"Hays II"*) (noting that Louisiana "now concedes that [the original plan] was bizarre").

146. *Hunt*, 861 F. Supp. at 468.

147. *Vera*, 861 F. Supp. at 1321.

[State legislator Ted] Lyon attributed the "irregular" shape of District 30 in Oak Cliff and Grand Prairie to fighting between [white Democratic incumbent Congressman Martin] Frost and [State Senator Eddie Bernice] Johnson settled by essentially splitting the

> The [Texas] Legislature obligingly carved out districts of apparent sup-
> porters of incumbents, as suggested by incumbents, and then added
> appendages to connect their residences to those districts.... The final
> result seems not one in which the people select their representatives, but
> in which the representatives have selected the people.[148]

As the *Vera* court further observed, to suggest that Texas Districts 18,
29, and 30 are narrowly tailored "is also implicitly equating incumbent
protection with a compelling state interest, an utterly unjustifiable argument."[149] In this respect, the dissenter in *Shaw* v. *Hunt* rightly scorned
the majority's contention that the plaintiffs' alleged interests in racially-
neutral redistricting "can be readily subordinated when placed in competition with such relatively transitory interests as incumbency protection,
one of the admittedly pervasive primary goals" of the North Carolina
plan.[150]

In sum, to the extent that the oddities of the North Carolina and
Texas plans reflect partisan and incumbency concerns, as opposed to
considerations of racial fairness, those plans cannot be viewed as narrowly tailored.[151] Moreover, to the extent that all of the plans radically
depart from traditional redistricting criteria, they cannot be regarded as
narrowly tailored.[152] As the *Vera* court observed, "to be narrowly tai-

---

areas between Districts 24 and 30....Lyon also attributed in part some of the irregularity in the district's eastern shape to incumbency protection—namely keeping [white
Democratic Congressman John] Bryant's East Dallas neighborhood in District 5. *Id.*
State Senator Johnson, an African-American, was elected to Congress from the 30th District in 1992.

148. *Id.* at 1334.

149. *Id.* at 1343.

150. *Hunt*, 861 F. Supp. at 493 n.26 (Voorhees, C.J., dissenting).

151. *Id.* at 489 n.26 (Voorhees, C.J., dissenting); *Vera*, 861 F. Supp. at 1342. An
additional problem with the majority black districts at issue in *Shaw v. Hunt* is that they
only partially comprehend the forty North Carolina counties subject to Section 5 preclearance. District 12 takes in portions of ten counties, only two of which are subject to
Section 5. District 1 includes, in whole (8) or in part (14), some 22 counties covered by
Section 5. But 16, or 40 percent, of the 40 covered counties lay outside both Districts 1
and 12. *Hunt*, 861 F. Supp. at 488 (Voorhees, C.J., dissenting).

152. I do not deal at all herein with one element of narrow tailoring—whether the
racial or ethnic percentages of the districts at issue appropriately counteracted the negative effects of racially polarized voting on minority voting strength, without, at the same
time, making the districts overly safe. *See, e.g., Johnson v. Miller*, 867 F. Supp. 1354,
1392-93 (S.D. Ga. 1994); *Hays v. Louisiana*, 839 F. Supp. 1188, 1209 (W.D. La. 1993).

lored, a district must have the least possible amount of irregularity in shape, making allowances for traditional districting criteria."[153]

A Closer Look at the Maps: Shape on Trial?

The Contiguity Problem

A central contention in this analysis is that the districts under challenge in the four congressional redistricting cases are, indeed, a drastic departure from previous redistricting practice. Even in the realm of contiguity, a heretofore "relatively trivial" and usually "noncontroversial" aspect of redistricting,[154] this departure is evident. Contiguity is "trivial" because there is little debate about what it means, it is relatively easy to achieve, and there is little doubt about when a redistricting map achieves it. A venerable definition of the concept holds that a "contiguous district is one in which a person can go from any point within the district to any other point without leaving the district."[155]

The congressional districts contested in *Shaw*-type litigation in various ways either test the outer limits of contiguity or clearly breach the standard. The now-abandoned Fourth District in Louisiana, for instance, probably satisfied the contiguity standard, although barely, since "at some places" along its 600-mile length, it was "no more than 80 feet wide."[156] Georgia's Eleventh District consists of a large central core of overwhelmingly rural counties that sends narrow fingers outward to pick up large black population concentrations in DeKalb County at the northwest end of the district, Richmond County (Augusta) at the northeast end, and Chatham County (Savannah) at the southeast corner. The court, in *Johnson v. Miller*, described the connection between Savannah and the rest of the district.

> The Eleventh soars 18 stories over the water upon the spine of the suspension bridge at Savannah to spill itself over uninhabited Hutchinson Island.... From Hutchinson the district goes northwest across the marsh-

---

153. *Vera*, 861 F. Supp. at 1343.

154. Bernard Grofman, *Criteria for Districting: A Social Science Perspective*, 33 UCLA L. REV. 77, 84 (1985). "Sometimes, however, there can be disputes about whether districts whose parts are connected by water or bridges are genuinely contiguous." *Id.* at 84.

155. Note, *Reapportionment*, 79 HARV. L. REV. 1228, 1284 (1966).

156. *Hays*, 839 F. Supp. at 1200.

es, a wildlife refuge, and the river again (this time without a bridge) to a mere point of contiguity with Effingham County.[157]

"From Burke County," the court observed in describing the tentacle into Richmond County, "the Eleventh District suddenly narrows to a corridor, following the Central Georgia Railroad into the City of Augusta. The corridor, composed of wetlands and some industrial areas, is virtually unpopulated."[158] Similarly, the extension of the Eleventh District into DeKalb County depends on a land bridge that narrows at one point to less than "one half mile."[159]

The Texas districts contested in *Vera* also test the outer limits of contiguity. "Part of the [Thirtieth District] runs along the Trinity River bottom, using it to connect dispersed minority population."[160] The Twenty-ninth District exhibits a similar feature, intruding into "a largely white area via the San Jacinto River" in order to incorporate "453 Hispanics...at the other end."[161]

If districts in Texas and Georgia stretch the concept of contiguity, various districts in North Carolina plainly violate the standard. North Carolina's First and Third Districts intersect and overlap one another at what has become known as the "double cross-over" point—described so vividly in the exchange reported at the beginning of this article.[162] Under the theory of the "double cross-over," which the district court in *Shaw* v. *Hunt* artfully labeled "technical contiguity,"[163] the red squares of a checkerboard could be a single district, while the black squares could be another.

---

157. *Johnson*, 864 F. Supp. at 1374-76.

158. *Id.* at 1378.

159. *Id.* I walked this land bridge, which occurs at the western edge of the Eleventh District near the boundary between Henry and Rockdale Counties; the actual width is less than 300 yards.

160. *Vera*, 861 F. Supp. at 1338.

161. Tomasky, *supra* note 105, at 57.

162. *See* text accompanying *supra* note 1. The purpose of the so-called "double cross-over" of the First and Third Districts:

> was to retain critical portions of Sampson County lying to the west of this cross-over in [Democratic Congressman Martin] Lancaster's Third District, as part of a larger purpose to avoid pairing in the same district any of the incumbent Democratic Congressmen who could be affected by the First District's final configuration: [Congressman Tim] Valentine (Second), Lancaster (Third), [Congressman Charlie] Rose (Seventh), and [Congressman Bill] Hefner (Eighth).

Shaw, 861 F. Supp. at 468.

163. *Id.*

The configuration of North Carolina's Twelfth and Sixth Districts resembles something like a severely warped arrow (the Twelfth) piercing a badly distended heart (the Sixth). In fact, the asserted technical contiguity of these districts depends on at least three double cross-over points (in Guilford, Rowan, and Davidson counties).[164] The simple fact of the matter is that judged in light of the traditional definition of contiguity, these districts—and the First and the Third—are simply not contiguous.[165]

Geographical Compactness

While compactness may be said to be in the eye of the beholder, social science has provided various quantitative measures that permit one to compare the relative compactness of districts. While I do not believe that these measurements should be used to create a legally enforceable standard of compactness, they can serve to isolate districts that are extraordinarily uncompact. In a recent law review article,[166] Richard H. Pildes and Richard G. Niemi rank current congressional districts in terms of a dispersion score, which is "the ratio of the area of the district to the min-

---

164. Deposition of Gerry F. Cohen at vol. I, 65-71, *Shaw v. Hunt*, 861 F. Supp. 408 (E.D.N.C. 1994) (No. 92-202-CIV-5-BR) (on file with author).

165. *See* Bernard Grofman, *Would Vince Lombardi Have Been Right If He Had Said: "When It Comes to Redistricting, Race Isn't Everything, It's the Only Thing?"* 14 CARDOZO L. REV. 1237, 1257, 1261 (1993).

> Congressional District 12 appears to pass through one side of District 6 and emerge from out the other side. If that does not result in District 6 being bisected into discontiguous pieces, the State of North Carolina would appear to be exercising skills superior to those of the late Houdini's famous 'sawing a woman in half' trick.

Id. at 1261 n.99. *See also* BARONE & UJIFUSA, *supra* note 12, at 942, 950 (observing that the 12th District "violate[s] the age-old principle of contiguity" and that "the 3d [District] is not really contiguous.").

See Shaw, 861 F. Supp. at 468 (liberal use of "point contiguity"). For additional background, with some representative maps, see Timothy G. O'Rourke, *Shaw v. Reno and the Hunt for Double Cross-Overs*, 28 PS: POL. SCI. & POL., March 1995, at 36-41.

North Carolina's contiguity problems were avoidable. As the Court observed in *Karcher v. Daggett*, 462 U.S. 725, 733 (1983): "The rapid advances in computer technology and education during the last two decades *make it relatively simple to draw contiguous districts of equal population* and at the same time to further whatever secondary goals the State has." (emphasis added).

166. Richard H. Pildes & Richard G. Niemi, *Expressive Harms, "Bizarre Districts," and Voting Rights: Evaluating Election-District Appearances After* Shaw v. Reno, 92 MICH. L. REV. 483 (1993).

imum circumscribing circle," and in terms of a perimeter score, which "is the ratio of the district area to the area of a circle with the same perimeter."[167] Both scores range from zero to one, with a higher score indicating greater compactness. Taking the lowest scores on each measure, Pildes and Niemi go on to list the 28 least compact congressional districts in the nation among the 428 districts in states with two or more congressional districts.[168] Six Texas districts, including the Eighteenth, Twenty-ninth, and Thirtieth, take spots on this dubious list,[169] while Louisiana's Fourth and Sixth Districts, also claim places.[170] Four North Carolina districts, including the First and Twelfth, end up on the list, with the Twelfth District making a bid for number one.[171] As Pildes and Niemi observe, "If we rather crudely consider dispersion and perimeter scores simultaneously, by simply adding the two scores, North Carolina CD 12 turns out to be the worst in the nation."[172] While Georgia's Eleventh District does not show up on the list of the twenty-eight least compact, it comes close; on the dispersion measure, it ranks among the bottom 7 percent of least compact districts nationwide and among the bottom 11 percent according to the perimeter score.[173]

The compactness of congressional districts nationwide, Pildes and Niemi report, generally declined between 1982 and 1992. For the states of Georgia, Louisiana, North Carolina, and Texas, the post-1990 plans produced more extreme departures from compactness on both dispersion and perimeter scores than did the plans in effect in the 1980's.[174] Pildes and Niemi attribute the overall declines in compactness scores to the combined effect of the equal-population standard, the new redistricting technology, and the demands of the Voting Rights Act.[175] The statistical analyses of Pildes and Niemi provide numerical confirmation of what the congressional district maps reveal; districts in the 1990's are often more

---

167. *Id.* 554.

168. *Id.* at 565.

169. *Id.*

170. *Id.*

171. *Id.*

172. *Id.* at 566.

173. *Id.* at 570. These figures are extrapolated from data in Richard Niemi, et al., *Bright Lines and Tradeoffs: The Conflict Between Compactness and Minority Representation in the Congressional Districts of the 1990s*, Tables 1, 4, 5 (paper presented at the annual meeting of the Midwest Pol. Sci. Assoc., Chicago, Apr. 17, 1992). The percentages are based on 428 congressional districts, excluding those coterminous with whole states. I reported these numbers in *Report of Timothy G. O'Rourke, Ph.D., Johnson v. Miller*, No. CV-194-008 (S.D. Ga.) (on file with author).

174. *Id.* at 569-74.

175. *Id.* at 574.

bizarre-looking than their predecessors. For various reasons, however, district courts in the Georgia, North Carolina, and Texas cases apparently accorded little weight to the numerical measures of compactness.[176]

Integrity of Subdivision Boundaries

Whatever the utility of these measures of compactness, an examination of the treatment of subdivision boundaries in post-1990 congressional districting plans offers strong evidence for the proposition that the recent round of redistricting brought an obvious diminution in fidelity to readily recognizable borders. Until 1991, congressional district lines in North Carolina historically had adhered to county contours almost unfailingly. While the plan in force in the 1980's split only four of the state's 100 counties, the 1992 plan divides 44 counties; seven counties are divided among three districts.[177] Louisiana's 1992 plan split 28 of the State's 64 parishes; the Fourth District itself took in four whole parishes and portions of 24 others. By contrast, the 1980's congressional districts split only seven parishes.[178] In Texas, the plan in effect in the 1980's split

---

176. *See Johnson v. Miller,* 864 F. Supp. 1354, 1388 (S.D. Ga. 1994) ("Various mathematically based measures have been created, none of which yielded clear answers in this litigation."); *Shaw v. Hunt,* 861 F. Supp. 408, 470 (E.D.N.C.) (Recognizing Districts 1 and 12 to be among the least compact in the country according to mathematical measures, but minimizing the utility of numerical measures of compactness because "there is admittedly no consensus as to which of these is most valid" and because "these proposed measures of compactness are not 'judicially manageable.'"). *See also Vera v. Richards,* 861 F. Supp. 1304, 1328 (S.D. Tex. 1994).

177. Whether dictated by the pursuit of exact population equality, the pressure to create two black majority districts, or the need to respond to the special interests of state legislators and incumbent congressmen, some of the splits seem, for lack of a better label, immoderate. The plan divides Guilford (Greensboro) County's 347,420 people among three districts: 207,722 are placed in the Sixth; 135,759 in the Twelfth; and only 3,939 in the Fifth District.

Mecklenburg (Charlotte) County, with 511,433 people, is also split three ways; 346,167 in the Ninth, 162,189 in the Twelfth, and 3,077 in the Eighth. The plan slices up Orange (Chapel Hill) County, most of whose population of 93,851 is in the Fourth District, in order to give 2,836 people to the Twelfth District. The plan carves out 767 of Wake (Raleigh) County's 423,380 people and places them in the Second District; the other 99.8 percent of the county's population is placed in the Fourth District. The plan puts most of Wayne County's 104,666 people in the Third District, but surgically removes 131 Wayne Countians for inclusion in the First District. *See* Memorandum from Gerry F. Cohen, *supra* note 21.

178. *Hays v. Louisiana,* 839 F. Supp. 1188, 1200 (W.D. La. 1993). "[F]or the first time in Louisiana history,...a districting plan violates the boundaries of nearly all major municipalities in the state." *Id.* at 1201. In contrast to the Fourth District invalidated by

ten counties, while the 1991 plan splits 35 counties and more than 160 cities.[179] Georgia's 1980's congressional districts divided three counties, while the 1992 plan splits 26 counties.[180]

The disregard of county and municipal boundaries extends downward to precinct lines in post-1990 redistricting. In North Carolina, the plan adopted in 1992 created a "large number of divided precincts," many of them in order "to put black population concentrations from predominantly white precincts into the 1st or 12th Congressional District."[181] In Texas, so many precincts were divided that three-fifths of the voters in Districts 18 and 29 lived in split precincts.[182]

The division of counties and cities may make congressional districts less recognizable to both constituents and candidates. The division of precincts may not have same effect, since precinct lines do not enjoy the same level of recognition. At the same time, it is evident that divided precincts may create, at the least, some election-day confusion (as voters show up at the wrong polling place).[183] At the worst, split precincts and the arbitrary lines that give rise to them may create severe impediments to campaigning and representation. In Texas, a congressional candidate conducting a "walking" campaign in the 18th District had "to carry a map to identify the district lines, because so often the borders would move from block to block."[184]

Communities of Interest

Among the traditional criteria of redistricting practice is the notion that legislative districts ought to preserve "communities of interest." Achievement of this objective is difficult precisely because there is little

---

Hays I, the Fourth District under the revised plan at issue in *Hays II* encompasses 15 parishes, 12 of which are split; the revised Fourth also divides Shreveport, Baton Rouge, Lafayette, and Alexandria. Overall, the revised plan splits 16 parishes. *Hays v. Louisiana*, 862 F. Supp. 119, 126 (W.D. La. 1993) (Shaw, C.J., concurring).

179. *Vera*, 861 F. Supp. at 1334 n.41; Tomasky, *supra* note 105, at 56.

180. *Johnson*, 864 F. Supp. at 1367.

181. Memorandum to Members of the North Carolina General Assembly from Gerry F. Cohen, Director of Legislative Drafting, North Carolina General Assembly, 1992 Congressional Base Plan #10-Split Precincts, (January 23, 1992) (on file with author).

182. *Vera*, 861 F. Supp. at 1329.

183. In Texas' Eighteenth District, some precincts got the wrong ballots. *Vera*, 861 F. Supp. at 1340.

184. *Id.*

agreement on what constitutes a community of interest. As Bernard Grofman has observed:

> It is roughly synonymous with "recognition and maintenance of patterns of geography, social interaction, trade, political ties, and common interests." In practice, provisions which require preservation of communities of interest are hard to enforce because they are hard to interpret. Also, preserving communities of interest may conflict with the criterion of following political or other sub-unit boundaries.[185]

Communities of interest might also be defined in terms of the unique or prevailing characteristics of places or regions (such as urban or rural, coastal or mountain, agricultural or industrial) or in terms of patterns of social or economic intercourse that are geographically identifiable (such as metropolitan areas or media markets on a large scale or neighborhoods at a much smaller scale). In either case, however, community of interest is viewed in terms of the geography of often readily recognizable regions or areas.

A different approach to community of interest would focus on the characteristics, not of places, but of persons (classified, for instance, by race, or income, or occupation). On the one hand, viewing community in terms of people could be completely compatible with, or even the same as, a place-centered approach to community. A redistricting process that sought to bring together rural areas in a single district would arrive at the same result as one that sought to pull together people engaged in farming. On the other hand, a redistricting plan that sought to collect people of shared characteristics, without regard to place, would produce exactly the sort of oddly-shaped districts at issue in the Georgia, Louisiana, North Carolina, and Texas congressional redistricting cases. In each case, of course, it was clear that race was a driving force behind the creation of the challenged districts.

In the North Carolina case, however, the state argued that the majority black First and Twelfth Districts reflected an underlying rationale that paralleled or transcended race. After the Justice Department rejected the

---

185. Grofman, *supra* note 154, at 87, (quoting VT. STAT. ANN. tit. 17, § 1903 (1982)). Tellingly, *Shaw v. Reno* does not list "communities of interest" among the traditional criteria. *Shaw*, 113 S. Ct. at 2827 (noting "traditional districting principles such as compactness, contiguity, and respect for political subdivisions.") The Court also refers to "'sound districting principles such as compactness and population equality.'" *Id.* at 2829, (quoting *UJO*, 430 U.S. 144, 168 (1977)) (Opinion of White, J., joined by Stevens and Rehnquist, C.J.). *See also Vera*, 861 F. Supp. at 1334 (noting absence of incumbency protection from Reno's list of traditional criteria).

state's 1991 redistricting plan, the legislature set about the task of creating two majority-black districts, one of which would be primarily rural and one that would be principally urban. In fact, 58 percent of the population of the First District lives in rural areas, defined as places with a population of less than 2,500 people. In contrast, the Twelfth District's population is 86 percent urban (defined as those who live in places of 2,500 or more); moreover, 80 percent of the population lives in *urbanized* areas (which are densely populated areas in and around major cities).[186] The make-up of the Twelfth reflected the legislature's determination to build the district with people living in Piedmont Crescent cities with a population of 20,000 or more; the district included four of the state's largest cities (all but Raleigh). The *Hunt* court concluded that Districts 1 and 12 are, indeed, "distinctively 'rural' and distinctively 'urban' in character."[187] Each district, in the court's view, defined a community of interest—an agriculture—centered economy in the First, an urban—industrial economy in the Twelfth—incorporating both white and black residents.

The *Hunt* court apparently believed that the distinctive character of the First and Twelfth Districts supported the proposition that these districts were more than the mere "racial gerrymander[s]" that it conceded them to be. But the court's analysis of "community of interest" is refuted by its own treatment of other traditional redistricting criteria. As the *Hunt* court would have it, criteria such as contiguity and compactness no longer matter and are, in any case, judicially unmanageable. Yet the court gave credence to evidence on "community of interest," arguably the most subjective, and therefore least manageable, of the traditional criteria. In fact, the court might have made more out of the legislature's achievement than the plan merited. Almost any district drawn in eastern North Carolina would have a rural character (the Second District is 58 percent rural and the Third is 62 percent rural). A second black district such as the Twelfth, wherever drawn, would have to be notably, if not

---

186. The figures are calculated from data published by the Census Bureau. BUREAU OF THE CENSUS, U.S. DEP'T OF COMMERCE, PUB. NO. 1990 CPH-4-35, 1990 CENSUS OF POPULATION AND HOUSING, POPULATION AND HOUSING CHARACTERISTICS FOR CONGRESSIONAL DISTRICTS OF THE 103D CONGRESS: NORTH CAROLINA 39-40 table 13 (1993). Definitions of urban, rural, and urbanized are given in *Id.* at A-11, A-12. An urbanized area consists of one or more "central places" and the adjacent "urban fringe" which together have a population of 50,000 or more; the fringe has a minimum density of 1,000 persons per square mile. *Id.* at A-12.

187. *Shaw v. Hunt*, 861 F. Supp. 408, 473 (E.D.N.C. 1994).

decisively, more urban.[188] Moreover, it is one thing to suggest that voters in Durham and Charlotte have common interests, but quite another to intimate that it is sensible to connect a voter in Durham, not with a voter across the street, but with a voter across the state. Indeed, the *Hunt* court's treatment of community of interest begs the question of whether districts must be "geographical" at all.

District courts in the other congressional districting cases were less impressed by defendants' arguments that contested districts represented *bona fide* communities of interest explainable on grounds apart from race.[189] In the first *Hays* case, the court found that efforts to describe the Fourth District in terms of socioeconomic characteristics apart from race were misleading since these characteristics are "strongly correlated with race."[190] In the Georgia case, the district court dismissed as "shallow and offensive thinking" the notion that because "blacks live in Savannah, [and] blacks live in Atlanta,...there must be some deep cultural bond between them."[191]

Do Looks Hurt?

As noted above, the *Hunt* court contended that traditional redistricting criteria were largely irrelevant to the law of modern redistricting. The *Hunt* court also adopted the view that ill-shaped districts cause no demonstrable harm. Because the other district courts opined that bizarre

---

188. Interestingly, one of the problems with Georgia's Eleventh District is the extent to which it brings together decidedly unlike communities—connecting densely populated tentacles at the extreme edges of the district with a large and sparsely populated rural core. "Two-thirds of the population of the district is concentrated in urban DeKalb, Richmond and Chatham counties." *Johnson v. Miller*, 864 F. Supp. 1354, 1389 (S.D. Ga. 1994). These counties contain less than 4 percent of the land area of the district. While the populations of DeKalb, Richmond, and Chatham counties are more than 90 percent urbanized (meaning, in part, a minimum density of 1,000 persons per square mile), 18 of the other 19 counties in the district have no urbanized population; 8 are entirely rural (having no population in areas of 2,500 or more). Socioeconomic conditions vary widely across the district, with, for example, residents in the DeKalb County portion of the district having a median family income nearly twice as high as residents in the Chatham County portion. *Id.* at 1389. *Report of Timothy G. O'Rourke, Ph.D., Johnson v. Miller*, No. CV 194-008 (S.D. Ga.), 4, 13-15 (on file with Author).

189. *See Vera*, 861 F. Supp. at 1329-30.

190. *Hays v. Louisiana*, 839 F. Supp. 1188, 1203 n.48 (W.D. La. 1993).

191. *Johnson*, 864 F. Supp. at 1390.

districts plainly had a negative effect on representation, the *Hunt* court's approach to the evidence merits extended attention.

The *Hunt* court found "no convincing evidence" that the shapes of Districts 1 and 12 "have had or are having any significant adverse effect" on "effective representation."[192] The court dismissed as insignificant some testimony about voters' confusion over new lines and also found that the lines had no negative effect on voter turnout.[193] Discussing the contours of Districts 1 and 12, the court observed:

> The few physical facts of the districts' configurations in relation to transportation facilities, media markets, commuting patterns and volumes certainly do not support any finding that their irregularities of shape *necessarily will make* their representatives less accessible and responsive than those of other districts.[194]

In one sense, the court's observation is surely correct; irregular districts do not *necessarily* produce harmful effects. There is, however, good reason to expect that in practice they actually are harmful. Split precincts confuse both election officials and voters. Districts that transect cities and counties burden electioneering; and constituencies that stretch over several media markets raise campaign costs.[195] As Chief District Judge Voorhees observed in his dissenting opinion in *Shaw v. Hunt*:

> [N]otwithstanding the potentially self-serving testimonies of those congresspersons elected to represent Districts 1 and 12, it cannot be gainsaid that 160 miles is long for such a lanky district as District 12. Indeed, it is sufficiently long to be served no less than by three national airports and three television markets. District 1 is equally ungainly, spread-

---

192. *Shaw v. Hunt*, 861 F. Supp. 408, 471 (E.D.N.C. 1994).

193. *Id.* at 471. The court cited evidence that overall turnout in North Carolina was higher in 1992 than in 1988 and that ballot roll-off (the percentage of voters who vote for President but do not vote for Congress) was not convincingly related to odd lines. *Id.* Looking for the effects of district lines on turnout or roll-off is, at best, a problematic inquiry—albeit one I undertook as an expert in *Hunt*—since larger forces (such as national trends, the competitiveness of particular districts) may eliminate what are likely to be, at most, modest effects associated with district configurations.

194. *Id.* at 472 (emphasis added).

195. In *Hays II*, Chief District Judge Shaw noted that the revised version of District 4 covers "not only four major population centers of Louisiana, but includes four separate and major media centers of this state. Congressional candidates would be required to spend substantial amounts of money and time covering voters in four major areas of the state." *Hays v. Louisiana*, 862 F. Supp. 119, 126 n.2 (W.D. La. 1994).

eagled over a vast portion of Eastern North Carolina, from Virginia
to South Carolina. These facts make fair representation impossible.[196]

Even if Chief Judge Voorhees is correct, perhaps the majority in *Hunt*
was properly skeptical and therefore justified in demanding more elaborate,
or more concrete, evidence that contorted districts actually do undermine
the representative process.[197] Yet it is difficult to imagine what kind of evidence the court would have found dispositive. The court brushed aside
1993 polling data that showed that only 6 percent of the constituents in the
Twelfth District could name Melvin Watt as their Congressman,[198] a finding
that takes on additional importance in light of the fact that the same poll
found that 31 percent of First District residents could name Eva Clayton.[199]

The *Hunt* court's resistance to such evidence, in the end, appears to be
less a matter of skepticism than of conviction. For the court's majority,
district lines just do not make any difference—a proposition the court
viewed as counterintuitive, but ultimately "unsurprising."[200]

On the theory of the *Hunt* court, geographical districts serve no real
function at all: assign the voter a number, identify the candidate by number, and the "interested enough" citizen will match his number with that

---

196. *Hunt*, 861 F. Supp. at 493 (Voorhees, C.J., dissenting).

197. In this respect, it is useful to recall that the harmful effects of malapportionment,
on the one hand, and the positive impact of reapportionment, on the other, were a matter of considerable scholarly debate in the 1960's. *See, e.g.*, William E. Bicker, *The
Effects of Malapportionment in the States—A Mistrial, in* REAPPORTIONMENT IN THE
1970S at 151 (Nelson W. Polsby ed., 1971). *See also Tucker v. United States Dept. of
Commerce*, 958 F.2d 1411, 1416 (7th Cir. 1992) (noting that "actual consequences of
reapportionment for the welfare of particular classes of voter or of resident remain, after
many years of study, obscure").

198. *Hunt*, 861 F. Supp. at 471.

199. MARKETWISE, INC., 1993 ISSUES POLL: DATA TABULATIONS, question 16 (Charlotte, 1993). The polling results are consistent with more general research that indicates
that residents in cities divided between two or more congressional districts are less likely
to recall the name of either their incumbent congressman or a congressional challenger
than are residents in cities located in a single congressional district. Significantly it
appears that television plays a key role in the emergence of this relationship; where television markets correspond with congressional district boundaries, citizens are better able
to identify their congressman than when they do not. *See* Richard G. Niemi, et al., *The
Effects of Congruity Between Community and District on Salience of U.S. House Candidates*, 11 LEGIS. STUD. Q. 187-201 (1986).

200. *Hunt*, 861 F. Supp. at 472 n.60.

> [The districts'] perceived ugliness...is entirely a function of an artificial perspec-
> tive unrelated to the common goings and comings of the citizen-voter. From the
> mapmakers wholly imaginary vertical perspective at 1:25,000 or so range, a citi-

of the candidate.[201] But surely representation requires more than this lotto-style identity between voter and candidate.[202]

Toward Functional, "Cognizable" Districts

The Supreme Court's "one person, one vote" precedents clearly speak in favor of geographic districting. Implicitly, the commitment to geographic districting requires, at a minimum, the creation of districts that are, in fact, contiguous and that constitute identifiable constituencies. As Bernard Grofman has written, a district must possess, in some fundamental sense, "cognizability," defined as "the ability to characterize the district boundaries in a manner that can be readily communicated to ordinary citizens of the district in common sense terms based on geographic referents."[203] Grofman elaborates:

---

zen may well find his district's one-dimensional, featureless shape aesthetically "bizarre."...But back down at ground or eye-level,...the irregularity of outline or exact volume of the district in which he resides surely is not a matter of any great consequence to his conduct as citizen-voter....What happens is that after every re-drawing of the lines of any of the various overlapping electoral districts in which he resides, he learns quickly enough (if interested enough), either by official notice or unofficially, that he is now in the same or a new district that is identified by a number. He has no idea where exactly on the earth's surface the lines of the district—mostly invisible from this live perspective—run throughout their course.

Id.

201. In truth, of course, the assignment is not so much by number but by color. As one court described Georgia's 11th District: "[B]eyond the general assumption in cities that 'if you are black you are in the Eleventh [District], and if you are white you are not,' the erratic lines and split counties and precincts do not afford voters ready indications of the district in which they reside." *Johnson v. Miller*, 864 F. Supp. 1354, 1389 (S.D. Ga. 1994).

202. Some number of citizens will regard bizarre lines, drawn in order to create safe minority districts, to be inherently stigmatic. As Chief District Judge Voorhees noted in his dissenting opinion:

A citizenry's perceptions of its political process can be as critical in a democracy as the process itself, and factors that can adversely affect such perceptions should not be dismissed. Thus, the majority's conclusion that certain facts outside the normal, "earth-bound, horizontal workaday world" of the citizen-voter, such as the irregularity of the district in which he or she resides, are not a matter of any great practical consequence,...seriously underestimates the intellectual grasp of those voters....[T]hey know when race is energizing the affairs of state.

Hunt, 861 F. Supp. at 494 (Voorhees, C.J., dissenting).

203. Grofman, *supra* note 165, at 1262.

> Central to American politics is the notion that representation should be based on geographically defined districts. The link between a representative and his or her constituents is facilitated by a candidate's ability to campaign in geographically defined areas, where door-to-door campaigning is possible, and where access to constituents via media channels—newspapers, radio, and television stations—is made easier by the existence of common sources of information.[204]

Grofman's concept of cognizability, then, encompasses at least two basic elements: identifiability and functionality. District lines should make sense and they should work. In redistricting cases involving the application of the Voting Rights Act and traditional redistricting criteria, some courts have embraced the notion of "functional compactness," which means, in effect, whether "a proposed district will provide effective political representation."[205] Although this is a usual approach to assessing the fairness of legislative districts, it is clear, as the district court observed in *Johnson v. Miller*, that "[t]his view of compactness will occasionally conflict with *Shaw v. Reno*, which places renewed emphasis on actual district shape; post-*Shaw*, the functional approach may improperly devalue geographical measurements."[206] The district court in *Shaw v. Hunt* committed this error, by holding that two congressional districts, which collected widely dispersed populations of similar demographic and socioeconomic characteristics, could satisfy some elemental

---

204. *Id.* at 1262.

205. *Marylanders for Fair Representation v. Shaffer*, 849 F. Supp. 1022, (D. Md. 1994). *See also Dillard v. Baldwin County Bd. of Educ.*, 686 F. Supp. 1459, 1465 (M.D. Ala. 1988); *Burton v. Sheheen*, 793 F. Supp. 1329, 1356 (D.S.C. 1992) (holding that the *Dillard* decision was a sound approach to problems of compactness). *Dillard* is often cited for the proposition that the compactness component of Section 2 of the Voting Rights Act, as articulated in *Thornburg v. Gingles*, 478 U.S. 30 (1986), "is a 'practical' or 'functional' concept, which must be considered in relation to § 2's laudatory national mission of opening up the political process to those minorities that have been historically denied such." *Dillard*, 686 F. Supp. at 1465. It follows that "[t]he degree of geographical symmetry or attractiveness is therefore a desirable consideration for districting, but only to the extent that it facilitates the political process." *Id.*; *see also DeWitt v. Wilson*, 856 F. Supp. 1409, 1413 (E.D. Cal. 1994) (rejecting challenge where districts bore shapes suggesting adherence to traditional districting criteria).

206. *Johnson v. Miller*, 864 F. Supp. 1354, 1389 n.43 (S.D. Ga. 1994). *See also Dillard*, 686 F. Supp. at 1465. *Dillard* observed, in part:

> [A] district is sufficiently geographically compact if it allows for effective representation. For example, a district would not be sufficiently compact if it was so spread out that there was no sense of community, that is, if its members and its representative could not effectively and efficiently stay in touch with each other;

test of "shared interests."[207] Geography does matter, because recognizable contours surely affect the ability of citizens to identify with a district. Geography matters, as well, for just the reason that *Shaw v. Reno* identified: bizarre districts, detached from meaningful geographic referents, are transparently racial classifications.

While state legislatures are not obligated to create districts that neatly conform to objective standards of compactness or to some preconceived model of community, neither are they utterly free to disregard the core values of geographic districting. It should be emphasized that the creation of functional, cognizable districts is not inconsistent with the establishment of majority-minority districts that conform to traditional redistricting principles and that, indeed, may be required by the Voting Rights Act.[208]

Concluding Comments

In the final analysis, the problem with the districts at issue in *Shaw v. Hunt* and in the other congressional redistricting cases is not merely that they effectuate a racial classification predicated on a dubious legal rationale. Such districts depend, ultimately, on a rejection of geographic dis-

---

> or if it was so convoluted that there was no sense of community, that is, if its members and representative could not easily tell who actually lived within the district. Also of importance, of course, is the compactness of neighboring districts.

Id. at 1466. The *Dillard* court was dealing with redistricting in a single county, as opposed to the typical multicounty congressional district. *Id.* at 1460. Thus, it is especially noteworthy that *Dillard*'s flexible view of compactness had both geographical and aesthetic outer limits: a district could be so spread out that "there was no sense of community" and/or its lines could be so bizarre that constituents could not tell who lived in the district. *Id.* at 1466; *cf. Shaw v. Hunt*, 861 F. Supp. 408, 482 n.12 (Voorhees, C.J., dissenting) (noting that "geographic" at least connotes physical location, and the word "community" implies some sense of physical proximity as well).

Shaw v. Reno, at the very least, adds this gloss to *Dillard*: the creation of a racial community of interest cannot make a sprawling, bizarrely-shaped district into a functionally compact one. District lines must have a persuasive justification in traditional redistricting principles apart from the fact that they agglomerate minority voters into a majority-minority district. Moreover, the fact that the election of a minority candidate may make a legislative body more representative does not mean that otherwise irrational district lines provide for "effective representation" in terms of legislator-constituency interaction. As one three-judge court observed, a district "must be 'manageable' from the standpoint of constituent services." *Burton*, 793 F. Supp. at 1356.

207. *Hunt*, 461 F. Supp. at 470.
208. *DeWitt*, 856 F. Supp. at 1413.

tricting itself. As the Supreme Court intimated, the conjunction of these two elements, racial classification and dysfunctional districting, creates an evident constitutional violation.[209] At the same time, it is clear that either racial classification or dysfunctional districting, taken separately, raises important constitutional issues.[210]

Observers of the 1994 elections might well conclude that gerrymandering is largely ineffective or self-limiting. In North Carolina, Republicans made a net gain of four congressional seats (and now have an 8-4 advantage) under a plan that they had challenged as a partisan gerrymander. Results across the South and the nation indicate that affirmative action racial gerrymandering has aided individual black and Hispanic candidates, but only at some cost to the overall strength of their preferred political party. In the end, however, who wins individual congressional contests may be less important than the fact that contemporary redistricting, unconstrained by fidelity to traditional redistricting standards, may make losers of us all.

---

209. At this time, I do not think it necessary to set out a comprehensive test or standard for the identification of impermissible racial gerrymanders. As Justice Clark suggested in *Lucas v. Colorado General Assembly*, 377 U.S. 713 (1964), a general rule may sweep aside otherwise rational districting policies. *Id.* at 742 (Clark, J., dissenting). It is enough to say, as did Justice Clark in *Reynolds v. Sims*, that some districts simply go too far, "clearly revealing invidious discrimination." *Id.* at 587-88 (Clark, J., concurring). *Shaw's* guidance, allowing for both the possibility of race-based redistricting and prohibiting racial gerrymandering that abjures traditional redistricting principles, certainly provides a workable framework that can be refined in subsequent cases. To the objection that *Shaw* invites unwarranted judicial intrusion into the redistricting process, the answer is that given by the three-judge court in *Vera*. The degree of judicial discretion or discernment required by *Shaw* is no greater than that required by vote dilution cases under Section 2 of the Voting Rights Act. *Vera v. Richards*, 861 F. Supp. 1304, 1343 n.55 (S.D. Tex. 1994). For a thoughtful explication of a contrary view—that *Shaw* leaves us "with an unsatisfactory theory that yields an unsatisfactory standard for its implementation," see Thomas C. Goldstein, *Unpacking and Applying* Shaw v. Reno, 43 Am. U. L. Rev. 1135 (1994).

210. With respect to dysfunctional districting more generally, I find much merit in Gordon Baker's call for federal legislation that would establish standards to govern congressional redistricting. "Formulation of [these] standards should include consideration of such issues as contiguity, compactness, communities of interest, and attention to local subdivision boundaries whenever possible. A reasonable population variance [also] should be specified...." Gordon E. Baker, *Whatever Happened to the Reapportionment Revolution in the United States?* in ELECTORAL LAWS AND THEIR POLITICAL CONSEQUENCES 257, 275-76 (Bernard Grofman and Arend Lijphart eds., 1986).

EPILOGUE

In the nearly two years since I completed the original piece, the Supreme Court has ruled on the Georgia, Louisiana, North Carolina, and Texas congressional districts examined in "The Shape of Things to Come."[1] In 1995, the Court struck down Georgia's 11th Congressional District in *Miller v. Johnson*, 63 U.S.L.W. 4726. The following year, the Court invalidated North Carolina's 12th District and Texas's 18th, 29th, and 30th Districts in *Shaw v. Hunt*, 64 U.S.L.W. 4437 (hereafter *Shaw II*) and *Bush v. Vera*, 64 U.S.L.W. 4452, respectively. *Shaw II* rejected the challenge to North Carolina's 1st District on the grounds of standing since no plaintiff resided in the district. The rule on standing carried forward from *United States v. Hays*, 63 U.S.L.W. 4679 (1995), in which the Court overturned the district court's invalidation of the 4th District on the ground that no plaintiff lived in the 4th. In subsequent litigation, however, the district court again struck down both the original 4th and the Louisiana legislature's proposed substitute and imposed its own plan; the Supreme Court, in 1996, allowed the district court actions to stand.[2]

In view of the argument I advanced in "The Shape of Things," the reader will not be surprised to learn that I regard these legal developments as salutary. While a full account of the Supreme Court holdings in *Miller*, *Hays*, *Shaw II*, and *Bush* is beyond the scope of this epilogue, I do wish to offer a few observations on the significance of these cases.

---

1. The title, as I should have noted in the original article, is, in part, a reference to the H.G. Wells book of the same name.

2. *Louisiana v. Hays*, 116 S.Ct. 2542 (June 24, 1996), appeals dismissed as moot. See also Juliana Gruenwald, *Minority Districts Fate Uncertain Following Supreme Court Ruling*, 54 Congressional Quarterly Weekly Report 1705–1706 (June 15, 1996) for a summary of the Louisiana and other recent congressional districting cases. In the aftermath of *Bush* and *Shaw II*, a three-judge panel in Texas has imposed a new plan for the 1996 congressional elections in that state, while a federal court in North Carolina has postponed a remedy in that state until 1998. Juliana Gruenwald, *New Districts to Stay in Place; Tougher Races for Candidates*, 54 Congressional Quarterly Weekly Report 2542 (September 7, 1996). Following the Supreme Court's Miller decision in 1995, a three-judge court invalidated Georgia's 2d Congressional District (in addition to the 11th) and ultimately imposed a remedial plan with only one majority black district. See *Johnson v. Miller*, 922 F.Supp. 1552 (S.D. Ga. 1995). The Supreme Court will hear an appeal of the remedial plan in its October 1996 Term. *Abrams v. Johnson, United States v. Johnson*, 116 S.Ct. 1823 (1996), noting probable jurisdiction and allotting one hour of oral argument.

First, despite complaints that the Court has failed to offer clear guidance on the standard for assessing racial gerrymanders,[3] the Court's basic directive is clear enough: a redistricting plan motivated primarily by race is subject to strict scrutiny; to the extent that a state adheres to traditional districting principles, it reduces its exposure to a *Shaw*-type charge of racial gerrymandering.[4] This rule is certainly sufficient to deal with "the egregious, unjustified race-based districting"[5] in Georgia, Louisiana, North Carolina, and Texas. The Court, quite properly, has postponed the elucidation of a more elaborate standard until it takes up more problematic cases.[6]

Second, the rulings in *Miller* and *Shaw I* and *II* have restored a more sensible reading of the Voting Rights Act and, at the same time, confirmed that for much of the past decade the Justice Department has been acting outside the law. The Court has confirmed that retrogression is the measure of "effect" under Section 5 and that neither Section 5 nor Section 2 require the sort of maximization policy pursued by the Department in Georgia and North Carolina.[7]

---

3. Holly Idelson, *Minority-District Decisions Lay No Clear Guidelines*, 54 *Congressional Quarterly Weekly Report* 1679–81 (June 15, 1996).

4. *Miller v. Johnson*, 63 U.S.L.W. at 4730; *Shaw II*, 64 U.S.L.W. 4439–40; *Bush v. Vera*, 64 U.S.L.W. at 4464 (O'Connor, J., concurring).

5. *Bush v. Vera*, 64 U.S.L.W. at 4466 (Kennedy, J., concurring).

6. While the Court's general approach is sound, the majority (consisting of Chief Justice Rehnquist and Justices O'Connor, Scalia, Kennedy, and Thomas) continues to be pulled in somewhat different directions because racial gerrymandering involves both the right to vote and the right to be free from racial discrimination. (On this point, see James F. Blumstein, *Racial Gerrymandering and Vote Dilution: Shaw v. Reno in Doctrinal Context*, 26 RUTGERS LAW JOURNAL 517, at 518, 543–48, 593 (1995).) Justice Kennedy, in his majority opinion in *Miller*, 63 U.S.L.W. at 4729, asserted that "bizarreness" of district shape is an indication that race may have been an overriding factor in redistricting, but "bizarreness" is not "a necessary element of the constitutional wrong or a threshold requirement of proof." In *Bush*, Justices Thomas and Scalia contended that strict scrutiny applied to the intentional creation of any minority district, however shaped. 64 U.S.L.W. at 4466 (Thomas, J., concurring). Justice O'Connor, the author of the majority opinion in *Shaw I*, has adhered to a seemingly different rationale, one that sees shape and motive as inextricably connected. Thus, she argued in *Miller* that her concern was with "extreme instances of gerrymandering." 63 U.S.L.W. at 4736 (O'Connor, J., concurring). In *Bush*, she contended that states may purposely draw majority-minority districts without triggering strict scrutiny, so long as they adhere to "traditional districting criteria." 64 U.S.L.W. 4464 (O'Connor, J., concurring).

7. See *Shaw I*, 509 U.S. 630, at 654–55 (1993); *Miller*, 64 U.S.L.W. at 4732–33; and *Shaw II*, 64 U.S.L.W. at 4441.

Third, attention to the deficiencies in the majority's racial gerrymandering jurisprudence should not obscure the very real flaws infecting the dissenters' legal analyses.[8] The dissenters in *Shaw II* and *Bush*, like the dissenters in *Shaw II*, have again recurred to the position of Justice Frankfurter in *Baker v. Carr*—essentially claiming that plaintiffs in racial gerrymandering cases have suffered only theoretical injury and complaining about the costs of judicial intrusiveness into traditional state legislative control over redistricting. Indeed, Justice Stevens, in *Shaw II*, dismisses the grievance of the plaintiffs as equivalent to the injury "to the polity" that Justice Frankfurter ridiculed in *Colegrove v. Green*.[9] But Justice Frankfurter made the case for keeping the Court out of the political thicket altogether, not for sealing off a portion of the thicket once entered.[10] In the specific context of the *Miller*, *Shaw II*, and *Bush*, the dissenters' avowed concern, à la Frankfurter, with protecting the states against unwarranted judicial oversight of the redistricting process is, not to put it too harshly, astounding.[11] Since virtually any congressional districting plan can be challenged on grounds of "one person, one vote," section 2 of the Voting Rights Act, or partisan gerrymandering, it is hard to understand what sort of protection the dissenters intend to offer the states. In actuality, one could argue that the Court's holdings in *Shaw II* and *Bush* will serve to protect state legislatures against the unbounded discretion of the Justice Department to object to legislatively-enacted plans. Surely, it is better to have state legislatures

---

8. The same four justices—Stevens, Souter, Ruth Bader Ginsburg (who replaced Justice White, and Stephen G. Breyer (who replaced Justice Blackmun)—dissented in *Miller*, *Shaw II*, and *Bush*.

9. 64 U.S.L.W. at 4444 (Stevens, J., dissenting), citing *Colegrove*, 328 U.S. 549 at 552.

10. As Martin Shapiro has argued, once one allows the legitimacy of the Court's intervention to ensure "one person, one vote" and to protect against racial vote dilution, it is difficult, if not impossible, to erect a barrier, based on principle or logic, against further judicial intervention in the redistricting field. See his "Gerrymandering, Unfairness, and the Supreme Court," 33 UCLA LAW REVIEW 227, at 229–32 (1985). Professor Shapiro's immediate concern was the question of whether the Court should adjudicate claims of partisan gerrymandering, but I believe his argument applies to the *Shaw*-type cases as well. Interestingly, while Justice Stevens railed against the Court's new racial gerrymandering jurisprudence in *Bush*, he reiterated his own well-established view that the Court ought to take a harder look at partisan and incumbent gerrymandering—contending that "[t]he real problem is the politically motivated gerrymandering that occurred in Texas." 64 U.S.L.W. at 4477 (Stevens, J., dissenting).

11. For the complaints about judicial interference, see *Shaw II*, 64 U.S.L.W. at 4452 (Stevens, J., dissenting); *Bush*, 64 U.S.L.W. at 4483, 4489 (Souter, J., dissenting).

second-guessed by the Supreme Court than by the Assistant Attorney General for Civil Rights.

Finally, while increased minority representation in Congress and in state and local legislative bodies is a very worthy goal, it matters a great deal how that goal is achieved. The attempt to secure minority representation by the creation of wildly contorted districts designed virtually to guarantee the election of minority candidates is a policy that the Supreme Court has rightly viewed as at odds with the Constitution and with commonsense.

CHAPTER 4

More Notes from a Political Thicket

Abigail Thernstrom

Introduction[1]

Cases involving minority voting rights are only partly about voting rights. At issue between the opposing sides are radically different views of American society and the place of blacks and Hispanics in it.[2] That makes them tough to resolve, and it makes them unusually important. The Supreme Court decided two redistricting cases this past June and has agreed to review two next term; these cases force the Court to take a stand on questions that lie at the very heart of our definition of ourselves as a multiethnic, multiracial society.

This past term's cases involved the constitutionality of majority-black congressional districts in Louisiana[3] and Georgia.[4] Both districts were drawn with the explicit purpose of creating safe black constituencies, and were thus subsequently challenged as unconstitutional racial gerrymanders—racial classifications that violate the Fourteenth Amendment.

The plans were defended by the two states, however, as reasonable: race-conscious but not race-driven. But even if viewed as a racial classification, and thus subject to strict judicial scrutiny, the states argued, they could meet the test; they were narrowly tailored to remedy past discrimina-

---

1. Much of the analysis of *Shaw v. Reno* is contained in Abigail Thernstrom, *Shaw v. Reno: Notes from a Political Thicket*, THE PUBLIC INTEREST LAW REVIEW 1994, 35; a number of other sections of the article are drawn from Abigail Thernstrom, WHOSE VOTES COUNT? AFFIRMATIVE ACTION AND MINORITY VOTING RIGHTS (Harvard University Press, 1987).

2. The Voting Rights Act actually covers members of five protected groups, the most important of which are blacks and Hispanics. The cases I discuss below, however, only involve blacks.

3. *Hayes v. Louisiana*, 862 F. Supp. 119(W.D.La.1994), vacated, 115 S. Ct.2431 (1995).

4. *Miller v. Johnson*, 115 S.Ct.2475 (1995).

tion and to further a compelling state interest in complying with the Voting Rights Act.

Although ostensibly constitutional cases, two intertwined questions were in fact before the Supreme Court: What does the Fourteenth Amendment allow, and what does the Voting Rights Act demand? For even if the districting lines were race-driven, the Court could not resolve the question of their constitutional legitimacy without deciding what the Voting Rights Act requires. The states had a compelling interest in complying with the law, but not—obviously—with an erroneously interpreted statute.[5]

These are legal issues that involve basic questions about the nature of American society, the direction in which we want to go, and how we get there. Are blacks still (in Lani Guinier's words) a "pariah group"?[6] Is a color-blind Constitution the wrong idea?[7] Does race consciousness, permitted or encouraged by the law, just harden the lines of race and ethnicity that already divide us? Or is that consciousness a necessity in a society in which true racial equality is still a dream deferred?[8]

These are just some of the issues that have run through the line of decisions that began in 1993 with *Shaw v. Reno*[9], which held that plaintiffs who challenged race-based districts did indeed have a claim upon which

---

5. Nor, clearly, can the Supreme Court blindly accept as a compelling interest justifying a racial classification compliance with the law as interpreted by an executive department—whatever the merits of that interpretation. As Justice Kennedy, writing for the Court in *Miller*, said: "Were we to accept the Justice Department's objection itself as a compelling interest adequate to insulate racial districting from constitutional review, we would be surrendering to the Executive Branch our role in enforcing the constitutional limits on race-based official action. We may not do so." (*Id.* at 2491)

6. Lani Guinier, THE TYRANNY OF THE MAJORITY (The Free Press, 1994), 37.

7. The Rev. Jesse Jackson has recently suggested substituting "color-caring" leadership for that which is color-blind—implying the two are mutually exclusive. "The Week with David Brinkley," July 23, 1995. Jackson is of course not alone in rejected that traditional civil rights ideal. On the history of that ideal, see Andrew Kull, THE COLORBLIND CONSTITUTION (Harvard University Press, 1992).

8. The inseparability of legal and political issues in voting rights cases has led Justice Thomas to argue—with respect, at least, to the question of vote dilution—that "[t]he matters the Court has set out to resolve in [these] cases are questions of political philosophy, not questions of law. As such, they are not readily subjected to any judicially manageable standards that can guide courts in attempting to select between competing theories." Thus, he would have the Court ends its "disastrous misadventure in judicial policymaking" and embark on a "systematic reexamination" of its interpretation of the act. *Holder v. Hall*, concurring opinion.

9. 113 S.Ct. 2816 (1993).

relief could be granted. This past term, in *Miller v. Johnson*[10], the Court struck down Georgia's Eleventh Congressional District as an impermissible racial classification, while in *Hays v. Louisiana*[11], it threw out the challenge to Louisiana's Fourth Congressional District on the ground that the white plaintiffs, who lived outside the district, lacked standing to sue. Nevertheless, because *Hays* is likely to return with a new set of plaintiffs, both that case and *Miller v. Johnson*, in addition to *Shaw*, are discussed below.

What Does the Fourteenth Amendment Allow?

Voting Rights and the Fourteenth Amendment

The Fourteenth Amendment is no stranger to voting rights cases. From 1965 to 1982 a series of constitutional rulings explored the meaning of equal protection in the electoral context. When did a multimember district unconstitutionally "dilute" the voting power of blacks and Hispanics? Were minority citizens denied an equal opportunity to elect the representatives of their choice when black Democratic candidates regularly lost in a Republican-dominated county? Every method of voting affects the distribution of seats among partisan, ethnic, and other groups. And none can promise every citizen equal power; inevitably, some individuals, like some groups, will be better positioned and more politically skillful than others. But a democracy promises not that power itself will be shared, but only that every citizen is "a potential participant, a potential politician."[12] Democracies guarantee a fair political process, but no particular results. Opportunity, not outcome. But how to recognize proper electoral opportunity? How to know when adequate potential is there? That was the hard question that only the constitutional cases directly and legitimately raised in the years 1965 to 1982.[13]

---

10. 115 S.Ct. 2475 (1995).

11. 862 F. Supp. 119 (W.D. La. 1994), vacated, 115 S. Ct. 2431 (1995).

12. Michael Walzer, Spheres of Justice: A Defense of Pluralism and Equality 310 (Basic Books, 1983).

13. Indirectly and illegitimately, particularly after 1980, the question was also addressed by the Justice Department in its review of submitted electoral changes in jurisdictions "covered" by section 5 of the Voting Rights Act. See Thernstrom, Whose Votes Count?, ch. 8.

Raised but did not resolve. And in 1982 that important line of cases came to an end. In that year the Voting Rights Act was amended to allow minority plaintiffs to ignore the demands of Fourteenth Amendment litigation. Two years earlier, in 1980, the Supreme Court had held in *City of Mobile, Alabama v. Bolden* that a successful constitutional attack on an at-large or other method of voting would have to demonstrate invidious intent in the adoption or maintenance of the electoral procedure in use.[14] As long as the method of voting had not been designed or perpetuated to keep minorities from public office, blacks and whites stood on equal electoral footing, the Court concluded.[15] Their votes were not diluted. Ballots cast in an electoral system uncontaminated by racial purpose carried their full, constitutionally-guaranteed weight. In the view of the civil rights groups, it was an unacceptable ruling, and representatives of those groups went to work immediately on a statutory amendment that would allow plaintiffs to circumvent the need to prove discriminatory intent. The fruit of their labor was a bold and radical revision of the Voting Rights Act.

Prior to 1982, the revised provision, section 2, was a seemingly insignificant preamble to the act. It introduced a statute resting on the Fifteenth Amendment by simply restating the core of that amendment, and with its clear link to the Constitution, it implicitly contained an intent test for electoral discrimination. A minor alteration in wording, however, solved the problem of proving racist intent. The provision was rephrased to contain a "results" test, allowing plaintiffs to challenge at-large elections, district lines, or other voting-related arrangements as discriminatory in their "result." The change left the constitutional test standing— yet idle.

To this day, vote dilution remains a question that now arises only in section 2 cases; minority plaintiffs who challenge a districting plan or other electoral arrangement on the ground of unequal electoral opportunity predictably choose to rest their case on statutory, not constitutional, grounds.[16] But in 1993, in *Shaw v. Reno*, Fourteenth Amendment voting rights suits made a remarkable, unexpected comeback. In revised form, however. The constitutional question re-emerged—radically changed. The issue was no longer fair and effective representation for members of racial and ethnic minority groups. It had become instead the limits im-

---

14. 446 U.S. 55 (1980)

15. 11. *Id.* at 66.

16. And indeed the impact of section 2 is greater than almost anyone in 1982 imagined possible. Its impact has been greatly heightened by the distorted reading given the provision by the Justice Department and courts. The revised section 2 was a gift to minority plaintiffs, but not initially of the magnitude it came to have.

posed by the Fourteenth Amendment on precisely that race-conscious districting that had been the remedy of choice in both Fourteenth Amendment and (after 1982) section 2 suits.

Until 1993, plaintiffs in voting rights cases had gone to court to assert the right of members of minority groups to have their race or ethnicity explicitly acknowledged. They demanded race-driven electoral arrangements, most often race-based single-member districts that ensured minority officeholding. But *Shaw* raised a new question: Was not that remedial arrangement itself constitutionally suspect? Race-based districting sorts citizens out by race. Didn't such sorting raise equal protection issues?

Race-based districting, the Court held in *Shaw*, is actually no different than other forms of discriminatory state action. "A plaintiff challenging a reapportionment statute under the Equal Protection Clause may state a claim by alleging that the legislation, though race-neutral on its face, rationally cannot be understood as anything other than an attempt to separate voters into different districts on the basis of race, and that the separation lacks sufficient justification."[17] Districts that constitute race-based classifications, in short, are not distinctive; they too are subject to strict judicial scrutiny.[18]

"In order to get beyond racism, we must first take account of race," Justice Blackmun had said in 1978.[19] It was that highly dubious—and, by 1978, unoriginal—notion that had informed the first line of Fourteenth Amendment decisions. And it was that idea that *Shaw* implicitly challenged. Taking race into account—drawing race-conscious legislative districting lines—may not get us beyond race at all, O'Connor suggested. In fact, race-consciousness may widen the racial divide, heightening our sense of racial identity.[20] It was a point reiterated this past term by Justice Kennedy in *Miller v. Johnson*, who quoted at length from *Shaw*.[21]

If the very remedy for electoral discrimination so frequently ordered by courts and the Justice Department has now been questioned, the

---

17. *Shaw v. Reno*, 113 S.Ct at 2828.

18. *Id.* at 2830–32.

19. *Regents of the University of California v. Bakke*, 438 U.S. 265, 407 (1978), Blackmun, J. concurring.

20. Karlan and Goldstein argue that the Voting Rights Act "is explicitly race-conscious," and thus the Court's new found concern over the constitutionality of race-conscious districting pits the statute against the Constitution. *On a Collision Course*, LEGAL TIMES (April 17, 1995), 24. But the point assumes that the race-based districting that plaintiffs in *Shaw* and subsequent cases challenged is mandated by the Voting Rights Act; that is far from the case.

21. *Miller v. Johnson*, 115 S.Ct. 2475, 2483(1995).

switch has to be seen as a sign of changed times. For roughly thirty years after the passage of the Voting Rights Act in 1965, the primary concern on the part of those who enforced the law was racial exclusion.[22] White racial attitudes, however, have been transformed in the intervening years, and the majority of blacks have joined the social and economic mainstream. Today, racism may not be our main problem, the Court implicitly acknowledged in *Shaw*; racial and ethnic fragmentation, driven in part by racial districting and other public policies, may have become the greater danger.

A Racial Classification

Race-based districting raises constitutional questions, the Court held in *Shaw*. But when is a state in fact racially classifying voters in violation of the equal protection clause? O'Connor's answer in 1993 was neither altogether reassuring nor entirely clear. "This Court never has held that race-conscious redistricting is impermissible in *all* circumstances," O'-Connor wrote.[23] Sometimes it's okay, in other words—just your everyday, garden-variety "reasonable" racial classification. But problems clearly arise when a district is "so extremely irregular on its face that it rationally can be viewed only as an effort to segregate the races for purposes of voting, without regard for traditional districting principles and without sufficiently compelling justification."[24] "Bizarre" districts, "unexplainable on grounds other than race," were thus a source of concern.

Districts that look bad, in other words, are bad, O'Connor seemed to suggest. "[R]eapportionment is one area in which appearances to matter," the majority opinion concluded.[25] Highly irregular contours obviously drawn with race in mind suggest racial stereotyping, reinforcing "the perception that members of the same racial group...think alike..."[26]

And yet surely contours less "highly irregular" could also be drawn "with race in mind." Shape, as Justice Kennedy acknowledged in *Miller*, could not be the only test. In both the Louisiana and Georgia cases, the "looks bad" test was supplemented by essentially uncontroverted direct

---

22. The primary concern of the Justice Department and the federal courts has racial exclusion, but finding that exclusion they have relied on legal standards that are, in my view, highly questionable. Thus they have frequently ordered remedies for an imagined wrong. See Thernstrom, WHOSE VOTES COUNT? Supra note 1, Ch.8.

23. 113 S.Ct at 2824.

24. *Id.*

25. *Id.*

26. Id. at 2827.

trial evidence that clearly established the overriding importance of race. In *Hays*, the contours of District Four could "only be explained credibly as the product of race-conscious decisionmaking," the trial court concluded;[27] twelve of the fifteen parishes the district contained had been split, as had four of the top seven cities in the state.[28] In the Georgia case, too, the contours of the Eleventh District were determined by "a far-flung search for black voters," as the trial court put it.[29] Its population was drawn from "four discrete, widely spaced urban centers that [had] absolutely nothing to do with each other, and stretch[ed] the district hundreds of miles across rural counties and narrow swamp corridors."[30]

Majority-black districts like those in Louisiana and Georgia are of course far from 100 percent black, and as a consequence the Congressional Black Caucus (the "CBC"), in its brief, described them as "among the *least* segregated districts in the Nation."[31] The point was very misleading. Majority-minority districts are not "integrated." The white voters they contain are merely "filler people," as two proponents of race-based districting have acknowledged with refreshing candor[32] Whites are simply included so as not to waste black ballots by excessive "packing."

That is, these are districts in which only black ballots are meant to count. They are designed to be safe black constituencies.[33] In effect, they have a sign pasted on them: no white candidates need apply. And in fact, almost no white candidates do come forward. None in the newly-created majority-minority congressional districts. Whites who think of running in a majority-black constituency are informed in no uncertain terms that

27. 862 F. Supp. 119 (W.D. La. 1994), vacated, 115 S. Ct. 2431 (1995).

28. *Id.* at 121.

29. *Johnson v. Miller*, 864 F. Supp. 1354, 1377 (S.D. Ga 1994), aff'd, 115 S. Ct. 2475 (1995).

30. *Id.* at 1389. In her dissent, Justice Ginsburg argues that "[e]vidence at trial... shows that considerations other than race went into determining the Eleventh District's boundaries." (*Id.* at 2503) Her denial that race was the overwhelming consideration in the configuration of that district is—given the evidence—truly puzzling.

31. Brief for the Congressional Black Caucus as Amicus Curiae, 19–20.

32. T. Alexander Aleinikoff and Samuel Issacharoff, *Race and Redistricting: Drawing Constitutional Lines After Shaw v. Reno*, 92 MICHIGAN LAW REVIEW, 588, 630–631. Whites in majority-black districts, the authors write, "should not be expected to compete in any genuine sense for electoral representation" in those districts, "lest they undo the preference given to the specified minority group."(631).

33. It is hardly a coincidence that the present occupant of the Congressional seat from District 4 was the chairman of the Louisiana State Senate reapportionment committee that drew its convoluted boundaries. The district he mapped out was designed as a safe black seat—for him. CONGRESSIONAL QUARTERLY'S POLITICS IN AMERICA, 1994: THE 103RD CONGRESS 650 (Duncan, ed., 1993).

the color of their skin disqualifies them; they are treading where they do not belong. Thus, as Lublin has pointed out, in 1992 several members of the U.S. House of Representatives chose to retire or move to other districts under pressure from black leaders to let blacks run racially uncontested races in the districts designed for them.[34]

As the Court made clear in *Miller*, Georgia's District Eleven and other majority-black constituencies thus constitutes racial classifications not because they look bizarre (the emphasis in *Shaw*), but because the classification of voters by race is precisely their point.[35] Race, not community, has determined their contours. Race was "the predominant factor motivating the legislature's decision to place a significant number of voters within or without a particular district."[36] Indeed, these districts are intentionally race-based for a goal their proponents believe in: maximizing black officeholding.

What Does the Voting Rights Act Demand?

The Court in *Shaw* referred to the possibility that the state of North Carolina "went beyond what was reasonably necessary to avoid retrogression"—the discriminatory effect against which section 5 of the Vot-

---

34. David Lublin, *Gerrymander for Justice? Racial Redistricting and Black and Latino Representation, unpublished manuscript* (1994), 48 and 90.

35. (115 S. Ct. 2475, 2487 (1995): "Our observation in *Shaw* of the consequences of racial stereotyping was not meant to suggest that a district must be bizarre on its face before there is a constitutional violation...Shape is relevant not because bizarreness is a necessary element of the constitutional wrong or a threshold requirement of proof, but because it may be persuasive circumstantial evidence that race for its own sake, and not other districting principles, was the legislature's dominant and controlling rationale in drawing its districting...[P]arties may rely on evidence other than bizarreness to reestablish race-based districting." In her dissent, Justice Ginsburg argues that "[o]ur Nation's cities are full of districts identified by their ethnic character—Chinese, Irish, Italian, Jewish, Polish, Russian, for example." *Id.* at 2505. What can be wrong, then, with black districts? The analogy doesn't hold. No legislature has strung Polish voters together from widely dispersed residential pockets in order to ensure Polish officeholding; nor has the Justice Department ever suggested than any legislature should.

36. *Miller v. Johnson* (*Id.* at 2488). The Court in *Miller* made it very clear that plaintiffs must prove that "the legislature subordinated traditional race-neutral districting principles...to racial considerations." It is thus not sufficient to assert that a legislature was "aware of racial demographics"; such awareness is normally be part of "the complex interplay of forces that enter a legislature's redistricting calculus." (*Id.* at 14)

ing Rights Act guards.[37] But, in fact, it was not the state that was out of bounds; it was the Department of Justice, which had directed North Carolina to create a second majority-black district. In the redistricting processes in Louisiana and Georgia as well the Attorney General insisted the states draw a maximum number of safe black districts.[38] In the case of Georgia, in fact, it was the American Civil Liberties Union's "max-black" plan—described by the trial court as a "triumph of demographic manipulation"—that became the DOJ's "guiding light."[39] At a meeting with voting section attorneys in Washington, Georgia legislators were "told to subordinate their economic and political concerns to the quest for racial percentages."[40] It is "disingenuous" to argue that DOJ's objections to the proposed districting plans proposing fewer districts than the ACLU's max-black plan contained "were anything less than implicit commands," the district court concluded.[41] "No one in the General Assembly (including the Black Caucus) thought so, and DOJ lawyers did nothing to dissuade legislators of that notion."[42]

And yet neither sections 5 nor 2 of the Voting Rights Act, the relevant statutory provisions, required the drawing of every last possible majority-minority constituency, as the Supreme Court said in *Miller* and on numerous previous occasions.[43] The Department of Justice enforces a law entirely of its own making.[44] This is not a new story; since the early 1980s, the voting rights section of the civil rights division has been distorting the statute it is supposed to enforce.

Section 5: The Retrogression Test

The statute that Congress passed in 1965 set limits on the authority of the Justice Department that, in the main, remain in place today. Those limits were (and are) integral to the integrity of the act. The powers of

---

37. 113 S.Ct at 2831.

38. See, e.g., *Johnson v. Miller*, Jt App. 229 (letter from Deval L. Patrick, Assistant Attorney General, Civil Rights Division to Brenda Wright and Robert B. McDuff, dated April 29, 1994).

39. *Johnson v. Miller*, (864 F. Supp. at 1363–64.)

40. *Id.* at 1364 n.8.

41. *Id.* at 1264.

42. *Id.* at 1364 n.16.

43. See, e.g., *Beer v. United States* 425 U.S. 130 (1976); *City of Lockhart, Tx v. United States* 460 U.S. 125 (1983); *Thornburg v. Gingles*, 438 U.S. 30 (1986).

44. In *Shaw* the Court noted (113 S.Ct at 2830) that states have an interest in complying with laws, but only those that are constitutionally valid "as interpreted and applied."

the Attorney General under section 5 were extraordinary. Envisioned as an emergency measure, the provision allowed federal intrusion on constitutionally sanctioned local prerogatives and thus fundamentally altered federal-state relations. A town in a "covered" state could make no change affecting voting—not even a change in the location of a polling place—without Justice Department approval. Moreover, the burden was on jurisdiction to prove the racial neutrality of its action beyond any doubt. Only a provision so narrowly drawn and carefully circumscribed could have withstood constitutional scrutiny.

The limits of section 5, in 1965, were set by section 4. The one banned literacy tests in states and counties with a bad record on black enfranchisement.[45] The other made sure that the effect of that ban stuck. The demand that federal authorities preclear any new voting procedure in counties and states in which literacy tests had been suspended thus had an unambiguous and limited aim: guarding against renewed disfranchisement, the use of the back door once the front one was blocked.

The ingenuity of racists had kept litigators attempting to secure the basic franchise always running and always behind, and those who shaped the Voting Rights Act could not be sure that eliminating the literacy test would do the trick. As the distinguished civil rights attorney, Joseph Rauh explained, stopping southern states from inventing new ways around the basic enfranchising provisions of the act was the point of preclearance; its aim was simply "self-defense."[46]

In *Allen v. State Board of Elections* (1969), a broader view of the provision did emerge—one that protected against vote "dilution" and thus allowed the Justice Department to review annexations, new district lines, and other changes affecting minority voting strength.[47] That broader view did somewhat muddy the legal waters. In 1965 the reference in section 5 to the discriminatory "effect" of a change in the method of voting was innocuous and thus unnoticed; "effect" and "purpose" were basically interchangeable terms. That is, the disfranchising impact of a sudden change in the method of registration or voting in a southern jurisdiction with a rotten history of civil rights violations made its purpose clear. But once annexations, redistrictings, and at-large voting were also subject to preclearance, effect and intent became two quite separate ques-

---

45. Jurisdictions subject to the ban were identified by a statistical test. States and counties in which total registration or turnout in the presidential election of 1964 had fallen below 50 percent and a literacy test had been used to screen potential registrants were assumed to have engaged in electoral discrimination.

46. Hearings before Subcommittee No. 5 of the Committee on the Judiciary, U.S. House of Representatives, 89th Congress, March–April 1965, 399.

47. *Allen v. State Board of Elections*, 393 U.S. 544 (1969).

tions. A municipal annexation, for instance, may be undertaken for perfectly normal, nonracial reasons, even though its impact is to add proportionally more white voters to the city, thus "diluting" the black vote. The Court's decision in *Allen*, in short, in allowing section 5 objections to rest on disparate racial impact alone, began the process by which the statute became an instrument for affirmative action in the electoral sphere.

Not only the Court, but in both 1970 and 1975 when the temporary provisions of the statute were extended and revised, Congress too partially remade the preclearance provision. In extending the extraordinary protection of section 5 to ethnic groups without the extraordinary history of southern blacks, in covering places outside the South that had no comparable history of racism, and in agreeing to ignore the difference between disfranchisement and dilution, Congress gave the provision independent validity as an instrument to promote the election of minorities to public office in both South and North.[48] Moreover the District Court for the District of Columbia, which has sole jurisdiction in section 5 cases, made a consistent attempt to amend the statute through the process of judicial enforcement.[49] Nevertheless, the Supreme Court, in its decisions interpreting the preclearance provision, never abandoned the "self-defense" rationale. The point of section 5 remained protection from backsliding—from "retrogression." It was to protect electoral gains already in place—to stop measures that left blacks worse off, deprived of political power they already had.[50]

With respect to districting, the Court's no-retrogression test could not be simpler.[51] If there had been two majority-black congressional districts

---

48. This complicated history of the way in which subtle and seemingly small statutory changes had big consequences is explored in Thernstrom, WHOSE VOTES COUNT?, chs. 2 and 3.

49. The lower court simply ignored Supreme Court rulings, and few of its decisions were appealed. In doing so, it was joined by the Justice Department and civil rights groups, both of which disliked the High Court's refusal to insist on the promise of proportional racial and ethnic representation as the standard jurisdictions had to meet in submitting electoral changes for preclearance. See Thernstrom, WHOSE VOTES COUNT?, chs. 7 and 8.

50. See *Beer v. United States*, 425 U.S. 130 (1976); *City of Lockhart v. United States*, 460 U.S. 125 (1983)

51. Annexations were a different question; a jurisdictional expansion that added more white than black voters to a city's electoral roll, forced the municipality to adopt single-member districts that ensured (to the extent possible) minority officeholding in proportion to the minority population. The result was a double standard—one for districting, another for annexations—that encouraged the Justice Department (which needed little encouragement) to ignore the *Beer* test and simply, without explanation, lift the

in Louisiana prior to the 1990 census, for instance, the state could not have chosen to eliminate one. But if the state had only one—as was the case—it was not legally obligated, under the effects test in section 5, to create another. As the Supreme Court stated in *Beer*, "It is...apparent that a legislative reapportionment that enhances the position of racial minorities with respect to their effective exercise of the electoral franchise can hardly have the 'effect' of diluting or abriding the right to vote on account of race within the meaning of section 5."[52]

In short, while neither Georgia nor Louisiana (nor other states that have engaged in race-based districting) misread the clear signals from the Department of Justice, those signals were at odds with the law. In insisting, in the post-1990 redistricting process, that states draw a maximum number of majority-minority districts, the Department ignored both the clear meaning of discriminatory "effect" under section 5 and the Supreme Court's decisions interpreting that provision.[53]

Discriminatory Purpose: More Definitional Games

In its correspondence with Louisiana over an earlier districting plan for the state board of education, the Department of Justice acknowledged that the proposed lines "appear[ed] to have no retrogressive effect" and thus in large measure met the section 5 requirement. But it refused to preclear the plan because an allegedly better one could be drawn.[54] That "better" one contained another, bizarrely-shaped majority-black district, and the failure to draw that district was viewed as a sin of omission that betrayed discriminatory intent. Louisiana thus logically assumed that the same rules would apply to congressional redistricting—that the Justice Department would refused to preclear a proposed plan as long as another majority-black constituency could still be created. In the

---

annexation standard out of context and apply it to redistricting submissions. The act was pulled in conflicting directions as well by other Supreme Court decisions. See, e.g. *City of Rome, Georgia v. United States*, 446 U.S. 156 (1980). Nevertheless, the Court has never abandoned the *Beer* standard in a redistricting case. On the record of the D.C. court and the Supreme Court's partial complicity in sanctioning an entitlement to proportionate racial and ethnic officeholding, see Thernstrom, WHOSE VOTES COUNT?, ch. 7.

52. 425 U.S. at 141.

53. Justice White in *Shaw* states that the "Attorney General's interposition of a § 5 objection 'properly is viewed' as 'an administrative finding of discrimination'" 113 S.Ct at 2838. But that finding rested on standards that the Supreme Court has never sanctioned.

54. *Hays v. Louisiana*, 839 F. Supp. 1188 (W.D. La. 1993) (three-judge court), vacated, 114 S. Ct. 2731 (1994).

case of Georgia too, the state's allegedly inadequate explanation for "its refusal in the first two submissions [of districting plans] to take the steps necessary to create a third majority-minority district" was read by the federal government as a violation of section 5's prohibition against purposefully discriminatory plans.[55]

In fact, the government's policy was legally indefensible.[56] Section 5 does contain both an effects and an intent test. In reviewing submissions, the Department of Justice is expected to ask two quite different questions: Will the proposed change leave minority voters with reduced electoral power? Or, alternatively, does it suggest hostility to minority voters? The latter question, clearly, could not be answered by counting the number of safe black districts. If such a count told the Justice Department all it needed to know, the question of discriminatory effect—to which the provision separately refers—would be superfluous. Every electoral plan with an allegedly insufficient number of safe black districts could be viewed as infected with racist intent.[57]

Moreover, the Department's position turns the enforcement of a federal law over to civil rights groups and their allies. It gives every organization with a "preferable" districting scheme—one that seems to ensure more black officeholding—the power to veto a proposed districting plan. And, in the case of Georgia, as noted above, the Justice Department did in effect allow the American Civil Liberties Union to assume

---

55. *Miller v. Johnson* (115 S. Ct. 2475, 2492 (1995).

56. *New York v. United States*, 874 F. Supp, 394, 401 (D.D.C. 1994); *Georgia v. Reno*, 881 F. Supp. 7, 14 (D.D.C. 1995). The District Court for the District of Columbia's interpretation of the purpose prong of section 5 squares with legislative history; see Thernstrom at WHOSE VOTES COUNT?, supra note 1, ch. 8.

57. As O'Rourke has noted, "[i]n essence, what the Justice Department appears to be doing is dressing a results analysis in the clothes of purpose." And, among other things, that strategy allows the Department to ignore the retrogression test, which (if properly applied) will often legitimize districting plans that do not guarantee a maximum number of safe minority seats. Timothy G. O'Rourke, *Shaw v. Reno: The Shape of Things to Come*, 26 RUTGERS LAW JOURNAL, 723, 752 (1995). This is not to say, of course, that there can be no circumstantial evidence of invidious purpose. As Butler points out, if a state has failed to recognize concentrations of minority voters that would naturally produce majority-minority districts using standard districting criteria, it could legitimately be said to have failed to carry its burden of proving an absence of discriminatory intent. But unless a rejected plan clearly meets the state's own stated redistricting criteria and is superior in that regard to the plan actually adopted, the argument that rejection itself is a sign of unacceptable purpose amounts to nothing more than an insistence on a maximum number of majority-minority districts. Katharine Inglis Butler, *Affirmative Racial Gerrymandering: Fair Representation for Minorities or a Dangerous Recognition of Group Rights*, 26 RUTGERS LAW JOURNAL 498, 510–11 (1995).

the government's job. Federal policy was literally driven by the ACLU: "an embarrassment," as the district court put it.[58]

The Georgia case provides the fullest record to date of the cozy relationship between the Justice Department's voting section and the civil rights community. But the basic facts of that relationship have been evident for some time. For instance, in 1984, in a section 5 case involving state senate redistricting in South Carolina, the NAACP came tried to suggest that the plan it offered was the one a jurisdiction had to adopt — that the failure to do so would constitute evidence of discriminatory purpose in violation of the preclearance provision.[59] Throughout the 1980s, it was an argument that both the D.C. district court and the Justice Department came close to embracing.[60]

Section 2: A Different Question

The Justice Department led Louisiana and Georgia to believe that preclearance required meeting the demands of both sections 5 and 2. Again, the policy is not new but it's wrong. By administrative fiat the preclearance provision has been rewritten.

Sections 2 and 5 "differ in structure, purpose, and application," the Supreme Court noted in *Holder v. Hall*.[61] As the D.C. district court explained at length in two recent decisions, the two are quite separate provisions.[62] It's an overdue insight. In 1982, when section 2 was transformed from an inconsequential preamble into a powerful instrument for ridding the nation of methods of election with a discriminatory "result," there was literally no discussion of a consequent change in section 5. In fact, during the debates of 1981 and 1982, civil rights spokesmen

---

58. "Succinctly put, the considerable influence of ACLU advocacy on the voting rights decisions of the United States Attorney General is an embarrassment," the district court concluded. That influence was evident even in the process by which the federal government notified the state of its decision. DOJ told the ACLU of its impending objection; and the ACLU notified the Black Caucus, before the letter of objection arrived at the office of the Georgia Attorney General. *Johnson v. Miller*, 864 F. Supp at 1360–63.

59. *South Carolina v. United States and the NAACP, Inc.* Civil Action No. 83-3626, District Court for the District of Columbia, 1984, NAACP's-Defendant's Supplemental Response to Interrogatories, April 2, 1984, 3–4: "The redistricting plan as drawn avoidable and deliberately denies Blacks the equal opportunity to elect a candidate of their choice...Moreover, the State...failed and or refused to implement suggestions for redistricting made by the NAACP Defendants, as well as other minority organizations."

60. See Thernstrom, WHOSE VOTES COUNT?, ch. 8.

61. 114 S.Ct 2581, 2587 (1994).

62. *New York. v. United States*, supra; *Georgia v. Reno*, supra, n.56.

directly and indirectly assured members of Congress that the amendment of section 2 would not alter the preclearance provision.[63]

Those assurances fell on deaf administrative ears. In January, 1987, the Justice Department "incorporated" section 2 into section 5. Revised districting lines, a new polling place and other electoral changes submitted for federal review under section 5, were henceforth judged by section 2 standards as well. An objections would lodged if the proposed change was arguably discriminatory in purpose, effect, or "result" (the latter being section 2 question), with the burden on the submitting jurisdiction to prove the racial neutrality of its proposed action. Section 5 was thus changed—on the assumption, evidently, that Congress had acted without debate to give dramatic new force to a central provision in the act.[64] And yet, in justifying such a radical overhaul of a key provision—one whose limits were clearly understood—the Department could point only to one footnote, buried in the 1982 Senate Judiciary Committee Report and unsupported by the text to which it was appended.[65]

The change in section 5 not only had no basis in legislative history. The Justice Department had assumed an inappropriate role. Federal administrators, remote from the scene, became plaintiff, defendant and judge, all rolled into one, with no reliable way of gathering information on race and politics in the local jurisdiction remotely comparable to that which opposing attorneys present at a trial. Cases resting on section 2 involve complex questions of electoral opportunity; courts are asked to judge whether the "totality of circumstances," for instance, in the city of Detroit suggest electoral inequality between minority and white citizens. Adjudicating competing claims about racial fairness requires, as the Supreme Court has noted, an "intensely local appraisal"—the specific detailed knowledge that only a court can obtain.[66] It was for that reason precisely that section 2 (as written and understood at the time) did not

---

63. See, e.g., 128 CONGRESSIONAL RECORD 14,938 (1982) (exchange between Reps. Don Edwards and Elliott H. Levitas).

64. See Procedures for the Administration of Section 5 of the Voting Rights Act, 28 C.F.R., § 51.55: "In those instances in which the Attorney General concludes that, as proposed, the submitted change is free of discriminatory purpose and retrogressive effect, but also concludes that a bar to implementation of the change is necessary to prevent a clear violation of amended Section 2, the Attorney General shall withhold Section 5 preclearance."

65. That footnote states that "[i]n light of the amendment to section 2, it is intended that a section 5 objection also follow if a new voting procedure itself so discriminates as to violate Section 2." S. Rep. No. 417, 97th Cong, 2nd sess. 12, n. 31 (1982) (hereinafter "1982 Senate report').

66. *White v. Regester*, 412 U.S. 755, 769 (1973).

offer—as section 5 did—the option of administrative preclearance as an alternative to a full-scale court proceeding in which evidence and rebuttal evidence is fully presented.[67] Administrative procedures are no substitute for a trial.

Access, Not Outcome

There is another, perhaps more important point. Attached or unattached to section 5, section 2 does not mean what the Justice Department says it means. That is, compliance with section 2 does not, in any case, necessitate the drawing of any particular number of majority-minority districts. The provision guarantees equal electoral access not racially fair outcomes. Opportunity is the "result" it ensures. And indeed, as Justice Kennedy noted in *Miller*, if the act did in fact compel race-based districting, by definition it would raise a serious constitutional question; such an interpretation would jeopardize the entire statute.[68]

The intimate link between section 2 and the pre-1980 legal standards established in Fourteenth Amendment cases should alone make that clear. In amending section 2, Congress lifted language directly from two constitutional rulings: *Whitcomb v. Chavis*[69] and White v. Regester.[70] In both, the Court had directed trial courts judging the level of electoral opportunity in a jurisdiction to assess the political environment: the setting in which the voting took place. Judges had been asked to distinguish the failure of minority voters to elect candidates of their choice for reasons of race from normal electoral defeat—that to which every group, however defined, was vulnerable. It was, however, a very tall order. What were the criteria that distinguished the one setting from the other?

Unequal electoral opportunity was inevitably an elusive concept. Were black voters distinctively entitled to some degree of representation? Was black officeholding an important measure of opportunity? As Justice Frankfurter observed (dissenting in *Baker v. Carr*), we can only know if voters are improperly represented if we know what it means to be properly represented.[71] And yet we lack a theoretical framework to decide. The point still held twenty years later.

---

67. The Justice Department itself, in its "comments" introducing the new 1987 guidelines, admitted that administrative review did not remotely resemble a judicial proceeding. Procedures for the Administration of Section 5.

68. *Miller v. Johnson*, 115 S. Ct. 2475, 2492 (1995).

69. 403 U.S. 124 (1971)

70. 412 U.S. 755 (1973)

71. 369 U.S. 186 (1962), dissenting opinion.

Nevertheless, if section 2 asked courts to measure an inadequately defined phenomenon—electoral inequality—it did not leave judges entirely clueless. Some guidance was provided. In *Whitcomb*, for instance, the Supreme Court unequivocally rejected the view that a showing of disproportionately low minority officeholding and evidence of black residential clustering would suffice to establish electoral discrimination.

By lifting language directly from that decision and from *White*, Congress thus rejected the notion that black voters had a right to even one legislative seat reserved for a black representative. Section 2, as Butler notes, is nothing but "standard remedial legislation."[72] Plaintiffs must establish a violation of their statutory right to an electoral process open to black political aspirations; only then are they entitled to a race-conscious remedy. Minority voters were guaranteed not their "fair share" of political offices, but only a "fair shake," a chance to play the electoral game by fair rules.[73] In fact, the language of section 2—guaranteeing minority voters an equal opportunity "to elect representatives of their choice"—plainly suggested a definition of representation broader than that which would have been conveyed had the phrase read, "minority representatives of their choice."

In addition, the concern was clearly with election contests in racist settings. Blacks, Congress concluded, lacked an equal chance to elect representatives of their choice where race had left them politically isolated—without potential allies in electoral contests. That focus was spelled out by numerous witnesses at the 1982 hearings and in the Senate Judiciary Committee Report as well.

The report thus listed "factors" to which courts were instructed to refer in judging the merits of a vote dilution suit. Those factors included a history of discrimination, racial polarization, a candidate slating process to which minorities were denied access, political campaigns characterized by racial appeals, and a lack of responsiveness on the part of public officials to minority interests.[74] The point of the list was clear: to help judges identify those situations in which either a history of discrimination or ongoing racism had left minority voters at a distinctive disadvantage in the electoral process. Not only the list, but other lan-

---

72. As Butler points out, "A jurisdiction that adopts extreme measures [stringing together black residential pockets] to create majority-black districts is akin to a manufacturer paying punitive damages to potential purchasers of its product prior to anyone suffering an injury or establishing a defect in the product." Butler, 26 RUTGERS LAW JOURNAL, at 516.

73. The "fair share," "fair shake" distinction is taken from Blumstein, *Defining Discrimination: Intent vs. Impact,* NEW PERSPECTIVES (Summer 1984), at 29, 30.

74. 1982 Senate Report at 28–29; Thernstrom, Supra n.1, at 192–197.

guage in the report signaled the importance of past and present racism. The concern, it noted, was with those exceptional communities in which racial politics still dominated the electoral process.[75]

That was the message as well of a number of civil rights advocates who testified at the 1982 hearings. For instance, Armand Derfner, a leading civil rights attorney and key witness, argued that single-member districts had no "precisely correct racial mix." The entitlement was not to districts that were, say, two-thirds black. Section 2 only promised an electoral process that was fluid—open to racial change, and thus not "frozen." Courts were expected to ask if minority voters would have "some influence."[76] Claims of dilution would rest, Derfner said, on "evidence that voters of a racial minority [were] isolated within a political system...'shut out,' i.e. denied access...[without] the opportunity to participate in the electoral process.[77]

When were minorities "frozen" out, however? No witness offered a definition of that total electoral exclusion against which the act protected, except to say that the test had been met when a group had "really been unfairly throttled."[78] "Unfairly throttled," that is, by racism, the Senate report—and the entire history of the act—made clear.

Some will argue that an interpretation of section 2 that makes racist exclusion the test of electoral discrimination is at odds with the stated intent in 1982 to create a way around the demand that plaintiffs provide evidence of discriminatory intent. Not at all. The objection in 1982 to the decision in *Mobile* was to the demand that plaintiffs produce a "smoking gun." Advocates did not object, in other words, to the focus

---

75. 1982 Senate Report at 32. The report also cited a South Carolina district court decision in *McCain v. Lybrand*, No 74-281, slip op. (D.D.C., April 17, 1980), as an illustration of the faithful application of the already familiar "results" test. The plaintiffs had prevailed in that decision because black candidates, the court found, tended to lose elections "not on their merits but solely because of their race." A report issued by the Subcommittee on the Constitution to the Senate committee on the Judiciary expressed concern that precisely that distinction would be lost. Not so, retorted the full committee's own report. In "most" jurisdictions white voters give substantial support to black candidates. But "unfortunately...there are still some communities...where racial politics do dominate the electoral process." And in such communities "a particular election method can deny minority voters equal opportunities to participate meaningfully in elections." 1982 Senate Report at 33.

76. *Voting Rights Act: Hearings on S. 1992 Before the Subcommittee on the Constitution of the Committee on the Judiciary*, 97th Cong., 2nd sess.(testimony of Armand Derfner) at 803 and 810.

77. *Id.* at 810 (prepared statement of Armand Derfner).

78. *Id.* at 803.

on racism, but only to the Court's alleged insistence on direct evidence of racist intent.

In sum, in revising section 2 Congress unequivocally and properly rejected the notion of group entitlement to even one legislative seat—however concentrated or dispersed black residential patterns were found to be. Had witnesses at the 1982 congressional hearings lobbied for an amended statute that would mandate race-based districting and thus guarantee legislative seats for members of designated minority groups, their arguments would have certainly fallen on deaf ears. Such a demand was not even remotely politically possible.

There is thus never any necessity on the part of a state (or its subdivisions) to maximize black officeholding by means of race-based districting. Race-conscious districting is available only as a remedy for a proven section 2 violation, and then only if adheres to standard districting criteria.[79] In the Louisiana and Georgia cases, both states (in creating a maximum number of safe black constituencies) hoped to avoid a costly and disruptive battle with the Department of Justice. Redistricting is a politically complex and laborious process, and to present a plan that won't be precleared is a waste of extensive political effort. That both states sought to avoid that rejection is understandable, but in their eagerness to do so, they engaged in a racial classification of voters that raised serious Fourteenth Amendment questions. A compelling state interest justifies a racial classification, but a preference for smooth bureaucratic sailing does not meet that test.

A Coercive Distortion of the Law: Business as Usual

The district courts in both the Louisiana and Georgia cases raised serious concerns over the Justice Department's coercive role in bending local jurisdictions to its will.[80] The circumstances were particularly egregious in the Georgia case, where Justice Department lawyers who have the responsibility to make impartial preclearance determinations worked in active concern with an outside group that wanted a maximum number of race-driven districts. As the trial court noted, the ACLU's attorney, Ms. Kathleen Wilde, developed a relationship with the voting section that was "in-

---

79. As Butler notes, only geographically compact minority groups may claim that a districting scheme dilutes their voting strength (*Thornburg v. Gingles*, 478 U.S. 30, 50 (1986). It thus cannot be possible that a district that runs down an interstate highway collecting residentially scattered black voters is necessary if a state wishes to avoid violating the act. 26 RUTGERS LAW J. at 518.

80. See, e.g., *Hays v. Louisiana*, 839 F. Supp. 1188, 1196 n. 21 (W.D. La. 1993), vacated, 114 S. Ct. 2731 (1994).

formal and familiar; the dynamics were that of peers working together, not of an advocate submitting proposals to higher authorities."[81]

As noted above, the record of the Justice Department in these two cases is not abberational. The voting section of the Justice Department's Civil Rights Division has long assumed freewheeling power to object to districting plans that did not seem "right"—that is, racially "fair."[82] In 1981, for instance, a Justice Department memo on county council districts for Barbour County, Alabama, explained that calculating what was "fair" was simple. "Since blacks constitute 40.5 percent of the voting age population, they would be entitled to 2.8 districts [that is, two viable districts plus a third influence district]." The voting section itself drew up the right plan. Such calculations—in Democratic and Republican administrations alike—became a routine part of the preclearance process.[83] Only one thing is new: with the post-1990 availability of sophisticated census software, the racial sorting of voters has become exquisitely precise.[84]

What is routine is obviously not necessarily right. The voting section of the Department of Justice has long had the aura of a law office; its files suggest attorneys at work constructing a case for minority plaintiffs.[85] And yet the interests of minority plaintiffs are not necessarily those of either the minority voters whom the Department purports to represent or the American public, its only legitimate client.

The Real Issue

At the heart of voting rights disputes, I noted at the outset, is an argument about the nature of American society. It is true of all conflicts over affirmative action policies. Deliberately drawn majority-minority districts are racial classifications for familiar affirmative action ends. The point of the race-conscious districting is precisely that of most such policies: to provide maximum protection for black candidates from white competition. Law school affirmative action programs, by setting separate admissions standards, pit black applicants primarily (sometimes only)

---

81. *Id.* at 1362.

82. This criticism is developed in detail in Thernstrom, WHOSE VOTES COUNT?, chapter 8; and in Katharine Inglis Butler, *Reapportionment, the Courts, and the Voting Rights Act: A Resegregation of the Political Process?* 56 UNIV. OF COLO. L. REV. 21 (1984).

83. Thernstrom, WHOSE VOTES COUNT? at 171–2.

84. On the impact of the changed technology on the crafting of districts, see, e.g., *Shaw v. Hunt*, 861 F. Supp. 408 (E.D.N.C. 1994).

85. See Thernstrom, WHOSE VOTES COUNT?, ch. 8.

against other blacks. Likewise, "safe" black legislative districts amount to protective racial sorting. Their aim is to ensure electoral contests in which black candidates compete only against other black candidates, eliminating potential white competitors.

Questions involving affirmative action in the electoral sphere are thus not simply about who ends up where in a districting map. At issue between the opposing sides are entirely different views of white racial attitudes, black opportunity, the nature of democratic representation, and the costs of race-conscious policies.

Bleak and Wrong

Black candidates cannot get elected in majority-white settings, the brief for the Congressional Black Caucus argued in the Louisiana case. That is "contemporary reality."[86] The doors of political opportunity are still closed. Black candidates remain at the mercy of racist white opposition. Hence the need for protective policies—for race-based districts drawn to ensure black officeholding, an implicit statutory promise.

From the outset the Voting Rights Act did clearly promise more than simple access to the polling booth; the architects of the statute believed black ballots would mean black power. Not just black political influence, but blacks elected to public office. But the statute contained no guarantee of such electoral success, and, equally important, the CBC's portrait of the American racial landscape is much too bleak.[87]

Whites not only say they will vote for black candidates; they do so, often casting their ballots for an African American running against a white opponent. That choice is most often available in mayoral contests. Conventional wisdom has it that the overwhelming majority of black mayors have been elected from majority-black cities. This is true but misleading. Most of those black "cities" are in fact tiny majority-black towns in the South. Eliminate those small urban dots on the southern map, focus on cities of 50,000 or more in population, and quite a different picture emerges. Sixty-seven percent of the black mayors elected in such

---

86. Brief for the Congressional Black Caucus at 1.

87. A concern that preferential policies rest on the arguably demeaning assumption that blacks require extraordinary protection from white competition in order to succeed in American society runs through a number of affirmative action cases. See, e.g., *Regents of the Univ. of California v. Bakke*, 438 U.S. 265, 298: "preferential programs may only reinforce common stereotypes holding that certain groups are unable to achieve success without special protection based on a factor bearing no relationship to individual worth."

cities over the last thirty years have not had the benefit of a majority-black constituency.[88]

Even in Maine, with a black population of just 0.4 percent, the mayors of two important cities are black. In the 1989 mayoral race in New York City (29 percent black), Rudolph Guiliani lost between 25 and 30 percent of the white vote to David Dinkins. At least 38 percent of whites deserted Jon Derus in Minneapolis (13 percent black) in 1993, and cast their ballots for the victor, Sharon Sayles Belton, the black president of the city council. That same year, 31 percent of the white electorate in St. Louis (48 percent African American) voted for Freeman Bosely Jr, despite the availability of three white candidates on the ballot; in fact, Bosely's overall vote total was precisely that of his white predecessor. Belton and Bosley were making their first try; incumbents (although not David Dinkins) generally do even better.

It is not only in races for a mayor's seat that white voters choose black candidates over those who are white. L. Douglas Wilder, in his successful gubernatorial run in 1989, got an estimated 40 to 43 percent of Virginia's white vote. Sceptics will say that figure still represents only a minority of the white electorate, but Charles Robb, the white Democratic governor who preceded Wilder, did only a shade better: 45 percent. Illinois (11.6 percent black) elected Carol Moseley-Braun as its U.S. Senator in 1992. In 1994, Ohio elected J. Kenneth Blackwell as state treasurer and New York chose H. Carl McCall as state comptroller. Also in 1994, J.C. Watts won a congressional seat in an 93 percent white Oklahoma district.

But what about Georgia and other southern states? Was Wilder's election in Virginia a fluke? Georgia, in fact, was one of the first states to send an African American to Congress from a majority-white district; Andrew Young, elected in 1972, did not have the benefit of a majority-black constituency. Young, however, was the first and last from his state, and in Louisiana no black congressman from a majority-white constituency has ever been elected. Hence the need, the CBC argues, for safe black constituencies. In fact, for three reasons the record in neither state is particularly telling.

To begin with, the past is not the future. White racial attitudes have been changing fast, and the record of black electoral success in 1975 tells us little about the prospects for such success today. In addition, black candidates cannot win contests they do not enter. And scholars who attempt to assess white willingness to support black candidacies on the basis of election returns cannot learn anything from elections in which no black candidate has been in the race.

---

88. The data are contained in Abigail Thernstrom and Stephan Thernstrom, *The Promise of Racial Equality*, in Lamar Alexander and Chester E. Finn, Jr., eds., THE NEW PROMISE OF AMERICAN LIFE (The Hudson Institute, 1995), ch. 5.

Finally, congressional candidates—whatever their color—cannot win elections if their political views are at odds with the majority of voters in their district. California Rep. Ronald V. Dellums gets elected from a constituency that includes Berkeley and like-minded suburbs, but few majority-white districts are as left-leaning as his. Particularly in the South, centrist and conservative candidates (whether white or black) will do better than those who are militantly liberal. J.C. Watts, a black Republican, would not have been elected in Oklahoma had he run as a liberal Democrat. As the Supreme Court recognized in *Whitcomb*, when black Democratic candidates lose in conservative districts, it is not their race but their ideology that white voters are rejecting.[89]

Guinier, among others, has argued that centrist or conservative black candidates who can attract strong white support are not "authentically" black.[90] There is a political test for "blackness"; black constituents can lack representation even with blacks in office. If (in Guinier's words) those officeholders are not "community-based," "culturally-rooted," and "politically, psychologically, and culturally black,"[91] then they're tokens—contaminated by white support. In her view, as mayor of Atlanta, Andrew Young did not count as a black advocate;[92] the "authentic" leader need not "appeal to white voters in order to get elected."[93] "Authenticity" has "a distinctive voice"[94] and a level of group consciousness incompatible with white enthusiasm.

It's an accusation with a familiar ring. White civil rights sympathizers in the South were once regularly called "nigger-lovers." Governor Wilder, Andrew Young, Justice Clarence Thomas and other African Americans against whom the charge of inauthenticity has been leveled are, in effect, "honky-lovers," and as such racial renegades.

But by that definition, a number of recently elected black mayors do not count as "black" for purposes of representation. Many are fiscal conservatives, tough on crime, and opposed to busing. Moreover, Jesse Jackson, whom the media treat as the authentic voice of black America,

---

89. Since blacks in Indiana's Marion County—largely Republican—were Democrats, the Court concluded, the "dilution" of their voting strength were a "mere euphemism for political defeat." It was not race but party that had determined electoral outcome. 403 U.S. at 153.

90. Guinier, THE TYRANNY OF THE MAJORITY at 55–58.

91. Lani Guinier, *The Triumph of Tokenism: The Voting Rights Act and the Theory of Black Electoral Success*, 89 MICHIGAN LAW REVIEW 1077, 1103.

92. Andrew Young's record, Guinier asserts, was not much different from that of Atlanta's white business-oriented mayors. *Id* at 1118 n. 196.

93. *Id.* at 1103–4.

94. *Id* at 1108.

is actually to the left of the majority of black voters, recent polling data suggest.[95] If the data are correct, the point applies as well to the Congressional Black Caucus.

Conservative and moderate blacks can represent black voters—and so can elected whites. The Voting Rights Act was designed to protect black voters, not officeholders with a particular color or those who hold only certain political views. The members of the CBC and other black politicians are strong advocates of racial gerrymandering; such districting is in their interest. All elected officials like safe constituencies from which to run, and majority-black districts are safe constituencies. Almost inevitably, they elect a black legislator. In part, that is because white candidates, as discussed above, are not welcome in such districts, but in part it is the consequence of the fact that black voters, whose electoral power is still relatively novel, tend to vote as a bloc.

If safe black districts are a gift to black politicians, they are not so clearly in the interest of black voters. Such districts may marginalize the black elected officials upon whom the voters count to represent their interests effectively.[96] In fact, arguably, a greater dispersion of black voters over more "influence districts" would result in a better representation of black interests, since more public officials, both black and white, would owe their election in part to black support.[97]

That greater dispersion, however, depends on judicial action. Majority-minority districts are here to stay, unless courts intervene. In this important sense, legislative plans that protect black candidates from white competition are a distinctive form of affirmative action. Separate lists for black and white candidates for spots on a police force or for seats in a medical school class are, at least in theory, temporary measures; their life is due to expire when the need for such protective racial sorting ends.

The racial gerrymandering of legislative districts, on the other hand, if allowed to stand, is likely to be permanent for two reasons. Black incumbents are politically secure; few white political aspirants would want to risk a media thrashing for attempting allegedly to "disfranchise" black

---

95. Michael C. Dawson, BEHIND THE MULE: RACE AND CLASS IN AFRICAN-AMERICAN POLITICS (Princeton Univ. Press, 1994), p. 137, figure 6.3.

96. See James F. Blumstein, *Racial Gerrymandering and Vote Dilution: Shaw v. Reno in Doctrinal Context*, 26 RUTGERS LAW JOURNAL #3, 515, 522. As Blumstein points out, in *Wright v. Rockefeller* (376 U.S. 52 [1964]), two groups of black plaintiffs were at odds as to what would be in the best interests of African American in Manhattan and thus urged different districting plans.

97. See *Voinovich v. Quilter,* 113 S.Ct 1075 (1993), in which plaintiffs argued that black voters were being "packed" into districts in such a way as to lessen their overall influence. *Id.* at 1153.

voters.[98] In addition, in the covered jurisdictions of the South and else-where, the retrogression test of section 5 forbids backsliding—a drop in the number of secure black legislative seats. Plans approved today be-come the absolute baselines against which subsequent districting changes are measured through at least 2007, when section 5 is now scheduled to expire.[99]

A People Apart

That in a racially fair political system blacks would hold office in pro-portion to their numbers in the population is a conviction that runs through all the writings by advocates of race-based districting.[100] In part, these advocates simply believe that disproportionately low minority of-ficeholding can have only one explanation: white racism. In part, pro-portionality is the logical legal standard once a distinction is made be-tween "meaningful" and "meaningless" black ballots.[101] For that distinction necessitates a determination as to when black votes "fully count," and the phrase itself invites a definition that gives those ballots maximum weight, defined as proportionate racial and ethnic officehold-ing. Anything less suggests a compromised right.

In addition, disproportionately low black officeholding, proponents of race-conscious districting clearly believe, denies representation to a group for whom members of no other group can speak.[102] "[B]lacks live

---

98. And indeed, as the district court noted in the Georgia case, it had "been placed in the unenviable position of depriving black citizens of a privilege [although one] the Justice Department never had the right to grant: maximization of the black vote, what-ever the cost." It was a politically uncomfortable position for federal judges with lifetime job tenure, and clearly would have been even more so had they been up for election. *Miller v. Johnson,* 864 F. Supp. 1354, 1369 (S.D. Ga. 1994), aff'd, 115 S. Ct. 2475 (1995).

99. "[A]ny redistricting plan designed for proportionality, that is upheld by the Court today, will not be easily uprooted in the foreseeable future." *Johnson v. Miller Id.* at 1386.

100. See, for instance, *Minority Vote Dilution, An Overview* in Chandler Davidson, ed., MINORITY VOTE DILUTION (Howard University Press, 1984), p. 12 ("about one-fifth as many blacks hold office as would be likely in a nonracist society"), and more recently, the Brief for the United States in U.S. v. Hays, 12, *U.S. v. Hays,* 115 S. Ct. 231 (1995).

101. The problem of definition meaningful votes did not of course first surface in the minority vote dilution cases. It had been fully apparent in the reapportionment decisions: *Baker v. Carr,* (369 U.S. 186 (1962) and *Reynolds v. Sims* 377 U.S. 533 (1964).

102. The notion that blacks are a group apart, sharing distinctive views, was directly attacked by Justice Kennedy in *Miller.* If redistricting, he wrote, often involves racial

in a different world from whites,"[103] Lani Guinier argues; "disagreements among blacks pale by comparison with the differences in political interest and philosophy between blacks and whites."[104] In severely divided societies, of which the United States is one, whites cannot speak for blacks, or (by logical extension) blacks for whites. Blacks—the assumption runs—are a nation within our nation, a people apart. And as such, they are entitled, as a matter of elementary fairness, to representation in proportion to their population strength.[105]

It may have been a legitimate argument in 1945; it isn't today. Fifty years ago, the novelist and social critic Richard Wright described his boyhood days in a South in which "whites had drawn a line over which we dared not step."[106] But that South has disappeared, and the position of African Americans within American society has been transformed. More than 80 percent of blacks polled in national surveys report having whites as neighbors.[107] Few whites say that they wouldn't want to live next door to a black family, while 30 percent object to having a Fundamentalist as a neighbor.[108] African Americans are permanent and influential political players in both North and South. They are partners in powerful law firms, and doctors at distinguished hospitals. An African American model in an upscale Bloomingdale's clothing ad is now busi-

---

considerations, "it does not follow...that individuals of the same race share a single political interest. The view that they do is 'based on the demeaning notion that members of the defined racial groups ascribe to certain 'minority views' that must be different from those of other citizens,' Metro Broadcasting..., the precise use of race as a proxy the Constitution prohibits." (*Miller* 115 S. Ct. at 2487). See also Thomas, J., concurring in *Holder v Hall*: "[I]n resolving vote dilution actions we have given credence to the view that race defines political interest. We have acted on the implicit assumption that members of racial and ethnic groups must all think alike on important matters of public policy and must have their own 'minority preferred' representatives holding seats in elected bodies if they are to be considered represented at all." 114 S. Ct. 2581, 2597 (1994).

103. Lani Guinier, *No Two Seats: The Elusive Quest for Racial Equality*, 77 VIRGINIA LAW REV. 1413, 1468, quoting Hochschild and Herk.

104. *Id.* at 1468.

105. Justice Ginsburg comes close to embracing this view in her dissent in *Miller*: "But ethnicity itself can tie people together, as volumes of social science literature have documented—even people with divergent economic interests." 1155 Ct. at 2504. (Ginsburg, J., dissenting, slip op 12)

106. Richard Wright, BLACK BOY (1945), 251.

107. William Feigelman and Bernard S. Gorman, *Blacks Who Live Near Whites: 1982 and 1987*, 74 SOCIOLOGY AND SOCIAL RESEARCH, (July, 1990), 202–207.

108. Howard Schuman, Charlotte Steenh, and Lawrence Bobo, RACIAL ATTITUDES IN AMERICA: TRENDS AND INTERPRETATIONS, (Harvard University Press, 1985), 106–107; 1989 Gallup poll cited in Stephen Bates, BATTLEGROUND (Poseidon Press, 1993), 64.

ness as usual; as are black faces in TV commercials selling every sort of product. The Bill Cosby show, watched by 20 million viewers, earned NBC a billion dollars.

African Americans still have incomes below the national average, are less likely than whites to have a college degree, have higher poverty rates, and rank behind whites in most measures of socioeconomic status. But they are no longer a people apart in the way that they arguably were as recently as the early 1960s, before the Civil Rights Revolution. Since then they have become part of the American mainstream. As the district court noted in *Johnson v. Miller*, "[B]lacks in Georgia did indeed rise from a common heritage of slavery and oppression, but with the shedding of those burdens they have begun to follow myriad, distinctive paths."[109]

Until the 1960s almost all of the small numbers of blacks students attending college were to be found in historically black institutions; today the number in higher education has grown explosively, and six out of seven of them attend predominantly white institutions. "Buy Black" campaigns routinely flop. Black separatist parties go nowhere. This picture could obviously be enlarged, but the point should be clear. The United States is not yet a fully integrated society, but it has moved in that direction with impressive speed in the four decades since *Brown v. Board*. A separate and excluded people may be entitled to legislative set-asides, seats reserved to ensure their political inclusion. In 1995, blacks no longer need such an extraordinarily protective arrangement.

African Americans are not a racially-defined nation within our nation. And yet if both they and whites believe they are, it may well become true. This is especially the case if that perception informs the law. Separate admissions procedures for whites and blacks, separate hiring processes, separate legislative districts: given a stamp of approval by Congress and the courts, they paint an official, influential and perverse portrait of American society.

Two societies—one white and one black—is not a fact; it is what the columnist Robert J. Samuelson has called (in another context) a psycho-fact: it is not true, but we feel it is and thus it threatens to become so.[110] Perceptions can take on a life of their own, shaping the society that they purport to describe.

Racially gerrymandered districts are an attempt to provide racial and ethnic minorities, and only them, with representation free from the con-

---

109. *Johnson v. Miller*, 864 F. Supp. 1354, 1390 (S.D. Ga. 1994), aff'd., 115 S. Ct. 2475 (1995).

110. "The Triumph of the Psycho-Fact" WASHINGTON POST, 4 May 1994, A25.

straints that our geographically-based districting system places on the representation of all group interests.[111] To impute to Congress an intent to permanently remove one group from the pluralism of American politics not only misreads the basic objectives of the Voting Rights Act, but would ensure the very segregation the act was intended to cure.

A Shared Danger

"All citizens are stigmatized by the notion that their 'interests' can be defined by race or will be represented adequately only if a member of their racial 'group' holds a particular office," the district court in the Louisiana case concluded.[112] It was true as well of the segregated institutions of the Jim Crow South. Blacks and whites were both harmed when drinking fountains carried "white" and "colored" signs.[113]

Racial classifications, in short, deliver the message that skin color matters—profoundly. They suggest that white folks and black folks just are not the same, that race and ethnicity are the qualities that really matter. Individuals are defined by blood—not by character, social class, religious sentiments, age, or education. But categories appropriate to a caste system are a poor basis on which to build that community of equal citizens upon which democratic government depends. Equal citizens are free to define themselves, and do so differently in different contexts. A voter whose choice of a candidate in a presidential primary is shaped primarily by racial considerations might react to the issues in a school board contest as parents of other races do. It is precisely that fluidity of individual political identity that prevents the formation of castes, which are rigid and hierarchical by nature.

The danger posed by racial classifications, as the Court said in *Shaw*, is especially serious when the question is the distribution of political

---

111. See Butler, 26 RUTGERS LAW JOURNAL at 523–24. As she notes, Justice Stevens' observation in *Shaw* that "African Americans may be the only group to which it is unconstitutional to offer specific benefits from redistricting" (115 S.Ct. at 2845 n. 4, Stevens, J., dissenting) is simply backwards. The Constitution permits the states to recognize group interests, but only those that can be furthered with a geographically-based representational structure.

112. *Hays v. Louisiana,* 862 F. Supp. 119, 125 (W.D. La. 1994), vacated, 115 S. Ct. 2431 (1995).

113. Or as Justice Thomas put it in his concurring opinion in *Adarand Constructors, Inc. v. Pena,* it is "irrelevant whether a government's racial classifications are drawn by those who wish to oppress a race or by those who have a sincere desire to help those thought to be disadvantaged." 115 Ct. 2097, 2119 (1995), concurring. Blumstein's article, supra, contains a good discussion of the point that racial classifications are, in themselves, an evil; their impact is not the issue. *Racial Gerrymandering, Shaw v. Reno,* Supra n. 96 at 522.

power—the good that ultimately determines the allocation of all other social goods. "Racial classifications" with respect to voting carry particular dangers," O'Connor noted. "Racial gerrymandering, even for remedial purposes, may balkanize us into competing racial factions...[carrying] us further from the goal of a political system in which race no longer matters."[114] It is a point that Justice Thomas reiterated at length in *Holder v. Hall.* "Our drive to segregate political districts by race," he said, "can only serve to deepen racial divisions by destroying any need for voters or candidates to build bridges between racial groups or to form voting coalitions."[115]

No decisions this past term were more important than those involving race-driven districting. If the Supreme Court had overturned the judgments of the lower courts in the Louisiana and Georgia cases, it would have signed on to a badly mistaken notion of American society—one that sees white racial attitudes as little changed since the 1960s; a racial divide that creates two nations, separate and unequal; blacks as politically excluded and thus in need of extraordinary protection from white competition. If embraced by the law in subsequent decisions, that view will perpetuate and encourage group-think. Ours is still a nation of individual citizens, not a confederation of racial and ethnic groups. But we need the Court's help to stay the course.

---

114. 113 S.Ct at 2816, 2832 (1993).
115. 114 S.Ct 2581, 114 S. Ct. 2584, 2599. (Thomas J. concurring.)

CHAPTER 5

Shaw v. Reno and the Voting Rights Conundrum: Equality, The Public Interest, and the Politics of Representation[1]

Anthony A. Peacock

Writing in the *Chicago Tribune* July 9, 1993, Bernard Grofman remarked that "The 5–4 majority opinion in *Shaw v. Reno*[2] is about as tortuous and hard to make sense of as the North Carolina 12th itself."[3] Grofman's statement was not far from the truth. In *Shaw*, the Supreme Court was asked to determine whether two North Carolina congressional districts, CD 1 and CD 12, were unconstitutional racial gerrymanders. Both were drafted to create majority-minority districts following the 1990 census, when North Carolina was granted an additional congressional seat, bringing its total delegation in Congress to twelve.

The focus of attention in *Shaw* was CD 12, described by Richard Pildes and Richard Niemi as the "worst district in the nation"[4] in terms of dispersion and perimeter measures of congressional district shape.[5]

---

1. Preliminary versions of this chapter were presented at the Western Political Science Association annual meeting in Albuquerque, March 12, 1994, and the Canadian Political Science Association annual meeting in Montreal, June 6, 1995. I would like to thank Ralph A. Rossum, Joseph M. Bessette, Charles R. Kesler, Mark E. Rush, Samuel Issacharoff, Patrick James, and George T. Felkenes for comments on earlier drafts of this chapter.

2. 113 S.Ct. 2816 (1993).

3. Bernard Grofman, *High Court Ruling Won't Doom Racial Gerrymandering*, CHICAGO TRIBUNE, Friday, July 9, 1993, Section 1, 19.

4. Richard H. Pildes and Richard G. Niemi, *Expressive Harms, "Bizarre Districts," and Voting Rights: Evaluating Election-District Appearances After Shaw v. Reno,"* MICHIGAN L. REV. 92 (1993): 483, 566.

5. "Dispersion" refers to capturing "'how tightly packed or spread out the geography of a district is'" (*id.*, 554). "Perimeter" examines "the extent to which district borders wander in irregular ways" (*id.*, 555).

CD 12 stretched some 160 miles along Interstate 85, incorporating to-bacco farms, urban financial and manufacturing centers, and linking Durham, Greensboro, Winston-Salem, Charlotte, and bits and pieces of 10 counties, until it strung together black communities sufficient to form a majority-black congressional district.[6]

The 12th District was drawn in response to an objection by the Justice Department that a previous North Carolina redistricting plan had, con-trary to section 5 of the Voting Rights Act (VRA),[7] created an inadequate number of majority-black districts following the 1990 census. (The orig-inal plan had created only one majority-black district, CD 1.) The North Carolina legislature responded by adding the 12th District. The 12th's unusual, elongated shape, however, seemed to ignore accepted principles of districting such as contiguity and compactness.[8] Five North Carolina voters, claiming that CD 1 and CD 12 violated the provisions of the Equal Protection Clause (EPC), appealed to the Supreme Court to have the second North Carolina redistricting plan declared unconstitutional. The Court was placed once again, as it had been on a number of occa-sions in the past, in the delicate position of having to reconcile the VRA with the EPC.

To suggest that the VRA and the EPC had to be reconciled, of course, implies that the two equality rights initiatives are incompatible—at least in some respects. My first contention, in this chapter, is that the VRA and the EPC are incompatible in the most fundamental respect: they are predicated upon competing, irreconcilable conceptions of equality. The VRA is informed by an affirmative action, equal "results" understanding of equality. The EPC is moved by an equal opportunity, race neutral un-derstanding of equality. The difficulty of reconciling these two concep-tions of equality goes a long way to explaining the split between the ma-jority and minority in *Shaw*—a split repeated in every voting rights case since—and also goes some distance to explaining why the Court has been unable to expound a theory of representation consistent with VRA-EPC jurisprudence. In simple terms, as long as the VRA and the EPC re-

---

6. See *Shaw*, 113 S.Ct. at 2820–21, and Pildes and Niemi, *Election-District Appear-ances*, 490–91.

7. Voting Rights Act of 1965, Pub. L. No. 89-110, 79 Stat. 445 (codified as amended at 42 U.S.C. §§ 1971, 1973 to 1973bb-1 (1988)).

8. For a discussion of these principles, see Pildes and Niemi, *Election-District Appearances*, esp. 536–57; Daniel D. Polsby and Robert D. Popper, *The Third Criteri-on: Compactness as a Procedural Safeguard Against Partisan Gerrymandering*, YALE L. AND POLY. REV. 9 (1991): 301; and Richard G. Niemi, Bernard Grofman, Carl Carlucci, and Thomas Hofeller, *Measuring Compactness and the Role of a Compactness Standard in a Test for Partisan and Racial Gerrymandering*, J. POL. 52 (1990): 1155.

main incongruous, any attempt to reconcile them in a theory of representation will be futile and we should expect judicial reasoning in such cases to be "tortuous."

My second contention is that if the conflict between the VRA and the EPC—the impasse between the majority and minority in recent VRA litigation—is to be overcome, the Supreme Court will have to settle upon a single constitutional understanding of equality. To date, it has not done so.

Third, I contend that even if the Court did do this, it would not resolve the problem of representation in voting rights litigation since the dominant theories of representation, prevalent in academic literature and generally accepted by the federal judiciary and federal administrators, restricts the role of representation to the representing of constituent interests and the fulfilling of an ombudsman's role. An adequate account of representation, while accommodating the demands of group interests and individual constituents, must also account for the role of the public interest in American representative government. American democracy is a deliberative democracy and the focus of redistricting and reapportionment litigation on group interests is symptomatic of assumptions dominant in modern social science, as well as modern jurisprudence and public administration.

As was pointed out in the introduction to this book, contrary to early prognostications, *Shaw* turned out to be a bellwether in equal protection litigation, undermining the very foundation of earlier voting rights law and inaugurating a widespread reassessment of the VRA's purposes and constitutionality. *Shaw* and its legacy are unique in the history of voting rights. For the first time in that long history, as Abigail Thernstrom suggests in her contribution to this volume, the Court was no longer concerned with racial discrimination so much as with the racial and ethnic fragmentation of American society. In this respect, *Shaw* initiated a reorientation in the types of questions and concerns that would now occupy federal judges. In particular, the structures or forms of representation would be scrutinized in a way that they seldom were before *Shaw* since it was these structures or forms that were the focus of the Court's attention rather than political or electoral results, the focus of attention in vote dilution jurisprudence.

My third contention then is that if the Court is to address the issue of representation seriously, that is, comprehensively, it is going to have to look beyond group or constituent interests to the public interest that is served by the forms of representation that are created by the VRA. Specifically, courts are going to have to examine the putative requirement of race-conscious districting and the underlying assumption of that requirement, that voters are most effectively represented when they elect representatives who mirror their interests in the legislative process. The logical endpoint of such forms of representation are proportional or semi-proportional representational systems, schemes typically requiring the partial or complete abandonment of territorial districting and winner-take-all elections. Proportional representation may better provide for minority officeholding, as it better provides for the officeholding of other groups submerged by winner-take-all systems. It is unclear, however, whether such systems of representation serve the broader purposes of the representational form of government that the Constitution contemplates. In the long term, and perhaps even in the short term, proportional representation may disserve minority interests, as it disserves other interests in the representational scheme.

Shaw's uniqueness lay in its concerns for the structural or formal problems posed by the VRA prior to 1993, problems extending beyond the strict legal issue of whether or not race-conscious districting was constitutional. If *Shaw* was an anomaly in voting rights jurisprudence, as many contend, it was nevertheless consistent with the spirit of recent equality rights litigation before the Supreme Court that had attempted to rein in affirmative action.[9] Like many of these other cases, *Shaw* signalled an attempt by the Court to clarify an equality rights jurisprudence that had become all too murky over the last generation. Yet, the very fact that the Court could be so divided on the purposes of the VRA as late as 1993 was an indication of how ambivalent the VRA's history had become, how confused its moving principles had remained since the dyspeptic attempts at clarifying them during the 1981–82 congressional hearings on the VRA extension and amendments.[10] How, after almost thirty years, could VRA jurisprudence have become so shrouded in ambiguity as to allow for such a decisive majority-minority split as occurred

---

9. See, for example, *Grove City College v. Bell*, 465 U.S. 555 (1984), where the Court narrowly construed Title VI of the 1964 Civil Rights Act; *Wards Cove Packing Co. v. Antonio*, 490 U.S. 642 (1989), where the Court reined in the disparate impact test applicable to Title VII cases under the Civil Rights Act; and *City of Richmond v. J.A. Croson Co.*, 488 U.S. 469 (1989), where the Court rejected the "benign" purposes of a Richmond set-aside program for businesses, maintaining that strict scrutiny under the EPC applied equally to all groups, regardless of race. After *Shaw*, the Court applied the *Croson* rule to a federal "benign" set aside program in *Adarand Constructors, Inc. v. Pena*, 115 S.Ct. 2097 (1995), overruling *Metro Broadcasting, Inc. v. FCC*, 497 U.S. 547 (1990), which had permitted the application of a lesser standard of scrutiny to federal set asides than applied to state set asides.

10. See Thomas M. Boyd and Stephen J. Markman, *The 1982 Amendments to the Voting Rights Act: A Legislative History*, WASHINGTON AND LEE L. REV. 40 (1983): 1347; and James F. Blumstein, *Defining and Proving Race Discrimination: Perspectives on the Purpose vs. Results Approach from the Voting Rights Act*, VIRGINIA L. REV. 69 (1983): 633.

in *Shaw*? How did the Supreme Court get itself into this conundrum? As we see, the Court is not entirely free from blame for its predicament.

Shaw and the VRA-EPC Tension

What exactly was at issue in *Shaw*? As has been noted, *Shaw* was not a vote dilution case. Rather, the plaintiffs were alleging an analytically distinct type of claim, one based on the bizarre shape of the North Carolina 1st and 12th CDs. As Justice O'Connor, writing for the Court, highlighted, the plaintiffs were alleging "that the deliberate segregation of voters into separate districts on the basis of race violated their constitutional right to participate in a 'color-blind' electoral process."[11] This was not the same as alleging that the North Carolina "General Assembly's reapportionment plan unconstitutionally 'diluted' white voting strength."[12]

In a strict sense, then, *Shaw* was not a vote dilution claim. The plaintiffs were not alleging that their votes were being submerged within a district comprised of an opposing majority. Yet if *Shaw* was not, strictly speaking, a vote dilution claim, its facts and issues nevertheless had been framed by the legacy of vote dilution jurisprudence. Without this legacy, the tortuously shaped 12th CD would never have appeared (even if its bizarre shape was due, in large measure, to partisan, political influences in addition to considerations of race[13]). Similarly, the Court in *Shaw* was not spared the task of addressing the perennial issues. Quite the contrary. The same difficult questions that had confronted the Court in vote dilution jurisprudence in the past would confront the Court in *Shaw*.

Reconciling the Past and Present

According to Justice O'Connor, *Shaw* involved "two of the most complex and sensitive issues the Court has faced in recent years: the meaning of the constitutional 'right' to vote, and the propriety of race-based state legislation designed to benefit members of historically disadvantaged groups."[14] The latter question had become particularly acute since 1989,

---

11. 113 S.Ct. 2816, 2824 (1993).

12. *Id.*

13. See *Shaw*, 113 S.Ct. at 2841, n.10, White, J., dissenting; and Bernard Grofman, *Would Vince Lombardi Have Been Right If He Had Said: "When It Comes to Redistricting, Race Isn't Everything, It's the Only Thing?*, CARDOZO L. REV. 14 (1993): 1237, 1257–58.

14. 113 S.Ct. at 2819.

when all state affirmative action programs were surreptitiously challenged in *City of Richmond v. J.A. Croson Co.*,[15] a case involving a business set aside program requiring of all prime contractors awarded City of Richmond construction contracts that they subcontract at least thirty percent of the dollar amount of each contract to minority business enterprises. Examining the record in *Croson*, Justice O'Connor could find no legitimate purpose for the plan. In her words, there was "*absolutely no evidence* of past discrimination" against the intended beneficiaries, Spanish-speaking, Oriental, Indian, Eskimo, and Aleut contractors. In addition, there was a serious question whether some of the groups had ever lived in Richmond[16] and the case had a strong aura of political self-dealing. Five of the nine members of the Richmond City Council, which had devised the plan, were members of a minority group.[17]

Croson presented a fact scenario ripe for judicial attack. The "benign" purposes doctrine, championing a standard less exacting than strict scrutiny for race-conscious affirmative action programs, had enjoyed prominence in equality rights litigation since the early 1970s. The doctrine had divided the Supreme Court in *University of California Regents v. Bakke* (1978).[18] As a result, however, of Justice Powell's famous compromise opinion, the Court in *Bakke* was able to settle upon an equal protection test allowing race to be used as one, but not the sole, criterion in government sponsored affirmative action. The tough question, never answered in *Bakke*, was just how much race could be considered in such programs? What was the level of scrutiny that was to be applied in later cases which allowed for race-conscious measures justified as remedies for historically disadvantaged groups?

Clarifying the issue in *Croson*, O'Connor affirmed that the provisions of the Fourteenth Amendment were "personal rights" guaranteed to the individual and not to groups.[19] The "standard of review under the Equal Protection Clause," she demurred, "is not dependent on the race of those burdened or benefited by a particular classification."[20] To assume that the mere recitation of a "benign" purpose for a race-conscious program

---

15. 488 U.S. 469 (1989).

16. *Id.*, 506, opinion of the Court, emphasis in original.

17. *Id.*, 495–96. See also, T. Alexander Aleinikoff and Samuel Issacharoff, *Race and Redistricting: Drawing Constitutional Lines After* Shaw v. Reno, MICHIGAN L. REV. 92 (1993): 588, 597–98.

18. 438 U.S. 265.

19. 488 U.S. at 493, quoting *Shelley v. Kraemer*, 334 U.S. 1, 22 (1948).

20. 488 U.S. at 494. The same standard now applies to federal affirmative action programs as applies to state affirmative action programs, such as the one at issue in *Croson*. See *Adarand Constructors, Inc. v. Pena*, 115 S.Ct. 2097 (1995).

was sufficient to save a program from strict scrutiny was tantamount to accepting a watered down version of equal protection analysis and to effectively emasculating the strict scrutiny standard, depriving it of any probative value.

> Absent searching judicial inquiry into the justification for such race-based measures, there is simply no way of determining what classifications are "benign" or "remedial" and what classifications are in fact motivated by illegitimate notions of racial inferiority or simple racial politics.[21]

Moreover,

> Classifications based on race carry a danger of stigmatic harm. Unless they are strictly reserved for remedial settings, they may in fact promote notions of racial inferiority and lead to a politics of hostility.[22]

The invidiousness of racial classifications and their sequelae could not be tolerated. A strict reading of strict scrutiny meant that the same test would have to be applied to all groups, no matter who benefited from a preferential policy. *Croson*, on its face a clarification of *Bakke*, in fact transformed it. As Alexander Aleinikoff and Samuel Issacharoff write:

> *Croson* is *Bakke* with a twist. It represents a new model of equal protection that narrowly limits the use of race-conscious measures based on a norm of equal treatment of individuals rather than the raising up of disadvantaged groups—a model that is dedicated to the pursuit of social peace rather than social justice.[23]

However we characterize *Croson*, it was clear the decision did not augur well for the defendants in *Shaw*. *Croson* broke with the status quo, subjecting the assumptions of affirmative action to unprecedented judicial scrutiny. It further assisted the plaintiffs in *Shaw*, three of whom lived outside the challenged districts and who were not directly affected by North Carolina's alleged racial gerrymandering, by loosening the standing requirements for plaintiffs in equal protection cases, invalidating the Richmond set-aside program absent proof of any direct or cognizable injury to any of the plaintiffs.[24]

---

21. *Croson*, 488 U.S. at 493, O'Connor, J., opinion of the Court.

22. *Id.*

23. Aleinikoff and Issacharoff, *Race and Redistricting*, 600.

24. See Aleinikoff and Issacharoff, *Race and Redistricting*, 599. As it would turn out, these three plaintiffs, granted standing in *Shaw v. Reno*, would lose that status in *Shaw v. Hunt* (*Shaw II*), 64 U.S.L.W. 4437 (1996). *Shaw II* applied the rule from *United States v. Hays*, 115 S.Ct. 2431 (1995), decided in the period between *Shaw* and *Shaw II*. In *Hays*, the Court ruled that plaintiffs residing outside racially gerrymandered districts did

Despite this, the facts in *Croson* were not the facts in *Shaw* and applying *Croson* to the VRA would not be an easy task. Cases prior to *Shaw* had made clear that racial considerations pertaining to redistricting legislation were not *per se* unconstitutional.[25] The issue was just how far could such considerations be taken? At what point did race-conscious districting become unconstitutional?

The appellants (plaintiffs) in *Shaw* were aware of the distinctive nature of voting rights litigation and framed their pleadings accordingly. It was implicit in the appellants' argument that were considerations of race mixed with other considerations, such as the preservation of communities of interest, county boundary lines, district compactness, and other non-racial factors, their constitutional claim might well fail.[26] Recent cases had made clear that the EPC required legislation distinguishing between citizens on the basis of race to be narrowly tailored to the government interest alleged to be served by such distinctions.[27] But legislative reapportionment, Justice O'Connor acknowledged, was unlike other legislative action.

> [R]edistricting differs from other kinds of state decisionmaking in that the legislature always is *aware* of race when it draws district lines, just as it is aware of age, economic status, religious and political persuasion, and a variety of other demographic factors. That sort of race consciousness does not lead inevitably to impermissible race discrimination.[28]

If it did not, what type of race consciousness did? What was the constitutional cut off point?

O'Connor never answered this question. She did, however, find that the North Carolina 12th was unconstitutional on its face: its irregular

---

not suffer "special harms" and did not therefore have standing to challenge Louisiana's redistricting plan (115 S.Ct. at 2436).

25. See, for instance, *Whitcomb v. Chavis*, 403 U.S. 124 (1971); *White v. Regester*, 412 U.S. 755 (1973); *Mobile v. Bolden*, 446 U.S. 55 (1980); *Rogers v. Lodge*, 458 U.S. 613 (1982); and *United Jewish Organizations of Williamsburg, Inc. v. Carey*, 430 U.S. 144 (1977).

26. As O'Connor observed:

> What appellants object to is redistricting legislation that is so extremely irregular on its face that it rationally can be viewed only as an effort to segregate the races for purposes of voting, without regard for traditional districting principles and without sufficiently compelling justification (*Shaw*, 113 S.Ct. at 2824).

27. See, for instance, *Arlington Heights v. Metropolitan Housing Development Corp.*, 429 U.S. 252. (1977); *Wygant v. Jackson Board of Education*, 476 U.S. 267 (1986); and *Croson*.

28. *Shaw*, 113 S.Ct. at 2826, emphasis in original.

shape bore "an uncomfortable resemblance to political apartheid."[29] Prima facie, the district appeared to segregate voters on the basis of race. Whether the 12th CD violated the Fourteenth Amendment and whether North Carolina could meet the stringent test of strict scrutiny, should it have to, was left to a lower court to decide on remand.

In allowing a potential claim based on the contorted shape of the 12th CD, the Supreme Court appeared to offer up a new litmus test for vote discrimination. Pildes and Niemi have argued that at no point in the Court's history had it ever suggested that an electoral district could violate the Constitution because its shape was too bizarre. *Shaw*, in their words, created a "new, geography-based challenge [that] might be called a *district appearance claim*," one in which, "at some point, too much becomes too much."[30] Daniel Polsby and Robert Popper have similarly observed that *Shaw* placed courts in the difficult position of having to respond to the unseemly and intractable question, "[h]ow ugly is too ugly?"[31]

Whether bizarre geography was a necessary condition for a successful equal protection claim or whether it was just one indicia of many that might point to a potential claim was not resolved until the Court's ruling two years later in *Miller v. Johnson*. In *Miller*, Justice Kennedy clarified that the "logical implication" of the reasoning in *Shaw* was "that parties may rely on evidence other than bizarreness to establish race-based districting."[32] Did this clarification bring the post-*Shaw* voting rights jurisprudence into conflict with earlier voting rights law which appeared to accept, as constitutionally permissible, race-conscious districting engaged to comply with the VRA?

In *Shaw* O'Connor had neither rejected nor accepted the state's defense that it had a compelling interest in meeting the terms of the VRA, in particular, the preclearance requirement of section 5.[33] The repercussions of O'Connor's suggestion that complying with the VRA would not necessarily immunize jurisdictions from equal protection scrutiny were significant, particularly in light of the motives most states advance to defend districts drawn with the VRA and the enhancement of minority

29. *Id.*, 2827.

30. Pildes and Niemi, *Election-District Appearances*, 484, emphasis in original.

31. Daniel D. Polsby and Robert D. Popper, *Ugly: An Inquiry into the Problem of Racial Gerrymandering under the Voting Rights Act*, MICHIGAN L. REV. 92 (1993): 652, 652.

32. *Miller v. Johnson*, 115 S.Ct. 2475, 2486 (1995), opinion of the Court.

33. As I discuss in the postscript, O'Connor has now made clear, at least with respect to the "results" test of section 2, that compliance with this test is a compelling state interest. The significance of this concession is discussed in the postscript.

electoral strength in mind. Would this lean construction of the Fourteenth Amendment drive state redistrictors underground, force them to find new reasons for drafting VRA inspired districts?

The original districting plan submitted by North Carolina following the 1990 census was rejected by the Attorney General's office on grounds that the state could have created a second majority-minority district in the southcentral to southeastern area of the state. Alleging noncompliance with section 5, the Attorney General's office demanded that the North Carolina Legislature amend its original redistricting plan to enhance minority electoral strength. Rather than seek a declaratory judgment approving the plan from the D.C. District Court, the only other option available to it, the North Carolina Legislature chose instead to amend the plan, which would now include the 12th CD. Arguably the hardest question in *Shaw*, whether compliance with the Attorney General's demands was sufficient to meet the provisions of the Fourteenth Amendment, was left in abeyance. But why? Earlier litigation had suggested that such compliance was indeed sufficient to meet the conditions of equal protection. Or had it?

In a 1977 decision, *United Jewish Organizations of Williamsburg, Inc. v. Carey (UJO)*,[34] the Supreme Court seemed to construe the VRA differently than had the Court in *Shaw*. Perhaps "the most important voting rights case of this era,"[35] *UJO* presented the most significant challenge to the majority's interpretation in *Shaw* and would have to be confronted. The ensuing debate over the signification of the case marked the most poignant division between the majority and minority, and sparked a heated rhetorical flourish.

In *UJO*, a divided Court affirmed a New York Court of Appeals decision, the plurality accepting the lower court's reasoning:

> "so long as a districting, even though based on racial considerations, is in conformity with the unchallenged directive of and has the approval of the Attorney General of the United States under the Act, at least absent a clear showing that the resultant legislative reapportionment is unfairly prejudicial to white or nonwhite, that districting is not subject to challenge."[36]

In *Shaw*, compliance with the Attorney General's demands did not insulate a reapportionment plan from a constitutional challenge. Speculating on the potential defense North Carolina might advance on re-

---

34. 430 U.S. 144.

35. Aleinikoff and Issacharoff, *Race and Redistricting*, 593.

36. 430 U.S. at 155.

mand—that it had to comply with the *Beer* nonretrogression principle[37]—O'Connor clarified:

> [W]e do not read *Beer* or any of our other § 5 cases to give covered jurisdictions *carte blanche* to engage in racial gerrymandering in the name of nonretrogression. A reapportionment plan would not be narrowly tailored to the goal of avoiding retrogression if the state went beyond what was reasonably necessary to avoid retrogression.[38]

What was "reasonably necessary" in *Shaw* and what was "unfairly prejudicial" in *UJO* were not the same thing. The statement in *UJO* referred to an unfair dilution of votes. The statement in *Shaw* referred to an unacceptable configuring of an electoral district.

In *UJO*, New York had submitted a state redistricting plan to the U.S. Attorney General for preclearance in 1972. Similar to the facts in *Shaw*, the plan was rejected for failing to provide for adequate minority electoral strength. In 1974, New York submitted a second, revised plan. As a result of this plan, the plaintiffs, members of an Hasidic Jewish community, were split into two assembly and two senatorial districts. Previously they had been part of a single assembly and single senatorial district. They brought suit, alleging that New York's revised plan was unconstitutional on two grounds. First, by splitting the Hasidic community's votes "solely for the purpose of achieving a racial quota," the 1974 plan diluted the community's vote by halving its effectiveness contrary to the Fourteenth Amendment.[39] Second, by assigning the members of the Hasidic community to different electoral districts "solely on the basis of race," the revised plan diluted the community's vote contrary to the Fifteenth Amendment.[40]

The plurality rejected both of the plaintiffs' claims. The New York plan, it determined, had neither the purpose nor the effect of disfranchising the Hasidic community. New York had demonstrated that its redistricting plan had the intent and would likely have the effect of enhancing minority electoral strength, thus satisfying the threshold requirements of section 5. Writing for the plurality, Justice White observed that New

---

37. In *Beer v. United States*, 425 U.S. 130, 141 (1976), the Court required the denial of all proposed voting changes in covered jurisdictions if they led "to a retrogression in the position of racial minorities with respect to their effective exercise of the electoral franchise" (opinion of the Court).

38. 113 S.Ct. at 2831.

39. 430 U.S. at 152.

40. *Id.*, 153.

York had "deliberately revis[ed] its reapportionment plan along racial lines."[41] The state

> adopted the 1974 plan because it sought to comply with the Voting Rights Act. This has been its primary defense of the plan, which was sustained on *that* basis by the Court of Appeals.[42]

The plaintiffs' allegations in *UJO* were not without foundation. New York had divided the Hasidic community on the basis of race. But the plurality insisted that this was what the VRA required. The Act "'necessarily deals with race or color,'" as the Court of Appeals recognized. Hence "'corrective action under it must do the same.'"[43] Race-conscious legislation was permissible under the VRA because the VRA was a constitutionally permissible exception to the rule with respect to race-based legislative classifications. "Implicit in *Beer* and *City of Richmond v. United States*[44]," White declared,

> is the proposition that the Constitution does *not* prevent a State subject to the Voting Rights Act from *deliberately* creating or preserving black majorities in particular districts in order to ensure that its reapportionment plan complies with § 5.... Contrary to petitioners' first argument ["that racial criteria may never be used in redistricting"], neither the Fourteenth nor the Fifteenth Amendment mandates any *per se* rule against using racial factors in districting and apportionment. Nor is petitioners' second argument [that racial criteria "may be used, if at all, only as a specific remedy for past unconstitutional apportionments"] valid. The permissible use of racial criteria is not confined to eliminating the effects of past discriminatory districting or apportionment.[45]

The VRA was not limited to remedying past harms.[46] No proof of past discriminatory actions was necessary to invoke the requirements of section 5. In addition, VRA remedies could be forward looking as well as backward looking, and could extend beyond equal opportunity to provide for equal electoral results. "[A] reapportionment," White proclaimed, "cannot violate the Fourteenth and Fifteenth Amendment merely because a State uses specific numerical quotas in establishing a certain number of black majority districts."[47] Quotas were specifically contem-

---

41. *Id.*, 155.
42. *Id.*, 164–65, emphasis added.
43. *Id.*, 155.
44. 422 U.S. 358 (1975).
45. *UJO*, 430 U.S. at 161, emphasis added.
46. This was recently affirmed in *Voinovich v. Quilter*, 113 S.Ct. 1149 (1993).
47. 430 U.S. at 162.

plated by the effects test of section 5 and could be used as an antidote to underrepresentation.

The crux of the decision in *UJO* then was that there could be no discrimination against the Hasidim because it was part of a larger, white majority.[48] Statistics indicated that although the 1974 reapportionment would change the racial balance within the districts comprising the Hasidic community, across the county and across the state the proportional representation of whites would remain more or less the same. The Hasidim could not prevail because, as the plurality was quick to affirm, it "enjoyed no constitutional right in reapportionment to separate community recognition."[49]

> [A]s long as whites in Kings County, *as a group*, were provided with fair representation, we cannot conclude that there was a cognizable discrimination against whites or an abridgment of their right to vote on the grounds of race.[50]

Clearly, *UJO* presented difficulties for the majority in *Shaw*. Contrary to Justice O'Connor's earlier admonition, the plurality in *UJO* had suggested that legislation racially segregating voters in order to comply with the preclearance requirements of section 5 was not unconstitutional. This was not lost on the *Shaw* minority, who acrimoniously dismissed O'Connor's attempt to distinguish *UJO* on the basis that the plaintiffs there "did not allege that the [reapportionment] plan, on its face, was so highly irregular that it rationally could be understood only as an effort to segregate voters by race."[51]

At one level, O'Connor's interpretation was not without justification. Three justices in *UJO* did qualify that remedying minority electoral ineffectiveness was permissible only in cases in which "districting principles such as compactness and population equality" could be maintained and "residential patterns afford[ed] the opportunity of creating districts in which [racial minorities] will be in the majority."[52] District shape was apparently important to the plurality in *UJO*.

---

48. See Aleinikoff and Issacharoff:
    the baseline assumption [for the analysis in *UJO* is] that the Hasidic community of Williamsburg could take solace for its electoral exclusion from the fact that it was "virtually represented" by white legislators from other parts of Brooklyn or from other parts of the state (*Race and Redistricting*, 595–96).
49. 430 U.S. at 153.
50. *Id.*, 166, White, J., emphasis added.
51. *Shaw*, 113 S.Ct. at 2829, O'Connor, J.
52. *UJO*, 430 U.S. at 168.

The distinction between *UJO* as a vote dilution claim and *Shaw* as an "analytically distinct" electoral segregation claim, however, was less tenable in the face of the Hasidic plaintiffs' explicit allegation that New York had "violated the Fourteenth and Fifteenth Amendments by *deliberately revising its reapportionment plan along racial lines*,"[53] that "'there could be—and in fact was—*no reason other than race* to divide the community at this time.'"[54] Further exacerbating O'Connor's position in *Shaw* was her recognition that "districting principles such as compactness, contiguity, and respect for political subdivisions" were not "constitutionally required."[55] Conceding this, how could the majority in *Shaw* take the position it did, particularly in light of O'Connor's earlier admission that legislative reapportionment was different from, and perhaps more acceptable than, other legislative racial classifications? Was acknowledging this not tantamount to endorsing the plurality's position in *UJO* and the minority's position in *Shaw*?

Affirmative Action and Voting Rights: Individual v. Group Claims

There was, no doubt, a certain paradoxical quality to the *Shaw* majority's opinion. By accepting the argument advanced in *Allen* that the VRA proscribed vote dilution in addition to outright bars to the right to vote, the majority had entered the political thicket into which previous courts had entered without ever exiting with a coherent theory of representation. The impossibility of achieving a coherent theory of representation, the intractable tension between individual and group rights, and the fractious consequences of racial politics brought about by vote dilution jurisprudence, was reflected in O'Connor's opinion itself. On the one hand, O'Connor acknowledged that states could take race into consideration when redistricting, as long as they did not go "beyond what was reasonably necessary to avoid retrogression." On the other hand, she proclaimed that the pathology associated with segregating voters into racially distinct districts could not be tolerated. In language that echoed, almost verbatim, her austere remarks in *Croson*, O'Connor insisted:

> Racial gerrymandering, even for remedial purposes, may balkanize us into competing racial factions; it threatens to carry us further from the goal of a political system in which race no longer matters—a goal that

---

53. *Id.*, 155, emphasis added.
54. *Id.*, 154, n. 14, citing the Brief for Petitioners, emphasis in original.
55. *Shaw*, 113 S.Ct. at 2827.

the Fourteenth and Fifteenth Amendments embody, and to which the Nation continues to aspire.[56]

Reapportioning on the basis of race

reinforces the perception that members of the same racial group—regardless of their age, education, economic status, or the community in which they live—think alike, share the same political interests, and will prefer the same candidates at the polls.[57]

Yet this commonality of interests, similar way of thinking, and preference for the same candidates, is apparently what the VRA contemplates. O'Connor was probably right. The Fourteenth and Fifteenth Amendments may embody a political system in which race no longer matters. But the VRA, the ostensible codification of the Fifteenth Amendment, apparently embodies no such goal. Under the terms of the VRA, race very much matters. In fact, it may be the only thing that matters. This was the substance of the *Shaw* dissenting opinions.

What difference in principle did it make whether electoral reapportionment resulted in districts that were compact or districts that snaked through a variety of counties when the determinative condition in all cases was race? The only difference between the North Carolina districts and more compact districts in other states was the accidental fact that blacks happened to be more scattered in North Carolina. The majority's decision, in the words of Justice White's dissent, would simply result in the hinderance of state efforts at redistricting "in areas where the minority population is geographically dispersed."[58] Focusing on the different shapes of districts was to focus on "surface differences."[59] Why? Because it was the effect of a reapportionment that mattered, not its appearance.

By focusing on looks rather than impact, the majority "immediately casts attention in the wrong direction—toward superficialities of shape and size, rather than toward the political realities of district composition."[60]

The type of claim purported to be "analytically distinct" in *Shaw* was, in White's opinion, indistinguishable from the claim in *UJO*.

Given two districts drawn on similar, race-based grounds, the one does not become more injurious than the other simply by virtue of being snake-like, at least so far as the Constitution is concerned and absent any evi-

---

56. *Id.*, 2832.

57. *Id.*, 2827.

58. *Id.*, 2841, White, J., dissenting.

59. *Id.*, 2834.

60. *Id.*, 2841, paraphrasing from Robert G. Dixon, Jr.'s Democratic Representation: Reapportionment in Law and Politics (Oxford University Press, 1968), 459.

dence of differential racial impact. The majority's contrary view is perplexing in light of its concession that "compactness or attractiveness has never been held to constitute an independent federal constitutional requirement for state legislative districts."[61]

According to the majority, legislative distinctions based on race were invidious and attracted strict scrutiny. It made no difference whether the distinctions advantaged blacks or whites.[62] Group characteristics were irrelevant, except in cases where racial bloc voting had been proved, a question not at issue in *Shaw*.[63]

For the minority, on the other hand, group characteristics—in particular the impact of legislative decisions on groups—were determinative in every case involving the VRA. The serious question for the minority was who was being advantaged by the reapportionment? Was there a differential racial impact such that minority voting strength would be diluted?[64]

For Justice White, the North Carolina 1st and 12th CDs could not discriminate against whites because whites, as a group, still constituted a voting majority in 10 of the state's 12 congressional districts. There could be no "discriminatory effects," no denial of "equal access to the political process" for whites because Districts 1 and 12 could not affect their "voting strength" as a group.[65] White went so far as to suggest that "State efforts to remedy minority vote dilution are wholly unlike what typically has been labeled 'affirmative action' [because to] the extent that no other racial group is injured, remedying a Voting Rights Act violation does not involve preferential treatment." Rather, it represents "an at-

---

61. *Shaw*, 113 S.Ct. at 2841, paraphrasing from *Gaffney v. Cummings*, 412 U.S. 735, 752 (1973).

62. "Justice Stevens," O'Connor remarked, "argues that racial gerrymandering poses no constitutional difficulties when district lines are drawn to favor the minority, rather than the majority.... We have made clear, however, that equal protection analysis 'is not dependent on the race of those burdened or benefited by a particular classification'" (113 S.Ct. at 2829, quoting *Croson*, 488 U.S. at 494).

63. See *Shaw*, 113 S.Ct. at 2832.

64. Quoting from his plurality opinion in *Davis v. Bandemer*, 478 U.S. 109, 132 (1986), Justice White contended:

> Because districting inevitably is the expression of interest group politics, and because "the power to influence the political process is not limited to winning elections" ... the question in gerrymandering cases is "whether a particular group has been unconstitutionally denied its chance to effectively influence the political process...Thus, "an equal protection violation may be found only where the electoral system *substantially disadvantages certain voters in their opportunity to influence the political process effectively. (Shaw*, 113 S.Ct. at 2836, dissenting, emphasis added in *Shaw*).

65. 113 S.Ct. at 2837.

tempt to *equalize* treatment, and to provide minority voters with an effective voice in the political process."[66] A number of voting rights commentators have argued a similar line. Bernard Grofman, for instance, has written:

> [I]f "affirmative action" means, as it often has come to mean, not just *equal* treatment, but that the claims of minorities are given *more* weight than those of identically situated whites, then it is clearly inaccurate to characterize voting rights remedies as affirmative action.[67]

Voting rights remedies are not affirmative action because they involve the raising of minority political effectiveness to a level closer, although never equal, to the political majority. How can such legislative action constitute preferential treatment when it never results in any disadvantage to the majority?

The response here is plain enough. If electoral reapportionment to enhance minority voting strength is not preferential treatment, what is? If we assume that minorities who can never attain the power of the majority can never, by virtue of that fact, be preferentially treated, no policy protecting minorities could ever constitute affirmative action because the statistical majority will always remain the statistical majority: it will always retain its power and, by definition, could therefore never be "injured." The only way the minority could ever be preferentially treated, on White's and Grofman's reading, is if it became the majority. In which case, there would be no need for affirmative action.

The second response to White and Grofman—and this is the more important point—relates to the issue of individual versus group claims. What White and Grofman focus on is the effect on the group, not the individual. Perhaps more accurately, the individual is considered, but only insofar as he or she is part of an identifiable group. Grofman laments this point, but qualifies that it is necessary given the sad facts of American life:

> I wish to distinguish the "ideal" Voting Rights Act from the Act that is "required" given a world in which racial divisions are all too real. The former would presumably be color-blind; the latter cannot be.[68]

Reapportionment politics is of necessity group politics. To ignore this fact, White reasoned, is not only contrary to the provisions of the VRA and the EPC but is both unrealistic and hypocritical. Writing in dissent, Justice Stevens concurred:

---

66. *Id.*, 2842–43, emphasis in original.

67. Bernard Grofman, *Would Vince Lombardi Have Been Right?*, 1247, emphasis in original.

68. *Id.*, 1269.

> If it is permissible to draw boundaries to provide adequate representation
> for rural voters, for union members, for Hasidic Jews, for Polish Amer-
> icans, or for Republicans, it necessarily follows that it is permissible to
> do the same thing for members of the very minority group whose histo-
> ry in the United States gave birth to the Equal Protection Clause.[69]

Here then we have the nub of the dispute in *Shaw*—in fact for virtually all voting rights disputes today. For the majority, the Constitution is
color-blind. Legislative distinctions that differentiate between individuals
on the basis of race are invidious. In O'Connor's words, racial classifications "threaten to stigmatize individuals by reason of their membership
in a racial group." They "incite racial hostility."[70] In the case of racial
reapportionment, they threaten "to undermine our system of representative democracy by signaling to elected officials that they represent a particular racial group rather than their constituency as a whole."[71]

But is race-conscious decisionmaking not the engine of the VRA? In
UJO, the plurality highlighted that the House and Senate reports recom-
mending extension of the VRA in 1975 emphasized that "the Attorney
General's role in screening redistricting plans [is] to protect opportunities
for nonwhites to be elected to public office."[72] The Department of Justice
operates on these assumptions. In North Carolina, Grofman notes,
"once a second black majority district had been drawn by the state, the
DOJ had little choice but to accept it, since the *only* criteria used by the
DOJ in its preclearance review is whether or not the plan [at issue] has
either the effect or purpose of diluting minority voting strength."[73] Members of the Supreme Court and voting rights scholars have questioned
the DOJ's interpretation of the VRA and have disputed the constitutionality of its requirement that majority-minority districts be maximized
under section 5. In *Miller v. Johnson*, Justice Kennedy animadverted that

> In utilizing § 5 to require States to create majority-minority districts
> wherever possible, the Department of Justice expanded its authority
> under the statute beyond what Congress intended and we have upheld.
> .... [T]he Justice Department's implicit command that States engage
> in presumptively unconstitutional race-based districting brings the Vot-
> ing Rights Act, once upheld as a proper exercise of Congress' authority

---

69. 113 S.Ct. at 2844–45.
70. *Id.*, 2824.
71. *Id.*, 2828.
72. 430 U.S. at 158–59.
73. *Would Vince Lombardi Have Been Right?*, 1267, emphasis in original.

under § 2 of the Fifteenth Amendment...into tension with the Fourteenth Amendment.[74]

Kennedy is not alone in his apprehension concerning the compatibility of the VRA with the principles of equal protection. In *Bush v. Vera* (1996), Justice O'Connor noted the apparent tension between the VRA, requiring that "the States and the courts...take action to remedy the reality of racial inequality in our political system, sometimes necessitating race-based action," and "the Fourteenth Amendment," which "requires us to look with suspicion on the excessive use of racial considerations by the government."[75]

The serious question is whether race-based action is necessary only some of the time under the VRA and not all of the time.[76] Does redistricting engaged under the auspices of the act not have to be crafted with a view to enhancing or diminishing the racial content of specific districts? Is there any instance in which remedial action undertaken to satisfy either section 2 or section 5 would not raise a Fourteenth Amendment issue? In *Miller v. Johnson*, the threshold for equal protection violations, derived from *Shaw*, was whether "race was the *predominant* factor motivating the legislature's decision to place a significant number of voters within or without a particular district."[77] This standard will likely be met in most if not every case involving the VRA.[78] Perhaps an indication of this is voting rights cases that have been decided since

---

74. 115 S.Ct. 2475, 2493 (1995).

75. 64 LW 4452, 4465, O'Connor, J., concurring.

76. See Pildes and Niemi, *Election-District Appearances*, 582, n.270: "Because the VRA prohibits electoral arrangements that discriminate in intent as well as result, policy-makers must be aware of—rather than indifferent to—the racial distribution of political power that different electoral structures will produce."

77. 115 S.Ct at 2488, Kennedy, J., opinion of the Court, emphasis added.

78. See Thomas, J., concurring, in *Bush v. Vera*, 64 U.S.L.W. 4452, 4466 (1996):
[T]he intentional creation of a majority-minority district certainly means more than mere awareness that application of traditional, race-neutral districting principles will result in the creation of a district in which a majority of the district's residents are members of a particular minority group....In my view, it means that the legislature affirmatively undertakes to create a majority-minority district that would not have existed but for the express use of racial classifications—in other words, that a majority-minority district is created "because of," and not merely "in spite of," racial demographics....When that occurs, traditional race-neutral districting principles are necessarily subordinated (and race necessarily predominates), and the legislature has classified persons on the basis of race. The resulting redistricting must be viewed as a racial gerrymander.

1993. Of the three cases brought to the Supreme Court and the one case brought before a federal court invoking the *Shaw* and *Miller* tests— cases involving Louisiana,[79] Georgia,[80] North Carolina,[81] and Texas[82]— not one of the states has succeeded in meeting the equal protection requirements. In none of the cases have the courts even had to proceed so far as to address the question left unanswered by *Shaw*: whether compliance with the VRA, standing on its own and independently of any concern with remedying past discrimination, constitutes a compelling state interest.[83] Although this has been assumed, *arguendo*, for the purposes of assessing whether any of the plans at issue were narrowly tailored, none of the districting plans survived the narrow tailoring requirement of the strict scrutiny test, the precondition, in these cases, to proceeding to answer whether compliance with the VRA constitutes a compelling state interest.

In the 1990s, the important question then is whether every VRA inspired redistricting plan is now susceptible to a Fourteenth Amendment challenge. Are the VRA and the EPC, in their present incarnations, compatible? Is the VRA constitutional?

Shaw and the Voting Rights Conundrum

The majority in *Shaw* began its reasoning by accepting the principle from *Allen* "that '[t]he right to vote can be affected by a *dilution* of voting power as well as by an absolute prohibition on casting a ballot.'"[84] Once this principle was accepted, the Court had entered the Pandora's box of racial group politics. Or had it?

In his contribution to this volume, Timothy O'Rourke maintains that the dissenters in *Shaw* got things wrong in suggesting that representation was a group-based right. In *Shaw*, as in *Baker v. Carr*, the issues had centered on standing and justiciability.[85] On the dissents' reading, the plaintiffs in *Shaw* as a group had suffered no injury because as a group they had not been treated unfairly in the electoral process. Consequently,

---

79. *Hays v. Louisiana*, 839 F.Supp. 1188 (WD La.1993), vacated and remanded on different grounds, 115 S.Ct. 2431 (1995).

80. *Miller v. Johnson*, 115 S.Ct. 2475 (1995).

81. *Shaw v. Hunt (Shaw II)*, 64 U.S.L.W. 4437 (1996).

82. *Bush v. Vera*, 64 U.S.L.W. 4452 (1996).

83. As I have indicated, Justice O'Connor does address this issue in her concurring opinion in *Bush v. Vera*, discussed in the postscript.

84. *Shaw*, 113 S.Ct. at 2823, O'Connor, J., emphasis in original.

85. See Timothy G. O'Rourke, "The Shape of Things to Come," 52.

the plaintiffs had failed to meet the threshold for standing. According to O'Rourke, the *Shaw* minority erred in its assumption that the right to representation under the VRA was a group-based right with a logical end-point of proportional representation.

> There is no right to proportional representation because the protection against vote dilution is an individual right with a group dimension, but not a group right. An election system cannot discriminate against individuals because of their membership in a protected group, but the group has no presumptive claim on some share of legislative seats.[86]

At least not until racial bloc voting is established. If, following *Thornburg v. Gingles* (1986), the only thing that counts in cases involving racial bloc voting is "the correlation between race of voter and the selection of certain candidates,"[87] not the reasons for those selections, as Justice Brennan affirmed, then the necessary consequence, as Justice O'Connor pointed out in *Gingles* and as Justice Thomas pointed out in *Holder*, is a right to usual, roughly proportional representation.[88] It would seem that the idea that there is no presumptive claim on a specific share of legislative seats is undermined once the Court allows discriminatory results, as established in *Gingles*, to guide its analysis of racially polarized voting. In other words, in cases involving potential claims for racial bloc voting or actual proof of racial bloc voting, even if one accepts *Shaw*'s requirements of contiguity and compactness in legislative redistricting, the consequences of the Court's interpretation of section 2—and now its analysis under section 5, which is guided by potential claims under section 2[89] and, by implication, *Gingles*—will be proportional representation.

The attempt to avoid this eventuality by loosening the *Gingles* preconditions in favor of a more flexible "totality of circumstances" approach, which the Court attempted in *Johnson v. De Grandy* (1994),[90] will likely have little effect on mitigating the inclination of judges and federal ad-

---

86. *Id.*, 54.

87. *Thornburg v. Gingles*, 478 U.S. 30, 63, Brennan, J., opinion of the Court.

88. See *id.*, 2787, O'Connor, J., concurring; and *Holder*, 114 S.Ct. at 2597 and 2616, Thomas, J., concurring.

89. See C.F.R. § 51.55(b)(2) (1994), originally adopted by the Department of Justice in 1987, which states must now comply with:

> In those instances in which the Attorney General concludes that, as proposed, the submitted change [in electoral practices or procedures] is free of discriminatory purpose and retrogressive effect, but also concludes that a bar to implementation of the change is necessary to prevent a clear violation of amended Section 2, the Attorney General will withhold Section 5 preclearance.

90. 114 S.Ct. 2647.

ministrators in demanding proportional representation as a remedy to voting rights violations. As Justice Thomas pointed out in *Holder*:

> [In *De Grandy*,] the Court assures us that proportionality does not provide the principle for deciding vote dilution claims. . . . Rather, the result in each case must depend on a searching inquiry into the ever-nebulously-defined "totality of circumstances". . . .
>
> But after the *Gingles* preconditions have been established . . . and after *White* factors such as a history of discrimination have been found . . . where does the Court turn for a deciding principle to give some meaning to these multifarious facts, which taken individually would each appear to count in favor of a finding of vote dilution? Quite simply, the Court turns to proportionality. . . . [91]

It is difficult to see how such an outcome could be avoided given, on the one hand, the reduction of the evidentiary burden on plaintiffs in section 2 cases from a test of intent to a test of results, and, on the other hand, the complexity of the fact-finding process involved in any vote dilution action (whether a results or an intent test is used).

Shaw, although curbing the cartographical excesses produced by the demands for equipopulous congressional districts, the maximization of majority-minority districts, and the availability of sophisticated computer technology in the 1990s,[92] nonetheless left the door open for further racial redistricting. Subsequent opinions denying the group-based nature of vote dilution claims should therefore be approached with caution. In *Shaw v. Hunt* (1996), for instance, Justice Rehnquist affirmed that plaintiffs may allege section 2 violations in single-member districts "if the manipulation of districting lines fragments politically cohesive minority voters among several districts or packs them into one district or a small number of districts, and thereby dilutes the voting strength of members of the minority population."[93] The test to be used in such cases remains the test set out in *Gingles*, as revisited by *De Grandy*.[94] Rehn-

---

91. 114 S.Ct. 2581, 2616 (1994), Thomas, J., concurring.
92. See O'Rourke, "The Shape of Things to Come," 66:
> The contested districts [challenged in post-Shaw jurisprudence in Georgia, Louisiana, North Carolina, and Texas] reflect the confluence of three forces. First is the constitutional mandate to create congressional districts that are, as nearly as practicable, equal in population. . . . Second is the prevailing view . . . that the Voting Rights Act requires the creation of majority-minority districts. Third is the impact of a new redistricting technology that has revolutionized the task of political cartography.
93. *Shaw v. Hunt*, 64 U.S.L.W. at 4442, opinion of the Court.
94. *Id.*

quist qualified that the creation of majority-minority districts must remedy a specific injury and applies only to individuals, not groups:

> To accept that the [majority-minority] district [provided as a remedy to a voting rights violation] may be placed anywhere implies that the claim, and hence the coordinate right to an undiluted vote (to cast a ballot equal among voters), belongs to the minority as a group and not to its individual members. It does not.[95]

But it is difficult to see how compact, cohesive districts change the nature of a section 2 vote dilution claim. Such claims adhere to individuals not as individuals but as members of specific, legally identifiable groups. The requirement of geographic compactness would not appear to change the nature of the *claim* so much as the nature of the *remedy*; the remedy is restricted to minorities who are geographically compact, as Justice White pointed out in *Shaw*. Again, despite intensifying the scrutiny applicable to race-conscious districting, a laudable enterprise, *Shaw*, like pre-*Shaw* voting rights jurisprudence and like *Gingles*, will have the effect of rewarding, not discouraging, residential segregation.

To summarize, even if *Shaw* and its legacy make vote dilution claims more difficult, restricting them to minorities consolidated within specific geographic regions, it does not appear to overcome the race essentialism that is at the heart of vote dilution jurisprudence. In *Bush v. Vera*, Justices Kennedy, Thomas, and Scalia expressed concern about this. All three departed from Justice O'Connor's plurality opinion that strict scrutiny does not "apply to all cases of intentional creation of majority-minority districts."[96] "In my view," Kennedy responded, "we would no doubt apply strict scrutiny if a State decreed that certain districts had to be at least 50 percent white, and our analysis should be no different if the State so favors minority races."[97] Thomas, joined by Scalia, wrote that in *Adarand Constructors, Inc. v. Pena* (1995),[98] "we vigorously asserted that all governmental racial classifications must be strictly scrutinized." Indeed, "[s]trict scrutiny applies to all governmental classifications based on race, and we have expressly held that there is no exception for race-based redistricting."[99] According to Justice O'Connor, however, this is not the case.[100] And the four dissenting justices in *Shaw* and subsequent voting rights cases would likely embrace her assessment.

---

95. *Id.*, 4443.
96. *Bush*, 64 U.S.L.W. at 4454, O'Connor, J., plurality opinion.
97. *Id.*, 4465, concurring.
98. 115 S.Ct. 2097.
99. *Bush*, 4466, concurring.
100. See *Bush v. Vera*, 64 U.S.L.W. at 4463, O'Connor, J., concurring.

Strict scrutiny, in a strict sense, cannot be applied to vote dilution cases because the approach adopted in *Gingles*, effectively prohibiting as a precondition to a vote dilution claim inquiries into the reasons why voters behave the way they do, requires only the establishment of correlations between voter preferences and candidates chosen, not the causes of those preferences or choices. *Gingles*, in other words, does not allow judges, or redistrictors faced with potential vote dilution claims, to inquire into whether intentional discrimination was the reason for racial bloc voting, what would likely become the litmus test in cases subject to equal protection review.[101] If the "narrow tailoring" and "compelling state interest" components of the strict scrutiny test necessitate a more searching inquiry for why voters voted the way they did or why states have engaged in racial redistricting than the mere recitation of the existence of racially polarized voting, then either *Gingles* inoculates against the application of strict scrutiny to vote dilution cases, making an exception for racial redistricting in such cases, or *Gingles* itself represents an unconstitutional exception to the Court's equal protection jurisprudence. Perhaps it was the realization of this latter possibility that caused the split among the majority justices in *Bush*. Did the plurality and concurring contingents in *Bush* recognize that the application of strict scrutiny to all cases involving the creation of majority-minority districts would effectively spell the end to vote dilution jurisprudence as we know it, requiring the abandonment of the *Gingles* results test and the application of an intent test that would produce little, if any, fruit for minority plaintiffs in the new South? That would mean the end of the VRA in other regions of the country with even less history of racial disfranchisement?

If the VRA, following *Gingles* and *Shaw*, continues to promote a right to proportional representation in cases where racial bloc voting exists or is potential, how is this to be squared with the Court's individualist equal protection jurisprudence, which requires proof of prior intentional discrimination as the precondition for race-conscious remedies? How is it, in fact, to be reconciled with the VRA's section 2 proviso that nothing in the section grants a right to proportional representation? The proviso, included in 1982, was an indication of just how far the meaning of discrimination under the VRA had been transformed by that time, when the new "results" test was incorporated into section 2. The section 2 results test effectively displaced the concern under the act for racial discrimination with a concern for racial disadvantage and the promotion of minority officeholding. As James Blumstein has underlined, a theoretical shift

---

101. See *City of Richmond v. Croson*, where the Court recognized the authority of the City of Richmond to remedy private discrimination "*if* it identifies that discrimination with the particularity required by the Fourteenth Amendment" (488 U.S. at 492, emphasis added).

had occurred with the 1982 amendments to section 2, even if the subtlety and importance of these changes, often not identified in the political arena, was lost on many members of Congress.[102] With these changes, the VRA had become an unequivocal tool of affirmative action, nationwide in scope[103] and effectively shifting the focus of concern from electoral discrimination to an evolving principle of distributive justice centering on an amorphous concept of electoral "fairness."

Although the right to numerically equal representation that designated minorities enjoy under the VRA may apply more conditionally and perhaps less surreptitiously after *Shaw*, the requirement that majority-minority districts be more cohesive and geographically compact has done little to change the nature of this right.[104] Despite *Shaw*, we are still left with the seminal question posed after *Allen v. State Board of Elections* in 1969, a question that became increasingly acute after 1982 and, again, after *Gingles* in 1986: has the VRA altered the nature of American representative democracy? If so, has that alteration been salutary?

Ultimately, what exactly is at issue under the VRA? Is it the protection of voting rights? Or is it the protection of a specific policy of affirmative representation maintained under the pretext of protecting minority electoral opportunity, a policy that stands to challenge the very bedrock principles of American liberal democracy?

---

102. See James F. Blumstein, *Defining and Proving Race Discrimination*, 647, 689–701, 707–14. See, also, *id.*, 635:

> Because only purposefully discriminatory conduct can violate the principle of nondiscrimination, disproportional racial impact by itself merely highlights the existence of racial disadvantage. If society considers such disadvantage undesirable because of independent principles of distributive justice, it can use the evidence of disproportional impact as a basis for some form of relief. Such relief furthers the independent, affirmative value of improving the political influence of blacks and necessarily encompasses some notion of race-based entitlements to political influence or representation; such relief does not, however, rest on the nondiscrimination norm embodied in the fourteenth and fifteenth amendments.
>
> Despite this clear conceptual distinction, prohibiting discrimination and overcoming disadvantage are often lumped together in debates over civil rights legislation and enforcement policies.

103. See Abigail M. Thernstrom, WHOSE VOTES COUNT? AFFIRMATIVE ACTION AND MINORITY VOTING RIGHTS (Harvard University Press, 1987), 81–82.

104. See Justice Thomas' remark in *Holder*, decided the year after *Shaw*:

> [T]he framework established by this Court for evaluating vote dilution claims in *Gingles* was at its inception frankly, and in my view correctly, labeled as setting a rule of roughly proportional representation.... Nothing has happened in the intervening years to change the basic import of the *Gingles* test (114 S.Ct. at 2616, concurring).

These questions and the implications of the VRA for representative government in the United States, and American politics generally, are examined in the remaining sections of this chapter.

Constitutional Forms and the Problem of Representation

Even if the VRA does promote proportional representation in some form, why is this necessarily undesirable? Does the VRA seriously undermine American representative democracy in any substantive sense? Does it genuinely threaten political principles or political legitimacy, subvert the integrity of the public understanding respecting liberal democratic institutions? On the other hand, as a tool of affirmative action, might it not promote more responsible government, provide a greater recognition of the needs and interests of groups that have for too long been left out of the mainstream of the American political process?

When we consider the effects of the VRA on state and federal legislative elections, as well as judicial elections, also now governed by sections 2 and 5 of the VRA,[105] a threshold question must be: what is the purpose of representative government and why are "bizarre" districts, such as CD 12 in *Shaw*, so offensive to our public or political understanding? Is there an unnecessary or irrational attachment to geographic or territorial representation that precludes Americans from considering more effective, more equitable systems of representation?

Pildes and Niemi suggest that the move toward proportional minority representation under the VRA may not necessarily be a bad thing. *Shaw*, which they describe as functioning, in some respects, "as the *Baker v. Carr* of the Voting Rights era,"[106] not only raised the specter of the incompatibility of the VRA with equal protection jurisprudence but the incongruence of vote dilution jurisprudence with the new claim developed in *Shaw*. "Critically," the authors write, "we might say *Shaw* elevates trivial concerns for 'pretty' districts over substantive values of effective minority representation."[107] If there are no such things as "naturally shaped" districts, why should constitutional impediments be erected "at the extremes of the districting process,"[108] particularly at the very mo-

---

105. See *Clark v. Roemer*, 111 S.Ct. 2096 (1991); *Chisom v. Roemer*, 111 S.Ct. 2354 (1991); and *Houston Lawyers' Ass'n v. Attorney Gen.*, 111 S.Ct. 2376 (1991).

106. *Expressive Harms, "Bizarre Districts," and Voting Rights: Evaluating Election-District Appearances After* Shaw v. Reno, MICHIGAN L. REV. 92 (1993): 483, 586.

107. *Id.*, 501.

108. *Id.*

ment minorities appear to be gaining a foothold in the legislative door? Providing minority groups a more proportionate share of electoral offices may be both equitable and prudent, putting minorities on a more auspicious footing with the majority while enhancing the legitimacy of political representation. "If urban residents or rural residents can be assumed to have cohesive political interests, perhaps racial groups can as well—particularly when this cohesiveness is not assumed, but demonstrated in fact [by the *Gingles* criteria]."[109] Aleinikoff and Issacharoff, in a similar vein, offer diversity as a possible compelling state interest justifying oddly shaped districts drafted to enhance minority representation:

> A more diverse legislature or congressional delegation would better represent the various interests of the state, as well as improve deliberations in the legislature, by adding to the debate a point of view that is frequently ignored by majority legislators.[110]

> A more defensible version [of the diversity justification] would focus on *legitimacy* rather than *voice*: a legislature without minority representation is less likely to be perceived as legitimate by the polity in general, or by the minority groups over whom it exercises power.[111]

These comments address the purposes of representation. What are the functions of representative government and what obligations do representatives have to their constituents? The VRA, and the exposition of its principal provisions in cases such as *Gingles* and *Shaw*, invite speculation on what forms of representation are best suited to American politics.

Two alternatives dominant in voting rights scholarship, proportional and semi-proportional systems of representation, have been proposed as an antidote to territorial, winner-take-all districting systems. Advocates of these alternatives share a desire to accommodate more political interests, specifically minority political interests, within the electoral process. In winner-take-all systems, votes are wasted. Most importantly, minority votes get submerged beneath the preferences of the majority. The concern with wasted minority votes is not only at the heart of proposals for proportional representation but vote dilution jurisprudence, where courts focus on the fair or equitable distribution of political power among groups.

According to one proponent of proportional representation, Andrea Bierstein, "The fundamental issue underlying voting rights cases is: How

---

109. *Id.*, 577.
110. Aleinikoff and Issacharoff, *Race and Redistricting*, 647.
111. *Id.*, 649.

should representation be allocated?"[112] Bierstein suggests that if we accept this as the fundamental question at the center of voting rights disputes, an initial set of questions that might be asked concerns electoral results: what results from elections would be best, how should they be reached, and does the Fifteenth Amendment or the VRA have anything to say about these results? A second, more fundamental set of questions would ask whether we should even occupy ourselves with results: "[S]hould courts, legislatures, the Justice Department, or society as a whole...try to control the outcome [of elections]?"[113]

For Bierstein, the "districting conundrum" concerns how much representation a group ought to receive, a substantive question that assesses the fairness of a districting proposal by the *results* it produces. An alternative approach to voting rights, which avoids the districting conundrum, a procedurally-oriented approach, would assess the fairness of a districting proposal by its rules of *process*. According to Bierstein, the Supreme Court first engaged in the results-oriented approach to voting rights jurisprudence in *Allen v. State Board of Elections*. It continued addressing the districting conundrum, more or less uninterrupted, until *Shaw*. *Shaw*, *De Grandy*, and *Holder* represented an increasing discomfort with a results-oriented approach to voting rights and a reticence about addressing questions of what constitutes fair electoral outcomes. These three cases marked the beginning of a reassessment of the VRA and whether federal courts should be addressing the districting conundrum at all, a position taken most emphatically by Justice Thomas in *Holder* who suggested that the Court abandon vote dilution jurisprudence altogether.[114]

Bierstein is correct that in *Shaw* and post-*Shaw* jurisprudence the purposes of the VRA were being reassessed. They were being reassessed because, following *Shaw*, the nature of the issues had been transformed. As Pildes and Niemi observe, the theory of voting rights endorsed by the novel "district appearance claim" developed in *Shaw*

> centers on the perceived legitimacy of structures of political representation, rather than on the distribution of actual political power between racial or political groups. Vote-dilution and-district-appearance claims share no common conceptual elements. They recognize distinct kinds of

---

112. *Millennium Approaches: The Future of the Voting Rights Act After Shaw, De Grandy, and Holder*, HASTINGS L. J. 46 (1995): 1457, 1462.

113. *Id.*, 1463.

114. *Id.*, 1466–69. See also, *Holder v. Hall*, 114 S.Ct. 2581, 2591 (1994), Thomas, J., concurring.

injuries, implicate different constitutional values, and reflect differing conceptions of the relationship between law and politics.[115]

The focus on structures or process rather than on the results of districting or the distribution of political power that occurred in *Shaw* was an indication of the Court's concern that the desire to achieve certain electoral results had corrupted the process or structure of political representation itself. In other words, the very procedures that had developed to give minorities more political power through guaranteed electoral outcomes were themselves creating political or structural inequalities. The districting process, and the form of representation it produced, was being distorted. This often happens when legal structures are modified to provide for specific substantive outcomes in addition to, or instead of, procedural fairness. Thomas Sowell has observed that equality of process is distinct from equality of results because equality of process is within our capabilities whereas equality of results requires vastly more intellectual and moral capacity than we have.[116] Although it is possible to reduce or eliminate certain instances of inequality, the processes involved in achieving equality of results may create other inequalities, in particular, inequalities of political power.[117]

Was this the concern of the majority in *Shaw* and post-*Shaw* jurisprudence? In the name of electoral equality were greater political inequalities being created, were the structures of government being transformed, democracy itself being undermined? In *Holder*, Justice Thomas was acerbic in reminding his colleagues:

> [U]nder our constitutional system, this Court is not a centralized politburo appointed for life to dictate to the provinces the "correct" theories of democratic representation, the "best" electoral systems for securing truly "representative" government, the "fairest" proportions of minority political influence, or, as respondents would have us hold today, the "proper" sizes for local governing bodies.[118]

The guiding principle of voting rights jurisprudence had been proportional or close to proportional representation, "a political choice, not a

115. *Election-District Appearances*, 493.

116. Thomas Sowell, A Conflict of Visions: Ideological Origins of Political Struggles (William Morrow, 1987), 122.

117. *Id.*, 128. See, also, Anthony A. Peacock, *Strange Brew: Tocqueville, Rights, and the Technology of Equality*, in Rethinking the Constitution: Perpsectives on Canadian Constitutional Reform, Interpretation, and Theory, ed. Anthony A. Peacock (Oxford University Press, 1996), 122, 151.

118. 114 S.Ct. at 2602, concurring opinion.

result required by any principle of law;"[119] neither the section 5 retrogression test nor section 2, which specifically provided that there was no right to proportional representation, required this. But, in Thomas' opinion, proportional representation had become the mantra of voting rights administration and adjudication.

Yet this was not the worst aspect of vote dilution jurisprudence on Thomas' reading. The worst aspect of vote dilution jurisprudence was the underlying assumption that the group asserting a vote dilution claim was not merely a racial or ethnic group but a group that had distinct political interests as well; that race defined political interest. This is what the *Gingles* test, content with the correlation between racial group identity and candidate preference, not requiring a search for the causes of those preferences, implied. *Gingles* did state that whether a racial group was politically cohesive could not be assumed and had to be proved, but the standards employed in "determining political cohesion have proved so insubstantial that this 'precondition' does not present much of a barrier to the assertion of vote dilution claims on behalf of any racial group."[120] The demand for expanding substantive equality, understood as a numerical parity between racial group size and the potential to hold legislative office, had translated, in Thomas' opinion, into an immoderate politics of racial group entitlement that "segregat[ed] the races into political homelands"[121] and that undermined the institutional structure of American government.[122]

This should have been expected. Judicial politics is an immoderate form of politics: it is developed around incomplete facts, adversarial advantage, judicial incapacity, and formal legal rules that impede political negotiation, all of which make the judicial forum a bad place for developing broad issues of policy.[123] With its focus on winning and losing, and the simplification of complex political questions into analytically neat legal categories, the judicial process does not lend itself easily to compromise or flexibility. This applies to *Shaw* itself, despite the good intentions of the Court. *Shaw* was intended to pierce the veil of an overly simplistic

---

119. *Id.*, 2597.

120. *Id.*

121. *Id.*, 2598.

122. See *id.*, esp. 2602.

123. See Donald L. Horowitz, THE COURTS AND SOCIAL POLICY (Brookings, 1977), 17–62; Eleanor P. Wolf, TRIAL AND ERROR: THE DETROIT SCHOOL SEGREGATION CASE (Wayne State, 1981), 251–82; Mary Ann Glendon, RIGHTS TALK: THE IMPOVERISHMENT OF POLITICAL DISCOURSE (Free Press, 1991), 18–46 and 171–83; and Peter W. Huber, GALILEO'S REVENGE: JUNK SCIENCE IN THE COURTROOM (Basic Books, 1991), 9–23 and 194–228.

politics of racial group entitlement. Ironically, it arguably complicated rather than simplified the issues judges would have to deal with by requiring the judiciary to single out whether race was the principal motive behind a specific districting configuration. As Pildes and Niemi note, "To ask about the reason behind the design of any one particular district is typically to implicate the entire pattern of purposes and trade-offs behind a district plan as a whole."[124] The problem is that the political task of redistricting is labyrinthine. "[T]o require a coherent explanation for the specific shape of even one district is to impose a model of legalistic decision-making on the one political process that least resembles that model."[125]

Yet for many the solution to this problem is not the abandonment of the model of legalistic decision-making that voting rights jurisprudence has imposed on politics, but rather—and perhaps incredibly—the abandonment of the political process itself and the geographic districting that forms its basis. This is what advocates of proportional and semi-proportional representation recommend. Bierstein, for instance, concludes her critique of *Shaw* and the post-*Shaw* jurisprudence with an invocation not to be *less*, but *more*, responsive to the legal rule that has become the *sine qua non* of VRA litigation and its racial group politics:

> If *Shaw*, *Holder*, *De Grandy* and *Miller* are a signal that communal representation is faltering, then their message is that we have two choices: We can follow Justice Thomas, back to an individual approach to representation that didn't work thirty years ago, or we can move forward to the twenty-first century with a new vision of representation and democracy by way of some form of proportional representation.

Rather than pull the judiciary out of vote dilution jurisprudence altogether and leave it to decide simple issues of ballot access (Justice Thomas' recommendation), something clearly within the judiciary's capacity, even if it would mean little work for judges, the suggestion here goes the opposite direction, inviting the judiciary to go to even greater lengths in reinventing the political process. The proposed "move forward" to proportional representation would indeed present "a new vision of representation and democracy" because it would require the overturning of one of the cornerstones of American republicanism: territorial districting and what most Americans identify with their federal and state governments.

Territorial districting is essential to the American republican form. As O'Rourke observes, compact, geographic districts facilitate communica-

---

124. *Election-District Appearances*, 585.
125. *Id.*, 586.

tion between representatives and the represented. "Split precincts confuse both election officials and voters. Districts that transect cities and counties burden electioneering; and constituencies that stretch over several media markets raise campaign costs."[126] Americans no doubt identify with social and economic interests. These interests consume a significant part of their lives. But Americans also, and perhaps in the main, identify with place: with urban and rural neighborhoods; mountainous, coastal, and prairie regions; state and federal constituencies. Bizarre districts, such as the North Carolina 12th at issue in *Shaw*, are bizarre precisely because they are unnatural and uncommon, not just dysfunctional.[127]

Geographic districting preserves the variegated communities of interest that extend beyond the single, formal interests that are the foci of attention for proponents of proportional representation. By requiring representatives to consider a multiplicity of interests, something they would not have to do or would have less necessity of doing under a model of proportional representation, territorial districting inclines representatives toward the general interest of the community. It is this, perhaps above all, that territorial districting achieves, compelling representatives to disregard individual or isolated interests in view of the public good.

In contrast to this, proportional representation, as Ward Elliott points out, discourages the compromise and coordination necessary for political action.[128] The palladium of a mechanistic democracy,[129] elegant "in its logic, symmetry, and representational accuracy,"[130] and capturing "every shade of difference of individual opinion," proportional representation nonetheless "sacrifices democratic substance for democratic form."[131] Although it promotes a uniform, formal equality that overcomes problems of gerrymandering by obviating the need to district, this simple formalism translates poorly into practice and, if implemented, would likely eliminate the American "party system as we know it."[132]

Elliott elaborates that by discouraging compromise proportional representation encourages schismatism. Intensely responsive to every ripple of public sentiment, proportional representation is unresponsive to tides. It gives everyone a voice but does nothing to gather those voices into an

---

126. *The Shape of Things to Come*, 86.

127. *Id.*, 58.

128. Ward E.Y. Elliott, THE RISE OF GUARDIAN DEMOCRACY: THE SUPREME COURT'S ROLE IN VOTING RIGHTS DISPUTES, 1865–1969 (Harvard University Press, 1974), 25.

129. *Id.*, 199.

130. *Id.*, 25.

131. *Id.* 199–200.

132. *Id.*, 210. See also, *id.*, 167.

effective, stable coalition. A clear choice of alternatives is available to people, but the alternatives tend to be impracticable.[133] Contrary to Bierstein's suggestion, a move toward proportional representation would not be a step toward the twenty-first century so much as a step backward to the halcyon days of proportional representation as an intellectual movement in the early twentieth-century. As the brainchild of Western and American intellectuals, proportional representation was utilized in Weimar Germany and the Fourth French Republic, both experiments failing disastrously. Weimar remains, to this day, a monument to the surreality of its principal architects, political scientists.[134]

Again, this failure should have been expected. Dissociation from reality is the hallmark of the intellectual world, as it is frequently the hallmark of judicial politics. Not only does judicial politics promote polarization rather than compromise, creating winners and losers instead of coalitions. Perhaps above all, it is prone to being hijacked by academic models of justice and fairness that make for tidy, sanitized legal theory, but dysfunctional political practice. Christopher Lasch has described America's new knowledge class as an immoderate, socially isolated elite, opposed to the more conservative middle class and generally disaffected with democracy. "The thinking classes are fatally removed from the physical side of life," living "in a world of abstractions and images" in contradistinction to "the palpable, immediate, physical reality inhabited by ordinary men and women." The new elites'

> belief in the "social construction of reality"—the central dogma of postmodernist thought—reflects the experience of living in an artificial environment from which everything that resists human control...has been rigorously excluded.... In their drive to insulate themselves against risk and contingency—against the unpredictable hazards that afflict human life—the thinking classes have seceded not just from the common world around them but from reality itself.[135]

Voting rights advocacy, with its demand for guarantees of minority officeholding, its invocations for modifications of the political process that would alter the very foundation of American republican government, and its insistence on administrative and judicial control over the electoral process, conform to Lasch's description of the elite-driven, postmodernist era. Proposals to implement proportional or semi-proportional representation are consumed with a single idea: that the representative

133. *Id.*, 200.
134. *Id.*, 25 and 94.
135. Christopher Lasch, THE REVOLT OF THE ELITES AND THE BETRAYAL OF DEMOCRACY (W.W. Norton, 1995), 20–21.

process must better accommodate group, and in particular minority group, interests. The almost blind obsession with this issue has obscured, in the minds of many advocates of alternative forms of representation, the other objects of republican government. The repercussions of this solitary focus have become obvious in VRA jurisprudence itself. In a recent attempt to accommodate minority complainants in Maryland, for instance, a federal district court judge ordered cumulative voting throughout Worcester County, overturning a system of government that had been in place since 1798.[136] Responding to this case in *Holder*, Justice Thomas admonished:

> If such a system can be ordered on a county-wide basis, we should recognize that there is no limiting principle under the [Voting Rights] Act that would prevent federal courts from requiring it for elections to state legislatures as well.[137]

Although the Fourth Circuit Court of Appeals overturned the district court judge's order, citing Thomas' opinion in *Holder* and the lower court's failure to respect the wishes of the County government, there was no assurance that other courts within the Circuit would not order a similar remedy where legislative intent was ambiguous or a legislative proposal failed to comply with section 2. And there was no assurance other federal courts would respect the Fourth Circuit's ruling.

In the rarefied world of academic theory and judicial politics, perhaps the most serious deficiency of voting rights advocacy and jurisprudence is not merely their immoderation but the idea that animates this immoderation: a doctrinaire, attenuated interpretation of the role of representative government in American politics. Instead of asking the question "How should representation be allocated?" perhaps the more fundamental question is: What is the ultimate purpose of representation? What is the public good that it serves, and how does mandating minority electoral officeholding further this goal, if at all?

Deliberative Democracy and the American Republican Form

Theories of representation dominant in voting rights commentary tend to restrict the role of representation to two functions: that of representing constituent interests and that of fulfilling an ombudsman's role.

---

136. *Cane v. Worcester County*, 847 F.Supp. 369 (Md. 1194), affirmed in part, reversed in part, 35 F.3d 921 (4th Cir. 1994).

137. 114 S.Ct. 2581, 2602, concurring opinion.

Of these, the former occupies the bulk of attention in voting rights scholarship. In a recent essay, Bernard Grofman observes that

> An important part of the history of representation has been the ongoing struggle between those who argue for representation of persons and those who argue for representation of interests.[138]

The federal Constitution and the majority of state constitutions, prior to *Baker v. Carr* (1962),[139] reflected a compromise between these two ideas of representation. At stake in reconciling them

> is whether voters ought to be regarded as faceless and interchangeable (one person-one vote carried to its most mindless extreme) or, whether, instead (or more plausibly, in addition) they should be seen as appropriately distinguishable on the basis of key characteristics such as place of residence, ethnicity, race, or political beliefs or affiliations.[140]

The most comprehensive and politically feasible concept of representation, Grofman suggests, will blend representation by population, which recognizes the equality of voters, with considerations that account for voter characteristics such as geography, ethnicity, race, political beliefs, and so on. On this reading, the representation of interests reflects voter characteristics: geographic place, ethnic or racial background, party affiliation, and the like.

Although academic commentary on the problem of representation focuses on voter equality and the necessity of accommodating constituency interests, perspectives, and needs, American political history, as well as the British constitutional tradition which developed prior to and contemporaneously with American republican government, suggest that other considerations may be equally important in the calculus of representation. Specifically, what of the role of the public interest?

When "interest" is spoken of in political science and legal literature, it tends to refer to limited or specific group interests. If the public interest is referred to at all, it is typically defined in terms of these more limited interests and the necessity of accommodating them. Arguably, however, it is the very impossibility of accommodating these interests in any absolute sense that makes representative democracy, and the deliberative

---

138. *What Happens After One Person-One Vote? Implications of the United States Experience for Canada*, in Drawing Boundaries: Legislatures, Courts, and Electoral Values, eds. John C. Courtney, Peter McKinnon, and David E. Smith (Fifth House, 1992), 156, 156.

139. 369 U.S. 186.

140. Grofman, *What Happens After One Person-One Vote?*, 156.

forum it facilitates, imperative. "Those who created the American constitutional system," Joseph Bessette remarks,

> believed that on most issues, most of the time, deliberative majorities would not exist independently outside of government, but rather would be formed through the operation of the governmental institutions, as the representatives of the people reasoned about public policy for their constituents.[141]

The public good, many of the Founders believed, extended beyond the interests of individuals, groups, and even constituencies, frequently requiring representatives not only to disregard the inclinations of their constituents but to act against them.[142] It required that representatives act not on the basis of a general *will*, on the mere wishes or opinions of the people, but on the basis of a general *wisdom*, on the basis of the true interests of the people, which may require little, if any, consultation with constituent wishes. As James Madison emphasized in *Federalist 10*, under a republican regime "it may well happen that the public voice, pronounced by the representatives of the people, will be more consonant to the public good than if pronounced by the people themselves, convened for the purpose."[143]

Edmund Burke referred to the essence of deliberative government as a concern with the public good best facilitated by representative institutions. Representative government could mediate and refine popular opinion. "[M]an is a most unwise and a most wise being," Burke observed. "The individual is foolish; the multitude, for the moment, is foolish, when they act without deliberation; but the species is wise, and, when time is given to it, as a species, it almost always acts right."[144] Representative government buys the time necessary to allow human wisdom to prevail. It facilitates that deliberation without which the momentary passions of the multitude, invariably "foolish," dominate. What counted in the legislative forum was not so much the voting of members mirroring

---

141. Joseph M. Bessette, The Mild Voice of Reason: Deliberative Democracy and American National Government (University of Chicago Press, 1994), 212.

142. See generally, *id.*, 13–26. See also, Alexander Hamilton, James Madison, and John Jay, The Federalist Papers, ed. Clinton Rossiter (New American, 1961), *No. 71*, 432:

> When occasions present themselves in which the interests of the people are at variance with their inclinations, it is the duty of the persons whom they have appointed to be the guardians of those interests to withstand the temporary delusion in order to give them time and opportunity for more cool and sedate reflection.

143. The Federalist, *No. 10*, 82.

144. Edmund Burke, *The State of the Representation*, in Burke's Politics, eds. Ross J.S. Hoffman and Paul Levack (Alfred A. Knopf, 1949), 224, 227.

the wishes of electors but prudence and sound judgment.[145] Representatives were not to be "personal representatives," subservient to the will of their constituents.[146] They were to look after the broad, substantive interests of the nation, interests that were independent of the particular, often illusory, interests of individuals and groups.[147] In a famous passage, Burke admonished the voters of Bristol:

> Parliament is not a *congress* of ambassadors from different and hostile interests, which interests each must maintain, as an agent and advocate, against other agents and advocates; but Parliament is a *deliberative* assembly of *one* nation, with *one* interest, that of the whole—where not local purposes, not local prejudices, ought to guide, but the general good, resulting from the general reason of the whole.[148]

The general reason of the whole led to the general good. The reason of particular interests was prone to be factious and divisive. Representative government was intended to remedy the effects of faction and division, mediating particular, incompatible interests through the machinery of representative institutions.[149]

If, however, representatives did not have to consult the wishes or opinions of their constituents and if the elected acted in the best interests of the nation independently of the demands of the electors, why have elections in the first place? Could the representation of interests, as Burke understood it, not be served by non-electoral means, by appointment for instance? In addition, what about the problem raised by Madison immediately following the passage cited above? How do we know the effects of representative government will not be the opposite of what we presume? Is it not possible that "Men of factious tempers, of local prejudices, or of sinister designs, may, by intrigue, by corruption, or by

---

145. See *id., Letter to Langriche*, 494–95.

146. *Id., The State of the Representation*, 229–30.

147. See Hanna Fenichel Pitkin, THE CONCEPT OF REPRESENTATION (University of California Press, 1967), 174:

> Burke almost never speaks of an individual's interest, or of the interest of a group, or of one group or locality as having more than one interest. His concept is thus very different from the subjective, personal interests of Utilitarian thought, and from the modern idea of a multiplicity of self-defined, changing interests at all levels of society.

148. *Speech to the Electors of Bristol (November 3, 1774)*, in BURKE'S POLITICS, 114, 116, emphasis in original.

149. Burke and the authors of *The Federalist* parted company on many significant issues respecting the role of representation in government. They did not depart, however, on the role of representative government in mollifying the effects of faction. The most succinct formulation of this in *The Federalist* is provided in *Federalist 10*.

other means, first obtain the suffrages, and then betray the interests of the people"?[150]

Madison's famous solutions to the latter problem were, on the one hand, institutional—federalism and separation of powers—and, on the other hand, noninstitutional—extending the sphere of government to incorporate enough interests and sects that none would dominate public forums. For Burke, the solutions to the problems of unresponsive and corrupt representation were different because the problems, referred to above, were not quite as they have been framed.

Burke's defense of Britain's mixed constitutional regime was not unlike Madison's defense of separation of powers and federal government: the idea of playing interest off against interest with a view to promoting the public good. Although the short term interests of representatives were not necessarily tied to the short term desires of constituents, the long term interests of representatives were tied to the long term desires of constituents. Representatives could ignore the wishes of constituents over the short term, but doing so over the long term was likely an indication of malevolent motives; "the species is wise, and, when time is given to it, as a species, it almost always acts right." When representatives consistently act contrary to the desires of constituents, they are in all likelihood—as the people suspect—corrupt. Elections are a good precaution against corrupt representation.

Failing to follow constituent wishes, however, is not merely a matter of unresponsive or corrupt representation. Debates in deliberative government take place in legislative assemblies, in committees, and in the chambers of legislative members. They occur, in other words, where the representative, not the constituent, appears. For this reason alone, it may make little sense for representatives to consult constituents about what to do with respect to specific legislation because constituents are not in the deliberative assembly. More importantly, however, the true nature of constituent interests is usually determined only *after* elections, only once legislative objects have been established and submitted to deliberation. It is only in the deliberative forum, in other words, that the true interests of the people are discovered.[151] Prior to, or even during, the electoral

---

150. THE FEDERALIST, *No. 10*, 82.
151. See Bessette, THE MILD VOICE OF REASON, 41:

> Although representatives have an obligation to prefer the interests of their constituents to their own personal interests, they have an equally important obligation to exercise their independent judgment as to what policies would best promote the good of their constituents and of the nation. This judgment will be informed by the discussion and debate that occur *within* the legislative body; for only those who are directly exposed to the arguments can reach wise decisions.

process the people's interests cannot be discerned with any certainty because political problems and prospective solutions have not been fully canvassed.

> The fundamental premise, or central proposition, of deliberative democracy...is that there are two kinds of public voice in a democracy—one more immediate or spontaneous, less well informed, and less reflective; the other more deliberative, taking longer to develop, and resting on a fuller consideration of information and arguments.[152]

The deliberative process is not only intended to facilitate "the general reason of the whole." It is only through such process that the general reason of the whole can be discovered.

Deliberative Democracy and Reapportionment

What does deliberative democracy have to do with the problem of voting rights and the drawing of electoral districts?

First, the potential irrelevance of the representation of particular interests in reapportionment, especially as this applies to federal redistricting. If the deliberative process involves members of legislative assemblies arguing about the general desirability or undesirability of legislative initiatives, focusing on broad interests rather than particular constituent interests, what does this imply for the reapportionment process? This issue speaks not so much to *whether* constituent interests need be accounted for; no one would deny that representatives need address them from time to time. Rather the concern here is the *weight* that is to be given them. If things such as geography, community interest, community history, or the voices of minorities must be accounted for, *how much* need they to be taken into account? It would seem that the response to this question depends, among other things, on what weight we give such interests in the legislative process. Do representatives mirror their constituents' interests to an extent mandating a high degree of scrutiny to ensure particular interests are reflected in the reapportionment process? Or does representation in the deliberative process largely ignore constituency interests, thus suggesting a lower standard of scrutiny be applied? No doubt what we are discussing here is deliberative *democracy*, not mere deliberative *government*;

Burke, like the framers of the U.S. Constitution, believed that people's inclinations and interests do not necessarily coincide. The task of representatives is to reason together to ascertain and foster the people's true interests.

152. *Id.*, 212.

an intimate tie between the representative and his or her constituent interests must exist.[153] But how far that tie reaches depends on the nature of the representative institutions and the level of attachment to constituency interests.

Federalism also factors into the representational calculus. The federal government looks after the general interests of the nation as a whole, while state and local governments look after state and local interests.[154] There is a qualitative difference between what federal representatives do and what state representatives do.

Models of representation that regard the legislative functions of federal and state representatives as mere quantitative distinctions and not qualitative distinctions, may then disregard an essential facet of American federalism that bears significantly on electoral boundary disputes. In addition, the relationship of federal and state interests may determine how we measure effective representation. For instance, if minority interests or racial and ethnic identity are more effectively represented in certain state assemblies than in the deliberations of Congress, what does this mean for federal reapportionments in those states? Can they be less representative of these interests? How exactly does state redistricting bear, if at all, on federal redistricting? And what about the division of federal and state powers outlined in the federal Constitution and the various state constitutions? If certain levels of government enjoy prerogatives that affect minorities more than other levels of government, such as control over inner city housing or education, does minority representation have to be proportionately higher at those levels of government? Conversely, can it be lower at the other levels of government? If some states, such as New York and Florida, send a proportionately higher number of minority representatives to Congress, does this mean that other states, such as Georgia and Louisiana, can send fewer; can they redistrict in such a way as to provide for less minority representation? Is there good reason, in law or in principle, why calculating proportional representation has to be restricted to state boundary lines?

In addition, do minorities necessarily need to hold office to be effectively represented, or is their representation more effective if they can influence a larger number of elected officials, even if this means holding fewer offices? As Justice Harlan noted respecting the difference between the influence of blacks under a multimember at-large electoral system versus their influence under a single-member districting system: "Under one system, Negroes have *some* influence in the election of *all* officers; under the other, minority groups have *more* influence in the selection of

---

153. *Id.*, 46.
154. See THE FEDERALIST, *No. 10*, 83.

fewer officers."[155] Which is the better form of representation and how is this question to be answered?

Related to the problem of what weight attaches to interests at the level of federal and state redistricting is the further problem of which groups count in the redistricting process. The problem of providing for minority representation is complicated by the further question regarding the dubious permanency of minority interests and how they are to be measured. Criticizing the Supreme Court's "discrete and insular minority" doctrine, Edward Erler has objected:

> American politics has never produced monolithic majorities and insular minorities. . . .
>
> Majorities in American life are formed from the diverse elements and groups that make up society as a whole. These majorities have been accurately described as, in reality, shifting coalitions of minorities. The constituent elements change from election to election so that, over the long run, there is no *permanent* majority and, hence, no *permanent* minority.[156]

If Erler's assessment is accurate and applicable to redistricting, this raises a host of problems with respect to preserving minority (or even majority) identities in reapportionment politics. The most obvious problem is that such minorities do not exist, at least not in any politically significant sense. Even if they do exist, how are they to be measured? If group "identities" fluctuate, if political alliances between individuals and groups continuously shift, particularly during federal and state electoral terms, how can such interests be accurately measured for the purpose of reapportionment after every decennial census?

In addition, there is the problem of "racial" interests. What are these? Are such interests legitimate? Are they as tangible as other interests, such as economic or geographic interests? It is clearly the case that prior to the VRA and the Civil Rights Act of 1964, and for some time thereafter, blacks had racial group interests. The egregious history of segregation and discrimination that blacks suffered was inseparable from their race. But can that still be said today? Do "racial" interests today attach to race or do they transcend race, fixing to non-racial phenomena, rendering race something only accidentally associated with the real interest at issue? If blacks have similar social or economic interests, for instance, does that make these interests racial or are they interests that are non-racial because of their potential to be shared with other races, such as whites or Asians?

---

155. *Allen v. State Board of Elections*, 393 U.S. 544, 586, dissenting opinion.

156. Edward Erler, *The Return to "Separate but Equal"*, in THE NEW FEDERALIST PAPERS, eds. J. Jackson Barlow, Dennis J. Mahoney, and John G. West, Jr. (University Press of America, 1988), 310, 312, emphasis in original.

If racial groups or minority groups do not exist or exist only in a politically peripheral sense, does inviting legislative districtors, or the Department of Justice and federal courts, to promote minority representation, as the VRA presently does, not risk accentuating or exaggerating differences between Americans that are politically irrelevant and potentially divisive? Is there not the danger, as Justice O'Connor complained in *Shaw*, that "Racial gerrymandering, even for remedial purposes, may balkanize us into competing racial factions,"[157] or as Justice Thomas complained in *Holder*, that "in pursuing the ideal measure of voting strength [under section 2 of the VRA, the Court has] devised a remedial mechanism that encourages federal courts to segregate voters into racially designated districts to ensure minority electoral success"?[158]

Deliberative democracy invites speculation on the process of representative reasoning and the importance of interests in the legislative forum. Theories of representation, typical of voting rights commentary, and generally accepted by federal judges and administrators, tend to overlook the significance of the public interest in American representational politics or identify this with the necessity of mirroring minority interests in American legislatures. Minority interests are clearly an important component of any representational scheme to the extent that such interests exist. However, exaggerating them or concentrating them in one or a few districts may undermine the moderating function and deliberative sense of broad community that geographic districting and America's constitutional form of representation were intended to serve. Justice O'Connor remarked in *Shaw* that

> When a district obviously is created solely to effectuate the perceived common interests of one racial group, elected officials are more likely to believe that their primary obligation is to represent only the members of that group, rather than their constituency as a whole.[159]

It is this whole and the broader "whole" of the state and nation—"a more perfect Union"—that deliberative democracy is intended to facilitate. To the extent that race-conscious districting undermines this concern with the broader community it erodes the representational form of government essential to American politics.

In *Federalist 10*, Publius highlighted that "Among the numerous advantages promised by a well-constructed Union, none deserves to be more accurately developed than its tendency to break and control the vi-

---

157. 113 S.Ct. 2816, 2832 (1993), opinion of the Court.

158. 114 S.Ct. 2581, 2592 (1994), concurring opinion.

159. 113 S.Ct. at 2827, opinion of the Court.

olence of faction." [160] The scheme of representation outlined in the Constitution was intended to provide the structural means by which the effects of faction would be controlled. Factious division, specifically, racial and ethnic balkanization, was at the center of controversy in *Shaw*. In both *Shaw* and the voting rights cases that followed it, the Court displayed an underlying discomfort with what had apparently become the reigning orthodoxy of VRA administration and adjudication: the imperative of proportional minority officeholding. The Court's discomfort reflected a shift in its priorities. No longer would the Court assess districting plans, such as the one at issue in *Shaw*, from the point of view—or solely from the point of view—of whether or not they enhanced minority representation. Rather, the new emphasis appeared to be on whether or not the overall effect of such plans on American politics was salutary. The guiding light for the Court appeared to be the public interest—the political system as a whole—not minority representation or minority representation solely or principally. Although providing for the representation of minority interests is essential to republican government, there is little evidence that alternative electoral schemes, such as proportional representation, would curb the factious excesses and racial politics that consumed the Court's attention in *Shaw*. To the contrary, the disproportionate emphasis such schemes place on representing group or minority interests may render them deficient both in theory and in practice, aggravating those very extremes in the representational process that the Court in *Shaw* seemed intent on curbing.

John Stuart Mill, an advocate of representative government and universal suffrage, declared that it was "important that everyone of the governed have a voice in the government, because it can hardly be expected that those who have no voice will not be unjustly postponed to those who have." [161] Although providing a voice in government is a critical factor in the calculus of representation, collective deliberation may make candidate ideology, party affiliation, and other considerations, more important in the scheme of representation, particularly at the level of national politics.

Has this public interest component of representation been sufficiently accounted for in voting rights jurisprudence and commentary to date? If it has not, perhaps this is one more element that needs to be added into

---

160. The Federalist, No. 10, 77.

161. John Stuart Mill, *Thoughts on Parliamentary Reform*, in Dissertations and Discussions (New York, 1874), IV, 21, quoted in Pitkin, The Concept of Representation, 202.

the already confusing mix of considerations that go to make up effective representation.

Conclusion

In *Mexican Americans*, Peter Skerry referred to the VRA as "the single strongest incentive for Mexican Americans and their leaders to define themselves as racial minority claimants."[162] As an elite initiative of national magnitude, the VRA has crystallized the problem of equality in American constitutionalism perhaps better than any other federal legislation over the last generation. It reflects the tension between equal opportunity and affirmative action; between individual rights and group rights; government protecting the rights of individuals versus government exercising those rights for certain designated groups;[163] between the public and the private, the state and society, liberalism and democracy; between maintaining constitutional forms and the demands for immediate political results that eschew constitutional forms in favor of constitutional substance. Tocqueville admonished that the "desire for equality always becomes more insatiable as equality becomes greater."[164] Modern democrats are anxious, impatient people, aspiring "only to facile and immediate pleasures," throwing "themselves impetuously toward the object of each of their desires, the least delays making them desperate."[165] Of all peoples, democratic peoples have the least respect for the utility of forms. Yet it is especially among democratic peoples that the preservation of forms is necessary to maintaining that wall of separation that it is imperative to maintain between those who are weak and those who are strong, between the governed and the government. The principal challenge to democracies is to respect the sanctity of their constitutional forms.[166]

Ironically, the VRA, although intended to preserve the constitutional forms of equality and representation, arguably now threatens them.

---

162. MEXICAN AMERICANS: THE AMBIVALENT MINORITY (Harvard University Press, 1993), 330–31.

163. See Harvey C. Mansfield, Jr., AMERICA'S CONSTITUTIONAL SOUL (Johns Hopkins University Press, 1991), 93.

164. Alexis de Tocqueville, DE LA DÉMOCRATIE EN AMÉRIQUE (Garnier-Flammarion, 1981), II, 174. The translation here and at n.165 are my own.

165. *Id.*, II, 393.

166. *Id.* See, also, Anthony A. Peacock, *Introduction: The Necessity of Rethinking the Constitution*, in RETHINKING THE CONSTITUTION, vii, xiii.

Having contributed to the transformation of the meaning of equality in American constitutionalism and the language in which the politics of representation is transacted, the VRA has caused, in a sense, a reversal of fortunes for minority claimants. The central concern of the Supreme Court is no longer racial discrimination, an issue that can only seriously be contended to exist at the periphery of American society. The issue today, as Thernstrom has pointed out, is racial and ethnic fragmentation, specifically how to avoid it. The Court must now reconcile the VRA with the principles of equal protection. What happens next will have to await further judicial clarification.

Whatever happens, it is clear that the VRA has displaced the source of decisionmaking power with respect to such fundamental political issues as the meaning of constitutional equality and the role of representation in American politics. By judicializing these issues, the VRA has not only upset the traditional separation of powers and disrupted the balance between federal and state governments. It has also contributed to that immoderation that is synonymous with judicial politics: dividing parties into irreconcilable, hostile camps; imposing an inflexible and impractical formalism on the political process; rewarding residential segregation at the very time other initiatives have attempted to restrain it; and compelling communities to engage in a high-stakes game of political roulette, gambling on all-or-nothing solutions to problems that require delicate political compromise but that cannot be otherwise addressed because of the demands of federal administrators and the federal judiciary.

At the heart of the new, affirmative understanding of equality and representation that has, till recently, been the moving principle of the VRA, lies a deeper confusion. In the final analysis, we can attribute this confusion to the indiscriminateness of modern social science. Modern social science has attempted to impose on the practice of politics a model of reform that formalizes what cannot be formalized and that simplifies what will always remain complex. It has misunderstood human freedom and its role in political action. Its credo, as Rainer Knopff has pointed out, is "that human beings do not *act* freely and spontaneously but *behave* predictably."[167] Hannah Arendt made a similar observation almost 40 years ago, that what started off in economics as an attempt to substitute "patterns of behavior only in this rather limited field of human activity, was finally followed by the all comprehensive pretension of the social sciences which, as 'behavioral sciences,' aim to reduce man as a whole, in

167. Rainer Knopff, with Thomas Flanagan, HUMAN RIGHTS AND SOCIAL TECHNOLOGY: THE NEW WAR ON DISCRIMINATION (Carleton University Press, 1990), 205, emphasis in original.

all his activities, to the level of a conditioned and behaving animal."[168] Whereas liberal thought had originally understood individuals to be free and the consequences of their actions to be unpredictable, modern social science assumes the opposite: that human action is predictable and thus controllable. It presumes to possess the knowledge necessary to understand, and therefore to reconstruct, social and political life.[169]

The credo of modern social science is also the credo of affirmative action, of the substantive understanding of equality and representation that has informed VRA jurisprudence and its administration until very recently. VRA advocacy is a paradigm of reconstructive politics. The application of a simple mathematical model of proportional representation for the benefit of designated minority groups; a statutory construction that deems correlation between minority group preferences and minority group identities, rather than causality, to be sufficient to warrant minority group entitlements; and the assumption that discrimination exists where it has not been conclusively proved, are consistent with a behavioral understanding of American politics that presumes to know more than it does; that sacrifices procedural fairness on the alter of substantive equal results and theoretical nicety.

The VRA presents a challenge not merely to American government, confronting the old order with a new understanding of equality, representation, separation of powers, and federalism. It presents, perhaps above all, a challenge to the fundamental preconditions of American liberal democracy—its freedom and its equality. In this sense, the VRA, as it has been administered and interpreted through the 1990s, should not be approached as one choice among many about how to deal with the problem of voting rights, given a fixed constitutional regime. Rather, it represents a choice between regime types themselves.[170] Recognition of this will be critical to any future administration or adjudication of the act, and to any reassessment of its purposes for maintaining political equality.

---

168. Hannah Arendt, THE HUMAN CONDITION (University of Chicago Press, 1958), 45.

169. See Peacock, *Strange Brew*, 124–25.

170. See *id.*, 137.

CHAPTER 6

The Supreme Court, The Voting Rights Act, and Minority Representation

Bernard Grofman *

Four key factors affected the initial phase of 1990's congressional and legislative districting: (1) The continued insistence by federal courts on strict standards of population equality (especially for congressional districts) that frequently forced state legislatures to cross city and county lines for the purpose of population equalization.[1] (2) The Supreme Court's upholding in 1986 of the constitutionality of the "effects test" language added to Section 2 of the Voting Rights Act of 1965 (VRA) when the Act was renewed in 1982, and the way in which the Court interpreted the new language of Section 2 to create a dramatically simplified three-pronged test of minority vote dilution.[2] (3) Vigorous enforcement by the Voting Rights Section of the Civil Rights Division of the Department of Justice of Section 5 of the VRA (preclearance provisions that apply to 16 states in whole or part). (4) The computer revolution, which has made it easy to rapidly draw alternative districting plans whose partisan and racial characteristics can be immediately assessed.

The combination of Section 2 and Section 5 made the Voting Rights Act "a brooding omnipresence" in the decision calculus of legislators anticipating voting rights challenges to the plans they draw during the

---

* I am indebted to Dorothy Green and Chau Tran for library assistance. An earlier version of this article appeared in PS (March, 1995) under the title "*Shaw v. Reno* and the Future of Voting Rights." This version, in addition to being somewhat longer, differs from the earlier one in several ways, including the discussion of additional cases.

1. Bernard Grofman. VOTING RIGHTS, VOTING WRONGS: THE LEGACY OF BAKER V. CARR. A REPORT OF THE TWENTIETH CENTURY FUND. *New York:Priority Press* (distributed through the Brookings Institution), 1991.

2. Bernard Grofman, Lisa Handley and Richard G. Niemi. 1992. MINORITY REPRESENTATION AND THE QUEST FOR VOTING EQUALITY. New York: *Cambridge University Press*; Bernard Grofman and Lisa Handley. 1992b. *Identifying and Remedying Racial Gerrymandering*. JOURNAL OF LAW AND POLITICS, Vol. 8, No. 2 (Winter), 345–404.

1990s round of redistricting.[3] Fear of voting rights litigation that would delay implementation of new plans and/or leave open the possibility that a plan would be totally redrawn by a court (with unforeseeable consequences for incumbents), as well as the far greater black presence in legislative halls due to earlier redistrictings, has led legislatures to draw many more black majority seats in the 1990s than ever before, especially in the South. As a consequence, 1992 saw dramatic gains in black legislative representation in the South, especially at the congressional level. Computer-drawn districts, built from units as small as census blocks and sometimes even splitting blocks, have raised the potential for gerrymandering to a new level, and given rise to some remarkably creative cartography.

The Voting Rights Backlash

There has been a public, scholarly, and legal backlash against the creation of majority-minority districts and against the judicial and administrative implementation of the VRA more generally.[4] There are three key factors in this backlash.[5]

One factor is the peculiar shapes of a number of majority-minority districts. Many of the new minority seat gains have occurred in tortuously shaped districts.[6] This is especially true of some of the majority-black congressional districts that were drawn in the South. These districts were carefully crafted to agglomerate enough minority population to assure a seat that a minority member might have a realistic chance to win given patterns of polarized voting. Arguably, standard redistricting criteria such as preservation of city and county boundaries, compactness, and even contiguity, have been given less weight in the 1990s, especially in areas where there was potential for drawing minority districts, than at any time in the past.[7] While black and Hispanic seats are certainly not the only strange-looking ones, they constitute a disproportionate share

---

3. Bernard Grofman. 1993. Would Vince Lombardi Have Been Right If He Had Said, 'When It Comes to Redistricting, Race isn't Everything, It's the Only Thing'? CARDOZO LAW REVIEW, Volume 14, No. 5 (April 1993), 1237–1276.

4. Paula McClain and Joseph Stewart Jr.(eds) Minisymposium: The Voting Rights Act After Shaw. PS (March 1995): 24–56.

5. Also see discussion of Shaw v. Reno and Miller v. Johnson below.

6. See e.g. Pildes and Niemi (1993).

7. Richard H. Pildes and Richard G. Niemi. 1993. Expressive Harms, Bizarre Districts, and Voting Rights: Evaluating Election District Appearances After Shaw v. Reno. MICHIGAN LAW REVIEW Vol. 92, No. 3, (December), 483-587.

of the most egregiously irregular shapes—at least for Congress.[8] Also, some of the irregularities in non majority-minority districts can be attributed to borders they share with minority districts.

Some critics object to districts like the North Carolina 12th congressional district on the grounds that a substantial disregarding of geographic criteria—whether in the interest of creating seats with black or Hispanic majorities or for any other purpose—harms a geographic-based notion of representation. For example, Ehrenhalt[9] asserts that the "main casualty... is the erosion of the geographical community-of-place as the basis for political representation.... If a district is nothing more than two pockets of separate white voters strung together..., then it is fair to ask whether the notion of a "district" is gradually ceasing to have any geographical meaning at all." Similarly, in my declaration in *Pope v. Blue* I wrote:[10]

> The notion that representation should be based on geographically defined districts presumes that the link between a representative and his or her constituents is facilitated by candidates being able to campaign in geographically defined areas where door to door campaigning is possible and/or where access to constants via media channels (e.g., newspapers and radio and TV stations) is made easier by the existence of common sources of information.... Permitting districts to be constructed whose boundaries are simply not definable in commonsense terms vitiates the principle that representatives are to be elected from geographically defined districts and vitiates the advantages of such districts as the basis of electoral choice. Also, [in such] districts, it may be especially hard to dislodge incumbents,

---

8. Richard H. Pildes and Richard G. Niemi. 1993. Expressive Harms, *Bizarre Districts, and Voting Rights: Evaluating Election District Appearances After Shaw v. Reno.* MICHIGAN LAW REVIEW Vol. 92, No. 3, (December), 483–587. For example, a 1992 editorial in the WALL STREET JOURNAL (February 4, 1992) refers to North Carolina's congressional plan as *Political Pornography.* An Editorial in the CHARLOTTE NEWS AND OBSERVER (January 13, 1992) said that it "plays hell with common sense and community." An editorial in the RALEIGH NEWS AND OBSERVER (January 21, 1992) says: "If a psychiatrist substituted North Carolina's proposed congressional redistricting maps for Rorschach inkblot tests, diagnoses of wackiness would jump dramatically. The maps... don't make any sense—to people who have any sense."

9. Ehrenhalt, Alan. 1993. *Redistricting and the Erosion of Community.* LEGISLATIVE STUDIES SECTION NEWSLETTER (APSA), (June) 18, 20.

10. Bernard Grofman. March 15, 1992. Expert Witness Declaration in *Pope v. Blue,* Civ. No. 3: 92CV71-P (W.D., Charlotte Division). *Pope v. Blue* was a challenge to the North Carolina congressional plan that was dismissed by a federal court. Indirectly, it led to *Shaw v. Reno,* as litigants sought other grounds on which to invalidate the North Carolina congressional plan.

because there is no straightforward geographical basis of electoral organization for change and the costs of campaigning are increased.

However, it is not district shapes, per se, that are at the root of the concerns expressed by many other critics. These critics would not be molli-
fied even if the shapes of majority-minority districts were less irregular.

A second major factor in the backlash to the use of the Voting Rights Act
to motivate/compel the creation of majority-minority districts is the belief
that, in Abigail Thernstrom's phrase, this is simply a new form of enforced
"political segregation." Many critics of VRA enforcement object to any use
of racial criteria as improper, on the grounds that racially motivated districting inexorably moves us away from a color-blind society to one of separate groups each making its own claim for a proportional part of the pie.

A third factor responsible for a backlash to newly drawn majority-minority districts is the concern of white Democratic legislators in the
South for the fate of the Democratic party in the South (as well as for
their own political safety) when black voters loyal to the Democratic
party are stripped away into heavily black seats.[11] These fears were reinforced by the visible evidence that Republican party officials throughout
the South were joining with black Democrats in voting rights lawsuits in
the 1990s round of districting; by allegations that the Republican-run
Department of Justice in the early 1990s was enforcing Section 5 of the
Voting Rights Act in a harsh and unreasonable manner in which "maximizing" the electoral success of black and Hispanic candidates had replaced "equal opportunity" as the prerequisite for a plan's preclearance;[12] and by the fact of Democratic legislative and congressional losses
in the South in 1992 and again in 1994, with white Democratic members
of Congress threatening to become an endangered species in several of
the Southern states.[13]

---

11. Kimball Brace, Bernard Grofman, and Lisa Handley. 1987. *Does Redistricting Aimed to Help Blacks Necessarily Help Republicans?* JOURNAL OF POLITICS, Vol. 49, 143–156.

12. Bernard Grofman. 1993. Would Vince Lombardi Have Been Right If He Had Said, *'When It Comes to Redistricting, Race isn't Everything, It's the Only Thing'?* CAR-DOZO LAW REVIEW, Volume 14, No. 5 (April 1993), 1237–1276.

13. Indeed, in 1994 this group was extinguished, at least for the nonce, from Geor-gia's congressional delegation, which went from nine of ten seats held by Democrats in 1990 to seven out of eleven Democratic in 1992 (when Georgia gained one new congres-sional seat) to only three out of eleven Democratically held seats in 1994—with those three seats being the black majority districts, each electing a Democrat of African-Ameri-can heritage, thus eliminating white Democrats from the Georgia congressional delega-tion. However, the contributions of the VRA to the Democratic congressional debacle of 1994 are often exaggerated. Democratic congressional losses (in percentage terms) were

The present battleground for the fight about race-conscious districting is the courts. The opening shot was fired in a North Carolina case. In *Shaw v. Reno*, a challenge to North Carolina's congressional plan was brought by white voters on the grounds that the plan unconstitutionally separated voters according to their race.[14] North Carolina is a state the bulk of whose black population is found in counties covered by Section 5 of the Voting Rights Act. In 1990, North Carolina had no black congressional districts and the last black member of Congress elected from that state was during Reconstruction. The congressional plan passed by the North Carolina legislature in 1991 contained one black majority seat. That plan was rejected by the Department of Justice, which indicated that the state had failed to demonstrate that the plan had neither the purpose nor the effect of diluting minority voting strength. DOJ suggested that a second black majority district could be drawn in the *southeastern* portion of the state. The state instead proposed a new plan, but with the second black majority district drawn *elsewhere* in the state. The lines of that second district, the elongated and snakelike 12th CD, are bizarre in the extreme.

The *Shaw* challenge to the North Carolina plan was initially rejected by a three-judge federal district court by a 2–1 vote. That court noted that district compactness was not a federal requirement.[15] An appeal to the Supreme Court led to a 5–4 decision in which the Supreme Court majority enunciated a new test for an equal protection violation. The Court held that the North Carolina redistricting scheme did not violate white voters' rights because it did not lead to unfairly diluting or canceling out the votes of white voters but, while avowing that lack of compactness, per se, was not a constitutional violation, the *Shaw* majority nonetheless asserted that equal protection can be violated if redistricting legislation "is so extremely irregular on its face that it rationally can be viewed only as an effort to segregate the races for purposes of voting,

---

as great, on average, in the states where no new black majority seats had been drawn, as in those where they had. Nonetheless, my own ongoing joint work with Lisa Handley and Wayne Arden does suggest that Democratic congressional losses in the South in 1992 and 1994 would have been somewhat curtailed had fewer black majority seats been drawn.

14. An earlier challenge to the North Carolina congressional plan, *Pope v. Blue*, in which I was to have served as an expert witness (Grofman, 1992), had been dismissed by a three-judge court for want of a federal question.

15. A compactness requirement for congressional districts was dropped from the decennial congressional apportionment legislation early in this century. Some states have compactness provisions for legislative districts written into their state constitutions (Grofman, 1983: Table 2).

without regard for traditional districting principles and without sufficiently compelling state justification." The Supreme Court then remanded *Shaw* back to the district court for a rehearing on the merits based on this new legal test.

When the case was heard again on remand (under the name *Shaw v. Hunt*), the lower court had by a 2–1 vote decided that the plan was constitutional. The appeal of that decision will be heard by the Supreme Court in Fall 1995. However, in the meantime, in the Spring 1995 term, the Court heard two other *Shaw*-like challenges to congressional plans, *Miller v. Johnson* (Georgia)[16] and *DeWitt v. Wilson* (California).[17] We will first review the holding in *Shaw v. Reno*, then briefly consider the subsequent Georgia and California cases, and then consider the broader questions of the likely long-run impact of *Shaw* on redistricting and on civil rights jurisprudence.[18]

Shaw v. Reno

The Supreme Court's somewhat muddled 1993 majority opinion in *Shaw v. Reno* was written by Justice O'Connor, joined by Justices Rehnquist, Scalia, Kennedy and Thomas. It bears internal evidence that strongly suggests compromises among the views of these Justices in forging a majority. There were four separate dissents, one by Justice White (joined by Justices Blackmun and Stevens), one by Justice Souter, and one by Justice Blackmun, and one by Justice Stevens. *Shaw* directly raised what Justice O'Connor refers to as "two of the most complex and sensitive issues this Court has faced in recent years: the meaning of the 'right' to vote and the propriety of race-based state legislation designed to benefit members of historically disadvantaged racial minority groups."

Reacting to the contorted shape of North Carolina's 12th CD with outrage, Justice O'Connor, wrote on behalf of the Court majority:

> (W)e believe that reapportionment is one area in which appearances do matter. A reapportionment plan that includes in one district individuals

---

16. *Johnson v. Miller*, CIV No. 194-008 (S.D. Georgia, 1994)

17. *DeWitt v. Wilson*, 1994 WL 325415 (E.D. Cal., June 27, 1994).

18. In the latter discussion I will speculate about the probable fate of the presently (August 1995) pending appeal of the district court decision in the remanded North Carolina challenge (*Shaw v. Hunt*). That case will be heard along with a challenge from Texas. Also, a challenge to Louisiana's congressional districts that was dismissed by the Supreme Court on purely procedural grounds has been reinstated and is likely to be considered by the Court in the not too distant future.

who belong to the same race, but who are otherwise widely separated by geographical and political boundaries, and who may have little in common with one another but the color of their skin, bears an uncomfortable resemblance to political apartheid.... For these reasons, we conclude that a plaintiff may challenge a reapportionment statute under the Equal Protection Clause and may state a claim by alleging that the legislation, though race-neutral on its face, rationally cannot be understood as anything other than an effort to separate voters into different districts on the basis of race, and that the separation lacks sufficient justification.

While Justice O'Connor's opinion in *Shaw* is hostile to race-based classifications, it does not make the use of race-conscious districting per se, unconstitutional. Indeed, Justice O'Connor is careful to say that "this Court has never held that race-conscious decision making is impermissible in all circumstances." Rather, her opinion draws on earlier cases making race a suspect classification such that allocations that make use of racial categories will be subject to strict scrutiny and must pass a test of being "narrowly tailored to further a compelling governmental interest."

Classifications of citizens solely on the basis of race 'are by their very nature odious to a free people whose institutions are founded upon the doctrine of equality.' They threaten to stigmatize individuals by reason of their membership in a racial group and to incite racial hostility. 'Even in the pursuit of remedial objectives, an explicit policy of assignment by race may serve to stimulate our society's latent race-consciousness, suggesting the utility and propriety of basing decisions on a factor that ideally bears no relationship to an individual's worth or needs.' (Justice O'Connor's opinion in *Shaw v. Reno, internal cites to other cases omitted*).

However, contrary to the way in which *Shaw* is commonly summarized in newspaper accounts, *Shaw* is not a reverse discrimination case.[19] *Shaw* is not about the rights of white voters to not have their voting strength diluted by the creation of black majority districts.[20] To the contrary, Justice O'Connor made it explicit that there was no claim being made by the *Shaw* plaintiffs that white voting strength had been diluted—white voters were not being underrepresented (ten of the twelve districts had clear white majorities, slightly more than the white proportion of state population). Both plaintiffs, and the court majority, in effect, conceded that the North Carolina plan was fair in racial outcome terms.

19. Remarkably, even academic commentators who ought to know better repeat this mischaracterization.
20. The same is true of *Miller v. Johnson*.

The four Justices who dissented from the majority opinion in *Shaw* did so for a number of reasons, and did so with vehemence.

The main arguments raised by the dissenters were based on the vagueness of the new equal protection test laid down in *Shaw,* and the lack of grounding of that test in criteria related to equal protection, given that no claim that white voting strength was being diluted had been made or could be sustained.

> Given two districts drawn on similar, race-based grounds, the one does not become more injurious than the other simply by virtue of being snake-like, at least so far as the Constitution is concerned and absent any evidence of differential racial impact. (Justice White in dissent, joined by Justices Blackmun and Stevens).

Justice Souter (in dissent), similarly, could not understand how a plan could be a violation of equal protection when there was no group whose rights had been violated.

> The Court offers no adequate justification for treating the narrow category of bizarrely shaped district claims differently from other districting claims....I would not respond to the seeming egregiousness of the redistricting now before us by untethering the concept of racial gerrymander in such a case from the concept of harm exemplified by dilution.

One other important argument raised by the dissenters was the claim that the peculiarities of North Carolina congressional plan could, in fact, be accounted for, at least in part, in non-racial terms. Justice White approvingly quoted the views of one political scientist (myself) that

> Understanding why the [North Carolina] configurations are shaped as they are requires us to know at least as much about the interests of incumbent Democratic politicians, as it does knowledge of the Voting Rights Act.[21]

---

21. Bernard Grofman. 1993. Would Vince Lombardi Have Been Right If He Had Said, '*When It Comes to Redistricting, Race isn't Everything, It's the Only Thing*'? CARDOZO LAW REVIEW, Volume 14, No. 5 (April 1993), 1237–1276. Another quote from my 1993 CARDOZO LAW REVIEW article is found in the majority opinion, wherein Justice O'Connor observes (quoting from Grofman, 1993: 1258): "The district has even inspired poetry: 'Ask not for whom the line is drawn, it is drawn to avoid thee.' "

There are at least two elements of this citation to my article by Justice O'Connor that deserve attention. First , it is very likely that this is the first time poetry (sic!) by a political scientist has ever been quoted by the Supreme Court. Second, this is the only instance with which I am familiar where an article by a social scientist is quoted in a Supreme Court case in both the majority opinion and in a dissenting opinion. (On a still more personal note, the reader is alerted to the fact that the poetry in question is not one for which I am allowed to take credit. It is found in a citation internal to my 1993 article.

However, we cannot really understand the reasons for the vehemence of the dissenters without understanding the context of historical injustices against African-Americans and other minorities.

As Justice Blackmun said in his dissent in *Shaw*:

> It is particularly ironic that the case in which today's majority chooses to abandon settled law...is a challenge by white voters to the plan under which North Carolina has sent black representatives to Congress for the first time since Reconstruction.

The legal scholar Pamela Karlan (personal communication, September 1993) has made this point in an elegant rhetorical question: "Which makes an uglier picture, the lines of the North Carolina 12th CD, or a North Carolina congressional delegation that remains without any black faces for 100 years."

Miller v. Johnson (Georgia)

Miller was a challenge to the Georgia congressional plan. In June 1995, affirming a lower court decision, the plan was struck down by the Supreme Court as unconstitutional under the *Shaw v. Reno* test. There was a majority opinion (joined by five Justices) and a dissent (joined by four members). Justice Sandra Day O'Connor also wrote a several paragraph concurring opinion. Short as it is, hers is the critical opinion in the case because it makes it clear that O'Connor will pursue a case-specific and fact-specific approach and, judging from the majority and minority positions in the case and the vehemence which they were held, she will be the swing-vote in future cases decided under *Shaw*.

In Miller, as in *Shaw v. Reno*, the court majority took the opportunity to slam the Department of Justice for overzealousness in enforcing the Voting Rights Act. DOJ had insisted in its Section 5 preclearance review that three black majority congressional districts be drawn in Georgia lest the plan be seen as having either the purpose or effect of diluting minority voting strength; the Court majority clearly disagreed that either the Constitution or the Voting Rights Act required that a third black majority seat be drawn. Moreover, the Court majority was especially attentive to the fact that the State of Georgia made no real affirmative defense of the redesigned majority black district other than to

---

The author is my "colleague" A Wuffle, and was personally communicated to me. The internal cite to Wuffle is omitted from the Supreme Court opinion for reasons of space. I might also note that some Justices liked this quote so much that they chose to cite the portion of the *Shaw* opinion containing it in *Miller v. Johnson*.)

say that it had been told that DOJ required it; furthermore, the record showed that the State took the view that the redrawn district clearly violated standard redistricting criteria. Thus, *Miller* became, for the court majority, an easy case under *Shaw*.

In contrast, the dissenters in *Miller* continued to affirm their view that *Shaw v. Reno* had been wrongly decided in that its limits on legislative discretion in districting matters had no clear constitutional justification, and further attacked the *Shaw* standard as ill-conceived (and perhaps even unconstitutional as a failure of equal protection) because it made it harder for legislatures to act for good reasons (e.g., remedying a past history of districting) than for bad ones (e.g., protecting a particular incumbent) and because it subjected black majority districts to a different standard than white majority ones.

DeWitt v. Wilson (California)

The California challenge was to plans drawn by Special Masters (retired judges) under the orders of the California Supreme Court, which had been given responsibility for drawing legislative and congressional plans under the California Constitution when the State failed to enact a plan in a timely fashion because of deadlock between the Democratically controlled legislature and the Republican governor. Like the 1970s California districting that had also been done by special masters, the 1990s plans were drawn with great attention to standard districting criteria and with great concern for the topography of the state. Although voting rights concerns were certainly taken into account, they were not overriding, and the plan could not be regarded as a "maximizing" plan, even though a substantial number of majority black and majority Hispanic seats were created. Indeed, the Mexican American Legal Defense and Educational Fund (MALDEF) unsuccessfully challenged the plans under Section 2 to require, i.a., the creation of an additional Hispanic majority legislative seat in the northern part of the state. When, in 1995, the Supreme Court validated the California Masters' work against a *Shaw*-type challenge, the Court opinion was unanimous and per curiam.

Was *Shaw* Necessary?

If fear by legislators of the costs in time and uncertainty in challenging overbroad DOJ preclearance denials, or anticipation by legislators of potential Section 2 lawsuits (or, in a few cases, a zeal for racial fairness and/or partisan lust) has led to some tortuous districts that could not be justified as having been required under the Voting Rights Act as remedies for vote dilution, there are more direct ways to address that problem than what the Court did in *Shaw*. *Shaw* reflects an activist conservative judiciary that, when confronted with a relatively minor problem, some bizarrely shaped majority-minority districts, proceeded to carve out a new "right" that had no clear standard for its enforcement. The decision, moreover, opens a can of worms vis a vis its potential threat to recent black (and Hispanic) electoral gains in descriptive representation— leading to a concern that we might end up throwing away the baby (minority representation) with the bathwater (tortuously shaped districts that lack any non-racial justification).

What could the Court have done? In my view, they could have decided *Shaw v. Reno* on non-racial grounds, holding that the penumbra of geographic-based representation required districts that were (a) contiguous in more than just a pro forma way, and/or (b) linked to some meaningful sense of place, i.e., (re)cognizable, and/or (c) not forming a crazy-quilt lacking rational state purpose. Thus, rather than the exclusive focus on the evils of race-conscious districting found in *Shaw*, the facts in North Carolina would have permitted its congressional plan to have been rejected on any one (or all) of the three tests above.[22] In so doing, since the case facts in *Shaw* are so egregious as to be near unique, especially with respect to contiguity, the court could have crafted a narrow standard that would protect against excesses without really threatening minority gains in representation. Such a holding would have raised no potential inconsistencies with *Thornburg* and would have permitted *Shaw* to be disposed in a way that did not raise a racial red flag. Of course, now that *Miller* has been decided, that avenue has been completely blocked off.

Why should it be unconstitutional for a legislature to seek to more fairly represent previously underrepresented minorities, especially in a state that has a long history of discrimination? In my view, the best attempt to provide a clear rationale for Justice O'Connor's views in Shaw is found in Pildes and Niemi's notion of "expressive harm" that they trace back to *Brown v. Board of Education*.[23] Nonetheless, it is not that easy to see exactly what is the problem to which *Shaw* is the solution. And, if there is a problem to which *Shaw* is the solution, it clearly does not appear to offer a "narrowly tailored" remedy. In particular, to the extent the problem is DOJ going "too far" in using its preclearance denial threat to force jurisdictions to draw tortuous majority-minority

---

22. Of course, taking this legal tack might have lost Justices Scalia and Thomas and resulted in no majority opinion.

23. For more critical views see Aleinikoff and Issacharoff (1993) and Karlan (1994).

seats, that problem could have been much more simply addressed by the Court simply laying down clearer standards for Section 5 (and also Section 2). Doing so might not have affected that many present majority-minority districts, but would have dramatically changed the decision calculus in the next round of redistricting and affected Section 2 litigation the rest of this decade... Did the Court really need to create a new constitutional districting standard?

The Jurisprudence of *Shaw v. Reno* and Its Progeny

Even if we accept the desirability of *Shaw v. Reno's* bar on drawing districts in ways that are essentially exclusively driven by racial considerations, there are some major unresolved questions about the standards for defining and measuring a constitutional violation under the guidelines of *Shaw v. Reno*.[24]

First, how exactly are we to operationalize the threshold test laid down in *Shaw v. Reno* for when there is a prima facie case that a district (or districts) should be subject to strict scrutiny? How do you prove that a district is too bizarre? Is this just a matter of visual inspection? In *Miller*, the Georgia district that was struck down was not that especially ill-compact, even relative to the other Georgia districts (a point emphasized by the four Supreme Court dissenters).[25] In any case, compactness, per se, is not a particularly useful test because some districts may appear ill-compact because they follow natural geographic boundaries (such as coastlines), or use as building blocks whole cities (or whole units of census geography) that are themselves not especially compact, and yet still be readily "recognizable" to their voters and to their legislators.[26]

---

24. The question of who has standing to bring a *Shaw*-type challenge has been clarified by the Court's initial dismissal of the appeal of the Louisiana congressional case on the grounds that plaintiffs lacked standing since none lived in the majority-minority district.

25. Ill-compactness of particular district lines or general failure to satisfy standard redistricting criteria does not becomes unconstitutional, *per se*, but is only relevant to the extent that it supports the inference that race was the sole or predominant motive in drawing a plan to aid disadvantaged minorities.

26. Bernard Grofman. 1993. Would Vince Lombardi Have Been Right If He Had Said, *'When It Comes to Redistricting, Race isn't Everything, It's the Only Thing'*? CARDOZO LAW REVIEW, Volume 14, No. 5 (April 1993), 1237–1276; Karlan, Pamela S..1989. *Maps and Misreadings: The Role of Geographic Compactness in Racial Vote Dilution Litigation.* HARVARD CIVIL RIGHTS - CIVIL LIBERTIES LAW REVIEW. Vol. 24,

My own view is that if we are to impose a *Shaw*-like test for district shape, the criteria of "contiguity" (Grofman, 1985) and "recognizability" are more important than that of compactness. By "recognizability" I refer to the ability of a legislator to define, *in commonsense terms, based on geographical referents*, the characteristics of his or her geographic constituency.[27]

Second, how do we decide when race is the predominant or exclusive factor responsible for the configuration of a challenged district or districts? In *Miller*, it was not shape alone. In *Miller*, the Supreme Court had "smoking gun" evidence that the Georgia plan had been drawn by the legislature only because the Department of Justice had insisted on a third black majority congressional district before they would agree to preclear any plan; and the legislature openly admitted that it had completely neglected standard districting criteria in drawing the revised plan

---

No. (Winter), 173–248; Niemi, Richard G., Bernard Grofman, Carl Carlucci and Thomas Hofeller. 1990. *Measuring Compactness and the Role of a Competent Standard in a Test for Partisan and Racial Gerrymandering.* JOURNAL OF POLITICS, Vol. 52, No. 4, 1155–1181; Bernard Grofman and Lisa Handley. *Minority Population Proportion and Black and Hispanic Congressional Success in the 1970s and 1980s.* AMERICAN POLITICS QUARTERLY, Vol. 17, No. 4 (October 1989), 436-445; reprinted in revised and updated form under the title "PRECONDITIONS FOR BLACK AND HISPANIC CONGRESSIONAL SUCCESS," in Wilma Rule and Joseph Zimmerman (Eds.) THE ELECTION OF WOMEN AND MINORITIES. New York. *Greenwood Press*, 1992a; Cain, Bruce. 1984. THE REAPPORTIONMENT PUZZLE. Berkeley: *University of California Press*; Butler, David and Bruce Cain. 1992. CONGRESSIONAL REDISTRICTING. New York: *Macmillan*. When *Shaw*-related issues have been raised in recent voting rights cases, testimony about district lines by plaintiffs' social science expert witnesses have tended to focus on geometric measures of compactness. While something can be learned from such measures, I would put little weight on them, and I would never use compactness, per se, as the test for a *Shaw* violation. Still, I might use compactness tests to help pick out districts whose peculiar features seem to require explanation.

27. In earlier writings (Grofman, 1992, 1993), I referred to this concept as "cognizability." Because that term is not as clear in its referents as recognizability and because it also has the defect of having an alternative legal meaning, at the suggestion of Barbara Phillips (University of Mississippi Law School), I have been using the term 'recognizability' for this concept. (Re)cognizability, per se, has not been the subject of previous case law, but egregious violations of the recognizability principle can be identified by making use of standard criteria of districting such as violation of natural geographic boundaries, grossly unnecessary splitting of local sub-unit boundaries (such as city and county lines), and sunderings of proximate and contiguous natural communities of interests (cf. Grofman, 1985). I should also emphasize that, in my view, the appropriate test of (re)cognizability is not whether the voters do know the boundaries of the district in which they reside, but whether those boundaries could, in principle, be explained to them in simple commonsense terms.

to create that third district. Moreover, since Georgia had two black majority CDs in the plan it submitted that was denied DOJ preclearance, compared to only one such district in the 1980s it was impossible to say that Georgia's initial proposal was retrogressive in the sense of *Beer v. U.S.* It was also hard to argue that the plan was intentionally discriminatory, given the contortions needed to create the third black majority district.[28] Thus, the Court majority felt itself on completely safe ground in saying both that race was the predominant or sole factor in creating the third black majority district in Georgia and in rejecting the view that the Voting Rights Act *required* that third Georgia district to be drawn. [29]

Rarely, however, will the factual record be that clear as it was in *Miller*. Certainly, in most redistricting, race is not the only consideration taken into account by line-drawers. For example, in the trial in *Shaw v. Hunt*, the North Carolina legislature argued that the North Carolina 12th CD could be justified on non-racial grounds in terms of its demography (urban, poor), and because of historical facts about patterns of migration and patterns of segregation that created communities of interest among its parts, and because partisan and incumbency preservation factors as well as racial concerns entered into the decisions as to how districts were to be configured. If the Supreme Court majority does decide that the North Carolina congressional plan is unconstitutional, will the Court regard these district court findings as "clearly erroneous," or can the Court accept these findings and then decide that the remedy was not "narrowly tailored?"[30]

---

28. Even though that district was not as unusual as the North Carolina 12th, it certainly displayed a number of pseudopodia whose presence was hard to explain except in terms of a desire to incorporate all available black voters.

29. Similarly, in the first post-*Shaw* case to be decided on the merits, *Hayes v. Louisiana*, No 92-CV-1522 (W.D. La., Shreveport Division), the district court did not decide the exact evidentiary test, because it held that "(I)f everyone—or nearly everyone—involved in the design and passage of a redistricting plans asserts or concedes that design of the plan was driven by race, then racial gerrymandering may be found without resorting to the inferential approach approved by the court in *Shaw*" (slip op. at p. 13, with internal cites omitted).

30. Judge Phillips, writing for the majority in *Shaw v. Hunt*, takes the view that district shape is but an indicator of potential unconstitutionality, and not unconstitutional *per se.* He argues that, once it can be shown the State of North Carolina had adequate grounds to believe that the Voting Rights Act required it to draw *two* black majority congressional districts, the State had discretion on how to balance off competing considerations in drawing such districts as long as no group had its voting strength diluted in the process. It is unlikely that the Supreme Court majority will agree with this view.

Third, how do we determine whether a plan is narrowly tailored to fulfill a compelling state interest? The "narrow tailoring" issue did not come up in *Miller*, because the court majority held, in effect, that there was no Voting Rights Act violation for which that Georgia needed to have provided a remedy.[31]

Another interesting question has to do with the racial composition of the majority-minority districts. Some of the black majority districts that have been created, such as the North Carolina 12th CD, are only barely majority-minority. Thus, they are among the handful of most integrated legislative districts in the country. Can such districts be justified in terms of "narrow tailoring"?[32] Alternatively, if a district that is 51 percent black is found unconstitutional, does turning it into a district that is 51 percent white now render it constitutional?

Lastly, can *Shaw* be reconciled with *Thornburg* and subsequent Voting Rights Act enforcement? In 1986, in *Thornburg v. Gingles*, in upholding the constitutionality of the new Section 2 language of the Voting Rights Act, the Supreme Court sanctioned Congress' right to require the creation of majority black districts in situations where black voting strength had been submerged in multimember districts with white majorities, *if* it could be shown that the presence of racially polarized voting minimized or canceled out the potential for a political cohesive set of black voters to elect candidates of choice (of their own race) *and* it also

---

31. The *Hayes* court, however, in a Louisiana congressional decision now again on appeal to the Supreme Court, held that both the shape and the size of the majority population may be no more than what is narrowly required to address voting rights concerns. In contrast, DOJ takes the position that threatened denial of Section 5 preclearance can itself constitute a compelling state purpose and that, to satisfy that end, jurisdictions should be given a considerable degree of latitude in balancing off competing considerations about districting.

The *Shaw v. Hunt* district court majority opinion expresses a rather similar, but somewhat more restrained, view. For example, in its amicus brief before the Supreme Court in *Hayes* (*State of Louisiana v. Hayes* No 83-1539, April 29, 1994), the DOJ argues that the original Louisiana congressional plan should not have been held to be unconstitutional because it was not motivated solely by race and because it was drawn primarily to serve a compelling state purpose, namely satisfying the Voting Rights Act. DOJ also makes the pragmatic argument in its amicus brief (p. 18) that the standards laid down in *Hayes* would be counterproductive because "state and local governments may well opt for litigation if their efforts are so narrowly circumscribed," and thus "the ultimate effect could be a serious disincentive to settlements and voluntary compliance with the law." However, DOJ made very similar arguments in amicus brief in *Miller*, and was unsuccessful in persuading the Court majority.

32. See discussion of *Schaefer* below.

could be shown that black population was sufficiently geographically concentrated that a black majority district could be drawn.[33] While *Shaw* does not overrule *Thornburg*, there is some reason to believe that two are on a potential collision course. A sentence late in Justice O'Connor's opinion, "(W)e express no view as to whether 'the intentional creation of majority-minority districts without more' always gives rise to an equal protection claim," reminds us that some Justices (led by Justices Scalia and Thomas) would like to revisit the whole question of color-conscious districting and perhaps even the constitutionality of Section 2 of the Voting Rights Act.[34]

Thornburg v, Gingles talks about a remedy for vote dilution being required if and only if the minority population is sufficiently geographically compact to form the majority in a single district. All the Supreme Court would need do to discourage jurisdictions (and lower courts) from going to extremes in crafting voting rights remedies under Section 2 is to tighten up slightly[35] on the standards for what level of geographical compactness is appropriate for a remedy plan. It is pressure from DOJ or threat of lawsuit that led many jurisdictions to create black or Hispanic districts that violated contiguity or recognizability standards. If the Supreme Court tightened up its interpretation of geographic compactness, certainly some majority-minority districts would not get drawn that might have been drawn under the previous legal regime, but remedies under Section 2 (or Section 5) could still be pursued exactly as be-

---

33. Here we are simplifying the complex legal issues in *Thornburg*. For discussion of how the *Thornburg* three-pronged test for vote dilution under Section 2 of the VRA ((a) a cohesive black vote, (b) usual defeat of black-sponsored candidates as a result of white bloc voting, and (c) a potential for remedy based on the drawing of a single-member-district plan) has been interpreted by federal courts since 1986 and of how it relates to the standards for vote dilution in earlier case law see Grofman, Handley and Niemi (1992).

34. See discussion of *Holder v. Hall* in Karlan (1993).

35. I use the term "slightly" because I share the view of Karlan (1989) that "a functional approach to Gingles' geographic compactness requirement is best suited to the inclusive spirit of Section 2" (this apt summary of Karlan's central argument is found in *Marylanders for Fair Representation v. Schaefer*, 1994, slip op. at p. 74, where it is quoted approvingly). (See discussion of *Schaefer* below.) Moreover, just as I would not use compactness as the test for *Shaw*, I would never use compactness, per se, as the test for whether a remedy existed under *Thornburg*. Rather, I would define the standard in terms of contiguity and of (re)cognizability in the fashion discussed above. It seems to me that this interpretation captures quite well the spirit of Justice Brennan's discussion of this prong of the *Thornburg* three-pronged test, and it is consistent with the way most federal courts have interpreted this prong (see discussion of relevant case law in Grofman and Handley, 1992a).

fore when it could be shown that minority voting strength had been fragmented, packed, or submerged.[36]

Direct evidence that *Gingles* and *Shaw* can be reconciled is found in the ruling by a three-judge panel in the combined cases of *Marylanders for Fair Representation v. Schaefer*, Civ, N. S-92-510 and *NAACP v. Schaefer*, Civ S-92-1409, decided on January 14, 1994. This is a post-*Shaw* redistricting challenge that offers a very commonsensical approach to *Shaw*-like issues. In this case, the Maryland Assembly plan was being challenged, because (a) it allegedly did not go far enough in drawing black districts, (b) as a partisan gerrymander, and (c) on other grounds, such as alleged inadequate attention to one person, one vote considerations. Space does not permit a full consideration of this decision; suffice it to say that the court rejected most claims, but held that plaintiffs had met their burden under *Gingles* in one part of the state, and that an additional black majority district needed to be drawn in the area of the Eastern Shore.

In affirming the need to draw this district, after reviewing case law showing that the *Gingles* requirement of geographical compactness should not be construed rigidly, the court held that the proposed district was geographically compact under *Gingles*. Then it rejected the claim that the proposed district was so ill-compact that it should be rejected under *Shaw*. It compared the shape of the proposed new district to that of other districts in the plan and concluded that it did not stretch further than that of some other non-majority-minority districts; and that it was not alone in being relatively irregular in shape. "In short, if District 54-9 is not sufficiently compact, then the same can be said of many districts in the State's new legislative districting plan".[37]

---

36. Recall that The *Thornburg* test determine what a jurisdiction *must* do; that test does not decide the question of the extent to which a jurisdiction could choose to go beyond what Section 2 or Section 5 of the Voting Rights Act requires in the way of color-conscious districting. If the DOJ position on *Shaw* had been adopted by the Supreme Court, it would make *Shaw* largely a dead letter, since it is a rare plan indeed where no factors other than race are involved or where a Voting Rights defense might not plausibly be raised. But the position taken by the majority in *Hayes* would dramatically limit what a legislature might choose to do to remedy previous racial inequities. I believe that there can be an appropriate middle ground between these two positions that reconciles *Shaw* and *Thornburg*, while still permitting line-drawers greater latitude in addressing concerns for racial fairness than what might be *required* of them under the Voting Rights Act.

37. In Maryland, a compactness challenge to the plan as a whole had already been brought in state court on state law grounds, and had been rejected (*Legislative Redistricting Cases*, 331 Md. at 580, 590–92) (slip op. at p.66).

In adjudicating the question of whether or not the new district could rationally be understood only "as an effort to classify and separate voters as to race"[38], the Maryland court found that alternative plans had even higher black populations and concluded that "District 54-9 could not have been merely the result of an effort to maximize the number of black voters and to minimize the number of white voters in the proposed district. Other considerations must have come into play".[39] The court also held that the proposed district did satisfy traditional districting criteria to a substantial extent, e.g., in terms of contiguity, population equality, regard for "natural [geographic] boundaries," and due regard to the "boundaries of political subdivisions," and that it met the state constitutional requirement that Assembly districts be nested inside Senate districts.[40] The district court also accepted as credible testimony by legislators that the district was one whose various parts could be traversed by a representative with no particular difficulty and could be effectively represented.[41]

Is DOJ Out of Control?
Part of a Republican Plot?

It has been claimed that the Republican-run Department of Justice in the early 1990s was enforcing Section 5 of the Voting Rights Act in a harsh and unreasonable manner in which "maximizing" the electoral success of black and Hispanic candidates had replaced "equal opportunity" as the prerequisite for a plan's preclearance. I find this characterization of Voting Rights enforcement to be largely mistaken, but space limits do not permit me to deal with that controversy here.[42] As for the claim that DOJ voting rights enforcement under Bush had been a Repub-

---

38. *Shaw*, 113 S. Ct. at 2828.

39. slip op. at p. 68.

40. slip op. at pp. 69–72.

41. slip op. at 73–74.

42. Bernard Grofman and Chandler Davidson. POSTSCRIPT: WHAT IS THE BEST ROUTE TO A COLOR-BLIND SOCIETY? In Bernard Grofman and Chandler Davidson (Eds.), CONTROVERSIES IN MINORITY VOTING: THE VOTING RIGHTS ACT IN PERSPECTIVE. Washington, D.C.: *The Brookings Institution*, 1992, 300–317; Bernard Grofman. 1993. Would Vince Lombardi Have Been Right If He Had Said, *When It Comes to Redistricting, Race isn't Everything, It's the Only Thing*? CARDOZO LAW REVIEW, Volume 14, No. 5 (April 1993), 1237–1276; Davidson, Chandler and Bernard Grofman (Eds.). 1994. QUIET REVOLUTION IN THE SOUTH: THE IMPACT OF THE VOTING RIGHTS ACT, 1965–1990. Princeton NJ: *Princeton University Press*.

lican plot to "whiten" districts by pulling off minority population into heavily minority districts for purposes of Republican advantage, it is easy to see that such a claim is undercut by the simple fact that voting rights enforcement policies under Clinton have been virtually indistinguishable from those under Bush.[43]

Implications of *Shaw v. Reno* and Its Progeny for Political Representation

How Important is *Shaw v. Reno?*

Shaw is widely viewed as the most important districting case of the 1990s both because of the scope of its opinion in creating a new constitutional cause for action in challenges to districting plans and because of the possible implications of the decision—namely an end to black gains (and perhaps also Hispanic gains) in representation, and the seeming potential of a stark reversal of precious dramatic gains in minority representation. What civil rights activists most fear about *Shaw v. Reno* (and now *Miller v. Johnson*) is that these are but the opening wedges to reversal of the great representational gains for blacks and Hispanics brought about by Voting Rights Act-inspired concerns for the drawing of black and Hispanic majority districts.

In the South, for example, the number of black members of Congress went from four to seventeen as a result of the 1990s round of districting. Hispanics, also under special Voting Rights Act protection, have made congressional and legislative gains as well. Handley, Grofman and Arden (1996 forthcoming)[44] show that black and Hispanic gains in representation in the 1990s, like minority legislative gains in the 1970s and 1980s[45] can be attributed almost entirely to the creation of black and Hispanic majority districts. Will those gains be wiped out by post-*Shaw* litigation

---

43. Moreover, just as the DOJ under Bush challenged some plans that created Republican advantage (e.g., that for the Los Angeles County Board of Supervisors), so has the DOJ under Clinton precleared plans that arguably help Republicans (e.g. in South Carolina). For further discussion see Grofman (1993).

44. Lisa Handley, Bernard Grofman and Wayne Arden. 1996. *Electing Minority Preferred Candidates to Legislative Office: the Relationship between Minority Percentages in Districts and the Election of Minority Preferred Candidates.* NATIONAL POLITICAL SCIENCE REVIEW.

45. Grofman and Handley, 1991, 1992; Grofman and Davidson, 1994; Handley and Grofman, 1994.

as the majority-minority districts that created the gains are restructured to be ones with greater esthetic appeal and a lower minority proportion?

Two congressional cases are already pending before the Supreme Court, with more on the way. Other challenges at all levels of government are in the process of being filed, and these are likely to gain in number if plaintiffs are ultimately victorious in more of the cases now pending and if Georgia significantly redraws its congressional lines in the aftermath of *Miller*. Moreover, as I have learned from conversations with voting rights attorneys around the country, *Shaw* has already begun to have an important indirect effect in triggering a greater unwillingness of jurisdictions to settle voting rights cases because they argue that the remedies that are being requested violate Shaw.

Just as *Baker v. Carr* simply upheld the justiciability of federal courts hearing challenges to the failure to redistrict, and left to subsequent cases the gradual evolution of standards of "one person, one vote," *Shaw v. Reno* did not strike down the North Carolina plan under challenge but simply enunciated new ground under which it could be constitutionally challenged. By striking down a black majority district in Georgia and upholding black and Hispanic districts in California, the Court majority will, at least if Justice O'Connor has her way, be weaving a fact-specific trial through subsequent *Shaw*-type challenges. I'm not even prepared to be confident about what will happen when the Supreme Court hears *Shaw v. Hunt* (see below).[46]

Also, while *Shaw* has the potential for totally changing the rules of the redistricting game,[47] I do not view its likely consequences as being as far-reaching as do some other voting rights experts.

First, given the degree of residential segregation in the U.S., drawing relatively compact and clearly contiguous black districts at the local level (or even for most state legislatures) is not that difficult. Only highly populous congressional districts may need to include minority population from considerably more than one city or county in such a fashion that snakes and amoebas would seem required if we wish to craft additional districts with majority black populations.[48]

---

46. In any case, my crystal ball has been known to have some cracks in it. I thought *Shaw v. Reno* would go 5–4 or 6–3 the other way.

47. For example, by creating a constitutional cause of action, the door is now open for district courts other than that of the District of Columbia, to, in effect, implicitly review Section 5 preclearance decisions—in the way that the district court did in *Miller*.

48. The situation is somewhat different for Hispanics, who are not as residentially segregated as blacks, but space does not permit a full elaboration.

Second, given the vehemence of the four-member minority in *Miller*, I do not see the votes on the U.S. Supreme Court to turn back the clock by overturning or substantially limiting *Thornburg v. Gingles*. As emphasized above, Justice O'Connor remains the critical swing vote, and she is clearly unwilling to take a uniformly extreme stance.

Third, it is a simply a misconception (albeit a common one) that *Shaw* held race-conscious districting to be prima facie unconstitutional.

Thornburg laid out minimal requirements for what a jurisdiction in which there were geographically concentrated pockets of minority voters must do in the way of race-conscious districting if voting was polarized along racial lines to the point that minority candidates usually lost; i.e. it provides a fact-contingent standard for race-conscious remedies. *Shaw v. Reno*, in contrast, addresses the question of what a jurisdiction may do, i.e., whether a concern for racial fairness can be carried too far in advance of any need shown for a race-conscious remedy. *Shaw* does not overturn *Thornburg*. Nor will the *Shaw* standards invalidate all majority-minority districts. For example, the black majority and Hispanic majority districts that were created by the California Supreme Court were sheltered from attack under a *Shaw*-like challenge by evidence that the plan-makers were very attentive to standard districting criteria and concerned with the topography and regional breakdown of the state.[49]

Fourth, I expect that even when majority-minority districts need to be considerably redrawn because of *Shaw*, many of the redrawn black majority districts will still elect minority candidates. Here I would anticipate that what will probably happen as lines are redrawn can be analogized to liposuction of some of the most unsightly bulges. Also, when districts have a high enough black registration that African-American voters have a virtual certainty of being able to control the Democratic primary if they are united, and a reasonable expectation of holding enough white Democratic votes in the general election to allow the minority candidate to win, then black population even less than fifty percent may be sufficient to create a district in which a black-supported candidate can win.[50]

---

49. As noted earlier, this plan sailed through Supreme Court scrutiny with flying colors in a unanimous per curiam decision.

50. Kimball Brace, Bernard Grofman, Lisa Handley, and Richard Niemi. *Minority Voting Equality: The 65 Percent Rule in Theory and Practice*. LAW AND POLICY, Vol. 10, No. 1 (January 1988), 43-62; Bernard Grofman and Lisa Handley. 1992b. *Identifying and Remedying Racial Gerrymandering*. JOURNAL OF LAW AND POLITICS, Vol. 8, No. 2 (Winter), 345–404.

Finally, the chief impact of *Shaw* will be on the next redistricting round, and a lot can happen on the Supreme Court (and in the country) between now and then.

Shaw v. Hunt

It might appear that Justice O'Connor's views about the unacceptability of the North Carolina 12th CD are so obvious from what she wrote in *Shaw v. Reno* that the plan is doomed despite its having been upheld by a 2–1 vote of the three-judge panel that heard the remand. However, in rejecting the Georgia plan the Supreme Court majority used the phrase "not clearly erroneous" with respect to the *Miller* trial court's findings about the challenged district having been created for purely racial reasons. In reversing *Shaw v. Hunt* the Supreme Court will either have to reverse lower court findings that race was *not* the sole or even the preponderant motivation for the way in which NC CD 12 was configured, or conclude that the remedy was not sufficiently narrowly tailored. In particular, DOJ may have insisted on a second black majority CD in North Carolina in order to give preclearance, but North Carolina was not compelled by the Department of Justice to configure the 12th CD in the way that it did.[51]

I am skeptical that the Supreme Court majority will accept the North Carolina 12th CD as sufficiently narrowly tailored under *Shaw*. As I wrote in my declaration in *Pope v. Blue*):[52]

> By any reasonable test, North Carolina's 12th Congressional District would appear to violate a [re]cognizability standard. The district stretches like a slender snake with unsightly bulges,[53] over a significant portion

---

51. "(T)he proposed configuration of the district boundary lines in the *south central to southeastern* part of the state appears to minimize minority voting strength given the significant minority population in this area of the state. In general, it appears that the state chose not to give effect to black and Native American voting strength *in this area*, even though it seems that boundary lines that were no more irregular than found elsewhere in the proposed plan could have been drawn to recognize such minority concentration *in this area of the state*" (Dunne letter of December 18, 1991 at p. 5, emphasis added). More recently, in its amicus brief in the remand of *Shaw*, the DOJ took the position that North Carolina had good reason to believe that any plan without a second black district would not be precleared, and argued that the most peculiar features of the North Carolina plan owe more to incumbency preservation considerations than to racial considerations, per se.

52. 1992.

53. My characterization of the Congressional District 12 as a snake with unsightly bulges is mild compared to the way the plan was characterized by North Carolina political observers. My own personal favorite is the description of the district by political

of the state, encompassing isolated pieces of diverse counties and political communities, involving multiple media markets, and connected over part of the district only by a corridor along I-85.

I should also note that Pildes and Niemi[54] find the North Carolina 12th the most ill-compact congressional district whether we look at perimeter-based or area-based measures of compactness.[55]

Moreover, with respect to contiguity, even though I would simply require that satisfaction of that standard be more than *pro forma.*, as I wrote in my declaration in *Pope v. Blue:*[56]

> The claim to contiguity of Districts 6 and 12 is based in large part on using the southbound lanes of I-85 to connect otherwise disjoint pieces of District 6, while using the northbound lanes of I-85 to connect otherwise disjoint pieces of District 12 in one county, with the pattern reversed in an adjacent county. . . . If contiguity is permitted via only one lane of a road, then it is possible to draw districts from one end of a state to the other that pick up dispersed populations without any regard for geographical proximity. Indeed, virtually any pieces of territory in a state can be simultaneously connected to one another in such a fashion. This is an open invitation to the most blatant and egregious form of gerrymandering, and makes a mockery of the notion of territorially based districting.

Do We Really Still Need to Draw Majority-Minority Districts?

Justice O'Connor's opinion in Shaw seeks a moral high ground by attacking districts for whites and districts for blacks as tantamount to apartheid. However, if voting is polarized along racial lines and minority

---

columnist Mark Barrett (January 12, 1992, reproduced in Appendix to Wright Affidavit in *Pope v. Blue*). Apparently the initial map showing the plan colored District 12 yellow, leading Barrett to say that "the district resembles the stain that might be left if a giant with yellow blood were stabbed in Charlotte, staggered across the Piedmont and fell to the ground and bled to death on the Virginia line." Of course, as I emphasize below it is not the visual esthetics of the plan, as such, that is at issue, but rather whether: (1) The plan a whole does not satisfy contiguity requirements, and/or (2) contains districts at least one of which fails any reasonable cognizability test, and/or (3) can be characterized as a crazy quilt lacking rational purpose.

54. 1993.

55. For an extensive discussion of the different type of compactness measures see Niemi, Grofman, Hofeller and Carlucci (1990); Niemi and Pildes (1993).

56. 1992

candidates usually lose—the preconditions for the Voting Rights Act to apply—then failure to draw a district plan that is fair to both groups perpetuates situations where, for all practical purposes, the districts are only districts for whites, i.e., districts that only whites can be expected to win. Abigail Thernstrom[57] and other revisionist scholars[58] argue that whites (even southern whites) are now acceptant of qualified black candidates.

Virginia is often cited as an example of where the Voting Rights Act has been misapplied. According to Thernstrom,[59] "Virginia's voters have proved beyond a shadow of a doubt that blacks can win in majority-white jurisdictions.... L. Douglas Wilder being the proof of that particular pudding." Taking nothing away from Governor Wilder, to regard his election as indicative of a general ability of blacks to get elected to state legislative office from majority white areas in the deep South, or even in Virginia, itself, is to completely disregard the evidence.

The number of black state legislators who are elected from majority white districts in the South can still be counted on one's fingers. Lisa Handley and I[60] found that, in the 1980s, in every southern state, the percentage of majority white state legislative districts that elected a black was either zero (in most deep South states) or near zero. This near complete absence of black electoral success in white majority districts occurred despite the fact that, even in the deep South, most blacks lived in white majority districts. Virginia is 19% black. It had no black members of Congress, and in 1990, no black legislators elected from majority white districts. In Virginia, the only black ever elected to the state legislature from a white majority district was Douglas Wilder—and his election (with a plurality) was made possible only because a half dozen white candidates in the Democratic primary split the white vote and Virginia does not have a majority vote requirement.

---

57. Abigail Thernstrom. WHOSE VOTES COUNT? AFFIRMATIVE ACTION AND MINORITY VOTING RIGHTS. Cambridge, MA: *Harvard University Press*, 1987; Abigail Thernstrom. *Op-Ed: A Republican-Civil Rights Conspiracy*. WASHINGTON POST (September 1991).

58. Carol Swain. BLACK FACES, BLACK INTERESTS: THE REPRESENTATION OF AFRICAN AMERICANS IN CONGRESS. Cambridge MA: *Harvard University Press*, 1993.

59. Abigail Thernstrom. *Op-Ed: A Republican-Civil Rights Conspiracy*. WASHINGTON POST (September 1991).

60. Bernard Grofman and Lisa Handley. 1991. *The Impact of the Voting Rights Act on Black Representation in Southern State Legislatures*. LEGISLATIVE STUDIES QUARTERLY, Vol. 16, No. 1 (February), 111–127; Lisa Handley, Bernard Grofman and Wayne Arden. 1996. *Electing Minority Preferred Candidates to Legislative Office: the Relationship between Minority Percentages in Districts and the Election of Minority Preferred Candidates*. NATIONAL POLITICAL SCIENCE REVIEW, forthcoming.

Handley, Grofman and Arden[61] updated earlier findings on the link between non-Hispanic white population proportion and electoral success of black candidates using data from the 1990s districting round. For the 23 states with greatest black and Hispanic population whose 1992 legislative and congressional elections they reviewed, they find that most of the black and Hispanic gains (especially those in Congress) came from new majority-minority districts. They also find that the probability that a black majority seat would elect a black legislator had gone up slightly; while in the South the likelihood that a minority candidate would be elected from a legislative or congressional district a majority of whose voters were white had not increased from the minuscule probability found in previous decades.

But what about Carol Swain's well known finding that, as of 1990, 40 percent of all black members of Congress were elected from non-majority black districts?[62] According to Swain, this shows that blacks can be elected from districts where blacks are in the minority. However, a closer look at the cases where blacks are elected to Congress from non-majority black districts gives us a much more pessimistic picture of the likelihood of black success in white districts than Swain would have one believe. While the forty percent figure given by Swain is technically correct, it is also fundamentally misleading and should best be regarded as a "factoid."

There were 25 black members of Congress elected in 1990. Of the 10 elected from districts that are not majority black, six are elected from districts that are majority black plus Hispanic.[63] That leaves *only four black congressmen elected from districts where non-Hispanic whites are in the majority.* Of the four black members of Congress who are elected from such districts, one (Rep. Franks, Conn.) was a Republican conservative who almost certainly was elected over the opposition of the black members of his district; one (Rep. Jefferson, Louisiana) is in a district that was 44.5% back and 49% minority using 1980 population figures but is now 66% black according to 1990 population figures—and he

---

61. Lisa Handley, Bernard Grofman and Wayne Arden. 1996. *Electing Minority Preferred Candidates to Legislative Office: the Relationship between Minority Percentages in Districts and the Election of Minority Preferred Candidates.* NATIONAL POLITICAL SCIENCE REVIEW, forthcoming.

62. Carol Swain. BLACK FACES, BLACK INTERESTS: THE REPRESENTATION OF AFRICAN AMERICANS IN CONGRESS. Cambridge MA: *Harvard University Press*, 1993.

63. Bernard Grofman and Lisa Handley. 1992b. *Identifying and Remedying Racial Gerrymandering.* JOURNAL OF LAW AND POLITICS, Vol. 8, No. 2 (Winter), 345–404. In all of these districts blacks make up the plurality of the minority electorate, and in all but one of these districts blacks make up the plurality of the minority population.

wasn't elected until 1990; one (Rep. Wheat, Missouri) runs with the advantage of incumbency in a district where he won the Democratic primary which first selected him as the Democratic nominee with only 32% of the vote[64]—a primary where he received almost no white support and which he won only because whites had divided their vote among seven white candidates; and the last (Rep. Dellums, California) was elected from perhaps the most liberal district in the nation (combining blacks in Oakland with the ultra-liberal city of Berkeley).

In short, one of the four exceptions really isn't one using 1990 population figures, one is a black Republican who doesn't enjoy that much black support, and the other two exceptions to the rule that blacks win only in majority-minority districts are very unusual cases that cannot be taken as the basis for reasonable expectations for the success of black-endorsed black candidates in majority (non-Hispanic) white districts.[65] Moreover, in 1990 (or for that matter, in 1992 and 1994) no black member of Congress from the South was elected from a non-black majority district, and the Mississippi 4th, 45% black according to 1980 population figures, failed to elect a black candidate.

Referencing the work on the political geography of minority electoral success that Lisa Handley and I have done jointly[66];[67] observes that creating additional black majority districts can have only limited payoffs for gains in the number of blacks elected to Congress because geographical constraints limit the number of such districts that can be drawn. *Black*

---

64. The state has no runoff requirement.

65. The facts I refer to above are all ones found in Swain (1993), but she fails to draw the proper inferences from them about how special are the circumstances under which blacks are elected to Congress from non-black majority districts, and how unlikely those circumstances are to be applicable to future black contests is white majority districts. Swain does provide data on Hispanic population and does discuss these majority-minority districts as a separate category from the other districts where blacks constitute less than half of the population, but her concluding chapter is, in my view, not sufficiently sensitive to the implications of this distinction as a limitation on what we can expect in the way of further black gains in district where blacks do not constitute the majority. For example, we are unlikely to see many new congressional districts with a black plurality and a combined black plus Hispanic majority in the South!

66. Bernard Grofman and Lisa Handley. *Minority Population Proportion and Black and Hispanic Congressional Success in the 1970s and 1980s*. AMERICAN POLITICS QUARTERLY, Vol. 17, No. 4 (October 1989), 436-445; reprinted in revised and updated form under the title "Preconditions for Black and Hispanic Congressional Success," in Wilma Rule and Joseph Zimmerman (Eds.) THE ELECTION OF WOMEN AND MINORITIES. New York. *Greenwood Press*, 1992a.

67. Carol Swain. BLACK FACES, BLACK INTERESTS: THE REPRESENTATION OF AFRICAN AMERICANS IN CONGRESS. Cambridge MA: *Harvard University Press*, 1993.

Faces, Black Interests was written before the results of the 1990's round of districting were known. If Swain were right in her expectations, then we should have seen black congressional gains primarily in non-black majority districts and we should have seen few black gains in the South. Yet, in the 1992 round of districting there were thirteen new black members of Congress, the largest gain in any single redistricting period. All of the thirteen new black members were elected from black majority districts. Moreover, all were elected from the South.[68] *Thus, in 1992 no new black members of Congress came from non-black-majority districts.* In 1994 all black members of Congress from the South were elected from black majority districts, and the one new black member not elected from a black majority district was a Republican who won without majority black support.

In a world of race-conscious voting, race-conscious remedies are needed. But we must be careful that a zeal to purge race from the districting process not retard the integration of the halls of our legislatures.[69]

---

68. Of course, with blacks a declining share of total U.S. population, virtually all of the black-majority congressional seats that might be drawn have already have been created in the 1990's round of districting. Thus, in the long run, the election of substantial numbers of new black members of Congress in succeeding decades can come only from black success in white majority districts.

69. Bernard Grofman and Chandler Davidson. "Postscript: What is the Best Route to a Color-Blind Society?" In Bernard Grofman and Chandler Davidson (Eds.), CONTROVERSIES IN MINORITY VOTING: THE VOTING RIGHTS ACT IN PERSPECTIVE. Washington, D.C.: *The Brookings Institution*, 1992, 300–317.

CHAPTER 7

The Redistricting Morass

Samuel Issacharoff[1]

In a democratic society, the purpose of voting is to allow the electors to select their governors. Once a decade, however, that process is inverted and the governors and their political agents are permitted to select their electors. Through the process of redistricting, incumbent political actors choose what configuration of voters is most suitable to their political agenda. The decennial redistricting battles reveal the bloodsport of politics, shorn of the claims of ideology, social purpose, or broad policy goals. Redistricting is politics pure, fraught with the capacity for self-dealing and cynical manipulation.

That different configurations of electors will yield different electoral results is hardly new or noteworthy; the pejorative term "gerrymander" stems from the creative linedrawing of Massachusetts Governor Gerry and the founding strokes of the American republic. What is still relatively new is the attempt to constrain, under the aegis of the federal Constitution, the most wanton excesses of the process. It was only thirty years ago that the Supreme Court required rural legislators in Tennessee and Alabama to redistrict their states to reflect the growing urban population centers and thereby undermine their stranglehold on state political power.

The commands of the one-person, one-vote rule of redistricting are by now so ingrained as to obscure what else is new in the 1990s round of redistricting. For the first time since the great Supreme Court reapportionment decisions of the 1960s, redistricting authorities had to contend not only with equipopulational districting, but with vigilant protections of minority representation as well. Only after the passage of the 1982 amendments to the Voting Rights Act and the Supreme Court's expansive endorsement of the amended Act in the 1986 North Carolina redistricting case, *Thornburg v. Gingles*,[2] did the issue of minority-controlled

---

1. Charles Tilford McCormick Professor of Law, The University of Texas School of Law. This chapter includes work that has previously appeared as T. Alexander Aleinikoff & Samuel Issacharoff, *Race and Redistricting: Drawing Constitutional Lines After Shaw v. Reno*, 92 MICH. L. REV. 588 (1993), and Samuel Issacharoff, *Race and Redistricting*, 2 RECONSTRUCTION 118 (1994).

2. 478 U.S. 30 (1986).

districts emerge front and center in the decennial battles over representation. In state after state, the question of minority districts became the most visible and debated issue after the 1990 Census, oftentimes joining an uncomfortable alliance of minority incumbents, aspirants for political office, and the Republican Party, the latter armed with the oversight powers of the federal Justice Department. Particularly for moderate Republicans without ideological opposition to race-conscious politics, the prospect of concentrating (or "packing," as the practice is known in the redistricting trade) the traditional Democratic votes of racial and ethnic minorities into minority-dominated districts offered the possibility of eviscerating the biracial power bases of many liberal Democrats—thereby realizing the long-term strategy of the late Lee Atwater, who early on saw in the redistricting battles of the 1990s the chance to weaken, if not destroy, Democratic control of state legislators and the House of Representatives.

Despite the centrality of minority representation to post-1990 redistricting, the process took place in the absence of any well-defined standards of law, particularly with regard to the application of the Voting rights Act. The leading cases under Section 2 of the Voting Rights Act—the section that prohibits diminishing of minority voting influence—were forged in the battles against at-large or multimember electoral districts. These electoral systems allow all members of a given jurisdiction to vote separately on each candidate for office, and thereby allow a voting majority to control every seat in an election. For example, if a community were 60 percent white and 40 percent black, and if the races had consistently different voting preferences, the result of an at-large election for a city council in which black and white candidates vied head-to-head for each of five council positions would likely be that the white candidate would prevail in each contest with about 60 percent of the vote. In such cases, the perceived harm was the capacity of majority communities to capture a disproportionate share of representation by the ability to vote serially for each candidate for local office. The principal remedy has been the creation of electoral subdistricts in which minority voters, acting in concert, are able to select a representative of their choice.

Unfortunately, the post-1982 vote dilution case law gave little guidance to measuring alternative electoral arrangements following a decennial reapportionment. In the context of such decennial redrawing of district lines, the stakes are far more complicated than in the binary decision of should there be single-member districts or at-large elections. Rather, redistricting poses the question of choosing among competing plans in which all jurisdictional lines are up for grabs. Nor did the prior cases articulate the conditions under which state redistricting entities are either permitted or required to resort to race-conscious practices. These were the issues presented to the Supreme Court initially in cases arising from the redistricting battles in Minnesota, Ohio, Florida, and most notably, North Carolina, the setting for *Shaw v. Reno*.[3] Whereas the prior cases had addressed the remedial use of race-conscious districting to alleviate proven exclusion, the 1990s redistricting cases concerned the affirmative use of race in the quintessentially political process of dividing electoral spoils.

Racial Classifications in Redistricting

Shaw v. Reno provided the Court with a combustible mix of race, politics and undisguised self-dealing. As a result of the 1990 Census, North Carolina was entitled to an additional congressional seat, bringing its delegation to twelve. Despite the growing political power of blacks in North Carolina and the absence of any black congressional representation since the turn of the century, the State initially apportioned itself to create only one district likely to elect a black representative, although its population was twenty percent black. The plan was presented for approval to the Justice Department under the preclearance provisions of the Voting Rights Act. The Justice Department objected to the State's refusal to create a second district in the southeastern section of the state, which contained a significant concentration of blacks, and the state's decision instead to disperse black voters among a number of majority-white congressional districts. Following the Department's objection, the state was forced to redraw its congressional districts with the avowed aim of increasing black representation.

Unfortunately, the creation of a black congressional district in the southeastern portion of the State would have disrupted the power bases of incumbent Democratic congressmen. Consequently, the Legislature decided instead to create the now-notorious I-85 district in the north-central region of the State, stretching 160 miles in length and often barely wider than the highway that it followed. Indeed, contiguity was maintained at one spot only because two parts of the district intersected at a single point. The plan divided towns, counties and even precincts among as many as three congressional districts with almost surgical precision to capture sufficient numbers of black voters to satisfy the Justice Department objection. The plan earned the sobriquet of "political pornography" from the *Wall Street Journal* before being dubbed the "snake" district and struck down as "political apartheid" by the Supreme Court.

---

3. 113 S.Ct. 2816 (1993).

It should go without saying that North Carolina is hardly unique in its recourse to geographically contorted districts to enhance not only minority electoral prospects but every fashion of controlling political whim. Although redistricting is constrained by the one-person, one-vote principle and by some notion of geographic units of representation, the process remains rife with capacity for self-interested manipulation. State redistricting bodies have frequently created oddly-shaped districts for a variety of purposes, including, but not limited to, the creation of minority-dominated districts.

This inevitably raises the question of the extent to which states undertaking reapportionment and redistricting are required, or even permitted, to use race as a driving factor in drawing district lines. The significance of these cases lies in the fact that, as the Court has recognized on several occasions, it is impossible to insulate the highly politicized process of redistricting and reapportionment from the exquisite awareness on the part of all participants of the likely consequences of each decision. At each point where a precinct line is drawn to include one block but not another, where a district is created through the reshuffling of precincts, or where an additional legislative seat is assigned to one region rather than another, sophisticated political actors take every step with the knowledge of who stands to benefit and who does not, who will be the beneficiaries and who will bear the cost. Since one of the factors that will clearly be weighed into the redistricting balance will be the racial and ethnic composition of the newly constituted districts, an immediate constitutional problem presents itself: When may state redistricting bodies legitimately use explicit racial and ethnic criteria in drawing district lines?

This is a perplexing issue from the standpoint of constitutional doctrine. Since *Brown v. Board of Education*[4] the use of racial and ethnic classifications by state bodies had been strongly discouraged; in the legal terminology, they are subject to strict scrutiny, and will be permitted only where they advance some compelling governmental interest. Yet redistricting is an area in which classifications of all kinds—most notably partisan, socioeconomic, racial, and ethnic—are the lifeblood of the process. No state actors in a politically charged redistricting fight could credibly claim that they did not take account of demographic information concerning proposed districting alignments and, as racially polarized voting patterns are well-documented, race will invariably be a crucial demographic variable. Moreover, the open nature of political horsetrading involved in redistricting battle leaves state actors open to the charge not only that they used racial classifications in drawing the

---

4. 347 U.S. 483 (1954).

lines, but that they used such classifications expressly to reward one racial group but not another. Despite the Court's expressed aversion to using racial criteria, it has continued to do so in a complex and wavering fashion. The unevenness of the Supreme Court's treatment of race is captured most clearly in its treatment of the claimed benign or even benevolent use of race as a classification intended not to stigmatize, as per the Jim Crow segregation, but to raise the horizons of the historically disadvantaged. At one pole are the views of former Justices Brennan and Marshall (often joined by Justice Blackmun) which held the use of "benign" classifications to be constitutionally tolerable so long as they were designed with some degree of care and were aimed at benefiting historically disadvantaged minorities. At the other extreme is the view that virtually any departure from color-blindness is invidious and thus invalid. While expressed primarily in the dissents of Justices Rehnquist and Scalia through the 1980s, this view occasionally rose to the fore in challenges to hard and unyielding racial categories, as in the 1989 decision, *City of Richmond v. J.A. Croson*,[5] striking down minority set-asides in construction contracts in Richmond, Virginia.

For well over a decade, however, the predominant view on the Court has reflected, albeit shakily, a middle zone in which classifications are tolerated so long as they do not excessively divide citizens into inescapable categories and so long as the costs imposed on non-benefitted social groups do not seem excessive. This is best shown by the complex and unsatisfying reasoning of *Regents of California v. Bakke*,[6] which upheld the benign use of racial classifications but imposed unresolved limits on the forms that racial preferences could take. This jurisprudential approach was largely the inheritance of a deeply divided Supreme Court, unable to come together in official "Opinions of the Court" in the major affirmative action cases of the 1980s. The alignment of views placed decisive votes in the fact-specific, centrist approach of Justices Powell and O'Connor, and resulted in race-conscious state action being approved or disapproved for a variety of almost idiosyncratic reasons.

Under the extreme contextualism of *Bakke* and its doctrinal descendants, racial classifications or preferences are usually subject to strict scrutiny regardless of their motivations and designated beneficiaries, but are allowed so long as they are found necessary to achieve some "compelling" interest asserted by the state, which has included, for example, achieving diversity in public institutions. At the same time, the Court's jurisprudence in this area remains unsettled as a result of strong lan-

---

5. 488 U.S. 469 (1989).
6. 438 U.S. 265 (1978).

guage in *Bakke* and some of the following decisions that suggests that it is always invalid to allow race to be the *dispositive*, rather than an ostensibly "contributing," factor in decision making. To put it mildly, this distinction is problematic. At the margins, race *must* be the dispositive make-or-break factor in a preferential decision-making process or else it would be meaningless. The result of *Bakke* has been a highly stylized selection process in public institutions that seek to soften the edges of racial classifications while maintaining the viability of preferences necessary for minority advancement.

The question for the redistricting context posed by *Shaw* was whether it would "*Crosonize*" the process of decennial line-drawing, or whether it would broadly tolerate preferences on behalf of historically marginalized groups, or finally whether it would allow for a *Bakke*-like middle ground. The clearest answer is that the majority of the current Court is completely uninterested in arguments echoing the commitment of Brennan and Marshall to advance the fortunes of the historically excluded. The fact that the beneficiaries of the race-conscious line-drawing were black did not detain the Court at all. Nor does the opinion analyze the use of racial preferences in terms of disproportionate benefits to the preferred group or excessive burdens imposed on the dispreferred groups. The various dissents in *Shaw* argue in vain that even under the challenged plan, whites would still retain control of ten of the twelve districts in the state, or presumptively more than their 78 percent of the population would entitle them to.

At the same time, the Court's opinion retains the combined and unstable strains of both *Croson* and *Bakke*. While the Court's rhetoric is powerful and lasting—castigating extensive reliance on racial classifications as an invitation to "balkanization"—the opinion bears the characteristic fact-specific qualities favored by its compromise author, Justice O'Connor. The Court is careful to emphasize that racial classifications are not an unconstitutional evil *per se*. In the Court's words, "race consciousness does not lead inevitably to impermissible race discrimination." Rather, in the Court's view, the potential for constitutional harm stems from an excessive reliance on race. Excessiveness is defined not in terms of process or even of harms suffered by dispreferred groups, but rather in the use of racial classifications as opposed to other criteria to create electoral districts. Thus, the Court concludes by condemning only the use of an "extremely irregular" district that is "so bizarre on its face" and "irrational" as to be presumptively invalid for its disregard of "traditional districting principles such as compactness, contiguity, and respect for political subdivisions." Even here, the Court is careful to emphasize that it is not enunciating a new constitutional principle so much as explicating the facts underlying its reasoning: "We emphasize that these criteria are important not because they are constitutionally required—they are not . . .—but because they are objective factors that may serve to defeat a claim that a district has been gerrymandered on racial lines."[7]

Shaw is therefore best understood as a case which makes explicit in the complex jurisprudence of racial distinctions the conception of "yes, but not too much." For all the harshness of rhetoric, the opinion announces only that there are limits to the state-imposed use of racial classifications, even if these limits are so contextually specific as to be incapable of articulation to a generalized principle. Not for naught does the Court sheepishly disavow any analogy to another failed area of judicial line-drawing, the "I know it when I see it" definition of actual, as opposed to metaphorical, pornography.[8]

What is Not Too Much?

The fact-specific holding of *Shaw* is unsatisfying at both a practical and theoretical level. In the first place, it is unclear what the confines of traditional districting principles should be. There are any number of oddly configured jurisdictions in the United States, including such foundational building blocks as the states of Maryland, West Virginia, and Michigan. There is no evidence that oddly configured congressional districts are a significant departure from either the current norm or from tradition, nor that they are restricted to districts drawn to satisfy minority voting concerns. Even the widely quoted witticism used to ridicule North Carolina's newest majority black jurisdiction—"if you drove down the interstate with both car doors open, you'd kill most of the people in the district"—was coined to describe an oddly configured congressional district drawn in Texas in the 1970s, to benefit white incumbents. Does prior use of oddly shaped districts thereby grandfather non-compactness into the ambit of traditional line-drawing, at least in Texas?

There is little in the Court's prior experience with gerrymanders that provides answers. In general, the Court has looked at oddly-configured jurisdictional lines in the past to infer the purpose of the political actors responsible for drawing those lines. For example, in the landmark case challenging the racial exclusion of blacks from the municipal boundaries of Tuskegee, Alabama, *Gomillion v. Lightfoot*,[9] the Court found the City's alteration of its boundaries from a square to "an uncouth twenty-

---

7. 113 S.Ct. at 2827.

8. 113 S.Ct. at 2827 (alluding to Justice Stewart's famous concurrence in *Jacobellis v. Ohio*, 378 U.S. 184, 197 (1964)).

9. 364 U.S. 339 (1960).

eight-sided figure" to be probative of an impermissible effort to exclude black voters, and only black voters, from the municipal electorate. But this sheds little light on the converse situation where the racial reasons for line drawing are express, rather than covert. What would the Court do with a perfectly geometric district drawn for the stated purpose of guaranteeing minority representation? Will geometry serve not only as a sword to condemn excessive reliance on race, but as a shield to protect an otherwise suspect racial classification?

The Court's attempt to create a *Bakke*-like standard may well prove more unstable in the new context than in previous incarnations in academic settings or in employment. In prior situations, there were neutral baselines by which the Court could appear to measure the extent of the preferences and their disruption to settled expectations. Thus, in college admissions racial preferences could be set against grades or scores on standardized tests to see the extent to which race was serving as a "plus". Similarly, in employment, prior measures of job performance or seniority or examination results could demarcate the extent of the racial preference to distinguish, at least in theory, race as "a" factor from race as "the" dispositive factor.

There is little support for a neutral baseline in redistricting. Even within the confines of one-person, one-vote the number of redistricting configurations in a large state such as California borders on the infinite. If *Shaw* is to have meaning as a working definition of permissible boundaries in redistricting, the lower federal courts will have to move in one of two directions. One possibility is to reify the concept of compactness by imposing absolute constraints on the shape districts may take. For years, various groups such as Common Cause have tried to devise compactness formulae to limit the amount of discretion available to state redistricting authorities. One example prohibits the creation of districts in which the aggregate length of the boundaries of all districts exceeds by more than five percent the aggregate length of all districts under any alternative plan. Such strategies would regiment the redistricting process and ultimately create a presumption of unconstitutionality whenever there are significant deviations from absolutely maximal compactness. The result would be the use of legal presumptions in much the same fashion as the one-person, one-vote rule works to create a presumption of invalidity in the case of population disparities between districts. The major problem, however, remains that unlike the Court's constitutionalization of the equipopulation principle, the Court in *Shaw* insisted that it was not seeking to make compactness an independent constitutional requirement.

Alternatively, *Shaw* could propel states to redistrict at some remove from the immediate demands of the political process—in effect to abandon the most traditional districting practices of all. This could take the form of either independent redistricting commissions or the nascent technology of computer-automated redistricting. In either case states could capitalize on the Court's apparent discomfort in *Shaw* with the *exclusive* use of race in creating the I-85 district. If race or some proxy for racially-defined communities could be one of the factors utilized by a redistricting authority, such as is the case in states such as Hawaii and Montana that assign redistricting to independent bodies, then race-dependent state decisions that do not use race as the "exclusive factor" to bring about minority representation would presumably not run afoul of *Shaw*. While it is unlikely that such independent redistricting bodies would create a district quite so convoluted as that in North Carolina, that may not be so significant for minority representation. Recall that a major impetus in the creation of the I-85 district appeared to be the desire to protect *white* incumbents in other parts of the state, an objective that would likely diminish in importance if redistricting is removed from partisan hands.

Finally, it is also entirely conceivable that *Shaw* will remain as an invitation to *ad hoc* judicial review of the political process. If so, each decade will inaugurate an impressionistic course of litigation following the developmental structure of the animal kingdom. While snake-like districts will clearly fall, "bug-splats" will stay on the margin and, conceivably, districts labeled amoebas or octopi may survive.

The Problem of Filler People

At a more fundamental level, *Shaw* really turns on the problems inherent in any process by which state entities assign the terms under which citizens will participate in the political process. Shaw rejects the restorative justice principle that race-consciousness to benefit historically disadvantaged groups is in itself a permissible state objective. *Shaw* then leads to a confrontation with voting rights law developed over the past twenty years for the reasons that follow.

The Voting Rights Act and the early constitutional voting cases of the 1960s successfully dismantled what have been termed the "first generation" of overt barriers to minority exercise of the franchise. This early struggle targeted the literacy tests, grandfather clauses, poll taxes, and voter registration barriers that served as the initial political armor of Jim Crow. As blacks began to exercise the franchise, a second layer of barriers emerged in the form of electoral systems that frustrated the electoral opportunities of minority-supported candidates and led to the "dilution" of minority electoral strength. It was the successes of this "second generation" of voting rights cases in dismantling at-large or multimember electoral systems and erecting single-member systems that created pressures toward districting not only in the legislative setting, but in smaller units of local governance as well, including city councils, county commissions, and school boards.

The impetus toward districting to promote minority representation then immersed the courts and the Department of Justice in the delicate task of determining the proper standards for ensuring minority voters a meaningful chance to elect representatives of their choice. On the one hand, if minorities are distributed among newly created single-member districts (or among congressional or legislative districts) in a more-or less even manner, then a districting system may be drawn to subordinate minorities mathematically within each of the electoral districts and effectively deny them the opportunity to elect any representatives of choice. For example, in a city that is 40 percent minority, little is accomplished by moving from at-large elections to single-member districts each of which is also 40 percent minority. If the same patterns of polarized voting that resulted in minority exclusion from representation in at-large elections persist, the shift from at-large to single-member districts can be expected to yield the same result in terms of the ethnic composition of elected representatives. The same processes of majority overrepresentation could be reproduced across even single-member districts in a large jurisdiction if the districting process resulted in a proportion of minorities in any given district lacking the critical mass for electoral success.

On the other hand, the overconcentration of minority voters, known in the trade as "packing," could similarly limit the opportunity for minority electoral representation. Take, for example, a city that is forty percent black, in which the creation of two seventy percent black city council districts would likely result in the election of two black city councilors. If the council districting lines were instead drawn to create one district that was one hundred percent black and another that was forty percent black, black voters would likely complain that their electoral influence had been diminished. Voting rights law seeks to steer districting officials away from the wasting of potential minority voting strength through either dilution or packing.

Lost in the shuffle, however, are persons assigned to such non-diluted/non-packed districts to balance out the numerical mandates of one-person, one-vote. Under current law, these additional individuals must not be of the relevant demographic group in order to avoid claims of packing, and should not be expected to compete in any genuine sense for electoral representation in the district to which they are assigned, lest they undo the redistricting assignment of that district to the specified minority group. It is the status of this precarious group, which I shall term the "filler people," that raises extraordinarily troubling problems under current voting rights jurisprudence. Indeed, it is the plight of the filler people to which the Court ultimately reacted in *Shaw*.

The Court's critique of redistricting in *Shaw* reopens the issues that appeared to have been resolved in 1977 in *United Jewish Organizations v. Carey*.[10] The *UJO* case involved the redistricting of Brooklyn state legislative districts so as to create an additional black majority district. The redistricting divided the Hasidic community of Williamsburgh, using a portion of that population to fill in the majority black district and to satisfy the equipopulation requirement for the reapportionment scheme as a whole. Responding to a lawsuit launched by the affected Hasidic community, the Supreme Court upheld the redistricting of Brooklyn on what in hindsight appear to be two different grounds.

First, the Court decided that the Voting Rights Act was not simply a remedial tool for proven willful violations of minority voting rights, but that it is also a device for redistributing political power to improve the lot of protected groups, particularly black voters. Under this theory, the conscious decision of the state redistricting authorities to augment the representation of previously underrepresented blacks could be sustained even where the jurisdiction in question did not wait to be affirmatively sued by black voters. Moreover, the Court reasoned that the racial element in redistricting cases was likely to be inescapable:

> Where it occurs, voting for or against a candidate because of his race is an unfortunate practice. But it is not rare; and in any district where it regularly happens, it is unlikely that any candidate will be elected who is a member of the race that is in the minority in that district. However disagreeable this result may be, there is no authority for the proposition that the candidates who are found racially unacceptable by the majority, and the minority voters supporting those candidates, have had their Fourteenth or Fifteenth Amendment rights infringed by this process. Their position is similar to that of the Democratic or Republican minority that is submerged year after year by the adherents to the majority party who tend to vote a straight party line.[11]

The second justification for the outcome in *UJO* is more problematic and presages many of the most controversial aspects of current voting rights law. According to the Supreme Court, the challenged districting plan did not have an adverse impact on white voters since by any analysis, whites would still control roughly their proportionate share of legislative districts—an approach expressly rejected in *Shaw*. Hence, in *UJO* the Supreme Court reasoned that "even if voting in the county oc-

---

10. 430 U.S. 144, 166–67 (1977).
11. 430 U.S. 144, 166–67 (1977).

curred strictly according to race, whites would not be underrepresented relative to their share of the population."[12] As should be apparent, the Court's baseline assumption in *UJO* was that the Hasidic community of Williamsburgh could take heart despite the dilution of its electoral power because it was "virtually represented"[13] in the state legislature by white Gentile legislators from other parts of Brooklyn or other parts of the state. Apart from the assumption that representatives from outside a community's electoral district could be counted on to advance the interests of that community, the Court also indulged in the highly troubling assumption that the Hasidim were, at bottom, an undifferentiated group of white people who were as likely to be well represented by elected officials from Italian or Norwegian areas of Brooklyn, or for that matter, by white politicians from upstate New York as by officials elected, at least in part, by the Hasidim themselves. Yet, it would be difficult to imagine a more "discrete and insular" minority than the Hasidim of Brooklyn to use the Supreme Court's traditional terms for those societal groups that should be afforded an extra measure of judicial protection from abusive political decisions.

To the extent that *Shaw* turns on the unseemliness of "essentialism,"— that is, state action based on the assumption that individuals will share outlooks and interests simply on the basis of a single characteristic, such as race—the opinion threatens to invalidate any district that creates a seat with an identified beneficiary based on anticipated voting patterns, be it a racially-or ethnically-defined seat or one created to protect the flanks of an incumbent politician. Nor does the Court's reliance on traditional districting principles resolve the increasingly explosive claims advanced by those assigned the role of providing numerical chaff to the representational wheat of another group. Such cases pose both the claim that such immersion violates some rights inherent to their community (the resurrection of the principal argument in *UJO*) and a second claim rejecting the purported adequacy of virtual representation by representatives not of their choosing. These arguments are made all the more volatile in the racial context by the tendency of proponents on each side to advance their claims in the language of entitlement, with representation assumed more as a grant to dispense patronage than to facilitate political self-expression.

A typical example arose with the creation of the last additional congressional district in Florida, although similar controversies have brewed

---

12. *Id.* at 166.

13. This is the term applied to the concept of representatives for whom one could not vote being assigned the job of serving as a surrogate representative. The most trenchant application of this concept comes from the now well-known writings of Professor Lani Guinier.

at the congressional and state legislative levels in Texas, New York City, and a number of other jurisdictions. In Florida, two alternative plans were contemplated: One would have created a district that would likely have elected a black to Congress; the other would have rearranged the lines to create an additional Hispanic seat. Each plan laid the foundation for the enhanced representation of one group by using the other as numerical filler. As the reapportionment battles in Florida heated up, the never quite amicable relations between black and Hispanic political leaders became increasingly frayed. According to one newspaper, some black spokespersons claimed a preferential stake on the last congressional seat on the grounds of being the group for whom the Voting Rights Act was truly intended. As one black state legislator commented, "If the basis of an extra minority seat is the Voting Rights Act, then we ought to look and see who it was standing on the Edmund Pettus Bridge in Selma getting trampled."[14] For their part, Hispanics countered that they were the most excluded group in terms of actual representation and that black interests were secured by, among other things, the depths of black political power in Atlanta.

Balkanization

The Court's concern with racial essentialism forces an unfortunate confrontation with voting rights law as it has developed through almost three decades of litigation. Unlike the other civil rights statutes, the Voting Rights Act is notably passive in its treatment of the core operational pattern that it addresses, once the issues of complete exclusion from the franchise are removed by the first generation cases. Specifically, the Act's strictures are triggered by the fact of racial bloc voting which, given otherwise nondiscriminatory electoral structures, defeat the electoral aspirations of the minority community. For reasons having to do with the nature of voting as a fundamental individual right, the Act makes no attempt to alter the underlying conduct. In the aftermath of a successful voting rights lawsuit, individual voters are as free to vote along racial lines as they were before. This sets the Voting Rights Act apart from statutes governing employment or housing discrimination. In those contexts, legal intervention is designed to break down patterns of workplace

---

14. Larry Rohter, *A Black-Hispanic Struggle Over Florida Redistricting*, NEW YORK TIMES, May 30, 1992, at A6 (quoting State Representative James C. Burke; the reference to Selma concerns the well-publicized beating of civil rights demonstrators on March 7, 1965, the broadcast of which garnered support for the passage of the Voting Rights Act).

or residential segregation. While the Voting Rights Act does seek to alter the consequences of such voting patterns in terms of the opportunity of minorities to elect candidates of choice to office, the primary conduct—the racial patterns in voting—is left unaffected.

The inability to address the primary conduct in claims of abridgment of voting rights stems directly from the complex quality of the right to vote. Whereas most civil rights in this country are defined in terms of state treatment of individuals, this model is of limited utility in the voting context. An individual's right to vote is, while indispensable, nonetheless of secondary value in defining a democratic electoral system. An individual citizen can be guaranteed only a right to go to the ballot box and cast a vote of roughly equal weight without needless encumbrances, such as a literacy test or a poll tax or overly burdensome registration requirements. At this level, however, there is little that distinguishes a democratic electoral system from a system that engages in show elections for predetermined outcomes, such as in the former Soviet Union.

Nor can the problem of identifying individual voting rights be packaged as the right to vote for a winning candidate. In any contested electoral system this condition cannot be satisfied. Some voters will fail to have their electoral preferences satisfied if elections are to have any meaning. Indeed, if the right to vote for a winning candidate were a genuine condition for democratic rule, the former Soviet Union would have the upper hand since all voters in a one-party election system are guaranteed the ability to vote for the winning candidate—and only the winning candidate.

Once the conditions of equal weight and access to the ballot are satisfied, there is little in the way of individual rights that concerns the electoral process. Attention must at this point shift to group rights to differentiate a fair from an unfair system. It is only as collective partisans of the same political preference, be it defined by party or race or any other measure, that voters can assert rights of meaningful participation in the political process. Once the collective quality of the right surfaces, however, there emerges the compounding problem of identifying the groups that are entitled to claim such rights. In the individual context this problem is relatively straightforward. The ballot is guaranteed to all citizens who meet rules of simple application, such as age and residency requirements. No such rule of simple application exists with regard to the determination of which groups merit representation. At some point, some state authority is going to have to determine which group controls a district and which group does not.

The inability of the Voting Rights Act to reach the primary act of racially defined voting patterns gives rise to a paradox. The Act recognizes protected rights of participation for only one characteristic, race, and only under one condition, where there is no substantial integration. Under the test for liability set forth in *Thornburg v. Gingles*, the threshold requirement for a minority group seeking the protection of the courts is to establish that under a single-member districting plan it could create its own district in which it could constitute a majority of the voting age population. This has the effect of protecting those minority communities that are most segregated residentially, and leaving the more geographically integrated communities without access to any remedy should they also suffer routine defeat of their candidates of choice. This feature of voting rights litigation was picked up by Justice O'Connor in *Shaw* through her argument that race-conscious remedies in the electoral arena may actually promote balkanization.

Although *Shaw* fails to explicate this point, the Act as currently interpreted is incomplete, if not defective, for reasons both descriptive and normative. As a descriptive matter, implementation of the Act suffers from a failure to incorporate the features of an increasingly multihued society. While blacks are still remarkably segregated throughout American society, the presumption of geographically-confined minorities is less justified for Hispanics or Asians, particularly those outside the ranks of first-generation immigrants. As a result, voting rights claims seeking to satisfy the first prong of the *Gingles* test—the ability to create a "majority-minority" district—are increasingly being brought in the name of more than one minority group, aggregated so as to achieve the numerical threshold established by *Gingles*. This leads to two separate problems. First, these aggregated claims are subject to the charge that they merely seek statutory reinforcement of coalition-building as opposed to protection against racial exclusion from political life.[15] Second, while these aggregate districts may have distinct political lives from the broader nonminority community, this distinctiveness does not necessarily translate into internal political coherence. Blacks and Hispanics often have very different political agendas, as is clearly evident in the current Florida redistricting battles, and these differences may surface as well where competing Latino communities are combined, as with the creation of a Chicago Hispanic congressional seat comprised of distinct Mexican-American and Puerto Rican communities.

At a more fundamental level, the focus on districting limits the transformative aspirations of political integration. One of the aims of broadening political participation was to open the halls of elective office to representatives of and from the diverse communities that make up American society.

---

15. This charge is raised most vociferously by Judge Patrick Higginbotham of the Fifth Circuit. *See Campos v. City of Baytown*, 849 F.2d 943 (5th Cir. 1988)(Higginbotham, J., dissenting from denial of rehearing en banc).

If such integration of elective office is an independent good, a goal that merits promotion in a democratic society, then the narrow focus on geographically isolated districts is at the very least problematic. To the extent that a minority community integrates residentially, the potential benefits of the Voting Rights Act are withdrawn, regardless whether the first stages of integration have been accompanied by political advancement. Moreover, to the extent that the core minority area may very well be marked by depressed socio-economic levels, and to the extent that more educated and technically skilled members of the minority community may be found outside the core minority area, the focus on geographic representation removes a cadre of potentially skilled advocates from the minority group's political base, as geographically defined by *Gingles*. The importance of access to leadership—the group that W.E.B. DuBois termed the "talented tenth"—should not be disregarded as a cost of districting. As Arthur Schlesinger, Jr. recently noted in *The New York Review of Books*, "All government known to history has been government by minorities, and it is in the interests of everyone, most especially the poor and powerless, to have the governing minority composed of able, intelligent, responsive, and decent persons with a large view of the general welfare."[16]

This in turn leads to the third major issue awaiting on the voting rights horizon: the entire premise of virtual representation and the ongoing pressures for proportionality as the measure of political fairness. At a fundamental level, the conceptual difficulty with *UJO* turns on the idea of assigning the right to representation to one community but not another. The Court in *Shaw* is ultimately responding to this problem, presented in a particularly crude and visually graphic form. In the process of assigning representation, an external authority such as a state redistricting body is determining how access to electoral power will be allocated. To the non-minorities in a designated minority district, or to those minorities not of the group expected to determine representation—the fillers in the district—representation over district-specific issues is to be delegated to representatives about whose selection they will likely have little say. On broader policy matters external to the district, the assumption is that their interests will be represented by elected officials from elsewhere, as was posited by the Supreme Court in *UJO*. For minorities of the designated ethnic group but not living in that group's district, say blacks living outside a core inner city neighborhood, the presumption must be that their interests will effectively be served by representatives elected from the core neighborhood for whom they cannot vote and with whom they may share neither socio-economic status nor political outlook.

---

16. Arthur Schlesinger, Jr., "The Radical," THE NEW YORK REVIEW OF BOOKS, February 11, 1993, at 6.

Dissatisfaction with districting patterns becomes most acute each ten years when legislators bowing to a variety of political pressures create oddly-shaped districts such as the bar-bell district in Chicago or the I-85 district in North Carolina. One of the responses is to try to cabin the clear manipulation of the redistricting process by imposing compactness constraints on the process or by elevating geographic proximity to be the primary concern in redistricting. While *Shaw* gave a significant boost to such constricting principles for redistricting, the Court was careful not to elevate these concerns to the level of constitutional principles.

The focus on geographic proximity in districting emerges from a time when communities were smaller and transportation more difficult. While tortured district lines may make it more difficult for individual citizens to identify their representatives, the problem goes beyond simply the compactness of the district. In today's society, lines of affiliation may be more markedly affected by proximity to an interstate or the common use of one shopping mall as opposed to another. But the concept of "geographical coherence" has far less meaning in a technologically-sophisticated society. The Census demographic data reveal a highly fluid society in which changes of residence are far from unexpected and in which the growth of "exurbs" defined by proximity to the highway networks have replaced any preexisting sense of geography.

Neighborhood identity has always been subject to manipulation in order to reap the benefits of political linedrawing. On the other hand, there is increasing attention to the issue of geography not for its own sake, but as a check on the increasingly naked use of governmental power to dispense electoral patronage through the redistricting process. It is the visual image of the gerrymander, from the "uncouth" figure in *Gomillion* to the "bug splattered on a windshield" description of the districts under review in *Shaw*, that suggest a districting system run amok, even though in the last round of redistricting many of the most "creatively" drawn districts were those designed to benefit dispersed minority communities.

The real issue is not "community" or "geography" but the inherent unseemliness of using governmental power to draw lines that are expressly designed to confer power to one group and suppress another. The problem is compounded by the narrowness of the categories that give rise to geographic districting. There are many forms of political self-identification, some of which may indeed be an individual's primary political affiliation, that are not readily reducible to the narrow confines of a geographic district. Such identity may turn on environmental issues, foreign policy concerns, or feminist causes, to name but a few in which geographic concentrations are unlikely. Under the Voting Rights Act, providing representation through geographically-based districting served best as the primary response to the complete exclusion of a severely segregated black community from any form of local representation. Thus, in communities such as Mobile, Alabama, or Jackson, Mississippi, one found a pattern of complete exclusion of blacks from city council positions, in towns with significant black populations, easily clustered in districts in which the vast majority of the local black population could be fitted. On the other hand, the more diverse and dispersed the local population, as with multiethnic communities, or the less legislative the office in question, as with the election of state court judges, the more ill-suited the districting remedy.

One response to the realization of these problems has been renewed attention to non-districted concepts of representation, both as remedial tools in voting rights litigation and as a more substantively fair mechanism of allocating electoral power. The basic insight is that all districting necessarily imposes an ordering of permissible electoral alliances based on the geographic proximity of the individuals who are to be aggregated into the district. Non-districted elections, on the other hand, allow individuals to aggregate themselves according to interests that are of moment to them, be those interests territorially centered or rooted in some ideological stance. This then leads to the critical question. If the problem with district-based elections is that they restrict the ability of voters to choose how to aggregate on whatever basis is important to them, what is to prevent individuals who are free to aggregate as they wish from coming together on the basis of racial identity and replicating the pattern of minority exclusion from elective office that prompted the second generation of voting rights challenges?

This question may not be intractable, for it turns out that there are a number of voting mechanisms that can both allow intermediate groups to form based on voter self-identification and at the same time prevent the complete capture of all representation by a strongly-motivated, racial majority voting bloc. Two of the most promising of these systems use modified at-large elections, termed semi-proportional election systems by political scientists, that alter some of the voting rules to preclude majority tyranny at the polls. These systems came into national prominence during the controversy surrounding the failed nomination of Lani Guinier as Assistant Attorney General for Civil Rights. One method is called limited voting; the other, cumulative voting. Both modify the way in which a voter may cast votes, as the following example illustrates.

In a five-member city council election under at-large voting, each voter is allowed to cast one vote for each of the five positions to be filled. Because the election turns into a sequence of single elections for each position, the same voting majority controls the outcome in each election and thereby reproduces its preference for each council position. Districting systems cure this problem by allowing each voter to elect only one of the five council members by restricting each voter's participation to one designated electoral subdistrict. The same result of depriving a majority of the opportunity to exercise a monopoly on representation may be achieved within the at-large system, so as to avoid some of the problems with districting described above.

Limited voting accomplishes this by allowing each voter to vote across the entire slate of candidates for office, but to cast fewer votes than there are positions to be filled. Thus, voting is "limited" in the sense that each voter casts fewer votes than the total number of open positions. Each voter is still allowed to pass on each candidate in that electoral district. Each voter would be permitted, for instance, to vote for only three candidates for five city council positions. The limited voting system therefore preserves the accountability of each candidate to all voters in the district but takes away from a cohesive majority voting bloc the ability to have its candidates fill all the contested offices.[17]

The same benefits can be obtained through cumulative voting, a common form of corporate governance. Cumulative voting shares with limited voting the ability to allow greater minority participation within a multi-member district election system. The difference is that in cumulative voting each voter is given a number of votes equal to the positions to be filled. Thus, if there were five city council positions to be filled, each voter would have five votes. Each voter would then be allowed to concentrate his or her votes (also referred to as "plumping" or "bulleting") among the candidates in any fashion desired. A voter could cast one vote for each of five candidates, five votes for only one candidate, three for one candidate and two for another, or any other aggregation chosen by the voter.[18]

While there are real benefits to districted election systems, most no-

---

17. The amount of support necessary for a group of voters to achieve electoral success is expressed as the threshold of exclusion. If the number of votes each voter may cast is divided by the number of votes each voter may cast plus the number of seats to be filled, the threshold can be calculated. For example, if each voter could cast three ballots in a five seat election the threshold of exclusion would be 3/8 or 37.5 percent. This means that any candidate getting over 37.5 percent of the votes could not be denied election whatever the configuration of remaining votes. This in turn means that any candidate who is the choice of 37.5 percent of the voters would be elected. This contrasts with the current multimember election districts in which candidates of choice of 49 percent of the voters may be defeated if the majority 51 percent bloc votes cohesively for a slate of candidates. The threshold of exclusion can be raised or lowered by the number of votes given to each voter.

18. Cumulative voting shares with limited voting the feature of a mathematically obtainable "threshold of exclusion" that would identify the voting patterns necessary for a cohesive minority to guarantee the selection of at least one of its candidates. Unlike limited voting, however, the "threshold of exclusion" in cumulative voting is at least in part dependent on the level of organization of voters to insure that they maximize the return on their votes.

tably the individual accountability of representatives to an easily identifiable constituency, there are also significant drawbacks. Once the door is opened to considerations of impermissible essentialism by state bodies, or the unseemliness of the cruder forms of state line-drawing, it is unclear whether the Court can stop short of inviting a re-examination of the premises of districts. The logic of *Shaw* reaches far into the construction of the building blocks of the American political order. The renewed interest in alternative voting systems, particularly in cases involving state courts or other non-legislative bodies, reflects the desire to preserve and extend the integrative effects of voting rights law while challenging the effectiveness of district-based elections in providing the most wide-open, robust mechanisms for political participation.

Pandora's Box

There is nothing quite so destructive to the legitimacy of a representative political system as a challenge to the integrity of the process by which representatives are chosen. The Court in *Shaw* attempted to preserve institutional legitimacy by questioning what it viewed as perhaps an excessively wanton manipulation of traditional forms of political accommodation. This attempt at surgical repair is problematic for several reasons. In the first place, it is unclear whether the problems underlying the Court's discomfiture are quite so readily confined to the excesses rather than the essence of districting. Second, to the extent that the problems of essentialism and state manipulation are inherent to the districting process, the Court is vulnerable to the charge that it was willing to tolerate the inescapable evils of districting until minorities developed sufficient political clout to claim their spoils as well. This, then, raises a serious point of institutional integrity for the Supreme Court, especially since the effect of its ruling in *Shaw* was to strike down a congressional district that elected only the second North Carolina African American to Congress since Reconstruction. In the absence of any real content to the Court's repeated invocation of the "traditional principles of districting," there remains the gnawing impression that the rules of the game were changed only when minorities started to figure out how to play.

Part III

ALTERNATIVE SYSTEMS OF REPRESENTATION

CHAPTER 8

Groups, Representation, and Race-Conscious Districting: A Case of the Emperor's Clothes

Lani Guinier[*]

> [N]ow that the first round of reapportionment has been accomplished, there is need to talk "one man-one vote" a little less and to talk a little more of "political equity," and of functional components of effective representation. *A mathematically equal vote which is politically worthless because of gerrymandering or winner-take-all districting is as deceiving as "emperor's clothes."*[1]

With voices pitched in the high decibel range, critics of race-conscious districting[2] are blasting the Voting Rights Act[3] and its 1982 amendments.

---

[*] Reprinted with the permission of The Free Press, a division of Simon & Schuster, from THE TYRANNY OF THE MAJORITY: FUNDAMENTAL FAIRNESS IN REPRESENTATIVE DEMOCRACY, by Lani Guinier. Copyright © 1994 by Lani Guinier. I thank all those who read this article and encouraged me to pursue my ideas, despite the apparent political costs. I greatly benefitted from my participation in the November 1992 University of Texas School of Law Symposium on Redistricting; in the September 1992 American Political Science Association Annual Meeting, Chicago, Illinois; and in the October 1992 Legal Studies Workshop at the University of Minnesota Law School. For their particularly valuable comments and criticisms, I thank Alex Aleinikoff, Phil Frickey, Sam Issacharoff, Pamela Karlan, Randy Kennedy, Dan Lowenstein, Frank Michelman, Rick Pildes, Susan Sturm, Gerald Torres, and Larry Tribe. Ann Bartow, Anthony Gay, and Robert Tintner provided very helpful research assistance.

1. ROBERT G. DIXON, JR., DEMOCRATIC REPRESENTATION: REAPPORTIONMENT IN LAW AND POLITICS 22 (1968) (emphasis added).

2. I use the term "race-conscious districting" to describe the practice of consolidating the number of minority group members in a single or a few winner-take-all subdistricts. Yet, in a racially polarized environment, the process of districting is inevitably race-conscious. *See* Lani Guinier, *The Representation of Minority Interests: The Question of Single-Member Districts*, 14 CARDOZO L. REV. 1135, 1135 n.2 (1993) (arguing that winner-take-all districts ultimately enable one group or another to dominate, meaning there is a racial consequence to the demographic constitution of all racially mixed districts if voting is racially polarized). *See also infra* notes 116–117 and accompanying text.

3. 42 U.S.C. §§ 1971–1974 (1988).

A recent *Wall Street Journal* headline declares that voting is now "rigged by race."[4] Ethnic activists, the writer asserts, are collaborating with GOP operatives in an unholy political alliance to herd minorities into their own convoluted urban districts in order to improve GOP prospects in majority white suburban areas.[5] According to such critics, this is a "political one-night stand" made possible by misguided federal courts and Department of Justice officials construing the 1982 Act to create majority minority districts, the newest form of "racial packaging."[6]

My students inform me that Cokie Roberts, as part of ABC News's election night coverage, dramatically illustrated the concerns of critics when she traced on a map of the Chicago area the "earmuff" district, allegedly carved out of two noncontiguous Chicago neighborhoods joined by a narrow rod to maximize the possibility that the Latino residents would be able to elect a representative of their choice to Congress.[7] And in June 1993, the Supreme Court discovered a new constitutional right enabling white voters in North Carolina to challenge, based on its odd and irregular shapes, a "highway" district that narrowly tracks the path of an interstate, creating a swatch of voters on either side of the highway from one end of the state to the other.[8] This fifty-four percent black district, the most integrated in the state, elected Melvin Watt, one of the first two blacks elected to Congress from that state in this century.[9]

---

4. Jim Sleeper, *Rigging the Vote by Race*, WALL ST. J., Aug. 4, 1992, at A14. Sleeper admits he has taken many of his ideas about the Voting Rights Act from ABIGAIL M. THERNSTROM, WHOSE VOTES COUNT? (1987). *Id.*

5. Sleeper, *supra* note 4, at A14.

6. *Id.*

7. *See ABC News Special: The '92 Vote* (ABC television broadcast, Nov. 3, 1992), *available in* LEXIS, CMPGN Library, ABCNEW File. It may be worth noting for the record that Ms. Roberts's mother, Lindey Boggs, was arguably "redistricted" out of a seat in Congress in response to a successful lawsuit under the Voting Rights Act. *See* Major v. Treen, 574 F. Supp. 325 (E.D. La. 1983).

8. *See* Shaw v. Reno, 113 S. Ct. 2816, 2828 (1993) ("For these reasons, we conclude that a plaintiff challenging a reapportionment statute under the Equal Protection Clause may state a claim by alleging that the legislation, though race-neutral on its face, rationally cannot be understood as anything other than an effort to separate voters into different jurisdictions on the basis of race, and that the separation lacks sufficient justification.").

9. Major Garrett, *Frosh Planning to Clean House*, WASH. TIMES, Nov. 22, 1992, at A1, *available in* LEXIS, Nexis Library, WTIMES File; *see* Kenneth J. Cooper, *New Member Seen Boosting Urban Caucus*, WASH. POST, Nov. 13, 1992, at A11. I use the term "integrated" to describe a racial composition close to 50% black and 50% white.

The Voting Rights Act codified the right of protected minority groups to an equal opportunity to elect candidates of their choice, although its language disclaims the right to racial representation by members of the racial group in direct proportion to population.[10] The critics now claim this is special and unwarranted protection for racial and language minority groups.[11] In the name of liberal individualism, these critics assert that the statute effected a radical transformation in the allocation and nature of representation.[12]

Although race-conscious districting[13] is their apparent target, these critics have fixed their aim on a deeper message—that pressing claims of racial identity and racial disadvantage diminishes democracy. We all lose, the theory goes, when some of us identify in racial or ethnic group terms.[14]

In my view, critics of race-conscious districting have misdirected their fire. Their emperor has no clothes. Their dissatisfaction with racial-group representation ignores the essentially group nature of political participation. In this regard, the critics fail to confront directly the group nature of representation itself, especially in a system of geographic districting. Perhaps unwittingly, they also reveal a bias toward the representation of a particular racial group rather than their discomfort with group representation itself.[15] In a society as deeply cleaved by issues of racial identity as ours, there is no one race.[16] In the presence of such

---

10. See 42 U.S.C. § 1973(b) (1988) (prohibiting representation where racial groups are given "less opportunity than other members of the electorate to participate").

11. See, e.g., THERNSTROM, supra note 4, at 237–38 (arguing that efforts to compensate for every potential source of inequality can only lead to a covert system of reserved seats comparable to India's system for caste representation).

12. See JIM SLEEPER, THE CLOSEST OF STRANGERS 159 (1990) ("Liberals and black civil rights activists thus shifted from demanding equality of individual opportunity which entails color-blind respect for a person's merits and rights beneath the skin, to demanding equality of condition, which submerges individual dignity beneath a color-based emphasis on the putative 'rights' of historically deprived ethnic groups.").

13. See supra note 2.

14. See Sleeper, supra note 4, at A14.

15. This is essentially the argument that there is a dominant "culture of whiteness" that is a unifying—even if unconscious—experience for some and an exclusionary experience for those who are not white. See Patricia J. Williams, Metro Broadcasting, Inc. v. FCC: Regrouping in Singular Times, 104 HARV. L. REV. 525, 529–31 (1990).

16. Cf. Lena Williams, Blacks Reject Gay Rights Fight as Equal to Theirs, N.Y. TIMES, June 28, 1993, at A1, A10 (quoting Andrew Hacker, professor of political science and author of TWO NATIONS: BLACK AND WHITE, SEPARATE, HOSTILE, UNEQUAL, as saying that "[b]y every measure I have seen, race runs deeper and does more damage than any other bias").

Many recent court decisions document the racial tension that exists in this country. *See, e.g.*, Lac du Flambeau Band of Lake Superior Chippewa Indians v. Stop Treaty Abuse—Wisconsin, Inc., 991 F.2d 1249, 1254 (7th Cir. 1993) (stating that race pervaded a conflict between Native Americans and Wisconsin residents over fishing rights, with Wisconsin protestors "hurl[ing] vile racial insults" and mocking "Indian culture and traditions"); Cella v. United States, 1993 U.S. App. LEXIS 15124 (7th Cir. 1993) (finding that a sailor experienced emotional stress arising out of racial tensions on board ship); Holthaus v. Board of Educ., 986 F.2d 1044, 1045 (6th Cir. 1993) (recounting the history of racial tension and race relations problems at a Cincinnati-area high school where the football coach was dismissed for telling the team that they were "starting to act like a bunch of niggers"); Woods v. Graphic Communications, 925 F.2d 1195 (9th Cir. 1991) (upholding the district court's finding that Woods, a worker at a packaging plant, was subject to racial hostility and physical abuse and that the Graphic Communications Union intentionally failed to take any action to alleviate the problem).

Recent articles in newspapers across the nation detail the depth and extent of these tensions. *See, e.g.*, Adelle M. Banks, *Pastor Shows His True Faith in Integration; New Hope Community Church Leaders Practiced What They Preached by Moving to Eatonville and Offering Services That Appeal to Many Cultures*, ORLANDO SENTINEL, June 27, 1993, at B1 (relating the observation by clergy that cross-cultural churches often revert to one culture after struggling with racial tensions); Dennis Duggan, *Shrug Is City's Bomb Shelter*, NEWSDAY (Long Island, N.Y.), June 29, 1993, at 18 (describing New York as a city that is "living at the edge of explosive racial tensions"); Shelley Emling, *Parrish Says He's Paying Dues To Run for Governor*, ATLANTA CONST., July 2, 1993, EXTRA, at A3 (mentioning attempts by a state senator to diffuse racial tension in Lincoln County, Georgia, after allegations were made that children were segregated on school buses); Denise Hamilton, *Tension Between Asian and Latino Students in the Alhambra School District Has Climbed to a Fever Pitch. Occasional Violence Has Officials Scrambling to Bridge Racial Rifts on Campus*, L.A. TIMES, June 10, 1993, at J1 (describing racial tensions between Asian and Latino students in the Alhambra, California school district); John Hiscock, *Mushroom Rustlers Shoot It Out*, DAILY TELEGRAPH (London), July 1, 1993, at 14 (stating that much of the tension sparking war among Oregon's rare mushroom pickers is racial); Sari Horwitz, *No Reprieve for Schools*, WASH. POST, June 16, 1993, at A1, A29 (describing a hearing leading up to the recommendation to close 40 Washington, D.C. schools that pitted neighborhoods against neighborhoods in a painful public display of racial and socioeconomic tensions); Melanie Lewis, *Teachers Cite Woes in Poll*, DALLAS MORNING NEWS, June 11, 1993, at 34A (noting that 40% of Texas teachers identify student gangs, racial tensions, and drug abuse as significant problems); Larry Rohter, *As Hispanic Presence Grows, So Does Black Anger*, N.Y. TIMES, June 20, 1993, at 1, 27 (discussing the growing economic, racial, and ethnic barriers between blacks and hispanics in Miami); Leonel Sanchez, *Racial Tensions Simmering in Ramona*, SAN DIEGO UNION-TRIBUNE, June 13, 1993, at B1 (reporting the racial tensions brewing at a San Diego area high school); *Selma City Council Soon to Show Black Majority* (NPR radio broadcast, June 16, 1993) (observing that racial conflict in Selma, Alabama is far from over); Richard Simon, *Anglo Vote Carried Riordan to Victory*, L.A. TIMES, June 10, 1993, at A25 (indicating poll among voters in Los Angeles mayoral race showed deep racial divisions); Mary Lynn Smith, *The*

racial differences, a system of representation that fails to provide group representation loses legitimacy.[17]

Yet these critics have, in fact, accurately identified a problem with a system of representation based on winner-take-all territorial districts. There is an emperor wearing his clothes, but not as they describe. Rather than expressing a fundamental failure of democratic theory based on group representation per se, the critics have identified a problem with one particular solution. It is districting in general—not race-conscious districting in particular—that is the problem.

Winner-take-all territorial districting imperfectly distributes representation based on group attributes and disproportionately rewards those who win the representational lottery. Territorial districting uses an aggregating rule that inevitably groups people by virtue of some set of externally observed characteristics such as geographic proximity or racial identity. In addition, the winner-take-all principle inevitably wastes some votes. The dominant group within the district gets all the power; the votes of supporters of nondominant groups or of disaffected voters within the dominant group are wasted. Their votes lose significance because they are consistently cast for political losers.

The essential unfairness of districting is a result, therefore, of two assumptions: (1) that a majority of voters within a given geographic community can be configured to constitute a "group"; and (2) that incumbent politicians, federal courts, or some other independent set of actors can fairly determine which group to advantage by giving it all the power

---

Long Arm of the Law Gets Some Feet As Well, STAR TRIBUNE (Minneapolis), June 12, 1993, at 1B (quoting a city council member as saying that there are "racial and people tensions" in a St. Paul, Minnesota neighborhood); Jason Vest, *Pushing Buttons on the Phone*, WASH. POST, June 24, 1993, at C1 (describing calls "in which phone pranksters pose as Asian social workers and play off the bigotry of residents in Garden Grove, Calif., a community wrought with racial tension"); Dean K. Wong, *4 Arraigned in Fight at S. Boston Project*, BOSTON GLOBE, June 30, 1993, at 23 (stating that racial tensions at a Boston housing development increased after black and white students clashed outside South Boston High School); Iris Yokoi, *Rights Panel to Focus on L.A. Strife*, L.A. TIMES, June 13, 1993, City Times section, at 3 (announcing that the U.S. Commission on Civil Rights was convening public hearings to discuss racial and ethnic tensions in Los Angeles as part of the Commission's nationwide investigation into what federal officials call a "resurgence of racial and ethnic tensions in the United States" over the past ten years); Lee Hancock & Doris Quan, *Corsicana Rally by KKK Sparks Fights; Five Arrested*, DALLAS MORNING NEWS, June 20, 1993, at 1A (reporting that a Ku Klux Klan rally spawned fistfights and shouting matches between blacks and whites).

17. By legitimacy I mean the perception that the process is fair, even from the perspective of adversely affected parties.

within the district. When either of these assumptions is not accurate, as is most often the case, the districting is necessarily unfair.

Another effect of these assumptions is gerrymandering, which results from the arbitrary allocation of disproportionate political power to one group.[18] Districting breeds gerrymandering as a means of allocating group benefits; the operative principle is deciding whose votes get wasted. Whether it is racially or politically motivated, gerrymandering is the inevitable by-product of an electoral system that aggregates people by virtue of assumptions about their group characteristics and then inflates the winning group's power by allowing it to represent *all* voters in a regional unit.

Given a system of winner-take-all territorial districts and working within the limitations of this particular election method, the courts have sought to achieve political fairness for racial minorities. As a result, there is some truth to the assertion that minority groups, unlike other voters, enjoy a special representational relationship under the Voting Rights Act's 1982 amendments to remedy their continued exclusion

---

18. By this definition, the majority in *Shaw* misuses the term gerrymandering to describe a 54% black district that, as the majority concedes, was drawn to remedy a century of racial exclusion and that, as the majority also acknowledges, did not arbitrarily enhance or diminish the political power of any group. *See* Shaw v. Reno, 113 S. Ct. 2816, 2824, 2832 (1993) (mentioning North Carolina's checkered race-relations past and noting that the plaintiffs did not claim that the redistricting would lead to the dilution of the European-American vote). Calling the district a racial gerrymander is simply inaccurate since it does not "arbitrarily allocate disproportionate political power" to any group. As the majority recognizes, all districting takes race into account. *Id.* at 2826. Thus, this district, by its very terms, did nothing more than take race into account to create a racially competitive or racially integrated district. Its offense, to the extent the Court identifies the nature of the new constitutional injury, was that its "bizarre" shape was aesthetically unappealing to white voters and "stigmatizing" to black voters. *Id.* at 2824–25. Although Justice O'Connor thundered against "political apartheid," the claim that the district separated voters by race is not supported by the district's own racial composition, which is the most integrated district in the state. *Id.* at 2827; *see supra* note 9.

In terms of aesthetics, O'Connor is quite correct that drawn on a map, the shape of the district is "bizarre." *Id.* But the relevant inquiry is not the district's shape but its feel: does it reflect an effort to connect voters who have a relevant community of interests? *Cf.* Dillard v. Baldwin County Bd. of Educ., 686 F. Supp. 1459 (M.D. Ala. 1988) (concluding that a district is sufficiently compact if it has a "sense of community"). The evidence in this case and others demonstrates that blacks in North Carolina are politically cohesive. Thus, the evidence of persistent racial bloc voting and racial appeals in North Carolina means that it is not an assumption, but a fact, that blacks function as a racial as well as a political group. To call this fact a racial stereotype takes all meaning from the term, which is about prejudging, not observing.

from effective political participation in some jurisdictions. But the proper response is not to deny minority voters that protection. The answer should be to extend that special relationship to *all* voters by endorsing *the equal opportunity to vote for a winning candidate* as a universal principle of political fairness.

I use the term "one-vote, one-value" to describe the principle of political fairness that as many votes as possible should count in the election of representatives.[19] One-vote, one-value is realized when everyone's vote counts for someone's election. The only system with the potential to realize this principle for *all* voters is one in which the unit of representation is political rather than regional, and the aggregating rule is proportionality rather than winner-take-all. Semiproportional systems, such as cumulative voting, can approximate the one-vote, one-value principle by minimizing the problem of wasted votes.

One-vote, one-value systems transcend the gerrymandering problem because each vote has an equal worth independent of decisions made by those who drew district lines. Votes are allocated based on decisions made by the voters themselves. These systems revive the connection between voting and representation, whether the participant consciously associates with a group of voters or chooses to participate on a fiercely individual basis. Candidates are elected in proportion to the intensity of their political support within the electorate itself rather than as a result of decisions made by incumbent politicians or federal courts once every ten years.[20]

My project in this Paper is to defend the representation of racial groups while reconsidering whether race-conscious districting is the most effective way of representing these groups or their interests.[21] My claim

---

19. *See* U.P. Auerbach, *The Reapportionment Cases: One Person, One Vote—One Vote, One Value*, 1964 SUP. CT. REV. 1, 55, 56. One-vote, one-value means each voter should enjoy the opportunity to vote for someone who gets elected. Each voter should be able to choose, by the way she casts her votes, who represents her.

20. A recent example is Chilton County, Alabama, where the first Republican and the first black were elected to the county commission when the county implemented a modified at-large system of election using cumulative voting. Jim Yardley, *1 Voter, 7 Votes? County Boosts Minority Clout*, ATLANTA J. & CONST., Oct. 23, 1992, at G5. Because the balance of power on the commission is now closely divided between white Republicans and white Democrats, even if voting is racially polarized the black Democrat may become an influential swing vote.

21. By representation of racial groups, I do not mean to suggest that only members of a group can represent its interests, that members of a group are necessarily racially similar, or that racial group members are necessarily homogeneous in thinking or interest. *See infra* note 123 and accompanying text.

is that racial-group representation is important, but it is only imperfectly realized through an electoral system based on territorial districting or through the limited concept of racially "descriptive" representation.[22]

In Part I, I describe current doctrinal approaches, such as the jurisprudence of one-person, one-vote, on which some critics of race-conscious districting rely to emphasize the individual rather than the group nature of voting. I suggest that the one-person, one-vote doctrine is consistent with both group and individual conceptions of voting, but in the context of winner-take-all territorial districting, it is a limited principle of political equality. In Part II, I argue that racial-group representation is a natural response to historical and current reality, but it is one best realized in electoral systems employing proportional or semiproportional aggregating rules. Proportional or semiproportional aggregating rules are primarily a proxy for the aspirational concept of procedural or political fairness.[23] In such systems, the unit of representation is political rather than regional, and almost all votes count in the election of officials. In this way, systems such as cumulative voting are consistent with principles of both one-person, one-vote *and* one-vote, one-value.

In contrast to winner-take-all districting systems, cumulative voting may—in appropriate, fact-specific circumstances—be an expedient, and more politically fair, election method. Cumulative voting promotes a concept of racial group identity that is interest-based rather than biological.[24] In light of the controversy surrounding race-conscious districting,

---

22. Descriptive representation defines representation as based solely on representative physical characteristics or representative identity. It does not envision an interactive or a dynamic view of the representational relationship. *Cf. infra* notes 106–15 and accompanying text.

23. *See infra* notes 168–74 and accompanying text. I employ the term "proportional" to mean fairness rather than an unduly numerical or strictly quantitative measure of political equality. *See* Lani Guinier, *No Two Seats: The Elusive Quest for Political Equality*, 77 Va. L. Rev. 1413, 1459 n.170 (1991) (finding the "spirit of the proportionality principle" in my son's conclusion that the proper result of a four-to-two vote against hide-and-seek in favor of tag is that "[t]hey will play both," tag coming first).

24. In this sense I take issue with Judge Chapman's dissent in Collins v. City of Norfolk, 883 F.2d 1232, 1244–51 (4th Cir. 1989) (Chapman, J., dissenting), *cert. denied*, 498 U.S. 938 (1990). Judge Chapman suggests that vote dilution, which he defines exclusively in terms of electoral access, has nothing to do with the *ideas* of certain candidates. For him, "[r]epresentativeness in a Voting Rights context concerns access, and it does not create a right to the representation of certain ideologies." *Id.* at 1246. Chapman seems to suggest that ideological representation necessarily requires a "political litmus test" of minority-preferred candidates in which "there are 'proper' black political attitudes, and therefore under the Voting Rights Act some ideas are worth more than others." *Id.*

where circumstances dictate, it is at least worth considering this alternative, thereby attempting to tailor the emperor with some real clothes by putting the principles of political equality into practice.

I.

For many liberal reformers, the one-person, one-vote principle is politically fair because its ideal of universal suffrage incorporates the respect due and the responsibilities owed to each citizen in a democracy.[25] The one-person, one-vote cases attempt to equalize the purely formal opportunity to cast a ballot through a system of population-based apportionment.[26] Under this rationale, each district contains approximately the same number of people; each person within the district has the same opportunity to vote for someone to represent the district; and each district representative represents the same number of constituents.

The one-person, one-vote principle thus assures all voters the right to cast a theoretically equal ballot. In this Part, I argue that this theoretical possibility is unlikely to be realized in an electoral system using winner-take-all districts. I further suggest that neither groups of voters nor individuals are fairly represented under such a system.

There are two issues at stake. One raises the question of whether voting is constitutionally protected because it implicates individual rights. If voting is an individual right, the second question asks whether the one-person, one-vote principles that operate within the confines of geographic districts adequately protect the right to vote. I concede that voting has garnered its highest constitutional protection when presented as an individual rights issue, but the widespread use of winner-take-all dis-

---

The one-vote, one-value standard does employ a political rather than a racial litmus test, but it allows the voters themselves to determine, at each election, what political attitudes they want represented.

25. *See* Sanford Levinson, *Gerrymandering and the Brooding Omnipresence of Proportional Representation: Why Won't It Go Away?*, 33 UCLA L. REV. 257, 263 (1985) ("The liberal side is manifested by [Chief Justice Warren's] statement that '[t]he right to vote freely for the candidate of one's choice is the essence of a democratic society, and any restrictions on that right strike at the heart of representative government.'" (quoting Reynolds v. Sims, 377 U.S. 533, 555 (1964))).

26. *See, e.g.*, Wesberry v. Sanders, 376 U.S. 1, 18 (1964) ("While it may not be possible to draw congressional districts with mathematical precision, that is no excuse for ignoring our Constitution's plain objective of making equal representation for equal numbers of people the fundamental goal for the House of Representatives.").

tricts undermines the validity of this characterization. The fact that constitutional rules about voting evolved within a system of regional representation suggests that posing the problem as one of individual rather than group rights has been a distraction. I claim that the heavy reliance on one-person, one-vote jurisprudence to develop a theory of democracy fails both as a theory and as an adequate doctrinal protection of either individual or group rights.

One-Person, One-Vote and the Limits of Liberal Individualism

In this subpart, I examine the assumption that allocation of representatives through winner-take-all districting is a form of representation of individuals. The heart of this assumption is that citizenship is the ultimate reflection of individual dignity and autonomy and that voting is the means for individual citizens to realize this personal and social standing. Under this theory, voters realize the fullest meaning of citizenship by the individual act of voting for representatives who, once elected, participate on the voters' behalf in the process of self-government.[27] Indeed the very terminology employed in the Supreme Court's one-person, one-vote constitutional principle suggests that voting is an individual right.[28] For these reasons, some assume that the right at stake is the individual right to an equally weighted vote or an equally powerful vote.[29]

---

27. For the liberal, "the ultimate unit is not class, estate, rank or interest, but the independent, rational man.... The people are a mass, an entity, and, ideally, act as one. Yet they achieve that unity of action by a series of individual acts of mind stimulated by common discussion." Samuel H. Beer, *The Representation of Interests in British Government: Historical Background*, 51 AM. POL. SCI. REV. 613, 634 (1957). But even those who argue that it is the individual who is being represented concede that the individual's vote is influenced by group affiliations. *See, e.g.*, Auerbach, *supra* note 19, at 55, 56.

The right to vote also bears purely symbolic significance. *See* JUDITH N. SHKLAR, AMERICAN CITIZENSHIP: THE QUEST FOR INCLUSION 27 (1991) (arguing that civic significance comes from having the right to vote, not from actually casting a ballot).

28. The Court has described voting rights as "individual and personal in nature." *Reynolds*, 377 U.S. at 561. The Court continued, "Legislators represent people, not trees or acres. Legislators are elected by voters, not farms or cities or economic interests." *Id.* at 562.

29. John Low-Beer has distinguished the right to an equally weighted vote, which is implicated in reapportionment cases, from the right to an equally meaningful vote, which is implicated in gerrymandering cases. John R. Low-Beer, *The Constitutional Imperative of Proportional Representation*, 94 YALE L.J. 163, 164 n.3 (1984); *cf. Reynolds*, 377 U.S. at 579 (defining the "equal-population principle" as the standard for equal weighting); Terry v. Adams, 345 U.S. 461, 484 (1953) (finding that "an empty

The assumption is that constitutional protection for voting is exclusively about protecting an individual right, not necessarily about ensuring equal voting rights. At first, the connection between the two concepts seems plausible because every citizen has the right to vote and every citizen has the right to an equally weighted vote.[30] But the one-person, one-vote principle of voting is primarily about equal, not individual, representation.[31] Under this equality norm, the right to "fair and effective representation" subsumes concerns about equal voting and equal access. As the Court stated in one of its early reapportionment cases, the principle of equal representation for equal numbers of people is "designed to prevent debasement of voting power and diminution of access to elected representatives."[32] Implicit in this equality norm is the moral proposition that every citizen has the right to equal legislative influence. This means an equal opportunity to influence legislative policy.[33]

---

vote cast after the real decisions are made" did not provide a meaningful right to vote).

The equal population principle is, however, an imperfect approximation of equally weighted voting because district size is based on population, rather than on voting age population or registered voters. *Cf.* Mahan v. Howell, 410 U.S. 315, 322 (1973) ("[P]opulation alone has been the sole criterion of constitutionality in congressional redistricting under Art. I, § 2."). If one-person, one-vote is satisfied by such population-based reapportionment, I would argue that this principle views representation as equal access to a representative, whether the voter voted for the representative or even voted at all. I have argued elsewhere that equally weighted voting really means an equal opportunity to influence the processes of government. *See* Guinier, *supra* note 23, at 1422. Under this view, the right to fair and effective representation subsumes both equally weighted voting and equally powerful voting.

30. *See* Alan Howard & Bruce Howard, *The Dilemma of the Voting Rights Act— Recognizing the Emerging Political Equality Norm*, 83 COLUM. L. REV. 1615, 1636 (1983) (arguing that the one-person, one-vote rule, which ensures each voter an equally weighted vote, is a fundamental requirement of representative democracy in the United States).

31. *See id.* at 1633 (discussing the reapportionment cases' articulation of a political equality norm). Fair and effective representation envisions an equality norm—the right of all citizens to equal treatment as citizens in a democracy. In addition, the equality norm says that every *person* has an equal right to government services. An equal right to government services is not the same as a right to equal government services. In this sense, I am equating the right to services with a right of access to the benefits of government.

32. Kirkpatrick v. Preisler, 394 U.S. 526, 531 (1969).

33. *See supra* note 29 and accompanying text; *see also* Garza v. County of Los Angeles, 918 F.2d 763, 766 (9th Cir. 1990), *cert. denied*, 498 U.S. 1028 (1991) (concluding that deliberately minimizing minority political power may violate both the Voting Rights Act and the Equal Protection Clause of the Fourteenth Amendment); Alex A. Yanos, Note, *Reconciling the Right to Vote with the Voting Rights Act*, 92 COLUM. L. REV. 1810, 1821 (1992) (arguing that the reapportionment cases, taken together, stand for a

The assumption that voting is an individual right is also unnecessary for the view that voting rights are a means of political empowerment. One-person, one-vote rules emerged in response to claims about population-based malapportionment and about the right of the majority of people to elect a proportionate share of representatives.[34] In announcing this principle, the Supreme Court recognized that the growing urban majority of the 1960s would never command its *fair share* of legislative power unless the Court intervened.[35] In conjunction with concern about both a

---

broad notion of equality among citizens' respective influence on the political process, encompassing both equality of participation through equipopulous districts and equality of success whereby each citizen has an equal shot at getting a satisfactory result).

34. The Supreme Court developed its one-person, one-vote jurisprudence in response to the disproportionate power exercised by a political minority. *See* Gray v. Sanders, 372 U.S. 368, 379 (1963) (expressing dissatisfaction with an electoral system that gives disproportionate weight to rural votes and to votes from less populous counties). The Court found a constitutional right to population-based apportionment on the theory that the majority of the population should have a majority voice in the legislature. *Cf.* Reynolds v. Sims, 377 U.S. 533, 565 (1964) (noting that denying the majority the right to control the legislature would far surpass the dangers of any possible denial of minority rights). Of course, minority interests should also be represented. In fact, concern with representing group interests was a major theme of Justice Stewart's famous dissent in Lucas v. Forty-Fourth Gen. Assembly, 377 U.S. 713, 744–65 (1964) (Stewart, J., dissenting). Stewart's group interests were determined by the state, not by the individual voter, in part because he perceived federalism concerns to be the missing element in the requirement of strict population equality. *Id.* at 744–45. Stewart's repeated references to the legitimacy of group interests as recognized by the state, *id.* at 748–49, 759, 765, reflect, however, an implicit faith in state government to provide a voice to minority interests.

Some argue, however, that the one-person, one-vote principle was designed primarily to restore a competing principle: majority rule or majority legislative power. *See* Gordon E. Baker, *The Unfinished Reapportionment Revolution, in* POLITICAL GERRYMANDERING AND THE COURTS 11, 14 (Bernard Grofman ed., 1990) (asserting that the outcome of an insistence on voter equality is "conditioned majoritarianism"). Yet majority rule need not mean that a simple majority inexorably prevails. Even if it does, there is a big difference between the majority winning legislative power and the majority controlling *all* the legislative power. I have argued elsewhere that winner-take-all majority rule is often fundamentally at odds with traditional notions of democracy. *See* Guinier, *supra* note 23, at 1441–43 (arguing that winner-take-all majority rule based on a prejudiced majority is itself illegitimate).

35. *See* Baker v. Carr, 369 U.S. 186, 299 (1962) (Frankfurter, J., dissenting) ("[T]he discrimination relied on is the deprivation of what appellants conceive to be their proportionate share of political influence."). A recent essay by a political science scholar makes the same point: "[W]hen disproportionality is great and when attitudes and interests differ radically across groups—as with rural/urban differences of the 1950s or current racial/ethnic differences—corrective steps must be taken if our system is to be

fair share of power and developments in the law of minority vote dilution, the Court also adopted an instrumental view of voting. People would participate when and if they thought their vote mattered. Under this empowerment norm, the primary purpose of voting rights is to empower citizens to participate in the political process.[36]

I take the position that the right of the individual to participate politically is a right best realized in association with other individuals, *i.e.*, as a group.[37] As Justice Powell recognized, "[t]he concept of 'representation' necessarily applies to groups: groups of voters elect representatives, individual voters do not."[38] This is a bottom-up view of representation in which voters are empowered by their collective participation in the process of self-government. Under this view, voters engage in collective action to choose someone to represent their interests within the govern-

---

regarded as fair." BERNARD GROFMAN ET AL., MINORITY REPRESENTATION AND THE QUEST FOR VOTING EQUALITY 133 (1992).

36. The empowerment norm is also explicated in the Voting Rights Act of 1965, as amended in 1982. *See* 42 U.S.C. § 1971(b) (1988) (protecting voting rights for racial minorities against intimidation, threats, or coercion). As such, the Act is informed by the goals and strategies of the civil rights movement, which pushed for its passage in 1965 and which has been successful in extending and amending the Act in 1970, 1975, and 1982. The empowerment norm views political participation and *the right to participate throughout the political process* as critical to democratic legitimacy. In other words, it is not enough that people get certain formal or symbolic rights. What is critical is that citizens are given the opportunity and incentive to exercise those rights to promote their interests. What legitimates representative government is the fact that citizens knowingly *choose* who represents them and that citizens have the opportunity not only to elect but to retire those who do not represent them effectively.

37. *See* Low-Beer, *supra* note 29, at 177. Low-Beer notes that individuals can be represented only insofar as they share certain interests:

No meaningful voting right can be defined exclusively in individual terms. A legislator inevitably votes on behalf of the collective as well as the individual interests of her constituents. Only the provision of personal services or the sponsoring of a private bill involves purely personal representation.

Id.; *see also* MARTIN SHAPIRO, LAW AND POLITICS IN THE SUPREME COURT 249 (1964) (asserting that "one person, one vote" ignores "the group nature of politics" by assuming that each individual exercises her whole political power by voting); Alexander M. Bickel, *The Supreme Court and Reapportionment, in* REAPPORTIONMENT IN THE 1970S, 57, 59 (Nelson W. Polsby ed., 1971) ("We have, since Madison, realized that people tend to act politically not so much as individuals as in groups...."). *See also* V.O. KEY, POLITICS, PARTIES, & PRESSURE GROUPS 589 (5th ed. 1969) (observing that because group affiliation is of special importance to political participation, persons with strong groups of organizational attachments are more likely to vote).

38. Davis v. Bandemer, 478 U.S. 109, 167 (1986) (Powell, J., concurring and dissenting).

ing body. The representative is charged with influencing public policy on behalf of constituents' collective interests.[39]

The Court's jurisprudence does not consistently express a bottom-up view of representation within either the equality or the empowerment norms.[40] On occasion, though, the Court implicitly assumes the value of collective participation and influence in opinions that do not articulate the bottom-up view. For example, the Court's discussion in *Reynolds v. Sims* of a fair share of representation for population majorities suggests that by equalizing the number of people for whom each representative is responsible, the election of a single individual can fairly represent what are in essence collective interests.[41] Another example is *Baker v. Carr*, where the plaintiffs' original complaint alleged a systematic plan to "discriminate against a *geographical class* of persons."[42]

The bottom-up view of representation is reflected in some of the Court's early language about the importance of having a voice—meaning a public policy vote—in the process of self-government.[43] It also is the basis for the Court's 1986 decision in *Davis v. Bandemer* that political gerrymandering claims are justiciable.[44] In his plurality opinion for the Court in *Davis*, Justice White suggests that the policy decision to represent groups fairly already had been made in the context of racial minorities.[45]

---

39. *See* Reynolds v. Sims, 377 U.S. 533, 565 (1964) (stating that legislative bodies should be "collectively responsive to the popular will").

40. *Compare* Thornburg v. Gingles, 478 U.S. 30, 77 (1986) (employing a top-down view to conclude that the presence of minority representatives would undercut a voting rights challenge) *with Davis*, 478 U.S. at 132 (implying a bottom-up approach by emphasizing the right to influence the political process rather than the right simply to win elections).

41. *See Reynolds*, 377 U.S. at 576 (holding that the right to equal representation ensures "adequate overall legislative representation to all of the state's citizens").

42. Baker v. Carr, 369 U.S. 186, 273 (1962) (Frankfurter, J., dissenting) (emphasis added). The dissenting opinions acknowledge the claim that the distribution of electoral strength among geographic units reflects a legislative judgment about the representation of interests. *See, e.g., id.* at 334 (Harlan, J., dissenting).

43. *See, e.g., Reynolds*, 377 U.S. at 555 ("The right to vote freely for the candidate of one's choice is of the essence of a democratic society....."); *see also* Terry v. Adams, 345 U.S. 461 (1953) (arguing that a county's white primary system "strip[ped] Negroes of every vestige of influence in selecting the officials who control the local county matters").

44. *See Davis*, 478 U.S. at 124.

45. *See id.* at 125 & n.9 (explaining that the racial gerrymandering cases established the objective of fair and adequate group representation). Justice O'Connor's majority opinion in Shaw v. Reno, 113 S. Ct. 2816 (1993), however, may suggest that the Court will revisit this policy decision. As Justice Stevens suggests in dissent, the only group no longer entitled to fair representation now may be African-Americans. *See id.* at 2844–45

Of course, one could counter that representation is essentially a process of providing individual constituents with individual service and that it is therefore an individual right. This is a top-down view of representation in which the representative reaches back to his or her district to return government benefits to district constituents.[46] In this sense, equalizing the number of constituents equalizes access for individuals, not groups of individuals. Representation becomes the formal opportunity to receive one's fair share of government benefits or to have access to one's representative for individual constituency service. Voting creates "a personal value," or a symbolic statement of belonging, by the mere act of casting a ballot.[47] A vote is meaningful because it is counted, whether or not it actually affects the outcome.

While this top-down view might rest on the assumption that the right to *representation* is an individual right, it does not mesh well with the assumption that the right to *vote* is an individual right. Indeed, a voter need not vote at all to be represented under this understanding.[48] Actually casting a vote is less important than establishing voting status. Representation becomes the process of initiating a relationship in which one need not ever participate except by moving into the district. Even nonvoters are represented vicariously by choices made on their behalf.

Proponents of the philosophy of individualism attempt to use the one-person, one-vote principle to locate voting in the status of individual or constituent. They rely on the fact that every individual has the *opportunity* to cast a potentially winning vote or to be represented vicariously by

---

(Stevens, J., dissenting). If Justice Stevens's observation proves correct, such a "perverse" consequence would not eliminate the concept of group representation, which would still be available for "Polish Americans, or for Republicans." *Id.*

46. *See* Harold F. Gosnell, *Representative Democracy, in* REPRESENTATION 98, 104–10 (Hanna F. Pitkin ed., 1969) (defining the process of representation as acting in accordance with the desires and needs of individual constituents).

47. *Cf. Reynolds*, 377 U.S. at 567 ("To the extent that a citizen's right to vote is debased, he is that much less a citizen."). This is the equal shares—as opposed to the equal probability of casting a decisive vote—condition of political equality. *See* Jonathan W. Still, *Political Equality and Election Systems*, 91 ETHICS 375, 378–79 (1981).

48. This follows, in part, from the purely symbolic significance attached to *being* a voter. *See* SHKLAR, *supra* note 27, at 27 (noting that "the denial of the suffrage to large groups of Americans . . . made the *right* to vote," and not the exercise of the right, "such a mark of social standing") (emphasis added); Gerald L. Neuman, *Rhetorical Slavery, Rhetorical Citizenship*, 90 MICH. L. REV. 1276, 1278 (1992) (reviewing SHKLAR, *supra* note 27) (concluding that Shklar attributes social standing and civic understanding of voting capacity as the key reasons that groups excluded from the franchise struggle to overcome that exclusion and then find that actually casting a vote is less important once voting status is established).

one who does. This approach camouflages the group nature of voting by emphasizing the personal aspects of representation.

Consistent with their prevailing political philosophy of individualism, some members of the Court have struggled mightily to use one-person, one-vote rules to avoid the concept of group representation.[49] However, even where its nexus to group activity remains disguised, the principle of one-person, one-vote is as consistent with group as it is with individual representation. Similarly, the one-person, one-vote principle is consistent with semiproportional representation systems. Even if voters each were awarded five votes to plump as they choose, the one-person, one-vote principle would be satisfied, since each voter would have the same voting power or voting weight.

In this Paper, I argue that despite the efforts of some members of the Court to characterize representation as an exclusively individual notion, the concept of group representation became unavoidable for two reasons. The first, which I develop in Part II, is that the concept of group voting was necessary to understand the political unfairness of excluding racial minorities in a racially polarized constituency. The second, to which I now turn, is that the one-person, one-vote principle was conceived and articulated within a construction of constituencies based on geography. It is districting itself that merges individual representation with the representation of groups of individuals. Thus, it always has been necessary to acknowledge, at least implicitly, the relationship between districts and interests. I already have explored some of the bottom-up interest representation aspects of the equality and empowerment claims elsewhere.[50] In the next subpart, I further develop the link between group representation and territorial districting.

Group Representation and Territorial Districting

In this subpart, I argue that because of our explicit and implicit recognition of constituencies of geography, we have never actually employed a system of individual representation. Indeed, the use of geographic districts as the basis for establishing representational constituencies is at its

---

49. *See, e.g.*, Whitcomb v. Chavis, 403 U.S. 124, 154–55 (1971) (holding that the simple fact that one interest group is outvoted and consequently unrepresented in the legislature "of its own provides no basis for invoking constitutional remedies where... there is no indication that this segment of the population is being denied access to the political system").

50. *See* Lani Guinier, *The Triumph of Tokenism: The Voting Rights Act and the Theory of Black Electoral Success*, 89 MICH. L. REV. 1077, 1081–91 (1991).

very heart a system of group-based representation. Moreover, even where districts comply with principles of one-person, one-vote, such districts dilute the voting strength of both individuals and groups.

The concept of representation necessarily applies to groups: groups of voters elect representatives; individuals do not.[51] Representation is more than the individual relationship between constituent and elected representative. Because representation is primarily about political influence, not political service, bottom-up representation becomes the essential link to a genuine voice in the process of self-government. Districting is a form of group-interest representation, albeit an imperfectly realized one.

Districting, by definition, assumes that each voter is a "'member' of a 'group' comprised of all the voters in her district."[52] As Justice Stewart noted, "The very fact of geographic districting . . . carries with it an ac-

---

51. In asserting the prominence of group identity and the necessity of collective action to political organization and efficiency, I do not set out a theory of group rights. Nor do I yet define the parameters of group representation. Group status could mean a collection of people with identifiable characteristics. It could also mean a collection of people with common interests. In this Paper I simply pose the preliminary issue that the concept of representation necessarily applies to the representation of a group. Once I pass this threshold question, I will need to explore the next set of questions, one of which will certainly be: What is a group?

There is in addition an important caveat to the claim here that the concept of representation necessarily applies to groups. I am not assigning value to groups over individuals. Individuals as the ultimate objects of concern do not disappear from view. Indeed, I attempt to recognize the individual by empowering each voter to choose her district, *i.e.*, her temporary group affiliation. Indeed, by advocating the benefits of modified-at-large elections, I seek to put in the hands of the voters the degree to which they want their race or other demographic characteristic to be represented, *i.e.*, the degree to which their group's status is salient or relevant.

52. Low-Beer, *supra* note 1, at 176 n.63; *see also* DIXON, *supra* note 1, at 48–49 (contrasting proportional representation with districting based upon residency). Geographic districting necessarily advantages some groups and disadvantages others. In this sense, "all districting is 'gerrymandering.'" *Id.* at 462. The Supreme Court has recognized the impact that districting has on opposing groups:

> It is not only obvious, but absolutely unavoidable, that the location and shape of districts may well determine the political complexion of the area. *District lines are rarely neutral phenomena.* They can well determine what district will be predominantly Democratic or predominantly Republican, or make a close race likely. Redistricting may pit incumbents against one another or make very difficult the election of the most experienced legislator. *The reality is that districting inevitably has and is intended to have substantial political consequences.*

Gaffney v. Cummings, 412 U.S. 735, 753 (1973) (emphasis added).

ceptance of the idea of legislative representation of regional needs and interests."[53] Regardless of whether other Justices of the Warren Court ever consciously adopted the idea of interest representation, in working within territorial districts they assumed that interests reflect where people live.[54]

The view that geography approximates political interests is not a new idea. Indeed, the idea that geographic units reflect a common or group identity is part of the historical explanation for the winner-take-all system of districts. The American system of winner-take-all districts was adapted from the system in Britain prior to 1832, which in turn can be traced to feudal origins.[55] The feudal tradition helped define the law of the franchise on the theory that "it was the land, and not men which should be represented."[56] It was the community, in theory, that was rep-

---

53. Lucas v. Forty-Fourth Gen. Assembly, 377 U.S. 713, 750 (1964) (Stewart, J., dissenting); *see also* Reynolds v. Sims, 377 U.S. 533, 623–24 (1964) (Harlan, J., dissenting) (stating that constituents' interests often reflect their geographic location). Other commentators agree that geographic districts ensure interest representation. *See* Alexander M. Bickel, *Reapportionment & Liberal Myths*, 35 COMMENTARY 483, 489 (1963); Jo Desha Lucas, *Legislative Apportionment and Representative Government*, 61 MICH. L. REV. 711, 756–66 (1963); Phil C. Neal, Baker v. Carr: *Politics in Search of Law*, 1962 SUP. CT. REV. 252, 277–86; *see also* ALFRED DE GRAZIA, ESSAY ON APPORTIONMENT AND REPRESENTATIVE GOVERNMENT 28 (1963) (stating that "a legislature based solely on territorial apportionment will represent something of a community"). There is very little actual individual representation, only community representation. "As it has developed historically, the territorial survey type of apportionment has granted emphasis to community representation and especially to local real property interests." *Id.*

54. For example, Justices Harlan, Clark, and White explicitly took this position. *See Reynolds*, 377 U.S. at 623–24 (Harlan, J., dissenting) (stating that the economic, social, and political interests of electors reflect the place where they live); *Lucas*, 377 U.S. at 742 (Clark, J., dissenting) (noting the indigenous interests and problems unique to Colorado's different geographic regions); *see also* Auerbach, *supra* note 19, at 37 (explaining that geographical districting is considered the most workable proxy for interest representation).

55. ENID LAKEMAN, HOW DEMOCRACIES VOTE 29–30 (4th ed. 1974).

56. A.F. POLLARD, THE EVOLUTION OF PARLIAMENT 164 (2d ed. 1926). The English Parliament was originally an assembly of the "estates" of the clergy, the baronage, and the commons. *See generally* WILLIAM STUBBS, 2 THE CONSTITUTIONAL HISTORY OF ENGLAND 166–203 (1875) (recounting the history of the system of estates under Edward I). Members of medieval parliaments were selected by common consent in order to represent the unanimous mind of the county or borough that was being represented. JENNIFER HART, PROPORTIONAL REPRESENTATION: CRITICS OF THE BRITISH ELECTORAL SYSTEM 1820–1945, at 5 (1992). When this method of membership selection became unmanageable, a rule of the bare majority was established by which members of parliament were elected by relative majorities if a poll was held. *Id.* Enid Lakeman suggests

resented, and therefore the qualification for voting was corporative, with the franchise varying between communities.[57] Functional groupings, not individuals, were the basic units of representation.[58]

The British system also created a link between political representation and geographically based interests. Elected representatives were not seen as representatives of individual constituencies; they were merely equal members of Parliament who represented all of Britain.[59] The parliamentary system of representation had evolved in Britain because of feudal duties and obligations; the lord and his vassals were literally tied to the land, and representation in Parliament was actually part of the lord's feudal service to the king.[60] Similarly, inhabitants of the medieval town were not separate, for representational purposes, from the town itself.[61] The town was a political association, and the status of its inhabitants was defined by the rights of the group to which they belonged, namely

---

that the system evolved to capture broadly the main trends of opinion rather than exact proportions of political interest. LAKEMAN, *supra* note 55, at 40.

57. PETER G.J. PULZER, POLITICAL REPRESENTATION AND ELECTIONS: PARTIES AND VOTING IN GREAT BRITAIN 32 (1967); *see* Beer, *supra* note 27, at 617 ("[The Old Whig theory, the dominant political theory of the eighteenth century,] conceived of representation as being not of individuals, but rather of corporate bodies, although not in the strict legal sense of the term."); *see also* PULZER, *supra*, at 14–15 ("In the eighteenth century, under the influence of Whig ideas, it was considered proper and desirable that representation should be by interest, even if these interests were no longer the corporations and estates of mediaeval society.").

58. Beer, *supra* note 27, at 618. In contrast to this Whig view, liberals assumed that representation was of individuals rather than of "corporate bodies" or interests and could best be realized by equal electoral districts. *Id.* at 629–30. But while liberals in America had a pronounced suspicion of interests, their fear was based primarily on the representation of special interests. *Id.* at 631. But as I argue, the liberal claim that rule by the majority would defeat special interests is in fact informed by Old Whig theories of virtual representation. *See infra* notes 85–87 and accompanying text.

59. "It was not merely Parliament collectively, but the individual MP who was considered autonomous." PULZER, *supra* note 57, at 22. Likewise, in 1774, Edmund Burke asserted: "Parliament is not a *congress* of ambassadors from different and hostile interests;... but parliament is a *deliberative* assembly of *one* nation, with *one* interest, that of the whole...." *Id.* (emphasis in original).

60. "[It] was the land rather than men that parliament represented.... Feudal service was always regarded as due from the land rather than from the individual tenant, and so long as the crown obtained its service it cared little who performed it." POLLARD, *supra* note 56, at 156.

61. *See* Gerald E. Frug, *The City as a Legal Concept*, 93 HARV. L. REV. 1057, 1083 (1980) ("The medieval town was not an artificial entity separate from its inhabitants; it was a group of people seeking protection against outsiders for the interests of the group as a whole.").

the town.[62] This link between political representation and economic or geographic ties was later carried over to the United States during the Colonial period.[63]

By the late eighteenth century, towns were directly represented in the American colonial legislatures by representatives with explicit instructions to represent the towns' interests.[64] The relevance of town representation is that colonial towns "exercised power as a group; as a group they had rights, as a group they had powers."[65] Representation by geographical groups became the norm, in part because there was often no practical distinction between occupational and territorial representation.[66]

Indeed, the word "representation" originated as a term used by medieval jurists to describe the personification of collectivities; the spokesperson for a community was its embodiment, the bearer of its representative personhood.[67] Even in its modern form, representation often connotes the activity of furthering the interests of an abstraction rather

---

62. *Id.* at 1084.

63. *See* GORDON E. BAKER, THE REAPPORTIONMENT REVOLUTION: REPRESENTATION, POLITICAL POWER, AND THE SUPREME COURT 16 (1966) ("In view of this English background, it is not surprising that representation in colonial America was originally based on localities."). This "representation by town" was illustrated in 1787 when the delegates gathered to create the United States Constitution and the smaller states were reluctant to yield their accustomed equality of status. *Id.* at 16–18; *see also* DE GRAZIA, *supra* note 53, at 26 ("Territorial representation, with equal representation to all men, was the ideal formula for a democratic rural society and was espoused as such...in America and elsewhere.").

Basing the franchise on the ownership of property also reflects this relationship. *Cf.* Minor v. Happersett, 88 U.S. (1 Wall.) 162, 172–73 (1874) (collecting state statutes that impose restrictions on the right to vote, some of which condition the franchise on property ownership); Beer, *supra* note 27, at 630 (discussing the importance of property in determining electoral participation in both Britain and the United States).

In other parts of Europe, systems developed in the nineteenth century that more directly represented political or group interests and better reflected modern notions of representation. The proportional representation systems that have gained prominence in continental Europe reflect differing voters' opinions "like a mirror image" by assigning the precise number of seats in the parliament to correspond to the number of votes cast. ELECTORAL SYSTEMS 12 (Wolfgang Adrian ed., 1987).

64. Frug, *supra* note 61, at 1096.

65. *Id.* at 1098.

66. Paul H. Douglas, *Occupational Versus Proportional Representation*, 29 AM. J. SOC. 129, 132 (1923).

67. Hanna F. Pitkin, *Introduction: The Concept of Representation*, *in* REPRESENTATION, *supra* note 46, at 1, 2.

than of an individual.[68] Although many liberal theorists of American democracy espouse the importance of representation of the rational individual,[69] this claim is at odds with the historical roots of an electoral system that relies on regional rather than political units of representation.

It is also at odds with the practice of districting. The process of geographic districting collects people into units of representation by virtue of certain group characteristics or assumptions about shared characteristics within geographic communities. Geographic districting grounds the representational relationship in the opportunity to vote for a candidate to represent the interests of voters within a regionally defined political unit. It is assumed that those voters who share the homogeneous characteristics that give the district its "identity" (its dominant political, regional, or racial affiliation) are in fact represented. Because *all* voters share at least a common regional identity—they all live within the district's geographic walls—all voters are therefore assumed to be represented without regard to their actual choice of a candidate.

But the geographic unit is not necessarily politically homogeneous or of one mind as to who should represent it. In any contested election, some voters will vote for someone other than the winning candidate. These votes do not lead to the election of any candidate. Although these voters reside in equally populated districts, they have not chosen someone to represent their interests. Their theoretically equal votes are, as a practical matter, wasted in that the casting of their vote did not lead to the selection of their representative. The term "wasted votes," therefore, refers to votes cast for a candidate who does not win. In addition, I use the term to refer to votes cast for someone who does not need the votes to win.

---

68. *Id.* at 14; *cf.* POLLARD, *supra* note 56, at 152 (arguing that modern notions of representation assume the representative is bound by the will of the represented, but asserting that the will of the people is largely fictitious). This is true whether the abstraction is defined by its political, regional, or racial group interests. *Cf.* Robert G. Bone, *Rethinking the "Day in Court" Ideal and Nonparty Preclusion*, 67 N.Y.U. L. REV. 193 (1992) (arguing that, because representation of an absent party can never be consistent with the "right to make one's own strategic choices," nonparty preclusion in civil litigation should be based on grounds other than a representation theory); Robert G. Bone, *Personal and Impersonal Litigative Forms: Reconceiving the History of Adjudicative Representation*, 70 B.U. L. REV. 213 (1990) (noting that American courts in the late nineteenth and early twentieth centuries viewed the representative of a class as a self-regarding litigant rather than a litigating agent with a fiduciary duty to consider group interests).

69. *See supra* notes 27–29 and accompanying text.

Perhaps for this reason, one commentator refers to the constituency of geography as an "artificial 'group.'"[70] Constituents do not consciously choose to become members of this group, since very few people move somewhere in recognition of their likely voting efficacy within particular election subdistricts. Similarly, when they move, few people know in advance the particular elected officials by whom they are likely to be represented.[71] In other words, voters do not move to an election district; they move to a neighborhood or community.

I am suggesting that constituents within a geographically districted group may be there involuntarily, without sharing the same interests as other community residents,[72] and despite pre-existing hierarchical relationships.[73] In this way, membership in the territorial constituency is like membership in a family, with the former imposed by residence and the latter by kinship. Like family, geographic districts may not reflect conscious choice; as "compulsory constituencies," they nevertheless reflect ties that bind.[74]

Moreover, even if this factual assumption is incorrect, voters who might move based on the likelihood that they will reside within a specific

---

70. *See* Low-Beer, *supra* note 29, at 176 n.63. *But cf.* Davis v. Bandemer, 478 U.S. 109, 173 n.13 (1986) (Powell, J., concurring and dissenting) (describing as "artificial communities" those district boundaries drawn with no rationality and finding that where district lines are irrational, they limit the opportunity of citizens "to become familiar with their voting districts, where they must focus their political activities" and "affect the ability of all voters to exercise their political influence").

71. *But cf.* Holt Civic Club v. City of Tuscaloosa, 439 U.S. 60, 82 (1978) (Brennan, J., dissenting) ("At the heart of our basic conception of a 'political community,' however, is the notion of a reciprocal relationship between the process of government and those who subject themselves to that process *by choosing to live within the area of its authoritative application.*" (emphasis added)). Brennan's claim that residence may be an appropriate proxy for political choices, however, seems primarily directed at political subunits, not at geographic election districts.

72. *Cf.* United Jewish Orgs. v. Carey, 430 U.S. 144, 158 (1977) (noting that minority communities may be divided among predominantly white geographic districts); Whitcomb v. Chavis, 403 U.S. 124, 176–77 (1971) (Douglas, J., concurring) (explaining that gerrymandering may be used "to defeat or circumvent the sentiments of the community").

73. Hierarchical relationships refer to associations or connections between people of unequal status and/or power. *See* Frug, *supra* note 61, at 1097 (describing the hierarchical relationships in early medieval towns); *cf.* Dunn v. Blumstein, 405 U.S. 330, 354–55 (1972) (striking down a durational residence requirement as an improper means of assuring that all residents share a local perspective); *see also infra* note 115 (describing the hierarchy of geography, which disadvantages those who live in poor neighborhoods).

74. WALTER BAGEHOT, THE ENGLISH CONSTITUTION 150–51 (Garland Publishing ed., 1978) (London, H.S. King 1872).

election district are not acting rationally. This is because the imperative of the one-person, one-vote rule mandates continual redistricting.[75] Even motivated voters may rely on existing district configurations for only limited lengths of time.

In addition, the level of mathematical equality now required by the courts[76] makes it hard to claim that many election districts are neighborhoods. The upshot of absolute population equality as the basis for representation is that equipopulous districts are more important than districts that preserve communities of interests or leave neighborhoods intact.[77] In this respect, districting under the one-person, one-vote rule is arbitrary. Indeed, this was Justice Stewart's complaint when he accused the Court of privileging the personal right to vote over the efforts of local government to represent regional needs, communities of interest, or political subunits.[78]

Districting justifies the representation of this artificial group using a theory of virtual representation.[79] "Virtual" representation works like "constructive" in "constructive possession." It means "as if" or "pretended" representation.[80] In contrast to direct representation or bottom-

---

75. *See* Mark T. Quinlivan, Comment, *One Person, One Vote Revisited: The Impending Necessity of Judicial Intervention in the Realm of Voter Registration*, 137 U. Pa. L. Rev. 2361, 2383 (1989) (explaining that the Supreme Court would probably view decennial redistricting as a minimum requirement under the one-person, one-vote rule).

76. *See* Karcher v. Daggett, 462 U.S. 725, 728 (1983) (holding that a congressional reapportionment plan with a maximum deviation of 0.7% was unconstitutional). *But cf.* Gaffney v. Cummings, 412 U.S. 735, 751 (1973) (establishing a lower standard for state and local plans and allowing a maximum deviation of 7.8% from mathematical equality).

77. The Court has rejected the argument that differing interests of independent political subdivisions such as counties are sufficient justification for departure from the one-person, one-vote rule. *See, e.g.*, Reynolds v. Sims, 377 U.S. 533, 581 (1964); Lucas v. Forty-Fourth Gen. Assembly, 377 U.S. 713, 725 (1964).

78. *See Lucas*, 377 U.S. at 750 (Stewart, J., dissenting) ("The Court today declines to give any recognition to these [local] considerations and countless others, tangible and intangible . . . .").

79. The concept of virtual representation describes how nonvoters or losing voters are represented in legislatures. *See* John P. Reid, The Concept of Representation in the Age of the American Revolution 50 (1989). The English used this theory to explain how the American colonists were represented in Parliament. *Id.*

80. *See* letter from Frank Michelman, Professor of Law, Harvard University, to Lani Guinier, Associate Professor of Law, University of Pennsylvania (Aug. 26, 1991) (on file with author) ("Virtual representation is a species of the genus disfranchisement. You are virtually represented when you are disfranchised—not procedurally counted either in the assembly or in the electoral constituency—and the excuse for the disfranchisement is some theory about how someone else will act on your behalf or in your interest.").

up representation, virtual representation relies on the concepts of (1) *indirect representation*, (2) representation of *similar interests* elsewhere, and (3) *top-down* representation.[81] While the theory of virtual representation theoretically could be justified by any one of these concepts, the three assumptions generally are interrelated. Each of these assumptions is critical to the validity of virtual representation.

First, virtual representation assumes that the district winner *indirectly* represents the district losers.[82] For this to hold true, the election winner must do an adequate job of representing all those who reside within the district, including his or her political opponents. This assumption is based on the golden-rule principle that the winner will not tyrannize the losers because the winner may become the loser in the next election. Because the winner realizes the value of political stability, the winner will also represent the losers. Thus, in the long run, the losers' votes are not permanently wasted because they operate to hold the winners in check.

The second assumption of virtual representation is that the district losers technically are represented by *similarly situated* voters elsewhere in the political system. In this assumption, voters are represented when other voters—who are like them—vote in other districts and succeed in electing their candidate of choice. This reasoning assumes that similarly situated voters are fungible and groups "district voters" by characteristics they share with "nondistrict voters." Because of these group characteristics, district losers are vicariously represented by winners in other

---

81. *See* Reid, *supra* note 79, at 58 ("[A]lthough nonelectors might share no interests with members of Parliament, they could nonetheless expect that their interests would be represented through interests shared with the electors."); *see also* Simon Sterne, *The Representational Likeness, in* REPRESENTATION, *supra* note 46, at 73, 74–77 (noting that even in a representative democracy voting for representatives can lead to wasted votes).

82. One difference between direct and indirect representation is the extent to which the voters' choice is considered paramount in defining the representational relationship. Direct representation is the representation by someone of the voters' choosing. Indirect representation, by contrast, is the representation of the voters' interests by someone for whom the voter did not vote. Another difference relates to the representative's role. Direct representation posits the representative as an agent or delegate who acts on behalf of, and at the direction of, those who selected her. Indirect representation, by contrast, incorporates a trustee concept of the representative. In a trustee relationship, the representative is public regarding and conscientious based on her own sense of the common good. For example, indirect representation assumes that the representative will act in the interests of political opponents to diffuse their opposition.

In sum, direct representation emphasizes the voters' participation and choice in initiating and terminating the relationship. Indirect representation focuses attention on the representative's capacity to negotiate consensus.

districts for whom they would have voted had they been given the chance. As a result, the second assumption sees voters as represented based on certain "group" characteristics that can be externally predetermined for a ten-year period (between census counts) at the time of reapportionment and that can be measured jurisdiction-wide, rather than district-wide.[83] Again, the district losers' votes technically are not wasted because district losers are represented by someone, albeit not someone for whom they voted.

The third virtual representation assumption is that the district itself is a cognizable group that is represented ultimately as a community of the whole. This incorporates the proposition that a district has some independent existence apart from the discrete individuals who form an electoral majority. This is the historical claim that the district itself has a political or group identity.[84]

This argument relies on a *top-down* view of representation.[85] Living in Pennsylvania, I am represented by two United States Senators even if I am under eighteen years old, mentally incompetent, or disenfranchised based on noncitizenship or a criminal conviction. The assumption is that the district, and hence all its residents, are serviced whenever anyone is elected to represent the district. The key element of representation is equal access to the elected representative who is available to each constituent as a result of her status as a district resident. Each of the voters within the district is represented, even those who voted for a losing candidate *as well as those who did not or could not vote*. Because voting is primarily symbolic of personal status within a coherent community, virtual representation argues that no one's vote is wasted.

Every voter in a district is presumed to be represented simply because her territorial constituency is represented. The voter within a territorial constituency is represented because she has someone to turn to in case of

---

83. *See* United Jewish Orgs. v. Carey, 430 U.S. 144, 166 n.24 (1977) ("[T]he white voter who as a result of the 1974 plan is in a district more likely to return a nonwhite representative will be represented . . . by legislators elected from majority white districts."); Karcher v. Daggett, 462 U.S. 725, 759–60 n.25 (1983) (Stevens, J., concurring) ("[I]f the plaintiffs' challenge is based on a particular district or districts, the State may be able to show that the group's voting strength is not diluted in the State as a whole."); Connor v. Finch, 431 U.S. 407, 427 (1977) (Blackmun, J., concurring in part and concurring in the judgment) ("Districts that disfavor a minority group in one part of the State may be counterbalanced by favorable districts elsewhere.").

84. *See* Sterne, *supra* note 81, at 77. *But cf.* Frug, *supra* note 61, at 1097 ("[W]e must be careful not to confuse the concept of association with that of democracy or equality.").

85. *See supra* text accompanying notes 46–48.

personal constituency service needs. She is presumed to be represented even if she did not vote for the winning candidate. The fact that she wasted her vote is ignored because she is nevertheless "geographically" present within the political subdivision. No stock is placed in the fact that she did not vote for the representative. She is simply represented through the direct representation of her needs and her geographic nexus to the representative's supporters.

If districting is to be justified by virtual representation, the entire theory of districting depends upon the juxtaposition of territorial constituencies and interest constituencies. Drawing district boundaries presumably defines communities of interest. District lines determine a set of associations between the voter and a particular representative as well as among the voters themselves. It is only because voters within a particular district are deemed unlikely to have opposing interests that the notion of a personal relationship between the voter and the representative can survive. Voters are presumed fungible, meaning they are essentially indistinguishable on some critical threshold issue. The representative otherwise would be unable to service disparate personal needs without compromising the interests of other constituents.

These virtual representation assumptions are related to two somewhat inconsistent premises of liberal individualism. One is the value of majority rule. The district majority governs with legitimacy because the district is a coalition of shifting "factions" whose multiplicity of interests will keep any one from dominating.[86] The factions demonstrate that the district is not homogeneous, but the winner will virtually represent the losers because the losers are not permanent; the winner may be the loser at the next election. The first premise of liberal individualism thus shares the first premise of virtual representation. It posits that individuals who vote for losing candidates are adequately represented by the winning candidate and have as much opportunity to influence that candidate as do other voters in the district.[87]

The second premise is that representation is primarily a personal relationship between the representative and her constituents. In this context, the representative does not know how a particular constituent voted and will service her needs in the hopes of recruiting or sustaining her alle-

---

86. *See* Auerbach, *supra* note 19, at 52.

87. *See* Davis v. Bandemer, 478 U.S. 109, 132 (1986) ("[P]ower to influence the political process is not limited to winning elections."). *But see id.* at 170 (Powell, J., concurring and dissenting) ("[I]t defies political reality to suppose that members of a losing party have as much political influence over state government as do members of the victorious party. Even the most conscientious state legislators do not disregard opportunities to reward persons or groups who were active supporters in their election campaigns.").

giance. Adherents of the personal relationship perspective do not deny that the representative is more likely to represent faithfully the interests of those who voted for her; they simply suggest that the *needs* of each constituent also will be met because a district constituency establishes a relationship between the voter and her personal representative without regard to the voter's actual electoral preference.[88]

This premise, however, unlike the majority-rule premise, is based on a view of relative homogeneity within the district. Because the district constituents have similar needs and interests, it is possible for one representative to service adequately all constituents.[89] If the constituency has such common interests, one would expect a relatively unanimous constituency. By contrast, the majority-rule assumption relies on a more fractured constituency to balance the majority's urge to dominate. The personal relationship perspective and the majority-rule premise are, therefore, in some tension. They define voting by reference to competing notions of fungibility and personal access on the one hand and distinct interests on the other.

As a consequence, the virtual representation assumptions do not fit neatly within a one-dimensional view of representation based on liberal individualism. In fact, the rational individual who serves as the focal point of individualism would often take actions that are wholly inconsistent with virtual representation. The most apparent inconsistency is the idea that one's interests can be effectively represented by someone whom the voter, when given the choice, rationally determined did not reflect her interests. There is something distinctly unliberal in the view that indirect representation of interests is preferable to direct representation of groups or interests as defined by the voters themselves.[90] If the voter who goes to

---

88. *See* Bruce Cain et al., The Personal Vote: Constituency Service and Electoral Independence 50–51 (1987).

89. *See* Gosnell, *supra* note 46, at 98, 105 (describing representative government as a mirroring of the constituents' characteristics).

90. *See supra* note 82 (identifying differences between direct and indirect representation). This critical view of direct representation of interests reflects a political judgment that interests, or factions, are the bane of democracy. Therefore, interests are suspect and expression of interests should be muted or counterbalanced wherever possible. *See* Hanna F. Pitkin, The Concept of Representation 186–90 (1967). However, some commentators hold the view that

> [t]he principle of representation is based upon the assumed right on the part of the citizen to take part in the business of making the laws which are to govern him; as there are practical difficulties in the way of his doing so, he must appear by deputy—each man is entitled thus to appear by deputy.... [If votes are wasted in the election process] it as effectually disfranchises the citizen as though a

the polls is represented by the person against whom he or she votes, then the representation of the majority of the people becomes a representation of the whole people.[91] The voter is defined not by a rational individual choice but by the majority's choice.

Another inconsistency is the notion that the voter will be motivated to participate when she will be adequately represented by whoever is elected. Voting will simply become a habit, a civic duty, although it yields no direct results. In such a scenario, the rational individual would choose not to vote because of the small likelihood of casting the decisive vote.[92]

Yet another inconsistency is produced by the virtual representation assumption that wasted votes—those cast for a losing candidate—do not reflect the absence of representation because the territory defines the community, the group *as well as its interests.* This view suggests that mere geographical subdivisions have interests distinct from those of the people who inhabit them.[93] Because individualism posits that the rational individual will act in her own self-interest, this external determination of the interests represented is inconsistent with individualism.

Perhaps most inconsistent with the theory of autonomous, rational individuals is virtual representation's notion of fungibility. Virtual representation, explicitly in the second assumption and implicitly in the third, assumes that individuals are interchangeable based on some externally observed characteristics. Accordingly, individual choice is subordinated to the choices made by the majority, and the individual must allow someone in another district to act on her behalf.

In these often unstated but related ways, districting conflates the view that territorial constituencies virtually represent discrete individuals who

---

positive law disqualified him from going to the polls; it gives him the semblance, but deprives him of the substance, of his right. Even the majorities that are represented are unfairly and improperly represented, as the voter is compelled to sink his individuality, and oftentimes his best political opinions, for the purpose of belonging to the represented class.

Sterne, *supra* note 81, at 76–77.

91. *See* Sterne, *supra* note 81, at 80 (criticizing the idea that the right of the majority to govern carries with it the right of the majority to sole representation).

92. *See* DIXON, *supra* note 1, at 53 (arguing that rational voters who did not expect their candidates to win would choose not to vote); Roger L. Faith & Robert D. Tollison, *Expressive Versus Economic Voting, in* PREDICTING POLITICS 231, 231 (W. Mark Crain & Robert D. Tollison eds., 1990) (explaining that in public choice theory, voting is an irrational act because it is costly and unlikely to influence the final outcome).

93. *See* Sterne, *supra* note 81, at 77; *supra* text accompanying notes 84–85.

reside therein with the view that territorial constituencies group like-minded voters. Related to each of the virtual representation assumptions, therefore, is the corollary that we can use proxies, in this case geography, for determining voter interests. Such proxies merge voters' own definitions of their interests with the self-interest of political incumbents or with the interests of a homogeneous territorial district majority. The use of such proxies reveals the fundamentally group-based nature of representation—a feature that is inherent in, but inadequately recognized by, our contemporary system of representation.

For example, where representation is only virtual rather than direct, those who vote for the losing candidate may find that their interests are not represented at all. The constituency is presumed to be a group based on a single choice—the decision where to reside. This one choice may not be a real choice for some; for others it may not satisfactorily carry all the weight being assigned. Or the assumption that the geographic constituency is not dominated by a highly organized majority may simply be wrong as a matter of fact.[94]

It is important to recognize, therefore, that the districting debate is not only about representing groups. It also may be about representing groups or individuals unfairly. If voting reflects the voter's conscious choice rather than simply representing the voter's state of belonging, then winner-take-all districting in fact *wastes* votes of both individuals and groups. First, it makes certain there are political losers in each district. Those who vote—as individuals or as a group—for the losing candidate do not obtain any direct political representation. They did not initiate, and they cannot alone terminate, the representational relationship.[95] In response, an individual-rights advocate might argue that the individual who votes for a losing candidate is adequately represented by the winning candidate and has "as much opportunity to influence that candidate as other voters in the district."[96] This, of course, only makes sense if one assumes both that election results count for very little

---

94. *See* Lucas v. Forty-Fourth General Assembly, 377 U.S. 713, 748–49 (1964) (Stewart, J., dissenting) (noting the possibility that within district systems of representation, diverse groups of people may be subjected to "absolute domination by a geographically concentrated or highly organized majority").

95. *See supra* note 82 (describing direct representation).

96. Davis v. Bandemer, 478 U.S. 109, 132 (1986). *But see id.* at 169–70 n.7 (Powell, J., concurring and dissenting) (arguing that the plurality's finding that a "losing" voter will be adequately represented was a "leap" from the conclusion that a redistricting plan is not unconstitutional merely because it makes it harder for a group to elect its own candidate).

and that representation is exclusively about individual access to representatives chosen by others.[97]

In response, districts could be made more homogeneous to reduce the number of wasted votes. But this alternative demonstrates the second way that winner-take-all districting wastes votes. When more people vote for the winning candidate than is necessary to carry the district, their votes are technically wasted because they were unnecessary to provide an electoral margin within the district *and* they could have been used to provide the necessary electoral margin for a like-minded partisan in another district. In other words, packing voters in homogeneous districts wastes votes because it dilutes their overall voting strength jurisdiction-wide.[98]

The third way districting wastes votes is apparent if we consider voting broadly. I have suggested that voting is not simply about winning elections. The purpose of voting is to influence public policy. Accordingly, I have elsewhere proposed a concept, which I labeled "proportionate interest representation," to describe the importance of an equal opportunity to influence public policy, not just to cast a ballot.[99] This concept reflects both the equality and empowerment norms that I discussed earlier, because the right to cast an equally powerful vote subsumes the right to participate directly in the choice of representatives who then presumably enjoy an equal opportunity to influence legislative policy.[100]

If voting is understood as a means of exercising policy influence, districting tends to limit that influence. Winner-take-all districting gives the district majority all the power. It creates an incentive, therefore, to seek electoral control of a district. But electoral control of a district may isolate minority partisans from potential allies in other districts. In this way, districting wastes votes because it forces minorities to concentrate their strength within a few electoral districts and thereby isolates them from potential legislative allies.

For example, race-conscious districting attempts to provide disadvantaged racial groups the equal opportunity to participate by drawing majority minority geographic districts. Proponents of this strategy assume that electoral control—becoming a district majority—works as a proxy

---

97. *See id.* (stating that "the plurality apparently believes that effects on election results are of little import, as long as the losers have some access to their representatives").

98. *See, e.g.,* LAURENCE H. TRIBE, AMERICAN CONSTITUTIONAL LAW 1075–76 (2d ed. 1988) ("Because any vote in excess of a majority (or a plurality) is in a sense wasted, such a plan would render essentially irrelevant the ballots of many minority voters.").

99. *See* Guinier, *supra* note 50, at 1136–44.

100. *See supra* notes 30–34 and accompanying text.

for interest. But creating majority black districts also means creating majority white districts in which the electoral success of white legislators is not dependent on black votes. In this way, race-conscious districting may simply reproduce within the legislature the disadvantaged numerical and racial isolation that the majority minority district attempted to cure at the electoral level.

Where blacks and whites are geographically separate, race-conscious districting isolates blacks from potential white allies—for example, white women—who are not geographically concentrated. It "wastes" the votes of white liberals who may be submerged within white, Republican districts. As a consequence, districting may suppress the development of cross-racial legislative coalition building. Because majority black districts are necessarily accompanied by majority white districts, black representatives may be disenfranchised in the governing body. In this third sense, districting wastes votes because it fails to ensure legislative influence.

The wasted-vote phenomenon makes gerrymandering inevitable.[101] Because winner-take-all districting awards disproportionate power to electoral majorities, it inflates the advantage of district control. This inflated power quotient drives the apportionment process and leads some, myself included, to conclude that on some level all districting is gerrymandering. Gerrymandering is inherent in the districting process, which in essence is the process of distributing wasted votes.[102]

Where incumbent politicians seek safe districts to ensure their re-election, they may be inclined to gerrymander, *i.e.*, waste the votes for their likely opponent. Where political or racial partisans seek legislative con-

---

101. Theoretically, of course, it might be possible to draw random, competitive districts in which no "group" was assured of electoral control. In such districts, electoral control would presumably shift depending on issues, candidates, and local electoral events. But this possibility rests on a different premise from the traditional justification for districting—that districting presumes some group characteristics—and simply assumes that the groups can be fairly distributed without wasting their votes in the second sense of packing. This assumption, however, still allows wasting votes in the first sense in that some voters, albeit different voters each election, waste votes by voting for a political loser. The possibility of a "political fairness" approach—measuring fairness based on proportionate jurisdiction-wide influence—cannot be realized without an accurate measure of group voting strength. *Cf.* Davis v. Bandemer, 478 U.S. 109, 155 (O'Connor, J., concurring) (stating that allowing a "waste" of individual votes through a bipartisan gerrymander is contrary to the meaning of the Equal Protection Clause in that it confers more rights to politically powerful groups than to individuals).

102. *See id.* at 117 n.6 (describing the "familiar techniques of political gerrymandering," "stacking," "cracking," and "wasting" votes); *see also supra* note 38 and accompanying text.

trol, they may be inclined to gerrymander, *i.e.*, pack the minority party or minority race into a few districts to diminish their overall influence.[103] Or they may fracture the likely supporters of the minority party or minority race, spreading out their votes among a number of districts and ensuring that they do not comprise an electoral majority in any district.[104] These votes are counted, but they are essentially irrelevant in influencing the electoral or governing process.

The gerrymandering phenomenon illustrates once again the group nature of districting. Gerrymandering depends on assumptions about voters' likely behavior based on externally observed or supposed group characteristics or perceived common interests. Although the use of electoral districting has been defended based on the virtues of individual representation, assumptions about the nature of groups likely form the theoretical underpinnings of this election method.

I have tried to show that district representation weakens the connection between the voters' votes and the voters' representative by wasting votes. Unless all the voters in the district vote for the winning candidate, some of their votes are wasted. In addition, if a candidate only needs fifty-one percent of the votes to win, but the district is homogeneous and electorally noncompetitive, then all votes for the winning candidate over fifty-one percent are also technically "wasted." The point is that the voter is deemed represented whether she votes for the losing candidate, is an unnecessary part of the winning candidate's victory margin, or fails to vote at all.

The concept of wasted voting reveals the one-dimensional quality of the virtual representation assumptions. Yet wasted voting is only one of the ways that district representation minimizes the connection between voting and representation. The winner-take-all aspect of territorial constituencies also tends to over-represent the winning party and to deny the losing party a voice on behalf of their specific interests in the legislative forum where public policy is finally fashioned. In addition, territorial constituencies both submerge and subsume the concept of group representation. They also subsume individual definitions of relevant group identity in favor of individual residential decisions.

The artificial nature of these geographic associations suggests the limitations of the view that individual representation is the cornerstone of the right to vote. Territorial constituencies do not realize individual autonomy for at least three reasons. First, many people do not exercise real

---

103. *See* TRIBE, *supra* note 98, at 1075 ("While minority voters might thus be assured of a controlling influence in those few districts, they would have no impact on the choice of representatives outside those districts.").

104. *Id.*

choice in deciding their place of residence.[105] Second, even where residential decisions are conscious and discretionary, they do not capture the range or salience of interests which voters may hold. Third, the one-person, one-vote requirement of equipopulous districting makes districting even more artificial. If the major constraint on the drawing of district lines is the number of people within each district, district lines cannot conform to naturally occurring areas of common interest. When incumbents exercise enormous control over the districting process, including the custody of census data and the access to computer technology, communities of interest may become mere re-election opportunities. This is the threat to functional interest representation that various Justices have predicted over the years in their dissents to strict population equality principles.[106]

The key point is that criticisms leveled at race-conscious districting as a means of group representation should in fact be directed at the process and the theory of geographic districting itself. In the next Part, I attempt to show that when commentators criticize race-conscious districting, they are really finding fault with the assumptions behind districting in general. It is districting itself which is anomalous, because geographic definitions of group identity, especially within subdistricts, are often so artificial.

II.

In this Part, I argue that race is as effective as geography in functioning as a political proxy, but neither is as effective as allowing voters the

---

105. People with low incomes are relegated to living in deteriorating neighborhoods; affluent and middle class residential areas are generally not accessible to them. *See, e.g., Housing and Urban Development Secretary Henry Cisneros' Remarks on "The Changing Federal Role in Urban Policy" at a Progressive Policy Institute Conference,* Reuter Transcript Rep., Apr. 19, 1993, *available in* LEXIS, Nexis Library, Wires File (noting that poverty is "geographically isolated, economically depressed, [and] racially segregated" and that cities "have become warehouses of our poorest"); *see also Destabilized Suburbs: Officials Confront the Shortcomings of Section 8,* 7 CENT. PA. BUS. J. 18 (Sept. 1992) (observing that families receiving subsidized housing are concentrated in "Section 8 corridor" in Cook County, Illinois).

106. *See, e.g.,* Davis v. Bandemer, 478 U.S. 109, 175 (1986) (Powell, J., dissenting) (warning that "[c]omputer technology now enables gerrymanderers to achieve their purpose while adhering perfectly to the requirements that districts be of equal population"); Whitcomb v. Chavis, 403 U.S. 124, 177–78 (1971) (Douglas, J., concurring and dissenting) (explaining that despite achieving "substantial equality of population within each district," lines may nevertheless be drawn so as to favor a particular political party).

opportunity to make their own *local* choices about the nature and salience of their interests. Semiproportional systems permit shifting coalitions to form based on voters' own determinations of their interests or their group identity. In other words, geography and race rely on representational assumptions about group association but do not suggest the necessity, standing alone, of either representing or defining group interests a particular way. Modified at-large systems, such as cumulative voting, could be viewed as preferable alternatives that allow members of racial groups, politically cohesive groups, and strategically motivated individuals to be both self-defined and represented, while minimizing the problem of wasted votes for *all* voters.

Race in this country has defined individual identities, opportunities, frames of reference, and relationships. Where race has been of historical importance and continues to play a significant role, racial-group membership often serves as a political proxy for shared experience and common interests.[107] At least to the extent that an overwhelming majority of group members experience a common "group identity,"[108] those who are group members are more likely to represent similar interests.[109] Group members also may share common cultural styles or operating assumptions.[110]

---

107. *See* City of Mobile v. Bolden, 446 U.S. 55, 88 (1980) (Stevens, J., concurring) (arguing that despite the questionable proposition that race and interests coincide, legislators necessarily predict voting patterns based on racial group membership); *see also supra* note 18.

108. By group identity, I mean the tendency to self-identify as a group member and to perceive one's group membership as a salient feature in relationships with group and nongroup members. In another context, Professor Gerald Torres has suggested that this concept is captured by the question: Does your cultural grouping determine the narrative structure through which you organize your life? *See* Gerald Torres & Kathryn Milun, *Translating* Yonnondio *by Precedent and Evidence: The Mashpee Indian Case*, 1990 DUKE L.J. 625, 657–58.

109. Studies of black and female politicians do show that they have somewhat different agendas. *See* Rufus P. Browning et al., *Racial Politics in American Cities: Blacks and Hispanics in the U.S., in* POLITICAL MOBILIZATION, POWER AND PROSPECTS (1990); *see also* R.W. Apple, Jr., *Steady Local Gains by Women Fuel More Runs for High Office*, N.Y. TIMES, May 24, 1992, § 4, at 5 (reporting on a survey of approximately half of all state legislators which found that "even when men and women shared the same party affiliation and ideology, women were much more likely to expend their energies on health care, children's and family questions and women's rights issues"); Gwen Ifill, *Female Lawmakers Wrestle with New Public Attitude on 'Women's' Issues*, N.Y. TIMES, Nov. 18, 1991, at B7 (describing a study done by the Center for American Women and Politics at Rutgers University which found huge gaps between male and female legislators over issues involving women's rights, health care, and children).

110. *See* Apple, *supra* note 109, § 4, at 5 (citing a survey that women public officials

Group members also are more likely to be perceived by their constituents as representing them. This definition of representative as descriptive likeness or racial compatriot has a psychological component. Just as the flag stands for the nation, the presence of racial group members symbolizes inclusion of a previously excluded group. The symbolic role results from both the personal characteristics of the racial-group member and the assumption that, because of those characteristics, the racial-group member has had experiences in common with her constituents. As Hanna Pitkin writes in her groundbreaking work on representation, "We tend to assume that people's characteristics are a guide to the actions they will take, and we are concerned with the characteristics of our legislators for just this reason."[111] Thus, many racial minorities do not feel represented unless members of their racial group are physically present in the legislature.[112]

As a result, traditional voting rights advocates comfortably rely on race as a proxy for interests. For example, in conventional voting rights litigation, election contests between black and white candidates help define the degree of racial polarization, i.e., the degree to which blacks and whites vote differently.[113] The idea is that the outcome would be different if elections were held only in one community or the other. The assumption of difference extends explicitly to the specific candidate elected, and implicitly to the issues that candidate, once elected, would emphasize.

The assumption of this difference between races rests in part on the claim that where black candidates enjoy protection from electoral competition with whites, black voters can ratify their choices to hold their representatives accountable. In this way, the association between race and interests is modified to the extent that voters are given a meaningful choice in both initiating *and* terminating a representational relationship. Voting rights advocates assume that minority group sponsorship is critical.[114] It is only where minority voters exercise electoral control, or have

---

tend more than their male counterparts of the same party and ideology to involve private citizens in the governmental process, to focus on needs of the poor, and to conduct public business in the open rather than behind closed doors).

111. PITKIN, *supra* note 90, at 89.

112. *Cf.* Guinier, *supra* note 50, at 1104 (describing the experience of black voters who consider blacks elected from other districts "their representatives").

113. *See* Thornburg v. Gingles, 478 U.S. 30, 53–55 & n.21 (1986); City of Mobile v. Bolden, 446 U.S. 55, 98 (1980) (White, J., dissenting).

114. *See* Evelyn E. Shockley, Note, *Voting Rights Act Section 2: Racially Polarized Voting and the Minority Community's Representative of Choice*, 89 MICH. L. REV. 1038, 1061–62 (1991) (explaining that in determining the relevance of a candidate's race, the "best [judicial] approach relies on *sponsorship*: the minority community's 'rep-

a meaningful opportunity to retire their representative, that race functions as a representational proxy. Thus, majority-black single-member districts take advantage of segregated housing patterns to use geography as a proxy for racial choice, racial control, and racial representation.[115]

I argued in Part I that the one-person, one-vote cases, with their focus on equalizing individual access through equalizing population, conceal the group nature of representation by districting.[116] The one-person, one-vote rule merges political interests and regional interests under the umbrella of equal access for equal numbers of people. In order to justify placing people with different political interests into one district with only one representative, the wasted vote problem is elided by discussing everything in terms of individual voters. In deference to a tradition of according individual rights a higher value, and relying on the access view of voting, adherents to population-based districting simply skip over geographic districting's implicit assumptions about group attributes.

Race-conscious districting confronts the group nature of representation more directly. It attempts to minimize the wasted vote problem for minority voters whose preferred candidates—because of racial bloc voting by the majority—experience consistent defeat at the polls. Where voting is racially polarized, white voters and black voters vote differently. Where blacks are a numerical minority, racial bloc voting means that the political choices of blacks rarely are successful. To remedy this problem of being a permanent loser, black political activists and voting rights litigants have sought majority black districts in which the electoral choices of a majority of blacks determined the electoral winner.[117]

Yet some commentators challenge race-conscious districting on the grounds that special protection throughout the political process for the rights of minority groups is unnecessary as long as individual minority

---

resentative of choice' can only be a candidate who was sponsored by that community," and that such an approach "will satisfy proponents of a focus on civil inclusion").

115. This use of geography as a proxy for "race" is not limited to voting rights. "Demographic red-lining" for marketing direct sales also relies on information about zip codes and housing tracts from census data. JEFFREY ROTHFEDER, PRIVACY FOR SALE 102–05 (1992) (describing how sales marketing companies rely on real estate data bases to portray "likely political leanings, tastes and lifestyle of each American by his address"). Such characterizations mean that if you "[t]ell me someone's zip code, . . . I can predict what they . . . even think." *Id.* at 102–03.

116. *See supra* text accompanying notes 47–49.

117. *Cf.* Samuel Issacharoff, *Polarized Voting and the Political Process: The Transformation of Voting Rights Jurisprudence*, 90 MICH. L. REV. 1833, 1856 (1992) ("[T]he increased number of minority elected officials is most directly attributable to the successes of redistricting and reapportionment litigation and the resulting creation of more minority-dominated electoral districts.").

group members have a fair chance to participate formally by voting in an election.[118] For these commentators, race-conscious districting is illegitimate because the right to vote is individual, not group-based.[119] Relying again on assumptions about fungibility and access, these observers challenge the right of minority groups to representative *or* responsive government.[120]

---

118. *Cf.* James F. Blumstein, *Defining and Proving Race Discrimination Perspectives on the Purpose vs. Results Approach from the Voting Rights Act*, 69 VA. L. REV. 633, 636 (1983) (concluding that while minorities have the right to ballot access, there is no corresponding entitlement to racial group representation).

119. *Id.* at 712 n.378; *see also* Michel Rosenfeld, *Affirmative Action, Justice, and Equalities: A Philosophical and Constitutional Appraisal*, 46 OHIO ST. L.J. 845, 912 (1985) ("The right to vote is a paradigmatic individual right. Each individual has only one vote, and absent any discrimination or unfair procedures, no group of voters has a right to complain that its candidate lost."); *cf.* Brian K. Landsberg, *Race and the Rehnquist Court*, 66 TUL. L. REV. 1267, 1305 (1992) (asserting that proponents of the individual-based model tend to oppose race-conscious affirmative action).

120. *See supra* notes 84–91 (employing the term "fungibility" to mean that voters are essentially indistinguishable, and the term "access" to define representation in terms of a personal relationship). Of course, some commentators challenge race-conscious districting on grounds unrelated to group representation principles. To some of these critics, requirements to maximize minority representation are a quota system that awards benefits, *i.e.*, votes, through a racial entitlement. They view the arguments for minority representation in proportion to minority population ominously because the arguments rely on the implicit belief that maximizing minority representation means accepting the assumption that only minorities should represent minorities. Abigail Thernstrom, for example, is quoted as denouncing this assumption because it reflects the divisive notion that "this is a deeply divided society of separate nations." Ronald Brownstein, *Minority Quotas in Elections?*, L.A. TIMES, Aug. 28, 1991, at A1, A14. Similarly, Judge Eisele asks, "Do we really believe in the idea of one political society or should this be a nation of separate racial, ethnic, and language political enclaves?" Jeffers v. Clinton, 730 F. Supp. 196, 227 (E.D. Ark. 1989) (Eisele, C.J., dissenting), *aff'd*, 498 U.S. 1019 (1991).

My response to this criticism is twofold. First, to some extent I agree that the current approach is divisive. Nevertheless, the right to vote is not a benefit but an essential element of our system's political legitimacy. Therefore, those who take issue with current approaches have a responsibility not just to criticize but to propose alternative solutions that protect the right of the minority to have its voice represented and heard in the legislative debate. Second, in light of recent events in Los Angeles, concerns about *unnecessarily* dividing society do not seem consistent with the divided society in which we already find ourselves. *See supra* note 16. These concerns fail to acknowledge the prediction from twenty years ago of the Kerner Commission Report, that unfortunately we *are* becoming two nations, separate and unequal. *See* NAT'L ADVISORY COMM'N ON CIVIL DISORDERS, REPORT OF THE NAT'L ADVISORY COMM'N ON CIVIL DISORDERS 1 (1968); *see also* Issacharoff, *supra* note 117 (documenting and analyzing the significance of racially polarized voting in contemporary political discourse). While concerns about balkanization are real, the solution to the problem of racial division is not to ignore the

Given the prominence of racial group identities, I am not persuaded by this criticism to abandon the concept of group representation. I am aware of, but not in accord with, those critics of race-conscious districting who object on moral grounds to the drawing of districts along racial lines.[121] As I suggested earlier, representation is a bottom-up process that ideally recognizes the importance of influencing public policy decisions on behalf of constituency interests.[122] Accordingly, we cannot define political fairness merely as electoral fairness that guarantees nonbiased conditions of voting eligibility and equally counted votes. Nor do I think the only issues are whether blacks have special claims for protection or whether whites can or should represent blacks, although I think they can and do.[123]

Yet, in making the argument that racial groups deserve representation, I do not rely primarily on the political, sociological, or cultural claims involved in racial-group identity, or even on the historic context of group disfranchisement. My principal argument rests on the distinction within the political process between a claim for group rights and a claim for group representation.[124] I argue for the latter based on the historic evi-

---

divisions but to attempt to heal them.

Other critics object to race-conscious districting on moral grounds. *See, e.g.*, T. Alexander Aleinikoff, *A Case for Race-Consciousness*, 91 COLUM. L. REV. 1060, 1063 (1991) ("[T]he race of a person tells us nothing about an individual's capabilities and certainly nothing about her moral worth. Race-consciousness, from this perspective, is disfavored because it assigns a value to what should be a meaningless variable. To categorize on the basis of race is to miss the individual."); Neil Gotanda, *A Critique of "Our Constitution is Color-Blind"*, 44 STAN. L. REV. 1, 16 (1991) (stating that opponents of race-conscious decisionmaking believe the approach is morally inferior to a technique which ignores race as a factor). My response to this objection rests, in part, on a claim that to a greater or lesser degree, all districting is gerrymandering. In other words, the criteria for drawing district lines are arbitrary and subject to the preferences of those drawing the districts.

121. Gotanda, *supra* note 120, at 16. In Shaw v. Reno, 113 S. Ct. 2816, 2827 (1993), the majority suggests that consciously drawing districts to represent black voters as a group is problematic, although in political terms the districting plan is "fair." This is essentially a moral claim which the Court then constitutionalizes. *See supra* text accompanying note 8.

122. *See supra* notes 37–39 and accompanying text.

123. This particular concern is primarily hypothetical. Blacks are very unlikely to be elected from any majority white districts, and all majority black congressional districts now elect black officeholders. Bernard Grofman & Lisa Handley, *The Impact of the Voting Rights Act on Black Representation in Southern State Legislatures*, 16 LEGIS. STUD. Q. 111, 117 (1991).

124. This is not to suggest that arguments for group rights can be ignored. *See, e.g.*, Williams, *supra* note 15, at 545–46 (arguing that the Court should advance the rights of

dence that representation within territorial districts is implicitly about recognition of group interests, not just individual access.[125] However, the future of such group representation—like the future of the group itself—lies less inside geographic boundaries and more within the cultural and political community forged by group consciousness and group identity. Empowerment—for a group as well as for an individual—comes from active assertion of self-defined interests. A group is represented where it has the opportunity to speak out and not just to be spoken for.

The argument for recognition of group interests makes three assumptions about representation. First, legislators should represent unanimous, not divided, constituencies.[126] Second, each voter's vote should count toward the election of a representative. Third, the unit of representation

---

minority groups to achieve the socially desirable goals of diversity and multiculturalism); Melissa Williams, Memory, History and Membership: The Moral Claims of Marginalized Groups in American Political Representation, paper delivered at the Annual Meeting of the American Political Science Association, Chicago, Illinois (Sept. 3, 1992). I simply choose not to make such an argument here.

125. *See supra* notes 37–48 and accompanying text.

126. Unanimous constituencies are those in which all voters agree on a basic definition of their interests. A unanimous constituency lets the voters choose which interest is salient and should be promoted. In a divided constituency, it is the legislator whose choice is important as she attempts to strike a balance among her supporters. Unanimous constituencies focus on the role of the voter; divided constituencies adopt a trustee view of representation. The former is a bottom-up view of representation; the latter is top-down.

The bottom-up view of unanimous constituencies assumes that voters, not legislators, should be empowered to make legislative choices, at least initially, for several reasons. First, it adopts a delegate or agency view of representation that suggests legislators represent the parts in order to avoid viewpoint monopoly. By encouraging the active assertion of diverse perspectives, the legislative process is infused with more and different ideas. This discourages monolithic control of legislative agendas by assuring the active representation of unanimous, issue-oriented constituencies. The second assumption is that compromise should occur openly after an election as part of the deliberative process of legislative debate rather than behind closed doors, where office seekers pre-"position" themselves to camouflage mutually inconsistent or divergent philosophies. In this sense, it reflects a more participatory view of fairness as the balancing of perspectives rather than as the absence of a viewpoint.

Second, it assumes that issue-based, rather than candidate-based, constituencies will be mobilized to participate throughout the political process, not just on election day. In this way it responds to the increasing levels of alienation and passivity within the electorate. *Cf.* Burt Neuborne, *Of Sausage Factories and Syllogism Machines: Formalism, Realism, and Exclusionary Selection Techniques,* 67 N.Y.U. L. Rev. 419 (1992) (noting that allowing jurors to be excluded from juries because of their race leads the community to lose faith in the jury system).

should be psychological, cultural, and/or political rather than territorial.[127] In other words, groups should be represented, but in ways that permit automatic, self-defined apportionment based on shifting political or cultural affiliation and interests. This would enable voters to form voluntary affiliative districts without the need for prior authorization or formal recognition of the group as one which deserves special treatment. Because such group identity would be affiliative and interest-based, group representation would encourage both coalition building among racial and political factions and grass-roots political organization around issues, not just individual candidacies.

If the decision to represent groups already has been made in the adoption of geographic districting, then group representation based on racial-group association or historical oppression becomes less problematic. Whatever the alleged flaws in racial-group representation, it is racial representation within a system of geographic districts that must be analyzed. As one white Democratic congressman who represents a largely minority constituency is quoted as saying, "I'm torn about it. I do not believe you have to be of the exact same ethnic group to do a good job in representing that community. But, in the end, I think it's that community's choice."[128] Thus, it is important to emphasize the connection between choice, accountability, and group identification. Whoever represents minority interests (just as whoever represents majority interests) should be directly, not merely virtually, accountable to those interests.[129]

Yet some critics of race-conscious districting might attempt to distinguish race from geography as a useful political proxy. Such critics claim that geographic association, unlike race, is temporal, individualistic, and discretionary, at least for some people. There are two problems with this purported distinction. First, geography is neither discretionary nor individualized for members of disadvantaged racial groups.[130] Rather, it re-

---

127. Some suggest that state boundaries would not survive this approach. That question is beyond the scope of this Paper. Suffice it to say that retaining states as units of representation reflects deeply embedded constitutional and tradition-bound constraints.

128. Brownstein, *supra* note 120, at A1, A15.

129. *See supra* notes 90–91 and accompanying text; *see also* Martha Minow, *From Class Actions to Miss Saigon: The Concept of Representation in the Law*, 39 CLEV. ST. L. REV. 269, 280–84 (1991) (surveying contemporary views of political representation and accountability).

130. The decision to live next to someone may suggest some connection, kinship, or community of interest, but only if the decision to move was the exercise of choice within a range of options. *Cf. supra* note 63 (discussing the historic link between geographic and political ties); *see also supra* note 106.

flects the very essence of limitations on choice based on group identity. Race-conscious districting can capture racial communities of interest precisely because residential ghettos are often the result of racial discrimination. As Professor Pamela Karlan writes, residential segregation reflects racial discrimination in both the private and public housing markets.[131] Because residential segregation by definition results from the absence of choice, race-conscious districting "can serve as a proxy for a bundle of distinct political interests."[132]

A second problem is that this criticism applies only to race-conscious representation executed within a system of fixed district boundaries. Indeed, the concern can be avoided almost entirely where the voters themselves define their own interests using alternative, modified at-large systems of representation. Representation based on voluntary interest constituencies would unhitch racial-group representation from arbitrary, involuntary assignments.

The voluntary interest constituencies would be comparable to Professor Iris Marion Young's model of a "highly visible" social group with emotional, historical, and social salience defined by a sense of group identity, not just shared attributes.[133] According to Young, groups exist only in relation to other groups.[134] The social processes of affinity and differentiation produce groups.[135] Yet group differentiation is not necessarily oppressive nor homogeneous. Group differentiation is created by multiple, cross-cutting, and shifting differences.

---

131. Pamela S. Karlan, *Maps and Misreadings: The Role of Geographic Compactness in Racial Vote Dilution Litigation*, 24 HARV. C.R.-C.L. L. REV. 173, 177 (1989); *see also* Whitcomb v. Chavis, 403 U.S. 124, 131 n.8 (1971) (defining a ghetto as a residential area with a defined racial population of lower than average socioeconomic status "*whose residence in the area is often the result of a social, legal, or economic restriction or custom*" (emphasis added)); Wright v. Rockefeller, 376 U.S. 52, 59 (1964) (Douglas, J., dissenting) ("Neighborhoods in our larger cities often contain members of only one race; and those who draw the lines of Congressional Districts cannot be expected to disregard neighborhoods in an effort to make each district a multiracial one.").

132. Karlan, *supra* note 131, at 177; *see also* *Whitcomb*, 403 U.S. at 135 (finding that ghetto residents have interests "diverging significantly from interests of nonresidents of the ghetto" (paraphrasing language of the lower court opinion that the Court overruled)).

133. IRIS M. YOUNG, JUSTICE AND THE POLITICS OF DIFFERENCE 43–46 (1990) (arguing that "highly visible" groups—those who identify with a certain social status and have a common history produced by that status—are different from "mere 'combinations of people'"—such as voluntary clubs—which are defined by shared attributes).

134. *Id.* at 43.

135. *Id.*

The group differentiation of racial minorities is a function of historical oppression, shared experience, and present inequality.[136] Territorial configurations may track this phenomenon to the extent that disadvantaged racial groups are concentrated in substandard housing in urban ghettos, but differentiation by race cuts across geographic lines in many cases. Some racial-group members share a group consciousness without sharing group space. Others are dispersed in small barrios throughout the jurisdiction.[137] Still others may technically be group members in terms of their racial origin or current residence but not in terms of their racial identity.[138]

In addition, group differentiation by race subsumes gender, age, and class differences. A racial group that is politically cohesive on civil rights or welfare policy may have some members with interests that are not shared throughout the group. On these issues, the racial group members may have more in common with group members of another race living outside their immediate geographic area. In other words, racial groups are not monolithic, nor are they necessarily cohesive.

Race in conjunction with geography is a useful but limited proxy for defining the interests of those sharing a particular racial identity. But it is the assumption that a territorial district can accurately approximate a fixed racial-group identity—and not the assumption of a racial-group identity itself—that is problematic. Race-conscious districting—as opposed to racial-group representation—may be rigidly essentialist, presumptuously isolating, or politically divisive. For example, different groups may share the same residential space but not the same racial identity. A districting strategy requires these groups to compete for political power through the ability to elect only one representative.

Yet strategies for race-conscious districting respond to important deficits in a non-race-conscious geographic districting process. Proponents of racial-group representation confront on the jurisdiction-wide level the unfairness of the indirect, virtual representation claims. In justifying race-conscious districting, voting rights activists appropriately employ the concept of racial-group identity.[139] They can demonstrate that members of the racial group have distinctive interests that are often ig-

---

136. *See id.* at 44, 51–52; *see also supra* notes 16, 18, and 106.

137. *See id.* at 247 (describing the mechanisms by which this segregation is enforced).

138. *See supra* note 108 and accompanying text; *infra* note 171 and accompanying text.

139. *See* Frank R. Parker, *Racial Gerrymandering and Legislative Reapportionment, in* Minority Vote Dilution 85, 112 (Chandler Davidson ed., 1984) (concluding that the use of race-conscious remedies is "benign and beneficial to the minority community because it enhances their voting strength").

nored by elected officials who suffer no adverse consequences at the polls.[140] In this way, the activists challenge the view that voters are fungible, especially where minority group voters are consistent losers as a result of racial bloc voting by the jurisdiction majority.

Based on complaints about the way that virtual representation assumptions operate at the macro level to dilute minority voting strength, race-conscious strategies seek to control smaller, majority minority districts. By making the minority a district majority, race-conscious districting seeks to exercise the prerogatives of majority rule on behalf of a jurisdiction-wide minority. But while they challenge the fairness of jurisdiction-wide virtual representation of minority voters by the majority, proponents of race-conscious districts replicate many of the same fairness problems at the micro level.

The same assumptions about virtual representation that were the object of challenge at the macro level are now reproduced within subdistricts that the racial minority controls. The majority minority subdistrict operates on the same winner-take-all, majority rule principles. Even as an imperfect geometric "fractal"[141] of a larger jurisdiction-wide majority, it carries with it the assumptions of virtual representation to justify the minority group's domination. As a consequence, race-conscious districting raises in microcosm the theoretical questions I raised in Part I about districting itself.

An illustration of this fractal problem is a 1992 New York City congressional plan that included a Brooklyn/Queens district to represent the interests of a Latino minority.[142] This district concentrated Latinos in a new 12th Congressional District.[143] Several Latino activists filed as candidates in the Democratic primary. So did Representative Stephen Solarz, a white incumbent whose previous district was consolidated within one-fifth of the new "Latino" district.[144]

---

140. *Cf.* Chandler Davidson, *Minority Vote Dilution: An Overview*, *in* MINORITY VOTE DILUTION, *supra* note 139, at 1, 10 (arguing that elected officials are often unaware of the extent of minority support and therefore respond to strong pressure from white voters).

141. A fractal is a set of jagged curves or surfaces that has "the same index of jaggedness when examined at any level of minuteness or abstraction." *See* Louise Weinberg, *The Federal-State Conflict of Laws: "Actual" Conflicts*, 70 TEX. L. REV. 1743, 1777 n.120 (1992). Professor Pamela Karlan suggested the analogy to fractal geometry.

142. *See* Alison Mitchell, *In Politics, There Is Only One Language*, N.Y. TIMES, July 19, 1992, at A29.

143. Mary B.W. Tabor, *Loyalty and Labor*, N.Y. TIMES, Sept. 17, 1992, at B6.

144. Sam Roberts, *Does Politics of Fairness Mean Only Those from Minorities Should Apply?*, N.Y. TIMES, July 27, 1992, at B4.

The entry of a well-financed, nine-term incumbent from a largely Jewish section of Brooklyn shifted the political expectations. The primary, which had been expected to focus on issues of interest to a poor Latino constituency, turned into a debate over whether a minority group could be represented by someone of a different ethnicity.[145] According to a Latino community organizer, "The community is saying, 'Why is it that this Jewish person who has always represented other interests than ours, comes in now saying he's going to be our savior?'"[146] This complaint—that the white incumbent should not enter the race—rested on a complex, but misinformed, understanding of group representation.

The group is deemed represented where it has electoral control over the winner. The organizer's concern was that the sixteen percent white minority in the district—not the Latino majority—could have electoral control by consolidating their votes and converting their minority status into a plurality win.[147] Since there were at least four Latino candidates, the white candidate would most likely win if the Latino vote were split, even though Latinos are fifty-five percent of the district's voting-age population.[148] If the Latino majority was disaggregated into factions supporting different Latino candidates, it could have been white voters who chose the representative for the new district.

Latino activists complained that this did not give their community the choice they deserved. "The whole idea was to give our community some degree of choice, Latinos or non-Latinos who have some connection with the community. . . . [The well-financed white incumbent] doesn't fit that bill at all."[149] The white candidate answered, "The other candidates fear that I'll win, which somewhat belies their notion that the purpose of this district was to empower the people to make a choice."[150]

The nature of this controversy was captured by a *New York Times* headline that appeared before the primary: "Does Politics of Fairness

---

145. *Id.*

146. Mitchell, *supra* note 142, at A29 (quoting David Santiago).

147. *Id.*

148. *Id.*

149. *Id.* (quoting Angelo Falcon, President of the Institute for Puerto Rican Policy).

150. Roberts, *supra* note 144, at B4 (quoting Rep. Steven J. Solarz). Others suggest that politics, not principles of choice, motivated Solarz's decision. "When his polls showed he couldn't win against any incumbent," he ran in an open district created to enhance the power of Latino residents. *Id.* (quoting Fernando Ferrer, President of the Bronx Borough). Still others suggested that Solarz had an unfair advantage based not on his ethnic background but his financial foreground. "It's not a question of what background he is. It's the color of his money," said Herman Badillo, the city's first Latino congressman. *Id.*

Mean Only Those from Minorities Should Apply?"[151] I propose restating the problem as follows: Does politics of fairness mean that self-defined groups are best represented by territorial districts, even those they ostensibly control? So stated, the question shifts the issue from the candidate to the constituency. By asking this new question, we can see the three incongruous assumptions inherent in racial control of territorial constituencies.

The first assumption is that because they represent a majority of the district population, the fifty-five percent Latino voting-age population is appropriately empowered to represent the entire district, although eight percent of the district is black, twenty-one percent Asian, and sixteen percent white.[152] This assumption parallels the first virtual representation assumption: the district losers will be indirectly represented by majority winners.[153]

Race-conscious districting is arguably necessary because the jurisdiction-wide majority is organized racially and permanently.[154] This argument suggests that there is nothing inherently wrong with the principles of indirect representation underlying winner-take-all majoritarianism, except where the majority operates based on its prejudices. As long as the current pattern of racial bloc voting continues, the minority cannot become part of the jurisdiction-wide governing coalition.[155] Thus, "special" smaller majorities are warranted.

The second assumption is that a Latino majority in this district will choose a representative for all Latinos in the jurisdiction. This tracks the second vicarious representation assumption that similarly situated voters

---

151. *Id.*

152. Mitchell, *supra* note 142, at A29. *But see* Joseph Berger, *A Jagged Shard of Fairness Slices Apart Voting Communities*, N.Y. TIMES, Sept. 7, 1992, at A22 (citing slightly different percentages of racial populations in this District).

153. *See supra* note 81 and accompanying text; *see also* Guinier, *supra* note 23, at 1438.

154. The assumption is that race-conscious districting is necessary to remedy race-conscious exclusion. The exclusion is demonstrated by the unwillingness of the majority to include the minority in its governing coalition. Evidence of this premise is provided by patterns of racially polarized voting. *See* Guinier, *supra* note 23, at 1441 (explaining that virtual representation assumes that "[t]he 51% will look out for the 49% minority as their proxy" because majority self-interest is consistent with the common good; yet, where a permanent and homogeneous majority consistently exercises all the power, that fixed majority loses incentive to look out for or cooperate with the minority, because minority political support is unnecessary).

155. *Id.* at 1442 ("[T]he operation of prejudice in a winner-take-all system denies blacks elected from single-member districts the ability to exercise even minimal legislative power.").

can represent each other.[156] Because Latino interests are underrepresented in other winner-take-all congressional districts, their interests in the city as a whole are now fairly represented by virtue of their electoral control over this one district. Conversely, the Asian, black, and white minorities in this one district are *vicariously* represented by their electoral control over other districts in the city.

Thus, Latinos who do not live in the district are virtually represented by choices made by the Latinos who do live in the district. Race-conscious districting only approximates the diversity of voter identities in the *jurisdiction as a whole*, but not necessarily in each district.

With the second assumption, the race-conscious districting approach does not challenge political representation based on geography; it simply suggests that specific groups should dominate specific districts in proportion to their overall state-wide or jurisdiction-wide percentage. Here, the claim is that political fairness is measured by a jurisdiction-wide baseline rather than by reference to a critique of group rights or majority domination more generally. Majority domination is acceptable as long as each group gets a chance to be represented somewhere in the jurisdiction by its own localized majority.

The third assumption is that the 12th Congressional District is a minority district without regard to the actual intra- or inter-minority conflict within the district. The third assumption presumes political cohesion based on the fiction that the district has an identity independent of the actual constituents. It also presumes equal access for constituency service within the district and relies on the claim that a minority identity ensures a minority ideology. Minority group interests will define the district identity and anyone who represents it.

The Asian, black, and white minorities are presumed to be represented because of their choice to live near Latinos. Stated differently, because Latinos are not as residentially segregated as other racial groups, they can represent the interests of their multicultural neighborhood as a whole. Their neighbors' interests are represented both for personal constituency service and for their territorially defined common interests.

The third assumption is related to the top-down view of representation.[157] Like the virtual representation view that the district has an independent identity, the 12th Congressional District is a "Latino district." As a so-called minority district, it has an identity independent of the actual tensions present, the level of political cohesion, or the political participation rates of its constituents. In this way, race-conscious districting

---

156. *See supra* text accompanying note 83.
157. *See supra* notes 46–48 and accompanying text.

incorporates a static, somewhat monolithic, view of representation that, after the initial drawing of a majority minority district, diminishes the subsequent importance of broad authority from a consenting group of participants.[158]

For example, Latinos within the district arguably are represented by any one of the four Latino candidates, even where a majority of the Latino residents vote for a losing candidate. The issue of choice is submerged within a presumption of ethnic solidarity in the majority Latino population district, even if Representative Solarz did not compete. This is because the district is a Latino district, and the elected representative will therefore service all constituents equally, especially other Latinos.[159]

Yet a top-down view of representation does not encourage broad-based political participation among the district constituency. Nonvoters are represented equally with voters. Because representation is viewed primarily as a means of distributing constituency service and benefits and is primarily based on a common group identity, there is little incentive to monitor actively the public policy positions the representative takes within the governing body. Under this top-down view, elections serve not to initiate an interactive relationship, but to ratify an open-ended one.

In this way, the assumption of "minority district as independent identity" ignores issues of multiple, cross-cutting, and shifting differences. This is an empowerment strategy designed primarily to increase the proportion of minority-group legislators. Because of the success of individual minority-group members, the group as a whole is empowered. As I have argued elsewhere, however, empowerment is not based on assumptions about phenotypic representation.[160] Voters also must be directly given the opportunity and the information necessary to define their interests for themselves.

---

158. In the static view, representation is neither interactive nor engaging of the electorate. When the focus is on empowering voters by instantly emphasizing their opportunity to elect representatives of their choice, the result is that those choices are less important once the boundary lines of the district are set.

159. This virtual representation assumption is also reflected in psychological or filial terms used to describe a common cultural or ethnic heritage. Even where all members of the racial group did not actively support a racial group member, they each are nevertheless represented by someone who is a "role model," a source of pride, and a "sister or a brother."

160. See Guinier, *supra* note 50, at 1101–34 (discussing the assumptions made by the black electoral success model and concluding that the theory often leads to token representation).

These three assumptions, of course, invite the criticism that race-conscious districting arbitrarily reduces voters to their ethnic or racial identity and then only represents that characteristic in a way that isolates or balkanizes the population. But the real complaint is not with the race consciousness of the districting, but with the districting process itself. The race-conscious districting assumptions simply replay the same virtual representation assumptions that are used to justify territorial constituencies in the first place.

Thus, the race-conscious districting assumptions are neither unique nor necessarily contextual. For example, the winning candidate might be the one Latina who appeals to all the different ethnic and racial groups within the district, winning with a five-percent plurality of Latino support and a solid majority of white, black, and Asian votes. Although this individual might be Latina in identity, she would not in fact be elected directly by Latinos to represent their interests.

In fact, the successful candidate was Nydia Velazquez, a former representative of Puerto Rico to New York, who polled thirty-three percent of the vote, compared to twenty-seven percent for Mr. Solarz. According to *The New York Times*, Ms. Velazquez's margin of victory came from overwhelming Latino support in Brooklyn and from strong support from the black community.[161] She reportedly benefited from an endorsement by the city's black mayor, David Dinkins, and from the "firestorm" of criticism that erupted when Mr. Solarz decided to run in the newly drawn district.[162]

One might argue, then, that Ms. Velazquez's election affirmed the second and third assumptions of virtual representation. Because Latinos supported her within the 12th District, Latinos throughout New York City are now vicariously represented even though they could not vote for her. In addition, Ms. Velazquez's black support confirmed the viability of the third assumption that the 12th District is a bona fide "minority dis-

---

161. Tabor, *supra* note 143, at B6.

162. *See* Lindsey Gruson, *For Solarz, A Career Ends in Grief and Relief,* N.Y. TIMES, Oct. 7, 1992, at B3 (attributing Ms. Velazquez's 1869-vote margin primarily to criticism of Solarz's decision to run in a "Hispanic district"); *New York: The Race for the House,* N.Y. TIMES, Sept. 16, 1992, at B8 (listing the final election returns from the Democratic primary for the 12th district). Incidentally, Ms. Velazquez was heavily outspent. Solarz spent $2 million in the race, about $220 for each of the 9138 votes he won. Alison Mitchell, *Rep. Solarz Loses in a New District,* N.Y. TIMES, Sept. 16, 1992, at A1 (noting that Solarz had a "campaign fund of $2 million, more than all the other candidates combined").

trict." The first virtual representation assumption is not directly implicated by the election because it depends upon post-election behavior of the elected representative.

Four other Latino candidates competed in the primary. Elizabeth Colon polled twenty-six percent; Ruben Franco polled eight percent; Eric Ruano Melendez and Rafael Mendez each received three percent of the vote.[163] Although I do not have the actual precinct totals, these figures do not rebut the possibility that a majority of Latino voters (especially those living in Queens) actually preferred someone other than Ms. Velazquez. Similarly, they do not deny the possibility that blacks, who are only eight percent of the District, may have supported Ms. Velazquez, but Asians and whites may have preferred someone else.[164]

Because Asians, at twenty-one percent, are the second-largest group in the District,[165] it may not be appropriate to presume that interminority political cohesion extends to all of the District's minority voters. The other aspect of the third assumption—that this is a genuine Latino district—is also not clear, since a majority of Latinos may have preferred someone other than Ms. Velazquez.

The validity of the first assumption, that the electoral majority will now indirectly represent *all* the electoral minorities, also remains to be seen. It is currently a theoretical claim based on the operation of golden-rule reciprocity in conjunction with other assumptions about the individual nature of voting and representation. The District's political reality, however, may defy the theory that the district minority—those who wasted their votes—will act as a potent political check on a shifting district majority. For example, I noted the possibility that the election returns suggest dis- tinct group interests that exist among and within the Asian, black, and white district community. The votes of these subgroups may, as a practical matter, become permanently wasted.

Indeed, over the ten-year term of the District, the Latino majority may act cohesively and return the Latina incumbent to office. Re-election of the incumbent may occur with decreasing turnout as a percentage of all the District's population, but with increasing support among those who do vote simply because she is the incumbent. This is consistent with evidence that minority candidacies generate relatively high voter turnout the first time a viable minority candidate competes. Turnout, however,

---

163. *Tuesday's Primary Results*, N.Y. TIMES, Sept. 17, 1992, at B6.

164. *See* Tabor, *supra* note 143, at B6 (suggesting that Elizabeth Colon weakened Mr. Solarz by drawing Asian and white votes).

165. *See supra* text accompanying note 152.

tends to go down when constituents realize that the election of a single minority incumbent changes very little of their day-to-day lives.[166]

But the fact that the Latina is now an incumbent gives her tremendous resource advantages over any future opponents. Some may argue that her continued re-election reduces polarization within the district, as the other non-Latina voters see Ms. Velazquez work on their behalf. On the other hand, her predictable re-election success may exacerbate rather than reduce intergroup conflict. The District's complicated racial, ethnic, and linguistic mix is not reflected in the ethnic or racial group membership of its representative. The fact that the district winner in a multi-ethnic district has a psychological, cultural, and sociological connection primarily to one ethnic or racial group may alienate other groups over time.

If Asians, for example, feel consigned to permanent minority status within the minority district, they may bide their time until redistricting in the year 2000, when the legislature decides how many minority districts should be created and who should control them. The fight to be "the group" who gets the district, and with it all the power, pits minorities against each other. The fact that some members of the other minority groups in the 12th District can only cast wasted votes for ten years encourages each group ultimately to think in terms of its own moral, historical, and pragmatic claims to exclusive or primary district representation. Where representation becomes the lottery of competing oppression, no one wins.

Only the second assumption, at least on the psychological level of vicarious representation, is solidly supported by the election of Ms. Velazquez. This is based on evidence that those minority group members who do not vote for group members nevertheless feel "represented" by them.[167] This phenomenon reflects the continued vitality of racial group identity. Many group members feel most represented by one of their own.

Even if the second vicarious representation assumption is true, one could maintain that people are represented without regard for whom they choose to vote simply because of where they choose to live or who they are. Latinos in Queens living a few blocks outside the 12th District, who cannot vote for Ms. Velazquez, will continue to "waste" their votes within the districts in which they reside. Their votes, which under some other district configuration might help elect an additional, or simply a different, Latino, are submerged within their non-Latino district.

---

166. *See* Guinier, *supra* note 23, at 1434–37.
167. *See* Guinier, *supra* note 50, at 1102–09.

Because their votes will be wasted, nondistrict Latinos are not encouraged to participate directly in the process of self-government. The process of voting itself may become meaningless. Districting ignores this problem with wasted votes by embracing group representation based on territorial contiguity and indirect representation.

Because geographic districting wastes votes, neither minority groups nor majority voters are fairly represented. Districting fails to deliver on its virtual representation assumptions, even where districts are drawn to maximize minority voting strength. Districting is not justified by the individual representation value because each voter's vote does not count to the greatest extent possible toward the election of a representative. Districting is not supported by the group representation value because legislators do not represent unanimous constituencies, and they therefore find it either hard to govern or easy to excuse unaccountability. The tensions—between values of individual and group representation; between direct and indirect representation; between top-down and bottom-up representation; and between wasted and effective votes—permeate virtual representation, even within race-conscious geographic districting.

For this reason, modified at-large systems used in corporate governance, such as cumulative voting, should be considered.[168] Under a modified at-large system, each voter is given the same number of votes as open seats, and the voter may plump or cumulate her votes to reflect the

---

168. Under a cumulative voting mechanism, the shareholders of a corporation can multiply the number of votes they are entitled to cast by the number of directors on the ballot and then distribute these votes however they wish. For example, a shareholder could cast all of her votes for only one director in one race and forgo voting in the other elections. *See* REVISED MODEL BUSINESS CORP. ACT § 7.28 (1984). *See generally* Arthur T. Cole, Jr., *Legal and Mathematical Aspects of Cumulative Voting*, 2 S.C. L. Q. 225 (1949) (describing the cumulative voting process and analyzing a formula for calculating the maximum number of shares needed to elect a single or multiple director(s) under a cumulative voting arrangement); Amihai Glazer et al., *Cumulative Voting in Corporate Elections: Introducing Strategy into the Equation*, 35 S.C. L. REV. 295 (1984) (providing a modified formula for maximizing director representation where shareholders vote in blocs).

In raising the idea of alternative remedies, I am not advocating a grand moral theory of representation. I introduce the idea of cumulative voting primarily as a means of broadening the debate about solutions to the continuing problem of racial discrimination and polarization in the political process. I do not believe that cumulative voting is a panacea. Nor do I suggest that it should be imposed on nonconsenting jurisdictions nationwide, or that it should be considered in the absence of evidence that existing electoral arrangements are operating unfairly.

intensity of her preferences. Depending on the exclusion threshold,[169] politically cohesive minority groups are assured representation if they vote strategically.[170] Similarly, *all* voters have the potential to form voluntary constituencies based on their own assessment of their interests. As a consequence, semiproportional systems such as cumulative voting give more voters, not just racial minorities, the opportunity to vote for a winning candidate.

Racial-group interests become those self-identified, voluntary constituencies that choose to combine because of like minds, not like bodies. Legitimate interest constituencies are formed among groups of individuals who share similar opinions or identities. These interest constituencies are less fixed than under territorial districting. Nevertheless, racial minority groups may still choose collectively to elect representatives. But now the minority voters' choices are based on their own conception of identity, which may be defined in racial terms because it is either racially

---

169. The exclusion threshold is the minimum number of minority group members required to guarantee representation in a cumulative voting system. *See* Guinier, *supra* note 23, at 1483 n.250.

170. The following formula determines the minimum number of voters needed to guarantee the election of one representative:

$$\frac{V}{R + 1} + 1$$

See Cole, *supra* note 168, at 229. In this formula, V equals the total number of voters, and R equals the number of representatives to be elected. A minority group may assure itself of representation by having this number of voters plump their votes for a single candidate. In *No Two Seats*, I suggested the following example of a jurisdiction that is to elect ten representatives:

> [I]n a jurisdiction with 1000 voters, 250 of whom are black, a modified at-large plan would use a threshold of exclusion of 1/11th based on the formula of one divided by one plus the number of open seats, plus one. This means that 1/11th of the voters could not be denied representation. The threshold exclusion would work out to be 91 voters (91 is 1/11th of 1000, plus 1). Here, there are 250 black voters. Blacks are more than 2/11th, but short of 3/11th, of the population.
>
> If all voters had 10 votes and could plump them any way they wished, any candidate supported intensely (meaning receiving all 10 votes) by 91 voters would get elected.

Guinier, *supra* note 23, at 1466. Thus, by voting strategically and plumping their votes behind a single candidate, blacks in the scenario above could assure themselves of representation. If 182 black voters plumped their votes evenly behind two candidates, they could assure themselves of representation by two candidates.

apparent, racially derived, or a function of historical treatment by the numerically superior racial majority.[171]

Thus, even if voting is thought to be a concept of individual autonomy, the recognition of voluntary choices to affiliate or form associations minimizes wasted voting while transcending "artificial groups" based solely on residence or race. On the other hand, if voting is seen as a group-representation concept, representation systems should minimize wasted votes in order to realize maximum influence and empowerment. Under either view of voting and representation, a semiproportional system is preferable because it minimizes wasted votes and defines voting behavior based on choices exercised by the voters themselves.

Additionally, if racial group identity is a value that deserves representation, territorial constituencies are an imperfect proxy. If racial group membership is thought to be affiliative yet involuntary in the sense that history, culture, and social pressures combine to define one's membership, it is equally important to provide openings within the political process for self-defined group representation. Territorial constituencies do not do this, because they fail to maximize opportunities for group political empowerment and individual group members' participation and self-expression.

As a result, whether representation is considered essentially an individual *or* a group activity, the principle of one-vote, one-value is necessary to protect voters' interests.[172] Everybody's vote should count for

---

171. An interest constituency need not be racially homogeneous from a physiological standpoint. In other words, interests may be racially identifiable in that members of a particular racial group are more likely to hold certain views. But not all members of the group are assumed to agree on all issues for the group to form an interest constituency. In addition, nongroup members may be part of the interest group to the extent they identify with the group's primary agenda. In this sense, an interest constituency is defined by racial identification, not by racial origin. Blacks in the United States are an obvious minority interest group, despite the presence of a range of ideologies and class status. Whites in South Africa are also a minority interest, although their choice to self-define is a function of their historical treatment of—not by—the numerically superior racial majority. *See generally* LEONARD THOMPSON & ANDREW PRIOR, SOUTH AFRICAN POLITICS 108–80 (1982).

172. Although the concept of one-person, one-vote focuses on the importance of representing the individual, systems of semiproportional representation represent groups *and* individuals better than winner-take-all equipopulous districts. In such districts, one-person, one-vote has been fulfilled, but it has not led to one-vote, one-value. The party winning 51% of the votes actually would capture 100% of the legislature seats. *See* SHAPIRO, *supra* note 37, at 222. In that scenario, 49% of the votes are wasted or lost. The votes of the 49% then do not have equal values to the votes of the 51%, because only the latter votes led to the election of someone representing the voters' interests. More votes can have equal value in a proportional representation system where the seats

somebody's election. Voters are directly represented only if they actively choose who represents their interests.

In this sense, I am arguing for a more expansive account of the representational relationship for *all* voters. In order to achieve political equality and political fairness, an electoral system should give voters the direct opportunity to initiate and terminate their own representational relationship. It is not enough that some voters choose for everyone or that everyone has an equal chance to be the only electoral winner or electoral loser. Voting should become a positive-sum experience in which all voters actively participate in selecting their representative.

On the assumption that each participant should enjoy an equal opportunity both to participate and to influence, the concept of one-vote, one-value describes the idea that each voter should elect someone to represent her interests. This new view of the representational relationship draws on the concepts of equal opportunity to participate and equal opportunity to elect representatives of one's choice that are embodied in the 1982 Voting Rights Act amendments.[173] It arguably would expand the statutory view of the representational relationship in a way that benefits all voters.[174]

The courts, however, have been hesitant to employ a one-vote, one-value system as a remedy under the Voting Rights Act. In Granville

---

awarded are directly proportional to the votes cast. PULZER, *supra* note 57, at 48, 49; *see also* DIXON, *supra* note 1, at 525 ("Pure proportional representation maximizes the number of votes that 'count' and minimizes the number of votes that are 'lost.'").

I should reiterate that my use of the term "proportional representation" is not an effort to reduce political equality to numerical head-counting or numerical shares, but describes instead the goal of political fairness or democratic fair play. I disavow the idea that political fairness is simply a function of numerical proportions or shares. Indeed, my project involves efforts to avoid binary win/lose terminology. In this sense, politics is not necessarily a zero-sum game, but a continuous process of negotiation, compromise, and consensus building toward positive-sum solutions.

173. *See* 42 U.S.C. § 1973(b) (1988) (prohibiting practices that give minority groups "less opportunity than other members of the electorate to participate in the political process and to elect representatives of their choice").

174. Again, I do not argue that the 1982 amendments mandate this view. Especially in light of the Supreme Court's interpretation of the term "voting" in Presley v. Etowah County Comm'n, 112 S. Ct. 820 (1992), legislative action may be necessary in the context of § 5 to re-assert congressional intent about the scope of voting. At this point, I am simply suggesting an approach to curing political unfairness that builds on the themes that have been the subject of the debate surrounding the 1965 Act and especially its 1982 amendments: How can we ensure political equality and meaningful opportunities to participate for a group that has historically been excluded from the franchise without reinforcing the polarization the Act is designed to remedy?

County, North Carolina, black voters challenged the at-large method of electing the county commission.[175] Blacks, who comprised forty-four percent of the county's population, had never been able to elect any person to the five-member commission.[176] The defendant-commissioners conceded that black voters were not represented on the county's at-large commission.[177] They also admitted that if the county were districted, *and if two additional commissioner seats were added,* blacks would be able to elect one of seven commissioners, giving the forty-four percent black population "electoral control" over fourteen percent of the commission.[178] The single-member districting remedy failed to capture much of the black community, which was dispersed throughout the county.

The plaintiffs proposed, and the district court approved, retention of the staggered term, at-large method of election with a threshold lowering, semiproportional modification that allowed voters to cast only three votes for the five open seats.[179] When the modified system was employed, three blacks were elected to the seven-person commission.[180]

The Fourth Circuit in *McGhee v. Granville* reversed and restricted the relief granted based on a narrow definition of the causal relationship between what the plaintiffs challenged and the available relief.[181] The court ruled that single-member districts were the only appropriate remedy.[182] Since the plaintiffs challenged at-large elections that prevented black candidates from getting elected, the exclusive remedy was to create single-member districts in which black candidates were likely to get elected. Even if all or many black voters did not reside in the newly configured majority-black districts, their remedy was limited to the "virtual" representation[183] they received from districts that enjoy black electoral success.[184]

---

175. McGhee v. Granville County, 860 F.2d 110, 112 (4th Cir. 1988).

176. *Id.* at 113.

177. *Id.*

178. *Id.* at 114.

179. *Id.*

180. *Id.* at 114–15 n.5.

181. *See id.* at 118 (holding that if vote dilution is established, "the appropriate remedy is to restructure the districting system to eradicate, to the maximum extent possible *by that means,* the dilution proximately caused by that system; it is not to eradicate the dilution by altering other 'electoral laws, practices, and structures' that were not actually challenged by the claim as made" (emphasis in original)).

182. *Id.*

183. *See infra* notes 81–84 and accompanying text.

184. *See generally* Guinier, *supra* note 50 (offering a critique of black electoral success theory).

By articulating its analysis of vote dilution exclusively in terms of single-member districts, the courts have tended to promulgate single-member districts as a talismanic liability and remedial threshold.[185] At the same time that courts have moved closer to a single-member district, black electoral success standard, they have clearly established "descriptive" proportional representation as the *ceiling*.[186] The Court in *Thornburg v. Gingles*, for example, reversed a finding of dilution in District 23 where it appeared that black voters enjoyed "proportionate" representation because a black was consistently elected over a twelve-year period.[187] The Court did not discuss the fact that in District 23 black voters had to employ "bullet voting" to elect the black candidate and thus forfeited their chance to influence which whites would be elected.[188] Nor did the Court address the evidence that the black who was elected was actually chosen by the white voters and had to "sail trim"[189] his legislative positions accordingly.[190]

Despite judicial reluctance to adopt alternative remedies, the principle of one-vote, one-value satisfies the representational needs of voters in two ways that districting does not. First, it extracts the unfairness of wasted votes from winner-take-all solutions. Votes that would have been wasted in a winner-take-all system are redistributed to voluntary constituencies consistent with the actual level of their political support. Second, it allows voters to choose their representational identity. Rather than imposing a group identity on a given geographic constituency, this

---

185. *See, e.g.*, McNeil v. Springfield, 851 F.2d 937, 939, 942–43 (7th Cir. 1988) (holding, as a threshold requirement, that a minority must "demonstrate that it is sufficiently large and geographically compact to constitute a majority in a single-member district" (quoting Thornburg v. Gingles, 478 U.S. 30, 50 (1986)), *cert. denied*, 490 U.S. 1031 (1989).

186. *See Thornburg*, 478 U.S. at 77 (finding that the presence of minority representation would be inconsistent with an allegation of vote dilution); *see also supra* note 22.

187. *Thornburg*, 478 U.S. at 77.

188. Bullet voting is a technique employed in at-large elections whereby a politically cohesive minority strategically concentrates its voting strength. Guinier, *supra* note 50, at 1142 n.307. By voluntarily abnegating the right to vote for a full slate of candidates and casting instead only one ballot for the "black" candidate, the minority bloc can increase the probability of electing their favored candidate. *See id.* Bullet voting "forces a minority to limit its vote while the majority exercises control over the full state." *Id.*

189. Sail trimming refers to the phenomenon where blacks elected from majority-white multimember districts "defer to other blacks to introduce and promote controversial legislation that would affect black constituents." *Id.* at 1104 n.18.

190. White voters in District 23 thus elected *all* the legislative representatives; without some white cross-over voting, the black candidate would not have received enough support, even with bullet voting by blacks.

system gives voters the opportunity to associate with the identity that fits their own view of psychological, cultural, and historical reality. Thus, racial and other politically cohesive groups could be represented in proportion to their actual strength in the electorate rather than in proportion to their geographic concentration. As a result of political organization, voter education, and strategic voting, any politically cohesive group that is numerous enough to meet the local threshold of representation could mobilize to gain representation.[191]

Ultimately, what the one-vote, one-value principle does is to transform the unit of representation from a territorial or racial constituency to a political or psychological one.[192] This affirms Iris Young's view of the social group as one based on self- and historical-identification, and it rejects representational groups based simply on the joint possession of externally observable attributes or the choice of a residence.[193]

One-vote, one-value makes the assumption that each voter should enjoy the same opportunity to influence political outcomes. No one is entitled to absolutely equal influence; but by the same token, no one is entitled to grossly disproportionate influence or a monopoly on control.[194] The majority should enjoy a majority of the power, but the minority should also enjoy some power too. Thus, one-vote, one-value measures opportunities for fair participation using a baseline of actual participation and real political strength.

The principle of one-vote, one-value, as realized through cumulative voting, also restores the link between representation and voting by ensuring that legislators represent unanimous, not divided, constituencies. Representation becomes the process of bottom-up empowerment based on self-defined expressions of interest. Moreover, assuming voters vote strategically, votes are not wasted either by voting for losing candidates or by packing voters into safe districts. The legislative body can reflect fairly the range of opinions and interests within the public at large, including racial minorities who can be represented based on their electoral strength. Gerrymandering becomes unnecessary and can no longer be used to enhance the disproportionate power of incumbents to ensure their own re-election or to exaggerate the political control of the party in

---

191. This is true for conservative Republicans in Democratic communities or religious minorities within the larger white electorate.

192. *See* Douglas, *supra* note 66, at 155.

193. YOUNG, *supra* note 133, at 82.

194. *See* LoFrisco v. Schaffer, 341 F. Supp. 743, 750 (D. Conn. 1971) ("[I]t is hard to fault minority representation as non-democratic or impermissible as a legislative goal.... [I]t is not antimajoritarian to limit the power of the majority to command more power than its actual strength at the polls."), *aff'd*, 409 U.S. 972 (1972).

power. Finally, local political organizations may be given the space and the possibility of success. Such parties can fill the needs for political mobilization, voter education, and legislative monitoring that largely go unfilled in our current system.

Thus, by restoring the link between representation and voting, alternative election systems encourage voter participation. They also can broaden the range of debate by allowing local political organizations to emerge and interest-based political coalitions to form. These coalitions would not be limited to neighborhood communities of interest, certain racial groups, or particular elections, but would contain dynamic possibilities for regional, reciprocal, or cross-racial political cohesion. The race-conscious context of districting might be retained, but only on an election-by-election, issue-by-issue, voter-by-voter basis.

Of course, semiproportional systems of representation can be criticized for their tendency to destabilize the electorate by either promoting stalemate or creating chaos. I have elsewhere identified many of these concerns,[195] some of which still need to be addressed more fully. In brief, alternative election systems raise legitimacy concerns about paralysis, stability, and efficiency, all of which need to be taken seriously. On the other hand, for those who feel excluded, legitimacy is derived from broad-based consensual authority. Self-government by consensus that recognizes the views of minorities is legitimate and enduring.

In balancing the fears of balkanization against observations about existing alienation, I conclude that exclusiveness is a greater evil than controversy, that passivity does not equal contentment, and that differences need not be permanently enshrined in the electoral configuration. Modified at-large election systems encourage continuous redistricting by the voters themselves based on the way they cast their votes at each election. Whatever differences emerge, therefore, are those chosen by the voters rather than imposed externally on the voters based on assumptions about demographic characteristics or incumbent self-interest. These voter generated differences may infuse the process with new ideas; diversity of viewpoint can be enlightening. Finally, the modified at-large system may simply reflect a necessary transition phase from power politics to principled politics. But, whether it succeeds in that respect, it at least has the benefit of infusing the process with more legitimacy from the perspective of previously disenfranchised groups.[196]

---

195. *See* Guinier, *supra* note 23, at 1487–94.

196. For example, where local county governments, such as Chilton County, Alabama have adopted a modified at-large election system, new interest constituencies have been recognized. For the first time this century, white Republicans and a black Democrat were elected to the county school board and county commission. But, the process of self-

I do not mean to denigrate concerns that the proliferation of political interest constituencies may undermine consensus, exacerbate tension, and destabilize the political system. These concerns reflect a preference for conflict resolution that camouflages rather then identifies political differences. My preference, however, is first to recognize salient differences and then to work with those differences to achieve positive-sum solutions. My idea is that politics need not be a zero-sum game in which those who win, win it all. My idea is that where everyone can win something, genuine consensus is possible.

There is, in addition, a concern with one-vote, one-value principles that I have not previously considered. In my focus on wasted votes, I have not yet examined the effect of one-vote, one-value approaches on communities with large numbers of noncitizens, age-ineligible citizens, or people with other conditions that disable them from voting.[197] For example, concerns about the representation of noncitizens are prominent in the Latino community;[198] concerns about the disproportionate number of young citizens are also relevant to the black community.[199] Thus, each of these communities has a special profile in terms of the number of people each voting member of the community ultimately represents. This is a virtual representation problem within the electorate itself.

Since districting is based on population rather than on turnout or registration rates, people who do not vote at all are nevertheless represented. This idea is encompassed by the third virtual representation assumption— that the district identity is independent, yet consuming, of all constituents. Even if one cannot vote, one's interests are presumably represented by those who can. For minority communities whose population is in greater need of government service, access to representatives based on population may be more fair than access to representatives based on turnout. A voluntary interest constituency composed of like-minded voters devalues the interests of elements within the constituency who cannot or do not vote.

---

government has not broken down. In a county that is about one-sixth black, three white Republicans, three white Democrats and one black Democrat now sit on the school board and the commission. With the balance of power held so closely between Republican and Democratic commissioners, the black representative can be an influential swing vote.

197. Both Bernard Grofman and Pamela Karlan have helped me recognize the extent of this problem.

198. *See* Garza v. County of Los Angeles, 918 F.2d 763 (9th Cir. 1990), *cert. denied*, 111 S. Ct. 681 (1991).

199. Recognition of this fact was behind the development of the 65% rule. *See* United Jewish Orgs. v. Carey, 430 U.S. 144, 164 (1977) (noting that blacks generally constitute a smaller proportion of the voting-age population than of the total population).

Of course, the same criticism can be leveled at safe districting. Although its population base extends top-down representational access to nonvoters, these constituents are stuck with whomever the majority of district voters choose. In other words, safe districting assumes that nonvoters and voters are fungible in that the voters indirectly represent the interests of the nonvoters. Accordingly, children are only indirectly represented by the representatives chosen by adults on their behalf.

Admittedly, changing the structure of electoral units is an incomplete solution even to those problems on which I have previously focused. Because of its potential disruption, it is also a solution worth considering only where the existing election system unfairly distributes political power in a way that is itself disruptive or illegitimate. As for the problem of differential participation rates, I can speculate about three possible responses. First, like districting systems, one-vote, one-value election systems require some subdistricting. Except in very small cities or towns, some multimember subdistricts would be required both to reduce the complexity of the ballot and to promote access for local communities of interest. In New York City, for example, boroughs might be appropriate multimember districts for borough-wide cumulative voting. This might accommodate the concern that representatives have a local constituency for whom they are responsible without regard to who actually voted for them.

Second, although interest representation based on one-vote, one-value does not directly protect nonvoters any better than districts, it does create an environment in which they, as well as voters, are encouraged to participate directly. By participation I refer to the broad range of bottom-up activity relating to the political process. I specifically disavow an emphasis exclusively on election-day voting. Because semiproportional systems rely on *voluntary* interest-group constituencies, they reward local political organizing efforts more than systems with predetermined constituencies. Representation is earned in proportion to political activity and actual turnout rather than fixed population or majoritarian aggregating rules. This means that local political organizations, with an activated grass roots base, can actually win elections.

Nonvoters can participate in the organizing and monitoring efforts of local political organizations and thus actively assert their own interests. Nonvoters can participate in all the pre- and post-election day activities of the political organization. In this way, one-vote, one-value encourages representation directly of interests, not just of voters. Nonvoters can directly support a local organization that articulates their interests rather than passively rely on the presumption that they benefit from choices made by those who virtually vote their interests.

Third, the commitment to consensus politics implicit in the one-vote, one-value approach benefits voters and nonvoters, majorities and minorities. It infuses the process with receptivity to new ideas. It promotes a new definition of stability based on inclusiveness, not quietude. It creates positive-sum possibilities rather than limiting participation to winners and inevitable losers. With its focus on coalition-building and consensus, it does not assume that conflict is better suppressed than voiced. Nor does it assume that politics need always be zero-sum.

One-vote, one-value represents a new vision of political participation. It assumes that empowerment comes from opportunities for the active assertion of one's own interests—speaking out, not just being spoken for. One-vote, one-value attempts to mediate directly the tension between individual and group representation that characterizes the districting process at each level. Thus it is more fair both to individuals and to groups.

III. Conclusion

The controversy over racial-group representation offers us an opportunity to re-examine the political fairness of our district-based electoral system. I posit that a system is procedurally fair only to the extent that it gives each participant an equal opportunity to influence outcomes. I call this principle one-vote, one-value. This is a measure of procedural, not substantive, legitimacy. According to this principle, outcomes are relevant only to the extent that they enable us to measure degrees of input, not to the extent they achieve some objective, substantive notion of distributive justice.

The challenge to racial-group representation is actually a criticism of a different kind of group representation: representation based on homogeneous geographic constituencies. Race-conscious districting is simply one expression of a larger reality: winner-take-all districting. Both justify wasting votes with often unstated assumptions about the group characteristics of district voters. In other words, the criticism of racial-group representation is, at bottom, a criticism of winner-take-all districting in which the district boundaries and the incumbent politicians define the interests of the *entire* district constituency.

I conclude that group representation is as American as winner-take-all districting; that the two are conflated in criticisms of race-conscious districting; and that consideration of alternative means of representing racial groups can shift the debate about political fairness. By directly confronting the problem of wasted voting, we may make the system more legitimate from the perspective of previously disenfranchised groups, and more fairly representative of issue-based groups who previously have been aggregated and silenced within the majority.

I have proposed a new view of the representational relationship that is more protective of all voters' ability and more conducive to all voters' initiative to choose directly who represents them. By critically examining certain fundamental assumptions about representation, I hope to revive our political imagination. "Change the way people think," said South African civil-rights martyr Steven Biko, "and things will never be the same."[200] Or as Professor Robert Dixon declared almost 25 years ago:

> [N]ow that the first round of reapportionment has been accomplished, there is need to talk "one man-one vote" a little less and to talk a little more of "political equity," and of functional components of effective representation. *A mathematically equal vote which is politically worthless because of gerrymandering or winner-take-all districting is as deceiving as "emperor's clothes."*[201]

200. David Myers, *America's Social Recession*, CHI. TRIB., July 30, 1992, § 1, at 27.
201. DIXON, *supra* note 1, at 22 (emphasis added).

CHAPTER 9

One Person, Seven Votes: The Cumulative Voting Experience in Chilton County, Alabama

Richard L. Engstrom, Jason F. Kirksey, and Edward Still

> The time has come to contemplate more innovative means of ensuring minority representation in democratic institutions.
>
> United States District Court,
> Southern District of Georgia,
> *Johnson v. Miller*, 864 F. Supp.
> 1354, 1393 (September 12, 1994)

The typical medium in this country for providing racial and language minorities with an opportunity to elect representatives of their choice has been the single member district (SMD). Geographical districts are created that contain sufficient numbers of minority group members to provide voters of that group with a realistic opportunity to elect a candidate of their choice. In the redistricting that followed the 1990 census, this medium was manipulated for this purpose far more than ever before. District boundaries reflecting racial differences in residential patterns resulted in many odd-shaped configurations. Some districts, for example, contain finger-like extensions that capture additional minority voters. Others have narrow unpopulated, or lightly populated, "land bridges" connecting otherwise noncontiguous minority voters. The shapes of these contorted districts have been equated with a "bug splat," "ketchup splash," and an "angry snake."[1] The district that stimulated the popular

---

1. *See* Viteritti, Joseph P. 1994. *Unapportioned Justice: Local Elections, Social Science, and the Evolution of the Voting Rights Act* CORNELL JOURNAL OF LAW AND PUBLIC POLICY 4:199–271, p. 214.

expression "gerrymandering," a convex-shaped state senate district created in Massachusetts in 1812,[2] looks like a model of compactness compared to many of the electoral districts adopted in the 1990s.

This species of district may soon be extinct, however. The manipulation of the district format to enhance the electoral opportunities of minorities has provoked a hostile reaction among many whites. Contorted majority-minority districts are viewed as a form of racial entitlement or "affirmative action."[3] Despite the fact that these districts constitute only a small part of districting plans in which whites continue to be overrepresented, white voters have filed lawsuits alleging that these districts by themselves constitute impermissible "racial gerrymandering." The Supreme Court has established a standard for adjudicating these claims that leaves these districts in serious jeopardy.

While acknowledging that there are no federal constitutional or statutory requirements that districts conform to any particular shape criterion, the Supreme Court held in 1993, in *Shaw v. Reno*, that districts with "bizarre" or "extremely irregular" shapes may be constitutionally invalid if race is the only explanation for their appearance. Such districts, according to the Court, must be "strictly scrutinized" for possible violations of the equal protection clause of the Fourteenth Amendment. Under that test, if race is the only explanation for an otherwise "irrational" district, then the district violates that clause unless it was adopted to further a "compelling governmental interest" and was "narrowly tailored" to accomplish that interest (*Shaw*, at 642, 644, 657–658). In a subsequent case, *Miller v. Johnson* (1995), the Court held that strict scrutiny is required whenever "traditional race-neutral districting principles" are subordinated to racial considerations in the design of districts (*Miller*, sl. op. at 15). Strict scrutiny is a difficult standard to satisfy, and the number of majority-minority representational districts in this country could be reduced dramatically as a result of the *Shaw* and *Miller* rulings.[4]

---

2. *See* Griffith, Elmer C. 1907. THE RISE AND DEVELOPMENT OF THE GERRYMANDER. Chicago: Scott, Foresman and Company, pp. 16–18.

3. *See* Cain, Bruce E. 1992. *Voting Rights and Democratic Theory: Toward a Color-Blind Society?* In Bernard Grofman and Chandler Davidson, eds., CONTROVERSIES IN MINORITY VOTING: THE VOTING RIGHTS ACT IN PERSPECTIVE. Washington, D.C.: The Brookings Institution, p. 261 and, more generally, Sniderman, Paul M. and Thomas Piazza. 1993. THE SCAR OF RACE. Cambridge, MA: Harvard University Press.

4. Federal district courts in Louisiana, Texas, and Georgia invalidated majority African American congressional districts soon after the *Shaw* ruling [see *Hayes v. State of Louisiana*, 839 F. Supp. 1188 (W.D. La. 1993) and 862 F. Supp. 119 (W.D. La. 1994), *Vera v. Richards*, 861 F. Supp. 1304 (S.D. Tex. 1994), and *Johnson v. Miller*, 864 F. Supp

Extinguishing this particular medium for providing minorities with electoral opportunities should not become an excuse, however, for limiting the opportunities themselves. Democracy does not require that the voting strength of a politically cohesive minority group be devalued simply because the group's voters cannot form a majority within a nicely shaped election district. Indeed, democracy does not require SMDs at all. As Justice Clarence Thomas has noted, the use of SMDs in this country is "merely a political choice," not a constitutional mandate (*Holder v. Hall* sl op at 20). Accepting limitations on minority electoral opportunities imposed by that particular format, especially after *Shaw*, is also a political choice.

This was recognized explicitly in one of *Shaw*'s initial progeny, *Johnson v. Miller* (1994). A majority-African American congressional district in Georgia was invalidated in *Johnson* for failure to satisfy the strict scrutiny standard. The court made it clear that the goal of a more inclusive representational arrangement did not violate the Constitution, only the particular medium employed. While invalidating the district, the court admonished the state to find "more innovative means of ensuring minority representation" (see epigraph). It called upon the Georgia legislature to find "new solutions" to the problem of minority underrepresentation, noting that the law does not require "a wooden, mechanical application of one remedy while ignoring all alternatives" (at 1393).

A variety of election systems could be used in place of our system of geographical districts combined with a winner-take-all plurality or majority vote rule. Electoral opportunities within many of these other systems do not depend on, or depend much less on, where district lines are placed. These alternative systems are equally if not more democratic than our district arrangements. Indeed, almost all of the world's democracies employ one of these less district-dependent election systems.[5]

In this country, the alternative system that has received the most attention is cumulative voting. Electoral reformers generally, and voting rights

---

1354 (S.D. Ga. 1994)]. The congressional districts at issue in *Shaw* itself, however, were found on remand to satisfy the strict scrutiny standard [*Shaw v. Hunt*, 861 F. Supp. 408 (E.D. N.C. 1994), as were state legislative districts in California [*DeWitt v. Wilson*, 856 F. Supp. 1409 (E.D. Ca. 1994)].

5. *See*, e.g., Lijphart, Arend. 1994. ELECTORAL SYSTEMS AND PARTY SYSTEMS. Oxford: Oxford University Press, pp. 10–56; Rule, Wilma and Joseph F. Zimmerman, eds. 1994. ELECTORAL SYSTEMS IN COMPARATIVE PERSPECTIVE: THEIR IMPACT ON WOMEN AND MINORITIES. Westport, CT: Greenwood Press; Taagepera, Rein and Matthew Soberg Shugart. 1989. SEATS AND VOTES: THE EFFECTS AND DETERMINANTS OF ELECTORAL SYSTEMS. New Haven, CT: Yale University Press, pp. 19–37, and Bogdanor, Vernon and David Butler, eds. 1983. DEMOCRACY AND ELECTIONS: SYSTEMS AND THEIR POLITICAL CONSEQUENCES. Cambridge: Cambridge University Press.

advocates in particular, have shown increasing interest in the cumulative voting option.[6] Over 30 counties, municipalities, and school districts have recently adopted this system in response to lawsuits alleging minority vote dilution.[7]

The following reviews the cumulative voting alternative. The theoretical argument in support of its utility as a remedy for minority vote dilution will be identified and empirical evidence of its nondilutive nature examined. In addition, a major argument advanced against the use of the cumulative system, that it is too complex for voters to understand and to use effectively, will also be examined empirically. The source of this evidence will be an exit poll of voters in a recent cumulative voting election in Chilton County, Alabama. Chilton County is a rural county in the center of Alabama, about 30 miles south of Birmingham. The county adopted the cumulative system as part of the settlement of a vote dilution lawsuit brought by African Americans against its previous at-large

---

6. See e.g., Guinier, Lani. 1994. THE TYRANNY OF THE MAJORITY: FUNDAMENTAL FAIRNESS IN REPRESENTATIVE DEMOCRACY. New York: The Free Press, pp. 94–101; Reed, Judith. 1992. *Of Boroughs, Boundaries and Bullwinkles: The Limitations of Single-Member Districts in a Multiracial Context.* FORDHAM URBAN LAW JOURNAL 19:759–780; Richie, Rob. 1993. *Cumulative Voting Captures Imagination of Electoral Reformers.* NATIONAL CIVIC REVIEW XX:72–74; Vigil, Maurilio E. 1992. *A New Remedy for an Old Ailment: Cumulative Voting as an Alternative to the Single Member District in Minority Voting Rights.* LATINO STUDIES JOURNAL XX: 82–90, and Viteritti, 1994.

7. The first adoption of cumulative voting this century was in 1987 in Alamogordo, New Mexico (see generally Engstrom, Richard L., Delbert A. Taebel, and Richard L. Cole. 1989. *Cumulative Voting as a Remedy for Minority Vote Dilution: The Case of Alamogordo, New Mexico* JOURNAL OF LAW AND POLITICS 5:469–497; Cole, Richard L., Richard L. Engstrom, and Delbert Taebel. 1990. *Cumulative Voting in a Municipal Election: A Note on Voter Reactions and Electoral Consequences.* WESTERN POLITICAL QUARTERLY 43:191–199.; and Vigil, 1992). At least 34 other local governmental units had adopted the system by 1994, including 26 in Texas, six in Alabama, and one in Illinois and South Dakota.

A federal court ordered a mixed election system for the Worcester County Commission in Maryland, in which party primaries were to be held in single member districts and the subsequent general elections at-large with cumulative voting, was overturned on appeal when all parties objected to that arrangement. African American plaintiffs objected to the districting plan to be used for the primary elections, while the county objected to the cumulative voting system for the general elections. The mixed arrangement was replaced by a single member district scheme preferred by the plaintiffs, which is to be used in both elections. *Cane v. Worcester County, Maryland,* 59 F.3d 165 (4th Cir 1995).

election arrangement.[8] Voter understanding of, use of, and reactions to the option to cumulate seven votes in this election will be examined, as well as the electoral consequences of the cumulative system for racial and other political minorities.

Cumulative Voting

Cumulative voting is applicable to multi-seat elections. Its defining characteristic is voters are permitted to cast more than one vote for a candidate of their choice. Voters in this system are provided with as many votes as there are seats to be filled in an election, but they are not restricted, as is usually the case in this country, to casting only a single vote for any candidate or candidates that they may prefer. If a voter prefers one or a few of the candidates more than the others, under cumulative voting he or she is free to express the intensity of that preference by casting more than one vote for those candidates. In a three-seat election, for example, a voter could vote in the traditional way, casting one vote apiece for three different candidates, or cast two votes for one candidate and one for another, or "plump" all three of his or her votes for a single candidate. This system satisfies the basic "one person, one vote" rule because every individual voter is provided the same number of votes and the same options through which to cast them. The winning candidates are determined by a simple plurality vote rule; the top N candidates are awarded the N available seats.[9]

---

8. *Dillard v. Chilton County Commission*, Civ. No. 87-T-1179-N (M.D. Ala. 1988) (consent decree).

9. Cumulative voting has been a common feature of elections to corporate boards in this country (see Glazer, Amihai, Deborah Glazer, and Bernard Grofman. 1984. *Cumulative Voting in Corporate Elections*. SOUTH CAROLINA LAW REVIEW 35:295–309). Prior to 1987, however, its only use in elections to public offices this century had been for seats in the Illinois state House of Representative. That application was discontinued when a state constitutional amendment was adopted in 1980 that reduced the membership of that legislative chamber by one-third and required the smaller chamber to be elected by SMDs. The amendment was stimulated by a negative public reaction to a large legislative salary increase, and voter acceptance is believed to have been based on the desire to reduce the number of legislators rather than abandon cumulative voting (see Everson, David H. 1992. *The Effect of the 'Cutback' on the Representation of Women and Minorities in the Illinois General Assembly*. In Wilma Rule and Joseph F. Zimmerman, eds., UNITED STATES ELECTORAL SYSTEMS: THEIR IMPACT ON WOMEN AND MINORITIES. New York: Greenwood Press). On the experience with cumulative voting in Illinois generally, see Blair, George S. 1960. CUMULATIVE VOTING: AN EFFECTIVE ELECTORAL

Cumulative Voting And Minorities

Cumulative voting has been promoted as a remedy for minority vote dilution because it allows a politically cohesive minority group to concentrate its votes in a multi-seat election more effectively than it can when the one vote for candidates of choice restriction applies. The ability to cumulate votes can provide a minority of voters with the opportunity to elect a candidate or candidates favored by that group, even though other voters do not support those candidates.

The opportunity a minority group has to elect a candidate through cumulative voting can be demonstrated theoretically through a coefficient known as the threshold of exclusion.[10] This coefficient identifies the percentage of the actual electorate that a group must exceed in order to elect a candidate of its choice regardless of how the rest of the electorate votes. The coefficient is based on a set of "worst case" assumptions, from the minority group's perspective, about the behavior of the voters outside the group. These assumptions are: (1) the other voters cast all of the votes available to them, (2) none of their votes are cast for the minority group's preferred candidate, but rather (3) are concentrated entirely on a number of candidates equal to the number of seats to be filled, and (4) are divided evenly across those candidates. The other voters, in short, vote in the most efficient manner possible. They do not "waste" any of their votes by dispersing votes across too many candidates or overconcentrating votes on one or a few candidates.

In a three-seat three-vote cumulative election, for example, the threshold of exclusion is 25.0 percent. Any group that constitutes over 25 percent of the voters in that context can elect a candidate if all of the group's voters plump for that candidate. This can be illustrated by the following hypothetical. Assume that 1,000 people have voted and that

---

DEVICE IN Illinois Politics. Urbana: University of Illinois Press; Dunn, Charles W. 1972. *Cumulative Voting Problems in Illinois Legislative Elections.* HARVARD JOURNAL ON LEGISLATION 9:627–665; Kuklinski, James. 1973. *Cumulative and Plurality Voting: An Analysis of Illinois' Unique Electoral System.* WESTERN POLITICAL QUARTERLY 26:726–746; Broh, C. Anthony 1974. *Utility Theory and Partisan Decision-Making: Cumulative Voting in Illinois.* SOCIAL SCIENCE QUARTERLY 55:65–76; and Wiggins, Charles W. and Janice Petty. 1979. *Cumulative Voting and Electoral Competition: The Illinois House.* AMERICAN POLITICS QUARTERLY 7:345–365.

10. See generally Rae, Douglas, Victor Hanby, and John Loosemore. 1971. *Thresholds of Representation and Thresholds of Exclusion: An Analytic Note on Election Systems.* COMPARATIVE POLITICAL STUDIES 3: 479–488, and regarding cumulative voting more specifically, Engstrom, Taebel, and Cole, 1989: 478–80, and Still, Edward. 1984. *Alternatives to Single-Member Districts.* In Chandler Davidson, ed., MINORITY VOTE DILUTION. Washington,D.C.: Howard University Press, pp. 255–258.

25 percent plus one of them, or 251, have plumped for candidate A. Assume further that the remaining 749 voters have voted consistently with the worst case assumptions, that is, all 749 cast three votes, none of which are cast for candidate A but instead are divided evenly across candidates B, C, and D. Under these assumptions, A receives 753 votes while B, C, and D each receives 749, and therefore A is elected. If any of these assumptions about the behavior of the other voters is relaxed, candidate A's vote is still sufficient to win one of the three seats. (For example, if the other voters did not support B, C, and D evenly, but instead gave B and C 754 votes each, then D can receive at most 739 votes and A still wins one of the seats.) In the three-vote three-seat context, in short, any group that constitutes more than 25 percent of the voters and concentrates its support on one candidate can elect that candidate, regardless of how the rest of the voters cast their ballots.

The value of the threshold of exclusion varies inversely with the number of seats to be filled. As the number of seats increases, the value of the threshold decreases. The value can be calculated for any specific number of seats through the following formula:

$$\frac{1}{1 + \text{Number of seats}} \times 100$$

As noted above, the value for the three-seat context is 25 percent. When the number of seats is five, the value of the threshold is 16.7 percent. If the number of seats is seven, then the value is 12.5 percent (see Table 1). These

Table 1. Threshold of Exclusion Values for Cumulative Voting Systems

Number of Seats or Positions	Value (%) of Threshold of Exclusion
2	33.3
3	25.0
4	20.0
5	16.7
6	14.3
7	12.5
8	11.1
9	10.0

values illustrate that with cumulative voting rules a relatively small group of voters has an opportunity to elect a candidate of its choice in a multi-seat election, provided the group is politically cohesive. It must be remembered that the coefficient represents the percentage of the electorate that a group must exceed in order to elect a candidate regardless of how the other voters vote. If the behavior of the other voters deviates from any of the worst case assumptions, then the minority group may be smaller and/or less cohesive and still have a realistic opportunity to elect a candidate or candidates of its choice.

Cumulative voting obviously does not guarantee any particular election result. It simply provides a politically cohesive minority group with a better opportunity to elect a candidate than it has in the more traditional multi-seat election systems employed in this country.[11] In the more traditional systems, the largest group of voters often determine the winners of all of the seats.[12] Votes cast by minority group members tend to be submerged into those of the larger electorate and have little if any impact on the election outcome. This sweep effect is less likely to occur when cumulative voting rules are employed. The ability to cumulate votes provides minority voters, as a group, with an opportunity to cast a much larger vote for a candidate of its choice, thereby increasing that candidate's chances of being among those elected. This is the reason cumulative voting has been classified as a "semi-proportional" election system.[13] It does not employ a formula that converts votes into seats in a proportional manner. Nor are any seats reserved for candidates of any group. Winners are determined, as noted above, by a simple plurality rule.

This feature of cumulative voting makes election outcomes less district dependent. The cumulative system can be employed with an at-large format or with smaller multi-member districts, but when it is applied to multi-member districts, the importance of the district itself declines as the number of seats allocated to it increases. Districts in a cumulative voting election do not need to be majority-minority in order to provide minority groups with electoral opportunities. There is less need, therefore, to manipulate district lines for that purpose. The larger the number of seats allocated to a district, the smaller and/or more residentially dis-

11. See Engstrom, Richard L. and Michael D. McDonald. 1993. 'Enhancing' Factors in At-Large Plurality and Majority Systems: A Reconsideration. ELECTORAL STUDIES 12:385–401.

12. See, e.g., Niemi, Richard G., Jefferey S. Hill, and Bernard Grofman. 1985. The Impact of Multimember Districts on Party Representation in U.S. State Legislatures. LEGISLATIVE STUDIES QUARTERLY. 10:441–455, p. 447.

13. See, e.g., Lakeman, Enid. 1974. How DEMOCRACIES VOTE: A STUDY OF ELECTORAL SYSTEMS. London: Faber and Faber,pp. 87–90, and Weaver, Leon 1984. Semi-Proportional and Proportional Representation Systems in the United States. In Arend Lijphart and Bernard Grofman, eds., CHOOSING AND ELECTORAL SYSTEM: ISSUES AND ALTERNATIVES. New York: Praeger, pp. 198–199.

persed a minority can be and still have an opportunity to elect a candidate of its choice.

The electoral opportunities provided minorities by cumulative voting are not just theoretical. They have been verified empirically by the experiences of local government jurisdictions that have had cumulative voting elections recently. At least one minority candidate has been elected in almost all of the recent elections in which voters have had the option to cumulate votes.[14] Exit polls conducted at three of these elections, those to the Alamagordo, New Mexico city council in 1987 and 1990, and that to the Sisseton, South Dakota school board in 1989, have documented that the minority candidates elected were the candidates most preferred by the voters of the respective minority groups. The ability of minority voters to aggregate their votes on behalf of these candidates, a Latina in the Alamogordo elections and a Native American in the Sisseton case, contributed significantly to their electoral success.[15]

The electoral opportunities provided by cumulative voting are not limited to racial and language minorities. Any group of like-minded voters can take advantage of the option to cumulate votes. Indeed, one of the arguments advanced in favor of cumulative voting as a remedy for minority vote dilution is that it, unlike SMDs, is not a race-specific remedy.[16] Other voters that share interests and candidate preferences can employ the cumulative options to help elect candidates of their choice as well. These groups need not be bound by race or residence. Two groups in particular, political parties that do not attract a plurality of the votes, and women, are commonly identified as likely beneficiaries of the cumulative system.

The semi-proportional label has been attached to the cumulative voting system primarily because of its impact on political parties.[17] As noted above, when cumulative voting is allowed, the strongest party in a multi-

14. Engstrom, Richard L. 1992. *Modified Multi-Seat Election Systems as Remedies for Minority Vote Dilution.* STETSON LAW REVIEW 21:743–770, pp. 752–757; Engstrom, Richard L., Edward Still, and Jason F. Kirksey. Forthcoming. *Limited and Cumulative Voting in Alabama: An Assessment After Two Rounds of Elections.* NATIONAL POLITICAL SCIENCE REVIEW.

15. Engstrom, Richard L. and Charles J. Barrilleaux. 1991. *Native Americans and Cumulative Voting: The Case of the Sisseton-Wahpeton Sioux.* SOCIAL SCIENCE QUARTERLY 72:388–393; Cole, Richard L., and Delbert Taebel. 1992. *Cumulative Voting in Local Elections: Lessons from the Alamogordo Experience.* SOCIAL SCIENCE QUARTERLY 73:194–201; and Engstrom, Taebel, and Cole, 1989.

16. Guinier, Lani. 1994. *[E]racing Democracy: The Voting Rights Cases.* HARVARD LAW REVIEW. 108: 109–137.

17. See Lakeman, 1974: 87–90, and Weaver, 1984: 198–199.

seat election is less likely to win all of the seats. Seats are more likely to be shared between or among parties. It was this feature of cumulative voting that prompted its adoption in Illinois, where it was used to elect the lower chamber of the state legislature from 1872 to 1980. Cumulative voting was adopted in 1870 to offset the domination, at that time, of the Democratic Party in the southern part of the state and the Republican Party in the northern part. Single party domination within these regions was so complete that members of the weaker party within a region were rarely elected in SMDs. Cumulative voting was adopted to provide the supporters of the weaker parties in each region with a chance to be represented.[18]

Women are a second group expected to benefit from cumulative voting. Many advocates of more direct representation for women view the SMD as a major impediment to the election of women. When only one person is to be elected, they argue, women are disadvantaged both in terms of party nominations and voter reactions. Multi-seat formats have been favored, therefore, and the advantages of cumulative voting within that context noted.[19] If enough women voters have a preference for women candidates and cumulate votes on their behalf, the number of women elected will increase. Cumulative voting has been described, consequently, as a "woman-friendly" election system.[20]

The Complexity Criticism

A major criticism of cumulative voting has been its alleged complexity. The option to cumulate votes, it has been suggested, is too difficult for voters to understand and use effectively. Voters in this country have

---

18. See Cornelius, Janet. 1972. CONSTITUTION MAKING IN ILLINOIS, 1818–1970. Urbana, IL: University of Illinois Press, pp. 66–67 and Blair, 1960:1–10.

19. See, e.g., Rule, Wilma. 1992. *Multimember Legislative Districts: Minority and Anglo Women's and Men's Recruitment Opportunity*. In Wilma Rule and Joseph F. Zimmerman, eds., UNITED STATES ELECTORAL SYSTEMS: THEIR IMPACT ON WOMEN AND MINORITIES. New York: Greenwood Press; Rule, Wilma and Pippa Norris. 1992. *Anglo and Minority Women's Underrepresentation in Congress: Is the Electoral System the Culprit?* In Wilma Rule and Joseph F. Zimmerman, eds., UNITED STATES ELECTORAL SYSTEMS: THEIR IMPACT ON WOMEN AND MINORITIES. New York: Greenwood Press; and Darcy, R., Susan Welch, and Janet Clark. 1994. WOMEN, ELECTIONS, AND REPRESENTATION. 2d ed; Lincoln, NE: University of Nebraska Press, pp. 170–171.

20. Rule, Wilma. 1994. *Parliaments of, by, and for the People: Except for Women?* In Wilma Rule and Joseph F. Zimmerman, eds., ELECTORAL SYSTEMS IN COMPARATIVE PERSPECTIVE: THEIR IMPACT ON WOMEN AND MINORITIES. Westport, CT: Greenwood Press, pp. 26–28.

rarely been allowed to cast more than a single vote for any candidate of their choice, even in multi-seat, multi-vote elections, and the removal of this restriction, it is asserted, will create significant confusion for voters.[21]

The exit polls noted above have failed to substantiate these claims. In all three of the polls, very high percentages of voters (around 90 percent) indicated that they understood the system and did not find it any more difficult to use than the voting systems employed in other elections. This was true for minority voters as well as other voters.[22]

The actual use of the option to cumulate votes, however, was found to vary sharply with whether a voter was a member of the relevant minority. Minority group voters were found to have aggregated their votes behind one or a few candidates much more frequently than other voters. Overall evaluations of the cumulative system varied by group status as well, with minority voters far more positive in their evaluations of the system than the other voters.[23]

The Chilton County Context

The Chilton County exit poll provides another test of the understanding of, use of, and electoral consequences of cumulative voting. It was conducted during the 1992 November general election for the Chilton County Board of Commissioners. The 1990 census places the county's population at 32,458, of which only 11.3 percent is African American. The county's voting age population is 9.9 percent African American. Both the county commission and the county school board settled vote dilution lawsuits in 1988 by agreeing to the adoption of cumulative voting.[24] The commission was expanded from a four-member body elected

---

21. See, e.g., Dunn, 1972:655–658; Everson, David H., Joan A. Parker, William L. Day, Rita A. Harmony, and Kent D. Redfield. 1982. *The Cutback Amendment.* Illinois Issues Special Report. Sangamon State University, Springfield, Illinois, p. 23; and Note. 1982. Alternative Voting Systems as Remedies for Unlawful At-Large Systems. YALE LAW JOURNAL 92:144–160, pp. 155–156.

22. Cole, Engstrom, and Taebel, 1990:193–194; Engstrom and Barrilleaux, 1991: 391; and Cole and Taebel, 1992: 197.

23. Cole, Engstrom, and Taebel, 1990: 194–197; Engstrom and Barrilleaux, 1991: 391–392; and Cole and Taebel, 1992: 197–200.

24. Dillard v. Chilton County Commission, Civ. No. 87-T-1179-N (M.D. Ala. 1988) (consent decree) and Dillard v. Chilton County Board of Education, 699 F. Supp. 870 (MD Ala. 1988).

at-large through a place system[25] to a seven-member body elected at-large by cumulative voting. The school board, previously a five-member body elected at-large, likewise became a seven-member body elected countywide by cumulative voting.

This cumulative voting election was significantly different, in two respects, from those at which voters have been polled previously. The first concerns the number of votes available for cumulation. The previous exit polls have all been conducted at elections in which the voters had only three votes to cast. This limited voters to casting either one vote apiece for three separate candidates, two votes for one candidate and one for another, or plumping all three of their votes for a single candidate (assuming voters cast all three of their votes). This limited number of permutations may have been a reason for the voters not perceiving the system to be particularly complex. In the Chilton County election, in contrast, every voter had seven votes to cast. This allows all seven votes to be cast in 15 different combinations, e.g., 5-1-1, 4-3, 3-2-1-1, 2-2-2-1, a situation in which the voters might be expected to find exercising their cumulative options a much more complex task.

The previous elections at which polls were conducted were also non-partisan elections. Political party identifications of candidates did not appear on the ballots, and parties were not active in the campaigns. The Chilton County commission election, however, was a partisan contest. Both the Democratic and Republican parties presented a complete slate of candidates in this election, and the party endorsements appeared on the ballot along with the candidates' names.[26] This provided another potential source of complexity for voters. While voters committed to a party could cast all of their votes among candidates of that party, any cumulation of votes behind a candidate would be at the expense of one or more of the other candidates of that party.[27] Cumulating votes therefore

---

25. See Engstrom and McDonald, 1993: 387–388.

26. Party nominees were selected in a primary election. Nomination through primaries precludes a party from nominating less than a full slate of candidates unless fewer than seven candidates seek the nominations. This virtually eliminates the problem of noncompetitive general elections due to political parties not nominating a complete slate of candidates, which had been a pronounced feature of the Illinois experience with cumulative voting (see, e.g., Goldburg, Carol B. 1994. *The Accuracy of Game Theory Predictions for Political Behavior: Cumulative Voting in Illinois Revisited.* JOURNAL OF POLITICS 56:885–900; Wiggins and Petty, 1979: 358–359; Dunn, 1972: 646–647, 661; Sawyer, Jack and Duncan MacRae, Jr. 1962. *Game Theory and Cumulative Voting in Illinois: 1902–1954.* AMERICAN POLITICAL SCIENCE REVIEW 56:936–946.; and Blair, 1960: 41–44, 106).

27. See Goldburg 1994:886,890, n.9.

could conflict with a partisan commitment, adding additional complexity to the choices voters faced.

The partisan context in Chilton County also meant, of course, that a second identifiable minority, a partisan minority, could be advantaged by the option to cumulate votes. While cumulative voting had been adopted to enhance the opportunities of the county's African Americans to elect candidates of their choice, it could also serve as a medium through which voters attached to a minority political party would have a better chance to elect candidates. In Chilton County, the Republican Party is the minority party. No Republican had ever been elected to the county commission under the previous at-large arrangement. Voters identifying with the Republican Party, therefore, as well as African American voters, could be advantaged by the use of the system in this setting. This raises the distinct possibility that in Chilton County the use and evaluation of the system might vary not only along racial lines, but also along party lines, at least among the white voters.

There was one woman among the 14 commission candidates. Ann Bankston was a Republican Party nominee. This election therefore provides at least a limited opportunity to determine the extent to which the cumulative option was exercised on behalf of a woman candidate.

The following reports the results of the exit poll, in which 1,362 voters participated. The poll attempts to ascertain the extent to which voters understood and utilized the cumulative system in this seven-vote partisan context, and their overall evaluations of that system. Possible racial, partisan, and gender differences in the use of the system will be examined, as will the impact of the cumulative options on the electoral success of candidates favored by the respective groups.

The 1992 Election

The 1992 election was the second time cumulative voting was used to elect the county commission. The first cumulative voting election was in 1988. Democratic and Republican primary elections were held for both commission and school board seats in June of that year, followed by general elections in November. These cumulative voting elections resulted, for the first time, in the racial and partisan integration of both of these governing bodies. African American candidates were the leading vote recipients in each of the Democratic primaries. These candidates then finished first in the general election for the commission and second in the general election for the school board. Republicans were also elected for the first time, as Republican candidates finished second, third, and seventh in the general election for the commission seats, and first, third, and fourth in the school board contest.[28] Two of the successful Republican school board candidates were women. The only woman the Democrats nominated for the school board finished eighth. In the commission election, the only woman candidate in the general election was a Republican who finished next to last.

A second cumulative voting election was held for commission seats in 1992. (Commissioners serve four-year terms, whereas school board members serve six-year terms.) Two African Americans were nominated from a field of 16 candidates in the Democratic primary that year. Bobby L. Agee, the African American incumbent, was again the leading vote recipient in that party's June primary, while Robert R. (Shelby) Binion, another African American, finished third. Agee was subsequently reelected in the November general election, placing second with 9.69 percent of the votes cast, while Binion failed to win a seat, finishing eleventh with 5.78 percent of the votes. The number of Republicans on the commission declined from three to two as a result of the 1992 election. Incumbents Julius Kelley and Charles W. Bryant, who had been the top two vote recipients in the eight-candidate Republican primary, finished fourth and seventh respectively in the general election with 8.73 and 7.35 percent of the votes. The third Republican incumbent, Durward Plier, finished ninth with 6.68 percent of the votes. The only woman candidate, Bankston, finished twelfth, with 5.37 percent of the votes. The votes received by all of the candidates in the general election are reported in part A of Table 2, opposite.

Exit Poll

African Americans constituted only 11.6 percent of the registered voters in Chilton County at the time of the general election in 1992. Given that a primary purpose of the exit poll was to compare African American and white voters use of and reactions to the cumulative option, precincts were selected for the exit poll so that African American voters would be oversampled. This was accomplished by including among the sample precincts the four with the highest percentages of African Americans among the registered voters. These precincts had African American registration percentages of 45.4, 37.0, 32.4, and 29.0 individually, and 39.5 percent overall. These four precincts were supplemented by six others that were selected randomly from the remaining 23 precincts, with the

---

28. See Still, Edward. 1992. *Cumulative and Limited Voting in Alabama.* In Wilma Rule and Joseph F. Zimmerman, eds., UNITED STATES ELECTORAL SYSTEMS: THEIR IMPACT ON WOMEN AND MINORITIES. New York: Greenwood Press, pp. 185–190.

Table 2. 1992 Chilton County Commission Election and Exit Poll Results

CANDIDATE	(A) Official Vote Totals		(B) Vote in Exit Poll		(C) % Point Difference (B-A)	(D) Weighted Vote in Exit Poll		(E) % Point Difference (D-A)
	RANK	%	RANK	%		RANK	%	
Hayes(D)*	1	11.94	3	9.95	-1.99	2	10.76	-1.18
AGEE (D)**	2	9.69	1	15.73	6.04	3	10.64	0.95
Smitherman (D)	3	9.22	2	10.08	0.86	1	11.06	1.84
Kelley (R)	4	8.73	8	6.87	-1.86	7	7.58	-1.15
Culp (D)	5	8.52	4	7.60	-0.92	4	8.33	-0.19
Cost (D)	6	8.21	9	6.62	-1.59	8	7.23	-0.98
Bryant (R)	7	7.35	5	7.45	0.10	5	8.21	0.86
Clecker (D)	8	6.86	10	5.36	-1.50	9	5.86	-1.00
Plier (R)	9	6.68	6	7.19	0.51	6	7.93	1.25
Godbee (R)	10	5.83	11	5.08	-0.75	10	5.60	-0.23
BINION (D)**	11	5.78	7	7.05	1.27	13	4.66	-1.12
Bankston (R)***	12	5.37	12	4.46	-0.91	11	4.92	-0.45
Wallace (R)	13	3.56	13	4.27	0.71	12	4.71	1.15
Robinson (R)	14	2.25	14	2.28	0.03	14	2.52	0.27

* D or R in parentheses denotes partisan affiliation.

** African American candidates.

*** Female candidate.

probability of selection proportional to the total number of registered voters in the precincts. African American registration in these six precincts ranged from 0.0 percent to 13.2 percent, and was 8.1 percent overall. The 10 sample precincts therefore contained 82.8 percent of the county's African American registered voters, compared to 40.1 percent of the other registered voters. Registration overall in these 10 precincts was 21.4 percent African American.

An effort was made to invite all of the voters in the sample precincts to participate in the exit poll.[29] Unless assistance was requested, the poll was self-administered by each respondent. Participation in the exit poll was solicited the entire time the polls were open at all but one of the precincts. The exception was an all-white, rural precinct where, despite the fact that no laws had been violated, a county law enforcement officer made those administering the exit poll leave soon after voting began. Only 12 voters therefore participated in the poll at this precinct. (A similar effort to remove interviewers from a second polling place was aborted when the interviewers cited their legal rights to conduct the poll.)

A total of 1,362 voters participated in the exit poll, of which 270 (19.8 percent) were African Americans. In the nine precincts in which the poll was administered the entire day, 22.4 percent of the people signing in to vote participated in the poll. In the county overall, 9.3 percent

---

29. Skip intervals, which identify every kth person leaving a polling place as a potential respondent, were not employed because of the high refusal rates typical of exit polls [see, e.g., Lewis, I. A. (Bud). 1991. *Media Polls, the Los Angeles Times Poll, and the 1988 Presidential Election*. In Paul J. Lavrakas and Jack K. Holley, eds., POLLING AND PRESIDENTIAL ELECTION COVERAGE. Newbury Park, CA.: Sage Publications, and Frankovic, Kathleen A. 1992. *Technology and the Changing Landscape of Media Polls*. In Thomas E. Mann and Gary R. Orren, eds., MEDIA POLLS IN AMERICAN POLITICS. Washington, D.C.: The Brookings Institution]. Voters skipped through this procedure leave the polls and are not in any retrievable sample frame through which subsequent nonrespondents can be randomly replaced. This precludes a truly random procedure for replacing the large number of voters who either evade the interviewers or otherwise refuse to participate. Rather than skip potential respondents, therefore, we made an effort to reach all of the voters in each sample precinct. Two interviewers were assigned to every precinct. This approach provides every voter in a precinct with an equal probability of being asked to participate, and results in a larger number of actual respondents, thereby facilitating the analysis of different demographic or other categories of respondents.

One of the co-authors of this manuscript participated in the administration of the exit poll, along with an inter-racial group of students from Birmingham Southern University. The poll was conducted under the direction of Davis and Penfield, a polling firm located in Birmingham, Alabama.

of those signing in participated. Only 702 (51.5 percent) of the respondents, however, identified how they had cast their votes in the commission election, of which 143 (20.3 percent) were African Americans.

The votes reported in the exit poll are compared to the official count in Table 2. The exit poll vote is contained in part B of the table. Each candidate's percentage of votes in the poll was within 2 percentage points of the percentage they received in the actual election, with one exception. The vote in the exit poll for Agee, the African American incumbent, was 6.04 percentage points higher than his actual vote. This no doubt reflects the overrepresentation of African Americans in the poll. Among the top seven candidates in the exit poll, all but the sixth and seventh place finishers actually won seats on the commission. These were Plier (who finished ninth in the actual vote) and Binion (the other African American candidate, who finished eleventh in the actual vote), both of whom were among the top seven candidates in the actual vote in the sample precincts.

If the votes in the exit poll are weighted to reflect the oversampling of African Americans, then the percentage of votes received by Agee is reduced to 10.64, only 0.95 percentage points off his actual percentage, and the percentage for Binion drops to 4.66, which is likewise closer to his actual percentage.[30] Binion is also no longer among the top seven vote recipients when the votes are weighted. He is replaced in that group by Kelley, a candidate who was in fact elected. Weighting had little impact on the vote percentages of the white candidates. None had their percentage reduced as a consequence of weighting, and none gained as much as a percentage point. The weighted exit poll results are reported in part C of Table 2.

Voter Understanding

As noted above, a major criticism of cumulative voting concerns its alleged complexity. Voters may distribute their votes across candidates in more ways under the cumulative system than under the multi-member election systems more commonly used in this country. This has prompted predictions that voters will find cumulative voting to be confusing, and voting therefore more difficult under that system. Exit polls

---

30. African Americans constituted 11.8 percent of those signing in to vote in the county, but 23.6 percent in the sample precincts. They also constituted a similar 20.3 percent of the respondents reporting how they had voted in the exit poll. In this weighted analysis, the number of votes reported by African Americans has been deflated by weighting their votes by .523, which reproduces an electorate that is 11.8 percent African American.

in Alamogordo and Sisseton have not confirmed these expectations, but in each of those settings voters had only three votes to cast.[31] It is possible that the cumulative options are not particularly confusing in a three-vote context, given the limited permutations in which the votes can be cast, but will become more confusing when more votes are available for cumulation. It has also been suggested that this problem, if it is present, is likely to be most acute among the less educated voters, and therefore among those who are expected to be major beneficiaries of the system, minority voters.[32]

Despite having seven votes available to cumulate, the voters in Chilton County did not appear to find the cumulative system particularly confusing. When asked whether they knew they could cast all seven of their votes for a single candidate, 89.8 percent of the respondents answering the question indicated that they did (see Table 3, part A), a fig-

Table 3. Voter Understanding of Option to Cumulate

	Voter Knew Could Plump[a]			
	Yes		No	
	%	(n)	%	(n)
A. Overall	89.8	(1207)	10.2	(137)
B. Education				
<12 years	86.7	(235)	13.3	(36)
12 years	90.1	(556)	9.9	(61)
>12 years	91.6	(393)	8.4	(36)
C. Race				
White	88.2	(937)	11.8	(125)
African American	95.5	(252)	4.5	(12)

[a]Question: "In the county commission election today, you were allowed to cast seven votes. Did you know that you could cast all seven of your votes for the same candidate in the county commission election?" (Response options=no and yes.)

---

31. See Cole, Engstrom, and Taebel, 1989; 193–194; Engstrom and Barrilleaux, 1991: 391; and Cole and Taebel, 1992: 197.

32. See, e.g., Note, 1982: 155.

ure similar to that in the other exit polls. Answers did not vary greatly by either education or race. As revealed in part B of Table 3, among those with less than 12 years of formal education, 86.7 percent stated that they understood they could plump, compared to 90.1 percent of those who had completed 12 years of school and 91.6 percent of those with more than 12 years. While African American respondents, overall, had completed fewer years of formal education,[33] a higher percentage of African Americans than whites stated that they knew they could plump (95.5 percent compared to 88.2) (Table 3, part C). Indeed, over 90 percent (90.3) of the African Americans with fewer than 12 years of school understood they could plump, while among the white respondents, 85.2 percent of those with fewer than 12 years of school understood they had this option.

When asked whether the cumulative voting system was more difficult to understand than the voting systems employed in other local elections, a higher percentage of the respondents in Chilton County than in the other settings did answer that it was. Responses to this question are reported in part A of Table 4, p. 304. Whereas about 15 percent of the respondents in the other polls had found it more difficult, this was the case for 25.0 percent of the respondents in Chilton County. Among those completing fewer than 12 years of school, 27.2 percent found it more difficult, while among those with 12 years and those with more than 12 years, the percentages were 20.8 and 29.3 (Table 4, part B). African Americans again appeared to be the most comfortable with the system, despite their lower levels of education, as only 12.2 percent of them found it more difficult, compared to 28.1 percent of the whites (Table 4, part C.) Among the respondents with less than 12 years of school, 22.2 percent of the African Americans and 29.0 percent of the whites reported that they found the system to be more difficult.

Voter Use and Electoral Consequences

Among the respondents indicating how they had voted, over three-fourths (78.1 percent) reported casting more than one vote for at least one candidate. The largest number of votes cast for any of the candidates

---

33. Among the African American respondents reporting their education, 27.8 percent had completed fewer than 12 years of school, 43.0 percent completed 12 years, and 29.3 percent had completed more than 12 years. Among the white respondents reporting their education, 18.8 percent had completed fewer than 12 years, 48.0 percent 12 years, and 33.2 percent more than 12 years.

Table 4. Voter Perception of Relative Difficulty

	System Perceived as More Difficult[a]			
	Yes		No	
	%	(n)	%	(n)
A. Overall	25.0	(326)	75.0	(977)
B. Education				
<12 years	27.2	(71)	72.8	(190)
12 years	20.8	(124)	79.2	(472)
>12 years	29.3	(123)	70.7	(297)
C. Race				
White	28.1	(287)	71.9	(734)
African American	12.2	(32)	87.8	(231)

[a]Question: "Compared to other local elections in which you have voted, did you find this county commission election system any more difficult to understand?" (Response options=no and yes.)

by each respondent is reported in part A of Table 5, p. 305. The option to plump all seven votes for one candidate was by far the most popular option. Over half (53.6 percent) reported giving all seven votes to a single candidate. Other cumulative options were exercised by about one-fourth of the voters.

While more respondents in the Chilton County poll than other polls reported that the cumulative system was more difficult to understanding than the systems employed in other local elections, the increased difficulty did not appear to impede actual use of the cumulative options. Among those finding the system more difficult, over two-thirds (68.7 percent) reported cumulating votes, with 46.7 stating they plumped their votes for one candidate.[34] The actual exercise of the cumulative option was not strongly related to education, either. Among those who had completed less than 12 years of school, 81.6 percent cumulated votes,

34. A higher percentage of those finding the system to be more difficult, however, did decline to identify how they had voted. Among those reporting the system more difficult, 54.0 percent did not reveal their vote, compared to 46.1 percent of those who said the system was not more difficult.

Table 5. Use of the Cumulative Option

Largest Number of Votes Cast for Any Candidate	A Overall		B Whites		B African Americans		C Adjusted Overall	
	%	(n)	%	(n)	%	(n)	%	(n)
1	21.9	(154)	25.5	(140)	9.1	(13)	23.3	(148)
2	3.7	(26)	4.7	(26)	—	—	4.1	(26)
3	6.4	(45)	8.2	(45)	—	—	7.1	(45)
4	9.8	(69)	11.5	(63)	3.5	(5)	10.5	(67)
5	4.0	(28)	5.1	(28)	—	—	4.4	(28)
6	0.6	(4)	0.7	(4)	—	—	0.6	(4)
7	53.6	(376)	44.4	(244)	87.4	(125)	49.9	(316)
	100.0	(702)	100.1	(550)	100.0	(143)	99.9	(634)

compared to 78.9 percent of those completing 12 years and 75.8 percent completing more than 12. Indeed, the option to plump all seven votes was exercised more frequently by those with less education. Among those with less than 12 years of school, 62.7 percent reported plumping for a single candidate, whereas the corresponding percentages for those with 12 years and more than 12 years were 56.0 and 45.4.

There was a large racial difference in the use of the cumulative option, however. Over 90 percent (90.9) of the African Americans reporting how they had voted cast more than one vote for at least one candidate, compared to 74.5 percent of the whites (Table 5, part B). The difference was even larger when it came to plumping. Among African Americans, 87.4 percent reported casting all seven votes for a single candidate. The comparable figure for whites was 44.4. (Part C of Table 5 reports the overall percentages of voters exercising the various cumulative options, adjusted for the oversampling of African American voters.)

African American voters exercised the cumulative option to support the two African American candidates, Agee and Binion. Agee was their first choice, receiving 63.3 percent of their votes, and Binion their second choice, with 28.9 percent. No white candidate received as much as 2.0 percent of the votes cast by African Americans. Most of the African American support for Agee and Binion came in the form of plumping. Agee received seven votes from 57.3 percent of the African American voters, and Binion received seven from another 25.9 percent. Agee would not have been reelected without his African American support, as he was the twelfth choice of white voters, receiving only 3.2 percent of their votes. (Binion was the last choice of white voters, receiving 1.2 percent of their votes.) The ability to cumulate votes was extremely important to Agee's reelection. When the analysis is adjusted to reflect the oversampling of African American voters, Agee finished seventh in terms of the number of voters supporting him (rather than the number of votes received), only five voters ahead of the eighth place candidate.

Among the white respondents, there was very little difference in the use of the cumulative option between the Democratic and Republican party identifiers. About three-fourths (76.6 percent) of the Democrats gave more than one vote to at least one candidate, and 45.1 percent plumped (Table 6). The respective figures for Republicans were 71.9 and 43.6.[35] Democratic voters were more cohesive in their support of their

---

35. Straight party voting, defined in this context as casting one vote for each of the party's nominees, also differed little between identifiers. Whereas 9.7 percent of the white Democratic respondents reported supporting each Democratic nominee, 14.5 percent of the Republican identifiers cast a vote for each of the Republican candidates.

Table 6. Partisan and Gender
Differences in the Use of the Cumulative Option

White Respondents Only

Largest Number of Votes Cast for Any Candidates	Party				Gender			
	Democrat		Republican		Male		Female	
	%	(n)	%	(n)	%	(n)	%	(n)
1	23.4	(41)	29.1	(64)	27.1	(67)	23.7	(71)
2	5.1	(9)	3.2	(7)	5.3	(13)	4.3	(13)
3	9.7	(17)	7.3	(16)	8.1	(20)	8.3	(25)
4	11.4	(20)	10.9	(24)	13.4	(33)	10.0	(30)
5	5.1	(9)	4.5	(10)	4.5	(11)	5.7	(17)
6	—	—	1.4	(3)	0.8	(2)	0.7	(2)
7	45.1	(79)	43.6	(96)	40.9	(101)	47.3	(142)
	99.8	(175)	100.0	(220)	100.1	(247)	100.0	(300)

party candidates than Republican voters were of Republican candidates. The white Democrats gave 79.4 percent of their votes to Democratic candidates. Their first five choices were the five white Democratic nominees. Agee was their sixth choice, but a Republican rather than Binion was their seventh choice. Binion placed twelfth in the vote cast by white Democrats.

Republican voters were less cohesive, casting 69.2 percent of their votes for Republican candidates. The first five choices of the Republican voters were Republican candidates, but three Democratic candidates finished ahead of the two remaining Republican nominees. (Agee and Binion were the thirteenth and fourteenth choices of Republican voters.) While the cumulative option may have been critical to the initial election of Republican candidates in 1988,[36] it does not appear to have benefited the party's candidates in 1992. In the adjusted analysis, all of the Republican candidates placed better when the candidates are ranked by the number of voters supporting them rather than by the number of votes they received. The two Republican incumbents who were reelected finished first and fourth in the number of voters supporting them, but fifth and seventh in the number of votes received.

White women were slightly more likely than white men to cumulate votes. Among the women, 76.3 percent cast more than one vote for at least one candidate, and 47.3 percent plumped all of their votes for a single candidate (Table 6). The corresponding figures for white men were 72.9 and 40.9. This difference had little electoral consequence, however, as the two groups did not differ much in their candidate preferences. Both groups would have elected four Democrats and three Republicans, with the only disagreement being over one of the Democrats.

The cumulative option was rarely exercised in support of the only woman candidate in this election, Republican nominee Ann Bankston. Only 5.5 percent of the white voters cumulated votes on her behalf, and only 2.0 percent plumped for her. The respective figures for white women were 5.9 and 2.3. Not even Republican women were likely to cumulate votes for Bankston; only 8.0 percent of the Republican women gave her more than one vote, and only 3.2 percent plumped for her. Bankston was not among the top seven choices of either male or female voters, and was only the seventh choice of the Republican women. While cumulative voting may be a "woman friendly" election system, as Rule argues,[37] gender was not a salient variable in this election.

---

36. Still, 1992.
37. 1994: 26–28.

Voter Evaluations

The respondents evaluation of the cumulative system was mixed. Respondents were asked to provide a summary evaluation of the system, rating it as either excellent, good, fair, or poor. The distribution of responses is reported in part A of Table 7, p.310. While the modal response overall was poor, selected by 39.1 percent, more respondents gave the system a positive rating of either excellent (15.3 percent) or good (32.0).

Just as the exercise of the cumulative option varied by race, so did the evaluation of the system. Indeed, the racial gap was even more pronounced in the evaluations (Table 7, part B). African American voters were very positive about the system, with 37.4 percent saying the system was excellent and 39.2 percent saying it was good. Another 17.7 percent of the African Americans responded with fair, while only 5.7 percent rated the system as poor. This perception was not shared by white voters, however, more of whom rated the system as poor, 47.7 percent, than either excellent (9.7 percent) or good (30.1 percent). The remaining 12.5 percent of the whites rated it as fair. (Part C of Table 7 reports the distribution of responses when adjusted for the oversampling of African Americans.)

This racial division should not be surprising. Cumulative voting was a systemic change resulting from a lawsuit African Americans brought against the county. It was adopted for an explicit racial purpose, to give the county's African Americans a better chance to elect a candidate of their choice to two local governing bodies, the county commission and the school board. It has undoubtedly accomplished that purpose, and African American support for the system is to be expected.

In this context, white hostility to the system is not surprising either. Cumulative voting was adopted in Chilton County as a remedy for racial vote dilution, and like other race conscious remedies for discrimination, it can be expected to stimulate white resentment and resistance.[38] In other settings in which cumulative voting has been adopted in response to lawsuits, similar divisions between majorities and minorities have been present.[39] The candidate preferences registered in the exit poll reveal that race remains a major division in Chilton County politics. Racial division over a race-conscious remedy, therefore, should not be surprising. In the only setting in which polls have been conducted at more than one cumulative voting election, in each of which a minority candidate

---

38. See Cain, 1992: 261, 271, and more generally Sniderman and Piazza 1993.

39. See Cole, Engstrom, and Taebel, 1990; Engstrom and Barrilleaux, 1991; and Cole and Taebel, 1992.

Table 7. Evaluations of the Cumulative System

	Excellent		Good		Fair		Poor	
	%	(n)	%	(n)	%	(n)	%	(n)
A. Overall	15.3	(202)	32.0	(422)	13.6	(179)	39.1	(516)
B. Race								
White	9.7	(100)	30.1	(311)	12.5	(129)	47.7	(493)
African American	37.4	(99)	39.2	(104)	17.7	(47)	5.7	(15)
C. Adjusted Overall	12.9	(152)	31.3	(367)	13.1	(154)	42.8	(503)

Evaluation[a]

[a]Question: "How do you like this county commission election system?"
(Response options = excellent, good, fair, and poor.)

preferred by minority voters won a seat, majority group hostility toward the cumulative system did decline over time.[40]

Among the white voters, party identification had minimal impact on the evaluation of the system. While Republican identifiers could be expected to rate the system more favorably, given the minority status of that party in county politics, their evaluations differed only marginally from those of the white Democrats (see Table 8, p. 312). White women, however, while not a distinct voting group in this election, were much less negative toward the system than white men. Whereas 59.6 percent of the white men rated the system as poor, only 36.2 percent of the white women did (Table 8). Almost half of the white women gave the system a positive rating of excellent (12.4 percent) or good (36.2 percent).

Conclusion

Majority-minority districts have become an endangered species. According to the Supreme Court, those that do not conform to "traditional race-neutral districting principles" must satisfy the strict scrutiny standard for compliance with the Fourteenth Amendment (*Miller*, sl. op. at 15). While exactly what these principles entail is the subject of great confusion, as is how much deviation from them suffices to trigger strict scrutiny,[41] there can be little doubt that the number of such districts will decline in the near future. The popular description of the strict scrutiny test is, after all, "strict in theory but fatal in fact."

This new adjudication standard should not be allowed to become an excuse for limiting the opportunities that minority voters have to elect candidates of their choice. As the federal district court in Georgia noted, minority vote dilution does not have to be tolerated simply because nicely shaped majority-minority districts cannot be created. Additional remedies are available and should be considered (*Johnson v. Miller*, at 1393).

The alternative remedy that has received the most attention is cumulative voting. The nondilutive nature of this modified multi-seat election system has been documented on numerous occasions. The analysis reported above provides additional evidence of its efficacy. The Chilton County experience is especially important because it is the most potentially complex context in which cumulative voting has been employed in this country. Voters in Chilton County are allocated seven votes, over twice as many as the voters in any of the other cumulative voting settings in which exit polls

40. Cole and Taebel, 1992.
41. Engstrom, Richard L. 1995. *Shaw, Miller, and the Districting Thicket.* NATIONAL CIVIC REVIEW 84:323–336.

Table 8. Partisan and Gender
Differences in Evaluations of the Cumulative System
White Respondents Only

	Evaluation[a]							
	Excellent		Good		Fair		Poor	
	%	(n)	%	(n)	%	(n)	%	(n)
Party								
Democratic	12.7	(42)	27.2	(90)	13.3	(44)	46.8	(155)
Republican	9.1	(34)	34.9	(131)	13.6	(51)	42.4	(159)
Gender								
Male	7.2	(36)	23.9	(120)	9.4	(47)	59.6	(299)
Female	12.4	(64)	36.2	(187)	15.1	(78)	36.2	(187)

aQuestion: "How do you like this county commission election system?"
(Response options = excellent, good, fair, and poor.)

have been conducted. Chilton County voters are therefore presented with far more permutations through which to cast their votes. It is also the only partisan election setting so studied, with each party nominating a full-slate of candidates.

Despite this potential complexity, the voters in Chilton County did not find the cumulative system particularly confusing. Indeed, approximately 80 percent of the voters in Chilton County actually employed the option to aggregate votes behind a candidate or candidates in the November, 1992 election, reflecting the different intensity with which they preferred candidates. This ability to cumulate votes was critical to the re-election of the county's only African American commissioner. The Chilton County experience clearly illustrates that cumulative voting can provide minority voters with an opportunity to elect a candidate of their choice, while enhancing, rather than inhibiting, every voter's ability to express their candidate preferences through the ballot.

Part IV

JUDICIAL ELECTIONS AND THE VOTING RIGHTS ACT

Applying the Voting Rights Act to Judicial Elections: The Supreme Court's Misconstruction of Section 2 and Misconception of the Judicial Role

Ralph A. Rossum

In *Chisom v. Roemer*,[1] the Supreme Court held that § 2 of the Voting Rights Act of 1965, as amended in 1982, applied to judicial elections. In the original Voting Rights Act of 1965, § 2 was a restatement of the guarantees of the Fifteenth Amendment. In 1982, Congress amended the section to allow minority voters nationwide to challenge any "standard, practice, or procedure" of election (however long it may have been in place) on the ground of discriminatory "result."[2] Congress thereby circumvented the constitutional requirement laid out in *City of Mobile v. Bolden*[3] that minority plaintiffs must prove discriminatory intent behind a challenged electoral procedure. In amended § 2, a "standard, practice, or procedure" of election is said to have a discriminatory result when minority voters are found to have "less opportunity than other members of the electorate to participate in the political process and to elect representatives of their choice." The provision explicitly states, however, that "nothing in this section establishes a right to have members of the protected class elected in numbers equal to their proportion in the population."[4]

Chisom applied the results test of § 2, as amended, to the election of judges, thereby affecting the judicial selection systems of 29 states.[5] It

---

1. 501 U.S. 380 (1991)

2. See Abigail Thernstrom, WHOSE VOTES COUNT: AFFIRMATIVE ACTION AND MINORITY VOTING RIGHTS (*Harvard University Press*, 1987), 304.

3. 446 U.S. 55 (1980).

4. 42 U.S.C. § 1973 (b).

5. Judges are elected in partisan election in 11 states (Alabama, Arkansas, Illinois, Indiana, Mississippi, New York, North Carolina, Pennsylvania, Tennessee, Texas, and

barred these states from employing any "standard, practice, or procedure" that would result, whether intentionally or not, in the dilution of minority voting strength in the election of their judiciaries. *Chisom* has been "taken almost uncontroversially as correct" by voting rights activists.[6] I will argue, to the contrary, that *Chisom* was wrongly decided— the Supreme Court both misconstrued Section 2 and misconceived the judicial role—and should therefore be overturned.

I.

The specific language of § 2 at issue in *Chisom* provided that a voting rights violation exists when minority voters "have less opportunity than other members of the electorate to participate in the political process and *to elect representatives of their choice.*"[7] When the federal courts were first called upon to apply these words to judicial elections, they refused, insisting that judges are not representatives."[8]

a.

In *Chisom v. Edwards*,[9] Judge Charles Schwartz was asked by black plaintiffs in a class-action suit to find that the process of electing justices to the Louisiana Supreme Court violated § 2, as amended. The plaintiffs alleged that the election of two at-large justices from the Parishes of Or-

---

West Virginia) and in nonpartisan elections in 18 states (Arizona, California, Florida, Georgia, Idaho, Kentucky, Louisiana, Michigan, Minnesota, Montana, Nevada, North Dakota, Ohio, Oklahoma, Oregon, South Dakota, Washington, and Wisconsin). G. Alan Tarr, JUDICIAL PROCESS AND JUDICIAL POLICYMAKING (*West Publishing Company*, 1994), 67–68.

6. Kathryn Abrams, *Relationships of Representation in Voting Rights Jurisprudence*, 71 TEXAS LAW REVIEW 1409, 1411 (1993).

7. 42 U.S.C. § 1973(b). Emphasis added. While § 2 does not speak of "vote dilution," the Supreme Court in *Thornburg v. Gingles*, 478 U.S. 30 (1986), understood it to proscribe practices that produce that result, identifying as the statutory basis for a dilution claim the words, "to elect representatives of their choice."

8. This paper does not address the issue of whether judicial election systems are covered by § 5 of the Voting Rights Act, which requires preclearance by the U.S. Justice Department of any changes in voting procedures in areas of the country with a history of voting discrimination. Section 5 does not specifically restrict its application to election systems pertaining to "representatives," a restriction included in the 1982 amendments to § 2. See *Clark v. Roemer*, 500 U.S. 646 (1991)

9. 659 F. Supp. 183 (E.D. La. 1987).

leans, St. Bernard, Plaquemines, and Jefferson impermissibly diluted the voting strength of blacks who were registered to vote in Orleans Parish (Orleans Parish contained half the registered voters of the at-large district, and more than half of the registered voters in Orleans Parish were black) and thereby deprived them of the opportunity to "elect representatives of their choice." Judge Schwartz dismissed their claims.

He began by noting that, prior to the 1982 amendments to § 2, a three judge court in *Wells v. Edwards*[10] had rejected an earlier claim of discrimination in the election of the same two at-large justices based on an alleged violation of the one-man, one-vote principle. The three judge court held that "the concept of one-man, one-vote apportionment does not apply to the judicial branch of government,"[11] because "[J]udges do not represent people, they serve people. Thus, the rationale behind the one-man, one-vote principle, which evolved out of efforts to preserve a truly representative form of government is simply not relevant to the makeup of the judiciary."[12] Relying on *Wells*, Judge Schwartz argued that "[j]udges, by their very definition, do not represent voters but are 'appointed (or elected) to preside and to administer the law.'"[13] He noted that "the legislative history of the Voting Rights Act Amendments does not address the issue of § 2 applying to the judiciary," and that "most of the discussion concerning the application of the Voting Rights Act refers to legislative offices."[14] He closed this portion of his opinion by reflecting on the judicial role and how different judges are (and should be) from representatives:

> This Court recognizes the long-standing principle that the judiciary, on all levels, exists to interpret and apply the laws, that is, judge the applicability of laws in specific instances. Representatives of the people, on the other hand, write laws to encompass a wide range of situations. Therefore, decisions of representatives must occur in an environment which takes into account public opinion so that laws promulgated reflect the values of the represented society, as a whole. Judicial decisions which involve the individual or individuals must occur in an environment of impartiality so that courts render judgments which reflect the particular

---

10. 347 F. Supp. 453 (M D. La 1972).

11. 347 F. Supp. at 454.

12. 347 F. Supp. at 455. The Supreme Court affirmed *Wells v. Edwards* without opinion. 409 U.S. 1095 (1973). Justice White, joined by Justices Douglas and Marshall, vigorously dissented.

13. Judge Schwartz was quoting BLACK'S LAW DICTIONARY, 1968. 659 F. Supp. at 186.

14. 659 F. Supp. at 186–187.

facts and circumstances of distinct cases, and not the sweeping and sometimes undisciplined winds of public opinion.[15]

Judge Carl B. Rubin reached the same conclusion in *Mallory v.
Eyrich*,[16] an Ohio case concerning the election of municipal court
judges. Although he cited *Thornburg v. Gingles*[17] and conceded that
"the election of only two blacks to the Municipal Court of Hamilton
County Ohio and the election of no blacks to the Common Pleas
Court of Hamilton County Ohio is sufficient evidence to make a 'results' determination in favor of plaintiffs,"[18] Judge Rubin granted the
defendant's motion for summary judgment, because, he insisted, § 2
of the Voting Rights Act does not apply to the election of judges in
state courts. "A person performing a judicial function is not a representative of anyone."[19]

Judge Rubin distinguished a "representative legislature" from a
"court"—a distinction "noted as far back as in an essay by Hamilton in
The Federalist, No. 78" and based on the fact that they "simply perform
different functions." Moreover, he reasoned, only judges may be either
elected or appointed. The notion of an "appointed legislature" is "impossible in a democratic society;" a "nonrepresentative legislature" is "a
contradiction in terms." "An appointed judge, however, is not a contradiction in terms. In accordance with Article III. of the U.S. Constitution,
every United States judge is appointed and in varying degrees so are
judges in many states." If judges can be either elected or appointed but
legislatures can only be elected, he concluded that "there must be an inherent difference in their functions."[20]

For Judge Rubin, the function of the courts is to interpret and apply
the law while the function of the "representative legislature" is to re-present the views of the public.[21] He highlighted this difference by observing
that "a black or white legislator elected to represent the interests of his

---

15. 656 F. Supp. at 187.
16. 666 F. Supp. 1060 (S.D. Ohio 1987).
17. 478 U.S. 30 (1986).
18. 666 F. Supp. at 1062.
19. Judge Rubin cited *Buchanan v. Rhodes*, 249 F. Supp. 860 (1966), at this point in
his argument. 666 F. Supp. at 1064. Judge Rubin also invoked *Stokes v. Fortson*, 234 F.
Supp. 575 (1964): "[M]anifestly, judges and prosecutors are not representatives in the
same sense as are legislators or the executive. Their function is to administer the law, not
to espouse the cause of a particular constituency." 666 F. Supp. at 1062.
20. 666 F. Supp. at 1062.
21. Judge Rubin quoted from *New York State Association of Trial Lawyers v. Rockefeller*, 267 F. Supp. 148 (1961): "[T]he state judiciary unlike the legislature is not the
organ responsible for achieving representative government." 666 F. Supp. at 1063.

constituency is expected by that constituency to act at all times in accordance with its wishes. If he did not he might be violating their trust. He is their representative. To translate that concept to black and to white judges would reduce the judicial system to chaos," since no one could "seriously assert that white litigants should fare better before a white elected judge and black litigants fare better under a black elected judge." Underscoring his point, he concluded: "To refer to a 'partisan legislator' may be [a] mark of approval; to refer to a 'partisan judge' is a mark of condemnation and one which removes him completely from the role of an unbiased arbiter of social conflicts."[22]

b.

Judges Schwartz and Rubin denied that judges were representatives and thus refused to hold that judicial elections were covered by the results test of § 2.[23] Their method of interpreting § 2 was altogether straightforward and customary; they found the ordinary meaning of Congress's language in the statute's text and then applied that meaning, having first determined by use of the established canons of construction that Congress did not intend for some meaning other than the ordinary one to be applied.[24] Their appellate brethren on the Fifth and Sixth Circuits, however, found their methods of statutory construction too simple. In *Mallory v. Eyrich*, the Sixth Circuit refused to "believe the word 'representatives'...was used as a narrowing term of art."[25] Guided by what it was convinced that Congress intended (i.e., to proscribe all practices that resulted, whether intentionally or not, in the dilution of minority voting strength) rather than by what Congress actually said (i.e., the text of § 2 as amended), it rejected the argument that judges are not represen-

---

22. 666 F. Supp. at 1063. Judge Gee made much the same point for the *en banc* majority in *League of United Latin American Citizens Council No. 4434 (LULAC II) v. Clement*, 914 F. 2d 620, 628 (5th Cir. 1990): "To describe the judge's office merely as 'not a representative one' is a gross understatement; in truth, it is rather the precise antithesis of such an office. Just insofar as a judge *does* represent anyone, he is not a judge but a partisan." Emphasis supplied by Judge Gee.

23. See, however, Judge William Henry Barbour's opinion in *Martin v. Allain*, 658 F. Supp. 1183 (S.D. Miss, 1987), who conceded that "judges do not 'represent' those who elect them in the same context as legislators represent their constituents," but insisted that "[t]here is no legislative history of the Voting Rights Act or any racial vote dilution case law which distinguishes state judicial elections from any other type of elections." 685 F. Supp. at 1200.

24. See Justice Scalia's dissent in *Chisom v. Roemer*, 501 U.S. 380, 404 (1991).

25. 839 F. 2d 275, 280 (6th Cir. 1988).

tatives because that "would limit the application of the Act."[26] It invoked *Allen v. State Board of Elections*,[27] in which the Supreme Court

---

26. 839 F. 2d at 280.

27. 393 U.S.544 (1969). The Sixth Circuit's explicit reliance on *Allen v. State Board of Elections* is noteworthy, as *Allen* fundamentally altered the very purpose of the Voting Rights Act. See Thernstrom, *Whose Votes Count*, p. 22. At issue in Allen were proposed changes to state election laws in Mississippi and Virginia. None of the proposed changes related to access to registration or to the counting of ballots, which up until that time had been the only issues litigated under the Voting Rights Act; rather, they concerned switching from single-member districts to at-large districts, changing a school superintendent office from being elective to being appointive, and changing the procedures by which independent candidates were to be nominated. Chief Justice Warren, writing for the Court, argued that the remedial powers of the Voting Rights Act were not limited to protecting voter registration and ballot access. The "Act was aimed at the subtle, as well as the obvious, state regulations that had the effect of denying citizens their right to vote because of their race." This meant that electoral practices or procedures that might adversely affect the political effectiveness of black voters were subject to preclearance, not just direct bars to registration and polling booths.

> The right to vote can be affected by a dilution of voting power as well as by an absolute prohibition on casting a ballot.... Voters who are members of a racial minority might be in the majority in one district, but in a decided minority in the county as a whole. This type of change could therefore nullify their ability to elect the candidate of their choice just as would prohibiting some of them from voting. 393 U.S. 566–67.

Justice Warren determined that the intent of the Voting Rights Act was "to reach any state enactment which altered the election law of a covered State in even a minor way." It was to ensure that electoral practices neither prevented blacks from voting nor interfered with their ability to elect candidates of their choice. Just as the one-man, one-vote decisions transformed the Constitution's guarantee of the right to vote into the right to representation, so, too, *Allen* transformed the right to vote guaranteed to black citizens by the Voting Rights Act into the right to black representation.

Allen further enlarged the federal power of supervision over state electoral practices. When the Court itself subsequently attempted to curtail somewhat this federal supervisory power in *Mobile v. Bolden*, 446 U.S. 55 (1980), by holding that the Voting Rights Act applied only to purposeful or intention discrimination against the voting rights of blacks, the Congress responded in 1982 by amending the Voting Rights Act to allow black plaintiffs to show discrimination solely on the effects of a voting plan. In *Thornberg v. Gingles*, 478 U.S. 30 (1986), the Court accepted the amended Act's "results test" and Congress's decision to invalidate districting plans that have the effect (even if not the intention) of diluting the black vote. Addressing the issue of whether multimember districts are ever permissible or whether they invariably disadvantage minorities, the *Gingles* majority spelled out the circumstances under which it would conclude that multimember districts "operate to impair minority voters' ability to elect representatives of their choice."

had declared that the purpose of the Voting Rights Act was "to rid the country of racial discrimination in voting,"[28] and claimed that it was obligated to give the most "expansive interpretation" to the Act. Since it understood that Congress intended its 1982 amendments to expand the application of § 2 "without limiting it in any way,"[29] the Sixth Circuit interpreted the words of § 2 consistently with that understanding and applied them to judicial elections. That Congress used the word "representatives" in its formulation of the results test (which would seem to exclude its application to judges) rather than the word "candidates" (which would clearly include them, and which it used elsewhere in the 1982 amendments) was dismissed as of no consequence; what was important to the Sixth Circuit was its conviction that Congress had intended to protect minority groups from vote dilution in all circumstances, not the actual words that Congress used to express that intention.[30]

Likewise in *Chisom v. Edwards*, the Fifth Circuit found "untenable" Judge Schwartz's reliance on the plain meaning of the word "representatives" to support his assertion that judges are exempt from the Act..[31]In a sentence that is a model of obfuscation, it declared: "Judges, while not 'representative' in the traditional sense, do indeed reflect the sentiment of the majority of the people as to the individuals they choose to entrust with the responsibility of administering the law."[32]

---

28. 393 U.S. at 567 (1969). See April D. Dulaney, *A Judicial Exception for Judicial Elections: A Burning Scar on the Flesh of the Voting Rights Act*, 65 TULANE LAW REVIEW, 1230 (1991).

29. 839 F. 2d at 280.

30. 839 F. 2d at 278–279. Eager to be seen as serving Congress, the Sixth Circuit did Congress the grave disservice of not taking its words seriously; it simply believed it knew what Congress meant better than Congress knew how to express it.

31. 839 F. 2d 1056, 1063 (5th Cir. 1988).

32. 839 F. 2d at 1063. *Chisom* v. *Edwards* was itself overturned by the Fifth Circuit's *en banc* decision in *League of United Latin American Citizens Council No. 4434 (LULAC II)* v. *Clements*, 914 F. 2d 620 (5th Cir. 1990), which in turn was overturned by *Chisom* v. *Roemer*, 501 U.S. 380 (1991). On remand, the Fifth Circuit again denied relief to LULAC on the grounds that the divergent voting patterns between white and minority voters were best explained not by discriminatory intent but by "partisan affiliation"—Texas elects its judges in partisan elections—and that LULAC failed to establish the existence of racial bloc voting as required by *Thornburg v. Gingles*, 478 U.S. 30 (1986). See Judge Patrick Higgenbothan's majority opinion in *League of United Latin American Citizens Council No. 4434 (LULAC III) v. Clements*, 999 F. 2d 831, 861 (5th Cir. 1993), cert. denied, 114 S. Ct. 878 (1994). See also Ronald E. Weber, *The Voting Rights Act and Judicial Elections Litigation: The Defendant States' Perspective*, 73 JUDICATURE 85, 86 (1989).

c.

Justice Steven's majority opinion for the Supreme Court in *Chisom* repeated much of what the Fifth and Sixth Circuits had said in *Chisom* and *Mallory*. He likewise saw *Allen v. State Board of Elections* as compelling the Court to give the Voting Rights Act—and its objective of eradicating racial discrimination in voting—the most expansive interpretation.[33] Exempting judicial elections from the results test simply because Congress used the word "representatives," a term not ordinarily understood to include judges, was inconsistent with the obligation to give § 2 as amended "the broadest possible scope."[34] He found it "difficult to believe" that Congress, in "its express effort to broaden the protection afforded by the Voting Rights Act" through its 1982 amendments, would have intended to withdraw judicial elections from "the ambit of § 2 as amended."[35] "If Congress had such an intent," he was "convinced" that "Congress would have made it explicit in the statute, or at least some of the Members would have identified or mentioned it at some point in the unusually extensive legislative history of the 1982 amendment."[36] Use of the phrase, "to elect representatives of their choice," did not, for Justice Stevens, constitute such an "explicit" communication of congressional intent, for, he insisted, the word representatives" is "better read" as describing "the winners of representative, popular elections"[37] than as identifying the functions they perform.

---

33. 502 U.S. at 403.

34. 501 U.S. at 403. See Richard Saks, *Redemption or Exemption: Racial Discrimination in Judicial Elections Under the Voting Rights Act*, 66 CHICAGO KENT LAW REVIEW 245, 248 (1990): "Whether judges have been defined as 'representatives' for other doctrines is irrelevant to the heightened scrutiny required for racial discrimination claims in voting…The notion…that judges are not 'representatives' rests on a dated, formalist notion of jurisprudence and the role of the court." See also Dulaney, *A Judicial Exception for Judicial Elections*, 65 TULANE LAW REVIEW 1246: "Even if state judges are not' representatives' in the sense of accountability to the people, § 2 *should* nevertheless apply to judicial election because of the need for judges to be representative of the people within their jurisdictions." Emphasis added.

35. 501 U.S. at 404. See Frederick G. Slabach, *Equal Justice: Applying the Voting Rights Act to Judicial Elections*, chapter 11 herein.

36. 501 U.S. at 396.

37. 501 U.S. at 399. Justice Stevens' definition is, of course, circular—an individual is a representative because of winning a "representative, popular election"—and does nothing to support his contention that judges are representatives and hence covered by § 2. After all, is a judicial election a "representative popular election?" It may be a popular election, but is it also a representative election? Judges may be popularly elected, but not as representatives—i.e., as individuals whose function is to re-present their con-

His "'better reading' of the word representatives'" allowed Justice Stevens to rebut, to his satisfaction, Louisiana's argument that if Congress had intended to have the statute's prohibition against vote dilution apply to the election of judges, it would have used the word "candidates" instead of "representatives." That argument by Louisiana would seem to have considerably force, for the statute would then unquestionably apply to candidates for judicial office no less than to candidates for the legislature. According to Stevens, however, "that [argument] confuses the ordinary meaning of the words. The word 'representative' refers to someone who has prevailed in a popular election, whereas the word 'candidate' refers to someone who is seeking an office. Thus, a candidate is nominated, not elected."[38] The implicit conclusion for Stevens: since candidates are those who have been nominated but not yet elected, for Congress to have used the phrase "to elect candidates of their choice" would have been a contradiction in terms.

Justice Stevens further argued that judges must be considered representatives because, otherwise, judicial elections would be totally excluded from the coverage of the Voting Rights Act,[39] and even "a standard, practice, or procedure in a judicial election, such as a limit on the times that polls are open, which has a disparate impact on black voters' opportunity to cast their ballots," could not be challenged.[40] He noted that a violation of § 2, as amended, is established only if minority voters "have less 'opportunity' than others 'to participate in the political process *and* to elect representatives of their choice.'"[41] He insisted that it would "distort the plain meaning of the sentence to substitute the word 'or' for the word 'and.' Such radical surgery would be required to separate the opportunity to participate from the opportunity to elect."[42] He was unwilling to perform so radical a surgery and, therefore, was unwilling to hold that judges are not representatives, for, as he noted, if the

---

stituents—but as judges—i.e., as individuals whose function is to interpret and apply the laws that representative bodies and individuals adopt and enforce. The decision by a state to elect judges is one answer to the question of how judges should be selected; it is not an answer to the question of whether judges are representatives.

38. 501 U.S. at 399–400.

39. 501 U.S. at 398. Justice Stevens was not the only one to march in this "parade of imaginary horribles." See Brenda Wright, *The Bench and the Ballot: Applying the Protections of the Voting Rights Act of Judicial Elections,* 19 Florida State University Law Review 669, 680 (1992), and Dulaney, *A Judicial Exemption to Judicial Elections,* 65 Tulane Law Review 1235.

40. 501 U.S. at 396.

41. 501 U.S. at 397. Emphasis supplied by Justice Stevens.

42. 501 U.S. at 397.

word "representatives" did not include judges, "all claims" involving judicial elections would be excluded from the protection of § 2.[43]

Finally, Justice Stevens felt obliged to respond to the argument, first
made by Judge Schwartz in *Chisom v. Edwards*, that the Supreme
Court's refusal in *Wells v. Edwards*[44] to apply the one-man, one-vote
principle to judicial elections is further evidence of the fact that judges
are not representatives.[45] He dismissed *Wells* as irrelevant, for it involved
"a constitutional challenge based on the Equal Protection Clause of the
Fourteenth Amendment," whereas the instant case involved a statute
"enacted to protect voting rights that are not adequately protected by
the Constitution itself."[46] Of course, what was not irrelevant was that
Wells had held that judges were not representatives and therefore that judicial elections were not governed by the one-man, one-vote principle,
whose very objective was to ensure truly representative government. The
only problem that Justice Stevens was willing to concede was posed by
the Court's refusal to apply the one-man, one-vote principle to judicial
elections was the difficulty of fashioning "judicially-manageable standards for deciding vote dilution claims" in the absence of the one-man,
one-vote rule. He conceded that this was a "serious problem" but
bravely insisted that "difficult as it may prove to be," the Court must do
its duty rather than create a judicial "limitation on the coverage of the
broadly worded statute."[47]

II.

Justice Stevens' opinion, no less than the Fifth and Sixth Circuit opinions
he was affirming, represents a profound misconstruction of the language
of § 2 and a perverse misreading of its legislative history. He misconstrued the word "representatives" and misread the legislative history because, as Justice Scalia noted in his dissent in *Chisom*, he adopted a

---

43. 501 U.S. at 398. "For all such claims must allege an abridgment of the opportunity to participate in the political process *and* to elect representatives of one's choice."
Emphasis supplied by Justice Stevens.

44. 409 U.S. 1095 (1973), affirming 347 F. Supp. 453.

45. See Andrew S. Marovitz, *Casting a Meaningful Ballot: Applying the One-Person,
One-Vote Principle to Judicial Elections involving Racial Discrimination*, 98 YALE LAW
JOURNAL 1193 (1989). Marovitz surveyed the problem that Justice Stevens was to face
in *Chisom* and concluded that the only way to resolve the problem was for the Supreme
Court to overturn *Wells v. Edwards* 347 F. Supp. 453, and apply the one-man, one-vote
principle to judicial elections.

46. 501 U.S. at 403.

47. 501 U.S. at 402–403.

method of statutory construction that was "just backwards" of the usual practice.[48] Instead of beginning with "the text that Congress had passed and the President had signed," reading the words of that text "as any ordinary Member of Congress would have read them," and applying the "meaning so determined," Justice Stevens and his appellate brethren on the Fifth and Sixth Circuits began with an "expectation about what the statute must mean" and interpreted "the words of the statute to fulfill" their expectations.[49]

a.

Had Justice Stevens and those who shared in his conclusions read the words of § 2 as ordinary Members of Congress "would have read them," they would have recognized that judges, even elected judges, are not representatives. Elected judges may share with representatives the same mode of selection, but they do not serve the same function. Judges do not serve to re-present the views of the public; rather they serve to apply and interpret the laws that representative bodies and individuals adopt and enforce. The decision by a state to elect judges is one answer to the question of how judges should be selected, not an answer to the question of what judges should do—i.e., what should be the appropriate role of the judge.[50] A model of how properly to construe § 2 was provided by Judge Thomas Gee in his *en banc* opinion for the Fifth Circuit in *League of United Latin American Citizens Council 4434 [LULAC II] v. Clements,*[51] in which he rejected the contention that Texas's at-large method of electing trial court judges violated the Voting Rights Act.

Judge Gee began by invoking the "well-settled principle of statutory construction that the enacting Legislator is presumed to have been aware of the judicial construction of existing law;" he then noted that at the time of

---

48. 501 U.S. at 405. See Philip P. Frickey, *From the Big Sleep to the Big Heat: The Revival of Theory in Statutory Interpretation,* 77 MINNESOTA LAW REVIEW 241 (1992).

49. 501 U.S. at 405.

50. Dulaney argues that the language of § 2 "rejects a function-based inquiry. Although an elective judicial seat 'differs in certain respects' from a state or local legislative or executive position, the judicial post 'is exactly the same in the one crucial factor—these officials are elected by popular vote.' The process of electing officials constitutes the only relevant factor in determining the application of § 2." *A Judicial Exemption for Judicial Elections,* 65 TULANE LAW REVIEW 1232. Supporting her argument, she cited *Hadly v. Junior College District,* 397 U.S. 50, 52 (1970), the very case that the Supreme Court, by affirming *Wells v. Edwards,* 347 F. Supp. 453 (1972), 409 U.S. 1095 (1973), held inapplicable in judicial elections.

51. 914 F. 2d 620 (5th Cir. 1990).

Congress's adoption of the 1982 amendments to § 2 and its addition of the "explicit results test," "every federal court which had considered the question had concluded that judges were not 'representatives' and did not fall within the definition of that term."[52] From that, he drew the inevitable conclusion: "Had Congress, then, meant to exclude votes in judicial elections from the ambit of its new results test, it could scarcely have done so more plainly than by adopting the term 'representative' to describe that ambit."[53]

Judge Gee explored the ordinary meaning of the word "representatives" at length. Representatives, he wrote, "synthesize the opinions of their constituents and reflect them in the debate and deliberation of public issues." Judges, by contrast, serve "no representative function whatever: the judge represents no one."[54] They "have no constituents. Judges speak the voice of the law. In doing so they speak for and to the *entire* community, never for segments of it and still less for particular individuals."[55]

---

52. "[A]s of the time of Congress's adoption…[of the 1982 amendments to § 2], at least fifteen published opinions by federal courts…had held or observed that the judicial office is not a representative one, most often in the context of deciding whether the one-man, one-vote rubric applied to judicial elections. Not one had held the contrary." 914 F. 2d at 626.

53. 914 F. 2d at 623.

54. 914 F. 2d at 626. Judge Gee quoted Eugene Hickok: "The judiciary occupies a unique position in our system of separation of powers, and that is why the job of a judge differs in a fundamental way from that of a legislator or executive. The purpose of the judiciary is not to reflect public opinion in its deliberations or to satisfy public opinion with its decisions. Rather, it is to ensure that the ordinary laws do not run contrary to the more fundamental laws of the Constitution, to resolve disputes and controversies surrounding the law, and to resolve disputes among contesting parties over the meaning of the law and the Constitution." Eugene Hickok THE POLITICAL ROOTS OF ADVICE AND CONSENT IN JUDICIAL SELECTION: MERIT, IDEOLOGY, AND POLITICS (National Legal Center for the Public Interest, 1990). p. 5.

55. 914 F. 2d at 628. Emphasis supplied by Judge Gee. Contrast Judge Gee's understanding with Judge Patrick Higginbotham's in *League of United Latin American Citizens Council No 4434 (LULAC I) v. Clements*, 902 F. 2d 293 (5th Cir. 1990), where Higginbotham wrote the majority opinion, and in *League of United Latin American Citizens Council No. 4434 (LULAC II) v. Clements*, 914 F. 2d 620, 634–651 (5th Cir. 1990), where he filed an opinion concurring in the judgment. Judge Higginbotham accepted the contention that judges are representatives but argued that elections of district judgeships are exempt from § 2, because district court judges, unlike appellate judges who act as members of a collegial body, are single-office holders who have jurisdiction that is co-extensive with the geographical area from which they are elected and have authority to render final decisions independently of other judges serving in the same area or on the same court. In *Houston Lawyers Association v. Attorney General of*

Moreover, to the extent that "a judge does represent anyone, he is not a judge but a partisan."[56]

Judge Gee's understanding of the judicial function was wholly consistent with that of *Federalist* No. 10 and shows by contrast how much Justice Stevens and his colleagues in the *Chisom* majority abandoned the constitutional understanding of the Framers, who viewed judicial decisionmaking as the model of all governmental decisionmaking and who considered one of the major tasks of a constitution to make legislative decisions conform as closely as possible to judicial decisions. In *Federalist* No 10, Madison wrote: "No man is allowed to be a judge in his own cause; because his interest would certainly bias his judgment, and, not improbably, corrupt his integrity. With equal, nay with greater reason, a body of men, are unfit to be both judges and parties at the same time; yet, what are many of the most important acts of legislation but so many judicial determinations, not indeed concerning the rights of single persons, but concerning the rights of large bodies of citizens; and what are the different classes of legislators, but advocates and parties to the causes which they determine?"[57]

Madison compared legislative decisionmaking to judicial decisionmaking because he believed that through a properly-designed constitution—operating on either the federal or state level—it is possible to obtain results from the legislature that approximate the decisions that would be made by a judicial body. According to Madison, a constitution can be judged a success to the extent that it takes self-interested legislators and makes them act as wise and disinterested judges. By contrast, according to the *Chisom* majority, the Voting Rights Act can be judged a success to the extent that § 2 takes judges and treats them in the same way as self-interested legislators.[58] Given the Supreme Court's activist tendency to behave like a legislative body and its penchant freely to substitute its policy preferences for those of the popular branches, it was perhaps inevitable that Justice Stevens should

---

Texas, 501 U.S. 419 (1991), Justice Stevens held Judge Higginbotham's argument to be a legitimate factor to be considered by courts in determining whether, based on the "totality of circumstances, " a vote dilution violation has occurred and must be remedied. 501 U.S. at 426.

56. 916 F. 2d at 628.

57. Alexander Hamilton, James Madison, and John Jay, THE FEDERALIST. Ed. Jacob E. Cooke (World Publishing Company, 1961), 59.

58. See Michael Herz, *Choosing Between Normative and Descriptive Versions of the Judicial Role*, 75 MARQUETTE LAW REVIEW 725, 726 (1992): "If judges are 'policymakers' and 'representatives' who can change the law freely and prospectively like a legislature, then how can they be dispute resolvers who, lacking a constituency, decide questions of law rather than policy?"

come to equate judging with lawmaking and to identify the self-interested legislator as the model for judicial decision-making.[59]

Be that as it may, Justice Stevens does great violence to § 2, through his misconstruction of the word "representatives," as well as to our understanding of what it means to be a judge,[60] through his misconception of the judicial role. By so doing, however, he does even greater violence to the ends our federal and state constitutions were intended to achieve and to our ability to determine whether they are successful in achieving those ends.

b.

Justice Scalia built on Judge Gee's method for interpreting the word "representative" in his dissent in *Chisom*. He chided Justice Stevens for having "labored mightily to establish that there is *a* meaning of 'representatives' that would include judges." But, he insisted, "our job is not to scavenge the world of English usage to discover whether there is any possible meaning of 'representatives' which suits our preconception that the statute includes judges;"[61] rather, "our job is to determine whether the ordinary meaning includes them, and if it does not, to ask whether

---

59. Justice Stevens even justified treating judges as representatives by saying: "[T]his Court has recently recognized that judges do engage in policymaking at some level." 501 U.S. 399, n. 27.

60. See Dulaney, who confidently assures the reader that those who believe that judges should not make policy are in the grips of a "'mechanical theory of jurisprudence' that has been discredited for nearly a century.... 'Modern students of state courts recognize that judges do indeed make policy and that...the selection of judicial policymakers should, therefore be subjected to the same analysis as national, state, and local executives and legislators. *A Judicial Exemption for Judicial Election,* 65 TULANE LAW REVIEW 1240.

61. Examples of such scavengers include Abrams, *Relationships of Representation in Voting Rights Act Jurisprudence,* 71 TEXAS LAW REVIEW 1426; Dulaney, *A Judicial Exemption for Judicial Elections,* 65 TULANE LAW REVIEW 1233; and Judith Hayde, Section 2 of the *Voting Rights Act of 1965: A Challenge to State Judicial Election Systems,* 73 JUDICATURE 68 (1989). Hanna Pitkin's book, THE CONCEPT OF REPRESENTATION (University of California Press, 1967), is a favorite hunting ground for these scavengers, for, in Abrams' words, it explores the "many meanings and nuances" inherent in the word "representative." Abrams, *Relationships of Representation in Voting Rights Act Jurisprudence,* 71 TEXAS LAW REVIEW 1411. It is noteworthy, however, that Pitkin's book nowhere appears as a reference source for the Congress in what Justice Stevens described as the "unusually extensive legislative history of the 1982 amendment." 501 U.S. at 396.

there is any solid indication in the text or structure of the statute itself that something other than *ordinary* meaning was intended."[62]

Concerning the "ordinary meaning" of "representatives," Scalia cited *Webster's Second New International Dictionary* and declared "There is little doubt" that it "does not include judges." He ridiculed the majority's "feeble argument" that "representatives" means those who "are chosen by popular election." If that were the case, "the fan-*elected* members of the baseball all-star teams are 'representatives.'" For Scalia, the word "representative" "connotes one who is not only elected by the people, but who also, at a minimum, *acts on behalf* of the people.'[63] That clearly excludes judges. "As the captions of the pleadings in some States still display, it is the prosecutor who represents 'the People;' the judge represents the Law—which often requires him to rule against the People."[64] Moreover, he noted, it is "precisely because" judges are not ordinarily conceived to be representatives that the federal judiciary had refused to hold judges within the one-man, one-vote requirements of the Fourteenth Amendment.[65]

For Justice Scalia, the "ordinary meaning" of "representatives" clearly excluded judges; moreover, there was no indication whatsoever from Congress that the "ordinary meaning" was not to apply. He found altogether unpersuasive Justice Steven's attempt to explain why Congress used the word "representative" in an out-of-the-ordinary way rather than use the word "candidate," which would have been the more "natural choice." Stevens claimed that the word "candidate" could not be used for it referred to those who have been nominated but not yet elected, and that, therefore, the phrase "to elect candidates of their choice" would be a contradiction in terms. Scalia observed that "the only flaw in this argument is that it is not true, as repeated usage of the formulation 'to elect candidates' by this Court itself amply demonstrates."[66] For Scalia, "far from being an impermissible choice, 'candi-

---

62. 501 U.S. at 410. Emphasis supplied by Justice Scalia. See Antorin Scalia, *The Rule of Law as the Law of Rules*, 56 UNIVERSITY OF CHICAGO LAW REVIEW 1175 (1989). But see William D. Popkin, *An "Internal" Critique of Justice Scalia's Theory of Statutory Interpretation*, 76 MINNESOTA LAW REVIEW 1133, 1141 (May 1992), who is critical of Justice Scalia's statutory construction of "representatives" in *Chisom*.

63. 501 U.S. at 410. Emphasis supplied by Justice Scalia.

64. 501 U.S. at 410–411.

65. 501 U.S. at 411.

66. 501 U.S. at 413. Here Justice Scalia cited the following cases: "See, e.g., *Davis v. Bandemer*, 478 U. S. 109, 121 (1986); *Rogers v. Lodge*, 458 U.S. 613, 624 (1982); *id.*, at 639, n. 18, 641, n. 22, 649 (Stevens, J., dissenting); *Mobile v. Bolden*, 446 U.S. at 75; *United Jewish Organizations of Williamsburg, Inc. v. Carey*, 430 U.S. 144, 158 (1977);

dates' would have been the natural choice, even if it had not been used repeatedly elsewhere in the statute." He found it "quite absurd" to argue that Congress would have replaced the word "candidates" with the word "representatives" in order to convey "what 'candidates' naturally suggests (viz., coverage of *all* elections) and what 'representatives' naturally does not."[67]

Scalia also rejected as "unquestionably wrong"[68] Justice Stevens's contention that unless judges were considered to be "representatives," judicial elections would be totally excluded from the coverage of the Voting Rights Act. If a violation § 2 can occur only when minority voters "have less opportunity than others both "to participate in the political process *and* to elect representatives of their choice," then, Scalia noted, "minorities who form such a small part of the electorate in a particular jurisdiction that they could on no conceivable basis 'elect representatives of their choice' would be entirely without § 2 protection," and not only in judicial elections but in all elections—a conclusion hardly consistent with the Court's insistence that the Voting Rights Act (both as originally enacted in 1965 and as amended in 1982) is to be given the most expansive interpretation. This conclusion was also based on faulty statutory construction. Scalia explained why:

> The Court feels compelled to reach this implausible conclusion of a "singular right" because the "to participate" and the "to elect" clauses are joined by the conjunction "and." It is unclear to me why the rules of English usage require that conclusion here, any more than they do in the

---

Moore v. Ogilvie, 394 U.S. 814, 819 (1969); *Allen v. State Board of Elections*, 393 US. 544, 569 (1969). We even used the phrase repeatedly in *Thornburg. Thornburg v. Gingles*, 478 U.S. at 40, 44, 54, 80; *id.*, at 86, 103 (O'Connor, J., concurring in judgment); *Id.* at 107 (Stevens, J., concurring part and dissenting in part)."

67. 501 U.S. at 413. Emphasis supplied by Justice Scalia. See also Judge Gee's language in *League of United Latin American Citizens Council 4434 (LULAC II) v. Clements*, 914 F. 2d at 628: "Congress deliberately picked a term of art for use in amending § 2 that up to that time had been universally held, and which it *knew* had been universally held by every federal court that had considered it as of that date, neither to include judges nor to comprise judicial elections. In view of these circumstances, we find it all but impossible to avoid the conclusion that Congress intended to apply its newly imposed results test to elections for representative, political offices but not to vote dilution claims in judicial contests, leaving the matter to be regulated and controlled by state law, by the Constitution, or by other provisions of the Voting Rights Act. Given the mutual exclusiveness of the two terms, to suggest that Congress chose 'representative' with the intent of including judges is roughly on a par with suggesting that the term *night* may, in a given circumstance, properly be read to include *day*." Emphases supplied by Judge Gee.

68. 501 U.S. at 409.

case of the First Amendment - which reads "Congress shall make no law...abridging...the right of the people peaceably to assemble, and to petition the Government for a redress of grievances." This has not generally been thought to protect the right peaceably to assemble only when the purpose of the assembly is to petition the Government for a redress of grievances. So also here, one is deprived of an equal "opportunity...to participate...and to elect" if *either* the opportunity to participate *or* the opportunity to elect is unequal.[69]

c.

Judge Gee in *LULAC II* held that judges are not representatives not only because such a conclusion is contrary to "well-settled principle[s] of statutory construction"[70] but also because the one-man, one-vote principle had never been applied by the federal judiciary to judicial elections. It had not been applied for several reasons. Judge Gee identified one in *LULAC II*: The one-man, one-vote principle had "evolved out of efforts to preserve a truly representative form of government,"[71] and judges were not representatives. Another reason was "the importance of locating judges in areas where their services are required."[72] Judicial case loads, determined by the volume and nature of litigation arising in various parts of the state, are unrelated to population.[73] As the Federal District Court said in *Buchanan v. Rhodes*, judges must be "conveniently located to the people whom they serve. Location, then, is one of many significant factors which the legislature may properly consider when carrying out its constitutional mandate to create an effective judicial system."[74] These reasons were for Judge Gee dispositive of the question of whether the results test of § 2 applied to judicial elections: since the one-man, one-vote principle does not apply to the judiciary, "judicial elections cannot be attacked along lines that their processes result in unintentional dilution of the voting strength of minority members." According to Judge Gee, absent the one-person, one-vote rule—i.e., the

---

69. 501 U.S. at 409. Emphasis supplied by Justice Scalia

70. 914 F. 2d at 623.

71. 914 F. 2d at 627.

72. Marovitz, *Casting a Meaningful Ballot*, 98 YALE LAW JOURNAL 1210.

73. Pasquale A. Cipollone, *Section 2 of the Voting Rights Act and Judicial Elections: Application and Remedy*, 58 UNIVERSITY OF CHICAGO LAW REVIEW 733, 749 (1991).

74. 249 F. Supp. 860, 865 (N. D. Ohio, 1966). See also *Holshouser v. Scott*, 335 F. Supp. 928, 932 (M. D. N. C. 1971); *New York State Association of Trial Lawyers v. Rockefeller*, 267 F. Supp. 148, 153 (S. D. N. Y. 1967); and *Stokes v. Fortson*, 234 F. Supp. 575, 577 (N. D. Ga. 1964).

rule "that the vote of each individual voter must be roughly equal in weight to the vote of every other individual voter, regardless of race, religion, age, sex, or even the truly subjective and uniquely individual choice of where to reside—there is no requirement that any individual's vote weigh equally with that of anyone else."[75] Absent the one-man, one-vote rule, there "exists no yardstick by which to measure either the 'correct' magnitude of minority voting strength or the degree of minority vote dilution,"[76] and the court "can fashion no remedy to redress the nonexistent wrong complained of here."[77] Not only logic led Judge Gee to this conclusion, so, too, did the legislative history of the 1982 amendments to § 2:

> Congress knew that "the principle that the right to vote is denied or abridged by dilution of voting strength derives from the one-person, one-vote reapportionment case of *Reynolds v. Sims*." Given its awareness of

---

75. 914 F. 2d at 627.

76. 914 F. 2d at 628. Dulaney attempts to rebut this by arguing: "Unlike claims brought under the one-person, one-vote principle, minority groups challenging judicial elections under § 2 'do not challenge the number of judges within the various circuits and districts.' Instead, 'they accept the number of judges as a given and challenge only the relative weight of different voting blocs in electing those judges." Dulaney, *A Judicial Exemption for Judicial Elections*, 65 TULANE LAW REVIEW 1251. See also Haydel, *Section 2 of the Voting Rights Act of 1965*, 73 JUDICATURE 69: "These lawsuits are not concerned with population equality in election districts. Instead, plaintiffs seek full value for their votes. That is, plaintiffs seek assurance that their vote will not be diluted or weakened by the votes of whites." However, absent the principle that one vote is to count as much another (i.e., the one-man, one-vote principle that the Supreme Court in *Wells v. Edwards* held is not required in judicial elections), there is no basis for determining the relative weight of different voting blocs and therefore no basis for determining whether the votes of minority members have been diluted or weakened. Dulaney ultimately concedes as much, although with great apprehension: Judge Gee's "rationale is especially dangerous because it extends not only to the Voting Rights Act, but to the fourteenth and fifteenth amendments as well. If it were true that absent the one-person, one-vote mandate there is no requirement that any individual's vote weigh equally with that of anyone else, then dilution of the minority vote in judicial elections would not violate the Constitution. Such a result is contrary to the goals of racial equality manifested in the Civil War Amendments. Whatever uniqueness an elective judicial office may possess, the removal of judicial elections from the realm of protections arising from the fourteenth and fifteenth amendments and the Voting Rights Act is simply unjustified." Dulaney, *A Judicial Exemption for Judicial Elections*, 65 TULANE LAW REVIEW 1254. Her apprehensions would be considerably allayed if she were to recall that the only provision of the Voting Rights Act not applicable to judicial elections pertains to the ability of minority groups to elect "representatives of their choice," and that provision of § 2 is inapplicable only because judges are not "representatives."

77. 914 F. 2d at 627. See how this worried Slabach, "Equal Justice," 344.

the *Wells v. Edwards* holding that the one-person, one-vote rule does not apply to the judiciary—we must conclude that Congress, aware of the combined effect of *Reynolds* and *Wells*, limited the scope of amended Section 2 so as to rule out the judicial branch, an area within which the issue of the viability of minority vote dilution claims had been well settled."[78]

Here, too, Justice Scalia built on Judge Gee's argument. He noted that one person, one-vote "has been the premise and the necessary condition of a vote dilution claim, since it establishes the baseline for computing the voting strength that the minority bloc *ought to have*."[79] If, through its use of the word "representatives," Congress had intended to make vote dilution claims available with respect to the election of judges, it would have been, "for the first time, extending that remedy to a context in which 'one-person, one-vote' did not apply." Moreover, Congress would have brought about this "significant change in the law" solely through the use of an "extremely inapt" word, while leaving wholly unmentioned in the legislative history any expression of this intention or any suggestions concerning how the judiciary might identify some other baseline for computing vote dilution. If, on the other hand, through its use of the word "representatives," Congress was giving the word its "normal meaning" and expressing its wish to exempt the judiciary from its new results test, there was no significant change in the law, no need for Congress to identify a substitute baseline, and no reason to question the "entirely understandable" silence of the legislative history.[80]

d.

Justice Stevens and his colleagues in the *Chisom* majority engaged in the statutory misconstruction they did, because they adopted "a method that psychoanalyzes Congress rather than reads it laws." The "ordinary meaning" of § 2 did not fit their "conception of what Congress must have had in mind." Their psychoanalytic method "poison[ed] the well of future legislation, depriving legislators of the assurance that ordinary terms, used in their ordinary context, will be given a predictable meaning;"[81] it also turned the use of legislative history on its head. Stevens argued that if Congress had intended to exempt judicial elections from the results test of § 2, it would have "made it explicit in the statute," or at least some members of Congress would have addressed the issue somewhere "in the unusually extensive legislative history of the 1982 amend-

---

78. 914 F. 2d at 629.
79. 501 U.S. at 414. Emphasis supplied by Justice Scalia.
80. 501 U.S. at 415.
81. 501 U.S. at 417.

ment."[82] However, Justice Stevens gloated, there was nothing in the legislative history to indicate that Congress did not consider judges to be representatives. Waxing literary, Stevens observed: "Congress's silence in this regard can be likened to the dog that did not bark."[83]

Of course, as Justice Scalia pointed out in his dissent, there was nothing in the legislative history to indicate that Congress did consider judges to be representatives either. He criticized Stevens's mistaken "notion that Congress cannot be credited with having achieved anything of major importance by simply saying it, in ordinary language, in the text of a statute, 'without comment in the legislative history. As the Court colorfully puts it, if the dog of legislative history has not barked nothing of great significance can have transpired.... We have forcefully and explicitly rejected the Conan Doyle approach to statutory construction in the past.... We are here to apply the statute, not legislative history, and certainly not the absence of legislative history. Statutes are the law though sleeping dogs lie."[84] Justice Scalia characterized Justice Stevens's approach in *Chisom* as "psychoanalyz[ing] Congress." Basing its opinion not on what the law actually says, but rather on what those who framed the law can be psychoanalyzed to have intended, would seem a strange way to proceed for justices who "have made a career reading the disciples of Blackstone rather than of Freud."[85] However, Freud and his disciples apparently have their charms: Justice Stevens's method of relying on the absence of legislative history can, in fact, be compared to the trial court judge who is sympathetic to the claims of a criminal defendant seeking to establish diminished responsibility for his acts, and who accepts as evidence of the defendant's mental incapacitation the fact that he apparently believes the moon is made of green cheese—evidence of which is that the defendant has never been heard to declare that it is not.

III.

In his recent concurrence in *Holder v. Hall*,[86] Justice Thomas scraped away the incrustation of years of judicial precedents and interpretations concerning the Voting Rights Act and focused simply on what Congress had said in the statute, free of any judicial gloss. He courageously con-

---

82. 501 U.S. at 396.

83. 501 U.S. 396, n. 23. The phrase used by Stevens, "the dog that did not bark," came from Arthur C. Doyle's short story, "Silver Blaze."

84. 501 U.S. at 406.

85. *Lee v. Weisman*, 112 S. Ct. 2649, 2684 (1992). Justice Scalia dissenting.

86. 114 S. Ct. 2581, 2591–2619 (1994).

cluded that the Court has consistently misconstrued § 2, and not simply as it applies to judicial elections. He argued that at least since *Thornburg v. Gingles*, it has stretched the section's "standard, practice, or procedure" language so that it covers not just what Congress wanted (viz, state enactments that regulate citizens' access to the ballot or its processes for counting ballots) but also what Congress never intended to cover and, in fact, what it expressly declared was not and could not be covered (viz, claims of minority vote dilution predicated on the right to proportional representation).[87] The Court's decision in *Gingles* has placed the federal judiciary in the position of having to develop, in Justice Thomas's words, "some theory of the benchmark undiluted voting system that provides minorities with the 'fairest' or most 'equitable' share of political influence."[88] But, as Thomas continued, "in setting the benchmark of what 'undiluted' or fully 'effective' voting strength should be, a court must necessarily make some judgments based purely on an assessment of principles of political theory."[89] Thomas found no evidence whatsoever that Congress intended § 2 to serve as "a charter for federal courts to embark on the ambitious project of developing a theory of political equality to be imposed on the Nation;"[90] he therefore urged the Court to overturn *Gingles* and "reconsider whether the course we have charted for the Nation is the one set by the people through their representatives in Congress."[91] Justice Thomas accused the Court majority in *Gingles* of having employed the same "sort of statutory construction through divination"[92] that Justice Scalia accused the *Chisom* majority of employing.

> In approaching § 2, the *Gingles* Court, based on little more than a bald assertion that "the authoritative source for legislative intent lies in the Committee Reports of the bill," bypassed a consideration of the text of

---

87. "[O]ur understanding of what Congress purportedly 'wished to do'—that is, to allow claims of vote 'dilution'—depends solely on a selected reading of legislative history, whereas Congress' statement of what it 'wished to avoid' appears explicitly in § 2(b)'s disclaimer of a right to proportional representation. I can see no logical reason to import the 'inherent tension' between these two imperatives into the Act, when on its face the statute incorporates only one of two potentially contradictory commands. I would have thought the key to resolving any such conflict between the text and the legislative history obvious: the text of the statute must control, and the text of § 2 does not extend the Act to claims of dilution. 114 S. Ct. at 2613.

88. 114 S. Ct. at 2608.

89. 114 S. Ct. at 2594.

90. 114 S. Ct. at 2609.

91. 114 S. Ct. at 2619.

92. 114 S. Ct. at 2611.

the Act and proceeded to interpret the section based almost exclusively on its legislative history.... Contrary to the remarkable "legislative history first" method of statutory construction pursued in *Gingles*, however, I had thought it firmly established that the "authoritative source" for legislative intent was the text of the statute passed by both houses of Congress and presented to the President, not a series of partisan statements about purposes and objectives collected by congressional staffers and packaged into a Committee Report. "We have stated time and again that courts must presume that a legislature says what it means and means in a statute what it says there." Nevertheless, our analysis in *Gingles* was marked conspicuously by the absence of any attempt to pursue a close reading of the text of the Act.... [T]he legislative history of § 2 itself, and the Court's use of it in *Gingles*, aptly illustrate that legislative history is often used by this Court as "a forensic rather than an interpretive device."[93]

Justice Thomas's argument in *Holder* is twofold: First, the Court, by relying on partisan and misleading legislative history rather than on the words of the statute, flatly misconstrued § 2, leading it to conclude that "the terms of the Act" oblige the courts to address claims of vote dilution and to evaluate these claims based upon how closely electoral outcomes provide for proportional representation - all this, despite Congress's explicit "disclaimer of a right to proportional representation."[94] Second, the Court then compounds its error by entering the policy-making arena and establishing benchmarks for what the minority groups' undiluted voting strength should be—benchmarks that are based simply on the "principles of political theory"[95] of the justices. The justices may be learned in the law, but nothing in their training prepares them to pronounce on matters of political theory, and certainly nothing in their official capacity authorizes them to do so. Justice Thomas's two-fold argument, while true for elections in general, has special power when applied

---

93. 114 S. Ct. at 2612.

94. 114 S. Ct. at 2612, 2613. "I have endeavored to explain...that the core of any vote dilution claim is an assertion that the plaintiff group does not hold seats in the proportion they should. There is no logical way to avoid reliance on a simple ratio in evaluating such a claim. And allocation of seats in direct proportion to the minority group's percentage in the population provides the most logical ratio to apply as an 'undiluted' norm. But § 2 makes it clear that the Act does not create a right to proportional representation, and thus dictates that proportionality should not provide the rule of decision for § 2 claims. Nevertheless, despite the statutory command, in deciding claims of vote dilution, we have turned to proportionality as a guide, simply for lack of any better alternative." 114 S. Ct. 2614.

95. 114 S. Ot. at 2594.

to judicial elections, given their exemption from having to comply with the one-man, one-vote rule.

The decision to treat judges as "representatives" and to apply the *Gingles* results test to judicial elections poses daunting problems for the federal judiciary. The Supreme Court has held that the opportunity of minority voters to elect judges of their choice cannot be diluted. But, it has also held that judicial elections need not conform to the one-man, one-vote principle, the very principle that gives meaning to the concept of dilution. How are federal judges to determine whether there has been a dilution of minority voting strength in a judicial election when there is no benchmark or baseline for computing the voting strength that the minority group ought to have? If, as Justice Scalia queried in his dissent in *Chisom*, there is no requirement that "10,000 minority votes throughout the State should have as much practical 'electability' effect as 10,000 non-minority votes,"[96] how is a federal court to decide whether the effect of those minority votes has been diluted?

A solution offered by some to the problems of how to conduct judicial elections consistent with § 2—or to implement a remedy to cure prior discrimination—is for the states to abandon an elective judiciary altogether and replace it with an appointed system of judicial selection.[97] The irony present in this solution is palpable: by misconstruing § 2 and holding that judges are "representatives" and that judicial elections are covered by the 1982 amendments—all done in the name of *Allen v. State*

---

96. 501 U.S. at 415.

97. Cipollone, *Section 2 of the Voting Rights Act and Judicial Elections*, 58 UNIVERSITY OF CHICAGO LAW REVIEW 757. See Robert McDuff, *The Voting Rights Act and Judicial Elections Litigation: The Plaintiff's Perspective*, 73 JUDICATURE 82, 83: "[I]n a sense, appointive systems would not satisfy the key objective of § 2 of the Voting Rights Act, which is to increase the opportunity of minority voters to elect candidates [notice McDuff did not say "representatives"] of their choice, be those candidates black, Hispanic, or white." See also Slabach, "Equal Justice," 344, who is alarmed that the Supreme Court "has asserted [in *Chisom*], without justification or analysis, that states may avoid the application of the Voting Rights Act to the judicial selection process by simply altering their method of judicial selection from election to appointment." Slabach argues that any "switch from elective to appointive judicial selection methods" that would result in the selection of fewer minority judges than occur under the vigorous enforcement of the results test (i.e., something closely approaching proportional representation) should be challenged under "a new 'vicarious selection' analysis." *Id.* On the need for "affirmative action" in judicial selection, see Larry W. Yackle, *Choosing Judges the Democratic Way*, 69 BOSTON UNIVERSITY LAW REVIEW 273, 276 (1989): "Put bluntly, the Constitution mandates that members of constitutionally significant outgroups are included in the pool from which judges are taken."

Board of Elections and its call to the federal judiciary to give the Voting Rights Act the "broadest possible scope" in order to eradicate racial discrimination in voting, Justice Stevens and the others in the *Chisom* majority have introduced such difficulties for federal judges implementing *Chisom* (and for states attempting to conform to it), that the least problematic solution is to take away the right to vote for judges altogether.[98] In its effort to ensure that minorities have an opportunity equal to others to elect judges of their choice, it condemns both minorities and the electorate at large to having their judges appointed for them.[99]

With unbridled sarcasm, Jonathan Swift remarked: "As learned commentators view in Homer more than Homer knew."[100] He could have been writing about Justice Stevens and the *Chisom* majority. These learned commentators thought they knew better what Congress intended with its 1982 amendments to the Voting Rights Act than Congress itself

---

98. For those jurisdictions covered by § 5 of the Voting Rights Act, even that solution would have to be precleared. See Slabach, "Equal Justice," 344, 395–97, and 403.

99. "[A]ppointive systems are not likely to be acceptable as a remedy for § 2 violations in judicial elections. First of all, there is something rather sinister about taking away the power to vote for judges at the very time litigation under the Voting Rights Act promises that minorities will finally have their fair share of power." McDuff, *The Voting Rights Act and Judicial Elections Litigation*, 73 JUDICATURE 83. As an alternative to appointment, McDuff proposes remedying voting rights violations arising from multi-member judicial election districts by dividing those multimember districts into smatter subdistricts, with some having black or other minority-bloc majorities sufficient to elect judges of their choice. Once elected from the sub-district, the judges would serve the entire district, *Id.*, p. 84. This proposal, however, is also problematic: If judicial elections are covered by § 2 because judges are "representatives," it is difficult to see how judges elected from the various subdistricts are "representative" of those constituents who live outside those subdistricts. Such an arrangement would seem to violate the very premise in *Chisom* that judges are to "be representative of [i.e., elected by] the people within their jurisdiction." See Dulaney, *A Judicial Exemption for Judicial Elections*, 65 TULANE LAW REVIEW 1246. Subdistricts also raise the issue of judicial partiality. As Haydel queries: "What are the implications, for instance, of a judge hearing a case in which one of the litigants is from his or her judicial district and the other litigant is not? How impartial will that judge's decisions appear? If the judge rules against the litigant from his or her district, how will that ruling affect the judge's chances for re-election? Creation of smaller judicial districts could place undue pressure on the most ethical and impartial of judges." Haydel, *Section 2 of the Voting Rights Act of 1965*, 73 JUDICATURE 73. These difficulties prompt Shawn Fremstad, *State Judicial Elections and the Voting Rights Act: Defining the Proper Remedial Scheme*, 76 MINNESOTA LAW REVIEW 101, 115 (1991), to contend that subdistricting is appropriate only for appellate courts where decisions are made collectively and not individually.

100. Jonathan Swift, *On Poetry: A Rhapsody*, in Harold Williams (ed.), THE POEMS OF JONATHAN SWIFT (Clarendon Press, 1957), p. 643, line 103.

knew—or at least, knew better what Congress intended than Congress was able to express in the words of the statute. They construed what they imagined Congress meant, not what Congress said. The result is an decision that misconceived judges to be representatives and the judicial role to be indistinguishable from the policymaking role. Just as the reader is likely to profit more from reading Homer than from reading his "learned commentators," so too the public is likely to benefit more from being governed by the plain text of the laws Congress has passed than by what the Court imagines the Congress intended to pass. *Chisom v. Roemer* fails the minimal test of judicial craftsmanship: "the modest desire to protect our...legal system from ridicule."[101] It should be overturned.

---

101. *Grady v. Corbin*, 495 U.S. 529, 542 (1990). Justice Scalia dissenting.

CHAPTER 11

Equal Justice: Applying the Voting Rights Act to Judicial Elections

Frederick G. Slabach

Introduction

The application of recent United States Supreme Court decisions[1] could cause the most extensive restructuring of state judiciaries since popular sovereignty swept the country in the nineteenth century, making election the primary method of judicial selection.[2] A trio of decisions in the 1990 term ruled that section 2[3] and section 5[4] of the Voting Rights Act[5] (the "Act") apply to judicial elections.[6]

Far from resolving all the difficult issues surrounding the Voting Rights Act and elected judges, the Court's decisions invite confusion,

---

1. *Houston Lawyers' Ass'n v. Attorney Gen.*, 501 U.S. 419 (1991); *Chisom v. Roemer*, 501 U.S. 380 (1991); *Clark v. Roemer*, 501 U.S. 646 (1991).

2. See *infra* note 82.

3. *Houston Lawyers' Ass'n*, 501 U.S. at 125 (holding that § 2 applies to judicial elections for trial judges who exercise their authority independently); *Chisom*, 111 S. Ct. at 2368 (holding that § 2 applies to judicial elections).

4. *Clark*, 501 U.S. at 653 (holding that § 5 applies to changes in laws relating to judicial elections). *Clark* was the first United States Supreme Court decision on this subject following plenary review. Previously, the Court had summarily affirmed appeals from two lower court decisions. See *Brooks v. Georgia State Bd. of Elections*, 111 S. Ct. 288 (1990), *aff'g mem.* 775 F. Supp. 1470 (S.D. Ga. 1989) (holding that § 5 applies to judicial election changes); *Martin v. Haith*, 477 U.S. 901 (1986), *aff'g mem.* 618 F. Supp. 410 (E.D.N.C. 1985) (three-judge court) (same).

5. The Voting Rights Act of 1965, 42 U.S.C. §§ 1973–1973c (1988).

6. *Houston Lawyers' Ass'n*, 501 U.S. at 419 (holding that § 2 applies to elections for trial judges); *Chisom*, 111 S. Ct. at 2354 (holding that § 2 applies to elections for appellate judges).

threaten to dramatically change traditional Voting Rights Act analysis, and subvert the clear congressional mandate to eliminate the necessity of proving intentional discrimination. While the Court has answered the threshold question of whether the Act's provisions apply to judicial elections, it expressly has declined to consider whether the method for determining a violation of the Act is the same for judicial elections as for other types of elections.[7] Should courts use the same "totality of the circumstances" test in judicial election challenges as used in suits involving nonjudicial elections? Or, must courts abandon the totality of the circumstances test in favor of a "balancing test," which allows the state's interest to override liability even when a violation of the Act has been proven? Furthermore, if the one-person, one-vote principle embodied in the Fourteenth Amendment does not apply to judicial elections, how does this affect a court's ability to determine whether a violation of the Act has occurred?

In addition, the Court has asserted, without justification or analysis, that states may avoid the application of the Voting Rights Act to the judicial selection process by simply altering their method of judicial selection from election to appointment.[8] As a result, some states are considering changing their method of selecting judges.[9] The Court failed, however, to consider whether section 2 or section 5 of the Act would allow such a change in judicial selection schemes.

The effect of the Court's rulings has been confusion and, in some cases, a marked departure from established case law and statutory mandate. Some lower federal courts have entered remedial orders mandating the election of judges from single-member districts using the traditional totality of the circumstances test.[10] Other courts, however, have advanced a new "balancing test" that would, in some instances, allow the state's interest in the challenged election scheme to defeat Voting Rights Act liability even if the election scheme would have violated the Act

---

7. See *Houston Lawyers' Ass'n*, 111 S. Ct. at 2380 (expressly avoiding issues of proof and remedies); *Chisom*, 111 S. Ct. at 2361 (expressly refusing to address the question of what elements must be proved or what remedies might be appropriate for a violation of the Act).

8. *Chisom*, 111 S. Ct. at 2367.

9. See, e.g., Settlement Memorandum from Michael J. Bowers and Laughlin McDonald to Hon. Anthony A. Alaimo 1–3 (June 17, 1992) (proposing agreement to settle Georgia judicial election vote-dilution suit by changing to gubernatorial appointment with guarantee of a specific number of black judicial appointees) [hereinafter Settlement Memorandum] (on file with author).

10. See, e.g., *Martin v. Mabus*, 700 F. Supp. 327, 336–37 (S.D. Miss. 1988) (creating single-member subdistricts).

under the totality of the circumstances test.[11] The difficulty experienced by lower courts in attempting to resolve these issues is exacerbated by the Court's cursory analysis of the language, history, and application of the Voting Rights Act. Many of these issues may be revisited by the Court in the near future.

This Article identifies several problems engendered by the Court in its 1990 term and offers some possible solutions to them. Section II explores the legislative and judicial history of the Act, including the Court's recent decisions regarding judicial elections.[12] Section III considers whether the same standard for proving a violation of the Act that applies to other types of elections also applies to judicial elections.[13] It concludes that considering the state's interest in the challenged practice at the liability stage misconstrues the Act. Finally, Section IV asserts that states can be challenged pursuant to the Voting Rights Act if they switch from elective to appointive judicial selection methods and sets forth a new "vicarious selection" analysis for review of challenged appointment schemes.[14]

Legislative and Judicial History of the Voting Rights Act

Introduction to the Act

Congress adopted the Voting Rights Act of 1965 to protect minority voting.[15] Congress did not, however, establish separate rules for various kinds of elections based upon the purpose of the election. In fact, much of the debate surrounding the 1965 Act focused on barriers to registration and fraud and intimidation at polling places—practices that traditionally had prevented minorities from voting in all elections, regardless of their object.[16]

---

11. See League of *United Latin Am. Citizens v. Clements*, 986 F.2d 728, 764–72 (5th Cir.) (applying a proposed balancing of interests in judicial election challenge), *rev'd*, 999 F.2d 831 (5th Cir. 1993) (en banc), *cert. denied*, 114 S. Ct. 878 (1994).

12. See *infra* notes 15–114 and accompanying text. For another contemporary discussion of the Act's application to judicial elections, see Robert B. McDuff, *Judicial Elections and the Voting Rights Act*, 38 LOY. L. REV. 931 (1993).

13. See *infra* notes 115–296 and accompanying text.

14. See *infra* notes 297–334 and accompanying text.

15. 42 U.S.C. §§ 1973–1973bb (1988).

16. 111 CONG. REC. 19,187 (1965); see, e.g., H.R. Rep. No. 439, 89th Cong., 1st Sess. 6 (1965), reprinted in 1965 U.S.C.C.A.N. 2437, 2438 (suspending the use of tests

Statutory Provisions

To remedy these offenses and to protect the right to vote, Congress provided broad administrative and judicial relief.[17] The two most important provisions of the Act for purposes of this Article are section 2 and section 5. In certain jurisdictions with particularly egregious histories of disenfranchisement,[18] the Act suspends literacy tests and other practices used to prevent minorities from participating in the electoral process.[19] Section 5 requires administrative preclearance by the U.S. Department of Justice or the Federal District Court for the District of Columbia of any changes affecting voting in these jurisdictions.[20] The purpose of preclearance is to prevent states from replacing old disenfranchising procedures with new ones.[21] Section 2 applies to all jurisdictions and broadly prohibits procedures that deny or abridge the right to vote because of race or color.[22]

---

and devices in all elections where such tests and devices have been used to deny the right to vote on account of race or color); see also *Id.* at 13, reprinted in 1965 U.S.C.C.A.N. at 2443 (literacy tests and other devices); *Id.* at 43, reprinted in 1965 U.S.C.C.A.N. at 2471 (evidence of stuffing ballot boxes, votes cast for deceased persons, multiple casting of ballots, threats and coercion of voters, destruction of ballots, willful miscounting of ballots, and buying votes); *infra* note 72 and accompanying text.

17. *South Carolina v. Katzenbach*, 383 U.S. 301, 315 (1966) (stating that Act adopted for purpose of ridding country of racial discrimination in voting).

18. Originally, covered jurisdictions were defined as:

> any State or...any political subdivision of a state which (1) the Attorney General determines maintained on November 1, 1964, any test or device, and with respect to which (2) the Director of the Census determines that less than 50 per centum of the persons of voting age residing therein were registered on November 1, 1964, or that less than 50 per centum of such persons voted in the presidential election of November 1964.

The Voting Rights Act of 1965, Pub. L. No. 89-110, § 4(b), 79 Stat. 437, 438 (codified as amended at 42 U.S.C. § 1973b(b) (1988)).

19. 42 U.S.C. § 1973b(a) (suspending "test or device"); *Id.* § 1973b(c) (defining "test or device"); *Id.* § 1973b(d) (requiring frequent use of "test or device").

20. *Id.* § 1973c. These jurisdictions could seek either a declaratory judgment from the United States District Court for the District of Columbia or an affirmative indication from the Attorney General that no objection would be made. *Id.*

21. See *United Jewish Orgs. of Williamsburg, Inc. v. Carey*, 430 U.S. 144, 157 (1977) (finding that Act aimed at preventing use of new procedures until capacity for discrimination has been examined); *South Carolina v. Katzenbach*, 383 U.S. 301, 335 (1966) (finding that Act aimed at preventing states from evading remedies to discrimination).

22. 42 U.S.C. § 1973a.

The Concept of Vote Dilution

The courts lost no time in applying the Act to invalidate practices restricting minority voting rights.[23] The United States Supreme Court recognized that the Act requires more than the mere absence of practices and procedures designed to keep minorities from voting; the law also prohibits practices and procedures that dilute votes so as to prevent minorities from electing candidates of their choice.[24]

The 1982 Amendments to the Act

Nothing in the legislative history of the Act prior to 1979 supports the contention that different standards apply to different types of elections based on the purpose of the election. In *City of Mobile v. Bolden*, however, the Court set in motion a chain of events that would prompt Congress to amend the language of section 2.[25] States seized on this new statutory language to claim that the Act did not apply to judicial elections.[26]

In *Bolden*, the Court ruled that section 2 of the Act accomplished nothing more than codification of the Fifteenth Amendment's language.[27]

---

23. See *Katzenbach*, 383 U.S. at 301. The first case came before the Court on January 17, 1966, five months after the Act's passage. See *Id*.

24. The Court first recognized dilution claims under the Act in *Allen v. State Board of Elections*, a § 5 preclearance case. 393 U.S. 544 (1969). The Court adopted the Fifteenth Amendment concept of vote dilution to claims under the Voting Rights Act, stating that "[t]he right to vote can be affected by a dilution of voting power as well as by an absolute prohibition on casting a ballot." *Id*. at 569 (citing *Reynolds v. Sims*, 377 U.S. 533, 555 (1964)).

For a further discussion, see Chandler Davidson, *Minority Vote Dilution: An Overview*, in MINORITY VOTE DILUTION 4 (CHANDLER DAVIDSON ed., 1984); Lani Guinier, No Two Seats: The Elusive Quest for Political Equality, 77 VA. L. REV. 1413, 1424–26 (1991) (same); Lani Guinier, *The Triumph of Tokenism: The Voting Rights Act and the Theory of Black Electoral Success*, 89 MICH. L. REV. 1077, 1078 (1991) (discussing dilution as submergence of black votes in multi-member districts).

25. 446 U.S. 55 (1980); see also Frank R. Parker, *The "Results" Test of Section 2 of the Voting Rights Act: Abandoning the Intent Standard*, 69 VA. L. REV. 715, 729–46 (1983) (providing critical discussion of *Bolden*).

26. See *infra* note 77 and accompanying text.

27. *Bolden*, 446 U.S. at 60–61. The Fifteenth Amendment provides, in pertinent part, that "[t]he right of citizens of the United States to vote shall not be denied or abridged by the United States or by any State on account of race, color, or previous condition of servitude." U.S. Const. amend. XV, § 1.

According to the Court, to prevail on a claim for denial of the right to vote, whether under the Act or under the Constitution, a plaintiff must prove intent to discriminate on the basis of race, not just that an election scheme resulted in racial discrimination.[28]

In response to *Bolden*, Congress amended the Act in 1982[29] to make clear that section 2 does not require proof of discriminatory purpose or intent.[30] As was the case in 1965, the new language adopted by Congress still made no distinction between voting for judges and voting for other officials or ballot measures.[31] The new language in section 2, however, does include the phrase "representatives of their choice."[32] States, therefore, began claiming that judges are not "representatives" and, as a result, are not subject to the antidiscrimination requirements of section 2.[33]

---

28. *Bolden*, 446 U.S. at 65.

29. Voting Rights Act Amendments of 1982, Pub. L. No. 97-205, 96 Stat. 131 (1982). The language of the amended Act is as follows:

SEC. 2.(a) No voting qualification or prerequisite to voting or standard, practice, or procedure shall be imposed or applied by any State or political subdivision [to deny or abridge] *in a manner which results in a denial or abridgment of* the right of any citizen of the United States to vote on account of race or color, or in contravention of the guarantees set forth in section 1973b(f)(2) of this title, *as provided in subsection (b) of this section.*

(b) *A violation of subsection (a) is established if, based on the totality of circumstances, it is shown that the political processes leading to nomination or election in the State or political subdivision are not equally open to participation by members of a class of citizens protected by subsection (a) in that its members have less opportunity than other members of the electorate to participate in the political process and to elect representatives of their choice. The extent to which members of a protected class have been elected to office in the State or political subdivision is one circumstance which may be considered: Provided, That nothing in this section establishes a right to have members of a protected class elected in numbers equal to their proportion in the population.* Id. (pre-1982 language deleted by the 1982 amendment is in brackets, while new language is italicized).

30. S. Rep. No. 417, 97th Cong., 2d Sess. 2 (1982), reprinted in 1982 U.S.C.C.A.N. 177, 179.

31. On the contrary, the legislative history indicates the results test would apply to elections of all types, including elections for judges. See S. Rep. No. 417, *supra* note 30, at 151, reprinted in 1982 U.S.C.C.A.N. at 323–24 (report of the Senate Subcommittee on the Constitution providing that "political subdivision" test applies to all governmental units, including judicial districts, city and county councils, school boards, and state legislatures).

32. See *supra* note 29.

33. See *infra* note 77.

Application to Judicial Elections

Prior to 1990, the lower courts were nearly unanimous in holding that both section 2 and section 5 apply to judicial elections. The courts found no more difficulty in applying preclearance, antidiscriminatory, and vote-dilution concepts to judicial elections than to any other types of elections.

Section 5

The preclearance provision of section 5 originally was to expire in 1970.[34] Congress extended its life in 1970[35] and again in 1975.[36] When Congress amended section 2 in 1982, it further extended the life of section 5 for another twenty-five years.[37] At all times, the substantive provisions of section 5, requiring preclearance, remained unchanged.

History of Application

Prior to the October 1990 term, the United States Supreme Court had not considered whether the Voting Rights Act applied to judicial elections.[38] *Haith v. Martin* was the first case in which a lower court expressly held that any part of the Act applies to judicial elections.[39] In *Haith*, the plaintiffs alleged that North Carolina violated section 5 of the Act by failing to preclear changes in the number of and method for elect-

---

34. The Voting Rights Act of 1965, Pub. L. No. 89-110, § 5, 79 Stat. 437 (1965).

35. Voting Rights Act Amendments of 1970, Pub. L. No. 91-285, §§ 3-4, 84 Stat. 314 (1970), reprinted in 1970 U.S.C.C.A.N. 373 (extended for 10 years).

36. Voting Rights Act of 1965—Extension, Pub. L. No. 94-73, § 101, 89 Stat. 400 (1975), reprinted in 1975 U.S.C.C.A.N. 400 (extended for 17 years).

37. Voting Rights Act Amendments of 1982, Pub. L. No. 97-205, § 2, 96 Stat. 131, 131–34 (1982), reprinted in 1982 U.S.C.C.A.N. 131, 131–34. The 1982 amendments also provide a method by which an individual jurisdiction could prove compliance with the Act and "bail out" from § 5 coverage. *Id.*; see also S. Rep. No. 417, *supra* note 30, at 43–62, reprinted in 1982 U.S.C.C.A.N. at 221–40.

38. The Court had summarily affirmed two lower court cases applying the preclearance provisions of § 5 to judicial elections. See *Brooks v. Georgia State Bd. of Elections*, U.S. 916 (1990), *aff'g mem.* 775 F. Supp. 1470 (S.D. Ga. 1989) (holding that § 5 applies to judicial election changes); *Martin v. Haith*, 477 U.S. 901 (1986), *aff'g mem.* 618 F. Supp. 410 (E.D.N.C. 1985) (three-judge court) (same). *Clark v. Roemer*, however, was the Court's first opinion on the subject following full consideration of the issue. See 500 U.S. 646 (1991).

39. *Haith v. Martin*, 618 F. Supp. 410 (E.D.N.C. 1985) (three-judge court), *aff'd. mem.*, 477 U.S. 901 (1986).

ing state district court judges in counties subject to preclearance.[40] North Carolina admitted that certain changes had not been precleared, but contended that section 5 does not require preclearance of changes affecting the election of judges.[41] North Carolina noted that the Court had summarily affirmed cases refusing to apply the Fourteenth Amendment's one-person, one-vote requirement to the state judiciary.[42] The state asserted, therefore, that the Voting Rights Act could not apply to judicial elections.[43]

Rejecting this contention, the district court analyzed section 2 and held that "the Act applies to all voting without any limitation as to who, or what, is the object of the vote."[44] The court noted that the one-person, one-vote principle is a constitutional requirement, while the Voting Rights Act defines its own coverage.[45] The court also expressly held that "the fact that an election law deals with the election of members of the judiciary does not remove it from the ambit of [s]ection 5."[46] The United States Supreme Court affirmed the district court's decision without opinion.[47]

Because *Haith* was a summary affirmance, in *Brooks v. Georgia State Board of Elections*, a 1989 three-judge district court considered anew whether changes in laws affecting the election of judges are covered by section 5.[48] In holding that section 5 does apply to judicial elections, the district court relied on a number of factors. First, all the courts that had addressed the issue at that time had held that both section 5 and section

---

40. *Id.* at 411–12.

41. *Id.* at 412.

42. *Id.* (citing *Wells v. Edwards*, 409 U.S. 1095 (1973), *aff'g* 347 F. Supp. 453 (M.D. La. 1972)).

43. *Id.* at 412–13. These courts reasoned that the one-person, one-vote rule was designed to give equal representation to constituents and, because judges do not represent a constituency, the rule was inapplicable. *Id.*

44. *Id.* at 413 (emphasis in original). The court noted:

> [I]t is quite clear that no such distinction can be attributed to the Act. The Act provides: "No voting qualification or prerequisite to voting, or standard, practice, or procedure shall be imposed or applied by any State or political subdivision to deny or abridge the right…to vote on account of race or color.…" Id. (quoting 42 U.S.C. § 1973 (1988)).

45. *Id.*

46. *Id.*

47. *Martin v. Haith*, 477 U.S. 901 (1986), *aff'g mem.* 618 F. Supp. 410 (E.D.N.C. 1985) (three-judge court).

48. *Brooks v. Georgia State Bd. of Elections*, 775 F. Supp. 1470, 1474 (S.D. Ga. 1989), *aff'd mem.*, 111 S. Ct. 288 (1990).

2 apply to judicial elections.[49] Second, the phrase that delineates coverage—"any voting qualification or prerequisite to voting"—does not differentiate among types of elections.[50] Third, the United States Supreme Court had afforded the broadest possible interpretation to section 5, and the congressional intent was "to reach any state enactment which altered the election law."[51] Fourth, Congress had expressed its belief that the Act applies to the election of judges, because when it extended section 5 in 1982, the report accompanying the Senate bill noted the term political subdivision "encompasses all governmental units, including judicial districts."[52] The district court, therefore, concluded that the phrase "any voting qualification or prerequisite to voting, or standard, practice, or procedure..." includes laws affecting the election of judges.[53] The United States Supreme Court summarily affirmed the district court's decision in a memorandum opinion.[54]

1990 Supreme Court Term

In *Clark v. Roemer*,[55] the United States Supreme Court, in an unanimous opinion, made explicit what it had indicated through summary affirmances twice before: changes in laws affecting the election of judges in covered jurisdictions must be precleared under section 5 of the Act.[56] The Court's opinion gave short shrift to the district court's contention that section 5's applicability to judicial elections was uncertain. The Court, rather than engage in a lengthy explanation, simply cited its summary affirmances in *Brooks* and *Haith* for the proposition that the applicability of section 5 to judicial elections had been established as early as 1986.[57] *Clark*, therefore, explicitly established the fact that no distinc-

---

49. *Id.* at 1475 n.7 (citing *Chisom v. Edwards*, 839 F.2d 1056 (5th Cir.), *cert. denied*, 488 U.S. 955 (1988); *Mallory v. Eyrich*, 839 F.2d 275 (6th Cir. 1988); *Martin v. Mabus*, 700 F. Supp. 327 (S.D. Miss. 1988); *Kirksey v. Allain*, 635 F. Supp. 347 (S.D. Miss. 1986); *Haith*, 618 F. at 410).

50. *Id.* at 1476.

51. *Id.* (quoting *Allen v. State Bd. of Elections*, 393 U.S. 544, 566 (1969)).

52. *Id.* (quoting S. Rep. No. 417, *supra* note 30, at 151, reprinted in 1982 U.S.C.C.A.N. at 323–24 (report of the Subcommittee on the Constitution) (emphasis added by the Court)).

53. *Id.*

54. *Brooks v. Georgia State Bd. of Elections*, 111 S. Ct. 288 (1990), *aff'g mem.* 775 F. Supp. 1470 (S.D. Ga. 1989).

55. 500 U.S. 646 (1991).

56. *Id.* at 653

57. *Id.*

tion with respect to section 5's coverage may be made between practices used in judicial elections and those used in other types of elections.[58]

Section 2

History of Application

Martin v. Allain was the first reported decision that applied section 2 of the Voting Rights Act to judicial elections.[59] In *Martin*, the district court held that the at-large election of multiple judges by place designation in some of Mississippi's multi-member judicial election districts violated section 2.[60] The court, therefore, created single-member subdistricts with majority black voting populations.[61] In the next election, an increased number of African-Americans were elected judges.[62]

Subsequently, the United States Courts of Appeals for the Fifth and Sixth Circuits[63] and a federal district court in Alabama[64] also held that section 2 applies to judicial elections. Despite the near unanimity of court decisions, however, states continued to contend that the Act did not apply to judicial elections.[65] In 1990, the Fifth Circuit reversed field. In *League of United Latin American Citizens v. Clements*—an opinion that would have eliminated judicial election challenges based upon racially discriminatory results—the Fifth Circuit ruled that Congress' amendment to section 2 in 1982 excluded judicial elections from section 2 coverage.[66] As a result, with the circuits split, the United States Supreme Court granted certiorari in two cases from the Fifth Circuit to consider whether section 2 applies to judicial elections.

---

58. *Id.*

59. 658 F. Supp. 1183 (S.D. Miss. 1987); see also Brenda Wright, *The Bench and the Ballot: Applying the Protections of the Voting Rights Act to Judicial Elections*, 19 FLA. ST. U. L. REV. 669, 674–80 (1991) (discussing *Chisom* and *Clements*).

60. *Id.* at 1204–05. The court rejected the constitutional claims that the challenged statutes were adopted or maintained for a racially discriminatory purpose. *Id.* at 1196.

61. *Martin v. Mabus*, 700 F. Supp. 327, 336–37 (S.D. Miss. 1988).

62. *Slight Gain for Blacks*, NAT'L L.J., July 10, 1989, at 6 (finding an increase in number of elected judges in Mississippi).

63. *Chisom v. Edwards*, 839 F.2d 1056 (5th Cir.), *cert. denied*, 488 U.S. 955 (1988); *Mallory v. Eyrich*, 839 F.2d 275 (6th Cir. 1988).

64. *Southern Christian Leadership Conference v. Siegelman*, 714 F. Supp. 511 (M.D. Ala. 1989).

65. Prior to 1990, however, only one federal district court had actually found the Act inapplicable to judicial elections. *Mallory v. Eyrich*, 666 F. Supp. 1060 (S.D. Ohio 1987), *rev'd*, 839 F.2d 275 (6th Cir. 1988).

66. 914 F.2d 620, 622 (5th Cir. 1990) (en banc), *rev'd sub nom. Houston Lawyers' Ass'n v. Attorney Gen.*, 501 U.S. 419 (1991).

1990 Supreme Court Term

Because the language that defines the coverage in section 5 and section 2 is essentially identical, the conclusion that section 5 applies to judicial elections should have resolved the question of section 2 coverage.[67] Section 5, however, does not contain the phrase "representatives of their choice," which was added to section 2(b) by the 1982 amendment.[68] Perhaps for this reason, the Court provided a more detailed rationale for its decisions regarding section 2 applicability to judicial elections.

Applicability of Section 2 to Judicial Elections

In *Chisom v. Roemer*, Justice Stevens' majority opinion addressed the threshold question regarding the applicability of section 2 to judicial elections.[69] Justice Stevens began his analysis by noting that members of

---

67. Section 2 prohibits the denial or abridgment of the right to vote through the application of any "voting qualification or prerequisite to voting or standard, practice, or procedure...." 42 U.S.C. § 1973a (1988). Section 5 requires covered jurisdictions to preclear any "voting qualification or prerequisite to voting, or standard, practice, or procedure with respect to voting...." *Id.* § 1973c. Thus, § 5 and § 2 should apply to the same type of elections.

Once the Court determined that § 5 applies to judicial elections, there is little reason to question that § 2 applies to those same elections. Indeed, the basis of the *Haith* defendants' contention that § 5 is inapplicable was identical to that of the Fifth Circuit en banc decision in *Clements* that § 2 did not apply to judicial elections. Both argued that the United States Supreme Court had affirmed cases deciding that the one-person, one-vote rule did not apply to the state judiciary because judicial officers do not represent a constituency. Using the same analysis, therefore, the Voting Rights Act cannot apply to judicial officials. *Compare Haith v. Martin*, 618 F. Supp. 410, 412–13 (E.D.N.C. 1985) (three-judge court), *aff'd mem.*, 477 U.S. 901 (1986) *with Clements*, 914 F.2d at 625–27.

68. See *supra* note 29.

69. 501 U.S. 380 (1991) (joining in the majority opinion were Justices White, Marshall, Blackmun, O'Connor, and Souter). In *Chisom*, the plaintiffs—black registered voters in Orleans Parish of Louisiana—challenged the at-large system of electing Louisiana Supreme Court justices from the First Supreme Court District as a violation of § 2 of the Act and of the Fourteenth and Fifteenth Amendments because the system resulted in the dilution of minority voting rights. *Chisom v. Edwards*, 659 F. Supp. 183 (E.D. La. 1987), *rev'd*, 839 F.2d 1056 (5th Cir.), *cert. denied*, 488 U.S. 955 (1988). The First District consisted of four parishes and elected two justices at large; the other five districts elected one judge each. *Roemer*, 501 U.S. at 384. While Orleans Parish contained in excess of half of the registered voters of the First District and had a 52% black registered voter majority, the entire First District had a total population of only 34% black and 63% white. *Chisom*, 659 F. Supp. at 184.

Congress considered section 2, as originally enacted, to be a restatement of the Fifteenth Amendment.[70] Citing *City of Mobile v. Bolden*, he reiterated the fact that the coverage of the original section 2 was "unquestionably coextensive with the coverage provided by the Fifteenth Amendment."[71] Therefore, because the Fifteenth Amendment protected the right to vote without respect to the object of the vote, it followed that the original section 2 also protected the right to vote "without making any distinctions or imposing any limitations as to which elections would fall within its purview."[72]

With this premise established, the Court addressed whether the 1982 amendment to section 2 limits the original coverage to exclude judicial elections. The Court noted that Congress responded to the Court's deci-

---

The federal district court dismissed the plaintiffs' complaint, ruling that § 2 did not apply to judicial elections and that the plaintiffs failed to plead intentional discrimination by the state with specificity to support a constitutional claim. *Id.* at 184–89. The Fifth Circuit reversed, concluding that § 2 applies to judicial elections. *Chisom v. Edwards*, 839 F.2d 1056, 1065 (5th Cir.), *cert. denied*, 488 U.S. 955 (1988). On remand, the district court determined that the plaintiffs failed to establish a violation of § 2 and entered judgment for the state. *Chisom v. Roemer*, No. CIV.A.86-4057, 1989 WL 106485, at *16–*18 (E.D. La. Sept. 19, 1989). On the second appeal, the Fifth Circuit remanded the case with instructions to dismiss the complaint in light of its en banc decision in *Clements*. *Chisom v. Roemer*, 917 F.2d 187, 188 (5th Cir. 1990) (per curiam). The United States Supreme Court granted certiorari and set the case for argument with *Clements*. *Chisom v. Roemer*, 498 U.S. 1060 (1991).

70. *Chisom*, 501 U.S. at 392 at 2362 (citing S. Rep. No. 162, 89th Cong., 1st Sess., pt. 3, at 19–20 (1965), reprinted in 1965 U.S.C.C.A.N. 2508, 2540–42; H.R. Rep. No. 439, *supra* note 16, at 23, reprinted in 1965 U.S.C.C.A.N. at 2454).

71. *Id.* (citing City of Mobile v. Bolden, 446 U.S. 55, 60–61 (1980)).

72. *Id.* The Court also noted that, at the time Congress considered § 2, the Attorney General testified that every election in which registered voters participated would be subject to § 2 protection. *Id.* The Court could have reached the same conclusion by addressing the plain meaning of § 2 itself, which allows no limitation on the type of elections protected based on their purpose. See The Voting Rights Act of 1965, Pub. L. No. 89–110, § 2, 79 Stat. 438 (1965) (codified as amended at 42 U.S.C. § 1973 (1988)).

Even if the language of the original § 2 had been ambiguous, the legislative history of the Act shows that the purpose of § 2 is to protect voting in all elections, regardless of function. See, e.g., S. Rep. No. 162, *supra* note 70, at 1–16, apps. B, G, H, I, reprinted in 1965 U.S.C.C.A.N. at 2540–50 (discussing that the reasons to prohibit use of tests and other disenfranchising practices included registration for all elections regardless of function of the election); H.R. Rep. No. 439, *supra* note 16, at 6–16, reprinted in 1965 U.S.C.C.A.N. at 2440–44, 2464 (noting that subsection 14(c) of the Act applies to all elections); see also *Voter Info. Project Inc. v. City of Baton Rouge*, 612 F.2d 208, 211–12 (5th Cir. 1980) (stating that Fourteenth and Fifteenth Amendments may protect against racial discrimination in drawing of judicial election districts).

sion in *Bolden* by codifying a results test rather than an intent test.[73] Congress added a new subsection 2(b), which delineates how the results test is to be applied.[74] This new subsection borrows language from the Court's decision in *White v. Regester*, which states that a lack of proportional representation of racial groups is insufficient to show a violation of the Act:

> The plaintiff's burden is to produce evidence to support findings that the political processes leading to nomination and election were not equally open to participation by the group in question—that its members had less opportunity than did other residents in the district to participate in the political processes and to elect legislators of their choice.[75]

Congress incorporated this test into section 2(b) almost verbatim. The only significant difference is that Congress substituted the phrase "representatives of their choice" for the phrase "legislators of their choice."[76]

The Fifth Circuit, in holding that section 2 does not apply to judicial elections, based its decision largely on the assertion that the word "representative" could not be interpreted to include judges because judges do not represent anyone.[77] The Supreme Court, however, rejected this analysis.[78] It rejected the Fifth Circuit's conclusion that judges are not "representatives" for purposes of the Act.[79] Rather than adopt the Fifth Circuit's assertion that "representatives" are those officials who serve in the legislative and executive branches of government, the Court held that, for purposes of the Act, representatives are "the winners of representative, popular elections."[80] According to the Court, the belief that public opinion should be irrelevant to the function of a judge does not require the conclusion that judges are not representatives in the broader sense that they were chosen through the process of representative democracy.[81] In fact, ample evidence exists, although not mentioned by the Court, that many states changed their method of judicial selection from appointment to election during the nineteenth century specifically to

73. See *supra* notes 25–30 and accompanying text.

74. See *supra* notes 29, 31.

75. 412 U.S. 755, 766 (1973) (citing *Whitcomb v. Chavis*, 403 U.S. 124, 149–50 (1971)).

76. *Compare* 42 U.S.C. § 1973(b) (1988) *with Regester*, 412 U.S. at 766.

77. *League of United Latin Am. Citizens v. Clements*, 914 F.2d 620, 624–27 (5th Cir. 1990) (en banc), *rev'd sub nom. Houston Lawyers' Ass'n v. Attorney Gen.*, 501 U.S. 419 (1991).

78. *Chisom v. Roemer*, 501 U.S. 380, 396–404 (1991).

79. *Id.* at 400–401

80. *Id.* at 399

81. *Id.* at 400–401

make judges representatives of the people and responsive to the popular will.[82]

In addition, the Court refused to bifurcate the protections of section 2 and apply them differently to different types of elections.[83] The Fifth Circuit had held that section 2, as amended, protects two separate rights: the right "to participate in the electoral process" and the right "to elect representatives of their choice."[84] The Court refused to accept this participation/dilution dichotomy and stated: "Any abridgment of the opportunity of members of a protected class to participate in the political process inevitably impairs their ability to influence the outcome of an election.... The statute does not create two separate and distinct rights."[85] If the word "representatives" excludes judicial elections from any part of section 2, the Court concluded, it must exclude judges from section 2 entirely.[86] According to the Court, such a radical departure from the original section 2 would have occasioned at least some recogni-

---

82. See, e.g., HARRY P. STUMPF, AMERICAN JUDICIAL POLITICS 158–60 (1988) (noting that proponents of popular sovereignty led states to use direct election of judges); *Electing Judges by the People*, 19 AM. L. REV. 607, 607 (1885) (commenting that the judiciary should be subject to the popular will through direct elections); *Election of Judges*, 8 AM. L.J. 481, 482–85 (1849) (same); *Should the Judiciary Be Elective?*, 8 W. JURIST 523, 524–25 (1874) (same); see also *Kurowski v. Krajewski*, 848 F.2d 767, 770 (7th Cir. 1988) (noting that elected judges respond to political concerns).

Conversely, many legislative and executive branch officials also believe they should substitute their independent judgment for that of their constituents. See, e.g., EDMUND BURKE, *Speech to the Electors of Bristol*, in THE WORKS OF EDMUND BURKE 95 (3d ed. 1869) (asserting that representatives must ignore public opinion if to do otherwise would be inconsistent with the public good).

83. *Chisom*, 501 U.S. at 396–98.

84. *Id.* at 396. According to the Fifth Circuit, the former applied to judicial elections, but the latter did not because judges are not representatives. *Id.* at 396–98. Such a dichotomy would allow applying the results test to discriminatory procedures in judicial elections, such as early poll closings that deny "participation" in the electoral process to minorities. See *Id.* at 2365. Yet, it would not allow applying the results test to traditional vote "dilution" practices, such as multi-member districts, which limit minorities' ability to elect representatives of their choice. *Id.* Paradoxically, such dilution practices would be subject to the results test in all elections for offices other than judges. See *Id.* Using this analysis, plaintiffs challenging judicial elections schemes on the basis of dilution would be forced to prove intentional discrimination.

85. *Id.* at 397 (emphasis added) (citing *White v. Regester*, 412 U.S. 755, 766 (1973) (noting that opportunity to participate and opportunity to elect are inextricably linked); *Whitcomb v. Chavis*, 403 U.S. 124, 149–50 (1971)).

86. *Id.* at 398

tion by Congress at the time.[87] The Court concluded, however, that no such legislative history exists.[88]

Furthermore, the Court noted that interpreting section 2 to exclude judicial elections would make it inconsistent with section 5.[89] The two sections contain identical language to delineate coverage: "[any] voting qualification or prerequisite to voting, or standard, practice, or procedure with [respect to voting]."[90] If section 5 applies to judicial elections[91] and section 2 does not, a practice prohibited by the preclearance mechanism of section 5 may be permissible under section 2.[92] The Court believed that Congress could not have intended "such an anomalous result."[93]

The Court also concluded that whether the Fourteenth Amendment's one-person, one-vote requirement applies to judicial elections is irrelevant to the scope of section 2 coverage.[94] In *Clements*, the Fifth Circuit had reasoned that because the one-person, one-vote rule is the foundation for the concept of minority vote dilution,[95] and because the rule does not apply to judicial elections,[96] minority plaintiffs cannot challenge

---

87. *Id.* at 396.

88. *Id.*

89. *Id.* at 401–402

90. *Compare* 42 U.S.C. § 1973 (1988) *with Id.* § 1973c.

91. See *Clark v. Roemer*, 500 U.S. 646 (1991).

92. *Chisom*, 501 U.S. at 402. For example, the Attorney General would not preclear a change from 100 single-member judicial election districts to state-wide elections for all 100 judges if the effect would be to dilute minority voting strength. 42 U.S.C. § 1973c. However, if the same state-wide voting procedure for all 100 judges existed prior to November 1, 1964, the date after which changes must be precleared, the results test of § 2 would not apply, and courts considering a challenge under § 2 could not consider whether the effect of the scheme dilutes minority voting strength. Plaintiffs could, of course, bring an action under either the Constitution or § 2 and claim intentional discrimination.

93. *Chisom*, 501 U.S. 402.

94. *Id.* at 402–403.

95. *League of United Latin Am. Citizens v. Clements*, 914 F.2d 620, 627–28 (5th Cir. 1990) (en banc) (citing *Zimmer v. McKeithen*, 485 F.2d 1297, 1303 (5th Cir. 1973) (en banc), *aff'd on other grounds sub nom. East Carroll Parish Sch. Bd. v. Marshall*, 424 U.S. 636 (1976)), *rev'd sub nom. Houston Lawyers' Ass'n v. Attorney Gen.*, 501 U.S. 419 (1991).

96. As support for its position that vote-dilution claims may not be made against judges, the Fifth Circuit en banc opinion in *Clements* relied upon the Supreme Court's decision in *Wells v. Edwards*. *Clements*, 914 F.2d at 620 (citing *Wells v. Edwards*, 409 U.S. 1095 (1973), *aff'g* 347 F. Supp. 453 (M.D. La. 1972) (three-judge court). In *Wells*,

judicial election districting schemes through vote-dilution claims.[97] The Court dismissed this reasoning as a non sequitur. The Court noted that the application of the one-person, one-vote principle to judicial elections involves a constitutional challenge based on the Equal Protection Clause of the Fourteenth Amendment.[98] The issue in *Chisom*, however, is a question of statutory construction—whether the Voting Rights Act applies to judicial elections. As a result, the applicability of a constitutional standard is irrelevant to answering that question.[99]

Finally, the Court noted that the purpose of the 1982 amendment to section 2 is to broaden the protection of the Act.[100] The Fifth Circuit decision, however, would have required a conclusion that Congress withdrew, without comment, a category of elections, while at the same time expressly purporting to increase protection of minority voting rights.[101] The Court asserted that such a conclusion was "anomalous."[102]

Therefore, the Court concluded that, on its face, the statute applies to all elections, regardless of their purpose.[103] Since nothing in the 1982 amendment altered that coverage, judicial elections are subject to all of the Act's protections contained in section 2 and section 5.[104]

Independent Decisionmakers

In *Chisom*, the Court addressed the general applicability of the Act to judicial elections. In *Houston Lawyers' Ass'n v. Attorney General*, however, the Court addressed whether the Act's coverage is affected by the type of judicial office filled by the election—independent actor or collegial actor.[105] The Court considered whether section 2 of the Act excludes

---

the Court summarily affirmed a district court opinion which stated that the one-person, one-vote principle of the Fourteenth Amendment does not apply to judicial elections. *Wells*, 409 U.S. at 1095.

97. *Clements*, 914 F.2d at 627–29.

98. *Chisom*, 501 U.S. 403.

99. *Id.* According to the Court, "The statute was enacted to protect voting rights that are not adequately protected by the Constitution itself." *Id.* Thus, the inapplicability of the constitutional one-person, one-vote standard to judicial elections did not resolve the question of the applicability of § 2 to judicial elections. See *Id.*

100. *Id.*

101. *Id.*

102. *Id.* at 404

103. *Id.*

104. *Id.* at 401–404.

105. 501 U.S. 419 (1991), *rev'g* League of *United Latin Am. Citizens v. Clements*, 914 F.2d 620 (1990) (en banc). The plaintiffs, League of United Latin American Citizens Councils Nos. 4434 and 4451, challenged the at-large system of electing multiple state district judges in nine Texas counties as a violation of § 2 and the Fourteenth and Fif-

district court judges simply because they wield authority independently, as opposed to appellate court judges, who act collegially.

In his concurring opinion in *Clements*, Judge Higginbotham had agreed with the plaintiffs contention that section 2 of the Act applies to judicial elections.[106] Higginbotham, however, argued for a "single-member office" exemption to section 2's prohibition against vote dilution.[107] Like the *Chisom* en banc majority, Judge Higginbotham bifurcated section 2 into two types of claims: (1) participation, such as registration and poll closings, and (2) dilution, such as multi-member districts.[108] Higginbotham contended that the results test of section 2 protects minority participation in elections for single-member offices, but that minorities may not use the results test of section 2 to challenge vote-dilution mechanisms in elections for these offices.[109]

---

teenth Amendments because the system was designed to and resulted in the dilution of minority voting rights. *League of United Latin Am. Citizens v. Clements*, 902 F.2d 293, 293–94 (5th Cir.), *different result reached on reh'g*, 914 F.2d 620 (5th Cir. 1990) (en banc), *rev'd sub nom. Houston Lawyers' Ass'n v. Attorney Gen.*, 501 U.S. 419 (1991).

The federal district court found for the state on the claims of intentional discrimination, but held that the electoral system resulted in a violation of § 2 in each of the nine counties. *Id.* at 295. The district court enjoined elections for district judges, divided the counties into single-member election districts using state legislative districts and precinct lines as boundaries, and ordered nonpartisan elections with run-off elections. *Id.* The single-member districts were to be used for election purposes only. *Id.* Jurisdiction of each district court remained county-wide. *Id.*

A panel of the United States Court of Appeals for the Fifth Circuit reversed, reasoning that although the Act applied to judicial elections, it did not apply to district judges who act independently of each other. *Id.* at 303–08. On rehearing en banc, the Fifth Circuit ruled that § 2 did not apply at all to judicial elections. *League of United Latin Am. Citizens v. Clements*, 914 F.2d 620, 631 (1990), *rev'd sub nom. Houston Lawyers' Ass'n v. Attorney Gen.*, 501 U.S. 419 (1991).

106. *Clements*, 914 F.2d at 645 (Higginbotham, J., concurring). Judges Politz, King, and Davis joined in Judge Higginbotham's concurring opinion. *Id.*

107. *Id.* at 646–51 (Higginbotham, J., concurring). Judge Higginbotham defined single-member officers as those whose authority is coterminous with their election districts and who may exercise that authority independent of other office holders. *Id.*; see also Pamela D. Karlan, *Undoing the Right Thing: Single-Member Offices and the Voting Rights Act*, 77 VA. L. REV. 1, 14–39 (1991) (analyzing the single-member office exception to the Act).

108. See *supra* notes 84–87 and accompanying text.

109. *Clements*, 914 F.2d at 648–49 (Higginbotham, J., concurring). Judge Higginbotham reasoned that the concept of a minority group's impaired opportunity for equal representation makes sense for elections for multi-member bodies that reach decisions collegially. *Id.* According to Higginbotham, this concept is inapplicable to elections for officials who reach decisions independently of other officers. *Id.* at 646. Decisionmaking

The Court rejected Higginbotham's single-member office interpretation of section 2 coverage. It held, as in *Chisom v. Roemer*, that the protection of minority voters' rights to participate in the electoral process and to elect representatives of their choice is unitary.[110] Section 2's protection cannot be bifurcated and applied in some elections, while not in others.[111]

The Court also rejected Higginbotham's inverse logic that without a remedy there can be no right.[112] Because the statute requires protection of minority voters' rights in all elections, whether a particular office may be shared is irrelevant to the question of section 2 coverage.[113] The Court speculated that if courts considered such a concern at all, they must do so for purposes of determining liability or appropriate remedies, and not for the purpose of determining the coverage of the Act.[114]

C. *Summary of Supreme Court Decisions*

In the three decisions rendered during the October 1990 term, the United States Supreme Court erased any doubt that the scope of the Voting Rights Act includes judicial elections. Neither the language of the statute nor the purpose of the election exempts particular practices from the protections provided by the Act. Section 5 requires covered jurisdictions to preclear any change in laws affecting election practices regardless of the purpose of the election. Section 2 prohibits any jurisdiction from using racially discriminatory voting practices and procedures regardless of the purpose of the vote.

Proving Voting Rights Act
Violations in Judicial Elections

While the Court has made clear that section 2 and section 5 of the Act apply to judicial elections, it has expressly refused to consider the stan-

---

authority in a collegial body, such as a legislature or appellate court, may be "shared," but according to Higginbotham, there is no such thing as a "share" of a single-member office such as governor or district court judge. *Id.* at 649. Because there is no judicial remedy available to allow the office to be shared, Higginbotham concluded that the Act cannot recognize the right of minorities to be free from vote-dilution claims. *Id.* at 650–51.

110. *Houston Lawyers' Ass'n v. Attorney Gen.*, 501 U.S. at 425 (1991).
111. *Id.* (citing *Chisom v. Roemer*, 501 U.S. 380, 396–98 (1991)).
112. *Id.* at 426–28.
113. *Id.*
114. *Id.*

dards by which courts should determine whether the Act has been violated.[115] In fact, the Court suggested the possibility that the proof necessary to establish a violation of the Act may be different in cases involving judicial elections than in cases involving elections for other offices.[116] Therefore, the Court left two issues unresolved: (1) the standard for measuring minority vote dilution in judicial election challenges, and (2) whether the test for proving a violation of the Act is the same for judicial elections as for other types of elections.

Measuring Minority Vote Dilution: One-Person, One-Vote

In *Chisom*, the state contended that because the constitutional one-person, one-vote principle is inapplicable to judicial elections, it follows that the concept of vote dilution under the Voting Rights Act does not apply to judicial elections.[117] The state's contention was based upon two assumptions: first, that the Fourteenth Amendment's one-person, one-vote principle is inapplicable to judicial elections, and second, that this standard is the only standard by which vote dilution could be measured.[118] The United States Supreme Court, however, rejected these contentions and found them irrelevant to the question of Voting Rights Act coverage.[119]

In dissent, Justice Scalia agreed with the state's contention and claimed that the concept of "dilution" has no meaning if the principle of one-person, one-vote does not apply.[120] According to Scalia, this principle establishes the baseline for computing the strength that the voting minority ought to have.[121] If there is no requirement that 10,000 minority votes have the same ability to elect officials as 10,000 majority votes, courts cannot determine whether vote dilution has occurred.[122]

---

115. *Id.* at 428 (holding that § 2 applies to elected single-officer district court judges); *Chisom*, 501 U.S. at 404 (holding that § 2 applies to elected judges); *Clark v. Roemer*, 500 U.S. 646, 653–55 (1991) (holding that § 5 applies to changes in laws affecting election of judges).

116. *Houston Lawyers' Ass'n*, 111 S. Ct. at 2380–81 (expressly avoiding question of liability); *Chisom*, 111 S. Ct. at 2361 (refusing to consider the requirements for proving a § 2 violation).

117. *Chisom*, 501 U.S. at 402–403

118. See *Id.*

119. *Id.* at at 402–403.

120. *Id.* at 413–415 (Scalia, J., dissenting).

121. *Id.* at 413–416 (Scalia, J., dissenting).

122. *Id.* (Scalia, J., dissenting).

Although the Court rejected the state's contention, it failed to express whether courts may use the one-person, one-vote principle to measure minority vote dilution in judicial election challenges.[123] If courts may not use the one-person, one-vote principle in judicial election challenges, however, courts must determine how vote dilution can be measured. If a judicially manageable standard of measurement cannot be ascertained, plaintiffs may not be entitled to prevail in judicial vote-dilution claims.

Applicability of the One-Person, One-Vote Principle to Judicial Elections

The states may argue that because the Court summarily affirmed a lower court decision holding the principle of one-person, one-vote inapplicable to judicial elections, then it may not be used as a method of measuring vote dilution under the Voting Rights Act.[124] This argument assumes that the inapplicability of the one-person, one-vote principle to judicial elections remains valid law. Based upon the Court's analysis in *Chisom*, however, courts should re-examine whether the one-person, one-vote principle applies to judicial elections.[125] If the principle applies to judicial elections, the argument against its use in measuring minority vote dilution is inapposite.

Development of the One-Person, One-Vote Standard

The one-person, one-vote principle evolved from the United States Supreme Court's interpretation of the Fourteenth Amendment's Equal

---

123. See *Id.* at 403

124. See *Wells v. Edwards*, 347 F. Supp. 453 (M.D. La. 1972) (three-judge court), *aff'd mem.*, 409 U.S. 1095 (1973).

125. The Fourth Circuit has started this reconsideration. In *Republican Party v. Martin*, the Fourth Circuit reversed a district court's dismissal of the Republican Party's partisan group vote-dilution challenge to a state-wide multi-member judicial election scheme brought pursuant to the Equal Protection Clause of the Fourteenth Amendment. 980 F.2d 943 (4th Cir. 1992), *cert. denied*, 114 S. Ct. 93 (1993). The full Fourth Circuit Court of Appeals refused to rehear the case en banc, but, in dissent, Judge Phillips asserted that the Republican Party's claim was nonjusticiable because of the United States Supreme Court's summary affirmance of *Wells v. Edwards. Republican Party v. Hunt*, 991 F.2d 1202, 1203–10 (4th Cir. 1993) (Phillips, J., dissenting) (citing *Wells v. Edwards*, 409 U.S. 1095 (1973)). In *Wells*, the district court held that judicial elections are not subject to the Equal Protection Clause standard of one-person, one-vote. *Wells*, 347 F. Supp. at 455. Judge Phillips argued that if the one-person, one-vote standard of the Equal Protection Clause is not applicable to judicial elections, then the partisan group vote-dilution concept of the Equal Protection Clause recognized in *Davis v. Bandemer*, 478 U.S. 109 (1986), must not be applicable to judicial elections. *Hunt*, 991 F.2d at 1204 (Phillips, J., dissenting).

Protection Clause.[126] The Court developed the principle in *Baker v. Carr*[127] and *Reynolds v. Sims*.[128] In both cases, plaintiffs alleged abridgment of the right to vote based upon unequal population within election districts, not upon unequal treatment of racial minorities.[129] The one-person, one-vote rule, simply stated, is that the Equal Protection Clause requires that each voter have an equally effective voice in the election of members of a representative body. In order to obtain this result, the population of legislative districts must be substantially equal.[130]

In *Wells v. Edwards*, a three-judge district court ruled that the requirement of equal population does not apply to apportionment of judicial election districts.[131] The district court reasoned that judges, unlike legislators and other popularly elected officials, do not represent constituents in the formulation or execution of policy.[132] According to the district court, judges must render decisions according to the law, regardless of the opinions of the people who elect them.[133] For that reason, numerical equality based on population and geography is irrelevant to a person's ability to obtain equal protection of the law with respect to a judge's rulings.[134] Theoretically, regardless of the numerical composition or geographic area contained in an election district, a judge's rulings will be the same.

---

126. ~~The~~ Fourteenth Amendment provides, in pertinent part:

> No State shall make or enforce any law which shall abridge the privileges or immunities of citizens of the United States; nor shall any State deprive any person of life, liberty, or property, without due process of law; nor deny to any person within its ~~jurisdict~~ion the equal protection of the laws.

U.S. Const. amend. XIV, § 1.

127. 369 U.S. 186 (1962).

128. 377 U.S. 533 (1964); see also *Gray v. Sanders*, 372 U.S. 368, 379, 381 (1963) (concluding that concept of political equality requires one-person, one-vote).

129. *Reynolds*, 377 U.S. at 540 (plaintiffs alleging uneven population growth caused a citizen's vote in some districts to have less impact than a vote in other districts); *Baker*, 369 U.S. at 187–88 (redistribution of population without reapportionment alleged to be debasement of votes).

130. *Reynolds*, 377 U.S. at 565–68.

131. 347 F. Supp. 453, 454 (M.D. La. 1972) (three-judge court), *aff'd mem.*, 409 U.S. 1095 (1973) (three Justices dissenting).

132. *Id.* at 455 (relying on *Buchanan v. Rhodes*, 249 F. Supp. 860 (N.D. Ohio 1960)). But see *Chisom v. Roemer*, 501 U.S, 380, 399 n.27 (1991) (recognizing policy-making functions of the courts).

133. *Wells*, 347 F. Supp. at 455 (citing *Stokes v. Fortson*, 234 F. Supp. 575 (N.D. La. 1964)). But see *Chisom*, 501 U.S. at 400–401 (recognizing that judges may be influenced by the opinions of their constituents).

134. *Wells*, 347 F. Supp. at 455.

The United States Supreme Court summarily affirmed the district court's decision.[135] Justice White, however, dissented from the Court's decision, recognizing the incongruity of the district court's decision that the Equal Protection Clause applies to all popularly elected governmental officials except judges.[136] Justice White noted that the Court had already ruled that "whenever a state or local government decides to select persons by popular election to perform governmental functions, the Equal Protection Clause of the Fourteenth Amendment requires that each qualified voter must be given an equal opportunity to participate in that election."[137] Judges are state officials vested with state powers and elected to perform the state government's judicial functions. They most certainly "perform governmental functions."[138]

Justice White pointed out that even the Court itself had applied the one-person, one-vote principle to judicial election districts in *Gray v. Sanders*.[139] In *Gray*, the Court held unconstitutional the Georgia county unit system of counting votes for governor and for justices and judges of the state supreme court and court of appeals.[140] Justice White noted that nowhere in *Gray* did the Court "suggest that the county unit system was any less unconstitutional for the election of judges than for the election of governor."[141]

Subsequently, in *Chisom v. Roemer*, decided in 1991, the Court adopted Justice White's analysis and rejected the *Wells* decision, at least as it applies to the Voting Rights Act.[142] In *Chisom*, the Court rejected the state's argument, based on *Wells*, that elected judges do not serve a representative function for purposes of the Voting Rights Act.[143] Through an analysis strikingly similar to the Court's one-person, one-vote opinion in *Hadley*, the Court stated that when a state "decide[s] to elect its judges and to compel judicial candidates to vie for popular support just as other political candidates do...the winners [are] representa-

---

135. *Wells v. Edwards*, 409 U.S. 1095 (1973).

136. *Id.* at 1095–98 (White, J., dissenting). Justices Douglas and Marshall joined in Justice White's dissent. *Id.*

137. *Id.* at 1095–96 (White, J., dissenting) (quoting *Hadley v. Junior College Dist.*, 397 U.S. 50, 56 (1970)).

138. *Id.* at 1096–97 (White, J., dissenting).

139. *Id.* (White, J., dissenting) (citing *Gray v. Sanders*, 372 U.S. 368, 379–80 (1963)).

140. *Gray*, 372 U.S. at 370, 379–80.

141. *Wells*, 409 U.S. at 1097 (White, J., dissenting).

142. *Chisom v. Roemer*, 501 U.S. 380, 398–401 (1991).

143. *Id.*

tives of that district."[144] Although the question in *Chisom* involved statutory interpretation of the Voting Rights Act, the reasoning the Court adopted is identical to Justice White's Equal Protection Clause analysis in his dissent in *Wells*.

Given the *Chisom* Court's rejection of the *Wells* majority analysis, the applicability of the one-person, one-vote principle to judicial elections is ripe for plenary review. If the Court determines that the one-person, one-vote principle applies to judicial elections, opposition to its use in measuring judicial election minority vote dilution should diminish.

Measuring Minority Vote Dilution Without One-Person, One-Vote

If the one-person, one-vote rule remains inapplicable to judicial elections, states may argue that judicially manageable standards do not exist to measure vote dilution pursuant to the Act. Courts, however, should be able to create manageable standards. Two possibilities exist. First, courts can apply the one-person, one-vote rule as a statutory principle, even though *Wells v. Edwards* does not require it as a constitutional matter. Second, courts can use the totality of the circumstances test in section 2(b) of the Act, without resorting to the one-person, one-vote rule.

The One-Person, One-Vote Rule as a Principle of Statutory Analysis

Courts have long borrowed constitutional concepts as aids in Voting Rights Act analysis from the time of the Act's passage in 1965. The United States Supreme Court adopted the concept of vote dilution itself from Fifteenth Amendment jurisprudence for use in Voting Rights Act cases.[145] The Court enjoined minority vote-dilution schemes under the

---

144. *Id.* at 401. *Compare Id.* (holding that if state decides to select an office holder through popular elections, that election is subject to the prohibition of vote dilution contained in the Voting Rights Act) *with Hadley v. Junior College Dist.*, 397 U.S. 50, 56 (1970) (holding that where state selects persons by popular election to perform governmental functions, that election is subject to the vote-dilution prohibition of the Equal Protection Clause of the Fourteenth Amendment).

145. *See White v. Regester*, 412 U.S. 755, 765–66 (1973) (finding vote dilution under Constitution); *Allen v. State Bd. of Elections*, 393 U.S. 544, 569 (1969) (holding that right to vote can be affected by dilution of voting power and citing *Reynolds v. Sims*, 377 U.S. 533, 555 (1964)); *Zimmer v. McKeithen*, 485 F.2d 1297, 1302 (5th Cir. 1973) (en banc) (same), *aff'd on other grounds sub nom. East Carroll Parish Sch. Bd. v. Marshall*, 424 U.S. 636 (1976).

Act, not because the Constitution required it, but because adoption of the vote-dilution concept is necessary to give full effect to the Act.[146]

For purposes of creating useful standards of measurement, courts can adopt the one-person, one-vote rule for Voting Rights Act cases involving judicial elections. In *Martin v. Mabus*,[147] one lower federal court has already borrowed the constitutional one-person, one-vote standard to devise an appropriate remedy in a section 2 case involving judicial election minority vote dilution.[148] In *Martin*, the court, following *Wells*, held that the one-person, one-vote doctrine is not applicable to judicial election districts, but that "general equity requires that population variances should be minimized between subdistricts."[149]

Although *Martin* involved the fashioning of a remedy, nothing prohibits a court from using the one-person, one-vote standard to aid in determining whether an election practice violates the Act. As a result, the inapplicability of the one-person, one-vote standard to judicial elections is not a bar to the development of judicially manageable standards for measuring vote dilution pursuant to the Act.

Standard of Measuring Vote Dilution Without Resort to One-Person, One-Vote

While the adoption of the one-person, one-vote rule may be useful in determining whether an election scheme dilutes minority voting strength, it is not essential. Contrary to the state's assumption in *Chisom*,[150] the one-person, one-vote rule is not the only meaningful measure of minority vote dilution. Unequal population apportionment and minority vote dilution are distinct claims. To establish a violation of the one-person, one-vote rule, plaintiffs must prove that the state violated the racially neutral principle that each person's vote be counted equally.[151] To establish minority vote dilution, however, plaintiffs must prove that, regardless of substantial numerical equality, the election scheme minimizes the strength of voting minorities.[152] Plaintiffs can meet this burden even if no violation of the one-person, one-vote principle exists. The Court and Congress

---

146. *Allen*, 393 U.S. at 569.

147. 700 F. Supp. 327 (S.D. Miss. 1988).

148. *Id.* at 330–31.

149. *Id.*

150. *Chisom v. Roemer*, 501 U.S. 380, 402–403 (1991) (asserting that one-person, one-vote principle is only judicially manageable standard for deciding vote-dilution claims).

151. *Reynolds v. Sims*, 377 U.S. 533, 565 (1964).

152. *Zimmer v. McKeithen*, 485 F.2d 1297, 1303 (5th Cir. 1973) (en banc), *aff'd on other grounds sub nom. East Carroll Parish Sch. Bd. v. Marshall*, 424 U.S. 636 (1976).

have developed the "totality of the circumstances" test to determine when vote dilution occurs. This test is distinct from the one-person, one-vote analysis.

The Court recognized this distinction between the one-person, one-vote rule and minority vote dilution in the early case of *Fortson v. Dorsey*.[153] In *Fortson*, the plaintiffs challenged a Georgia scheme that apportioned the fifty-four seats of the state senate by electing thirty-three senators from single-member districts and twenty-one senators from multi-member districts.[154] Plaintiffs claimed that the multi-member districts violated the one-person, one-vote principle enunciated in *Reynolds v. Sims*.[155] The Court ruled that multi-member districts do not violate the one-person, one-vote requirement, so long as "the vote of any citizen is approximately equal in weight to that of any other citizen in the State."[156] The Court went on to note, however, that such a scheme might not withstand a different challenge based on a claim that a multi-member districting scheme "would operate to minimize or cancel out the voting strength of racial or political elements of the voting population."[157]

Thus, minority plaintiffs need not prove unequal apportionment under the one-person, one-vote principle to prove a claim of racial vote dilution. Cognizance of racial vote dilution cannot depend upon applicability of the equal population principle. If it did, a racial vote-dilution claim could not remain a live issue under the Georgia multi-member district scheme after the Court's decision in *Fortson*. The Court held, however, that the constitutional racial vote-dilution issue remained.[158]

In *White v. Regester*, the Court confirmed the possibility of finding racial vote dilution, even when no violation of the one-person, one-vote rule exists.[159] In *White*, the Court reversed the district court's finding that the Texas legislative apportionment plan violated the one-

---

153. 379 U.S. 433 (1965).

154. *Id.* at 434–35.

155. *Id.* at 435.

156. *Id.* at 436 (quoting *Reynolds v. Sims*, 377 U.S. 533, 579 (1964)). If one county has a population seven times as large as another and elects seven members of a legislative body and the smaller party elects one, the one-person, one-vote rule is not violated even though the larger county elects all seven members at-large. *Id.* at 437.

157. *Id.* at 439.

158. See also *Kilgarlin v. Hill*, 386 U.S. 120 (1967) (holding that plaintiffs failed to prove constitutional claim of racial vote dilution in multi-member districts); *Burns v. Richardson*, 384 U.S. 73, 88 (1966) (holding that although multi-member district scheme complied with the one-person, one-vote rule, it would violate the Equal Protection Clause if it diluted minority voting strength).

159. 412 U.S. 755 (1973).

person, one-vote rule because of a 9.9 percent population variance, but affirmed the district court's finding that the multi-member districts for Dallas and Bexar counties unconstitutionally diluted the voting strength of racial minorities.[160] *White* demonstrated, therefore, that courts can determine minority vote dilution without resorting to the one-person, one-vote standard.[161]

Furthermore, *Chisom* answered any remaining question as to whether the one-person, one-vote principle is the only way to measure vote dilution under section 2. The Court explicitly stated that "an analysis of a proper statutory standard under [section] 2 need not rely on the one-person, one-vote constitutional rule."[162]

Finally, *White* not only made clear that the one-person, one-vote rule is not the sine qua non of minority vote-dilution claims, it established the standard to be used in determining minority vote dilution—the totality of the circumstances test.[163] Significantly, Congress expressly borrowed this test and codified it as new section 2(b) of the Voting Rights Act.[164] This standard, as all other portions of the Act, applies equally to judicial elections as to other types of elections.[165]

If a court finds from a totality of the circumstances that the political processes in the state are not equally open to participation by members of a minority class (in that its members have less opportunity than other members of the electorate to participate in the political process and to elect representatives of their choice), then the challenged process or procedure violates the Act regardless of numerical equality in weighing a citizen's vote in one geographical area as compared to another. If the court finds (1) a history of racial discrimination; (2) the existence of procedures that enhance the opportunity for racial discrimination; (3) lack of minority electoral success; (4) use of racial campaign tactics to defeat minority backed candidates; or any combination of the Senate Report fac-

---

160. *Id.* at 763, 765–70.

161. See also *Zimmer v. McKeithen,* 485 F.2d 1297, 1303 (5th Cir. 1973) (en banc) (stating that United States Supreme Court has long differentiated between one-person, one-vote and minority vote dilution), *aff'd on other grounds sub nom. East Carroll Parish Sch. Bd. v. Marshall,* 424 U.S. 636 (1976).

162. *Chisom v. Roemer,* 501 U.S. 380, 403 n.32 (1991) (citing *Thornburg v. Gingles,* 478 U.S. 30, 88–89 (1986)); see also *Clark v. Roemer,* 500 U.S. 646,653 (1991) (holding that changes affecting voting in judicial election in § 5 case must be precleared); *White v. Regester,* 412 U.S. 755 (1973) (holding that multi-member districts are invalid, regardless of compliance with one-person, one-vote rule).

163. *White,* 412 U.S. at 765–67.

164. See *supra* notes 75–77 and accompanying text.

165. *Chisom,* 111 S. Ct. at 2368.

tors sufficient to determine that the political process is not equally open to minorities, then minority vote dilution has occurred[166] and numerical and geographical equality do not foreclose a finding that the scheme violates the Act.[167]

Thus, the courts and Congress have established standards to measure minority vote dilution in challenged judicial election plans. Courts may either adopt the Fourteenth Amendment's one-person, one-vote standard and determine whether a judicial plan dilutes a minority group's votes or they may apply the totality of the circumstances test without reference to population equality. In either case, the standards would apply to judicial elections in the same manner as in elections for other purposes.

Elements of Proof—Applying the Totality of the Circumstances Test to Judicial Elections

In both *Chisom* and *Houston Lawyers' Ass'n,* the Court expressly refused to consider what elements must be proven to determine whether a challenged judicial election practice violates the Act. At least one lower court has proposed a new "balancing test" to determine whether a practice violates the Act.[168] This balancing test would be a stark departure from the totality of the circumstances test and would allow the state's interest in a particular election practice to outweigh a finding of vote dilution.

This section concludes that the same elements of proof for the totality of the circumstances test apply to judicial elections as to any other challenged election practice. This section asserts that the congressional declaration of the elements of proof prevails against inconsistent judicial formulations and expressly rejects the proposed balancing test that allows a state's interest in a particular election scheme to validate an otherwise invalid judicial election practice.

Development of the Totality of the Circumstances Test

When Congress first enacted the Voting Rights Act in 1965, it did not address the elements required to show that a practice or procedure vio-

---

166. S. Rep. No. 417, *supra* note 30, at 28–29, reprinted in 1982 U.S.C.C.A.N. at 206–07.

167. *Chisom,* 111 S. Ct. at 2368 n.32.

168. See *League of United Latin Am. Citizens v. Clements,* 999 F.2d 831, 868–76 (5th Cir. 1993) (en banc) (holding that extent of vote dilution proved by the totality of the circumstances test should be weighed against the magnitude of the state's interest in the practice), *cert. denied,* 114 S. Ct. 878 (1994).

lates the Act.[169] After the Court determined that vote-dilution practices, as well as absolute prohibitions on casting ballots, violate the Act,[170] federal courts began to articulate elements necessary to prove vote dilution. The Court first expressed a test in *White v. Regester*.[171] *White's* test became known as the "totality of the circumstances" test. It listed a series of elements that courts could consider in determining whether a violation of section 2 exists.

Court Efforts to Express Elements of Proof Necessary to Establish a Violation of the Act

In large measure, the development of the totality of the circumstances test was the result of a judicial attempt to define "vote dilution" in the context of racial politics. In *White v. Regester*, the Court explained that vote dilution is not a simple lack of proportional representation; it is not simply that elected officials do not reflect, by a proportional basis, the racial group's voting potential.[172] Rather, the plaintiffs must prove, by a "totality of the circumstances," that the political processes leading to nomination and election are not equally open to participation by the minority group challenging the process.[173] A minority group must prove that its members have less opportunity than other groups to participate in the political process and to elect officials of their choice.[174]

In *White*, the Court listed several elements of this totality of the circumstances test: (1) a history of racial discrimination in education, employment, economics, health, and politics; (2) existence of procedures that, though not improper per se, enhance the opportunity for racial discrimination, such as majority run-off requirements and so-called "place" rules limiting candidacy for office from multi-member districts to a specified "place" on the ticket resulting in head-to-head contests for each position; (3) a history of insignificant numbers of minorities elected to office; (4) white-domination of party slating processes; (5) lack of responsiveness to the political and other needs and aspirations of the mi-

---

169. The Voting Rights Act of 1965, Pub. L. No. 89-110, § 2, 79 Stat. 437 (1965).

170. See *Allen v. State Bd. of Elections*, 393 U.S. 544, 569 (1969) (first case in which Court recognized that vote dilution is prohibited by Voting Rights Act).

171. 412 U.S. 755 (1973); see also Samuel Issacharoff, *Polarized Voting and the Political Process: The Transformation of Voting Rights Jurisprudence*, 90 MICH. L. REV. 1833, 1838–45 (1992) (discussing the test prior to Bolden); Parker, *supra* note 25, at 718–29 (same).

172. *White*, 412 U.S. at 765–66.

173. *Id.* at 769.

174. *Id.* at 766.

nority community; and (6) recent history of racial campaign tactics in white precincts to defeat minority-supported candidates.[175]

To this list of elements, in *Zimmer v. McKeithen,* the United States Court of Appeals for the Fifth Circuit added the state's purpose in adopting the challenged procedure.[176] According to the court in *Zimmer,* a court may consider the fact that a challenged procedure is "rooted in a strong state policy divorced from the maintenance of racial discrimination...."[177] On the one hand, this fact may counsel against a finding of vote dilution. On the other hand, if the state policy is tenuous or invidiously discriminatory, the policy may be used as evidence of vote dilution.[178]

Both *White* and *Zimmer,* however, decided constitutional claims of vote dilution that required proof of intent,[179] not challenges brought pursuant to the amended Voting Rights Act.[180] The Fifth Circuit's inclusion of the state's interest in the totality of the circumstances test articulated criteria to determine whether intentional discrimination occurred.[181] This determination, however, is no longer required in light of Congress' 1982 amendment to section 2, which eliminated intent as an element of proof.

Congressional Declaration of the Elements Necessary to Establish a Violation of the Act

The *White v. Regester* totality of the circumstances test remained the only authoritative vote-dilution test[182] until Congress amended section 2

---

175. *Id.* at 766–69.

176. 485 F.2d 1297 (5th Cir. 1973) (en banc), *aff'd on other grounds sub nom. East Carroll Parish Sch. Bd. v. Marshall,* 424 U.S. 636 (1976).

177. *Id.* at 1305 (citing *Whitcomb v. Chavis,* 403 U.S. 124 (1971)).

178. *Id.*

179. See *Washington v. Davis,* 426 U.S. 229, 239–48 (1976) (holding that proof of discriminatory intent, not merely disproportionate impact, is required for constitutional violation).

180. See *White v. Regester,* 412 U.S. 755, 765 (1973) (same); *Zimmer,* 485 F.2d at 1300–02 (discussing constitutional requirements).

181. See *Cross v. Baxter,* 604 F.2d 875, 884–85 (5th Cir. 1979) (stating that purpose of *Zimmer* state-policy inquiry is to determine whether challenged practice is racially motivated), *vacated,* 460 U.S. 1065 (1983); *Blacks United for Lasting Leadership, Inc. v. City of Shreveport,* 571 F.2d 248 (5th Cir. 1978) (finding gravamen of state policy issue to be whether state interest negates discriminatory purposes); *Nevett v. Sides,* 571 F.2d 209, 224 (5th Cir. 1978) (asserting that state policy behind districting plan is evidentiary consideration to determine whether plan is improperly motivated); *Wallace v. House,* 515 F.2d 619, 633 (5th Cir. 1975) (stating that *Zimmer* shows that tenuous state policy is good indication that the scheme is intended to dilute minority vote), *vacated,* 425 U.S. 947 (1976).

182. Prior to the 1982 amendment to the Voting Rights Act, most vote-dilution claims were brought pursuant to the Fourteenth and Fifteenth Amendments because § 2

in 1982 to eliminate intent as an element of proof in response to the Court's decision in *City of Mobile v. Bolden.*[183]

In its report accompanying the 1982 amendments to the Act, the Senate Judiciary Committee embraced the *White* approach and listed seven "typical" factors to be used in the totality of the circumstances test.[184] This list did not include the state's interest in the challenged practice. In fact, the report notes that prior to *Bolden*, the courts required no proof of the state's reason or purpose in adopting the practice at issue.[185] The committee report acknowledged that some lower federal court decisions gave probative value to evidence of the tenuous nature of the state's interest or policy underlying its use of a particular practice.[186] Even in those rare cases in which this issue is probative, however, "a consistently applied practice premised on a racially neutral policy would not negate a plaintiff's showing through other factors that the challenged practice denies minorities fair access to the process."[187] Thus, if plaintiffs proved by a totality of the circumstances that an election scheme dilutes minority voting strength, the state's interest in the illegal practice would not outweigh that proof. To the extent that earlier cases had allowed the state's nonracial interest in the challenged practice to avoid the application of the Act, the 1982 amendments clearly prohibited courts from continuing to use that analysis.

Thornburg v. Gingles

The United States Supreme Court placed its first interpretive gloss on section 2, as amended, in *Thornburg v. Gingles.*[188] In *Gingles*, African-

---

of the Act was considered a restatement of the Fifteenth Amendment. See *City of Mobile v. Bolden*, 446 U.S. 55, 60–61 (1980) (finding that § 2 was intended to have the same effect as Fifteenth Amendment).

183. *Bolden*, 446 U.S. at 60–61. For a full discussion of *Bolden*, see *supra* notes 25–28 and accompanying text.

184. S. Rep. No. 417, *supra* note 30, at 28, reprinted in 1982 U.S.C.C.A.N at 205–06. The Senate Judiciary Committee Report is the "authoritative expression of Congress' intent in amending section 2 of the Voting Rights Act." *League of United Latin Am. Citizens v. Clements*, 986 F.2d 728, 741 n.3 (5th Cir.) (citing *Thornburg v. Gingles*, 478 U.S. 30, 43–46 (1986)), *rev'd*, 999 F.2d 831 (5th Cir. 1993) (en banc), *cert. denied*, 114 S. Ct. 878 (1994); see also Issacharoff, *supra* note 171, at 1845–50 (discussing the Senate factors in the report); Parker, *supra* note 25, at 747–64 (same).

185. S. Rep. No. 417, *supra* note 30, at 37, reprinted in 1982 U.S.C.C.A.N. at 215.

186. *Id.* at 28–29, reprinted in 1982 U.S.C.C.A.N. at 206–07.

187. *Id.* at 29 n.117, reprinted in 1982 U.S.C.C.A.N. at 207 n.117.

188. *Gingles*, 478 U.S. at 30; see also Issacharoff, *supra* note 171, at 1850–53 (discussing *Bolden*).

American plaintiffs challenged certain single-member and multi-member state legislative districts as violating the Fourteenth and Fifteenth Amendments and section 2 of the Voting Rights Act.[189] Shortly after the suit was filed, Congress amended section 2 to eliminate the intent requirement.[190] The three-judge district court applied the results test of section 2, as amended, and found, based upon the totality of the circumstances, that the districting scheme diluted minority voting strength in violation of section 2.[191] The United States Supreme Court took this opportunity to consider the operation of the totality of the circumstances test, as codified in section 2, in cases challenging multi-member election districts.

The Court acknowledged the Senate Report as "the authoritative source" for legislative intent,[192] and embraced Congress' articulation of the totality of the circumstances test.[193] The Court also created a hierarchy of factors within those listed in the Senate Report. While the Court acknowledged that any inquiry into the question of minority vote dilution requires a searching, fact-based analysis of the Senate Report factors,[194] the Court proclaimed that three elements of the totality of the circumstances test are essential.[195] To prevail in a multi-member district vote-dilution claim, a minority group must demonstrate (1) that "it is sufficiently large and geographically compact to constitute a majority in a single-member district";[196] (2) that it is "politically cohesive";[197] and (3) "that the white majority votes sufficiently as a bloc to enable it... usually to defeat the minority's preferred candidate."[198] The Court noted that all other Senate Report factors are supportive of a claim of vote dilution, but are not "essential."[199]

---

189. *Gingles*, 478 U.S. at 35.

190. *Id.*; see *supra* notes 25–30 and accompanying text.

191. *Gingles v. Edmisten*, 590 F. Supp. 345 (E.D.N.C. 1984).

192. *Gingles*, 478 U.S. at 43 n.7; see also *League of United Latin Am. Citizens v. Clements*, 986 F.2d 728, 741 n.3 (5th Cir.) (asserting Senate Report as "authoritative expression of Congress' intent"), *rev'd*, 999 F.2d 831 (5th Cir. 1993) (en banc), *cert. denied*, 114 S. Ct. 878 (1994).

193. *Gingles*, 478 U.S. at 43–46.

194. *Id.* at 45.

195. *Id.* at 48 n.15.

196. *Id.* at 50.

197. *Id.* at 51.

198. *Id.*

199. *Id.* at 48 n.15.

Significantly, eight Justices[200] agreed that the state may not rebut the plaintiff's objective evidence that an element of the test exists with proof that the element was caused by factors other than racial animus.[201] Justice Brennan recognized that the language of section 2 and the Senate Report made clear that the critical question is whether the challenged structure "results" in vote dilution, not whether the dilution is "caused by race."[202] A court should look at whether the factors exist, not the reason for their existence.[203] "[U]nder the 'results test' of [section] 2, only the correlation between race of voter and selection of certain candidates,

---

200. Justice Brennan's opinion received support of a majority of Justices for its central holdings. *Id.* at 34. Part III-C of Justice Brennan's opinion was joined by Justices Marshall, Blackmun, and Stevens. *Id.* This section rejects the relevance of causation in determining whether racially polarized voting occurs in a particular jurisdiction. *Id.* at 61–74. Although only four Justices joined in support of this section, Justice O'Connor's concurring opinion agreed that defendants cannot rebut plaintiff's evidence of racially polarized voting "by offering evidence that the divergent racial voting patterns may be explained in part by causes other than race, such as an underlying divergence in the interests of minority and white voters." *Id.* at 100 (O'Connor, J., concurring). This opinion was joined by Chief Justice Burger, as well as Justices Powell and Rehnquist. *Id.* at 83.

Thus, eight Justices agreed with this basic proposition. Justice O'Connor's concurring opinion, however, was not prepared to concede that the reasons white voters reject the minority-preferred candidate could never affect the overall vote-dilution inquiry. *Id.* at 100 (O'Connor, J., concurring). Justice O'Connor could foresee a situation in which such evidence could be relevant to a different question: whether the racially polarized voting would consistently defeat minority candidates over time. *Id.* (O'Connor, J., concurring). According to O'Connor, evidence that white voters rejected a minority preferred candidate for reasons other than those that made the candidate the minority group's preference "would suggest that another candidate equally preferred by the minority group[] might be able to attract greater white vote support in future elections." *Id.* (O'Connor, J., concurring). Justice White's concurring opinion did not discuss this issue. *Id.* at 82–83 (White, J., concurring).

201. *Id.* at 63, 100; see also *League of United Latin Am. Citizens v. Clements*, 986 F.2d 728, 745 (5th Cir.) (holding that minority group not required to demonstrate that racial animus is responsible for white bloc voting), *rev'd*, 999 F.2d 831 (5th Cir. 1993) (en banc), *cert. denied*, 114 S. Ct. 878 (1994).

202. *Gingles*, 478 U.S. at 63.

203. See, e.g., *Clements*, 986 F.2d at 748 (declaring that racially polarized voting is not racially motivated voting, but rather an objective fact that voters vote along racial lines); *Westwego Citizens for Better Gov't v. City of Westwego*, 946 F.2d 1109, 1122 (5th Cir. 1991) (same); *Collins v. City of Norfolk*, 816 F.2d 932, 935 (4th Cir. 1987) (same), *rev'd*, 883 F.2d 1232 (4th Cir. 1989), *cert. denied*, 498 U.S. 938 (1990).

not the causes of the correlation, matters."[204] Any attempt by the state to explain the existence of the Senate factors through a back door re-intro-duction of causation or intent has "no relevance to the central inquiry of section 2."[205] As the Fifth Circuit noted, "Anecdotal testimony to the ef-fect that voters are pure of heart, by its very nature, will not bear much weight."[206]

The State's Interest in a Proposed Balancing Test for Judicial Elections

Justice Stevens' dictum in *Houston Lawyers' Ass'n* has prompted aggressive attempts to establish a new "balancing test" in vote-dilu-tion cases under the Voting Rights Act.[207] In the Fifth Circuit en banc decision on remand in *Houston Lawyers' Ass'n*, a majority of the judges agreed with the state that even if vote dilution is proved by ap-plying the totality of the circumstances test, the state's interest in the illegal scheme may require retention of the scheme if the interest is of great enough importance.[208]

---

204. *Gingles*, 478 U.S. at 63.

205. *Id.* Justice Brennan also noted other "serious flaws" in the state's attempt to avoid a violation of the Act by ascribing nonracial motives to racially polarized voting. *Id.* at 63–64. The state claimed that differences in voting choices were caused by "socioeconomic" characteristics, such as "income level, employment status, amount of education, housing and other living conditions, religion, language, and so forth." *Id.* at 64. Justice Brennan noted that these characteristics are shared by members of geographi-cally insular racial and ethnic groups and, in fact, these socioeconomic factors are often caused by racial and ethnic discrimination. *Id.* If the state were allowed to claim polar-ized voting is not "caused" by racial animus, the very evidence that the Senate Report said should be used to prove a challenged practice violates the Act could be used to vali-date what would otherwise be a clear violation of the Act. *Id.* at 64–67.

206. *Clements*, 986 F.2d at 754.

207. *Houston Lawyers' Ass'n v. Attorney Gen.*, 501 U.S. at 426–427 (1991). For the content of Justice Steven's dictum, see *infra* notes 252–53 and accompanying text; see also Wright, *supra* note 59, at 680–88 (discussing state interest in judicial election schemes as part of § 2 analysis).

208. *League of United Latin Am. Citizens v. Clements*, 999 F.2d 831, 868–76 (5th Cir. 1993) (en banc), *cert. denied*, 114 S. Ct. 878 (1994). Slightly different balancing tests were proposed by various defendants. See *Clements*, 986 F.2d at 756–57.

Defendant-intervenor Judge Sharolyn Wood proposed a three-part balancing test: (1) the court must determine the "existence and severity" of vote dilution; (2) the court must "assess" the state interests that would be affected; and (3) the court must then "balance the severity of the dilution against the intrusion on state interests necessary to cure it." *Id.* at 756. No violation of § 2 would exist if the state interests outweighed the severity

The supporters of a balancing test base their proposals on three legal theories. First, they assert that Congress intended the courts to balance the state's interests in a particular election practice against the severity of vote dilution. Second, they assert that notions of federalism rooted in the Constitution require application of a balancing test. And third, they assert that the United States Supreme Court mandated use of a balancing test in *Houston Lawyers' Ass'n.*

The Balancing Test and Congressional Intent

Balancing the state's interest in the challenged practice against evidence of racial vote dilution is at odds with the express language of the Act, with the legislative history of the 1982 amendment to section 2, and with prior judicial decisions.

The Language of Section 2

The express language of section 2 does not permit a court to use a balancing test that allows the state's interest to outweigh proof of vote dilution. Section 2(b) establishes the test to be used by courts to determine a violation of the Act:

> A violation of subsection (a) of this section is established if, based on the totality of circumstances, it is shown that the political processes leading to nomination or election in the State or political subdivision are not

---

of the dilution. *Id.*

Defendant-intervenor Judge F. Harold Entz proposed the following balancing test: (1) the minority group must first satisfy the three Gingles threshold factors; (2) if the *Gingles* factors are satisfied, the court must determine whether the state's interests are "legally compelling," that is, (a) "whether they relate to a central aspect of state sovereignty," and (b) "whether tampering with them would result in undue federal entanglement with the operations of state government." *Id.* at 756–57. A finding that the state interests are legally "compelling" would preclude a § 2 violation regardless of the severity of the vote dilution. *Id.* Even if not legally compelling, the state's interests must be balanced against the severity of vote dilution proved. *Id.*

The state of Texas proposed a third balancing test: the court must, before any consideration of proof of vote dilution, determine whether the challenged practice is necessary to achieve a compelling state interest (Fourteenth Amendment strict scrutiny). *Id.* at 757. If the practice survives strict scrutiny, no violation of § 2 exists regardless of the proof of the totality of the circumstances. *Id.* If the strict scrutiny standard is not met, the plaintiffs would be required to meet the *Gingles* factors, whereupon the burden shifts to the state to prove its interests and nondiscriminatory purposes. *Id.* At this point, the burden would revert to the plaintiffs to prove vote dilution by clear and convincing evidence. *Id.*

equally open to participation by members of a [protected] class... in that its members have less opportunity than other members of the electorate to participate in the political process and to elect representatives of their choice.[209]

The statute specifically provides that if the totality of the circumstances test is met, the practice violates the Act. It does not provide that if the totality of the circumstances test is met, the practice violates the Act unless the state had a "good reason" for the practice. As Judge King noted in the Fifth Circuit panel majority opinion in *League of United Latin American Citizens v. Clements*:

> On its face, section 2 does not allow a state to defeat proof of vote dilution by showing that it has a good reason for maintaining the challenged electoral practice. It provides, in absolute terms, that a violation is established if, "based on the totality of the circumstances, it is shown that the political processes leading to nomination or election in the state or political subdivision are not equally open to participation by members [of a racial or language minority]...." It makes no exceptions.[210]

Thus, congressional intent is clear from the express language of section 2: balancing the state's interest to validate an otherwise invalid practice is impermissible.

Legislative History

Even if congressional intent were not clear from the express language of the statute, a review of the legislative history of the 1982 amendment to the Act eliminates any claim that Congress intended to allow the state's interest to negate a finding of vote dilution using the totality of the circumstances test. The Senate Report clearly rejects this claim by stating: "Even a consistently applied practice premised on a racially neutral policy would not negate a plaintiff's showing through other factors that the challenged practice denies minorities fair access to the process."[211] Evidence of the tenuousness of the state's purported interest is a factor in the totality of the circumstances test for purposes of finding vote dilu-

---

209. Voting Rights Act Amendments of 1982, Pub. L. No. 97-205, § 3, 96 Stat. 131, 134 (1982).

210. *Clements*, 986 F.2d at 757 (emphasis added).

211. S. Rep. No. 417, *supra* note 30, at 29 n.117, reprinted in 1982 U.S.C.C.A.N. at 207 n.117.

tion.[212] A valid state interest, however, even a compelling one, will not save a procedure that dilutes minority voting strength.[213]

The legislative pronouncements contained in the Senate Report, which the Court in *Gingles* recognized as the authoritative source of congressional intent,[214] are in keeping with the primary purpose of the 1982 amendment to section 2. Congress amended section 2 to make clear that plaintiffs need not prove intent in establishing a violation of the Act.[215] Congress expressly recognized that, by eliminating the need to prove intent, it was eliminating the possibility that the state could negate a finding of vote dilution by stating a nonracial interest in the challenged practice.[216]

The rejection of the state's interest in a balancing test framework also makes practical sense from the perspective of eliminating the need to prove intent. If a court could consider the state's racially neutral interest in a particular procedure, plaintiffs could only counter that consideration by arguing that the state policy was motivated by racial animus. Such a formulation of the totality of the circumstances test would require consideration of intent.[217] Consideration of the state's interest, therefore, would undermine the 1982 amendment of section 2, which expressly rejects intent as an element. As the Senate Report accompanying the 1982 amendment makes clear, states abridge or deny minority voting

---

212. The Senate Report recognizes as one factor of the totality of the circumstances test "whether the policy underlying the state or political subdivision's use of such voting…practice or procedure is tenuous." *Id.* at 29, reprinted in 1982 U.S.C.C.A.N. at 207; see also *Zimmer v. McKeithern*, 485 F.2d 1297, 1305 (5th Cir. 1973) (en banc) (using state's interest in totality of the circumstances test), *aff'd on other grounds sub nom. East Carroll Parish Sch. Bd. v. Marshall,* 424 U.S. 636 (1976).

213. S. Rep. No. 417, *supra* note 30, at 29 n.117, reprinted in 1982 U.S.C.C.A.N. at 207 n.117; see also *Clements,* 986 F.2d at 758 (holding that legislative history of § 2 forecloses claim that state's interest will outweigh proof of vote dilution).

214. *Thornburg v. Gingles,* 478 U.S. 30, 43 n.7 (1986); see also *Clements,* 986 F.2d at 741 n.3 (finding Senate Report to be authoritative expression of Congress' intent).

215. See *supra* notes 25–30 and accompanying text.

216. S. Rep. No. 417, *supra* note 30, at 37, reprinted in 1982 U.S.C.C.A.N. at 215 ("The inherent danger in exclusive reliance on proof of motivation lies not only in the difficulties of plaintiff establishing a prima facie case of discrimination, but also in the fact that the defendants can attempt to rebut that circumstantial evidence by…eschewing any racial motive[] and advancing other governmental objectives.").

217. See *supra* notes 176–81 and accompanying text; see also Gregory G. Ballard, Note, *Application of Section 2 of the Voting Rights Act to Runoff Primary Election Laws,* 91 Colum. L. Rev. 1127, 1132–33 (1991) (asserting that Senate Report factors are relevant to discriminatory purpose, not effect).

rights regardless of the presence or absence of discriminatory intent.[218] The Senate Report expresses Congress' intent that the failure of a plaintiff to establish any particular factor is not rebuttal evidence of nondilution.[219] Thus, the tenuousness of a state's interest may be used to establish vote dilution, but a nontenuous state interest is irrelevant as to whether a procedure violates the Act.[220]

One argument that Congress did intend to incorporate a state interest balancing test is that the 1982 amendment to section 2 incorporated the totality of the circumstances test as articulated in *Zimmer*,[221] which allegedly used a state interest balancing test.[222] This argument, however, fails for three simple reasons. First, Congress incorporated the language from *White v. Regester* into the amended section 2, not *Zimmer*.[223] Second, *White* and *Zimmer* did not, in fact, use a state interest balancing test.[224] Third, even if a tortured reading of these cases lent support to a state interest balancing test, it would be irrelevant to the question at

---

218. S. Rep. No. 417, *supra* note 30, at 27–28, reprinted in 1982 U.S.C.C.A.N. at 204–06.

219. *Id.* at 29 n.118, reprinted in 1982 U.S.C.C.A.N. at 207 n.118; see also *Id.* at 194, reprinted in 1982 U.S.C.C.A.N. at 365 (statement of Senator Dole that plaintiffs need only establish discriminatory results). This treatment of the state's interest is no different from other factors of the totality of the circumstances test. For example, one factor to be considered as a part of this test is whether members of the minority group have been denied access to any candidate slating process. The absence of an exclusive slating process, however, will not mitigate evidence of an unequal opportunity to participate in the political process. *McMillan v. Escambia* County, 638 F.2d 1239, 1245 (5th Cir.), *cert. dismissed*, 453 U.S. 946 (1981).

220. See S. Rep. No. 417, *supra* note 30, at 27–29, 29 n.117, reprinted in 1982 U.S.C.C.A.N. at 204–07, 207 n.117; see also, e.g., *Jones v. City of Lubbock*, 727 F.2d 364, 383 (5th Cir. 1984) (holding that state policy has no probative value in determining results); Citizens for a Better *Gretna v. City of Gretna*, 636 F. Supp. 1113, 1135 (E.D. La. 1986) (same), aff'd, 834 F.2d 496 (5th Cir. 1987), *cert. denied*, 492 U.S. 905 (1989); *Gingles v. Edmisten*, 590 F. Supp. 345, 373 (E.D.N.C. 1984), *aff'd in part, rev'd in part on other grounds*, 478 U.S. 30 (1986).

221. *Zimmer v. McKeithern*, 485 F.2d 1297 (5th Cir. 1973) (en banc), *aff'd on other grounds sub nom. East Carroll Parish Sch. Bd. v. Marshall*, 424 U.S. 636 (1976).

222. See *League of United Latin Am. Citizens v. Clements*, 986 F.2d 728, 837 (5th Cir.) (Higginbotham, J., dissenting), *rev'd*, 999 F.2d 831, 868–76 (5th Cir. 1993) (en banc), *cert. denied*, 114 S. Ct. 878 (1994). Judge Higginbotham failed to repeat his argument in his majority en banc opinion. See *League of United Latin Am. Citizens v. Clements*, 999 F.2d 831, 868–76 (5th Cir. 1993) (en banc), *cert. denied*, 114 S. Ct. 878 (1994).

223. See *supra* notes 182–87 and accompanying text.

224. See *supra* notes 169–81 and accompanying text.

hand because any vote-dilution standard applied prior to the 1982 amendment would be superseded by the amendment itself.[225]

Judicial Interpretation of Congressional Intent

The United States Supreme Court's interpretation of the 1982 amendment also adds weight to the foregoing arguments. Justice Brennan's analysis in *Gingles,* rejecting causation of racially polarized voting as evidence to rebut a plaintiff's prima facie case, applies with even greater force to the state's interest in a challenged practice. The evidence excluded in *Gingles* related to the existence of only one factor—racially polarized voting.[226]

If a state is permitted to introduce evidence of its interest in the challenged practice as part of the balancing test, that evidence could rebut the ultimate finding of vote dilution. Surely, if the absence of one factor may not be used as rebuttal evidence of nondilution, then evidence that a state's interest is not tenuous may not be used as rebuttal evidence of the ultimate finding of vote dilution. As Justice Brennan observed in *Gingles,* "Both [section] 2 itself and the Senate Report make clear that the critical question in a [section] 2 claim is whether the use of a contested electoral practice or structure results in members of a protected group having less opportunity than other members of the electorate to participate in the political process and to elect representatives of their choice."[227]

If, in a multi-member district election scheme, the plaintiffs prove blacks vote sufficiently as a bloc to elect their preferred candidates in a black majority, single-member district, and if a white majority votes sufficiently as a bloc usually to defeat the candidates chosen by blacks, the scheme violates section 2 regardless of the cause.[228] This result is true regardless of whether the state has a bad reason, no reason, or a good reason for maintaining the practice that results in minority vote dilution.

Furthermore, some lower courts have allowed the plaintiff to use evidence of the tenuousness of the state's purported race-neutral policy, not to show discriminatory intent, but rather to show discriminatory results. These courts recognized that the 1982 amendment to section 2 made the state's policy underlying the challenged practice irrelevant for purposes of proving intent. These cases, however, use the tenuousness of the state policy as circumstantial evidence that the particular electoral device pro-

225. See *supra* notes 182–206 and accompanying text.
226. *Thornburg v. Gingles,* 478 U.S. 30, 61 (1986).
227. *Id.* at 63.
228. *Id.*

duces discriminatory results.[229] These cases, therefore, correctly conclude that a tenuous state policy can be used to prove discriminatory results, but cannot be used to rebut an ultimate finding of vote dilution.[230]

Finally, no reason exists for a different formulation of the totality of the circumstances test for judicial election procedures than for any other challenged procedures. Since the adoption of the 1982 amendments, most courts have interpreted the statute and congressional intent to disallow a racially neutral articulation of the policy behind a challenged practice in the election of nonjudicial officials to defeat a finding of vote dilution.[231] Once the Court has determined that the Act applies to judicial elections, proving a violation must be the same

---

229. See, e.g., *McMillan v. Escambia County*, 748 F.2d 1037, 1045 (5th Cir. 1984) (finding state interest to be circumstantial evidence that system has discriminatory results); *United States v. Marengo County Comm'n*, 731 F.2d 1546, 1571 (11th Cir.) (same), *cert. denied*, 469 U.S. 976 (1984); *Houston v. Haley*, 663 F. Supp. 346, 355–56 (N.D. Miss. 1987) (same), *aff'd*, 859 F.2d 341 (5th Cir. 1988), *and vacated* 869 F.2d 807 (5th Cir. 1989).

230. See *League of United Latin Am. Citizens v. Clements*, 986 F.2d 728, 753 (5th Cir.) (holding that tenuousness of state policy is evidence of discriminatory results, but existence of a legitimate state policy does not preclude a finding of vote dilution), *rev'd*, 999 F.2d 831 (5th Cir. 1993) (en banc), *cert. denied*, 114 S. Ct. 878 (1994); *Westwego Citizens for Better Gov't v. City of Westwego*, 872 F.2d 1201, 1211 (5th Cir. 1989) (holding that court must consider plaintiffs' contention that the state policy is tenuous, but state's evidence that challenged practice had race-neutral policy is irrelevant).

231. See, e.g., *Solomon v. Liberty County*, 899 F.2d 1012, 1016 n.3 (11th Cir. 1990) (en banc) (Kravitch, J., specially concurring) (holding that if challenged electoral practice has effect of diluting minority voting strength, defendants cannot use nondiscriminatory purpose as affirmative defense), *cert. denied*, 498 U.S. 1023 (1991); City of Westwego, 872 F.2d at 1210–12 (holding that nondiscriminatory purpose for adoption of at-large aldermanic districts and longevity of its use are irrelevant to finding of vote dilution); *Jones v. City of Lubbock*, 727 F.2d 364, 384 (5th Cir. 1984) (holding that state policy behind challenged practice is of diminished importance under results test); *Ward v. Columbus County*, 782 F. Supp. 1097, 1105 (E.D.N.C. 1991) (finding no compelling governmental need for use of at-large elections for county commissioners that would justify result of racial vote dilution); *Jordan v. Winter*, 604 F. Supp. 807, 813 (N.D. Miss.) (holding that legitimate state interest in congressional redistricting plan did not defeat finding of vote dilution), *aff'd sub. nom. Mississippi Republican Executive Comm. v. Brooks*, 469 U.S. 1002 (1984); *Gingles v. Edmisten*, 590 F. Supp. 345, 373 (E.D.N.C. 1984) (holding that state policy favoring whole counties in multi-member legislative districts is irrelevant to finding vote dilution under § 2 results test), *aff'd in part, rev'd in part on other grounds*, 478 U.S. 30 (1986); *Terrazas v. Clements*, 581 F. Supp. 1329, 1345 n.24 (N.D. Tex. 1984) (holding that state policy has less probative value under results test).

for judicial elections as for other types of elections because nothing in the statute, its legislative history, or in the totality of the circumstances test counsels in favor of a different test.

The Balancing Test as a Constitutional Mandate

Proponents of a balancing test argue that, even if the statute does not require the state's interest as a counterweight to a finding of vote dilution, the Constitution requires it. This theory relies primarily upon the Court's decision in *Gregory v. Ashcroft.*[232]

The Plain Statement Rule

Ashcroft, according to proponents, requires the courts to interpret the Voting Rights Act to include a state interest balancing test.[233] Traditional notions of federalism, they argue, allow the states the authority "to determine the qualifications of their most important government officials."[234] This notion lies at the very heart of representative government.[235] In order to disrupt this traditional state power, Congress must unmistakably express its intent to do so.[236]

No one doubts that traditional state powers are at stake any time an election practice is found to violate the Voting Rights Act.[237] Thus, *Ashcroft* would require a plain statement of congressional intent to disrupt these traditional state powers. This aspect of *Ashcroft* is not startlingly different from previous Court precedent. Judicial insistence upon

---

232. 501 U.S. 452 (1991).

233. See *League of United Latin Am. Citizens v. Clements,* 986 F.2d 728, 758–60 (5th Cir.) (arguing that principles of federalism require balancing test unless plain statement by Congress to disrupt traditional federal-state relationship), *rev'd,* 999 F.2d 831, 868–76 (5th Cir. 1993) (en banc) (holding weight of state's interest in judicial election districts coterminous with venue as compelling according to *Ashcroft*), *cert. denied,* 114 S. Ct. 878 (1994).

234. *Id.* at 758 (citing *Ashcroft,* 501 U.S. at 463).

235. *Id.* Ironically, the state originally argued that the election of judges was so far removed from notions of representative democracy that Congress could not have intended to include them in the coverage of the Voting Rights Act as reflected by the phrase in § 2, "representatives of one's choice." See *League of United Latin Am. Citizens v. Clements,* 914 F.2d 620, 624–25 (5th Cir. 1990) (en banc), *rev'd. sub nom. Houston Lawyers' Ass'n v. Attorney Gen.,* 111 S. Ct. 2376 (1991).

236. *Ashcroft,* 501 U.S. 419 (1991).

237. One lower court, however, has noted that *Ashcroft* spoke only to the qualifications of government officials. *Clements,* 986 F.2d at 759. Because vote-dilution cases did not address qualifications to hold office, the court found Ashcroft of no precedential value. *Id.*

a clear statement of congressional intent in areas affected by federalism concerns is a long-standing interpretive tool.[238]

One need not reject this aspect of *Ashcroft*, however, to reject the proposed state interest balancing test. With respect to the Voting Rights Act, it is difficult to imagine a more unequivocal expression of congressional intent to disrupt important state powers in order to remedy racial discrimination. Congress, in 1965, specifically indicated which states would be covered by the Act,[239] spelled out the extensive disruption in the traditional state power to govern its own election practices (perhaps the aspect of the Act most intrusive of state sovereignty), and clearly articulated what aspects of traditional state power would be affected.[240]

The 1982 amendment, mandating a results/totality of the circumstances test, also clearly illustrates Congress' intent to interfere with traditional state power by stating that "to enforce fully the Fourteenth and Fifteenth Amendments, it is necessary that [s]ection 2 ban election procedures and practices that result in a denial or abridgment of the right to vote."[241] In addition, as previously noted, Congress specifically stated that the state's interest may not rebut a finding of vote dilution and, thus, no balancing of the state's interest may be made.[242]

Congressional Authority to Disrupt Traditional State Powers with Respect to Elections

Even if congressional intent was clearly articulated to pass scrutiny of the plain statement rule, a separate but related argument can also be made on behalf of the proposed state interest balancing test. The Court

---

238. See, e.g., *Atascadero State Hosp. v. Scanlon*, 473 U.S. 234, 242 (1985) (holding that unequivocal expression of congressional intent is required to disturb fundamental state interests); *Pennhurst State Sch. and Hosp. v. Halderman*, 465 U.S. 89, 99 (1984) (same).

239. 42 U.S.C. § 1973b(b) (1988).

240. See, e.g., H.R. Rep. No. 439, *supra* note 16, at 22, reprinted in 1965 U.S.C.C.A.N. at 2449–50 (recognizing that traditional power of states to fix qualifications for voting is subject to disruption by Congress pursuant to Fifteenth Amendment); see also Republican views of Hon. William M. McCulloch, Hon. Richard H. Poff, Hon. William C. Cramer, Hon. Arch H. Moore, Jr., Hon. Clark MacGregor, Hon. Carleton J. King, Hon. Edward Hutchinson, and Hon. Robert McClory, *Id*. at 37, reprinted in 1965 U.S.C.C.A.N. at 2470–71 (noting that Act is suspension of state sovereignty over state voting laws); views of Hon. William M. Tuck in opposition to the Proposed Voting Rights Act, *Id*. at 72, reprinted in 1965 U.S.C.C.A.N. at 2491 (noting that Act reaches a crest in the flood of federal intrusions into matters constitutionally reserved to the states).

241. S. Rep. No. 417, *supra* note 30, at 40, reprinted in 1982 U.S.C.C.A.N. at 218.

242. See *supra* notes 182–87 and accompanying text.

in *Ashcroft* stated that "[a]s against Congress' powers [to] regulate Commerce...among the several States, U.S. Const. Art. I, § 8, cl. 3, the authority of the people to determine the qualifications of their government may be inviolate."[243] Therefore, one may contend that Congress lacks the authority to adopt a results standard that does not incorporate a state interest balancing test. Such an argument, however, relies upon a fundamental misreading of *Ashcroft* and congressional enforcement powers pursuant to the Fourteenth and Fifteenth Amendments.

If Congress had relied upon its Commerce Clause powers to adopt the Voting Rights Act or the 1982 amendment to section 2, *Ashcroft* would be a serious impediment to the constitutionality of the entire statute, not just to a test for liability which does not include the state's interest. Congress, however, did not rely upon its Commerce Clause powers. Rather, Congress specifically acted pursuant to its enforcement powers under the Fourteenth and Fifteenth Amendment.[244] The Court has repeatedly upheld the constitutionality of this exercise of congressional power.[245]

In *Mississippi Republican Executive Committee v. Brooks*, the Court summarily rejected the argument that Congress must require proof of intentional discrimination to constitutionally exercise Fifteenth Amendment enforcement powers.[246] The state had argued that Congress exceeded its authority by providing section 2 liability in the absence of intentional discrimination.[247] Using a state interest balancing test, however, would reintroduce the requirement of intent.[248] *Brooks* specifically recognized the authority of Congress to exercise its Fifteenth Amendment enforcement powers without proof of intent. *Ashcroft*, therefore,

---

243. *Gregory v. Ashcroft*, 501 U.S. 452, 464 (1991).

244. See *South Carolina v. Katzenbach*, 383 U.S. 301, 326 (1966) (stating that when Congress adopted the 1965 Act, it acted pursuant to its remedial powers to effectuate the Fourteenth and Fifteenth Amendments); S. Rep. No. 417, *supra* note 30, at 39, reprinted in 1982 U.S.C.C.A.N. at 217 (same).

245. See, e.g., *Thornburg v. Gingles*, 478 U.S. 30, 43–44 (1986) (finding proof of intent is not required); *Mississippi Republican Executive Comm. v. Brooks*, 469 U.S. 1002, 1002 (1984) (finding that Congress possesses power to premise Voting Rights Act violation on elements without reference to state's intent to discriminate); *Katzenbach*, 383 U.S. at 326–27 (finding that Congress has power to go beyond the specific mandates of § 1 of Fifteenth Amendment pursuant to its enforcement powers contained in § 2 of the Amendment). But see *Chisom v. Roemer*, 111 S. Ct. 2354, 2376 (1991) (Kennedy, J., dissenting) (stating that nothing in the Court's opinion addresses the constitutionality of the Voting Rights Act).

246. *Brooks*, 469 U.S. at 1002.

247. *Id.* at 1003 (Stevens, J., concurring).

248. See *supra* notes 200–06 and accompanying text.

did nothing to diminish congressional enforcement authority to disrupt traditional state powers with respect to elections.

The Balancing Test and the Houston Lawyers' Ass'n Dicta

In spite of the overwhelming statutory and judicial authority rejecting a state interest balancing test, some lower federal courts have held that a valid state interest in an election scheme defeats liability under the Voting Rights Act.[249] These decisions rely on two isolated passages in Justice Stevens' opinion in *Houston Lawyers' Ass'n*.[250] Those passages, however, are clearly dicta. Justice Stevens' opinion itself stated that questions concerning proof of section 2 violations in judicial elections were to be addressed at a later date.[251] In addition, regardless of their classification, the passages cited do not support a state interest balancing test.

The *Houston Lawyers' Ass'n* Dicta

Supporters of a state interest balancing test rely on two passages from *Houston Lawyers' Ass'n*. First, in rejecting the notion that judicial elections are not covered by the Voting Rights Act, Justice Stevens, writing for a majority of the Court, stated:

> Even if we assume, *arguendo*, that the State's interest in electing judges on a district-wide basis may preclude a remedy that involves redrawing boundaries or subdividing districts, or may even preclude a finding that vote dilution has occurred under the "totality of the circumstances" in a particular case, that interest does not justify excluding elections for single-member offices from the *coverage* of the [section] 2 results test. Rather, such a state interest is a factor to be considered by the court in

---

249. *League of United Latin Am. Citizens v. Clements*, 999 F.2d 831, 868–73 (5th Cir. 1993) (en banc) (finding state interest in coterminous election districts and venue), *cert. denied*, 114 S. Ct. 878 (1994); *Nipper v. Chiles*, 795 F. Supp. 1525, 1547–48 (M.D. Fla. 1992) (finding valid state interest in election district/jurisdiction and small number of minority lawyers), *rev'd sub nom. Nipper v. Smith*, 1 F.3d 1171 (11th Cir. 1993), *and vacated and reh'g granted*, No. 92-2588, 1994 WL 81683 (11th Cir. Mar. 10, 1994); *Magnolia Bar Ass'n v. Lee*, 793 F. Supp. 1386, 1412 (S.D. Miss. 1992) (finding that state's interest in independent supreme court outweighs violation of Act), *aff'd*, 994 F.2d 1143 (5th Cir.), *cert. denied*, 114 S. Ct. 555 (1993); *Southern Christian Leadership Conference v. Evans*, 785 F. Supp. 1469, 1478–80 (M.D. Ala. 1992) (finding valid state interest in election district/jurisdiction linkage and small number of minority lawyers), *vacated*, No. 92-6257, 1994 WL 57377 (11th Cir. Feb. 28, 1994), *and reh'g granted*, No. 92-6257, 1994 WL 93271 (11th Cir. Mar. 23, 1994).

250. *Houston Lawyers' Ass'n v. Attorney Gen.*, 501 U.S. 419 (1991).

251. *Id.* at 426.

evaluating whether the evidence in a particular case supports a finding of a vote-dilution violation in an election for a single-member office.[252]

Second, in disagreeing with the lower court's decision that Texas' interest in its judicial system precludes coverage of the Act, Justice Stevens stated:

> Rather, we believe that the State's interest in maintaining an electoral system...is a legitimate factor to be considered by courts among the "totality of circumstances" in determining whether a [section] 2 violation has occurred. A State's justification for its electoral system is a proper factor for the courts to assess in a racial vote-dilution inquiry, and the Fifth Circuit has expressly approved the use of this particular factor in the balance of considerations. Because the State's interest in maintaining an at-large, district-wide electoral scheme for single-member offices is merely one factor to be considered in evaluating the "totality of the circumstances," that interest does not automatically and in every case, outweigh proof of racial vote dilution.[253]

These passages, however, are clearly dicta. The opinion specifically stated that the Court granted certiorari "for the limited purpose of considering the *scope of coverage* of [section] 2."[254] The Court even expressly stated that questions of liability were not a part of its considerations.[255] Therefore, any language arguably supporting a state interest balancing test is purely dictum.

The Meaning of the Houston Lawyers' Ass'n Dicta

Even if the two passages from *Houston Lawyers' Ass'n* are not dicta, they still would not support a state interest balancing test. The first quoted passage assumes, for the sake of argument, that the state's interest may be taken into account to determine liability or to fashion a rem-

---

252. *Id.*

253. *Id.* at 426–27

254. *Id.* at 425 (emphasis added).

255. *Id.* In the Court's words:

> We deliberately avoid any evaluation of the [state interest] concerns expressed in Judge Higginbotham's concurring opinion because we believe they are matters that are relevant either to an analysis of the totality of the circumstances that must be considered in an application of the results test embodied in § 2, as amended, or to a consideration of possible remedies in the event a violation is proved, but not to be the threshold question of the Act's coverage.

edy, and finds that such an assumption would not remove single-member officers from the scope of the Act.[256] The language, however, does not require consideration of the state's interest. It implies only that if the state's interest must be considered, it will not change the scope of the Act.

The second passage does say that a state's justification for its electoral system is a proper factor "for the courts to assess in a racial vote dilution inquiry."[257] The Court cited *Zimmer* for this proposition.[258] *Zimmer* also was cited by the Senate Report accompanying the 1982 amendment to section 2.[259] The state's purported interest was an important factor prior to 1982 because section 2 required proof of intentional discrimination.[260] Prior to 1982, plaintiffs could establish proof of purposeful discrimination by showing that the state's justifications for the challenged election scheme were not, in fact, the reasons it adopted or maintained the scheme—the state justification was tenuous.[261] The state could then rebut this evidence of intentional discrimination with evidence of the validity of its race-neutral justifications.

However, after the 1982 amendment to section 2 eliminated the need to prove intentional discrimination, the state's interest becomes much less important and its relevance much more limited. Plaintiffs can still offer evidence of tenuousness as circumstantial evidence of discriminatory results, but the state's interest in the election practice is not relevant to whether the scheme results in vote dilution.[262] It is only relevant to whether the state intentionally discriminated in adopting or maintaining the challenged procedure. The Senate Report specifically provides that "even a consistently applied practice premised on a racially neutral policy would not negate a plaintiff's showing through other factors that the challenged practice denies minorities fair access to the process."[263] The opinion cannot be read in isolation with sections taken out of context

---

256. *Id.* at 426–27.

257. *Id.*

258. *Id.* at 427.

259. S. Rep. No. 417, *supra* note 30, at 28 n.113, 29 n.117, reprinted in 1982 U.S.C.C.A.N. at 206 n.113, 207 n.117.

260. City of *Mobile v. Bolden*, 446 U.S. 55, 62 (1980).

261. See S. Rep. No. 417, *supra* note 30, at 28 n.112, reprinted in 1982 U.S.C.C.A.N. at 206 n.112 (noting *White-Zimmer* factors allow courts to infer purposeful discrimination).

262. See *Id.* (noting that amended § 2 no longer requires inference of purposeful discrimination from totality of the circumstances factors).

263. *Id.* at 29 n.117, reprinted in 1982 U.S.C.C.A.N. at 207 n.117.

with the cases it cites and the statute it interprets. To do so fundamentally mischaracterizes the Court's opinion.[264]

State Policies Underlying Judicial Election Schemes

Although the state's ability to articulate a racially neutral policy should not be considered in determining liability under the Act,[265] some courts continue to claim that judicial elections are unique and that special consideration should be given to the state's interest in particular judicial election schemes.[266] Usually, the state claims a non-racial policy in favor of maintaining large multi-member election districts in which the court's jurisdiction is coterminous with the election district.[267] Far from justifying racial vote dilution, however, most interests offered by the states are tenuous, thinly veiled attempts to avoid minority control of election results.

---

264. See also *League of United Latin Am. Citizens v. Clements*, 986 F.2d 728, 760–63 (5th Cir.) (asserting that the Court's opinion in *Houston Lawyers' Ass'n* did not support a state interest balancing test), *rev'd*, 999 F.2d 831 (5th Cir. 1993) (en banc), *cert. denied*, 114 S. Ct. 878 (1994).

265. See *supra* notes 200–64 and accompanying text.

266. See, e.g., *Clements*, 986 F.2d at 764–65 (urging consideration of numerous interests in the challenged election procedure: preserving an elected judiciary; partisan judicial elections; a qualified judiciary; residency/jurisdiction linkage; prohibition of judges engaging in certain political activity; an informed electorate; administrative advantages in at-large elections; specialization of judges; residency/election district linkage; preservation of judge as sole decisionmaker; Texas' citizens' expression of self-government; avoid disenfranchisement of white as well as black voters; rights of criminal defendants; and protection of minority representation); *Magnolia Bar Ass'n v. Lee*, 793 F. Supp. 1386, 1410–12 (S.D. Miss. 1992) (finding that a valid state interest in districts that foster political and economic diversity forecloses vote-dilution claim), *aff'd*, 994 F.2d 1143 (5th Cir.), *cert. denied*, 114 S. Ct. 555 (1993); *Brooks v. Georgia State Bd. of Elections*, 790 F. Supp. 1156, 1161 (S.D. Ga. 1992) (Bowen, J., concurring) (asserting that judges should not have identifiable constituency to whom they owe allegiance); *Southern Christian Leadership Conference v. Evans*, 785 F. Supp. 1469, 1472 (M.D. Ala. 1992) (determining Voting Rights Act violation more difficult in judicial elections than in others), *vacated*, No. 92-6257, 1994 WL 57377 (11th Cir. Feb. 28, 1994), *and reh'g granted*, No. 92-6257, 1994 WL 93271 (11th Cir. Mar. 23, 1994).

267. *Clements*, 986 F.2d at 764–65; see also *Clark v. Roemer*, 777 F. Supp. 471, 475–77 (M.D. La. 1991) (stating that to ensure independence of judiciary, district must be large enough to avoid domination by voting group with special interest), *appeal dismissed*, 958 F.2d 614 (5th Cir. 1992).

Large Districts

The state's purportedly race-neutral policy favoring large multi-member districts is that judicial independence is greater in large districts than in small ones.[268] Local residents can be angered by a judge's ruling in a particular case.[269] If the judge is dependent upon only the votes from that local area for re-election, the judge may be forced to cater to the will of the people, rather than decide cases based on the law and the facts.[270] If, on the other hand, judicial election districts are large, the judge can be re-elected with votes from outside the area in which popular dissatisfaction with a ruling runs high.

As an extension of this large district logic, states argue that they must be free to add multiple judges to the same district in order to manage larger caseloads.[271] States even advance the novel notion that election districts must be sufficiently large to create a sufficient pool of qualified minority lawyers to offer as judicial candidates.[272] States also assert an interest in creating large districts to foster political and economic diversity.[273] In sum, the states argue that their interest in judicial independence

---

268. See, e.g., *Clements*, 986 F.2d at 769–71 (stating that small single-member districts would make judge beholden to particular racial group that elected him); *Magnolia Bar Ass'n*, 793 F. Supp. at 1411 (stating that judges are more independent in large districts than in small ones); *Evans*, 785 F. Supp. at 1479–80 (same).

269. *Evans*, 785 F. Supp. at 1479.

270. *Id.* States have also argued that to ensure independence of the judiciary, districts must be large enough to avoid domination by voting groups with special interests. *Clark*, 777 F. Supp. at 479 (considering state interest for purposes of designing remedy).

271. But see *Westwego Citizens for Better Gov't v. City of Westwego*, 872 F.2d 1201, 1211 (5th Cir. 1989) (determining that district court should not consider the potential disruption of reorganizing administrative structure in determining whether an at-large election scheme violates the Act).

272. *League of United Latin Am. Citizens v. Clements*, 999 F.2d 831, 868–76 (5th Cir. 1993) (en banc), *cert. denied*, 114 S. Ct. 878 (1994); *Evans*, 785 F. Supp. at 1485. Such a conclusion results from the erroneous focus on the race of the official, rather than the ability of the voters to elect officials of their choice. Even if no qualified black candidates exist, minority voters could elect a candidate of their choice. This is the mandate of the Voting Rights Act.

273. *Magnolia Bar Ass'n v. Lee*, 793 F. Supp. 1386, 1410–11 (S.D. Miss. 1992), *aff'd*, 994 F.2d 1143 (5th Cir.), *cert. denied*, 114 S. Ct. 555 (1993). This state interest is especially pernicious in light of the court's finding of a history of official discrimination at the time of the creation of the district lines, continuing disparity in socioeconomic status between blacks and whites, and racially polarized voting. *Id.* at 1408–09. If a state can defeat a claim of vote dilution by claiming a state interest in maintaining socioeconomic

and resource allocation should allow them to maintain large multi-member election districts that would otherwise violate the Act.[274]

Even if courts did consider the state's interest in determining a section 2 violation, these particular interests in judicial independence are extremely tenuous. Rather than rebutting a finding of racial vote dilution, the state's purported interest in large districts supports one.[275] In *Chisom*, the states argued that their concerns for judicial independence, objectivity, and resource allocation preclude applying the Act to judicial elections.[276] The Court recognized this argument as a value laden concern that judges should not be influenced by popular opinion.[277] The Court, however, recognized that this concern is a policy choice made by the states, not the federal courts.[278] If the states did not want judges to be influenced by popular opinion, they would not have chosen to elect their judges.[279] In fact, the Court noted that if states were truly concerned

---

and political diversity, the very facts that the Congress and the United States Supreme Court say prove a violation could be used to avoid a violation. A district that "cracks" minority voters among several districts in which whites are a majority could be defended on the basis of a desire for political and socioeconomic diversity. See *Thornburg v. Gingles*, 478 U.S. 30, 63–67 (1986) (holding that socioeconomic disparities between blacks and whites may not be used to defeat a finding of racially polarized voting because the very evidence that the Senate Report found probative of such a finding would be used to defeat that finding).

274. The independence argument is inherently suspect. In effect, the state would be forced to argue that so long as whites control the electoral process and elect white judges, the system produces fair, independent judges. But if blacks are allowed to elect judges of their choice, somehow those judges will not be fair and independent. As Judge Johnson noted in his dissent to the original panel decision in *Clements*, "Once a state decides to elect judges from areas smaller than the entire state, it has made a decision to permit the appearance that...judges are accountable to only part of the electorate." *League of United Latin Am. Citizens v. Clements*, 902 F.2d 293, 317 n.17 (5th Cir.) (Johnson, J., dissenting), *different result reached on reh'g*, 914 F.2d 620 (5th Cir. 1990), *rev'd sub nom.* Houston Lawyers' Ass'n v. Attorney Gen., 111 S. Ct. 2376 (1991); see also *League of United Latin Am. Citizens v. Clements*, 986 F.2d 728, 771 (5th Cir.) (noting the negative racial stereotyping inherent in this argument), *rev'd*, 999 F.2d 831 (5th Cir. 1993) (en banc), *cert. denied*, 114 S. Ct. 878 (1994).

275. If a state interest is tenuous, that fact must counsel in favor of plaintiff's contention that the challenged practice results in minority vote dilution. See *supra* note 186 and accompanying text.

276. See *Chisom v. Roemer*, 501 U.S. 380, 400–401 (1991).

277. *Id.* at 400.

278. *Id.*

279. *Id.*

with the independence of their judiciary, they may change their method of judicial selection from election to appointment.[280]

Other courts that have considered this issue have reached similar conclusions.[281] In many cases, the stated policy is simply inconsistent with the state's practice. For example, in *Clark v. Edwards*, the court of appeals districts in Louisiana ranged in size from the smallest, 350 square miles, to the largest, 19,344 square miles.[282] Therefore, the court found that the state's actual geographic districts were inconsistent with its stated policy of favoring large geographic districts.[283] In *Martin v. Allain*, some Mississippi judges were elected from large multi-member districts, while others were elected from small single-member districts.[284] Therefore, the court found that the state's interest in large multi-member districts was tenuous and inconsistent with its purported policy.[285] As Fifth Circuit Judge Sam Johnson noted in his dissent to the original panel decision in *Clements*: "Once a state decides to elect judges from areas smaller than the entire state, it has made a decision to permit the appearance that the lower court judges are accountable to only part of the electorate."[286]

Court Venue Coterminous with Election Districts

Similar problems exist when states claim an interest in maintaining court venue coterminous with election districts.[287] States claim that court venue and the election district must be coterminous because a perception

---

280. *Id.* at 401.

281. *Clark v. Edwards*, 725 F. Supp. 285, 301 (M.D. La. 1988) (asserting that state has no strong policy for maintaining current size of court of appeal districts); *Martin v. Allain*, 658 F. Supp. 1183, 1195–96 (S.D. Miss. 1987) (asserting that state policy in post system elections in large multi-judge districts is tenuous).

282. *Clark*, 725 F. Supp. at 300.

283. See *Id.*

284. *Martin*, 658 F. Supp. at 1183.

285. *Id.* at 1195–96.

286. *League of United Latin Am. Citizens v. Clements*, 902 F.2d 293, 317 n.17 (5th Cir.) (Johnson, J., dissenting), *different result reached on reh'g*, 914 F.2d 620 (5th Cir. 1990), *rev'd sub nom. Houston Lawyers' Ass'n v. Attorney Gen.*, 501 U.S. 419 (1991).

287. Although the states and some courts refer to "jurisdiction," what they actually mean is venue. For example, in Texas, the state argued that it had an interest in maintaining election districts that are coterminous with jurisdiction. *League of United Latin Am. Citizens v. Clements*, 986 F.2d 728, 767 (5th Cir.), *rev'd*, 999 F.2d 831 (5th Cir. 1993) (en banc), *cert. denied*, 114 S. Ct. 878 (1994). But, in Texas, the trial court's jurisdiction—the power to decide a controversy—is statewide. Venue—the proper place where that power is exercised—is limited. *Id.*

of unfairness would exist if one party to a lawsuit voted in the judge's election district and one did not.[288] Such a perception of unfairness, however, is also present in judicial election schemes in which venue and election districts are coterminous.[289] Most states use venue rules that allow a certain amount of forum shopping.[290] It is easy to imagine a scenario in which the parties to a lawsuit do not both reside in the same judicial district. Indeed, lawsuits involving contract disputes, tort actions, and most other civil litigation invariably will involve residents of two different judicial districts. The perception of "hometown justice" is a problem in any judicial election scheme. It is a function of judicial elections themselves, not the link between venue and election districts, that creates the perception of bias.[291]

In addition, courts have found that states inconsistently apply the purported policy favoring coterminous venue and election districts. For example, in *Martin v. Allain*,[292] Mississippi Supreme Court justices were elected from one of three districts, but heard cases state-wide. The court concluded, therefore, that the state's policy of coterminous venue and election districts was tenuous and inconsistently applied.[293]

---

288. See, e.g., *Clements*, 902 F.2d at 308 (finding state interest in avoiding appearance of bias); *Southern Christian Leadership Conference v. Evans*, 785 F. Supp. 1469, 1478 (M.D. Ala. 1992) (finding perception of unfairness if litigant from judge's election district opposed litigant from outside the district), *vacated*, No. 92-6257, 1994 WL 57377 (11th Cir. Feb. 28, 1994), *and reh'g granted*, No. 92-6257, 1994 WL 93271 (11th Cir. Mar. 23, 1994); Clark v. Roemer, 777 F. Supp. 471, 475 (M.D. La. 1991) (finding link between election district and jurisdiction district avoids "hometown justice" perception), *appeal dismissed*, 958 F.2d 614 (5th Cir. 1992).

289. *Clark*, 777 F. Supp. at 479 (state witnesses agreeing that perception of "hometown justice" exists in any judicial election scheme).

290. See, e.g., ALA. CODE § 6-3-7 (1975) (corporation may be sued in any county in which it does business); ARK. CODE ANN. § 16-60-105 (Michie 1987) (action against person, firm, co-partnership, or association may be brought in any county in which that party maintains an office); LA. CODE CIV. PROC. ANN. art. 71–83 (West 1960) (exceptions to general venue rules offering various venue choices); MISS. CODE ANN. § 11-11-5 (1972) (actions against railroads, transportation companies, and communications firms may be brought in any county in which any part of the company may be); TEX. CIV. PRAC. & REM. CODE ANN. § 15.001 (West 1986) (generally, all lawsuits may be brought in the county in which the cause of action accrued or in the county of defendant's residence).

291. *Clark*, 777 F. Supp. at 479.

292. 658 F. Supp. 1183 (S.D. Miss. 1987).

293. Id. at 1195; see also *League of United Latin Am. Citizens v. Clements*, 986 F.2d 728, 767–69 (5th Cir.) (finding that exceptions to coterminous venue/election districts render state's purported interest tenuous), *rev'd*, 999 F.2d 831 (5th Cir. 1993) (en banc), *cert. denied*, 114 S. Ct. 878 (1994).

Furthermore, the use of election or appointment as a method of judicial selection is a policy choice made by the states. Once a state chooses to subject its judiciary to the popular will, it is subject to the Voting Rights Act.[294] The state's interest in protecting against judicial control by a particular minority group is no defense to an otherwise invalid election practice.[295]

Finally, the Court's decisions clearly hold that the Voting Rights Act applies equally to all elections, regardless of the object of the vote. Courts should give a state's interest in a particular judicial election scheme no greater weight in determining whether a violation of the Act has occurred than a state's interest in procedures for electing legislators, city council members, or county supervisors. The fact that the state prefers large judicial districts over small ones or that it prefers election districts coterminous with jurisdiction is of no consequence for purposes of determining whether the election districts violate the Act. State preferences may be of some consequence in determining the appropriate remedy for a section 2 violation, but are not relevant in determining whether a violation has occurred.[296]

Method of Judicial Selection—A Change from Election to Appointment May Violate the Voting Rights Act

In *Chisom*, the Court rejected the notion that concerns for judicial independence and objectivity place judicial elections outside the coverage of the Voting Rights Act.[297] The Court noted that Louisiana had chosen to subject its judges to the popular will.[298] Once that decision was made, the state had an obligation under the Act to ensure that the procedures it

---

294. *Martin*, 658 F. Supp. at 1195.

295. See *supra* notes 249–64 and accompanying text.

296. *Houston Lawyers' Ass'n v. Attorney Gen.*, 501 U.S. 419, 426 (1991); see also *Whitcomb v. Chavis*, 403 U.S. 124, 160–61 (1971) (finding that courts may not ignore state apportionment policy in remedying dilutive election schemes); *Clements*, 986 F.2d at 756 (same); *Clark v. Roemer*, 777 F. Supp. 471, 479–80 (M.D. La. 1991) (finding that state interest in large districts does not obviate necessity for creating subdistricts in judicial elections to eliminate minority vote dilution), *appeal dismissed*, 958 F.2d 614 (5th Cir. 1992).

297. See *supra* notes 78–82 and accompanying text.

298. *Chisom v. Roemer*, 501 U.S. 380, 400 (1991).

uses do not dilute minority voting strength.[299] The Court also stated, however, as dictum, that "Louisiana could, of course, exclude its judiciary from the coverage of the Voting Rights Act by changing to a system in which judges are appointed...."[300]

Appointing judges, rather than electing them through single or multi-member districts, would solve many of the objections to Voting Rights Act coverage raised by the states. Primarily, judges would no longer be subject to the pressures of accountability inherent in democratic elections. In fact, since the time states first chose to select judges by election, opponents have argued against judicial elections on precisely that basis.[301]

A majority of the states use elections as at least one component of the judicial selection process.[302] If these states believe that applying the Act to judicial elections will lead to less independence on the part of the judiciary, they may consider changing the method of judicial selection from election to appointment.[303] The Court, however, curiously failed to point out a major hurdle in making this change. Any change from election of judges to appointment may still be subject to challenge under section 2 and section 5 of the Voting Rights Act.

---

299. See *Id.*

300. *Id* at 401. Indeed, the parties in *Brooks v. Georgia State Board of Elections*, 790 F. Supp. 1156 (S.D. Ga. 1992), have signed a memorandum that would settle Voting Rights Act litigation challenging an at-large judicial election scheme by changing the method of judicial selection from election to appointment by the Governor. Appointed judges would be subject only to "retention" elections—elections in which an appointed judge runs unopposed and voters support or oppose the incumbent. Settlement Memorandum, supra note 9, at 1–3. The agreement was sent to the Justice Department for approval. Rhonda Cook & Steve Harvey, *Georgia to Phase Out Judge Elections*, ATLANTA J. AND CONST., June 18, 1992 at A1; see also Wright, *supra* note 59, at 688–90 (discussing merit retention elections and Voting Rights Act coverage).

301. See *supra* note 82 and accompanying text.

302. See Roy Schotland, *Elective Judges' Campaign Financing: Are State Judges' Robes the Emperor's Clothes of American Democracy?*, 2 J.L. & POL. 57, 72–73 (1985) (noting that 39 states elect some or all of their judges in partisan, nonpartisan, or retention elections).

303. State witnesses have argued for appointment. On remand from the United States Supreme Court, the state in *Clark v. Roemer* presented witnesses advocating merit selection rather than election of judges from majority black districts. 777 F. Supp. 471, 475–76 (M.D. La. 1991), *appeal dismissed*, 958 F.2d 614 (5th Cir. 1992).

A Change From Election to Appointment Requires Preclearance Under Section 5

Section 5 of the Act requires jurisdictions subject to its provisions to preclear any change in voting practices or procedures.[304] A state that changes its method of choosing officials from election to appointment, therefore, must preclear that change. In *Burton v. Patterson*, a companion case to *Allen v. State Board of Elections*, the Court ruled that a state law changing the method of selecting a county superintendent of education from election to appointment affected a citizen's vote by eliminating the voter's ability to elect an officer formerly subject to the approval of the voters.[305] Thus, the change was subject to preclearance under section 5.[306] In *Clark v. Roemer*, the Court reaffirmed the fact that changes affecting judicial elections are subject to the same preclearance requirements as any other elections.[307] The requirement of preclearance, however, does not answer the more difficult question of whether the change will be approved.

In determining whether to approve the change, the U.S. Department of Justice or the Federal District Court for the District of Columbia must determine whether the submitted change has the purpose or effect of denying or abridging the right to vote based upon race.[308] Prior to the 1982 amendments to section 2, the Court had interpreted section 5 to require a standard of review for discriminatory effect called "retrogression." In *Beer v. United States*,[309] and again in *City of Lockhart v. United States*,[310] the Court interpreted section 5 to prohibit implementation of changes in election laws that, by their purpose or effect, "lead to a retrogression in the position of racial minorities with respect to their effective exercise of the electoral fran-

---

304. The Voting Rights Act of 1965, § 5, 42 U.S.C. § 1973c (1988).

305. 393 U.S. 544 (1969).

306. *Id.* at 569–70; see also *Presly v. Etowah County Comm'n*, 112 S. Ct. 820, 828, (1992) (holding that changes affecting creation or abolition of elective office are subject to § 5 review).

307. *Clark v. Roemer*, 500 U.S. 646, 652–55 (1991).

308. *Compare* 42 U.S.C. § 1973c (providing that court must determine whether practice has purpose or effect of denying or abridging the right to vote) *with* 28 C.F.R. §§ 51.52(a), 51.56 (1991) (providing that Attorney General shall make the same determination as court under § 5 and shall be guided by the relevant judicial decisions).

309. 425 U.S. 130 (1976).

310. 460 U.S. 125 (1983).

chise."[311] Thus, if a change in election procedures resulted in an effect on minority voting rights no worse than the procedure it replaced, and if it was not enacted for a racially discriminatory purpose, the Attorney General or the D.C. Federal District Court reviewing the change must preclear it.[312]

The 1982 amendments to the Act, however, altered the appropriate standard of review under section 5 from retrogression to the identical standard used in section 2. The Senate Report accompanying the 1982 amendments made clear that the amendments augmented the *Beer* non-retrogression standard of section 5 by providing that "[i]n light of the amendment to section 2, it is intended that a section 5 objection also follow if a new voting procedure itself so discriminates as to violate section 2."[313] Thus, regardless of whether a practice is challenged under section 5 or section 2, the same totality of the circumstances test should be applied.[314] Either the Attorney General[315] or the court, therefore, should deny section 5 preclearance if a change from an elected judiciary to an appointed one has the effect of diluting minority voting strength.[316]

Even before the 1982 amendments, the Justice Department, using the retrogression standard, refused to approve some changes making formerly elected positions subject to appointment. For example, in 1966 the state of Mississippi attempted to make elected county school superintendents in several majority black counties subject to appointment. The Justice Department interposed an objection under section 5, and the changes did not take place.[317] In addition, the United States Supreme Court had previously acknowledged that a change from elective to appointive office may result in a section 5 violation.[318]

---

311. *Beer*, 425 U.S. at 141; see also *City of Lockhart*, 460 U.S. at 133–36 (applying *Beer* nonretrogression standard).

312. See *City of Lockhart*, 460 U.S. at 133–36.

313. S. Rep. No. 417, *supra* note 30, at 12 n.31, reprinted in 1982 U.S.C.C.A.N. at 189 n.31 (emphasis added).

314. See Stephen L. Lapidus, *Note, Eradicating Racial Discrimination in Voter Registration: Rights and Remedies Under the Voting Rights Act Amendments of 1982*, 52 FORDHAM L. REV. 93, 116–19 (1983).

315. 28 C.F.R. § 51.55(2) (1991) (providing that Attorney General shall withhold § 5 preclearance if change would violate amended § 2).

316. Although no court has ruled on this issue, a court must reject clear legislative intent to reach a contrary conclusion.

317. Letter from the Assistant Attorney General, Civil Rights Division, U.S. Department of Justice to the Mississippi Attorney General (May 21, 1967), *cited in* Robert McDuff, *The Voting Rights Act and Judicial Elections Litigation: The Plaintiffs' Perspective*, 73 JUDICATURE 82, 83 n.13 (1989).

318. *See Perkins v. Matthews*, 400 U.S. 379, 389–90 n.8 (1971) (noting with approval the remarks of Representative McCulloch in debate on the Act that substantive

Therefore, because the Attorney General and the D.C. Federal District Court must refuse section 5 preclearance if a change from election to appointment fails the standard of amended section 2, they must now decide whether the change dilutes minority voting strength under the totality of the circumstances test. In addition, jurisdictions not subject to section 5 preclearance requirements must rely on section 2, which applies nationwide, to challenge shifts from election to appointment.[319]

Does a Change from Election to Appointment Dilute Minority Voting Strength?

Any practice that affects voting, regardless of the object of the election, is subject to the requirements of section 2.[320] This principle, enunciated in *Chisom*, leads to the conclusion that a change in the selection of public officials from election to appointment must meet the requirements of section 2. As the Court noted in *Bunton*, such a change affects voters by removing their direct opportunity to select the public official.[321]

---

provisions of § 5 were designed to prevent change from elective to appointive offices); *Allen v. State Bd. of Elections*, 393 U.S. 544, 569–70 (1969) (court reserved judgment on complicated issue of whether change from elective to appointive method of selection denied or abridged the right to vote).

319. See 42 U.S.C. § 1973 (1988) (providing that § 2 applies to any state or political subdivision).

320. See *Chisom v. Roemer*, 501 U.S. 380, 404 (1991); see also *Bradley v. Indiana State Election Bd.*, 797 F. Supp. 694, 697–98 (S.D. Ind. 1992) (holding retention elections of judges covered by Voting Rights Act).

321. *Bunton v. Patterson,* 393 U.S. 544 (1969). But see *Irby v. Virginia State Bd. of Elections,* 889 F.2d 1352, 1357–59 (4th Cir. 1989) (holding that appointed school board scheme in use from 1870 is violative of § 2), *cert. denied,* 496 U.S. 906 (1990); *Searcy v. Williams,* 656 F.2d 1003, 1010 (5th Cir. 1981) (holding that appointed school board scheme in use from 1915 is not subject to § 2 challenge), *aff'd mem. sub nom. Hightower v. Searcy,* 455 U.S. 984 (1982); *African-American Citizens for Change v. Robbins,* 825 F. Supp. 1156 (E.D. Mo. 1993) (holding that Voting Rights Act is inapplicable to appointed positions); *Bradley,* 797 F. Supp. at 697 (holding that Voting Rights Act covers retention election of judges, but not original appointments); *Williams v. State Bd. of Elections,* 696 F. Supp. 1563, 1568–69 (N.D. Ill. 1988) (holding that Voting Rights Act covers elected officials only, not appointed judges).

These cases involved challenges to appointive schemes that had been in existence for many decades, not changes from election to appointment. The question whether long-standing appointive schemes may be challenged under the Act is separate from the question whether withdrawing the right to vote for a particular office dilutes minority voting strength. At least one court, however, has ruled that a long-standing appointment scheme—when coupled with retention elections—is subject to § 2. *Bradley,* 797 F.

Under a section 2 analysis, courts must use the totality of the circumstances test codified in the 1982 amendments, and as applied in *Gingles*, to determine whether a switch from election to appointment impermissibly dilutes minority voting strength. The House Report accompanying the 1982 amendment to the Act is noteworthy in that it recognizes that "shifts from elective to appointive office" are one of many "practices or procedures in the electoral process" that singly or in combination with other practices may violate section 2.[322]

Using the seven typical factors of the totality of the circumstances test outlined in the Senate Report accompanying the 1982 amendments,[323] a court could determine in a particular factual situation whether a change from election to appointment violated section 2 and, by extension, whether it should be rejected under the preclearance provisions of section 5. If plaintiffs can prove a history of racial discrimination, the existence of procedures that enhance the opportunity for racial discrimination, a history of insignificant numbers of minorities elected to office, white domination of party-slating processes, lack of responsiveness to the minority community, a history of racial campaign tactics, or any combination of these factors that show minorities do not have an equal opportunity to participate in the political process and to elect representatives of their choice, the shift from elected to appointed judges would violate the substantive prohibitions of section 2 and should be rejected under the preclearance provision of section 5.[324]

Supp. at 694.

322. H.R. Rep. No. 227, 97th Cong., 1st Sess. 18 (1981).

323. S. Rep. No. 417, *supra* note 30, at 27–29, reprinted in 1982 U.S.C.C.A.N. at 205–07.

324. See *Id.* (noting totality of the circumstances factors to be considered in determining whether a particular practice violates the Act); see also *Thornburg v. Gingles*, 478 U.S. 30, 44–46 (1986) (citing Senate Report factors); *White v. Regester*, 412 U.S. 755, 766–69 (1973) (same).

The state may argue that a shift from an elected judiciary to an appointed one would provide minorities an opportunity to elect representatives of their choice equal to that of the majority—that is, no opportunity to elect. Such an argument misses the mark. Under a vote-dilution analysis, the fact that the state dilutes the votes of the minority is not negated by the fact that it dilutes the votes of the majority at the same time. As the Court noted in *Allen v. State Board of Elections*, the power of a citizen to vote is affected by a change in the method of selection from election to appointment and, depending upon the circumstances, may have a "discriminatory purpose or effect." 393 U.S. 544, 569–70 (1969).

Formulation of a Vicarious Selection Analysis for Review of Appointment Schemes

Opponents of appointment schemes may be tempted to argue for a per se rule that any switch from election to appointment dilutes minority voting strength. If minorities had an opportunity to elect the officer and the state takes that opportunity away, the state dilutes the former minority voting strength. Conversely, one could argue that appointment never dilutes minority voting strength because minorities have the same opportunity to participate in the political process and elect representatives of their choice as whites—none.[325]

Both arguments, however, misconstrue the Voting Rights Act. The Act requires a searching, practical assessment of the past and present realities in a given situation to determine what opportunities for minorities exist to select the official under the elective system and what opportunities would exist for minorities under the appointive system.[326] The correct analysis is one of vicarious selection. Such an analysis would permit a change from election to appointment only if minority voters have the same opportunity to elect the appointing authority that they had under the election scheme. If a minority group has less opportunity to elect its preferred candidate for the position of appointing authority than it had to elect its preferred candidate for the formerly elected position, its voting power has been diluted.[327]

Using this vicarious selection analysis, a change from election to appointment could withstand a challenge under the Voting Rights Act in

---

325. See *supra* note 327.

326. *Gingles*, 478 U.S. at 45 (quoting Senate Report to 1982 amendment to Voting Rights Act).

327. Such a dilution of voting power has consistently been held to violate the Act from its original enactment in 1965. See, e.g., *Houston Lawyers' Ass'n v. Attorney Gen.*, 501 U.S. 419, 425–26 (1991) (holding judicial election schemes subject to vote-dilution claims); *Chisom v. Roemer*, 501 U.S. 380 (1991) (same); *City of Pleasant Grove v. United States*, 479 U.S. 462, 467 (1987) (holding annexation plans subject to vote-dilution claims); *Gingles*, 478 U.S. at 46 (holding multi-member districts that submerge minority voting strength subject to vote-dilution claims).

Such an analysis would comport with either a retrogression standard by which the courts could measure whether minority voting strength is less than what it was before the change, see *Beer v. United States*, 425 U.S. 130, 133 (1975), or a disparate impact standard by which courts could measure whether minority voting strength is diluted vis-à-vis white voting strength. See *Gingles*, 478 U.S. at 46–51.

only two circumstances: (1) where the minority population in a given area is so small or so diffuse that it could not constitute a majority in an election district,[328] and (2) where the minority population is so large that it can elect the minority preferred candidates under the elected system and it can elect the authority(ies) who appoints the formerly elected official, such as the governor or the County Board of Supervisors.

One arguable exception to this analysis would be an appointment scheme that guarantees appointment of an equal number of minority officials that would have been chosen under an election scheme.[329] For example, if twenty percent of the judges under a valid election scheme would have been selected from districts in which blacks constitute a majority, then twenty percent of the judges appointed would be black. This scheme would theoretically avoid dilution if we assume black voters would choose black candidates.

Such an exception to the vicarious selection analysis, however, misconstrues the purpose and language of the Act. The Act requires minorities to elect candidates of their choice—not the selection of black candidates by officials elected by white majorities. One cannot assume that an official elected by a white majority who appoints a black to an office necessarily chooses the minority preferred candidate. For example, given a choice between Clarence Thomas and Thurgood Marshall for a seat on the United States Supreme Court, African-American voters would not necessarily choose President Bush's nominee, Clarence Thomas.[330] Thus, a numerical guarantee exception to the vicarious selection analysis would circumvent the purpose of the Voting Rights Act, which is the effectuation of minority voter choices.

---

328. See *Gingles*, 478 U.S. at 50 (finding that minority group must be sufficiently large and geographically compact to constitute majority in proposed remedial scheme or the challenged practice could not be responsible for dilution).

329. See, e.g., Settlement Memorandum, supra note 9, at 1–3 (proposing agreement to settle Georgia judicial election vote-dilution suit by changing to gubernatorial appointment with guarantee of specific number of black judicial appointees).

330. Although a poll indicated a majority of African-Americans supported Thomas' nomination, this support may have been a result of lack of a black progressive candidate. See George E. Curry, *Conservative Blacks Heartened by Thomas*, CHI. TRIB., Nov. 15, 1991, at C19. Given an alternative with a more positive record on civil rights, minority voters may well have chosen the alternative. See David C. Rudd & Steve Johnson, *Blacks Feel Painful Ambivalence on Thomas*, CHI. TRIB., Sept. 10, 1991, at C1 (reporting that many blacks favor Thomas only because fear of alternative); Ronald A. Taylor, *Blacks' Thomas Support Gives Leaders Pause*, WASH. TIMES, Oct. 20, 1991, at A6 (concluding that black support for Thomas based on racial solidarity, not ideology).

The following hypotheticals explain how a vicarious selection analysis would apply to various appointment schemes:

Multi-Member Appointing Authority—Appointment to Single-Member Office

(1) Majority black population: Assume the population of a given county is majority black. Assume further that evidence exists of racial bloc voting.[331] Would a change in selecting the Superintendent of Education from a county-wide election to appointment by a majority vote of the Board of Supervisors violate the Voting Rights Act? If a majority of the Board is elected from majority black single-member districts, the answer is no. No dilution occurs because minority voters retain voting strength to select vicariously the Superintendent of Education by electing a majority of the members of the appointing authority.

On the other hand, if the county as a whole is majority black, but a majority of the districts in that county are majority white,[332] minority votes would be diluted because blacks could elect the Superintendent if elected from the entire county (because a majority of the county's population is black), but could not exercise their voting strength vicariously by electing a majority of the members of the appointing authority. White voters could exercise vicarious selection power by electing a majority of the members of the appointing authority. Thus, under the election scheme, minority voters would be able to elect the candidate of their choice, while under the appointment scheme, the choice would be made on behalf of the white voters.

(2) Majority white population: If a county has a majority white population, blacks would not be able to elect a Superintendent of Education. Minority voting strength would not be sufficient to prevail in a county-wide election and would not be sufficient to prevail in a majority of the elections for the appointing authority. Thus, no vote dilution would

---

331. All factual situations in this section assume proof of racial bloc voting. Without such proof, a claim for minority vote dilution cannot be sustained in any Voting Rights Act suit. See *Gingles*, 478 U.S. at 54–61.

332. This situation could occur. For example, if the county is 55% black with 5,500 blacks and 3,500 whites, two majority black districts could be created with 1,500 blacks (75%) and 500 whites (25%) in each district, and three majority white districts could be created with 833 blacks (42%) and 1,167 whites (58%). Blacks could elect directly a Superintendent of Education of their choice, but could not select a superintendent of their choice if the Superintendent of Education was appointed by the Board of Supervisors.

occur in a change from election to appointment because the election is for only one person.[333]

Multi-Member Appointing Authority—Appointment of Multiple Officials

If a county attempted to change the selection of a five-member Board of Education from election to appointment, the analysis would be similar to the situations described above. The change would not violate the Act if each member of the Board of Supervisors elected pursuant to a valid districting plan appointed one member of the Board of Education. Minorities would have the same opportunity to participate as they had under the elective system. If minorities constituted a majority in a given single-member Board of Education election district, they would have the same voting strength in the Supervisor's district and could exercise vicarious selection power by electing the appointing authority. This result would be true whether the county is majority black or majority white, as long as the election districts for the members of the appointing authority do not themselves dilute minority voting strength.

If, on the other hand, the appointing authority must appoint all members of a multi-member board by majority vote, the result would be different. Assume a Board of Education has been elected from five single-member districts in a sixty-percent majority white county. Assume further that the five districts had populations as follows:

> Total Population—10,000: 6,000 white and 4,000 black.
> District 1—Total Population 2,000: 1,500 white, 600 black.
> District 2—Total Population 2,000: 1,500 white, 500 black
> District 3—Total Population 2,000: 1,400 white, 400 black
> District 4—Total Population 2,000: 800 white, 1200 black
> District 5—Total Population 2,000: 800 white, 1200 black

In Districts 4 and 5, blacks could elect the candidate of their choice even though they are not in a majority black county. If, however, the county changed to a method in which a majority vote of the Board of Supervisors appointed the Board of Education, blacks would not retain the same vicarious selection power in the appointment scheme. Although they would have a majority population in two of the districts, they would not be able to elect a majority of the Board of Supervisors. Therefore, they would have no power over the appointment of the

---

333. Cf. Butts v. City of New York, 779 F.2d 141, 148 (2d Cir. 1985) (finding no vote dilution of single-member office), cert. denied, 478 U.S. 1021 (1986).

Board of Education, because they are selected from a majority vote of the Board of Supervisors.

Single-Member Appointing Authority—Multiple Appointed Officials

A change to appointment by a state-wide elected official would dilute minority voting strength if multiple judicial offices are filled by election from majority black districts. For example, if a majority white state elects twenty district court judges from majority black districts and eighty from majority white districts, a change to gubernatorial appointment would dilute minority voting strength because blacks do not constitute a majority of the vote in the gubernatorial election. Even if the state guaranteed a number of black appointments, the official who appointed the black judges would not have been chosen by the black voters.[334]

Conclusion

A majority of the states currently select judges by election. Although the states continue to assert that the function of judges should remove them from the scope of the Voting Rights Act, the Court has made clear that the Act extends its protections to the vote and the voter, regardless of the object of the vote. If states choose to make their judges accountable to popular opinion through elections, the Act should and does protect minority voting rights with respect to those procedures.

In addition, the standard for proving a violation of the Act should be the same for judicial election challenges as for any other elections. If, by a totality of the circumstances, a court determines that a practice results in the dilution of minority voting rights, that practice is invalid regardless of the election in which it is used.

Now that the applicability of the Act to judicial elections is settled, states may attempt to avoid the Act by changing their method of judicial selection from election to appointment. States that choose this course, however, may be subjected to challenges under both section 2 and section 5 because a change from election to appointment may dilute minority voting rights.

---

334. Therefore, the proposed settlement to the Georgia judicial election challenge would itself violate the Act. See *supra* note 329 and accompanying text.

Part V

POSTSCRIPT

CHAPTER 12

The Supreme Court and the Future of Voting Rights

Anthony A. Peacock

Shortly before this book went to press, the Supreme Court released *Shaw v. Hunt (Shaw II)*[1] and *Bush v. Vera*.[2] Although a number of issues were raised in these cases which cannot be addressed here, perhaps the most important opinion in either case, indeed in any voting rights decision since *Shaw v. Reno (Shaw)*,[3] was Justice O'Connor's concurring opinion in *Bush*. There O'Connor spoke alone, asserting, among other things, that "compliance with the results test of § 2 of the Voting Rights Act (VRA) is a compelling state interest."[4] In light of earlier voting rights and equal protection law, which O'Connor frequently joined or authored, this proposition was curious, if not extraordinary. What are future courts to make of it? In addition, as Daniel Lowenstein has pointed out, the dissenters in *Shaw II* and *Bush* certainly agree with O'Connor on this issue.[5] What happens if they join O'Connor in her assessment, forming a majority on the question?

In *City of Richmond v. Croson* (1989), O'Connor had attacked the invidiousness of all race-based classifications, accusing the dissent of promoting a watered-down version of equal protection analysis for suggesting that the Court apply a lesser standard of scrutiny to racial classifications aimed at ameliorating the condition of historically disadvantaged groups. "[T]he standard of review under the Equal Protection Clause," O'Connor declared, "is not dependent on the race of those burdened or benefited by a particular classification."[6] In *Shaw*[7] and in

---

1. 64 U.S.L.W. 4437 (1996).

2. 64 U.S.L.W. 4452 (1996).

3. 113 S.Ct. 2816 (1993).

4. 64 U.S.L.W. at 4463.

5. Daniel Hays Lowenstein, Election Law: 1996–97 Supplement (Durham, NC: Carolina Academic Press, 1996), 13.

6. *City of Richmond v. J.A. Croson Co*, 488 U.S. 469, 494 (1989), O'Connor J.

7. See 113 S.Ct. at 2824, O'Connor, J., opinion of the Court:

Express racial classifications are immediately suspect because "[a]bsent search-

Adarand Constructors, Inc. v. Pena (1995),[8] O'Connor reaffirmed this holding. So did Justice Kennedy in *Miller v. Johnson* (1995), where he clarified that the equal protection claim recognized in *Shaw* was not limited to bizarre-shaped districts but applied to all cases in which race was used by a state to separate voters into electoral districts.[9]

This uniformity of opinion, still preserved in *Shaw II*, dissolved in *Bush*. In *Bush*, Justice Kennedy and Justice Thomas, joined by Justice Scalia, filed separate concurring opinions rejecting O'Connor's statement in her plurality opinion that strict scrutiny does not "apply to all cases of intentional creation of majority-minority districts."[10] Earlier equal protection law had made clear that strict scrutiny did apply to all such cases. In addition, Kennedy responded to O'Connor's concurring opinion that compliance with section 2 was a compelling state interest by emphasizing that this created a two-tier predominant factor review unique to redistricting cases. There was no authority in equal protection law for such a distinction.[11] Indeed, a principal theme throughout both Kennedy's and Thomas' opinions was that the equal protection doctrine promulgated by O'Connor in *Bush* was inconsistent with the current state of the law. But how exactly?

In *Shaw*, O'Connor had recognized that redistricting was distinct from other forms of state decisionmaking insofar as "the legislature always is *aware* of race when it draws district lines."[12] The examples O'Connor cited in support of this statement—maintenance of compact districts and political subdivisions that happened to contain racial or ethnic communities—appeared to presume that race could not be the predominant consideration in configuring such districts.[13] This, in any event, was the gloss on her opinion provided by the Court in *Miller*, where the "predominant factor" test was developed as the new threshold for a *Shaw*-type equal protection violation. In *Bush*, O'Connor appeared to change course from her more austere position in *Shaw*. There she reasoned that "so long as

---

ing judicial inquiry...there is simply no way of determining what classifications are 'benign' or 'remedial' and what classifications are in fact motivated by illegitimate notions of racial inferiority or simple racial politics" (quoting *Richmond v. J.A. Croson Co.*, 488 U.S. at 493).

8. See 115 S.Ct. 2097, 2110 and 2112 (1995), O'Connor, J., opinion of the Court.

9. 115 S.Ct. 2475, 2485–86, opinion of the Court.

10. 64 U.S.L.W. at 4454, plurality opinion.

11. *Id.* at 4466, Kennedy, J., concurring.

12. 113 S.Ct. at 2826, O'Connor, J., opinion of the Court, emphasis in original.

13. *Id.*

they do not subordinate traditional districting criteria to the use of race for its own sake or as a proxy, States may intentionally create majority-minority districts, and may otherwise take race into consideration, without coming under strict scrutiny."[14]

But how was this to be done? According to Justice Thomas, intentionally creating a majority-minority district had to mean more than mere *awareness* of race when drafting district lines. It had to mean that the district would not have existed *but for* the explicit use of a racial classification; that the district was created not "in spite of" but "because of" racial demographics. "When that occurs, traditional race-neutral districting principles are necessarily subordinated (and race necessarily predominates), and the legislature has classified persons on the basis of race."[15] Justice Kennedy appeared to agree with this assessment, adding: "In my view, we would no doubt apply strict scrutiny if a State decreed that certain districts had to be at least 50 percent white, and our analysis should be no different if the State so favors minority races."[16] The question of whether strict scrutiny was to be invoked every time a majority-minority district had been intentionally created, although not answered in *Shaw*, was definitively resolved by *Adarand* and *Miller*. The latter, in particular, had made clear that any governmental classification based on race was subject to strict scrutiny and that no exceptions were to be made for race-based districting.[17] Could O'Connor's contrary opinion in *Bush* be reconciled with *Adarand* and *Miller*, or her opinion in *Croson*? If so, how?

O'Connor defended her assertion that compliance with section 2 was a compelling state interest, first, on grounds that since 1982, when Congress incorporated the results test into section 2(a) of the VRA, the Court had frequently interpreted and enforced the obligations of the subsection, "assuming but never directly addressing its constitutionality."[18] In addition, lower courts had "unanimously affirmed" section 2's constitutionality.[19] In light of the Court's obligation to defer to Congress' authority under the Reconstruction Amendments where possible, and given the legacy of jurisprudence upholding the constitutionality of section 2, compliance with the results test should be accepted as a compelling state

---

14. *Bush*, 64 U.S.L.W. 4464, O'Connor, J., concurring.
15. *Id.*, 64 U.S.L.W. at 4466, Thomas, J., concurring.
16. 64 U.S.L.W. at 4465, Kennedy, J., concurring.
17. *Id.*, 4466, Thomas, J., concurring.
18. *Id.*, 4463, O'Connor, J., concurring.
19. *Id.*

interest, at least until lower court opinion was reversed and the test found unconstitutional. The Supremacy clause obliged states "to comply with all constitutional exercises of Congress' power" and the Court should therefore "allow States to assume the constitutionality of §2 of the Voting Rights Act, including the 1982 amendments."[20]

Compliance with the VRA had indeed been assumed, *arguendo*, to constitute a compelling state interest in voting rights cases that had considered the issue following *Shaw*. In none of these cases, however, had the Court suggested that such an assumption, *on its own*, provided a compelling state interest. The principles of judicial review and equal protection required otherwise. Whether compliance with the section 2 results test constituted a compelling state interest had not been determined in any of the post-*Shaw* cases not because the Court had accepted the section's constitutionality or had been deferential to Congress (if this was what O'Connor was suggesting) but because in none of the cases had any of the proposed districting plans survived the narrow tailoring requirements of equal protection review, the precondition, in all of the cases, to proceeding to the more delicate issue of whether the VRA was constitutional.

Was O'Connor's conclusion then a *non sequitur*? Did she get the logic of constitutional review perfectly backwards, assuming for the purposes of determining whether compliance with the VRA was constitutional the very constitutionality of the act that the Court had to assess as a precondition to determining whether compliance with the act was a compelling state interest? In *Miller v. Johnson*, Justice Kennedy declared that were the Court

> to accept the Justice Department's objection [to Georgia's redistricting plan] itself as a compelling interest adequate to insulate racial districting from constitutional review, we would be surrendering to the Executive Branch our role in enforcing the constitutional limits on race-based official action.[21]

Did Justice O'Connor in *Bush* not offer up such terms of surrender?

A central theme throughout this book has been that *Shaw* was a bellwether in equal protection litigation, inaugurating a new era in the constitutional adjudication of race-conscious redistricting. Justice O'Connor's plurality and concurring opinions in *Bush* suggest that we may be in for yet more surprises in equal protection review—and this in the not too distant future. Whether *Shaw* and its legacy survive this development, and if so exactly how it can, is a matter of significant speculation.

---

20. *Id.*, 4464.
21. 115 S.Ct. at 2491, opinion of the Court.

Table of Cases

Index